DOUBLE LIVES

By the Same Author

Women of the World: The Rise of the Female Diplomat
The British People and the League of Nations: Democracy,
Citizenship and Internationalism, c. 1918–1945

DOUBLE LIVES

A History of Working Motherhood
in Modern Britain

HELEN MCCARTHY

BLOOMSBURY PUBLISHING
LONDON · OXFORD · NEW YORK · NEW DELHI · SYDNEY

BLOOMSBURY PUBLISHING
Bloomsbury Publishing Plc
50 Bedford Square, London, WC1B 3DP, UK
BLOOMSBURY, BLOOMSBURY PUBLISHING and the Diana logo are trademarks of
Bloomsbury Publishing Plc

First published in Great Britain 2020

Page 1, top: Stefano Bianchetti/Getty Images; bottom: Mary Evans Image Library; Page 2, top and
bottom: Getty Images; Page 3, bottom: Getty Images; Page 4, top right: Hulton Deutsch / Getty
Images; Page 4, bottom left: Illustrated London News Ltd / Mary Evans Image Library; Page 4,
bottom right: Illustrated London News Ltd / Mary Evans Image Library; Page 5, top left: National
Portrait Gallery; Page 5, top right: National Trust; Page 5, bottom: Getty Images; Page 6, top: Getty
Images; Page 6, bottom: National Portrait Gallery; Page 7, top left: Getty Images; Page 7, top right:
British Library; Page 7, bottom: Getty Images; Page 8, top and bottom: Imperial War Museum;
Page 9, top and bottom: Getty Images; Page 10, top: National Portrait Gallery; Page 10, bottom:
Alamy Stock Library; Page 11, top and bottom: Imperial War Museum; Page 12: National Archives;
Page 13, top left: Alamy; Page 13, top right: University of Reading, Special Collections; Page 13,
bottom:; University of Reading, Special Collections; Page 14, top: Fairfax Media Archives / Getty
Images; Page 14, bottom: Larry Ellis / Getty Images; Page 15, top: London Metropolitan Archives;
Page 15, bottom: Graham Wood / Getty Images; Page 16: Photo by Kim Sayer / Pan Books

Material from Mass Observation is reproduced with permission of Curtis Brown Group Ltd,
London on behalf of The Trustees of the Mass Observation Archive © The Trustees of the Mass
Observation Archive

A catalogue record for this book is available from the British Library

ISBN: HB: 978-1-4088-7073-0; TPB: 978-1-4088-7074-7; eBook: 978-1-4088-7076-1

2 4 6 8 10 9 7 5 3 1

Typeset by Newgen KnowledgeWorks Pvt. Ltd., Chennai, India
Printed and bound in Great Britain by CPI Group (UK) Ltd, Croydon CR0 4YY

MIX
Paper from
responsible sources
FSC® C020471
FSC
www.fsc.org

To find out more about our authors and books visit www.bloomsbury.com
and sign up for our newsletters

To whom is her first duty, herself or the coming generation? We hold, her first, second, and third duty is to herself, and, that duty being fulfilled, she will have done her duty to the coming generation.

The Freewoman, 1912

Contents

Introduction

This is a book about mothers who worked for pay: what they have thought and felt and said about their lives, and what others have thought and felt and said about them over the past century and a half. It is not a universal history of women, for not all women are mothers, and not every mother works for pay. But it is, nonetheless, a story which lies at the heart of how women's everyday worlds have been shaped in modern societies like Britain.

There are no 'typical' lives in history, but the tale of Isabella Killick, a tailoress in Mile End, east London, reveals something of the struggles experienced by poor, working-class mothers in the late nineteenth century, when our story begins. Born in the neighbouring district of Stepney in the mid-1840s, as a girl Isabella was apprenticed to the tailoring trade and continued to work for wages after her marriage to a boiler-maker named William, fitting trouser-finishing in around her household and caring duties as mother to three children. William's health broke down in 1885, which made Isabella the family's main breadwinner, toiling at her needle from six in the morning until eight at night. Her earnings covered the rent and kept young mouths fed, but Isabella's own diet was woefully inadequate: a herring and a cup of tea was her 'chief living', she told a Parliamentary Committee in 1888, 'as for meat, I do not expect; I get meat once in six months'.

Three years later, William's condition deteriorated, prompting a temporary admission to the parish infirmary, and misfortune struck again in 1895, when both husband and wife entered the workhouse, the last resort of the destitute. After William's death in 1902, Isabella survived as best she could through earnings from needlework, charring and cleaning. In 1911, she returned to the workhouse and remained there until discharging herself in 1915, possibly because she was, by then, eligible for the modest old-age pension introduced by the Liberal government seven years earlier. It was not to be a lengthy or restful retirement. Isabella died in 1920 aged seventy-six, no more than a mile or two from her place of birth.[1]

Isabella Killick was one of 4 million girls and women working for wages in late Victorian Britain, as factory hands, domestic servants, shop assistants, clerical workers, agricultural labourers, small-business owners, teachers, nurses, midwives, writers and actresses.[2] They participated in the urban spectacle of the towns and cities in which the majority of Britons now lived, travelling to work on trams and trains, serving behind counters, populating office blocks, pacing hospital wards and scrubbing the floors of municipal buildings. They belonged, too, to the army of toilers cleaning and cooking in the basements and sculleries of private homes, tilling fields or slaving, like Isabella Killick, in their own modest dwellings as seamstresses, matchbox makers, childminders or washerwomen.

Many of these working women were mothers. According to the census, which forms the historian's chief guide to the composition of the Victorian workforce, 13 per cent of married women were engaged in waged occupations across Britain in 1901. To this must be added the busy wives of shopkeepers, pub landlords and farmers, as well as those employed in seasonal work such as hop-picking and harvest-gathering, all of whom were likely to have gone unrecorded in the decennial population count.[3] Not every occupied wife had children, but most did, and their ranks were further swelled by unknown numbers of unmarried mothers reliant on their own earnings for survival. We cannot be sure exactly how many mothers worked for pay at the end of the nineteenth century, but there is little doubt that working motherhood was a well-established feature of the late Victorian labour market and a daily reality for hundreds of thousands of British women.[4]

And yet it was not a social norm. The dominant ideal across all classes was that of the breadwinner family: a household headed by a male worker earning a wage large enough to keep his wife and children, typically through secure, skilled work. Many men never achieved this aspiration, thwarted by low pay, unemployment, disability or old age, leaving their wives little choice but to work in order to survive. Despite this reality, the 'family wage' retained its ideological power over British society.[5] The belief that fathers had a duty to provide justified men's higher wages as well as the exclusion of women from skilled trades and the restrictions on married women's employment, and it legitimised social welfare policies which assumed that all men had dependants whereas women had none. The labour market was structured so fundamentally around gender difference that only a few isolated voices saw, in the lives of wage-earning mothers, a template for women's economic independence beyond marriage and maternity. Instead, working motherhood was blamed for idleness amongst men, high infant death rates, and the evil of low-paid labour. For late Victorians, wage-earning by mothers was a warning that something had gone seriously wrong along Britain's pathway to industrial modernity. The working mother stood as a symbol of domestic and economic disorder, the antithesis of progress and civilisation.

Now consider the testimony of this thirty-four-year-old secondary school teacher from a town in north-east England, written for the Mass Observation archive in 2015:* 'For me there has never been any question about whether I would work and that is the same for virtually all of my friends … and indeed virtually all of the girls I teach expect to have a career of some sort.' Looking back to a 1980s and 1990s childhood, the writer recalled that 'whether

*Mass Observation is a research project recording the history of everyday life in Britain, first established in 1937 and now based at the University of Sussex. It regularly collects written testimonies from a panel of over 500 volunteers spread around the UK, typically in the form of responses to 'directives' on a range of subjects. See www.massobs.org.uk.

someone's mum worked or didn't work didn't seem to be a huge issue at the time'. Her own mother had returned to teaching when she and her sister were old enough to attend nursery school. Although currently single, the correspondent hoped to have a family one day and felt that under ideal circumstances one partner – she didn't specify which – would be in a position to work part-time while the children were very young: 'I think it is important for children to see their parents working and being good role models,' the writer concluded.[6]

These reflections signal how far norms regarding mothers and paid work changed over the course of the twentieth century. By the early 2000s, women made up half of Britain's workforce and the participation rate of mothers with dependent children was nearly two-thirds.[7] In 2018, it stood close to three-quarters.[8] Women in regular employment now enjoy a statutory entitlement to maternity leave and pay and to request flexible working hours to care for dependants. Today some progressive employers go even further, offering generous parental leave schemes, subsidised childcare places, job-share opportunities and programmes to support mothers making the transition back to work. These laws, policies and initiatives seem to affirm the proposition voiced by our schoolteacher to Mass Observation: that seeking to combine the care of children with paid work has become an ordinary and legitimate aspiration for women.

Despite this shift in values, workplace equality is still elusive. The gender pay gap stands at around 14 per cent, affordable childcare is hard to find, and occupational segregation, sexual harassment and discrimination against pregnant women remain rife.[9] Nor has attitudinal change been universal. Not everyone approves of parents who pay others to look after their children while they work, and attitudes and practices often vary according to differences of class, generation, ethnicity and religion – although never in wholly predictable or straightforward ways. Nonetheless, few would now describe, as late Victorians did, the employment of mothers as a 'social problem' or the sign of a dysfunctional economy. Nineteenth-century observers recognised that some mothers had to earn to secure their family's basic subsistence, but they lacked a vocabulary for describing the wider significance that paid work might hold in these women's lives. By the end of the twentieth century, it became possible to speak about other motives and desires propelling mothers into the workplace: for personal autonomy, professional achievement, mental stimulation, friendship and sociability, or to set a good example to sons and daughters. All are now broadly accepted as legitimate reasons for why mothers might stay in or re-enter the workforce.

This is the first and major claim of this book. The meaning of working motherhood has changed dramatically over the past century and a half. What was understood to be a social problem arising from economic pressure on families has become a social norm rooted in a more expansive set of needs, rights and preferences felt and asserted by mothers. This amounts to a profound transformation in the lives of British women and this book aims to describe and account for it.

*

Some of the voices we will hear over the following chapters looked back to an even earlier transformation as they sought to make sense of women's changing position in the economy and the family. The Industrial Revolution which remade Britain between 1750 and 1850 threw a long shadow over all subsequent debates about working motherhood. The enclosure of the common land, the coming of the factory system and the rise of the city had major consequences for women's economic status.[10] The claim that married women lost out as production moved from cottage to factory was frequently made by feminists in the early twentieth century. In 1911, the free-thinking author and intellectual Olive Schreiner argued that wives and mothers were dispossessed of their rightful share in the economic life of the community, describing in her book, *Woman and Labour*, the encroachment by men and machines upon women's traditional domain. No longer required to bake, brew or spin, and with children absent for many hours of the day at school, the modern woman, Schreiner feared, could sink easily into a state of moral and intellectual dissipation with disastrous results for the future race. It was, in her view, the desire to reclaim their former economic status which animated the contemporary women's movement and their demands for votes, legal equality and access to all occupations.

Writing three years later, the Fabian socialist Mabel Atkinson concurred with this analysis of the middle-class woman's revolt, but suggested that economic dispossession had assumed a different form for women of the labouring classes. The working-class housewife's grievance against the Industrial Revolution was not that it had given her too little to do but too much: eking out an inadequate male wage to feed a whole family, cleaning a dwelling which might be riddled with vermin and damp, nursing a baby while hoping that the next one didn't come too soon. 'The reforms she demands,' Atkinson observed, 'are not independence and the right to work, but rather protection against the unending burden of toil which has been laid upon her.'[11] Eleanor Rathbone, one of the leading British feminists of the 1920s and 1930s, shared this conviction that restitution for the disinherited working-class mother would not be achieved through greater access to waged work. Her campaign for State-funded payments to mothers, known as family allowances, rested on the belief that woman's role in sustaining the family as an economic unit – 'something which has its own claim, based on its own value to the nation, to its own share in the nation's wealth' – had been tragically forgotten.[12]

These early twentieth-century perspectives are worth recovering because they remind us that even feminists have never been united as to the desirability of wage-earning by mothers. By the 1970s, and under the influence of the Women's Liberation Movement, paid work was more consistently identified as the key to autonomy and independence, yet questions about how to value women's unpaid caring work and how 'stay-at-home' mothers ought to be supported remained very much live ones. These reflections also point to the ways in which women's relationship with paid work could be calibrated differently depending on class, educational background and, as Britain became an increasingly multicultural society, race and ethnicity too. If, in the later twentieth century, it became possible for mothers to talk about paid work as a fulfilling aspect of their lives and an important component of personal identity, for many its primary meaning continued to be defined by economic need. Wage-earning formed an integral part of women's strategies for 'getting by' throughout the entire period covered in this book. For mothers living on the edge of poverty, decision-making about paid work was always driven by calculations about how best to make ends meet. The presence or absence of other earners in the household; the number and ages of children and the options for their care; the availability of suitable jobs and the wages on offer; the workings of the local Poor Law and later of the welfare state – all these factors influenced women's thinking about what kind of work to do, where and when to do it, and indeed whether to do it at all.[13]

And yet, even when considering the poorest mothers, material survival did not determine everything about the place which wage-earning occupied in their lives. Beyond basic subsistence, economic needs are socially and culturally defined, and to say 'I work because I need the money' had different resonances in 1900, 1960 and 2020. This book does not start from the premise that paid work is emancipatory for mothers in all places and at all times, but nor does it assume that only privileged, middle- and upper-class white women could experience paid work as an arena for independence, self-expression and pride in skill. Working mothers from all walks of life have found meaning in their jobs which transcended the struggle for food and shelter, crucial though their earnings may have been in securing those resources for their families. We must not conspire, to quote the historian Carolyn Steedman, in 'the refusal of a complicated psychology to those living in conditions of material distress'.[14] Instead of making assumptions, as contemporaries often did, about what wage-earning meant to mothers based on their class, education or ethnic identity, this book tries to reconstruct those meanings in all their human complexity and track how they have changed over time.

This means writing a cultural history of working motherhood, as well as a social and economic one. As the following chapters set out, the pattern of women's employment was determined by multiple factors across the nineteenth and twentieth centuries, from developments in the economy and industrial relations, to reductions in family size, improvements in health and welfare and the impact of two world wars. These broad narratives of historical change move into sharper focus when viewed, as this book views them, through the lens of the working mother's day-to-day life and in light of prevailing ideas about women's relationships with family and work. Teasing out the interplay between structural forces, cultural attitudes and lived experience is never an easy task for the historian, but it is key to unlocking one of the major social revolutions of modern times. *Double Lives* takes women's feelings and desires as its central theme, not because these alone prompted growing numbers of mothers to enter the workplace from the middle of the twentieth century, but because they became crucial to the reimagining of working motherhood as a social norm. This transformation had many sources, but standing at its heart was women's changing conception of themselves and their growing determination to claim a life of their own.

*

How one might recover these feelings and desires at the beginning of the period covered in this book is no simple matter, given that most working mothers left no personal archives and appear only as names on the census form, the workhouse ledger or the register of births, marriages and deaths. I discovered Isabella Killick's story because she, alongside a handful of other women from east London, appeared before a House of Lords Select Committee in 1888 to give evidence about her wages and working conditions as a tailoress. Killick's brief testimony is a rare instance of a working-class mother speaking directly to us across time, but consider the setting: a poor, uneducated woman stands before an audience of aristocratic men in a lushly ornate committee room in Westminster, answering the questions they put before her. We hear her voice through the written record, but it is muffled by the glaring imbalances of power which determined who got to speak for themselves in late nineteenth- and early twentieth-century Britain.

Some working-class men narrated their lives by writing autobiographies, but few women put pen to paper in this way, lacking the necessary time or ego to do so.[15] More typically, the lived experience of working motherhood is mediated for us by Victorian reformers diagnosing the wider moral, social and physical condition of the nation. These self-styled experts formed their knowledge about wage-earning women through processes of inspection, observation and inference, entering factories and working-class homes and reporting what they saw to middle-class audiences. This way of 'seeing' the woman worker was reinforced by the images produced by artists and photographers and by living displays of bodies, such as the real flesh-and-blood women featured at the famous Sweated Industries Exhibition of 1906, an event staged to expose the problem of precarious, low-paid employment.

As well as looking, these investigators listened to their working-class subjects, often sympathetically, but what exactly did they hear? Studying women in the clothing trades in 1908, the trade unionist and suffragist Clementina Black felt it necessary to let her informants 'tell their story in their own way' if she were to obtain 'the industrial facts that one sets out to learn'. But this was evidently a frustrating experience. The personal testimony, Black wrote, 'is often very interesting – as a glimpse into any human life can hardly fail to be – but listening to it is apt to take a long time'.[16] Black, as we will see, was one of the more sensitive observers of working mothers' lives, but in prioritising the collation of 'facts' over the narratives told by poor women she was typical of the late Victorian reformer mindset. These encounters between middle-class experts and working-class mothers helped to shape official understandings of women's industrial labour, with important effects on public policy and in the workplace.

Those belonging to the modest but growing ranks of professional women were in a somewhat more fortunate position in the late nineteenth century. These educated women were able to articulate their demands for wider training and employment opportunities and to describe what paid work meant to them in letters, diaries, memoirs and autobiographies, which some published in later years.[17]

Yet only a fraction of this pioneer generation found it possible to combine the professional work they loved with motherhood, thwarted by regulations requiring resignation on marriage and wider codes of bourgeois respectability. Many middle- and upper-class mothers filled their time instead with voluntary work for charitable organisations or public service in local government.[18] Some women pursued these non-remunerated activities with astonishing levels of commitment and expertise, but this type of unofficial working motherhood remained firmly bounded by the middle-class traditions of female voluntary action. With some notable exceptions, women of education and means had to choose between professional careers and motherhood in late Victorian and Edwardian Britain.

From the middle of the twentieth century, it becomes easier for the historian to recover women's voices across all social classes, reflecting broader democratising forces at work in Britain – from universal suffrage and the founding of the welfare state to expanding educational opportunities and mass consumerism. Observers of women's employment from the 1940s and 1950s became interested in attitudes and orientations, especially those of working mothers, who were returning to the labour market in ever-increasing numbers following the completion of smaller, closely spaced families. A fundamentally new outlook seemed to be at large amongst British women, who now regarded paid employment as a lifelong pursuit, rather than one terminated by marriage or maternity. Policymakers and employers alike were keen to understand these changing aspirations as they wooed women into jobs in the expanding public services or booming consumer industries. Newspaper columnists and magazine editors were similarly intrigued, turning women's shifting expectations regarding home and work into topical material for an increasingly pervasive print and broadcast media. The working mother became a cultural figure who could channel all manner of post-war anxieties and fantasies about marriage, the family and the character of 'affluent' Britain.

None of this meant that working mothers ceased to be an object about which generalisations were made by experts professing authoritative knowledge of their lives. But it did create greater space for mothers to articulate their *own* feelings and desires about work and family, a move reinforced in the 1970s by second-wave feminists, who placed women's self-expression and self-determination at the heart of their radical sexual politics. As a result, mothers played a more active part in articulating the meanings which paid work held in their lives, rather than having others determine it for them, as had been the fate of most working mothers a century earlier.

*

Women's quest to become authors of their own lives in the later twentieth century was not achieved without costs. One major reason for why working motherhood had been framed as a problem by the Victorians was the fear that wage-earning made it impossible for women to fulfil their higher duty as nurturers of the 'race'. The tendency to reduce women to this reproductive function lingered on in social policy debates as late as the 1940s, when concerns about Britain's falling birth rate reached fever pitch. By the 1980s and 1990s, by contrast, politicians rarely talked about parenting as a 'service to the state', seeing it instead as a choice to be exercised freely by individuals. This undoubtedly meant greater autonomy for women in making decisions about childbearing, but it reinforced the assumption that reconciling the demands of work and family was a private matter for mothers to resolve for themselves. With career structures still predicated on the male norm of continuous employment and with childcare options limited, the freedom to 'choose' the life of the working mother translated into high levels of stress for women. Failure to achieve the 'Superwoman' ideal of combining career success with a fulfilling family life was personalised. A lack of willpower, an inability to multitask, insufficient commitment to the job – these became the explanations for why mothers could not compete with men in the workplace, rather than society's wider failure to support parents in meeting their economic and caring responsibilities. The disinherited family lived on.

Some contemporary commentators identify these dynamics as the product of 'neoliberalism', an ideology rooted in free markets and competitive individualism which became politically ascendant in Britain in the 1980s and 1990s.[19] There can be no doubt that the deregulatory policies and welfare cuts instigated by Margaret Thatcher and her Conservative successors adversely affected millions of women, including many working mothers. Yet, as this book shows, the gender inequalities produced by unregulated labour markets were not unique to the late twentieth century. Furthermore, even at the high point of social democracy between the 1940s and 1970s, mothers who needed or wanted to work for pay were poorly served by the welfare state and marginalised by male-led trade unions. For most of the post-war period, Labour and Conservative governments alike invested in maternity services and nursery education with a view to stabilising the family rather than promoting women's economic independence and choice through paid work. Despite sustained pressure from feminists in recent decades, the major political parties in Britain, alongside trade unions and employers, have been slow to devise policies which recognise society's responsibility to families in all their diverse forms, and which do not entrench women's dependence within them.

This raises a final question about the role of men. *Double Lives* is a history of working motherhood, but fathers played an important part in shaping women's employment trajectories throughout the nineteenth and twentieth centuries. The size of a husband's wage packet was often a key determinant in whether or not his wife would work, but men's attitudes were influential too. Some were staunchly opposed in principle and some were indifferent, but others encouraged their wives to seek waged work for a variety of reasons: because they appreciated the extra income, because they thought it was good for a wife to have interests beyond the family, or, more rarely, because they recognised their partners' career goals as equal in value to their own. A supportive stance towards certain forms of married women's work became increasingly common amongst husbands from the 1950s, when men were generally spending more time at home and marriages became increasingly 'companionate'.[20] Yet this had only a limited impact on men's primary identity as providers or on their working patterns: full-time employment pursued continuously over the course of their life remained the norm for British fathers – and, despite some growth in part-time and flexible working amongst men since the 1990s, it remains so today.[21] As the following chapters reveal, the meanings attached to working motherhood were transformed dramatically over the course of the past century and a half, but the cultural significance of fathers, who are always assumed to be in or looking for full-time paid work, remained much more stable.

A NOTE ON TERMINOLOGY AND THE SCOPE OF THIS BOOK

Throughout this book, the terms 'working mothers' and 'wage-earning mothers' are used more or less interchangeably to refer to women who work for pay whilst having parental responsibility for the care of at least one dependent child. I use 'paid work' to refer to regular waged or salaried employment, as well as casual or intermittent forms of earning inside and outside the home, and to self-employment in all its varieties. The huge volume of unpaid work performed by women, including the embodied labour of mothering itself, is integral to the story, but this book does not purport to provide a general history of motherhood in its every aspect.

Most of the women whose lives are described in this book were the biological mothers of their children, although stepmothers and adoptive mothers occasionally make an appearance. I have cast my net as widely as possible, exploring working motherhood across social classes, ethnicities, regions and occupational cultures, and amongst unmarried mothers, separated and divorced mothers as well as those in more conventional married-couple households. However, not every experience features here. The lives of working mothers in same-sex relationships, mothers with disabilities or caring for children with disabilities and the more recent phenomenon of trans-parenting all deserve space that I am unable to offer within the scope of this book. Those fascinating and complex subjects will, I am confident, find their historian before too long.

PART ONE

Disinheritance, 1840–1914

I

Bread and Butter

Consider this account of a gruelling day in the life of a mother employed in the cotton mills of early Victorian England:

> Half an hour to dress and suckle her infant and carry it out to nurse; one hour for household duties before leaving home; half an hour for actually travelling to the mill; twelve hours' actual labour; one and a half hours for meals; half an hour for returning home at night; one and a half hours for household duties and preparing for bed, leaving six and a half hours for recreation, seeing and visiting friends and sleep; and in winter, when it is dark, half an hour extra time on the road to the mill and half an hour extra on the road home from the mill.[1]

These words were spoken by William Ferrand, a Yorkshire MP and passionate advocate of factory reform, shortly before Parliament passed the Ten Hours Act in 1844 to limit women's working time in the textile industry. Even after this landmark measure, the average week for a textile operative stood at sixty-five hours, with most wage-earning mothers leaving the house before 6 a.m. and not returning until early evening.[2] The work itself, standing all day long amidst noisy machinery and in sweltering heat, was monotonous yet required sustained mental effort to keep machines correctly fed and safely running. The working-class suffragist Ada Nield Chew described the typical day of a weaver of her acquaintance, Mrs Bolt, as one punctuated by the relentless discipline of supplying the four power-looms in her charge, replenishing the cops of cotton inside the shuttles every three minutes.[3]

These punishing realities of industrial life were, of course, shared by male operatives, yet for wives and mothers, housework added a second shift to be squeezed in during the early morning hours or between getting home and bedtime. With no regular 'wash-day' during the week, laundry often took place late at night whilst the rest of the family slumbered. Some women stored up major chores for Saturday afternoons when the factory was shut. From midday, smartly suited men and mill girls in their finery could be seen in town making a 'real holiday', but for Lancashire wives, these were precious hours in which to clean the house, bake bread, mend clothes and buy provisions for the week ahead. Many mothers spent a portion of their wages paying others to do their washing, sew their dresses and even warm up their tea and coffee ready for the morning break. One visitor to Lancashire in the 1860s noticed the existence of 'a very large class of women [who] derive their maintenance entirely by providing for the wants of mill hands'.[4] This included meals: every factory district had numerous chippies or 'eating-shops' as well as a public bake-house where hotpots, the traditional dish of meat, onions and layered potatoes, could be heated during the morning shift and collected at dinner time. Some factories, like Samuel Courtauld's silk mill in Essex, allowed operatives the use of kitchen facilities, which gave mothers the opportunity to 'take home something for their own and their children's dinners'.[5]

Childcare was provided in the main by local networks of paid minders, often close relatives or neighbours. Mrs Bolt took her five-year-old and toddler each morning to a Mrs Earnshaw, who lived in 'an exact replica' of her own house on a nearby street. Sometimes a resident grandmother, sister or aunt might watch the children for payment or in return for bed and board.[6] A less satisfactory but cheaper option was to leave infants with an older sibling kept home from school, perhaps asking a friend to pop by to 'take a look' at intervals during the day. Very young babies were amongst those minded in this way, for many mothers returned to the factory within a few months or even a few weeks of giving birth. A survey in Preston found that two-thirds of new mothers were back at their looms within three months, and only a tiny proportion were away for longer than six.[7] Legislation passed in 1891 prevented factory owners from 'knowingly' employing women within four weeks of childbirth, but this law was widely evaded. Working into late pregnancy was also common. Amongst eighty-two cases studied by investigators in the Dundee jute industry, some forty-six worked to within a month of confinement, twenty-seven to within a week, and seven to within a few hours.[8]

If minders lived close to the factory gates, mothers might nurse their babies during the dinner hour, but this was not always possible. In 1844, the Tory peer Lord Ashley reported the case of 'M.H.', who left her newborn from five in the morning until eight at night: 'during the day milk runs from her breasts,' he luridly described, 'until her clothes have been wet as a sop.' Another married woman, 'H.W.', told the noble lord that her breasts gave her 'the most shocking pain, and I have been dripping wet with milk'.[9] From the 1850s, day nurseries were opened in factory areas offering care for babies from the age of one month, with breastfeeding encouraged during meal breaks. Yet many of these institutions closed when they failed to become self-supporting enterprises, whilst others, run on philanthropic lines by committees of middle-class ladies, were cold-shouldered by mothers who disliked accepting 'charity'. The nursery opened at Courtauld's in 1850 never filled its twenty places, partly because mothers were suspicious of its moralising motives and partly because they found local minders to be cheaper and more convenient.[10]

The picture was not dramatically different for mothers in factories outside the textiles districts, although few places had as sizeable a presence of occupied married women as the cotton towns of Lancashire.[11] The Staffordshire potteries probably came closest, where, according to an estimate from the early 1890s, married women accounted for just under a third of all female workers, whose jobs were carefully demarcated from men's and paid on a separate scale.[12] Laundries, which were increasingly mechanised in the later nineteenth century, also became well-known employers of married women, who represented nearly 30 per cent of the female workforce in 1911.[13] Wives and mothers were found in other industrial occupations, although generally in much lower proportions and always employed on tasks designated as 'women's work'. Of the Bristol factories investigated by the Royal Commission on Labour in 1892, wives and widows comprised 16 per cent of female employees at a boot and shoe firm, 13.4 per cent at a corset factory, but less than 1 per cent at a cocoa and chocolate works.[14] Female labour underground was banned by the 1842 Mines and Collieries Act, but 'pit-brow' women were discovered in the collieries of South Wales: 'roughly dressed, with their hair carefully protected from dust with a handkerchief', these women spent their days in the open air oiling trains, unloading coal, picking out bits of ironstone and carrying messages.[15]

Households with wage-earning mothers came in different shapes and sizes. Many were headed by widows. In 1901, just under a quarter of all married women aged between forty-five and sixty-five were widowed, a reflection of men's poorer life expectancy resulting from their greater susceptibility to acute illnesses and workplace accidents.[16] Some widows drew upon small pensions or the earnings of adult children, or supported themselves by continuing with their husband's small business, but many were left penniless and had to rely on the wages they earned, supplemented by the parish. In the later nineteenth century, Poor Law Guardians generally paid outdoor relief to widows if they had more than one dependent child, which allowed those families to stay out of the workhouse. Payments, however, were rarely made at a level adequate to live on and women were expected to add to this sum through waged work. Deserted and legally separated wives were similarly placed, unless aberrant husbands could be tracked down and forced to pay maintenance, which often proved impossible.[17]

Mothers with babies born out of wedlock were in a more difficult position, and were likely to be offered only the workhouse and refused places at day nurseries on moral grounds. Many unmarried mothers were cast out by parents and employers, although some factory owners adopted a more flexible policy. At Courtauld's, for example, reinstatement was possible for girls of otherwise good character who demonstrated sufficient penitence for their sin.[18] Families could be forgiving too. The diarist Arthur Munby recorded the story of Ellen Grounds, a young pit-brow worker whom he befriended in the 1870s. Her 'sweetheart', he learned, had died of smallpox – 'Ah never had a chance te marry him, yo know!' – leaving Ellen with a two-year-old son who was looked after by her mother while she worked at the pit. 'Neither she nor her parents were ashamed of the matter,' Munby mused, 'though they are all decent folk. Her father was evidently fond and proud of the child.'[19] It was a very different story for unmarried mothers who sold sex to survive. In Plymouth, women working as prostitutes often ended up in workhouse infirmaries for their confinement, where they were separated from 'those of a better character' and sometimes made to wear special clothing advertising their shame.[20]

In households with husbands present and in full-time regular work, the assumption that wives would see to domestic duties regardless of whether they also toiled for pay outside the home was firmly entrenched. Such men regarded wage-earning as their primary contribution to the household for which leisure – frequently taken at the pub, club or football ground – was their rightful reward. This masculine code did not preclude fathers from spending evenings by the fireside or building warm ties with their children, but it rarely translated into any significant shouldering of housework or childcare.[21] Relations seem to have been somewhat more egalitarian between dual-earning textile workers. One elderly ring-spinner from Preston remembered how her husband used to warm up the dinner, help get the children ready each morning and take charge of certain household tasks: 'I never wound up a clock in all my married life,' she recalled. 'I never made a fire and I never chopped wood and I never made a bed. He did all that whenever he had his tea and washed his hands.'[22]

The dynamics also differed in households where female breadwinners supported unemployed or disabled husbands. In 1893, the Royal Commission on Labour reported the case of an Acton shoemaker who, failing to find employment, stopped in to look after the children while his wife, a laundress, went out to work.[23] The Women's Industrial Council, a body of female social investigators specialising in the study of women's waged work, discovered a number of involuntarily domesticated husbands in its survey of married women's employment carried out in 1909–10. In London, one investigator encountered a consumptive father who was able to work only in the summer months, when he took the family hop-picking. The rest of the year this 'poor fellow was a devoted parent, who among other services cooked midday meals for all his children' while his wife worked.[24] Then there was the former rag-and-bone man, similarly stricken by consumption, who cared for his younger offspring on Saturdays when his wife and eldest daughter went out to sell flowers.[25] These families, as the survey's author Clementina Black noted, were in desperate circumstances, but the childcare provided by fathers had real value in freeing wives for wage-earning. 'Even an unemployed husband,' Black wrote, 'will keep toddling children from being run over, tumbling downstairs or setting themselves on fire.'[26] This role reversal released some mothers from the burden of attending to domestic chores on top of their waged work. One woman whose injured husband was well enough to take charge of the home told a member of the Fabian Women's Group: 'It is such a nice rest for me to go out to work.'[27]

*

Two questions loomed large whenever middle-class Victorians discussed the subject of mothers employed outside their homes: why did they seek wages, and did their wage-earning cause harm? Nearly everyone who publicly debated such questions agreed with the broad principle that married women's work was socially undesirable. Back in the 1840s, this consensus spanned a wide spectrum, from working-class Chartists demanding political democracy to Tory paternalists nostalgic for the old social hierarchies of pre-industrial times. One Chartist periodical argued that female factory labour 'deprives the poor man of a virtuous wife', whilst an orator from Stalybridge insisted that English men wanted their womenfolk running clean, well-ordered homes, and not 'polluted by lickspittles' in factories.[28] Middle-class advocates of shorter hours for female mill workers similarly dwelt upon the evils which they believed inevitably followed when mothers left their 'proper sphere' to enter factories and workshops. Richard Oastler, a leading agitator behind the Ten Hours Bill, declared his desire 'to see woman in her right place, on her own hearthstone, making it ready and comfortable for her industrious husband, when he returns to his meals and to his bed at night'.[29] Speaking in favour of the bill in Parliament, Lord Ashley told his colleagues that the employment of mothers disturbed 'the order of nature, and the rights of the labouring men'. He continued:

> It affects – nay, more, it absolutely annihilates, all the arrangements and provisions of domestic economy – thrift and management are altogether impossible ... everything runs to waste; the house and children are deserted; the wife can do nothing for her husband and family; she can neither cook, wash, repair clothes, or take charge of the infants ... Dirt, discomfort, ignorance, recklessness, are the portion of such households; the wife has no time for learning in her youth, and none for practice in her riper age; the females are most unequal to the duties of the men in the factories; and all things go to rack and ruin, because the men can discharge at home no one of the especial duties that Providence has assigned to the females.[30]

The claim that home life suffered when mothers engaged in wage-earning continued to dominate debates on the same subject half a century later. But by the 1880s and 1890s, the problem of working motherhood had become yoked to different and even higher stakes, as new questions were raised about the social, moral and physical condition of the British population.

This was the era of Charles Booth's mammoth survey, *Life and Labour of the People in London*, which mapped income and social status street by street, and of Seebohm Rowntree's famous study of conditions in York, which established the concept of the 'poverty line' as the earnings threshold below which basic subsistence was judged impossible. It was a moment when, as the Fabian socialist Beatrice Webb described it, the comfortably-off middle classes were gripped by a

> new consciousness of sin ... a growing uneasiness, amounting to conviction, that the industrial organisation, which had yielded rent, interest and profits on a stupendous scale, had failed to provide a decent livelihood and tolerable conditions for a majority of the inhabitants of Great Britain.[31]

In this climate of heightened concern for the poor, working-class mothers became targets for scrutiny and remedial action by a troubled bourgeois public. Fears about the link between the quality of population and British power and prosperity at home and abroad reconfigured mothering as a service to the State and a duty to the Empire.[32] If the nation was to be saved from physical degeneration, class revolution and moral decline, it was to the 'nurturers of the race' that reformers now increasingly turned their attention.

The qualities and habits of Britain's working-class mothers – earning and non-earning alike – were thus elucidated in the greatest possible detail by an expanding army of middle-class reformers colonising the national and municipal arena. Medical officers, health visitors, factory inspectors, sanitary inspectors, school attendance officers, lady rent-collectors, social workers from the formidable Charity Organisation Society, investigators of poverty following in the paths of Booth and Rowntree – all these, and more, weighed in on the question of who or what was to blame when families fell into destitution. Was it idleness and improvidence? Unscrupulous landlords and exploitative employers? Or was it the ordinary human risks which everyone ran when they started a family or became too old or sick to work? Between the 1880s and 1910s, the centre of gravity in these debates moved slowly and unevenly away from the moral chastisement of the poor and towards backing for State intervention to protect its citizens, a shift reflected in the introduction by the Liberal government of free school meals, old-age pensions, compulsory health insurance and unemployment benefits for workers in selected industries between 1906 and 1911.[33] Nonetheless, the question of where ultimate responsibility lay for the welfare of the working-class family would remain a fraught debate, and one in which the working mother and her earnings were directly implicated.

She was an object of concern, too, for those preoccupied with the closely linked problem of labour. The 1880s witnessed a sharp upswing in trade union membership and industrial action, often involving workers in unskilled or semi-skilled trades where low wages were endemic and employment insecure. Franchise reforms in 1867 and 1884 meant that millions of working men now had the vote, fuelling the growth of an independent Labour movement committed to achieving direct parliamentary representation for the working classes. This increasingly assertive spirit amongst workers prompted Lord Salisbury's Conservative government to appoint a Royal Commission in May 1891 with a broad remit to inquire into workplace conditions and relations between employers and their employees.[34] Women's industrial labour was identified as a key area of study, although the all-male Committee dealing with it was unsure as to how best to approach their subject and sought the views of Clementina Black and three working-class trade unionists, Amie Hicks, Elizabeth Mears and Clara James. These witnesses insisted that working women should be called to give their *own* evidence, for, as Mears put it, 'no one can speak for us as well as we can speak for ourselves'.[35] Black warned that factory girls, if accosted by an unknown 'lady' asking questions, 'would simply amuse themselves by telling tales, one more sensational and amusing than another, and in that way she would get a good deal of curious information'.[36]

The Committee, however, disregarded this advice and turned instead to the expertise of their next witness, the celebrated author of *Life and Labour*, Charles Booth. Booth had sent his secretary, the economist Clara Collet, to east London for three months in 1886 to collect data on women's wage-earning for his famous survey. Her method was to 'become acquainted with the girls and invite them to her house', Booth explained. 'She found it very difficult to get information that was satisfactory; but I think in the end that she did succeed with them.'[37] Despite this rather mixed endorsement, the Committee decided to replicate Booth's model and appointed Collet and three others, Eliza Orme, May Abraham and Margaret Irwin, as Lady Sub-Commissioners with a remit to report to the Committee on matters relating to women's employment. All thoughts of engaging working-class women for the job were put aside, a decision which proved consequential when the Commission later recommended the permanent addition of 'Lady Inspectors' to the existing Factory Inspectorate, and Collet found employment as Labour Investigator to the Board of Trade.[38]

This cadre of female experts in government formed the core of a new tradition of social investigation by middle-class women into working-class women's work. Their expertise played a major part in framing public debates about working mothers, supplemented by the fact-finding enquiries of the Women's Industrial Council and by the surveys, reports and studies carried out over the following decade by bodies like the Fabian Women's Group, the Women's Labour League, the Women's Co-operative Guild and the National Federation of Women Workers. These organisations offered some opportunities for wage-earning women to speak for themselves, as Mears insisted that they should to the Royal Commission, but in nearly all cases the leadership and direction was supplied by educated ladies of independent means. These middle-class inspectors, investigators and trade unionists did not, by any means, draw identical conclusions from the evidence they collected about wage-earning mothers in ever more voluminous quantities. But, nevertheless, they peered at their subjects through a lens calibrated by the ideologies and shared assumptions of their class and their times.[39]

*

What exactly did they see when they looked through this lens at the mother who worked outside the home? Perhaps more important was what they did *not* see, which was the ideal, well-ordered household headed by a male breadwinner in secure employment. Working mothers were nearly always defined in terms of this lack, as suggested by the list of circumstances leading to wage-earning by mothers compiled by the Principal Lady Inspector of Factories, Adelaide Anderson, in 1904. The primary causes were a husband who was deceased, unemployed or earning an inadequate wage, with desertion by her husband following close behind.[40] Some experts added a further, morally charged, category: 'idle and worthless husbands, who preferred', in the words of Lady Sub-Commissioner Margaret Irwin, 'to live on the earnings of their wives'.[41] Whatever the exact story behind the father's failure to provide for his household, the consequences seemed clear and were summarised neatly by Miss Sharples, a sanitary inspector from Leeds in 1906: 'My own experience,' she told a conference on infant welfare in London, 'is that the great majority of married women who work outside their own homes do so not from choice, but from necessity.'[42]

All mothers forced to earn wages were, then, identified as victims of one sort or another, although they evoked gradations of sympathy. Widows were regarded as the most blameless, their misfortune making them 'deserving' candidates for parish relief and for places on the work-schemes set up by local authorities under the 1905 Unemployed Workmen Act.[43] But their vulnerable position in the labour market was at the same time widely noted. Some employers treated taking on widows as a semi-philanthropic act and did not consider it necessary to pay a proper wage. One large manufacturer from Birmingham told a Select Committee in 1907 about a widowed mother with young children whom he employed in his wrapping department on eleven shillings a week. Parading his altruism, he added, 'I interested myself to get the parish relief as well, because I knew she would starve on that amount if she did not get it.' When pressed as to why he did not himself pay her enough to keep her family, the factory owner replied, 'It is not the place of any woman to support herself and three children. The man has to support the children.'[44] In other words, employers were not prepared to pay a female worker higher than the customary rate simply because she had unsupported dependants. This impossible position for women, suspended between the vicissitudes of the Poor Law and the intransigence of employers, gradually convinced policymakers that widows with young children had a legitimate claim to full State maintenance, although it was not until 1925 that a system of widows' pensions would be finally introduced.[45]

Wives with disabled husbands also tended to be judged kindly, whilst those with workless or under-employed husbands were viewed more ambiguously, which spoke to the concern voiced by Irwin – namely, that married women's employment was symptomatic of the fecklessness of working-class men. Some witnesses testifying before Parliament shared this belief that many fathers were unwilling, rather than unable, to provide for their families. An official from the Board of Trade investigating Black Country nail-making in the late 1880s expressed his fear that the numerous wives spotted toiling in workshops were 'the chief breadwinners of the households, many men taking advantage of the woman's ability to earn money by being comparatively idle themselves'.[46] The wife of a London laundry proprietor related to Collet the case of an employee whose husband appeared to be permanently unemployed right up to the day that she died, 'and then he seemed to find it quite easy to get work'.[47] Even Margaret MacDonald, co-founder of the Women's Labour League and a loyal defender of the working class, agreed that the employment of married women was damaging to men, because 'it lessens their feeling of responsibility as breadwinners; they are not so eager to get work, and not so careful to keep it when it is obtained'.[48]

MacDonald was quick to qualify this statement by noting that it was more often 'a bitter sorrow to a man that his wife is driven to do wage-earning work in his stead'. Yet her ambivalence reflected a wider uncertainty about the causes of male unemployment and low wages in this period. The very concept of 'unemployment' as a structural problem rather than a personalised masculine failing was itself relatively new.[49] Legislators slowly began to recognise that traditional forms of self-help such as Friendly Societies and sick clubs were plainly inadequate for protecting workers and their families from the cyclical fluctuations of the unregulated capitalist economy. They also became aware of the disquieting extent of low and irregular wage-earning amongst men and were more ready to admit the hopelessness of expecting a dock worker or general labourer to keep a large family respectably on a single pay packet. The middle-class investigators of women's work did a great deal to puncture the myth of the 'family wage' through their reports and surveys, piling up case upon case of married women compelled to go out or to take in work at home due to a husband's insufficient earnings. Clementina Black thought it 'clear that a man working in one of the numerous occupations which never supply an income adequate for the support of a family can never unaided fulfil that responsibility'.[50] Those who suggested that such men should abstain from marriage altogether, a position Black attributed to the stern political economists of the Charity Organisation Society, were simply evading a deeper problem.

The dominant picture to emerge from these debates presented working motherhood as, above all else, a response to dire economic need: women entered waged work to keep their families fed, sheltered and out of the workhouse. This was not a gross distortion of the reality. Wage-earning by mothers *was* a major strategy adopted by working-class families to avoid destitution and was always likeliest when a male breadwinning pay packet was, for whatever reason, unavailable.[51] Nonetheless, those studying married women's work in the later nineteenth century identified other dynamics, motives and behaviours which could not be easily accounted for by reference to pure economic pressure. For instance, nearly all surveys noted the existence of a class of wives who, despite being adequately supported by their husbands, went out to earn. Collet was surprised to see so many women engaged in bedstead-making in Birmingham, where factory conditions seemed to her 'most disagreeable'. She went on:

Curiously enough, however, this was a trade in which there seemed ample proof that women worked of their own free will. In the factory that I visited, nearly all the women were married, although in some cases their husbands were earning good wages. The Secretary of the Trade Union stated that out of about 2000 women and girls in the trade, fully 33 per cent, if not more, were married, and that frequently their husbands worked in the same trade and factory, and were quite able to support them.[52]

Miss Sharples, the Leeds sanitary inspector, was similarly confounded by wives and mothers who voluntarily added waged work to their unwaged labour in the home: 'when we realise what wage-earning means to a married woman,' she remarked, 'we wonder that any preference for it exists at all, for, in addition to the double burden of child-bearing and wage-earning, the time spent by the working man in amusements and recreation must be spent by her in trying to cope with the difficulties of housework, the washtub, and the kitchen oven.'[53]

Explanations were clearly needed for this seemingly irrational behaviour. One rather ambiguous answer touched upon by investigators of women's employment was 'custom'. This capacious term was frequently invoked in arguments over women's status as workers, deployed by employers to justify wage differentials and by trade unionists to keep women out of skilled occupations.[54] But it could also offer a rough kind of legitimacy to married women's labour in certain settings. Margaret Irwin suggested that the large number of mothers in the potteries and pipe factories of Glasgow was due to 'the custom among the men workers of employing their wives to finish for them'. The fragile materials required careful handling and many husbands seemed to trust their spouses to do this more competently than others – even though, as Irwin observed with some puzzlement, it meant 'leaving their homes and families to the care of strangers, while the money gain is small'.[55] 'Custom' seemed also to operate amongst jute workers in Dundee. An investigator for the Charity Organisation Society found that 'the public opinion of their class is in favour of the mother helping to support the family' through wage-earning, and she noted how this produced the peculiar effect whereby 'young couples calculate the family income on the basis of their *joint earnings*'.[56] This recognition of how married women's work contributed to distinctive regional or occupational cultures cropped up regularly in discussions about why mothers worked. It was referenced so routinely in relation to the Lancashire textile industry that 'custom' almost became an explanation in itself for that region's high maternal employment rates.

It was not the only way, however, of accounting for mothers who earned despite being under no obvious economic pressure to do so. Some appeared to be driven by the desire to enjoy a higher standard of living. In Blackburn, factory inspector Rose Squire discovered that 'comfortable houses and money to spend on excursions, holidays and amusements' were considered 'essentials' by textile operatives. In Hanley and Longton, her colleague Hilda Martindale quizzed twenty-four women with husbands in regular well-paid work on their reasons for going to the factory. In fourteen cases, she learned, the breadwinner's wage was judged too low to allow for saving or 'any additional comforts', and in the remaining ten, wives simply found the extra money 'very helpful'.[57] Neither Squire nor Martindale attributed great significance to these material aspirations, but Clementina Black did, having encountered mothers earning for a similar purpose in London. Black thoroughly approved:

> As a rule they are highly skilled and well remunerated; many of them pay for domestic help; the great majority buy educational advantages for their children; very often they are able to provide for health-giving holiday outings. Such women are nearly always conspicuously competent and marked by an independence of mind which I believe to be derived from the consciousness of their power of self-support.[58]

Ada Nield Chew painted a similarly favourable picture of the upwardly mobile working mother in the suffrage newspaper *Common Cause* in 1913. Chew related the story of Mrs Barton, a wage-earning mother from Manchester, whose acquaintance she made by chance at a seaside resort. Mrs Barton had given up her trade as a dressmaker upon marriage, but after a few years began to worry about how to provide for her daughter's education on the modest wage which her husband earned as a clerk. 'I can't bear to think of her going into a shop when she's fourteen,' she told her husband, 'I want to help in keeping her.' Despite her husband's initial resistance, Mrs Barton went ahead and hired a girl to help with housework, lined up her mother-in-law for after-school childcare and secured a job with her former employer. Her husband softened his stance and their daughter thrived, going on to win a scholarship to attend university. 'There is no prouder woman in England than Mrs Barton,' Chew wrote.[59] Decades later, these sorts of ambitions – for nicer homes, holidays away or educational opportunities for children – would be recognised as a major driving force behind the growing numbers of married women seeking to re-enter the workplace. In the 1890s and 1900s, however, Black and Chew were unusual for appreciating what wage-earning could mean to mothers who aspired to give their families a more hopeful future.

Clementina Black was also atypical in identifying paid work as a source of economic independence and perhaps even self-fulfilment for working-class mothers. She remarked upon the value which many informants in her 1909–10 survey placed on having money of their own: 'A shilling of your own is worth two that *he* gives you,' as one working mother put it. For the feminist-minded Black, this proved that the 'wave of desire for a personal working life which forms so marked an element in the general development of modern women touches and inspires even these humble and overdriven toilers'.[60] This was not, however, a widely held position in the years before the First World War. Middle-class feminists were increasingly vocal on the unequal distribution of resources within the working-class family, evoking images of selfish husbands handing over a fraction of their wage packets and keeping the rest for liquor and gambling. But whilst they believed married women had a right to keep their earnings (if they had any), they rarely recommended waged work outside the home as a positive solution for mothers.[61] The suffragist and settlement worker Anna Martin advocated instead giving wives a legal share of their husbands' wages, although the weight of opinion within bodies like the Women's Labour League and the Fabian Women's Group came to favour some system of State 'endowment', which would become family allowances after 1945 and child benefit after 1977.[62]

These debates accorded little priority to the question of whether mothers enjoyed their waged work or preferred it over housework. Where investigators noted a fondness for the workplace they viewed it as problematic, even pathological. On visiting the Staffordshire Potteries, Martindale recorded the 'universal preference' amongst married women for the factory and noted 'how depressed and out of health they became if they were obliged to remain at home'. This she explained in terms of the peculiar socialisation which women in manufacturing districts received in early life:

> At 13 years of age the majority of these women would have begun to work in a factory, to handle their own earnings, to mix with a large number of people with all the excitement and gossip of factory life. They would thus in most cases grow up entirely ignorant of everything pertaining to domesticity. After marriage, therefore, it is hardly probable that they would willingly relinquish this life to undertake work of which they are in so large measure ignorant, and which is robbed of all that is to them pleasant and exciting.[63]

It was the failure to prepare young women for marriage and motherhood which, in Martindale's view, produced this unhealthy 'preference' for wage-earning. Collet drew similar conclusions about the mothers she encountered in Birmingham. She thought the employment of married women was

> the worst feature in the industrial life of Birmingham ... The chief industries of the place necessitate the employment of girls in

processes absolutely useless to them in home life. After marriage they miss not only the cheerful society (for it is cheerful) of the factory, but also the steady work to which they have become accustomed, and for both reasons many of them persist in going to the factory.[64]

To compound matters, such wage-earning rarely brought any additional income into the household. Some of the married women Collet observed in Walsall 'went to the factory merely for company's sake, and hardly had any money over when they had paid for their washing and for looking after the children'. Margaret MacDonald offered an equally unfavourable pen-portrait of a young wife who had worked in a jam factory before marriage and now confessed herself horrified at the thought of staying 'at 'ome all dye [to] mind the blessed byby – it 'ud give me the bloomin' 'ump!' MacDonald closed her story on a disapproving note: 'So she earned 10/ a week in her jam factory instead, and paid her mother 5/ to mind and feed her poor little boy.'[65]

It is impossible to know what proportion of mothers employed in industry worked from choice rather than necessity, even allowing for the imprecision of these categories. Yet the ambiguous status of the voluntarily wage-earning mother in debates about women's work was of wider cultural and ideological significance. Mothers who worked for pay because they *wanted* to, rather than because they *had* to, imperilled the vision of domestic and economic order cherished by most middle-class Victorians. Women who earned, as Black put it, 'not for their own or their children's bread, but rather for butter for it', undermined the male breadwinner ideal and dishonoured the sacred duties of motherhood. These mothers stood apart from the widows, deserted wives and others genuinely facing destitution; wage-earning amongst those latter groups did harm, but less harm than the alternatives, which might be starvation, the workhouse or, worst of all, prostitution.[66] An invisible moral boundary-line separated those whose paid labour was regrettable but necessary from women whose reasons for going out were judged to be wholly without justification. A marker was set down in the late nineteenth century between the 'good' mother who earned only because she had to, and the 'bad' mother who went out because she wanted to. This dichotomy would prove enduring.

*

No issue did more to crystallise the distinctions between justified and unjustified wage-earning by mothers than the problem of infant mortality: the rate at which babies perished before their first birthday. The relationship between women's industrial labour and the loss of infant life was a subject of grave concern in the mid-nineteenth century, prompting much impassioned debate and statistical inquiry in the textile districts. The question moved sharply up the agenda of national policymakers in the 1880s when mortality figures revealed a shocking divergence between adult death rates, which were falling, and those of infants, which remained stubbornly high. Some of the highest rates were found in towns like Blackburn and Preston, where large numbers of mothers worked in factories. To the economist Stanley Jevons, this was nothing less than a national disgrace:

> Can such things be in a Christian country? Is the exclamation which rises to the lips in contemplating the mass of misery, and, especially, the infinite, irreparable wrong to helpless children, which is involved in the mother's employment at the mills.[67]

Over the next three decades, the crusade against infant mortality gathered apace, with a growing chorus of concerned citizens demanding legislative reform and municipal action. Prominent on their programme were measures to curb the wage-earning of mothers. As John Burns, President of the Local Government Board, told a national conference in 1906: 'We have got to restrict married women's labour as often and as soon as we can.'[68]

But why, exactly, were the offspring of wage-earning mothers believed to be at greater risk? To late Victorians, the causes appeared to be twofold. First, there were the effects on the unborn child of its mother performing heavy manual work late into pregnancy, which some medical authorities linked to premature labour, birth defects and an inability to suckle her infant. The second and, as contemporaries saw it, more serious problem, was the lamentable care received by babies sent out to nurse while the mother was at work. Horror stories surfaced of infants left in soapboxes and toddlers tied to bedsteads all day long; of 'old, worn-out, slatternly' women dozing inebriated whilst their charges played next to unguarded fires; of babies drugged with opiates so that minders could get on with their household chores undisturbed; and of tiny children being fed all manner of foodstuffs in place of their mother's breast. Investigators found contaminated cow's milk being habitually offered to babies and tins of condensed milk left open on a sideboard for days. Even where the milk was pure, it frequently reached the infant's mouth by means of 'dirty, fungus-bearing' bottles, sometimes via a long feeding tube which was impossible to keep clean. The children of factory mothers, it was routinely observed, were weaned too early, typically offered a 'taste of what's going' from the family table or a concoction of bread soaked in water and sweetened with sugar, known colloquially as 'pap'. One voluntary worker in Rochdale reported cases where babies under six months had been given raw tripe, fish and chips, pickled herrings and tinned salmon.[69] This diet wreaked havoc with babies' small, under-developed stomachs, and death by diarrhoea, typhoid or dysentery was often the result.[70]

Confronted with such a picture of neglect, it was not surprising that some voices within the infant life preservation movement felt moved to call for legislative reform. Jevons advocated the most drastic measure: a complete exclusion of all women with children under the age of three from factories and workshops. More commonplace were proposals to extend the 1891 law which already barred employers from 'knowingly' recruiting mothers within four weeks of giving birth, a regulation widely regarded as a dead letter. John Burns pushed for a period of compulsory withdrawal commencing six months into pregnancy and ending six months after birth, the hope being that women would use this time to rest and breastfeed their babies.

Interference with the worker's liberty to sell her labour was, in his view, wholly permissible given the enormity of the evil in question. The former lady factory inspector, May Tennant, agreed that 'the freedom to labour is no sacred right when its exercise involves injury to others'. There was, she argued, 'a danger to the race in the engagement in factory life of the mothers of young children ... sacrifice of infant life, failure of infant promise follow, have followed, and must follow, as surely as leaves fall to frost'.[71]

These proposals found a mixed response among policymakers, with whom the protestations of high-profile figures like Millicent Garrett Fawcett may have carried some weight. The suffragist leader was one of a number of well-connected feminists implacably opposed to restrictions on women's labour, who organised themselves through the provocatively named Women's Industrial Defence Committee and had the ear of leading Liberal politicians.[72] Yet Parliament had already passed the 1891 law, as well as legislation regulating women's employment in 'dangerous' trades such as white lead manufacturing, justified in part by purported risks to reproductive health.[73] Further measures to ban mothers from factories were thus inhibited not on principle but for more contingent reasons, including the lack of clear, conclusive evidence linking women's employment to infant death. Clara Collet's statistical expertise played an important role in casting doubt upon the case for legislative action. In an influential paper of 1898, she showed that the higher rates of infant mortality recorded in factory towns could be largely explained by the absence of better-off middle-class residents. When comparing infant deaths in manufacturing districts with working-class districts elsewhere, married women's employment paled in significance next to other factors, such as poor sanitation, insufficient household income and ignorance of proper infant care.[74] Adelaide Anderson endorsed this position in her submission to the Interdepartmental Committee on Physical Deterioration in 1904. She 'acknowledged the evil in evidence, but her appreciation of all the conditions of the problem led her to pause before subscribing to the prudence of any legislative change'.[75]

The investigations of the lady factory inspectors also alerted policymakers to the likely consequences of banning factory employment for mothers who relied on it for survival. In its final report, the Interdepartmental Committee advised against prohibition, largely taking its cue from Anderson's evidence. The Committee acknowledged that there existed 'a considerable number of unmarried mothers' whose 'main chance of rescue from degradation lies in the fact that they desire to labour and know they ought to labour in support of their infants', as well as the 'large proportion of married mothers who are necessarily the chief breadwinners of their families'. Given these pressures to earn, many new mothers would seek to evade any employment ban and some, it was suggested, might attempt to conceal their pregnancies or even to abort them. No one doubted that the presence of mothers in factories was 'attended by evil consequences both to themselves and their children', but in pursuing measures to reduce the harm caused the Committee advised 'extreme caution'.[76]

Mothers faced, then, no further restrictions on their factory employment, but hardly anyone was prepared to make a *positive* case for measures to support those mothers as they juggled their dual responsibilities. The infant lifesaving initiatives of the early twentieth century were overwhelmingly focused on educating the working-class mother in her 'proper' duties as full-time nurturer and homemaker. Municipal authorities and voluntary societies sent lady health visitors into slums to teach infant hygiene, opened sterilised milk depots and restaurants for breastfeeding mothers, and established welfare centres to weigh babies and distribute advice.[77] How working mothers fitted into these initiatives was not always clear. Some of the restaurants offered free meals on the express condition that recipients refrain from wage-earning, whilst the hours of baby clinics assumed that mothers were at home during the day. Attitudes towards nurseries and French-style workplace crèches were deeply ambivalent. Few doubted that, where properly run, these institutions saved infant life, but if provided on too wide a basis they risked encouraging more mothers to work. When one Medical Officer of Health, addressing a conference in 1906, tentatively proposed that employers fit out 'cradle-rooms' in their factories where mothers could suckle their babies throughout the day, he met with a hostile response from a Huddersfield delegate, who thought the idea 'absolutely ridiculous'. Employers would not do it, the delegate insisted, 'and what was more he, as a workman, did not want to see it done. The remedy was to keep the mother at home, and in order to keep the mothers at home the employers of the country must give the men more wages.'[78]

There was greater support for schemes of collective self-help modelled on the maternity funds which already existed in Germany. These were funded by regular insurance contributions from both employer and employee and allowed working mothers to take time off with pay after childbirth. But those advocating such arrangements in Britain did not do so out of any wish to place wage-earning by mothers on a more stable, institutionalised footing. George Newman, a Medical Officer in London and prominent authority on infant mortality, favoured the maternity fund model precisely because it would discourage mothers from making an early return to the factory. The Liberal MP Leo Chiozza Money similarly endorsed compulsory maternity insurance on the basis that it would prove inconvenient to the employer and hence result in fewer married women in the workforce: 'Thus penalised he will probably prefer not to employ them, to the very great advantage of the labour market and the nation.'[79]

The concept of maternity leave as a statutory period of withdrawal from employment followed by reinstatement did not figure in these debates in the way that it would in the later twentieth century.[80] The four-week exclusion period stipulated in the 1891 law did not bestow upon mothers any right to return to their jobs or to receive maternity pay. Under the 1911 National Insurance Act, married women workers became entitled to a one-off maternity benefit of £3, which was considerably more than the 30s received by non-earning wives, to cover such costs as doctors' fees, home helps and baby linen. But there is no evidence to suggest that this benefit was intended to normalise the employment status of married women, who, in most other respects, were shabbily treated in the

Act. Under its terms, women who had paid National Insurance contributions before marriage lost their entitlement to all benefits, including unemployment and sickness benefit, when they married. If they continued to earn, they had to build up their contributions again from scratch, a rule which was not applied to married men.

*

If any consensus existed between the 1880s and the outbreak of the First World War on the subject of wage-earning mothers, it was this: many mothers, through no fault of their own, *had* to go out to work and it was therefore better that they should be permitted to do so and that their children should not unduly suffer for it. Nonetheless, under ideal circumstances, a mother would be properly supported in her unwaged work inside the home, a full-time occupation of the highest possible value to the community. Bodies representing working-class housewives, like the Women's Labour League and the Women's Co-operative Guild, were especially insistent on this point because they wished to see lofty public rhetoric about the sacred duties of motherhood matched by positive State action to improve women's lives. This meant funding maternal and infant welfare centres, building higher quality housing and recognising that housewives, like working men, needed and deserved outlets for leisure and self-cultivation. As these organisations saw it, raising the status of the mother in the home, rather than adding to her burden the pressure of doing waged work outside it, was the surest way of securing women's welfare and well-being.[81]

There can be no doubt that these demands reflected the lived experience of many working-class mothers. Where their voices speak to us directly, as they do in the extraordinary collection of letters published by the Women's Co-operative Guild in 1915 on the subject of maternity, they describe strenuous lives marked by frequent childbearing, back-breaking housework and chronic poor health.[82] What these mothers craved most was rest, repose and tolerable conditions in which to bring up their children.[83] These aspirations were deeply felt, but when translated into policy positions by the Guild's leadership, they nonetheless shored up the ideology perpetuated by restrictive labour laws and male trade unionists, which specified mothering as women's work and breadwinning as the responsibility of men. The consequences for mothers employed in industry – both the 'good' mothers who did so from necessity and the 'bad' ones who went out of choice – were damaging. They were accorded an inferior status in the workplace and were denied the material support which might have actually helped them meet their dual responsibilities as workers and mothers.

There was one further effect of this broad agreement over the undesirability of employing mothers outside their homes. It pushed many women instead into the unregulated and anarchic universe of casual, low-paid work *inside* the home, which factory legislation could not touch nor trade unions apparently penetrate. Hundreds of thousands of women, including some of the respectable members of the Women's Co-operative Guild, took in needlework or washing, stitched tennis balls or assembled fancy boxes to earn a few much-needed shillings for the family. By not 'going out', they avoided much of the censure directed at women factory hands for neglecting their homes and children. But as investigators turned their gaze to the problem of so-called 'sweated' labour in the late nineteenth century, these home-working mothers were found guilty of causing a different kind of harm, and one potentially just as serious.

2

'The Essential Element of Evil'

Visitors to London's West End in May 1906 searching for a few hours' diversion might have found themselves drawn to the Queen's Hall, Langham Place, home to the Sweated Industries Exhibition. This high-minded attraction dedicated to exposing the plight of the low-paid home-worker had momentarily become the talk of the town. For one shilling, those gaining admittance could watch a collection of 'pale and bent women' and a couple of 'worn-looking men' toiling at their trades inside the hall, each showcasing items disturbingly familiar to the middle-class consumer, from smart overcoats and dainty baby linen to fancy chocolate boxes and colourful artificial flowers.

Placards hanging next to these human exhibits described the work being performed, the length of the average working day, the pitiful piece rates paid and the princely sum at which the item was typically sold on the market. Onlookers could also learn about the unenviable domestic circumstances of each worker. No. 15 had 'lost her husband, in a very tragical manner, some years ago', and was now maintaining herself and 'two weakly children' by making baby bonnets. No. 40 plied her trade of book-folding in order to support an unemployed husband and six children. Daily lantern shows arrested viewers with sombre photographic images of women sewing sacks or gluing matchboxes in dingy, cramped homes. In total, some 30,000 visitors passed through the exhibition hall, which stayed open an extra two weeks in June to meet popular demand. The *Daily News*, the liberal-leaning newspaper and the exhibition's chief sponsor, described the event as 'a great social object-lesson', and looked forward to the time when it would be remembered 'as the first stage in the great social movement which finally resulted in a Happy England'.[1]

Poor wage-earning mothers featured prominently in the crusade against sweated industries which gathered force in early twentieth-century Britain. But what exactly *was* a 'sweated' industry? For late Victorian and Edwardian observers, sweating occurred wherever workers laboured for excessively long hours in terrible conditions and for pay set too low even to support basic human subsistence. Many believed it to be a fundamental feature of unrestricted competition in the economy, giving rise to 'parasitic' industries which thrived, as one agitator put it, 'with the horrible rapidity and vigour of a poisonous creeper in a South American forest'.[2] Sweating had a long history stretching back to the 1840s, and was linked to male as well as female trades, but in the final decades of the nineteenth century it became closely identified with women employed in 'home-work', a category encompassing numerous forms of waged manual labour which could be performed by the worker in her own dwelling.[3] As we shall see, some observers extolled home-work as a flexible means by which mothers could contribute much-needed household income without neglecting their domestic duties. But most surveying the sweated nation judged such women to be 'the poorest of all' workers, toiling in ways which had no proper place in modern industry or a civilised society.[4]

One reason why home-work was framed as a backward labour practice was the fact that much of the waged work performed by women in or close to their homes appeared to be largely unchanged from earlier, pre-industrial times. Taking in lodgers, minding babies, washing or sewing for neighbours, hawking on the street or keeping small shops were strategies employed by wives and mothers to get by long before the coming of the Industrial Revolution. Furthermore, whilst a large portion of textile production moved from cottage to factory in the nineteenth century, many industries remained structured on the traditional 'putting out' system: this involved a skilled craftsman taking in work from a larger merchant, with the actual labour performed in a workshop by waged hands, some of whom might be family members. This kind of out-work was still common in industries employing large numbers of women in the early twentieth century, including hosiery, glove-making, lace-making, tailoring, dressmaking and millinery. The 1911 census counted over 650,000 needlewomen alone, of whom a significant proportion were married or widowed and hence likely to be mothers.[5] Most single women were employed in small workshops rather than at home, although their pay, status and conditions could vary dramatically across a spectrum which stretched from the smart fashion houses of Knightsbridge or Mayfair to the cramped sweatshops of Whitechapel and Stepney. Married women, by contrast, were more frequently home-workers confined to the lowest-grade 'slop-work', most typically stitching buttonholes on to shirts or finishing trousers for less than a shilling a day.[6]

Out-work also persisted in the small metal trades located in the villages of the Black Country, which had been a centre for the manufacture of locks, nails, nuts, bolts, screws, rivets, buckles, bits and stirrups since the eighteenth century. Visiting the district as an investigator for the Board of Trade in 1888, John Burnett estimated that some 15,000 nail-makers and perhaps a further 4,000 chain-makers were still practising their trade in small, brick workshops attached to their cottages, contracting with middlemen known locally as 'foggers'. Women and girls were widely employed in these crude, tumbledown structures, open, with their unglazed windows, 'to every wind that blows'.[7] They worked alongside husbands, brothers and fathers, beating rods of metal into shape with a few simple tools including the 'oliver' – a spring-tilt hammer operated by a treadle at the worker's foot. Burnett spied many mothers occupied at their anvils with small children playing nearby, dangling in slings suspended from the rafters or laid out to slumber on the bellows.

The toiling figure of the needlewoman in her dingy garret or the chain-maker at her humble forge might indeed have appeared utterly removed from the capital-intensive industries which Victorians believed had made their economy the envy of the world. Yet in truth, home-work was not a relic of the pre-industrial past but evolved hand in hand with the modern factory system. Employers could drive up productivity by investing in machinery and disciplining their operatives on the shop floor, but using home-workers was an effective strategy in sectors vulnerable to fluctuating demand, volatile consumer tastes and fierce competition. A great deal of home-work was found in firms manufacturing cheap articles – tennis balls, artificial flowers, umbrellas, tents, matchboxes, toothbrushes, beads, belts, neckties and ladies' fans – for the mass market. Rather than taking on extra hands or spending money on machines which might periodically stand idle, employers turned to home-workers, who could be engaged and dismissed as business required.

Charles Watts, a box manufacturer, told a group of MPs in 1907 that his firm had started using home-workers as far back as the 1840s and that he currently had between 300 and 400 names on his books, many of them former employees. 'When people leave us to get married,' he explained, 'they usually apply to us to be put on the list for home-work, if they should want it, and if we are satisfied with the way in which they have conducted themselves whilst with us, we put them on the list.'[8] Margaret Irwin noted a similar arrangement at the Glasgow rubber factory which she visited for the Royal Commission on Labour. Women who had worked 'inside' before marriage now formed a reserve force of home-workers, an arrangement which 'obviated the necessity for taking on fresh hands in the workrooms and paying them off when the slack time came on'.[9] Furthermore, in some factories, it was common for operatives to take work home to finish in the evenings, an employer's way of getting round statutory restrictions on women's working hours. Far from occupying a peripheral space outside the 'real' economy, home-work was integral to the organisation of production within Britain's expanding consumer industries.

*

It was hard for policymakers to comprehend how pervasive home-work was in industry, in part because so many home-workers were invisible to official statisticians. Women who regularly took in work but happened to have none at the time of the census were usually recorded as unoccupied, which casts doubt on the tentative estimate of 450,000 home-workers across England and Wales offered by a Home Office official in 1907.[10] The lists which local authorities had been obliged to keep since the early 1890s were practically useless, as firms could not be relied upon to submit accurate returns of the home-workers they employed every six months. This left a vacuum which was filled by impressionistic evidence, colourful anecdote and information peculiar to particular districts or trades. Irwin described home-work as 'an unknown country, without chart or beaten tracks, and in which the boundaries and landmarks are constantly shifting'.[11]

Mapping this strange territory was no simple task when conditions could vary so dramatically. Calculating the average length of the home-worker's day was complicated because her waged labour was frequently interrupted by unwaged chores, particularly if there were small children underfoot or other family members appearing at dinner time expecting to be fed. Some home-workers received the work from a middleman – or woman. In Birmingham a gaggle of old women operated as contractors for six major hook-and-eye firms, loading up their wheelbarrows and perambulators daily and dispersing the work amongst their regulars.[12] Others had to fetch the materials and deliver the finished goods themselves. This could take ten minutes if the factory was nearby, or it could consume several hours if the journey was long and the worker was made to wait upon arrival. Children were often sent instead, lugging large parcels of carefully wrapped boxes or bundles of freshly lined trousers through the streets.

Some women worked steadily all year round, but for others the work was intermittent or seasonal. Dressmakers always expected to be unemployed for several months of the year, usually after Christmas when trade was slack. At these times, many home-workers turned to other sources of income. A trouser-finisher told parliamentarians in 1888 that when business was slow she was 'glad to get anything to do, a bit of cleaning or washing. I cannot be without work, as I have three little ones to support.'[13] Investigators in east London observed the energy and resourcefulness with which mothers filled in the year

> with few gaps, between the jam and ginger beer factories, with the addition of indefinite charing and mending. The baby will be out at a subsidised crèche or in charge of a subsidised grandmother. The same person at different times may be found at matchbox-making, hopping, step-cleaning and hawking.[14]

Despite this astonishing variety, observers of home-work in the 1890s and 1900s believed that these trades had one feature in common: sweating. Curiously, given its ubiquitous presence in public debate, this term lacked a precise definition. Some associated it with the practice of sub-contracting, in which the much-hated middleman stood as chief instigator of cut-throat competition and ever-falling wages. Following inquiries by a House of Lords Committee between 1888 and 1890, sweating came to be understood as potentially applicable to any industry in which wages were low, hours long and conditions insanitary. A prevalent theme before immigration restrictions were introduced by the Aliens Act of 1905 was the role played by 'foreign' or 'alien' labour, mostly Jewish migrants fleeing anti-Semitism in Russia and Eastern Europe and finding work in the clothing trades of London, Manchester and Leeds.[15] Yet concerns about these mostly male immigrants were overshadowed by fears about female home-workers as the debate over sweating intensified around 1906–7 and a House of Commons Select Committee was appointed to investigate the matter in depth.[16] Like married women in factories, home-working by mothers was believed to result from a male breadwinner's failure to provide. But because home-workers' earnings were so low – too low to maintain the individual worker, in many cases, let alone any dependants – it seemed important to identify the deeper reasons for the persistence of this monstrously exploitative form of labour. How was the sweater allowed to perpetuate his crime?

One answer lay in the erratic employment patterns of the home-working mother, which could expand and contract as needs required. 'The husband is out of work, and the wife at once goes round to the nearest place where she knows work is to be found,' noted the factory inspector Rose Squire in her testimony before the Commons Committee. It was the same story, she insisted, for women married to men in low-paid occupations:

> The casual labourer's wife, such as the dock labourer, is employed in home work in the same way as the man who is unemployed. He is a dock labourer, but that is casual work, and she goes backwards and forwards to the shop for work on the days when he comes home, saying there is no work at the docks.[17]

Margaret Irwin agreed that many women only took work in when male trades were slack: 'You may have an unemployed tailor's wife getting the work at one time of the year, and an unemployed shipbuilder's wife at another part of the year, and so on, and each will drop out again when her husband gets employment.'[18]

These irregular work habits stemmed also from the fact that mothers were often balancing wage-earning with the care of small children, which was a major factor preventing them from seeking better-paid employment in factories. The Commons Committee heard the story of Mrs T., who secured a factory job after her husband fell out of work but gave it up when her baby caught pneumonia, a result, the mother claimed, of being placed on a wet floor by the girl she had engaged on 3s 6d a week to look after her three children.[19] Some mothers judged that higher wages in the factory would be offset by the costs of domestic help, making home-work by comparison a more attractive option. Miss Nora Vynne of the National Home Workers' League relayed the view held by her 3,000 members, namely, that '9s earned at home is worth 14s earned in a factory':

> They say that what you earn in a factory you earn to give away. What you earn at home you earn for yourself. They explain that

if they go to the factory they must pay someone to look after
the children. They must pay for their washing to be done, and
they must buy cooked tinned meats, which are expensive ... If
they stay at home they can do their own house-work and their
own shopping; and they lay special stress on better meals for
their children, and the fact that they can get their children off
comfortably to school and know that they do go to school, and
can receive them properly when they come in, and see if they are
wet or dry.[20]

Miss Vynne's League was opposed on principle to any regulation of
home-work, which might have coloured this rather rosy presentation
of its advantages for women. By contrast, the trade unionist Mary
Macarthur claimed that the majority of home-workers 'would
prefer to have regular work in the factory' and that taking in work
was 'a kind of last resource of the unemployed woman in many
cases'.[21] In practice, the 'choice' for mothers between factory and
home-work was often an artificial one. Factory jobs for married
women were not available everywhere, and nor were affordable
baby-minders or 'subsidised grandmothers'. Similarly, the kind of
home-work on offer varied between regions and industries and was
determined by how different employers structured their businesses.

Yet those seeking to explain the persistence of home-work
downplayed this broader context of constraint and opportunity,
focusing instead on how domestic ties 'naturally' incapacitated
married women as workers. A revealing exchange between the MP
Stuart Samuel and the Chief Inspector of Factories for Birmingham,
Robert Graves, during a session of the 1907 Commons Committee
illustrates the point. Graves described the typical week of one home-
worker whom he had recently visited, a married woman and French
polisher by trade. Two days of the week she did 'housework of some
sort', but 'when she could spare time on four days she worked and
got 6s for her work'. Samuel seized on Graves' turn of phrase:

Samuel: That is what I want to get from you – 'when she could
spare time'. I suppose these women work intermittently; when

they have time not looking after the baby or their housework they sit and do this work?'

Graves: Yes ... the woman has probably left the factory in most cases to get married, and then she has her household duties to attend to.[22]

French polishing took several years to learn and normally had the status of a skilled trade, but in this case both men gave far greater weight to the woman's domestic circumstances. In their eyes, the fact she was a wife and mother defined her as a casual, irregular worker, regardless of the intricate work that she performed four days a week.

Many observers assumed that maintaining any sort of occupational proficiency was unlikely given the interrupted rhythm of the home-worker's day and the episodic nature of her employment. Policymakers found their eyes drawn towards 'hard' cases which exemplified how ill-equipped the home-worker was to compete with the more efficient – and often unmarried – factory worker. There was, for example, the tailoress and deserted mother in Glasgow who had pawned most of her possessions and was 'faint for want of food' when Irwin visited her.[23] There was Mrs S., discovered by Graves in Birmingham, who had a partially paralysed hand and could only card hooks and eyes for ten minutes at a time before needing to lie down.[24] And there were the careworn faces, undernourished bodies and pitiful stories of many of the home-workers who appeared before both the Lords Committee in 1888 and the Commons Committee two decades later. These women described their daily struggle to survive, shocking the parliamentarians with details of minuscule earnings, woefully inadequate diets and infirm family members in need of constant care. The trouser-finisher Mary Hayes struck an especially tragic figure. Widowed for nineteen years, she had picked up the trade after her husband's death but had never achieved speed or skill, having children to attend to and suffering from poor health herself. Her 'nerves', she said, stopped her from using a sewing machine, and the long-standing abscess on the back of her eye made it 'hard work sometimes to see to thread the needle'. Her 'ordinary food' was bread and a cup of tea, a piece of fried fish for dinner and perhaps some meat on a Sunday, 'if I can possibly at all'.[25]

It was self-evident to these policymakers that half-starved women stretched to their limit keeping their families alive would find it difficult, if not impossible, to command high wages in the labour market. The Lords Committee concluded in 1890 that the large numbers of married women 'working at unskilled labour in their homes' were a major contributor to sweating, a verdict echoed subsequently by the Commons Committee.[26] Home-work, the latter noted, was performed by women 'whose circumstances, household duties, feeble health, age, invalid husband, parents, or children, render it impossible or difficult for them to undertake regular work in factories'. Many of these women were, 'from one cause or another, industrial, physical, and social wrecks'.[27] All agreed that no human being could possibly survive on the piece rates typically paid by the sweater. So how, then, did home-workers manage to live?

*

One solution to the pitifully low income of home-workers was found in the use of child labour. Investigators noted that the home-worker's weekly wage was often the result of joint rather than individual effort, with help from other family members enabling the mother to produce a larger quantity of goods and therefore to push up her earnings just enough to make ends meet. Rose Squire witnessed children doing 'little incidental things' to help before and after school in the glove-making districts, whilst in the homes of Nottingham lace-makers at dinner time 'you find the children without having removed their hats or jackets busy at the lace work ... They will be at work in the evening on their return, and in the neighbours' houses as well as in their mothers' houses.'[28] Graves observed children assisting with hook-and-eye carding in Birmingham homes: 'They cannot sew,' he explained, 'but first of all the row of hooks is sewn on, and then the mother will pass that over to the tiny little child, and she hooks the eyes to it, and then the mother has to go over that card again and sew on those eyes.'[29] A few witnesses considered these tasks closer to 'play' than to work. A colleague of Miss Vynne's from the National League of Homeworkers described a little girl helping her mother 'snip' as she sewed on the hooks and eyes, 'doing it purely for pleasure'.[30] Yet most viewed the practice in the gravest possible terms. The factory employment of children had been largely eliminated by the end of the nineteenth century through a combination of restrictive legislation and compulsory education, the one exception being the 'half-timer' system still in operation in Lancashire. This allowed children aged twelve or older to work a daily shift in the mill, either morning or afternoon, with the rest of the day spent at school. Nonetheless, a Parliamentary Committee in 1903 estimated that some 200,000 children were wage-earning outside the textile districts, chiefly by delivering newspapers, errand-running for shopkeepers, street-hawking, baby-minding and helping mothers with home-work.[31]

There was no doubt that these children's schoolwork and health suffered as a result. The trade unionist Gertrude Tuckwell cited evidence from Trowbridge, where children kept home from school to sort dirty feathers had developed enlarged tonsils and serious breathing problems. One boy was asked by his teacher why he was late for school and had to confess that after finishing his newspaper round he had been up until midnight helping his mother with her work.[32] Yet the evils of child labour were not just moral and physical, they were also economic. As Clementina Black observed, 'When a mother is being paid at the rate of a penny to two-pence an hour and sees her children hungry, the temptation to add a few more pennies by setting the children to work grows overwhelming.' No woman could be blamed for taking such a step, Black conceded, yet the practice was ultimately 'suicidal' because the employer would never stop pressing to lower the piece rates.[33] Some claimed that *all* women workers suffered as a consequence, not just the home-worker. This was the view of one Glasgow factory hand quoted in 1897 in the periodical press:

Married women take the work home, and sit up half the night to do it; and lots of them get their children to help them after school hours. They can thus lift fairly good wages at the week-end, and when we complain, the manager says, 'Look at So-and-so's big pay. Why can't you make this with the same rates?' And in the end the rates are reduced for everybody.[34]

Many believed that the same pernicious effects resulted where home-workers received poor relief to bring their incomes up to subsistence level. Rose Squire discovered many matchbox-makers and glovers to be in receipt of outdoor relief during her enquiries for the Home Office, whilst Mary Macarthur referred to several cases where up to three-quarters of the home-worker's weekly income came from the parish. Tuckwell put it with characteristic bluntness: 'the inefficient woman ... has to have poor relief or starve. Sometimes she starves. She generally has poor relief.'[35] Some members of the Commons Committee feared that such practices subsidised unprofitable industries and dragged down wages more generally, although conclusive proof of this was lacking. Parallel investigations carried out for the Royal Commission on the Poor Laws (1906–9) found that the proportion of home-workers receiving relief at any one time was far too small to exert any general influence on wage-setting.[36] In Poplar, fewer than one in ten home-workers were found to be in receipt of relief, whilst in West Ham, the figure was even lower.[37] Furthermore, the effect of relief in individual cases was unpredictable. There were women who used the cushion of a regular parish income to continue with casualised low-paid work, but others felt able to demand *higher* wages because the threat of destitution had been removed.

The chief mainstay for the sweated home-worker was, undoubtedly, not the Poor Law but the wages brought in by other members of the family, to which her own precarious earnings made a fluctuating contribution. In its 1897 survey, the Women's Industrial Council noted the case of an artificial flower-maker in Clerkenwell, who took in only small quantities of work because piece rates in the trade had fallen and her eyes were bad. She and her unemployed husband survived primarily on six shillings a week earned by a fourteen-year-old son and another six from a nineteen-year-old daughter, who was also able to bring home spare scraps of food from her job as a cook. As well as making a few flowers, the woman added a shilling or so to the purse by cleaning the ground floor of the building in which the family rented their rooms.[38] A cardboard-box-maker visited by the same investigator received thirteen shillings from her husband's dock work plus a few shillings from an adult son, but there were three children still at school and the family were in real difficulties when her own work was slack, as it happened to be at the time of the survey.[39]

*

Examples of the kind given above exposed a fundamental ambiguity in the debate over home-work as it unfolded in the late nineteenth and early twentieth centuries. What exactly were the earnings of home-working wives and mothers *for*? Most experts cited poverty as the chief cause driving women into this kind of work, but some noted the existence, in Rose Squire's words, of a 'class of women whose husbands earn regularly a fair wage, but where the wife has a higher standard of living, and desires to have money over which she herself has control, and which she can spend in extra comforts for the children and herself'.[40] Clara Collet was insistent that a large portion of home-workers were manifestly *not* on the brink of starvation but rather wished to 'spend the money on all sorts of things that they desire to have in addition to the necessities of life that they have'.[41] A paper-box manufacturer confirmed that amongst his home-workers were 'respectable' women who 'make a point of having their summer holiday, and that is from what the wife has provided out of her earnings or savings'.[42]

Like the factory mothers earning for 'extras' in Lancashire, these aspirations were noted but quickly sidelined by experts debating the evils of sweating. Such women did not fit easily into their larger analysis of the economic harm caused by home-working. One especially prominent voice belonged to Beatrice Webb (or Beatrice Potter, as she was at the time), who spent a formative decade as a young woman in the 1880s visiting the poor for the Charity Organisation Society, rent collecting at a block of working-class dwellings, and going undercover as a tailoress whilst investigating the clothing trades for Charles Booth's survey of London.[43] In 1888, Webb was invited to address the Lords Committee on Sweating, whose members were impressed by her eloquent and concise remarks about the oversupply of unskilled labour in the garment industry, especially female home-workers, whom she described as 'the lowest channel of the trade'.[44] Webb was pleased to see this observation reproduced in the Committee's final report, which presented married women as posing an even graver danger than 'pauper immigration' when it came to the problem of low wages. As Webb wrote in her review of the report, the supply of foreign labour was limited, whereas the women who came knocking at the sweater's door, 'dragging in their rear semi-dependent husbands and a huge force of unprotected children, may be numbered by hundred thousands'.[45]

Over the next ten years, Beatrice Webb developed and advanced a case for the extension of State intervention into the lives of women workers. She wanted to protect the woman who toiled honestly for her livelihood in a skilled trade from the casual 'amateur', a category into which Webb placed wives and mothers who did home-work. She gave short shrift to arguments about the inalienable right of these workers to contract out their labour:

> The 'freedom' of the poor widow to work, in her own bedroom, 'all the hours that God made'; and the wife's privilege to supplement a drunken husband's wages by doing work at her own fireside, are, in sober truth, being purchased at the price of the exclusion from regular factory employment of thousands of 'independent women.'[46]

This claim that the sweated home-worker was an 'enemy to her sex' gained further firepower from the economist and socialist Sidney Webb, whom Beatrice married in 1892. Giving evidence to the Royal Commission on Labour, he described home-work as a 'demoralising form of employment' and 'the essential element of evil' within the sweating system.[47] He recommended making landlords and employers responsible for monitoring sanitary conditions in home-workers' dwellings, which he hoped would discourage factory owners from sending out work in the first place.

Five years later, the Webbs joined forces on their 900-page magnum opus, *Industrial Democracy*, which warned readers that 'parasitic' industries sustained by underpaid home-workers were 'subtly draining away the vital energy of the community'. Their chief prescription was a national minimum wage, which would destroy the sweater's power to undercut his competitors at a stroke and force the reorganisation of industries reliant on home-work along more rational lines. The Webbs acknowledged that such an intervention might make it impossible for the most inefficient workers, including many home-working mothers, to sell their labour at all. But, on the positive side, they argued, it would 'set free for domestic duties, an ever increasing proportion of the women having young children to attend to'.[48] For the Webbs, a modern industrial order was one in which able-bodied men and unmarried women worked in factories, whilst wives and mothers cared for their families and homes. As Sidney Webb replied when asked by the Royal Commission on Labour whether it was preferable for a mother to do waged work at home or in a factory, 'I would much prefer to bring about such a condition of society in which the mother of a family did not work for her living at all.'[49]

The Webbs were formative voices within a wider current of liberal, radical and socialist thought which reshaped progressive politics in Britain around the turn of the twentieth century.[50] Their diagnosis of home-working's ills fitted into a larger account of how the old orthodoxies of economic individualism were being displaced by new models of State-led collectivist action. Many of those behind the Sweated Industries Exhibition of 1906 subscribed to this broad prescription for social reform, even if they differed on points of theory and detail. The exhibition's organising committee included: G. P. Gooch, Charles Masterman and Leo Chiozza Money, all progressive Members of Parliament returned in the

Liberal election victory of that year; the economist and journalist J. A. Hobson, who had devoted an entire chapter to sweated women workers in his popular 1891 book, *Problems of Poverty*; and familiar figures from the women's trade union movement, including Gertrude Tuckwell, Mary Macarthur and Clementina Black. These individuals formed the core of the National Anti-Sweating League, established shortly after the exhibition had closed, and enjoyed a strong presence at the Commons Select Committee on Home Work, either as witnesses or, in the cases of Gooch, Masterman and Money, the parliamentarians asking the questions.[51]

These agitators against sweating also agreed on the need for legislative action. The League favoured Wages Boards (also known as Trade Boards), which had already been tried with some success in Australia and New Zealand and were intended to bring employers and workers together to agree minimum rates in trades where low wages were endemic. This model fell considerably short of the *universal* minimum wage advocated by the Webbs, but the dramatic political traction which it gained in the aftermath of the Exhibition marked, nonetheless, a new consensus in favour of State action to tackle low pay.[52] The close identification of home-working mothers with sweating was crucial in securing this consensus because it helped to convince nearly everyone concerned that the obvious alternative remedy – trade union organisation – was not a viable option. As the Commons Committee observed: 'Women home workers, because they are very poor and helpless, and work separately, are unorganised, and cannot act together to promote common interests and secure better and uniform rates of payment.'[53] For A. G. Gardiner, the radical editor of the *Daily News*, it was 'the State alone which can take care of them, protect them against the rapacity of the oppressor and, in protecting them, protect itself also'.[54]

*

The image of home-working mothers as a dangerously vulnerable element in the labour market gained further power from the many literary and visual representations which swirled around the public debate over sweating. Late nineteenth-century social investigation was itself a genre-crossing blend of statistics and sentiment, empiricism and emotionalism.[55] It was perhaps irresistible, when writing about the slum-dwelling shirt-finisher, to use the sensationalist narratives of the 'New Journalism' – a brash style of investigative reporting sweeping the popular press from the 1880s – or to adopt the language of colonial adventurism and cultural encounter characteristic of late Victorian travel literature.[56] In such texts, sweaters always resided in 'dens', breeding on 'decaying and disorganised matter', whilst home-workers were invariably 'slaves', hidden away in the 'holes and corners of our cities' and inhabiting the 'dark places of the earth'. The spectre of degeneration and social contamination was endlessly conjured by middle-class observers who were courageous (or voyeuristic) enough to descend into this dangerous underworld with its peculiar sights and nauseating smells. The Women's Industrial Council investigator, Edith Hogg, presented herself as one such intrepid explorer to the well-to-do readers of the Victorian periodical press. She described her search for the fur-pullers of Southwark: women who spent their days extracting coarse hairs from rabbit skins, which often arrived from the middle man unwashed and covered in congealed blood. This mission led Hogg through labyrinthine alleys and courts where 'the very flies seem to lose the power of flight and creep and crawl in sickly, loathsome adhesion to mouldering walls and ceilings'. There she found 'inert, exhausted' women plying their revolting trade in tiny, windowless attics. Their utter demoralisation was plain to see: 'want and filth and disease are the normal inevitable conditions of existence, against which they lack the will as well as the power to rebel.'[57]

Mary Macarthur similarly sought to stir the emotions in her many articles and speeches on sweating. She was a talented storyteller, well-known for her 'parables' on the benefits of trade unionism published in *The Woman Worker*, the newspaper Macarthur founded in September 1907. In one leading article, Macarthur wrote of a scam she had uncovered in London, whereby infant clothing produced by sweated home-workers was being misleadingly advertised and sold via mail-order as items lovingly crafted by a bereaved mother.[58] Macarthur tugged even harder on her readers' heart-strings with the image reproduced in a glossy insert for *The Woman Worker*'s inaugural issue. Drawn by the American illustrator and cartoonist Luther D. Bradley, 'Sacred Motherhood' depicted a grim-faced woman seated at her sewing machine, a tiny baby at her breast and two ragged children in the background. The picture, Macarthur wrote, 'is not an exaggerated one', but 'epitomises the pathos and tragedy of the life of the sweated home worker'.[59] It contained the same motifs as the disturbing drawing which adorned the cover of the catalogue for the Sweated Industries Exhibition: a female figure stooped over her work, forlorn children beside her, and dwellings which are cramped, under-furnished and insanitary.[60]

These images recalled an older artistic tradition stretching back to the 1840s, when the impoverished needlewoman in her garret became a popular subject for painters, inspired by Thomas Hood's famous poem, 'The Song of the Shirt'.[61] A lament to the unremitting toil of a destitute seamstress, Hood's verse was published anonymously in *Punch* in 1843 but remained a cultural reference point well into the twentieth century. Early visual depictions tended to feature pale but sweet-faced women working alone, sometimes bathed in light or with eyes cast upwards, hinting at the salvation that was to come in the afterlife. This spiritual dimension was missing later in the century, when artists such as Edward Radford and Albert Rutherston aimed for an unflinching realism in their treatments of the subject, and when the visual grammar of sweating was recast again by photography, a medium much used by late Victorians to document social problems and pathologies.[62]

With their documentary feel and static aesthetic, the photographs displayed at the Sweated Industries Exhibition and reproduced inside the visitor handbook contrasted strikingly with the grotesque, stylised figure on the cover. These sombre images portrayed women labouring in cramped and cluttered interiors disfigured by faded wallpaper, ill-fitting furniture and laundry lines traversing the walls. Eight had children present, sometimes loitering in shot, sometimes helping a mother with her work. In one especially arresting photograph, a wild-looking woman stares directly at the camera with haunted eyes, her face flanked by the distressed expression on the face of the little boy on her knee. Three other children, one with noticeably filthy hands and shirt, sit or stand at the table quietly carding the hooks and eyes. We know nothing about the identity of these families nor the exact circumstances in which the photographs were taken. The only information offered in the handbook was that flash-light had been used and images had 'not been in any way altered', with two exceptions, where a small amount of touching-up had been carried out. This statement affirming the truth-telling power of photography was no doubt designed to pre-empt any suggestion that images had been 'faked' for dramatic effect, a practice not unknown amongst crusading philanthropists in the late nineteenth century.[63]

Reinforcing this claim to authenticity was the human material on display in the exhibition hall itself, where forty-two women and two men demonstrated their lowly trades for the benefit of fee-paying visitors. Here, written on tired faces and broken bodies, was incontrovertible proof that the evil of sweating was real and present. Each worker had a story of suffering to tell, the details of which could be found on the display placards, in the handbook, or even via the testimony of the stall-holder herself, should she prove forthcoming under questioning. It is impossible to reconstruct the interactions which might have taken place between exhibition-goers and these living exhibits. Snippets of conversation were occasionally reproduced in newspaper reports, although the press dwelt mostly upon the stage-managed visits of distinguished personages. The *Daily Mirror*, for instance, paid tribute to the Princess of Wales's attempt at empathy when she came upon a home-worker nursing a 'peevish' infant: '"My babies cry sometimes," said the kindly royal lady.' We can only imagine what the harassed mother said (if anything) in return, as the newspaper did not see fit to record it.[64]

How did it feel to be under surveillance from these bejewelled ladies and smartly dressed men as they circulated the Queen's Hall? We should not assume that the workers at their stalls were necessarily intimidated or unable to return the well-meaning visitor's gaze with one of their own. 'It's like being at the seaside,' one worker whispered delightedly to a *Daily News* journalist, 'as she surveyed the well-dressed company'.[65] Nonetheless, it is hard not to conclude that the Sweated Industries Exhibition – and the smaller-scale versions which it inspired in other towns over the following months – played an important role in fixing the popular image of the home-worker as helpless victim. Despite appearing to offer workers a chance to bear witness, the Exhibition was at heart a visual spectacle for the socially conscientious middle and upper classes. Its aim was not to give sweated home-workers a platform but instead to gather heartbreaking examples of exploitation and suffering in one place and, as Tuckwell put it, 'confront the public with them'.[66] As was so often the case when the rich and comfortably off interpreted the lives of the poor, the degradation of the nameless women (and men) on show at the Queen's Hall was deduced not through listening to voices but by observing bodies. The lined faces, gnarled hands, stooped backs and shabby clothing were all eloquent testimony to hopeless, defeated lives.[67] One worker was, quite literally, unable to speak for herself, as she had lost her voice some years back following a bout of diphtheria.[68]

*

This way of seeing the home-working mother had become so ingrained by 1906–7 that it was difficult for MPs on the Commons Select Committee to look at the problem through any other lens. Nora Vynne of the Homeworkers League protested that the Sweated Industries Exhibition painted a misleadingly gloomy picture, whilst several of the working women giving evidence talked authoritatively about trades which, far from being picked up casually when misfortune struck, had been 'in their hands' for many years.[69] Mrs A., a mother of five, had worked in the clothing trade for eighteen years, 'so I ought to know how to make a blouse … I am very quick, and I have a very quick machine'.[70] Mrs Brophy, who made paper bags, similarly described herself as 'a skilled worker. Very few are more skilled.'[71] Clementina Black drove the point home by brandishing a dainty box for sending pieces of wedding cake through the post, explaining to the Committee that it had required fifteen separate operations for its assembly: 'That box,' she said, 'was made in a very grubby house, but by a very clever woman.'[72]

A more nuanced view emerges, too, from the cases compiled by Women's Industrial Council investigators for their home-work survey in 1897. Living alongside the deserted, chronically ill and desperately poor women inhabiting filthy hovels were 'nice', 'neat', 'respectable', 'bright', 'well-dressed' and 'cheerful' wives in their 'clean' and 'comfortable' homes. Some had husbands who loafed about or were in and out of the workhouse, but others had helpful spouses; in one instance, the husband was found at home singing lustily with his harmonium. A number of the home-workers visited were skilled and resourceful women employing assistants or even subcontracting work out themselves. One married woman who made bows for adorning shoes kept an apprentice and, according to the investigator, 'likes her work very much, pretty & interesting, she said'.[73] A mother of three in Islington ran a thriving artificial-flower-making enterprise with the help of an apprenticed girl: 'This woman is evidently a skilled worker,' the investigator noted. 'Her mother, aunts and sisters make flowers, and she has done so since childhood.'[74]

Such women might well have belonged to Nora Vynne's Homeworkers League, feeling themselves in little need of State intervention to regulate their trades. The seven witnesses selected by Vynne to give evidence to the Commons Committee obliged her by expressing strong concerns about the proposed Wages Boards. Several argued that quicker workers would lose out from fixed minimum rates, whilst others complained that employers would stop giving out home-work altogether. Unfortunately for Vynne, the women became muddled when quizzed on the more technical aspects of wage-setting, which made it easy for MPs to disregard their objections. But what appeared to parliamentarians as the irrational fears of poorly educated working women could be read against the grain as an assertion of self-reliance and pride in skill. In the words of Mrs Somerset, a file-cutter from Sheffield:

I say that I think it is right that every woman should have what she earns … I stick up for a right cause because I like my price. I think that everyone else would do the same. I do my work so that I do not care who looks at it. I think it is nothing but right that everyone should have justice done to them, but all the same many people tell me they get the same price as I do and I know that their work is inferior, and it has come to my knowledge that they allow the masters so much on purpose to find them work … The master I work for now is a good master and is a gentleman, and I should not like to do him any harm by punishing him for the sake of punishing others.[75]

*

No serious move was made by politicians to prohibit home-work in its entirety during the early twentieth-century agitation over sweating. As with mothers in factories, pragmatic considerations about the practicability of enforcement and the impact on the poorest workers overshadowed principled arguments about the liberty of the individual to sell her labour. Nonetheless it was widely expected – and hoped – by advocates of minimum wage legislation that their desired reform would discourage manufacturers from sending work out and push women to seek more regular employment outside their homes. When the Liberal government introduced a Trade Boards Bill in April 1909, its spokesmen in Parliament adopted the language of the anti-sweating reformers. Junior minister Harold Tennant told the House that it was 'to the morbid and diseased places – to the industrial diphtheritic spots' that his government intended to 'apply the anti-toxin' of wage regulations. Speaking as President of the Board of Trade, a relatively youthful Winston Churchill conjured similar imagery of 'degenerate and parasitical' industries and the 'broken', 'weak' and 'struggling' workers who depended upon them to live.[76] Whilst the final legislation did not single out home-working mothers, it covered four trades – tailoring, box-, lace- and chain-making – in which home-work was ubiquitous and 90 per cent of the 250,000-strong workforce was female.

Home-working mothers were always in view when sweating and its suggested remedies moved into focus between the 1880s and the First World War. They were never the only group of low-paid workers of concern to politicians and reformers, but they occupied a privileged position within visions of the sweated nation because it was in home-work that this 'evil' seemed to reveal itself in its darkest form. Middle-class observers of home-work were not misguided in highlighting the poverty and wretchedness of many of the women who did it, nor in lobbying for State action on low pay. Evidence suggests that wages did in fact increase for workers in the trades covered by the Act, whilst the machinery created by the boards stimulated organisation and strike action.[77] The most famous case was at Cradley Heath, where female chain-makers walked out for ten weeks in the late summer of 1910 following moves by employers to evade an agreed wage increase.[78]

The larger point is that the prominent place occupied by mothers in these debates, who were always assumed to be dependent and inferior workers, helps to explain how a liberal state could legitimise its intervention into wage-setting within private industry. A significant number of *male* workers benefited from the Trade Boards Act, but they did so shielded by the image of the helpless female home-worker. Even more consequentially, the agitation over sweating established a cultural script in which women's inability to behave like full-time, skilled workers – to behave more like men, in fact – provided the starting point for all conversations about why home-work existed, why it was so poorly paid, and why it was a problem for a 'modern' industrial nation like Britain. As we shall see, this script could be pressed into service to devalue married women's work later in the century, including home-work, which declined after 1909 but never disappeared. It continued to suit employers to offer home-work and it frequently suited mothers to accept it. This was not because those mothers were helpless or naturally fitted to perform low-paid labour in their homes, but rather because mothers had to make calculated choices about how to earn when employment opportunities were limited and the constraints on their time and physical and emotional energies were great. This burden was felt most heavily by women of the poorer classes, yet wives and mothers more fortunately placed might have recognised a version of it in their own lives. Middle- and upper-class women observed the sweated home-worker's precarious existence at a distance, but knew the realities of women's economic dependence only too well. Even if their class privilege protected them from the horrors of poverty, it did not ensure that, in seeking to earn beyond marriage and maternity, they would be judged any less harshly.

3

Serving Two Masters

When Beatrice Potter married Sidney Webb in July 1892, she felt she had 'passed the age when it is easy or natural for a woman to become a child-bearer'. She was only thirty-four, yet believed herself incapable of building a new identity as devoted wife and mother following ten years of 'purely brain-working and sexless life'.[1] The Webbs' union was instead to be a 'fellowship of comrades' which would not announce the end of Beatrice's well-established career in social investigation but rather 'raise it to a higher level of usefulness'.[2] Nonetheless, the decision against maternity haunted Beatrice in her darker moments, when she conjured up idealised images of an alternative maternal self. She wrote in her diary in 1895:

> To think of the many hours in each day which I idle and mope
> away simply because I can only work my tiny intellect for
> two or three hours at most; whereas I could be giving forth
> tenderness and judgment to my children hour after hour and
> day after day without effort or strain.[3]

She had no doubt as to the 'holiness of motherhood – its infinite superiority over any other occupation that a woman may take to', although she was pained by the thought that maternity inevitably meant a woman 'putting aside intellectual things as no longer pertinent to her daily life'. For Beatrice, it seemed that an absolute choice had to be made: either compete, childless, alongside men in the 'prize fight' for professional success, or embrace wholeheartedly the sacred feminine task of nurturing the next generation. Beatrice believed passionately in the work she and Sidney were doing to rebuild British society on collectivist principles – work which she knew would be compromised by the presence of children in their marriage. But the feeling of maternal joys forsworn prompted her to wonder, all the same, whether 'I had better not have risked it and taken my chance'.[4]

Had she done so, Beatrice Potter might never have become Beatrice Webb. Twelve years earlier she had met and become deeply infatuated with the politician Joseph Chamberlain, then yet to make his decisive break from the Liberal Party over Irish Home Rule. The attraction was more keenly felt on Beatrice's side, but it is possible that, had she shown greater willingness to play the role, in her own words, of 'walking gentlewoman' to Chamberlain's great man, the match might have been made.[5] Instead, Beatrice wrestled with her passions and sought distraction in social work, initially with the Charity Organisation Society in Soho, and then as a resident rent collector at St Katharine's dwellings, a block of flats erected in the docklands of east London to provide affordable housing for working-class families. Her presence there was modelled on an earlier scheme devised by the philanthropist Octavia Hill, who envisaged a legion of lady volunteers restoring order in the homes of the poor by imparting firm but benevolent advice on a weekly basis. For a brief period, Beatrice was drawn to the way of life being pioneered from the 1880s by women like Hill, who embodied a new generation of energetic and well-educated spinsters galvanised by a longing for useful service. Living and working within communities of like-minded colleagues and friends, such women embraced their single, childless status as an opportunity to do good in the world, whether through social reform and missionary work, or by carving out new fields of feminine professional endeavour.[6] Perhaps this celibate but noble existence would offer Beatrice a satisfying outlet for her unrequited maternal instincts?

It was not to be. Beatrice was quickly disillusioned with her work at St Katharine's and turned to social investigation – and eventually to Sidney Webb and socialism. She retained a certain affection for single-sex institutions and their doughty spinster inhabitants: Somerville, one of the first women's colleges at Oxford, which Beatrice visited in 1896, was 'a charming vision of intellectual girlhood' and 'a delightful modern analogue to the Convent',[7] but she was at the same time troubled by the cloistered life they created for women away from the outside world, an ambivalence which proved key to Beatrice's always complicated relationship with feminism and her animosity towards certain kinds of feminists. Beatrice Webb was not alone in believing that women must choose: between work and motherhood, career and family, duty and love. Most women of her class saw themselves confronted with this forked path, and most made their decision about which path to travel – either towards conventional marriage and maternity, or towards spinsterhood and the possibility of professional achievement.

Most women chose one of these paths, but a few searched instead for another way. Mothers who worked for pay existed in the Victorian middle classes, although they were relatively few in number and always had to tread carefully to preserve their respectability and social status. One of the most prominent was Elizabeth Garrett, some twenty years older than Webb and the first British-qualified woman to appear on the General Medical Council's Register. Following a long struggle to study and train, Elizabeth achieved this distinction in 1865 and immediately established a private practice at her London home on Upper Berkeley Street, Marylebone. Soon after, she opened a dispensary providing medical services to poor women in the neighbourhood, later adding a small ten-bed hospital on the floor above. In 1869, Elizabeth was appointed to an honorary post at the East London Children's Hospital, whilst in November of the following year she became one of the first women elected to the London School Board, newly created to oversee the provision of elementary schooling under the 1870 Education Act. It was through joining the hospital's management board that she met her future husband, James Skelton Anderson, two years her junior and partner at a thriving shipping firm. Their relationship blossomed when Anderson became Elizabeth's agent for the School Board elections in November, no doubt sharing in the sweet taste of victory when she topped the poll.[8]

Elizabeth was closely connected to the mid-Victorian feminist movement and identified passionately with its liberal ideas and values. Having delightedly accepted James's proposal of marriage in December 1870, Elizabeth's thoughts immediately turned to the implications for her medical work and public status as a pioneering professional woman. She wrote to her sister, Millicent Fawcett:

> I do hope, my dear, you will not think I have meanly deserted my post. I think it need not prove to be so and I believe that he would regret it as much as I or you. I am sure that the woman question will never be solved in any complete way so long as marriage is thought to be incompatible with freedom and with an independent career, and I think there is a very good chance that we may be able to do something to discourage this notion.[9]

This subject dominated Elizabeth's letters to her fiancé over the following days and weeks. She felt a powerful obligation to set a positive example to other women, confessing to James her 'dread lest I may be choosing my own happiness at the price of the duty I owe to women who need something which I as one of their leaders can give them'.[10] Elizabeth pressed him for agreement that they should live at Upper Berkeley Street so as to avoid the disruption which a change of address would cause to her medical work. 'I should not like to be seriously discouraged by loss of practice in the first year,' she wrote. 'I think it would be very depressing, and it would make me think I had been the deserter I do not wish or mean to be.'[11] A grand house with more servants would, she pointed out, place added burdens on her as mistress: 'I want so much not to fail, in any way, and it would tax me very much either to manage a much larger household well with many patients or to be cheerful in a big house, without them.'[12] Elizabeth was adamant that she would not be 'given away' at her wedding, nor promise 'to obey', and she told James that she wished their finances to be managed through a 'common purse to which each contributed and from which each could draw, better than any elaborate deed of partnership, and division of expenses'.[13] The idea of engaging a chaperone for the duration of their engagement was swiftly dismissed. 'My position <u>must</u> be accepted as an independent one,' Elizabeth wrote, 'and it would be injuring all other professional women a little to allow myself to be treated like a child.'[14]

Few of James Anderson's replies survive, but he was evidently attracted by Elizabeth Garrett's professional drive, possibly because it matched his own. 'I take a decided line in this matter,' he wrote to his wife-to-be. 'I mean to be if I can a successful man of business neither interfering with your pursuits nor being interfered with by you (but having our confidences at off times and mutually advising and fortifying one another).' Their marriage, he insisted, must be based on 'warm personal love and utter truth and out-spokenness'. Her celebrity did not intimidate him, quite the opposite: 'It is very pleasant to me that you are a distinguished person.'[15] Yet he must have been irritated, as Elizabeth was, by the tone adopted in some of the press coverage which followed the announcement of their nuptials. The *Daily Telegraph* expressed astonishment that the famous Miss Garrett was stooping 'to the old chains' by getting engaged, 'just as if she were any ordinary Kate or Julia who came out last year!' A Yorkshire paper similarly feigned surprise, having supposed that 'Dr Garrett and women like her were quite beyond the reach of Cupid's arrows'. And yet here she was, 'the standard-bearer of the sex, having a bad fall and tumbling from her high estate into vulgar matrimony!'[16]

More seriously, some commentators announced that Elizabeth was duty-bound to resign from the School Board, on the grounds that married women were not eligible to stand for election and that her wifely obligations would interfere with serving the voters of Marylebone. Elizabeth seems to have quashed this possibility fairly quickly, with one newspaper reporting that 'Miss Garrett has no intention of resigning her seat at the School Board in marrying, nor do her friends entertain any expectation that she will be called upon to do so'.[17] Opinion was divided as to whether retirement from medicine would inevitably follow should 'Master Baby' decide to put in an appearance. One press observer thought it unquestionably would, as 'Mr Anderson cannot then take the mother's place, and then the mother will discover that she *can* be nothing higher and nobler than a woman'.[18] A correspondent for the *Sheffield Telegraph*, however, took a different view, pointing out that actresses and singers frequently returned to their professions following maternity: 'In those periods of retirement which occur in the best-regulated families a substitute is provided, and after a proper interval the lady re-appears, and earns her living by her own industry as before. Why may not the same be possible in medicine?'[19]

Elizabeth Garrett could not have agreed more. She and James married on a fine February morning in 1871 'without millinery and almost without cookery'.[20] A low-key reception was hosted at Upper Berkeley Street before the couple departed for a brief honeymoon rambling in the hills of North Wales. Then it was back to work. On top of private consultations, School Board business and hospital duties in east London, Elizabeth kept herself busy by launching a series of lectures on anatomy and physiology for female students, performing operations for patients attending her dispensary, and lending support to the fundraising campaign for a new women's college at Girton, Cambridge. In July 1873, when she was thirty-seven, Elizabeth gave birth to her first child, a little girl whom she and James named Louisa. This happy event did not divert her from professional work, which continued although with some slackening of pace. Elizabeth did not seek re-election to the School Board and resigned from the East London Hospital, a decision she later sorely regretted when the post was filled by a male doctor.

Like other women of the upper middle classes, Elizabeth Garrett Anderson could count on the assistance of resident nursemaids and servants when it came to the care of children and the running of the home. The fourth floor at Upper Berkeley Street was converted

into a nursery where Louisa spent much of her infant days, attended
by both a wet nurse and a nanny. Elizabeth was not a sentimental
or overly involved mother. One friend recalled her remarking, 'I
never really know how to play with my own children,' and Louisa
later wrote that her mother 'hated noise and could not enter
readily into a child's mind or play with children'.[21] But nor was she
physically distant or emotionally unavailable. Louisa remembered
riding in the carriage as Elizabeth went on her home visits and
being allowed to 'romp about on the beds' at the New Hospital,
which moved from its location over the dispensary to a larger site
on the Marylebone Road in 1874.[22] Elizabeth was devastated when
her second child, Margaret, died at the age of fifteen months the
following winter, probably from cow's milk infected with bovine
tuberculosis. She ceased all work in order to nurse Margaret, pacing
the room hour after hour with the child in her arms. Towards the
end, Elizabeth shared this heartbreaking labour with her husband,
and it was in James's arms that Margaret peacefully passed away on
15 December 1875. Elizabeth plunged back into medicine, writing
to her father: 'I feel it is a great blessing not to be one of those poor
mothers who have nothing to do but to think of what they have
lost.'[23] The birth of their third and final child, Alan, in 1877, helped
to lift some of the sadness, but Elizabeth remained marked by her
tragic earlier loss. When Louisa recovered from a serious illness
ten years later, Elizabeth and James abandoned their work for six
months and sailed to Australia with both children, conscious of the
fragility of the health and happiness they enjoyed.

*

Elizabeth Garrett Anderson was unusual for living the life of
a professional working mother in the 1870s and 1880s. She was
aided by a comfortable income and plenty of servants, and she
enjoyed excellent health, including during and after her three
pregnancies. Elizabeth was further emboldened by a powerful
sense of breaking new ground for women, which helps to explain
why she was so determined to continue practising medicine after
marriage and childbirth. Yet it is curious, given the remarks in her

letter to Millicent Fawcett, that Elizabeth did not publicly advocate employment beyond maternity, nor speak or write about her own life as a working mother.

The reasons for this silence undoubtedly lie in the wider climate of bourgeois opinion, which held that wives and mothers of the middle classes ought not to work for pay. These prevailing norms dated back to the early industrial era, when men who amassed fortunes by building mills, digging mines and erecting railways were anxious to maintain their womenfolk in comfort and leisure as a mark of gentility. By the middle of the nineteenth century, a typical day for a 'lady' involved writing letters, playing the pianoforte, doing light needlework, reading religious texts, paying social calls and, if mistress of the household, supervising servants and overseeing the education of the children. Few conformed perfectly to the ideal of docile, devoted womanhood venerated in Coventry Patmore's famous poem of 1854, 'The Angel in the House', yet middle-class women were, nonetheless, constrained by a powerful ideology of male domestic authority. The harmony of the home was widely believed to rest upon feminine submission to the will and judgement of husbands and fathers, a position shored up by mainstream religious teaching and a huge volume of didactic advice literature.[24] Furthermore, the doctrine of 'coverture' dictated that a woman gave up her independent legal personality when she married, together with the right to own property, keep her earnings, make a will or enter into any kind of contract.[25] This combination of moral pressure and legal disabilities entrenched the expectation that middle-class women would not engage in remunerated work after marriage.[26] By carrying on with her practice in 1871, Elizabeth Garrett Anderson was thus flouting the prevailing norms of her class.

It was a different story for the minority who did not, or could not, marry.[27] These so-called 'redundant women' pined away in the parental home, found solace in alms-giving, or led a superficial existence of constant amusement. For those unfortunate enough to have to earn a living, the options for doing so without 'losing caste' were unenticing. Women in the lower rungs of the middle class – the daughters of poor clergymen, junior clerks or shopkeepers, for instance – might pursue respectability through dressmaking or running small businesses selling haberdashery, stationery or other tasteful items to a genteel clientele. Alternatively, ladies with education and the right social graces could find low-paid employment as governesses in private homes, where they were accorded an uneasy status somewhere between family member and servant.[28]

This precarious economic position was the result of an enormous oversupply of spinster labour in a tiny market of opportunities. At the time that Elizabeth Garrett set out to conquer the medical field for women, the most attractive and secure middle-class professions – law, the Church, the military and the Civil Service – were exclusively male preserves, whilst commerce and trade were not regarded as appropriate pursuits for ladies. Girls' schooling was vastly inferior to boys', whilst university education was entirely off limits to women. Long-standing scriptural notions of woman as the 'weaker vessel' were reinforced by new medical theories which held that intense cerebral activity interfered with the female reproductive organs, leading to physical and mental breakdown. According to the psychologist Henry Maudsley, excessive intellectual strain during puberty and in the years immediately following was harmful to women, a claim which he and like-minded colleagues deployed in arguments against the opening of university degrees to both sexes.[29]

Given the weight of male resistance to allowing women access to higher education, training and the professions, it was not surprising that Elizabeth Garrett Anderson was reluctant to press the case publicly for working wives and mothers. Her allies in the mid-Victorian feminist movement, figures like Bessie Rayner Parkes, Barbara Bodichon, Jessie Boucherett and Josephine Butler, believed emphatically in the spiritually redeeming nature of work for both sexes. Needless suffering resulted, in Butler's words, 'from the shutting up in artificial channels of those good gifts of God which are meant to flow forth freely and bless the world'.[30] Yet most of their campaigning efforts focused upon the struggles of *single* women who needed well-paid, respectable work to support themselves at a standard fitting to their social station. Boucherett founded the Society for Promoting the Employment of Women as a practical step to establish such women in new occupations, from printing and glass-engraving to bookkeeping and pharmacy.[31] The Society offered careers advice, matched candidates to positions and provided small loans to girls whose parents were unwilling or unable to fund a period of training.

The position of wives and mothers was, by contrast, more ambiguous. Education and training would secure independence for those who could not marry, or preferred not to, but should it equip women for earning *beyond* marriage and maternity? Here, opinion was divided. Some early feminist thinkers, such as Harriet Taylor, thought that motherhood did not spell the end of all other occupations for women. She wrote in 1851 that it was 'neither necessary nor just to make imperative on women, that they shall be either mothers or nothing; or that, if they have been mothers once, they shall be nothing else during the whole remainder of their lives'. Taylor wanted all artificial restrictions lifted so that women might choose for themselves:

> There is no need to make provision by law, that woman shall not carry on the active details of a household, or the education of children, and at the same time practice a profession or be elected to Parliament. Where incompatibility is real, it will take care of itself; but there is gross injustice in making the incompatibility a pretence for the exclusion of those in whose case it does not exist: and these, if they were free to choose, would be a very large proportion.[32]

Barbara Bodichon also envisaged scenarios in which a middle-class wife might continue to earn: if her husband were poor, for instance, or if she were widowed and had 'to act as both father and mother to children dependent on her for daily bread', or if she simply wished to carry on her business or profession. For Bodichon, whose own family background and marital arrangements were unconventional, useful toil for both partners was the formula for domestic harmony.

'The happiest married life we can recall ever to have seen,' she wrote in 1857, 'is the life of two workers, a man and a woman equal in intellectual gifts and loving hearts; the union between them being founded in their mutual work.'[33]

This egalitarian vision must have encouraged Elizabeth Garrett as she contemplated marriage to James Anderson thirteen years later. Yet in truth, only a small minority of feminists openly challenged middle-class orthodoxy on the employment of wives and mothers. Bessie Rayner Parkes, who co-founded Britain's first feminist periodical, *The English Woman's Journal*, with Bodichon in 1858, was deeply equivocal on this subject, which she viewed in class terms. Certain occupations, she conceded, were compatible with the duties of motherhood: 'A great singer, an artist, or an author, who keeps good servants,' Parkes wrote, 'may righteously afford the number of hours necessary to fulfil her profession, without any sacrifice of the welfare of her children.'[34] But it was a different matter when women of the labouring classes left their homes to earn wages. *Their* absence, in Parkes' view, 'should, in the majority of instances, be discouraged by every possible moral means, since the workman must be very wretched indeed before his wife's absence can be a source of real gain'.[35] More generally, Parkes did not wish to see any fundamental shift in public opinion which might make men of any class 'more unmindful of the material welfare of the women of their families. Once infuse into their minds the idea that they may fairly leave women to shift for themselves, and that which is now a necessity, or an accident, will become the natural rule.'[36]

The liberal philosopher John Stuart Mill, who was Harriet Taylor's second husband and co-authored a number of her published works, leaned towards Parkes' line of thought. In his influential 1869 tract, *The Subjection of Women*, Mill argued that when a woman marries, 'it may in general be understood that she makes a choice of the management of a household, and the bringing up of a family, as the first call upon her exertions, during as many years of her life as may be required for the purpose'.[37] Like Taylor, Mill believed that women should be free to develop their talents in any field of their choosing, but unlike Taylor, he assumed that most wives would continue to regard marriage and motherhood as an all-absorbing occupation in itself.[38]

Feminists of the mid-Victorian generation could agree, however, that gainful employment was beneficial for *all* women, regardless of whether they made it a lifelong career or ceased to earn upon marriage. They argued consistently that girls who had some training behind them were better equipped for married life because they would select their partners more judiciously and have greater wisdom to impart to their offspring: 'Activity of brain, heart, and limb, gives health and beauty, and makes women fit to be the mothers of children,' wrote Bodichon. 'A listless, idle, empty-brained, empty-hearted, ugly woman has no right to bear children.'[39] Work increased women's status in marriage because wives would now enter it from a position of higher economic standing and find themselves better able to demand respect and real companionship from their spouses. This belief in the power of paid employment to reduce women's dependence was linked to other demands concerning married women's property and child custody rights, divorce reform and parliamentary enfranchisement. Feminists hoped that such demands, once met, would transform marriage from the tyrannical relation of master and slave into a loving partnership of equals.[40]

*

Elizabeth Garrett Anderson might have felt she had achieved exactly such a partnership in her own marriage. A few brave souls, however, went further by forming 'free unions' wholly unsanctified by Church or State.[41] Elizabeth Wolstenholme, who was a secularist free-thinker, lived openly with her partner Ben Elmy until autumn 1874, when, visibly pregnant, she was persuaded to marry by feminist friends fearful that her behaviour was bringing the movement into disrepute.[42] The birth-control campaigner Annie Besant found herself viewed with suspicion by women's rights advocates because of her similarly unconventional ideas about Christianity and marriage. Besant separated from her clergyman husband and moved to London in 1874, having successfully secured the custody of her younger child, Mabel. Thereafter she lived on a small allowance plus her salary at the free-thought newspaper, the *National Reformer*. This work brought Besant into a close partnership with Charles Bradlaugh, President of the National Secular Society, and the two gained notoriety in 1877 by reissuing a controversial birth-control tract from the 1830s. Prosecuted for obscenity, Besant avoided imprisonment, but her public stance cost her dearly: Mabel's father successfully sued for custody, arguing that Besant was an unfit person to bring up his daughter. Besant recalled how the child was taken away, 'nearly frantic with fear and passionate resistance', while she was left to pace her empty house, the loneliness piercing her thoughts 'like an evil dream'.[43]

Compared to these unorthodox lives, Elizabeth Garrett Anderson was a paragon of respectability. She fiercely championed women's educational and professional freedoms, but took care never to overstep the bounds of bourgeois propriety. This balancing act was evident in the rebuke to Henry Maudsley which Elizabeth penned in May 1874, questioning his evidence of female intellectual inferiority and arguing that normal menstruation caused 'no loss of vigour to the woman'.[44] Given that Elizabeth was, at the time of writing, mother to ten-month-old Louisa and pregnant with Margaret, it seems inconceivable that her personal experience did not inform her thinking on the relationship between female biology and intellectual ability. Yet her own identity as a mother was wholly effaced in her public dressing-down of Maudsley. Elizabeth was similarly silent in her writings on the fractious topic of birth control, mindful perhaps from the later 1870s of Besant's status as a social pariah after adopting this as her cause. She would have been fully aware of how continuous childbearing hindered married women from pursuing careers, and it seems highly likely that she herself practised some form of family limitation after the birth of her third child. Yet Elizabeth always steered clear of the subject in her lectures to medical students, and was cautious when offering advice privately to patients.

Pioneering professional women might have been bolder on questions of motherhood and work in the later nineteenth century had they felt their position to be more secure. Conscious of the weight of hostile feeling within the male medical establishment, Elizabeth Garrett Anderson always favoured subtle methods to advance women's status over head-on confrontation.[45] As a first step, she advised aspiring female medics to qualify overseas and then return to Britain to practise, thus proving their skill and competence to sceptics. 'If we could point to a considerable number of medical women quietly making for themselves the reputation of being trustworthy and valuable members of the profession,' she wrote to *The Times* in 1873, 'the various forms which the present opposition now takes would insensibly disappear, and arrangements would be made for providing female medical students with the advantages which it appears hopeless to look for at present in this country.'[46] On this point Elizabeth Garrett Anderson clashed with another pioneering woman doctor, Sophia Jex-Blake, who had attracted press attention in November 1870 when she and six others were pelted with mud by a mob of angry male students on their way to a medical exam at the University of Edinburgh. Rejecting Garrett Anderson's gradualist approach, Jex-Blake campaigned ferociously for equal treatment and fought hard to open a separate medical school for women in London in 1874. Elizabeth reluctantly lent support to this initiative, suppressing her fears that the training on offer would be regarded by outsiders as second-rate.

In the long term, both strategies paid off, with the number of medically qualified women increasing significantly in the decades before the First World War. By 1911, there were over 900 female names on the Medical Register, whilst women's share of medical school places was approaching 10 per cent.[47] The majority of female students trained in single-sex institutions and were directed towards a narrow range of specialties treating mostly women and children, such as gynaecology, obstetrics and paediatrics. Nonetheless, it was a dramatic change from fifty years previously, when medicine was an almost exclusively masculine profession. Like Elizabeth Garrett Anderson, some of these graduates managed to balance work with family life. Mary Scharlieb, for example, pulled this off by starting her medical career *after* becoming a mother. She married a lawyer in 1865 and moved with him to Madras, gave birth to two sons and a daughter between 1866 and 1870, and only then began studying midwifery. Entrusting childcare duties to nannies, relatives and boarding schools, Scharlieb continued her training in London and Vienna and, with Garrett Anderson's patronage, built a successful and lucrative career in gynaecology.[48] Frances Morgan and Edith Pechey were two further early cases of medics who continued to work after marriage. Morgan wed a fellow doctor, George Hoggan, in 1874 and the couple set up their respective practices in the same building and co-authored papers in the *British Medical Journal*. Pechey helped to develop medical services for women in India, carrying on her public health work in Bombay after marriage to a British wine merchant in 1889.[49] Having trained with Garrett Anderson at the Marylebone Dispensary, both women shared her sense of professional vocation as well as her feminist politics.

Unlike their mentor, however, neither Morgan nor Pechey had children. This might have been the result of personal choice or, in Pechey's case, age (she was forty-four when she married), but it pointed to a pattern which was to become characteristic for medical women by the end of the century. As medical training and careers became more rigidly structured, girls choosing this profession tended to see it as one requiring a level of dedication incompatible with family life. Sophia Jex-Blake certainly regarded it in these terms. 'If a woman becomes a mother,' she wrote on hearing about a former student's engagement, 'I certainly think nothing outside her home can have, or ought to have, so much claim on her time.'[50] Jex-Blake regarded babies rather than husbands as the real problem, but the generation of women qualifying after 1890 were less likely to acquire either. Following Elizabeth Garrett Anderson's retirement in 1903, all women appointed deans at the London School of Medicine over the next twenty years were unmarried. Elizabeth's own daughter, Louisa, followed in her mother's footsteps by building a career as a highly regarded surgeon, but she rejected marriage and motherhood and chose instead to share her life with

Flora Murray, a fellow doctor. The two ran a hospital, built a house and fought together for women's suffrage, exemplifying an early twentieth-century form of intense female friendship which we today find difficult to define. When Murray dedicated a book to her devoted friend, the inscription read: 'Bold, cautious, true and my loving comrade.'[51]

*

Singleness offered a positive and emotionally fulfilling alternative to heterosexual marriage for some professional women, but for many others it was a necessity. Formal workplace policies prohibiting the employment of married women were on the rise in the late nineteenth century. A marriage bar was introduced at the General Post Office (GPO) in 1876, just six years after female clerks had first been appointed, and by the 1890s it was widespread across central and local government, covering many teaching and public health posts now open to women.[52] Private firms followed suit, hiring young women to carry out low-level office tasks and dismissing them on marriage. Employers saw great advantage in this arrangement, as women could be paid lower salaries and were assumed to cope better with monotonous and sedentary work. The number of women occupied in clerical work in private companies thus grew dramatically, from around 6,000 at the beginning of the 1880s to nearly 125,000 by 1911.[53] This compared to the 40,000 women employed by that date in central government, the vast majority by the GPO as telegraph operators or as general clerks.

Disciplining this swelling pool of female white-collar labour through the mechanism of the marriage bar allowed employers to maintain a healthy turnover of junior staff whilst keeping promotion ladders unblocked for men, who, it was believed, were better equipped for holding supervisory positions and required greater job security because of their breadwinning responsibilities. The ease with which these expanding state and corporate bureaucracies discriminated against married women undoubtedly reflected wider ingrained attitudes concerning the 'proper' place of wives and mothers in the home. But it also demonstrated how those attitudes could be repurposed by employers to serve their own interests. Managers commonly argued that female employees received lower pay and were confined to repetitive tasks because they were less committed and regarded their job as a 'stop-gap' between school and matrimony. Yet it could be equally argued that it was the imposition of policies like the marriage bar which institutionalised this short-termist outlook for female employees, rather than women's 'natural' preference for full-time home-making.[54]

Furthermore, when it suited employers to retain married women, exceptions could always be made. This was especially apparent above the clerical grades of the Civil Service, where it was easier to bend rules because the numbers of women involved were so tiny. The first woman to be appointed to a permanent government post was both married *and* a mother. Jane Senior was employed as Government Inspector of Workhouse Schools in January 1873 by the President of the Local Government Board, James Stansfeld, a radical Liberal MP and firm ally of the mid-Victorian women's movement. Her main task was to investigate and report on conditions in workhouse schools for girls, a remit for which Senior was well qualified following many years of voluntary social work pursued alongside her more artistic pastimes, which included singing and sculpting. Senior's marital status did not appear to have presented any obstacle to her appointment, whilst the relative autonomy she enjoyed in organising her work schedule meant that midway through her regional visits she was able to take a week off at short notice to tend to two sick children. Senior, who lacked Garrett Anderson's feminist convictions, felt guilty about leaving her post and mused privately that a mother's duty to drop everything in cases of family illness was 'the great drawback I suspect to women having work of this sort'.[55] Yet it was ultimately Senior's own seriously ailing health, rather than the conflicts of working motherhood, which brought her short Civil Service career to an abrupt end in November 1874.

No married woman was thereafter appointed to a permanent salaried post in government until the Second World War, although a few existing employees temporarily evaded the strictures of the marriage bar. The factory inspector May Abraham, for example, did not immediately resign when she married the Liberal MP Jack Tennant in July 1896, nor when she fell pregnant very soon after. Her colleague Lucy Deane admired May's determination to continue her work, but thought she was unlikely to remain in her job for long. 'After a year when social duties & her husband's friends and politics and Babies all crowd in she'll *have* to drop the Depart[ment],' Deane wrote in her diary, '[and] she will sell all the years of steady work & influence which she *might* give!'[56] Deane's instincts were correct. May Tennant retired in April 1897 shortly before the birth of her son, although it is intriguing to speculate as to what her experiences might have been had she stayed and become the first female civil servant to give birth in post. It seems likely that a few other wives and mothers in less visible roles also clung on to their jobs in the early era of the marriage bar. A Royal Commission looking at pay and pensions in 1903 reported that its members were 'not sure that the ineligibility of married women as Civil Servants has been universally regarded in the past', although they thought that variations from the rule in the future would be rare.[57] On that point at least, the commissioners were to be proved right.

The other major group affected by the marriage bar was teachers. This profession was utterly transformed from the 1870s by the introduction of universal elementary education and the growth of secondary schooling for girls. The number of female teachers ballooned from 80,000 to 183,000 between 1861 and 1911, driven by the rapid expansion of State-aided school places and new systems of training and promotion.[58] The job demanded long hours and women were typically offered lower salaries than their male colleagues, yet for many girls looking for a profession which offered some security and social esteem, teaching was an attractive option. In any case, as was remarked by Clara Collet, who taught in a girls' grammar school whilst studying for the University of London's external degree, 'it is the only brain-work offered them, and badly paid as it is, it is better paid than any other work done by women'.[59] The most highly sought appointments were at well-established institutions like Cheltenham Ladies' College, or on the staff of one of the smart new schools opened by the Girls' Public Day School Company after 1872. These posts generally went to graduates, whose numbers were slowly creeping up with the founding of women's colleges in London, Oxford and Cambridge and the admission of female undergraduates to a growing tally of universities across the rest of the country.[60] Most women entered the profession, however, through shorter courses of training or by learning on the job, and typically found work in the elementary schools which educated the mass of the population. This was especially the case for girls from lower-middle- or working-class backgrounds, for whom teaching could offer the promise of higher social status as well as much-needed income for themselves and their families.[61]

As in medicine and the Civil Service, most women teachers were unmarried and did not have children. The campaigners who fought for the expansion of girls' schooling from the mid-nineteenth century envisaged a new vocational field to which energetic, publicly spirited spinsters would dedicate their lives. Most mistresses in secondary schools were exactly that; resignation upon marriage was customary and many chose not to marry at all. There were always exceptions, like Marion Andrews, who retained her teaching post at Notting Hill High School for twelve years after her marriage in 1888, although the absence of children may have been a factor in her career longevity.[62] There were also occasional allowances made for the tiny number of women fortunate enough to secure a teaching post in a university. The scientist Margaret McKillop, for example, who was married and had a young child at the time, was appointed to a post in the Ladies Department at King's College London in 1897. Similarly, the historian Lilian Knowles was allowed to keep her job at the London School of Economics after both her marriage in 1907 and the birth of her son shortly afterwards.[63]

These cases were undoubtedly anomalous, and the picture was rather different in elementary schools, where significant numbers of wives and mothers were employed. In London, around a quarter of female teachers were married, sometimes to male colleagues or men working in other lower-middle-class occupations as clerks, commercial travellers or shop assistants. Lavinia Church, for example, taught at an elementary school in Westminster, commuting every day from her home in Battersea and leaving her two sons in the care of a local minder. Her income, combined with the salary which her husband earned as a postal sorter, enabled the family to get a mortgage, acquire such luxuries as a piano and a set of tandem bicycles, and later to move to a much larger house in leafy Herne Hill.[64]

Employed by the progressively minded London County Council, Lavinia was not subject to a marriage bar, but teachers in other parts of the country were less fortunate. By 1904 at least sixty Local Education Authorities had put formal regulations in place to limit or prohibit the employment of married women, mostly on the grounds that home duties interfered with schoolwork and that permanent salaried posts should be reserved for single women who sought lifelong careers in the profession. Municipal authorities were free to determine their own rules, which varied from a blanket bar on all married women regardless of maternal status to more specific policies concerning pregnancy. With echoes of the debate over mothers in the factory, some authorities stipulated compulsory periods of leave before and after birth, although a major difference from industry was the provision of maternity pay. In most cases this was pegged at half the teacher's regular salary, although London County Council offered the more generous package of full pay for eight weeks followed by half pay for nine.[65]

These policies were undoubtedly shaped by the realities of the expanding labour market for qualified elementary teachers, which gave women like Lavinia Church some wriggle-room to continue working after marriage and motherhood. But such women could never assert their absolute *right* to work; they were always at the mercy of (mostly male) decision-makers in town halls up and down the country. Attitudes towards married women teachers were already beginning to harden in the early twentieth century, and local authorities would enforce marriage bars on a near-universal basis after the First World War.[66]

*

The combination of prevailing social assumptions and formal workplace policies ensured that, with the partial exception of elementary school teaching, mothers were a rare species in the new landscape of middle-class women's professional employment. Yet there *were* a handful of occupations in which maternity was perceived to be less of a disability in the late nineteenth century. Prominent amongst these was writing. It was not considered transgressive for a woman, even a married woman, to take up the pen for a living if she confined herself to particular genres, such as novel writing. Elizabeth Gaskell, Margaret Oliphant and Mary Ward were all wives and mothers who achieved critical and commercial success, Ward earning an astonishing £7,000 for the US rights to her third novel, *The History of David Grieve*, published in 1892. Journalism offered further opportunities for female authors, whose contributions were eagerly sought by editors of an expanding list of periodicals aimed at a growing middle-class readership.[67] Bessie Rayner Parkes noted this phenomenon in 1865: 'The magazines demanded short, graphic papers, observation, wit, and moderate learning,' she wrote. 'Women demanded work such as they could perform at home, and ready pay upon performance; the two wants met, and the female sex has become a very important element in the fourth estate.'[68] Alice Meynell, who was known to her eight children as the 'pencilling mama', was a prime example of this new breed of Victorian woman of letters. She wrote poetry, published volumes of essays and produced huge quantities of journalism alongside her editor husband Wilfred between the 1870s and her death in 1922.[69]

Parkes' reference to writing in a domestic setting provides a clue as to why working mothers like Meynell largely avoided public censure. Female authorship did not remove women from their 'proper sphere' in the way that medicine or the Civil Service obviously did in the eyes of contemporary observers. Many women began their writing careers by penning nursery stories for younger siblings or privately circulating fragments of prose to friends and family, and only subsequently seized opportunities to publish their work to a wider audience – and to be paid for their trouble. Soon after her marriage, Annie Besant was thrilled to earn the first thirty shillings of her life when she sent a short story to the *Family Herald*, a twopenny weekly magazine 'of useful information & amusement'.[70] Money was always an important aspect of Alice Meynell's literary efforts, with her earnings helping to secure a comfortable lifestyle in smart houses in Kensington. Yet she kept a low public profile while her children were young and always worked from her desk at home. One son recalled how the Meynell tribe were permitted to play by their mother's feet while she was writing, but were expected to entertain themselves: 'Blandishments we had little of; we were taken to her arms, but briefly; exquisitely fondled, but with economy, as if there were work always to be resumed.'[71] Constance Garnett, a distinguished translator of Russian literature, was less successful in keeping distractions at bay when she worked at home in the 1890s. Her son David, who was allowed to sit by his mother's side while doing his lessons, remembered that 'even if I did not interrupt, there would soon be a knocking at the back door, or Edward [David's father] would come in with a letter in his hand, worried until he could read it to her and work off his irritation by a discussion'.[72]

The assumption that a woman writer would drop everything when domestic duties called and pick her work up again at leisure reflected the enduring stereotype of the dilettante lady author. The successful reporter and mother of four Emily Crawford advised aspiring female journalists to dispel this image by drawing a clear line between family and work. 'A press life need not disqualify a woman for home life,' she wrote in 1893. 'But she ought to have a good house-keeper, and will have to send her children to school.'[73] Yet lack of clarity as to whether writing was a remunerative female profession or a non-contentious feminine pastime could offer mothers some moral cover. Unlike doctors, lawyers and civil servants, writers did not join well-established professional associations, sit qualifying exams or negotiate bureaucratic career structures, which might explain why male resistance to female interlopers in the literary world was less pronounced than elsewhere. The writing career of Elizabeth Garrett's sister, Millicent, provides a good example of this. She married the Cambridge economist and Liberal MP Henry Fawcett in 1867, gave birth to their daughter Philippa the following year, and soon began to develop her own profile as a writer and lecturer alongside campaigning for women's rights. She authored two novels and a bestselling economics textbook over the course of the 1870s and became even more prolific as a writer after Henry's death in 1884. Despite earning a significant income from these literary outputs, Millicent Fawcett was not identified, nor did she identify herself, as a 'professional' career woman. Her writing simply formed an uncontentious element within her larger image as Mrs Henry Fawcett, one of Britain's most notable female public figures.[74]

Notions of acceptable employment for married women were strikingly elastic when it came to other 'artistic' occupations, as previously noted by Parkes and the *Sheffield Telegraph* reporter who observed in 1870 how actresses and singers frequently returned to their profession following a 'proper interval' after childbirth. The lucky few who won fame and fortune on the Victorian stage certainly found that a colourful personal life was not necessarily incompatible with critical and commercial success. One of the biggest stars of the age, actress Ellen Terry, was married three times and had two children (not, it might be added, by any of her three legal husbands), yet was adored by the British public throughout her long and triumphant career. Another example was mother-of-two Stella Campbell, who won plaudits for playing edgy heroines with dubious pasts in the 1890s, using her income from acting to finance an extravagant lifestyle. Some observers maintained that acting as a profession for middle-class women was not quite respectable, but their position was a minority one by the early twentieth century. The highly esteemed figure of Sybil Thorndike, born a little later than Terry or Campbell, bears this out. Thorndike enjoyed professional success alongside the pleasures of a conventional family life; she married fellow actor (and later director) Lewis Casson in 1908 and gave birth to four children, taking short breaks from her repertory theatre work for each. In short, if an actress had beauty, charisma and talent, and if her performances consistently attracted paying audiences, she could enjoy considerable latitude in how she arranged her domestic life.[75]

Alongside writing and performing, there were similarly accommodating occupations falling within the broad arena of business and enterprise. Spinsters and widows had run shops and alehouses, rented out property or land, and produced goods for the market on their own account for centuries. The position of wives was more constrained due to the law of coverture, but there is ample evidence from the seventeenth and eighteenth centuries of married women of the middling classes running businesses as shoemakers, watchmakers, milliners and coffee-house owners, to name but a few. Often these were carried out jointly with husbands, but in some places, most notably London, the survival of medieval borough customs enabled wives to operate their own going concerns.[76] In the countryside, the farmer's wife typically took charge of the dairy, poultry, garden and orchard, supervising workers and riding to market every week with produce to sell.[77] As the nineteenth century wore on, these hands-on business roles came into tension with new notions of genteel femininity, although many wives in the less secure lower middle class had no choice but to continue helping out behind the shop counter or in the field. These women formed the backbone of small-scale, family-run enterprise in Victorian Britain. Going undercover as an East End tailoress in 1888, for example, Beatrice Webb noted that her employer's wife and daughters were fully involved in hiring, firing and inspecting the work of the hands, while the proprietor himself dealt with customers in the front shop.[78]

Reforms to married women's property rights between 1870 and 1882 made it easier for wives to own and run businesses independently, although it was still questionable as to how far a lady could enter trade without 'losing caste'. Kate Cranston, who established a popular chain of tea-shops in Glasgow in the 1880s, ran this gauntlet successfully, expanding her business empire after her marriage in 1892. Cranston's devotion to the cause of temperance reform, her concern for the moral welfare of the girls she employed and her eye for stylish and appropriately 'feminine' interior decor all helped to secure her membership of the city's business establishment.[79] Ellen Rollaston offers another case of a working mother whose entrepreneurial skill earned her a respected position in civic life. Starting out as an actress, Rollaston married Henry Nye Chart, the proprietor of the Theatre Royal, Brighton, in 1867 and juggled caring for their son with managing the theatre single-handedly following Henry's death nine years later. Mrs Nye Chart, as she was always known, extended the season and diversified the repertoire, bringing in top-name performers from London and turning a sizeable profit for the theatre's shareholders. Her death in 1892 was widely mourned by the citizens of Brighton who had lost, as one newspaper put it, a 'busy and bustling spirit'.[80]

Wives and mothers could take a further, less visible role in business as investors and speculators. Women were full participants in the upswing in popular shareholding which took place in Britain from the 1850s as the spread of limited liability companies reduced risk and the range of securities on offer lured new investors to the market. By the 1880s, the financial press was addressing female readers directly, offering them advice and guidance on where to invest their money. Acquiring shares undoubtedly generated income for many middle-class women, although this activity was viewed as wholly distinct from remunerative work. Indeed, some spinsters invested explicitly as an *alternative* to taking up poorly paid posts in over-stocked occupations like teaching. For married women, these sorts of financial assets could offer a degree of economic independence, although wives varied in how energetically they managed their portfolios. Some were avid and attentive speculators, buying low and selling high for capital gain; others were largely passive beneficiaries of assets controlled by husbands or fathers.[81] Such female investors were not working mothers in the strict sense of toiling for pay, like Elizabeth Garrett Anderson in her consulting rooms, or Alice Meynell at her writing desk. They were, nonetheless, contributing to the economic well-being of their families, although few contemporaries – apart, perhaps, from a perceptive novelist like Elizabeth Gaskell or Anthony Trollope – recognised the full extent of this female contribution to the living standards and social power of the Victorian middle classes.

If it was difficult for contemporaries to see female investors as economic agents in their own right, what view was taken of the many thousands of middle-class women active in occupations outside their homes which drew no wages or salary? Voluntary service had long stood as a socially acceptable pursuit for ladies of private means, both before and after marriage. For some, visiting the homes of the poor, running a soup kitchen or leading a Bible class were pastimes undertaken to fill hours of the day not given over to household duties or entertaining. But for others, working unpaid for social or political causes was an absorbing interest or passion akin to a professional vocation. As the remit of the central and local State expanded, efforts by trained health visitors or social workers to draw a clear line between themselves and the 'amateur' lady volunteer were only partially successful. Social welfare in the late Victorian city was a mixed economy of State and voluntary action, and serious-minded volunteers attached to a body like the Charity Organisation Society could rival any public servant in terms of expertise and authority.[82]

So, too, could women who held elected office on School Boards, as Poor Law Guardians or later as local councillors, where they wielded real power to shape policy. The public career of Ruth Homan reveals some of the possibilities available to a middle-class wife and mother in the world of voluntary and municipal service, although it is perhaps significant that her activism post-dated her husband's death in 1880. As a widow with a young daughter, Homan became fascinated with elementary schooling and the problems facing the poorest families who used it. Elected to the London School Board in 1891, she devoted five days a week to Board business whilst additionally running charitable initiatives in the East End, including a boot and clothing club and a committee which served free hot meals to needy children during the harsh winter months. Homan was a keen Liberal and from the late 1890s was active in local politics, although she also belonged to the Women's Local Government Society, which helped female candidates from all parties seeking elected office. Homan was included in an 1895 collection of conversations with 'professional women', which described her working life alongside accounts by teachers, nurses, actresses, stockbrokers, photographers and librarians. The editor of the collection, journalist Margaret Bateson, was in no doubt that Homan deserved her place in such a book, as 'she spoke with conviction of the absorbing and increasing interest in her work which would repay a woman of any sacrifice of time and ease she might make in the cause of human helpfulness'. [83]

Another model of unwaged working motherhood was the socialist Margaret MacDonald, who started volunteering in Sunday Schools and boys' clubs and subsequently combined strenuous activity for the Women's Industrial Council and the Women's Labour League with bringing up her six children. MacDonald, as previously noted, was opposed on principle to married women's employment amongst the lower classes, but her own life was dominated by relentless organising, lobbying and campaigning. Her husband, the Labour leader James Ramsay MacDonald, remembered Margaret stretched out on the floor with papers and babies by her side, giving the latter 'now and again an encouraging nod or smile or word' as she read. This multitasking continued as the children grew older, one friend recalling how Margaret would 'look up from her Blue Books to watch the progress of a game, or to help with a sum, or to criticise or praise a drawing'.[84] A charwoman cleaned their flat on Lincoln's Inn Fields and a nursemaid took charge of the children when needed, allowing Margaret ample time to attend committees, address meetings or give evidence to parliamentary inquiries, as she did on the subject of home-work in 1907.

Neither Homan nor MacDonald drew salaries, yet both women led full working lives made possible by two factors. First, a private income enabled each to pursue her activities on a voluntary basis, commensurate with long-established traditions of female philanthropy and cushioned by the availability of paid domestic help at home. Second, both women focused their efforts in fields deemed appropriate to their class and sex: for Homan, the education of poor children; for MacDonald, the welfare and status of working-class housewives and women workers. Where these two conditions applied, male professional authority did not appear to be under threat, nor the sanctity of the home as woman's true domain. This, it would seem, was the most acceptable face of working motherhood for the late Victorian middle classes.

*

Most wives and mothers continued to play by these well-established rules as the nineteenth century gave way to the twentieth. If they had worked for pay before marriage, they dutifully retired and focused their energies on becoming efficient household managers, sympathetic helpmeets to their husbands and successful bearers and nurturers of the next generation. A minority continued to pursue their occupations, but doing so required exceptional self-belief, a keen awareness of where the boundaries of respectability lay, good health and good luck. The few women who achieved professional distinction did not make maternal status a central feature of their public identity: Beatrice Webb instead privately mourned her childlessness in her diary, whilst Elizabeth Garrett Anderson kept her pride at juggling motherhood and medicine firmly to herself. Lines were drawn less rigidly where a woman's 'work' appeared to blend harmlessly into the wider gamut of bourgeois feminine pastimes and accomplishments, such as writing or singing. And mothers had freest rein of all where their activities outside the home could be presented as an extension of their duties inside it, notably through social or public service which improved the lives of the poor. Here, it was widely believed, the middle-class mother was *not* overreaching herself: maternal sympathy, practical knowledge of domestic affairs and social superiority formed the ideal equipment with which to win the working-class housewife's trust and effect a moral transformation of her humble home.

This logic helped to entrench a view which identified women, regardless of their actual maternal status, as possessing special qualities which suited them to certain kinds of 'caring' occupations, such as nursing, teaching and social work. Those wishing to pursue careers in alternative, male-dominated fields would struggle against these gender stereotypes throughout the twentieth century (and into the twenty-first). Yet for some Edwardian feminists, this growing consensus around the public value of motherhood made it possible to advance new claims regarding women's professional status. Led by the literary scholar and suffragette Edith Morley, the Fabian Women's Group published a major study on this subject in 1914, *Women Workers in Seven Professions*. The contributors questioned existing norms which framed paid work and marriage as incompatible and argued instead that the trained mother had much to offer in occupations like teaching, where first-hand experience of caring for small children was a positive asset. As one headmistress put it:

> Often the most valuable years of a woman's life are lost to the school by her enforced retirement at marriage. She gives to it her younger, less experienced years, when she knows less of the world, less of the problems of the household, less of the outlook of the parents ... To the teacher-mother there will come an altogether new power of understanding, which should ultimately compensate the school for broken time during the earlier years of the life of her children.[85]

Another contributor made a similar point about medicine: 'The medical woman who is married can,' she wrote, 'better than any one else, render to society certain services in her profession, and it is desirable that these should not be lost.'[86]

Alongside these arguments about the special capabilities of mothers, the essayists also voiced concerns about the likely result of forcing this highly educated and physically fit population of women to lead celibate lives. Morley thought marriage bars 'racially dangerous' because they discouraged such women from having children and thus contributed to the alarming fall in the birth rate amongst the better-off middle classes. The point was echoed by a colleague later in the volume, who observed that 'the great need of society at the present day is that the most healthy and well-trained young men and women should be induced to found families, and public authorities by this bar put on the trained woman, are doing their best to hinder marriage'.[87]

Contributors to *Women Workers in Seven Professions* also objected to marriage bars on classic liberal grounds, arguing, as Harriet Taylor had in 1851, for the right of the individual to decide for herself about work after marriage. Giving mothers greater choice and control over their lives was also a fundamental objective of the 'cooperative housekeeping' schemes dreamed up by visionary feminists like Charlotte Perkins Gilman in the US, and an abiding concern of writers like Dora Marsden, who founded the avant-garde libertarian journal *The Freewoman* in 1912.[88] Yet the creeping language of eugenics was unmistakable in feminist reflections on the professional working mother by these years. It signalled a growing tendency to discard Victorian notions of moral duty or spiritual mission and to reframe motherhood as a social function necessary for the perpetuation of the 'race'. This tendency was not peculiar to Britain, but shaped debates about family and social welfare across Europe and North America, albeit with different emphases and consequences.[89] By 1914, observers of all ideological stripes viewed the problems and possibilities of working motherhood through this lens of citizenship, nationhood and population. It was a vision that was about to be dramatically sharpened by the political convulsions, social upheavals and economic shocks which swept Europe as the continent plunged into its first total war.

PART TWO

Citizens, 1914–1951

4

Temporary Patriots

On a dark night on the Western Front in June 1915, Major John MacLennan of the Gordon Highlanders was thrown violently from his horse. The creature had stumbled into a shell hole during a routine transportation of supplies to the trenches, causing MacLennan to fall heavily and sustain injuries which laid him up for several days. Over the coming weeks and months, the Major complained of severe shoulder pain and abdominal discomfort, but he stayed with his men until the following spring, when he was granted leave to visit his family in Aberdeen. MacLennan arrived home in March 1916 and by August he was dead, the official cause recorded as cancer of the liver. MacLennan's widow, Christina, did not accept this verdict, which had consequences for the level of pension she could expect from the army: deaths not directly attributable to military service were paid at a considerably lower rate. Convinced that her husband's condition originated in his earlier fall, she wrote many letters to the War Office requesting a more generous settlement, citing MacLennan's thirty years of loyal military service and the precarious financial position in which his family now found themselves. These forceful missives secured Mrs MacLennan £105 per annum plus £20 for each of her three younger children, but it was a modest sum from which to fund a comfortable lifestyle for a sizeable middle-class family. To make matters worse, tragedy struck again in May 1917, when MacLennan's eldest son,

Donald, was killed whilst fighting with his late father's battalion in France.

By November 1917, Mrs MacLennan could no longer manage on her pension and decided to look for paid employment. Despite her lack of experience (she had spent the years since marriage doing voluntary pastoral work for army wives), MacLennan secured a decoding post at the Royal Naval Office in Aberdeen with a salary of £150 per annum. In some respects, the job was ideal: she worked a manageable four-hour shift each day, was not required to move from her home into quarters, and the work was clean and respectable. Yet Christina MacLennan's expectations were set higher and in February 1918 she wrote to the Director of the Women's Royal Naval Service (WRNS), Dame Katharine Furse, asking for a private meeting at the organisation's headquarters in London. This was granted and Mrs MacLennan used it to request more responsibility at better pay. She later restated her case in July, during Furse's tour of Scotland. By persuading titled ladies of her acquaintance to write on her behalf, together with Sir Nevil Macready, the adjutant general of the British Expeditionary Force whom her husband had personally served before the war, MacLennan manoeuvred a transfer to the Admiralty in London. There she could live with her daughter, now studying music, and see her youngest son who, following family tradition, had enlisted and was soon to be despatched to France.

Christina MacLennan was evidently a resourceful and determined woman. The ranking officer at the Royal Naval Office thought her 'an excellent organizer' and 'quite capable of holding any position in the WRNS'. Yet she did not impress everyone. At their first meeting, Furse found her 'nice' but somewhat reserved and not of the 'first-class' quality needed for a high-level position. At their second encounter, Furse's impression of MacLennan was altered: she 'looked ambitious', was 'rather loud' and wore dangly gold earrings, which Furse asked her to remove. Furse doubted 'her getting on really well with women', and when MacLennan wrote asking for yet another meeting, she was palmed off on a colleague. MacLennan harmed her standing further by arranging the transfer to London without consulting the WRNS's chief in Scotland. By then, however, Christina MacLennan's life was falling apart. Her work at the Admiralty was full-time and far more intense than she had been used to in Aberdeen. She made three applications for sick leave during the first two months, prompted by the return of an 'old trouble' for which she had had an operation some years earlier. On 5 November, MacLennan requested further leave, telling her superior at the Admiralty that she was struggling to sleep and feared herself to be on the brink of a nervous breakdown. A medical examination confirmed she was suffering from insomnia and indigestion and was 'inclined to weep'. On 14 November, just a few days after the signing of the armistice, MacLennan was assessed as unfit for duty and, with her agreement, given discharge papers with a month's paid leave. It is not hard to imagine her state of mind: still grieving for the loss of John and Donald, anxious about her surviving sons now both in the field, and feeling the pressure as sole provider for her privately educated daughter. MacLennan, desperate for a less strenuous job, sought help from the WRNS's demobilisation department, but in January 1919 she was still looking. 'It is women of her type who will be difficult to place,' the WRNS officer wrote, '& she herself needs work very urgently.'[1]

*

Christina MacLennan's story captures the matrix of personal tragedy, unforeseen events, financial pressure and time-limited opportunities which determined so much of the working lives of British mothers during the First World War. The female workforce grew by 1.25 million between August 1914 and Armistice Day, by which time a record 7.3 million women were in paid employment.[2] As in pre-war days, the typical worker was young and unmarried, but substantial numbers of wives and mothers also poured into munitions factories, filled men's jobs on trains, buses and trams, laboured on the land or in the uniformed auxiliary services, or took up posts in central and local government, where marriage bars were suspended for the duration. The majority of working mothers were already wage-earners at the time war broke out or had been prior to marriage. What changed for them was therefore not the experience of paid work itself but the *kind* of paid work now on offer. The casual economy of charring, cleaning and taking in home-work did not disappear, but more mothers found themselves doing skilled or semi-skilled jobs for good wages than at any time previously. Some benefited further from vastly improved conditions, including well-ventilated workspaces, better toilet facilities, on-site canteens, day nurseries and regular medical care.[3]

To those who had been battling to improve woman's economic status and advance her claims for equality, the war seemed to present an unprecedented opportunity. The suffragist leader Millicent Fawcett wrote in March 1918 that the idea 'formerly very widely entertained that women were incapable of skilled work' had been 'shattered by experience since the outbreak of the war'.[4] The trade unionist Mary Macarthur believed the future to be 'great with promise for women workers. Not only had women changed, but men's conception of women had changed.'[5] Yet skilled work in industry was made available to women under strict conditions set out in the Treasury Agreement of March 1915, whereby government pledged to maintain established rates of pay in return for trade union cooperation over the temporary use of female labour and the relaxation of factory regulations. Male trade unionists were never in any doubt about the purpose of this deal: to protect men's wages and jobs when they returned to reclaim them after the war.

Casting a further shadow was the ambiguous position of mothers within the rousing wartime rhetoric of women's industrial mobilisation. Macarthur wished to secure 'as wide a sphere as is possible' for the woman in industry when peace returned, but only where 'consistent with the maintenance of health and the welfare of the race'.[6] By 1915, Macarthur was a married woman and mother to a young daughter, but she evidently did not regard her own decision to continue working for pay as a viable or desirable option for most working-class housewives. In this Macarthur spoke not only for the majority of her comrades in the labour and trade union movements, but for a wider body of opinion which called, with increasing volume, for measures to support mothers in their full-time occupation as homemakers to the nation. Not everyone agreed on the exact form of those measures, but the broad proposition that the State should do more to value women's unpaid caring work gained new adherents, including those galvanised by the spectre of death on the Western Front to improve life for those yet to be born.

The war thus created a peculiar ideological landscape for the working mother. She was welcomed into factories and celebrated publicly for her service, but at the same time became the object of intense official scrutiny in which her 'higher' duty as life-giver and nurturer was continually invoked. This lent an air of conditionality and temporariness to all debates about women's war work, because every woman was treated as a potential or actual mother.[7] It also masked the realities of life for hundreds of thousands of working women with children dependent upon them. They, like Christina MacLennan, were fighting their own personal battles for physical and emotional survival.

*

By far the greatest numbers of mothers found wartime employment in munitions, the vast array of industries which supplied Britain's fighting forces with ships, tanks, aeroplanes, armoured cars, machine guns, shells, bayonets, bullets, grenades, helmets, boots, tents, ropes, haversacks, gas masks, shaving kits, bandages, mess tins and everything else required to win a continental war. From May 1915, this massive machine was controlled by the Ministry of Munitions, which managed 200 national factories directly and oversaw production in more than 5,000 private firms. By 1918, nearly 5 million workers came within the Ministry's remit, 3.3 million of whom manufactured armaments for the front line.[8] In total, this workforce produced 4 million rifles, 250,000 machine guns, 52,000 aeroplanes, 2,800 tanks, 25,000 artillery pieces and over 170 million rounds of artillery shells.[9] Women made up just under a third of these metal, chemical and engineering operatives. They worked either as direct 'substitutes' for men or as 'dilutees' performing skilled jobs divided into semi-skilled processes with the aid of automatic machinery, and always under terms carefully hammered out with the unions, most notably the powerful Amalgamated Society of Engineers.

Women came to munitions work from occupations of all kinds. Mill hands, dressmakers, domestic servants, agricultural labourers, charwomen and shop girls mingled with the many thousands of women who had been employed in factories (although usually on unskilled work) before the war. Recruits arrived in droves from Ireland and volunteers travelled from Canada, Australia and other parts of the Commonwealth to do their bit. Even leisured ladies chose to go 'munitioneering', later writing vivid accounts of their wartime adventures on the shop floor.[10]

The exact nature of the work varied enormously. Some found themselves operating the overhead electric cranes which whirled loads around the factory; others mastered heavy machine tools to cut, drill and stamp metal into precise shapes; a select number examined finished products for imperfections, a task requiring accuracy and intense concentration. Many jobs simply needed strength and stamina, such as lifting or rolling shells onto trolleys, loading goods into vehicles and sweeping floors. In shell-filling factories, women worked with explosive chemicals in specially constructed 'danger sheds', where they were required to leave all jewellery and personal belongings at the door and don protective gowns and headgear. Known as 'canaries', these workers were universally recognised by their yellow-tinged skin and hair, an effect of the exposure to chemicals. The work was different again in aircraft factories, where women were employed as welders and carpenters, or as needlewomen stitching the linen which formed the 'skin' of the planes.

Munitions work took place in all manner of settings: long-established armament factories in congested urban areas, newly constructed plants in remote rural locations, hastily adapted workshops in tram depots, drill halls, cinemas and commercial premises used for different purposes before the war. The Royal Arsenal at Woolwich, south London, expanded to occupy a site sprawling over 600 acres and comprised multiple buildings producing shells, small arms, chemicals and guns, as well as thirty-one canteens, a hospital and an internal railway system. By November 1917, over 30,000 people worked there, the vast majority of them women. Penny Hamilton, a young middle-class volunteer who got a job in a Woolwich fuse factory in 1916, remembered rising at 5 a.m. from her lodgings in Blackheath and struggling to mount one of the overcrowded buses serving the Arsenal in order to arrive in time for her 7 a.m. shift. By contrast, when she moved to the Government Rolling Mills near Southampton the following year, Hamilton rented a cottage with friends and was able to cycle to work along pleasant country lanes, negotiating a tricky final stretch through the mud and clutter of the half-built site. Hamilton ended the war back in London in very different conditions, with a job in a dilapidated former rag factory that was riddled with bugs.[11]

In these workplaces women picked up the lingo of their trades, learning to refer to spoiled shells as 'scrap' and to the long aisle separating their machines as the 'street'. They got used to wearing boiler suits and overalls, and to getting splashed by the oil dripping constantly from their machines. Some customised work clothes by lacing their shoes with coloured ribbons, wearing their caps at a jaunty angle or swapping them altogether for bandanas or handkerchiefs. Rules on dress were generally strict, but Hamilton recalled one woman who insisted on wearing her own dungarees and a man's cap, and another who wore 'lacy openwork stockings and high-heeled shoes' while operating her crane.[12] Each worker brought a teapot for her personal use, and some fried bacon on charcoal braziers next to their machines during the morning break. It was common to go home for dinner or to bring provisions to consume at work, but over time more factories installed well-equipped canteens serving affordable hot meals. The writer Monica Cosens described the cheerful dining room operated by the Young Women's Christian Association at the shell-filling factory where she worked in 1916: a long, low building with colourful walls and counters piled high with buns, oranges, sweets, urns of boiling water and glasses of milk, above which hung blackboards advertising the day's menu.[13] At the Royal Small Arms Factory in Enfield, canteen facilities improved dramatically from the provision of bread and butter and cups of tea in cramped quarters to offering a full range of meat and fish dishes, fruit tarts, milk puddings and pastries in accommodation spacious enough to feed 500 women per sitting.[14] By September 1917, nearly a million munition workers were eating hot meals provided by factory canteens.[15]

Medical care was available in many workplaces (although varying in degree and quality), as were the ministrations of welfare supervisors, a group of mostly unmarried middle-class women employed to hire, fire and manage the female workforce.[16] This wartime innovation was not universally welcomed. The presence of 'lady' supervisors was resented where they adopted a high-handed manner or took too close an interest in a girl's home circumstances or romantic liaisons. But many, like the legendary figure of Lilian Barker at Woolwich Arsenal, won the trust of their workers by combining firmness with fairness and by making practical improvements regarding food, uniforms, washing facilities, restrooms, first-aid posts and the welfare of workers off sick.[17] Barker, it was said, was affectionately serenaded with her favourite tune, 'Pack Up Your Troubles in Your Old Kit Bag', wherever she went in the Arsenal.[18] Some supervisors encouraged women to put on concert parties during the dinner hour for their own entertainment, usually comprising popular songs, comic skits and silly costumes. A number of factories started up women's football teams, whose fixtures would often draw large crowds. At Woolwich, Barker started up drama groups, classes in gymnastics, fencing, painting, debating and embroidery, and mixed evening clubs to which girls were allowed to bring their sweethearts.[19]

Those writing about female munition workers for the wartime public usually painted an upbeat picture of a happy, well-looked-after workforce, remarking frequently upon the high spirits and camaraderie that pervaded the shop floor. Girls sang the latest ragtime ditties as they worked, back-chatted with male supervisors and each other, jostled for space by the cloakroom mirrors and fought and giggled their way to the tea urn during their breaks. They were a 'very jolly, noisy rollicking lot', according to one anonymous lady volunteer.[20] Such observations had obvious propaganda value and invariably glossed over the darker sides of munitions work: the risks of chemical exposure, industrial accidents and air raids, intrusive medical inspections, and the unpleasant behaviours of male co-workers, which might in some cases border on harassment or abuse. Yet the memories of munition workers when interviewed by historians in later decades tended to confirm the broadly positive portrait. Most women said they had enjoyed their war work, which they saw as a service to fathers, husbands and sons fighting on the front line. For those coming straight from school, from small villages, or from live-in posts as domestic servants or shop assistants, munitions work felt like a new type of freedom, as well as an opportunity to make a direct contribution to the winning of the war.[21]

*

Much of the contemporary comment and retrospective testimonies of women regarding their wartime work privilege the experiences of younger, unmarried women without children.[22] Reconstructing the lives of *mothers* employed in munitions is more difficult. The overall number of wives and mothers is unknown, but anecdotal accounts suggest that their presence in war factories varied from negligible to as high as 40 per cent, 50 per cent or even 60 per cent.[23] Some employers refused to take on married women in line with earlier practices, whilst the wartime State never explicitly targeted this group in its recruitment literature. Nonetheless, as the demand for armaments soared in the first months of 1915, it became clear that women's labour was needed on a far more ambitious scale than previously thought and that mothers could not be exempt from the moral pressure to serve.[24]

Like their younger co-workers, married women were attracted to jobs in munitions because of the high wages and their desire to help menfolk fighting overseas. They were far less likely, however, to take advantage of the opportunities for dancing, sports or cinema-going enjoyed by single girls after clocking off at the factory. Mothers had to shoulder a double shift of paid factory work and unpaid housework just as they had before, only war conditions now made this dual responsibility even harder to bear. Restrictions on working hours were lifted and food shortages in the later stages of the conflict turned cooking and shopping into an intolerable burden for many.[25] Inadequate public transport meant that a mother working a twelve-hour shift might be away from home for fourteen hours or more, drastically reducing the time available for cooking and cleaning, feeding and bathing children, and for her own recuperation and rest. Janet Campbell, Medical Officer at the Board of Education, remarked that 'even Sunday, which should bring relief, must often be spent doing the weekly washing, baking or cleaning, and if such a day is followed by a night shift it is small wonder if the output of work is not as good as it might be'.[26] A few married women preferred night-work precisely because it kept the day free for domestic tasks, but most discovered that it was impossible to function on so little sleep. At one factory in the north-east, it was common practice for married women to take an unauthorised day off once every few weeks when they felt 'just done up' or 'dead beat'.[27] This could nonetheless be risky, as serial absentees were often hauled before munitions tribunals and fined. One tribunal assessor noted sympathetically that when a working mother appeared, it was nearly always 'because she has failed to achieve the impossible, and has neglected her work for the sake of her family'.[28]

For mothers moving to factory areas to find work, securing lodgings could be difficult. Government hostels were designed to house single girls, whilst many private landladies refused to rent rooms to mothers with small children. Organising childcare was also a challenge. As before the war, the most common arrangement was to leave babies and toddlers with trusted minders and for school-age children to look after themselves until their parents returned from work. Some employers were flexible around time-keeping. At the Rolling Mills in Southampton, for example, Dorothy Haigh was given an extra half hour at dinner to breastfeed her baby, who was cared for at home by Dorothy's mother.[29] A different solution was described by a welfare supervisor at a National

Ordnance Factory, who allowed an unmarried mother employed in the canteen to bring her baby to work. In fine weather, the child lay in its cot on the sunny veranda, where, in the supervisor's words, 'it thrives and is a source of interest and joy to the factory girls'.[30] Other workplaces were less accommodating. A young mother who made mess tins for soldiers wrote to *The Woman Worker* in despair in May 1917 after being ordered to work longer hours. She was already struggling to start her shift on time after getting her baby dressed, fed and delivered to the minder. She kept losing her bonus due to lateness, but was denied permission to leave in order to find a job with less strenuous hours.[31]

The other option was to use a day nursery. Places expanded significantly during the war as a result of government subsidies and growing demand for women's labour in munitions districts. By mid-1918, there were over 160 State-funded crèches in operation with room for 7,000 children. Most were open from 8 a.m. to 7 p.m. five days a week, plus a half-day on Saturday, and some took children overnight. They tended to be located near women's homes rather than next to munitions works, which were targets for Zeppelin attacks and always at risk of accidental explosions. Some nurseries had comfortable, purpose-built premises with attractive outdoor space. The crèche serving the Woolwich Arsenal was in a centrally heated bungalow with large French windows and a veranda which led to a sizeable garden containing a sandpit.[32] The Canongate nursery in Edinburgh was similarly well equipped, with specially designed glass partitions between the cots for nap time.[33] More common, however, were adapted residential or commercial properties, such as the abandoned pub in Bow which the suffragette Sylvia Pankhurst turned into a nursery and infant welfare centre, or the three-storey building a few miles away in Whitechapel which catered exclusively for Jewish families.[34] The matrons in charge of these establishments placed heavy emphasis on good hygiene, fresh air and diet. Children were examined on arrival, bathed and dressed in nursery clothing, while their own garments were disinfected in time for pick-up. As much activity as possible took place outside. Toddlers at Pankhurst's nursery in Bow trotted daily

to nearby Victoria Park, 'each with a tiny hand grasping a rope'.[35]
In Whitechapel, children were let loose in the rooftop playground,
whilst at Dunsmoor, near Coventry, they spent most of their day
in a large open-air shed. Children were fed the same sort of fare on
offer to their mothers in factory canteens – typically meat, potatoes
and stewed fruit – plus milk, and lots of it. The Notting Hill Day
Nursery encouraged nursing mothers to breastfeed their babies
during the dinner hour and take a meal for themselves at the same
time.[36]

Not all working-class mothers were keen to use these facilities.
Many were deterred, as they had been before the war, by uppity
matrons, rigid rules and worries about outbreaks of infectious
diseases, such as measles, whooping cough and meningitis. This
latter fear was not wholly ungrounded, although in general the
physical health of children attending wartime nurseries was good
and in many cases actually improved. A more important reason
why the hot meals, milk and clean clothing on offer did not attract
more takers was the fact that munition workers were increasingly
able to provide these things through their own wage packet. Few
women in industry received equal pay, but most benefited from
a general rise in the level of wages and the temporary pledges
made under the Treasury Agreement of 1915 to protect men's jobs
after the war.[37] Those formerly earning a barely subsistence wage
of 12s or 15s on unskilled factory work could now take home £2
or £3 a week doing piece work in munitions. Employers in other
trades were forced to raise pay accordingly, leading to a reduction
in the overall differential between male and female wages, which
narrowed from a pre-war level of around 50 per cent to something
in the region of 30 to 35 per cent.[38] As female trade unionists had
always insisted, a better-paid workforce was easier to organise, and
women's union membership shot up from less than 500,000 to
1.25 million by the end of the war, with most joining general unions
or Mary Macarthur's National Federation of Women Workers.
Women remained excluded, however, from 'craft' unions like the
Amalgamated Society of Engineers, which jealously guarded the
interests of its male membership.[39]

For working-class mothers, the opportunity to earn decent wages made a real difference to their standard of living. This was particularly true of munition workers in receipt of an additional separation allowance (paid by the army to the dependants of soldiers serving overseas), although the most fortunately placed were undoubtedly those with husbands also earning high wages in industry.[40] Observers noted dramatic improvements in the diet of female factory workers, which they attributed not only to the availability of canteens but to changing habits as women realised that they needed, deserved and could afford to buy or cook solid, nutritious meals. Where men were away at the front, wives no longer had to make do with the scraps left after the male breadwinner had taken his pick. A welfare supervisor in Enfield noticed that workers stopped bringing stodgy provisions from home and ate the hot meals available at the canteen instead.[41] Medic Janet Campbell reported in 1918 that 'the bread and butter and tea dietary is practically a thing of the past as far as munition workers are concerned'.[42] This superior diet was especially beneficial to the health of pregnant women and probably contributed to the long-term fall in infant mortality.[43]

Set against these improvements were high rents, rising food prices and, from 1917, serious shortages of key staples including meat, sugar and butter, which all went on ration later that year. Most munition workers found that their income just about kept pace with the soaring cost of living, but better wages did not in themselves solve all problems and certainly could not ease women's anxieties about loved ones in harm's way at the front. Shopping, queuing, commuting, arranging childcare and attending to housework all took their toll. A doctor from Bolton reported the case of a soldier's wife who earned £4 a week in munitions but was too exhausted to prepare proper meals for her family. She instead gave her two children money each day to buy whatever they fancied from the local cook-shop.[44] The doctor cited the case as evidence of the evils of letting mothers do war work, but the fatigue he described was really not much different from that felt by mothers in industry before 1914. What *was* new was the fact that this mother, unlike her pre-war counterpart, was paid a breadwinning wage over which she had full control. Money did not eliminate the stresses and strains of the working mother's wartime life, but those able to earn it were undoubtedly better equipped to cope with them.

*

Munitions provided by far the largest number of jobs to wage-earning mothers, but it was not the only kind of war work available. Boosting agricultural production was an urgent priority, with over 100,000 agricultural labourers enlisted in the armed forces and, from 1917, imports severely disrupted by German submarine warfare. Married women tended not to join the chief recruiting bodies, the Women's National Land Service Corps and its successor, the Women's Land Army, both of which targeted young, well-educated women who could sign up for six or twelve months and move to wherever their labour was needed.[45] Older women living in rural areas preferred to make casual or part-time arrangements with local farmers, very much as they had before the war. The kind of work they did was also similar, mostly weeding, fruit picking, root-pulling, hoeing and spreading. Training for the more skilled work done by men, such as threshing, ploughing, hedging and caring for livestock, required attendance at residential courses and was primarily aimed at the more mobile Land Army recruits.[46] In some areas, however, local organisers made active efforts to attract mothers by establishing day nurseries. These had to open very early in order to cover the hours typically worked by farmhands. The nursery at Long Sutton in Lincolnshire, which was located close to the fields in a converted cottage, took children from 4 a.m. during strawberry-picking season and sometimes kept them as late as 9 p.m.[47]

Rural housewives who preferred not to take on regular waged work could instead join a Women's Institute (WI), the first of which appeared in Anglesey, North Wales, in September 1915. With support and funding from the Board of Agriculture, the movement to organise countrywomen quickly grew, with 199 Institutes in operation by the end of the war, soon to be united under a National

Federation. WI members did their bit to drive up food production by bottling fruit, keeping poultry, pigs, rabbits and goats, and growing vegetables for sale locally.[48] These were all activities which could be carried out at home, sometimes with the help of children, or through village cooperatives. In Wales, the Criccieth Women's Institute established a regular weekly market which sold goods from members' gardens, allotments and smallholdings on a wholesale basis. Other Institutes ran market stalls or held table-top sales in a more ad hoc style.[49]

The wartime State was slow to mobilise women for military service, but from 1917 further opportunities for employment opened up in the newly established Women's Army Auxiliary Corps (WAAC), Women's Royal Naval Service (WRNS) and Women's Royal Air Force (WRAF). These bodies aimed to free men for front-line soldiering by transferring as much non-combatant work as possible to women: cooking, cleaning, laundering, chauffeuring, portering, repairing vehicles, operating telegraphs, coding and decoding and carrying out routine clerical duties.[50] Some of the 80,000 women who joined one of the auxiliary services over the course of the war were posted to stations behind the lines in France, Belgium, Italy and Greece, but most served in army camps and airbases in Britain. The majority of recruits were young, unmarried women, although there was no formal bar on married women signing up and a small number did, some of whom were mothers. This group included former charwomen now employed in WAAC hostels, laundries and storehouses, but also the occasional middle-class widow fallen on hard times, like Christina MacLennan at the WRNS.[51]

As well as doing work which supplied the armed forces directly, women stepped into jobs in other parts of the economy left vacant by men serving on the front. It is not known exactly how many of the 85,000 women employed on Britain's railways and trams were mothers, but their presence was certainly not uncommon.[52] Three of the seven female railway workers who testified before the War Cabinet Committee on Women in Industry in 1918 were married, two of whom had dependent children.[53] Mrs Kidby was a ticket collector for the Central London Railway, working ten hours a day at the barrier, including Saturdays, to support her two children. Mrs Mullen, a widow and mother of six, cleaned engines for the London and North Western Railway, employed on a mix of day- and night-time shifts.[54] Municipal authorities and train companies often recruited employees' wives as direct substitutes and paid them the male rate, a practice to which trade unions agreed, presumably because such women could be relied upon to hand the jobs back to their menfolk without dispute at the end of the war.[55] The War Office encouraged this too, advising employers that substitution by family members 'helps to avoid domestic disturbance and the breaking up of homes'.[56] Propaganda sometimes played up this theme of whole-family war service, paying tribute to wives and mothers who freed their menfolk for soldiering overseas. One official gave a speech in which he cited the case of a Yorkshire mother, 'who early in the war sent her only son to the fighting line. The lad was a skilled mechanic, and she took his place at his lathe in the Leeds shop where he worked.' This courageous woman, he concluded, 'is not only keeping this job going, but her output on the job she is doing is a record for the whole country'.[57]

*

Opportunities for mothers in white-collar occupations were, compared to those in industry, far more limited. Government departments in Whitehall ballooned in size between 1914 and 1918, but the majority of new clerical workers were young and unmarried. One eyewitness in London recalled the 'vast army of girl clerks' which descended upon the capital's restaurants and tea-rooms during the dinner hour.[58] It was a similar sight in the City, where hundreds of young women filled jobs in banks and businesses vacated by serving soldiers.[59] Some married women did find office work, as the personal advertisement columns of the broadsheet press revealed. One advert was placed by a 'Lady, engaged at Whitehall' who was seeking lodgings for 'herself and little one, with people who will care for child during the day'.[60] With husbands swapping comfortable salaries for army pay, some middle-class wives were forced to seek work in order to pay school fees and maintain living standards. A number returned to teaching, where marriage bars were temporarily suspended and good salaries could be earned: pay for elementary school teachers rose by 44 per cent over the course of the war, whilst changes to the rules on superannuation meant that women with discontinuous service could now draw a pension.[61] It was not always easy, however, to find charwomen and nursery maids to do the necessary housework and childcare, given the more attractive options on offer in the war industries. One middle-class observer advocated the establishment of special boarding houses for 'better-class' working women under the charge of a 'communal mother', who would organise meals and supervise a shared crèche. (It was taken for granted by this writer that 'ladies by birth and education' would not consider placing their children in an ordinary day nursery.)[62]

A handful of educated women held posts of real responsibility. Adelaide Anderson continued to preside over the female factory inspectorate, now with a much extended remit, whilst Rose Squire was seconded to the Ministry of Munitions as Director of Women's Welfare. Their former colleague, May Tennant, headed the women's division at the Ministry of National Service, established in 1917 to manage labour supply to industry, with her friend, the imperialist and anti-suffragist Violet Markham, as her deputy. Tennant subsequently served next to Squire on the Health of Munition Workers Committee, which published numerous memoranda and reports on women's employment, including extensive evidence gathered by Janet Campbell and other female medics and inspectors. Edith Lyttelton was another prominent wartime public servant. Best known as an advocate of imperial federation and a writer of plays about the evils of sweating, Lyttelton was made deputy director of the women's branch of the Ministry of Agriculture in 1917, responsible for recruiting more women to work on the land. In this role she had dealings with Gertrude Denman, who oversaw the expansion of the Women's Institutes, first as an official of the Agricultural Organisation Society and later as honorary assistant director in the Ministry's Food Production Department. Other top female administrators included Mona Chalmers Watson, a trained doctor who became Chief Controller of the WAAC; her deputy, Helen Gwynne-Vaughan, who later took up the directorship of the WRAF; Katharine Furse, the first director of the WRNS; and Maud McCarthy, who, as matron-in-chief to the British Expeditionary Force (BEF) in France, was responsible for the work of thousands of nurses in the field.

Many of these high-profile women were unmarried, but a few were mothers of young children. Furse, Chalmers Watson and Denman all had offspring under the age of twelve when war broke out, whilst the youngest of Tennant's five children was not yet two.[63] Women of their social class could rely on maids, nannies and boarding schools to deal with the practical problems of household management and day-to-day childcare, although some did feel constrained in their work by a moral duty to home and family. Chalmers Watson committed herself to the WAAC for twelve months only, at the end of which she resigned in order to rejoin her husband and children in Edinburgh. She also insisted that she would not travel overseas. That Chalmers Watson felt able to dictate these terms was revealing of how far family connections could overcome any prejudice that might have existed towards her as a working wife and mother. She was greatly helped by the intervention of her brother, Auckland Geddes, then a senior official at the War Office, who arranged a private meeting for his sister with top army personnel, after which the WAAC job was safely hers.[64] Tennant and Denman benefited in similar ways from privileged backgrounds and well-developed networks. The wife of a government minister, Tennant was already widely known in Whitehall as a former factory inspector and authority on 'dangerous' trades, and she had served in 1909 on the Royal Commission on Divorce. Denman was the daughter of a successful businessman, whilst her husband was a Liberal peer and former governor general of Australia.

Another reason for the absence of internal opposition to these high-level appointments was the comforting fact that these ladies were engaged as temporary public servants only, and on work deemed appropriate to their sex, mostly to do with the mobilisation and management of other women. They were patriots doing their duty, not career women seeking permanent professional advancement. Much of the war work of middle- and upper-class women was cast in this non-threatening feminine mould, from those joining the Voluntary Aid Detachments run by the Red Cross to others turning their stately homes into military hospitals or knitting socks for the troops. Even where jobs were salaried, required training and were performed by women who very much needed to earn their living – as in the case of Christina MacLennan – this kind of work retained its voluntary and short-term character in the eyes of the wartime State. These activities bore a reassuring resemblance to the social, political and philanthropic traditions of earlier decades through which women had served the wider community without overtly challenging the basis of male power.[65]

Yet the high premium placed on notions of self-sacrifice and service after 1914 subtly altered the dynamics in play. Suffragists were especially keen to encourage displays of dutiful citizenship during the war, conscious of their likely effect in bolstering arguments for women's enfranchisement once peace was achieved. The Women's Social and Political Union suspended its militant campaign and led a 'Right to Serve' demonstration through rainswept London streets in July 1915, complete with marching bands and fluttering union jacks. The non-militant National Union of Women's Suffrage Societies included some prominent pacifists who resigned en masse in 1915, but other members, not least the fiercely patriotic Millicent Fawcett, threw themselves into war work on both the home and fighting fronts. These feminist initiatives, from roving hospital units to female police patrols, were pursued with a double purpose – not only would they aid Britain's cause and secure her eventual victory, but they would demonstrate women's loyalty to king and country and place their fitness for the vote beyond doubt.[66]

*

It is impossible to generalise about the extraordinarily varied forms of war work carried out by British women, but it is clear that mothers had a hand in nearly all of them. Where good wages, satisfactory childcare and adequate housing were available, the lives of working mothers materially improved. Yet for every well-paid munition worker or tram conductor, there were dozens more still trapped in the makeshift economy of charring, minding, letting out rooms and taking in home-work. This casualised labour market did not disappear, even if some women were able to escape it for more lucrative jobs in the war industries. Despite experiencing some decline since the great anti-sweating campaigns earlier in the century, home-work remained a significant source of employment in places like east London.[67] Sylvia Pankhurst recalled how poor home-working mothers in Bow came to her for help, including one widow who finished soldiers' trousers from five in the morning until late into the evening, her little son fetching the shopping and preparing meals after he returned home from school.[68] Pankhurst staged another sweated industries exhibition in May 1915 to draw attention to the shocking conditions in which soldiers' uniforms were being made, although it took an outbreak of measles amongst the troops – believed to have originated with infected garments – to convince the authorities to ban home-work on all army tailoring contracts.

Some needlewomen subsequently went into the factory, but not everyone could take this option, because they had no one to look after their children, were in poor health or lived too far from any munitions works. These mothers were the most reliant on separation allowances, which were paid on a weekly basis to around 1.5 million women with husbands serving in the army by the end of 1914.[69] The level of payments, which took into account any dependent children, was raised twice over the course of the war, prompting some to speculate that the poorest mothers were now better off and could even withdraw from waged labour and live on their allowances. But whilst it was true that the wife of an enlisted farm labourer with four or five children probably received a more adequate income from her allowance than she previously had from her husband, the system was designed to provide families with only basic subsistence.[70] Women's organisations complained repeatedly that rising rents, fuel and food prices made it impossible to live decently on allowances, and they criticised the inefficient and heartless bureaucracy which prevented many wives from receiving their payments promptly, or indeed at all.[71] Sylvia Pankhurst was incensed by the high-handed lady volunteers who told mothers in Bow to sell their furniture and move to cheaper lodgings before they could apply for a separation allowance.[72]

As Pankhurst and many others pointed out, the allowance was not a charitable handout but the wife's entitlement in lieu of the wages she would have received from her husband in normal times. Unfortunately, this substitute wage packet could be just as susceptible to the prior claims of the male breadwinner. Soldiers were required to sacrifice a portion of their pay towards the cost of the scheme but some chose not to do so, as a result of which their wives did not receive the full amount due to them. Other men paid up but wrote to their families asking for socks, underclothes, cigarettes, soap and other essential supplies. This was usually because the army failed to provide these basic items, but the added expenditure was a heavy blow for the housewife trying to house, feed and clothe herself and her children on a tight budget.[73] In many cases the earnings of grown-up children raised household income to a more comfortable level, but it was not surprising that mothers often sought their own ways of supplementing allowances through waged work.

Widows and unmarried mothers found it especially necessary to secure paid employment in order to make ends meet. Pensions were introduced at the beginning of the war for the wives of men killed in action, but because these payments represented a continuing budget commitment rather than a temporary benefit, the value was set very low, initially at only 5s per week. It was assumed, both by central government and local Poor Law unions, that widows would find other sources of income, whether from relatives, charity or their own earnings.[74] Unmarried mothers could claim neither allowances nor pensions unless they could show that the father of their child had supported them before the war; such women were referred to by officials in somewhat oxymoronic terms as 'unmarried wives'. Illegitimate births rose only slightly between 1914 and 1918, despite popular belief that sexual morals had lapsed as a result of greater mixing in the workplace and short-lived wartime romances. Nonetheless, young women who did have babies out of wedlock often faced prejudice, including from fellow workers. 'We thought it was disgusting for girls to be pregnant in those times,' was the recollection of one munition worker.[75] As in previous decades, some tried to procure abortions whilst others, desperate to conceal their shame, abandoned their babies at birth or, in extreme cases, even resorted to infanticide.[76]

Yet employers could be understanding, too. In Woolwich, Lilian Barker refused to sack unmarried girls who fell pregnant, insisting, 'I will only do it when the man in question, if he be an Arsenal employee, is also dismissed.'[77] Helen Gwynne-Vaughan took a similar stance towards WAAC employees who got themselves into trouble. She interviewed each girl individually, issued no penalties and discharged them on compassionate grounds.[78] In east London, Sylvia Pankhurst did her best to persuade errant soldiers to marry the mothers of their offspring or, failing that, attempted to find suitable employment for the women so as to keep them and their babies out of the workhouse.[79] The Women's Labour League argued for the establishment of hostels under the charge of 'wise and kindly matrons', where these so-called 'war babies' could be looked after during the day while their mothers worked.[80] Other sympathisers included the suffragist and social worker Lettice Fisher, who founded the National Council for the Unmarried Mother and Her Child in April 1918 after witnessing first-hand the difficult lives of girls who gave birth to illegitimate babies in wartime Sheffield. This body would play a major role in advocating for the needs of lone mothers – and, later on, lone parents – throughout the rest of the century.

*

These initiatives sprang from a larger groundswell of wartime anxiety about the health of mothers and infants. Such fears had been evident since at least the 1880s, but the loss of British lives in the trenches lent a new urgency to infant preservation efforts. Baby clinics were, according to the Labour Party periodical *Labour*

Woman, a form of 'race-building' needed to counter the 'race-suicide' of war.[81] As a male speaker at a conference on infant care in June 1915 remarked, 'every baby was a potential citizen, a fighting man or a mother of a fighting man'. It was society's 'duty', he argued, to look after these children: 'We might be sure that our enemies, from the Kaiser upwards, would care for theirs.'[82] Infant mortality rates had been falling steadily in the previous decade, due in part to better midwife care and in part to the availability of safer types of milk substitute. But a small increase in the rate of infant deaths in 1914–15 and 1916–17 prompted a revival of emotive pro-natalist rhetoric. The Bishop of London drew a powerful comparison with casualties in combat, noting that 'while nine soldiers died every hour in 1915, twelve babies died every hour, so that it was more dangerous to be a baby than a soldier'. The destruction of life on the Western Front 'made every baby's life doubly precious'.[83]

This climate of concern inspired action by both State and civil society. It was made compulsory for midwives to register births with local health authorities within thirty-six hours, so as to ensure that post-natal care could be provided in the crucial first days and weeks of life. Training for midwives became more rigorous, whilst the number of health visitors more than doubled, helped by grants from the Local Government Board. These improvements were consolidated by the 1918 Maternal and Infant Welfare Act, which extended the powers of local authorities to provide midwifery and health-visiting services, baby clinics and free milk supplies for the benefit of new mothers and their babies.[84] Much was done to rouse public opinion, with a National Baby Week organised in July 1917 comprising mass public meetings, film screenings, church sermons and exhibitions of 'mothercraft' aimed at educating women in good infant care.[85] The Women's Co-operative Guild seized the moment to argue for a major overhauling of the maternity benefit instituted in 1911 through the National Insurance Act. They demanded that the increased value of £3 be paid to every mother regardless of her employment status, as opposed to the 30s paid to non-earning mothers. *The Times* detected a new political mood in the country, which was willing at last to support 'motherhood in its just demands'.[86]

This heightened obsession with the conditions of maternity and infant welfare had mixed effects for working mothers. The government's Health of Munition Workers Committee spent much time worrying about the impact of 'industrial fatigue' on women's reproductive capacities, especially those who worked the longest shifts or at night. The female workforce deserved special attention, the Committee reasoned, because of 'those contributions which women alone can make to the welfare of the State'.[87] Activists in the labour movement voiced a similar fear that 'the women now working will feel their strength lessened in many instances for the remainder of their lives', with perilous results for 'the burden of motherhood which they may be bearing now or in the future'.[88] Yet withdrawing women from heavy industry was not an option, given the ongoing demand for munitions. Policymakers were therefore forced to consider measures to mitigate the harmful effects on women's health and that of their children, living or yet to be born.

As we have already seen, these measures – which included canteens, washrooms, day nurseries and regular medical care – actually helped many mothers to reconcile paid work with domestic responsibilities, at least temporarily. Some factories trialled special schemes for pregnant women, which enabled them to work in safe conditions right up to their confinement. At the National Ordnance Factory in Leeds, expectant mothers were moved onto lighter tasks and then relocated to a separate workroom in the final months of pregnancy where the hours were shorter and comfortable chairs and hot meals were available. Some women disliked being segregated from their workmates, but many were grateful for the opportunity to continue earning in a safe and congenial environment. The originator of the scheme, Dr Rhoda Adamson, pointed out that fear of dismissal had formerly caused women to conceal their condition for as long as possible. Under the new system, pregnant women notified employers at a much earlier stage and were therefore able to access antenatal care and could be moved off unsuitable heavy work.[89] Dr Mary Deacon, who ran a similar scheme at a rural filling factory, was convinced of

the benefits of keeping the expectant mother at work: 'She shares
the company and fellowship of her companions, so necessary to
keep her cheerful, and by walking a mile to work obtains plenty
of exercise and fresh air.' By continuing to earn, women could eat
heartily, pay for good medical care and stay at home for longer after
the birth. 'Several of the workers,' Deacon noted, 'are reported as
never having felt so well during former pregnancies or having had
such good confinements or such healthy babies.'[90]

Both Adamson and Deacon thought these experiments might
be useful in peacetime, whilst an admiring observer in the feminist
Englishwoman newspaper dwelt at length on the potential gains of
making such schemes a regular feature of industry. As she pointed
out, the Leeds example was not 'a dream factory in Utopia' but a
mutually advantageous arrangement made on a 'sound business'
basis.[91] A few others spoke positively about the wartime growth
in married women's employment, including the familiar voice
of Clementina Black. She reiterated her belief that wage-earning
gave women financial independence and told the War Cabinet
Committee that the homes of working mothers were 'better
kept than the homes of non-workers with insufficient means and
insufficient occupation'.[92] Black based her testimony in part upon
the findings of a fresh investigation carried out by the Women's
Industrial Council amongst the laundresses of Acton, west
London. It concluded that maternal and infant welfare was best
served not by pushing married women out of the labour market
but by ensuring they did safe, well-paid work: 'If the health of
the future generations were given that place of first importance
that it should have, we should secure to our mothers, both actual
and potential, the healthiest, the best paid, the best conditioned,
but not necessarily the lightest and easiest work, instead of leaving
to them the badly paid and sweated industries as we do now.'[93]
The middle-class suffragists behind the Women's Service Bureau, a
body founded in 1914 to help women find war work, also argued
against any future move to ban or limit the employment of married
women. They suggested, as the Fabian Women's Group had a few
years earlier, that mothers might be especially encouraged to take

up jobs in social work, teaching or public health, where their first-hand experience of raising a family would be a useful qualification.[94]

Yet these were not the dominant views expressed by the numerous committees which began, from around 1917, to consider the place of women workers in the post-war world. Trade unionists, feminists, medical experts and officials in government all agreed that women's health had improved as a result of higher wages, whilst arguments in favour of better training opportunities and equal pay for equal work began to gather real force. These demands tended to be made with school-leavers in mind, or older, unmarried women destined to support themselves for life. Married women's work, by contrast, retained much the same status as it had before the war: an unavoidable evil for women who lacked other breadwinners, but positively damaging under all other circumstances and not to be officially encouraged. Women's motives for seeking employment had momentarily seemed less important when millions of soldiers' lives depended upon the mobilisation of a large female workforce. But once the restoration of 'normal' conditions looked like a not so distant prospect, morally charged arguments about 'good' and 'bad' working mothers were quick to resurface. The rhetoric which had praised women war-workers as selfless patriots rapidly gave way to statements about the claims of returning soldiers to jobs and every woman's duty as 'home-maker for the nation'.[95]

This shift was signalled with especial clarity in debates about the future of the war nurseries. A few officials at the Local Government Board took the pragmatic view that demand for nursery places was likely to remain high in peacetime, but most of those weighing in on the subject expressed deep reservations about any permanent expansion of provision. Their chief fear was that nurseries, where readily available, would 'tempt' mothers back to the factory to earn wages instead of nursing their babies and looking after their homes. Medical experts were especially concerned about the impact on breastfeeding, which, they argued, would be interrupted by too early a return to work. One male doctor from Nottingham thought that mothers needed to be taught to 'appreciate the honour that it is to feed a baby by the breast'.[96] Infant welfare campaigners warned that feeding was 'apt to be indifferent' where infants attended nurseries 'and the mother's interest in some cases slackens' to the point of abdicating all responsibility for her child.[97] Mary Deacon noted that French employers got round these problems by opening workplace crèches where mothers could see and feed their babies throughout the day, but opinion in Whitehall was generally against such a solution. An official from the Board of Education opposed it on the grounds that nurseries too conveniently located 'would tend to render permanent the employment in factories of married women with young children'.[98] The Welfare Advisory Committee at the Ministry of Munitions accepted this view, stating in August 1918 that its members were 'unanimously of the opinion that the Crèche should be regarded purely as a temporary expedient for meeting conditions necessitated by the war'.[99] The Ministry discontinued all grants to day nurseries in November with only a short-term exemption to those still serving 'bona fide' munition workers.

This consensus against public investment in childcare provision encompassed a range of opinion. There were traditionalists, like the male Medical Officer of Health from Warrington who thought even the extension of school dinners was a step in the wrong direction because it weakened maternal responsibility: 'There is nobody like the mother for looking after the child at home,' he told the War Cabinet Committee in 1918, 'and if she is not doing it properly it is our fault. We must teach her to do it and get to the base of the whole thing.'[100] But there were others, like the trade unionist Mary Macarthur or the medic Janet Campbell, who lacked enthusiasm for day nurseries because they wished ultimately to see mothers better supported by the State in their occupation as homemakers. They, and many others, pressed this case whenever the question was raised of lengthening the period that mothers were formally excluded from employment following childbirth. The current law, which stipulated one month, was still regularly flouted because many women needed to earn wages. Any move to extend it would therefore prove fruitless unless, in Janet Campbell's words, 'financial assistance is given to the mother to enable her to remain at home without anxiety'.[101] As one welfare supervisor at a projectile factory in Yorkshire confirmed, mothers appeared in her office four, five or six weeks post-partum, 'obviously quite unfit, perspiring from weakness', but desperate for reinstatement. Their distress was 'heartrending' when she informed them that factory policy was to take women back no earlier than three months after giving birth.[102]

To meet this problem, a number of witnesses before the War Cabinet Committee suggested generous maternity grants to keep working mothers away from the factory for three, six or even nine months, emphasising the benefits to infants suckled during this period. A medical officer from Birmingham felt that 'the absence of employment during the feeding of the baby is so important that one would pay anything to get it'.[103] Others agreed that grants should be conditional on breastfeeding and could be withdrawn where health visitors or midwives believed the money was being misspent. In her final recommendations, however, Campbell rejected this prescriptive approach, agreeing instead with the Women's Co-operative Guild that an improved maternity benefit should be paid to *all* expectant mothers, regardless of employment status. Non-earning wives, she argued, also deserved relief – from heavy housework and childcare – in the weeks and months after confinement, and any scheme offering preferential treatment to those in employment might simply encourage more mothers to work.

This position entirely ignored any question of a mother's right to reinstatement or her job security in the longer term, but it did at least recognise that she had needs that were distinct from those of her child or the larger 'race'. Having worked in some of London's most deprived districts, Campbell was especially sensitive to the poor health and monotonous lives led by many working-class women. There was 'no reason', she argued in her memo to the War Cabinet Committee, 'why the nation should be content to allow its mothers to wear themselves out in a life of colourless drudgery' or endure the 'treble strain' of wage-earning, housework and looking after children.[104] It was for these reasons that Campbell, along with bodies like the Women's Co-operative Guild and the Women's Labour League, advocated for nursery schools and municipal play-schemes to give mothers a break from their childcare duties for a few hours a week. They also placed high priority on housing reform, arguing that housewives needed better conditions in which to do their 'work' properly, as well as opportunities for leisure and recreation. As the Labour activist Marion Phillips put it: 'we ... believe that mothers who have time to be thinking citizens would make infinitely better homes for their children than those whose hours are filled with the drudgery of working in overcrowded, inconvenient and ugly homes.'[105]

The most radical wartime expression of this vision was the campaign for family endowment. State-funded allowances to help parents meet the costs of raising a family already existed in France and had found some support in Britain amongst those alarmed by falling birth rates, including William Beveridge, future architect of the post-1945 welfare state. In 1918, however, endowment was championed most energetically by a group of feminists led by Eleanor Rathbone, the suffragist, social worker and first woman to be elected to Liverpool City Council. Rathbone had investigated married women's employment in her home city in the 1890s and later made a study of casual male labour at the Liverpool docks. These experiences convinced her that the welfare of the working-class family lay not in greater wage-earning by mothers nor in higher pay for men, but in a system of universal allowances, funded from general taxation and paid directly to mothers in proportion to the size of their families. Such an 'endowment' by the State would recognise the value of women's caring work to the community, target resources where they were most needed and, furthermore, remove all justification for wage differentials in the labour market. Equal pay was only a viable proposition, Rathbone contended, if accompanied by a system of family allowances. Once financial responsibility for children was removed entirely from the wage-setting process, men and women could compete on the basis of their efficiency as workers rather than their needs as breadwinners.[106] Beatrice Webb, the sole female member of the War

Cabinet Committee, strongly endorsed this logic in her minority report, arguing that endowment was the only 'practical way of ensuring anything like adequate provision for all the children that are born', and a vital measure if women workers were to secure the 'rate for the job'.[107]

Framed this way, family endowment was a policy which promised to meet the needs of mothers in the home after they retired from paid employment. Its starting point, as Maude Royden, one of Rathbone's collaborators, expressed it, was that housewives were already 'earning their living, and earning it hard' by caring for their families. The problem was 'that they sometimes do not get it, and never have a right to it that can be enforced'.[108] It was not just that male wage packets were frequently too small to support a family, but they remained the property of the husband, who determined how much of it his wife would receive. Rathbone pointed to the wartime system of separation allowances as proof that housewives benefited enormously from having full control over a regular, guaranteed income. Forgetting, or perhaps downplaying, how often allowances were supplemented by women's wages, Rathbone argued that large numbers of mothers 'have tasted for the first time the sense of security, of ease and dignity that comes from the enjoyment of a settled income, proportioned to the size of their families and paid directly to themselves'.[109] For Rathbone, it was vastly preferable that women's financial autonomy should come from the State, rather than from pushing mothers to compete with single women and men in the labour market. Family allowances, paid on a universal basis and pitched at a generous level, would reduce women's financial dependence on their husbands and enable them to do their job of rearing the next generation with the proper support.

Towards the end of the war, all those arguing for State investment in motherhood, whether in the form of nursery schools, baby clinics, enhanced maternity benefits or family allowances, made the basic assumption that full-time domesticity was the aspiration of most women after marriage. Female activists in the labour and trade union movement recognised that some mothers might still *need* to work, but their object was to reduce this need as far as possible. Freed from economic pressure, they argued, most women would choose to retire from wage-earning. Margaret Llewelyn Davies, the leader of the Women's Co-operative Guild, expected 'to see the withdrawal of most married women from the wage market' following the introduction of family endowment.[110] Royden agreed with this prediction, 'because a very large number of women prefer to run their homes and rear their children themselves, if they are given proper conditions to do it'.[111] As noted, some feminists took a more positive view of married women's work, arguing that higher wages, rather than family allowances, would give mothers a real choice. Witnesses from the National Union of Women's Suffrage Societies told the War Cabinet Committee that 'if women were properly paid they would be able to hire domestic assistance and could choose freely between domestic and industrial life' (although these middle-class suffragists did not dwell upon the domestic arrangements of the women providing the assistance).[112] This debate within feminism over how best to secure women's economic independence would continue into the 1920s and 1930s. Nonetheless, the legacy of the wartime agitation over maternal and infant welfare led many to privilege the needs of the full-time housewife over those of the working mother.

*

All predictions about what mothers might do when given a 'pure' choice between wage-earning and full-time housewifery proved, in the end, to be premature. When demobilisation commenced from the end of 1918, mothers who had been employed in the war industries lost their jobs but found no alternative utopia as full-time homemakers. The old breadwinner norm was rapidly rehabilitated, paradoxically enough by the system hastily devised to aid men left workless following the cessation of hostilities. The 'out of work' donation (as it was called) included allowances for men's dependants, but the single and married women who tried to claim it were assumed to have none, even where they had been supporting their families during the war. The benefit was withheld if female applicants refused to take positions in domestic service or low-paying jobs in the pre-war women's trades. One widow who had been the sole provider for her young child for over five years signed on at the labour exchange in Camberwell, south London, in early 1919 and was offered a job in a laundry at a paltry 15s a week. When she turned it down, explaining that she had no widow's pension and was entirely reliant on her wages, the manager remarked that she could put her child in a foster home and go into service instead, 'as it was nothing to do with them what children we had dependent on us, and if I did not take either of the jobs she would report me'.[113] Other mothers resorted to placing adverts in the press. Mrs O'Breyon of West Ealing sought work 'as caretaker, housekeeper, or any position of trust, where 7-year old girl not objected to'. A young widow from Fulham wanted clerical or nursing work, 'but cannot be parted from her 2½ year-old child'.[114]

Cases of this kind demonstrate how easily mothers slipped between the cracks in State welfare in the immediate aftermath of the war, even with the establishment of war widows' pensions and the extended system of unemployment benefit, which included support for the families of some 750,000 soldiers permanently disabled by their war service.[115] These measures were all designed, like separation allowances, to substitute for the wages of a male breadwinner. By contrast, the more comprehensive reforms suggested by women's organisations – for family allowances or universal maternity benefit – did not feature in post-war social policy, and nor did feminist proposals for equal pay. One reason for this was the pledges made by government under the Treasury Agreement to protect men's jobs and wages, which male trade unionists were determined to see honoured in full. Sure enough, the Restoration of Pre-war Practices Act, passed in October 1920, made those pledges binding across industry and the old demarcations reserving 'skilled' jobs for male workers were quickly resurrected. Union leaders looked with suspicion on any proposals which weakened their bargaining position with employers over wages. Independent entitlements for mothers *not* directly derived from a husband's National Insurance contributions threatened exactly this.[116] So too did Beatrice Webb's demand for standard rates of pay undifferentiated by sex. As Webb openly admitted, this demand was intended to attack 'the principle of the vested interest of the male', by which she meant the deeply entrenched assumption that all the better paid, publicly esteemed and intrinsically rewarding occupations across industry and the professions were and should remain 'the sacred preserve of men'.[117]

The other major factor shaping the post-war settlement was concern for the economy. Public expenditure on maintaining the civilian population had massively increased between 1914 and 1918, whilst demobilisation exposed the State further. Pension payouts to veterans alone cost £9.7 million in 1919 and over £21 million in 1920.[118] Returning to 'normal' fiscal rules and reducing the national debt was a high priority for the Liberal–Conservative coalition government, which remained in power until 1922. Despite the enfranchisement of 8.4 million women under the Representation of the People Act in February 1918, ministers were not minded to introduce expensive non-contributory schemes of family endowment, and officials in Whitehall advised caution. Spending on mothers and children instead increased in a piecemeal fashion at municipal level under the permissive – but not compulsory – provisions of the Maternity and Infant Welfare Act of 1918.

Perhaps the starkest proof of how pre-war assumptions about social and economic order trumped the claims of maternity was the position adopted by the British government at the first international labour conference held in Washington DC in November 1919. Under discussion was a convention which would give women the right to twelve weeks of paid maternity leave (six to be taken before birth and six afterwards) and the services of a trained midwife or doctor free of charge. The three British women present, Constance Smith as a government advisor and Mary Macarthur and Margaret Bondfield representing organised labour, strongly backed the proposal, which passed by sixty-seven votes to ten.[119] The official British delegate, however, abstained from voting, and no move was made to bring the convention before Parliament until February 1921, shortly after which the Minister of Health, Christopher

Addison, confirmed that the government did not intend to ratify it. The reason he gave was that mothers already enjoyed the 'double-insurance' of an existing maternity benefit and welfare services provided by local authorities. The results of this 'great system' were, according to Addison, 'brilliant; no other word is adequate to describe them'.[120] Mothers not covered by the National Insurance Act who were struggling to provide for large families or worrying about long-term job security might have found an alternative term of expression, although in truth Addison's statement was disingenuous. The deeper cause of his reluctance to ratify lay in the projected cost to the Exchequer and the risk of further expenditure. The government actuary, Sir Alfred Watson, estimated the initial bill at £1.7 million per year, but warned that this figure did not account for the additional numbers of married women who might be attracted into industry by the availability of the enhanced benefit, and nor did it reflect the pressure which would inevitably follow to extend the benefit to *all* mothers, not just wage-earning ones.[121] In other words, ratification was dangerous because it would legitimise married women's employment and lead to a major redistribution of national income to mothers. Avoiding both of these outcomes would remain a high priority for government, employers and the male-led labour movement between the wars.

5

Modern Mothers

On first impression, Claudia Winsloe, the chief protagonist of E. M. Delafield's 1936 novel, *Faster! Faster!*, jumps off the page as a vital, brilliant woman. Sole breadwinner since her husband lost his job at the end of the war, Claudia runs a successful business supplying miscellaneous services to middle-class clients, everything from escorting unaccompanied children at railway stations to proofreading manuscripts and finding reliable servants. Claudia works exceptionally long hours at her London office or in her study in the family's large country home, earning to pay the mortgage, school fees and a never-ending succession of bills. Yet she always finds time to be a moral guide and exemplary role model for her son and two daughters. She is bringing them up to be independent young people, unsentimental and able, as she puts it, 'to face facts'. Claudia is proud of her own capacity for clear-eyed self-criticism – 'I've been honest with myself all my life,' she reflects with satisfaction – and her calm resilience in the face of overwhelming financial and emotional pressure. Still handsome and dynamic in her early forties, Claudia strives to live up to her 'ideal of a woman achieving, by sheer force of will, the next-to-impossible'.

Yet in doing this, Claudia makes everyone around her anxious or unhappy. Her elderly mother frets that Claudia is heading for a breakdown: 'She's at it morning, noon, and night ... This house, and the children ... *and* her office work as well. Claudia is doing three full-time jobs at once.' Her husband, Copper, resents being usurped from his role as family provider and is sulky and petulant in his wife's presence. Maurice, the youngest child, adores Claudia but fears he will disappoint her. Sylvia, the eldest, secretly longs for a husband rather than the job her mother has planned. Taffy, the middle child, is openly belligerent and yearns for travel and adventure. At the office, Claudia is respected but disliked for working her staff as ruthlessly hard as she works herself.

Worst of all, Claudia Winsloe is a hypocrite. As the story unfolds, evidence of her self-deception piles up: her controlling behaviour towards Copper and the children, her studied martyrdom and her utter inability to recognise the self-serving motives underpinning her every decision. At a tense moment halfway through the book, Claudia's sister (whose rich husband, it transpires, is paying the Winsloe children's school fees) confronts her with the unvarnished truth: 'It's this awful picture that you've built up of yourself in your own mind, as a bread-winner, and a wife, and a mother – and it's all artificial and unreal. It never goes below the surface for one minute.' In a later scene, she really lets rip:

> Aren't you, all day and every day, acting as the perfect selfless mother, the sole support of them all, the woman who's gallantly working herself to death? I'll grant that you've taken yourself in pretty completely – I don't suppose you ever do see anything now, except just what you want to see.

Delafield resolves this psychological drama through a rather crude (and cruel) device: Claudia crashes her car after an especially fractious day at the office and dies. Life for the Winsloes improves greatly as a result. Copper gets a job and swaps the expensive country house for a smaller, more manageable property near his work. Sylvia pursues a romantic attachment. Taffy goes to America with her aunt. Maurice feels 'happier than he had felt for a long time'. The office is a calmer place without Claudia in it. It turns out that her 'rush-life' had been hurting everyone, with husband, children and employees all forced to operate at the accelerated pace dictated by Claudia's uncontrollable ego. She is truly a product of the times, a woman enabled by motor cars and telephones, self-consciously casting off tradition and living by new values. But it is a troubling portrait of the professional working mother that Delafield paints, a mother seemingly made monstrous by modernity.

In Delafield's better-known character, the Provincial Lady, we find a personality which is almost the exact psychological obverse of Claudia Winsloe. Delafield created the Lady (whose real name is never revealed to the reader) and her fictitious diaries in 1929 for *Time and Tide*, a weekly feminist periodical with a strong literary slant. She subsequently published four bestselling volumes featuring her scribbling heroine: *Diary of A Provincial Lady* (1930), *The Provincial Lady Goes Further* (1932), *The Provincial Lady in America* (1934) and *The Provincial Lady in Wartime* (1940). Like Claudia, the Lady is a middle-class woman living in a spacious house in the country with her school-aged children and emotionally unresponsive husband. But there the resemblance ends. The Lady's existence is anything but the 'rush-life'. Her day is punctuated instead by the unhurried routines of bourgeois housewifery: managing servants, answering letters, paying social calls and attending the monthly meeting of the Women's Institute. Excursions to London are infrequent, prompted by the search for a new parlour maid or the purchase of a hat. The Lady's life is 'modern' in its way, with book-club subscriptions and experimental permanent waves. But it is a different kind of modernity, centred not on the performance of superwoman feats but the pleasures of ordinariness, a theme much celebrated in the wider middlebrow literature of the period.[1] The Provincial Lady can laugh at herself, accept her limitations and take joy in small victories. Where Claudia Winsloe seeks to control and dominate others, the Lady wants only to master herself. Her diaries become a place for introspection and self-knowledge, for marshalling the inner resources necessary to live a more authentic life.

Delafield identified closely with her most beloved literary creation. Like the Lady, she lived with her family in rural Devon, and her husband, like the Lady's husband, worked as agent to a local landowner. Art moved even closer to life in 1932, when Delafield gave the Lady a part-time career as a published author. Her character's modest fame did not rival Delafield's own commercial success as novelist, journalist, playwright and broadcaster.[2] Nonetheless, the Provincial Lady's income from writing pays her daughter's school fees and the rent on a flat in London, from which she launches herself onto the metropolitan literary scene. (Delafield similarly got herself a flat on Doughty Street in 1931, where, according to the testimony of a shocked friend, she would repair to the nearest Lyons tea-shop for breakfast instead of cooking it herself.) Further excitement for the Lady came in the shape of a lecture tour of the US, in which her diaries recorded events inspired by Delafield's own travels to New York, Chicago, Boston and Washington DC in late 1933. Throughout, the Lady never loses her detached mirth at the absurdity of it all yet takes obvious delight in the new faces she meets and places she visits, as well as the welcome envelopes containing cheques from her publisher. The Provincial Lady was not so provincial after all.

Middle-class readers would doubtless have smiled in recognition at the gentle tribulations of the Lady's typical day, whilst the small but growing band of women pursuing careers in business and the professions might even have extended some sympathy for the egotistical Claudia Winsloe. Working-class mothers, by contrast, were less likely to find in Delafield's novels a mirror of their social experience, particularly those in households blighted by unemployment, as millions were in Depression-era Britain. Nonetheless, the 'modern' dilemmas given fictional form by writers like Delafield were creeping into real women's lives across social classes between the wars. The idea that mothers were entitled to interests and pastimes besides caring for their families became increasingly axiomatic by the later 1930s, often linked rhetorically to women's new status as fully enfranchised citizens and housewife-workers in the home. Women in the comfortably off middle classes were best placed to take advantage of expanding possibilities for leisure and self-cultivation, but these gradually came within wider reach as more working-class couples limited the size of their families and acquired houses which were easier to heat and keep clean. As a result, equipping the married woman to make constructive use of her spare time presented itself as a new problem of the contemporary age.

As yet, getting a job was not an attractive or practical solution for most mothers. There was limited demand for married women's labour in interwar industry and not everyone could start their own business or write novels from a Bloomsbury flat. Instead, women's organisations urged housewives to sign up for adult education classes, join voluntary associations, throw themselves into political activism, or read books and listen to improving talks on the radio. This vision of the active woman citizen did not challenge prevailing norms which anchored the wife and mother in the home. Yet it advanced a view which would prove transformative in the longer term. Housewifery was central to dominant notions of femininity in these decades, but the claim that women *needed more* than pure domesticity for marital happiness and personal fulfilment gained wide public acceptance. This idea, modest as it seemed, would play a crucial part in legitimising paid work for mothers through the rest of the twentieth century.

*

The First World War might have effected no permanent improvement in women's economic status, but it helped, nevertheless, to accelerate trends already evident in the female workforce before 1914. Domestic service remained by far the largest sector employing women, but opportunities in clerical and retail work grew rapidly: by 1931 there were over half a million female typists and office workers and more than 400,000 shop assistants and saleswomen. In industry, the expansion of firms producing consumer commodities – radios, electric lamps, canned food, pharmaceuticals – created semi-skilled jobs for young women in the Midlands, Home Counties and outer London. Gleaming new factories sprang up in places like Slough, Oxford, Perivale and Hayes, extending the trend towards mass-production assembly lines staffed exclusively by women. This type of labour, familiar from munitions work during the war, offered good wages and clean conditions for those who could get it, although men still prevailed in the skilled and managerial grades and were paid at higher rates. Traditional heavy industry, including coalmining, ship-building, railways and steel works, remained masculine preserves.[3]

For ambitious young women of the middle classes, the picture looked especially bright with the throwing open of new professions and the higher grades of the Civil Service following the passage of the Sex Disqualification (Removal) Act (SDA) of 1919. Following the franchise reforms of the previous year, which created over 8 million new female voters, the Act stipulated that 'a person shall not be disqualified by sex or marriage from the exercise of any public function, or from being appointed to holding any civil or judicial post, or from entering or assuming or carrying on any civil profession or vocation'. It enabled women to sit on juries, serve as magistrates and enter professions including architecture, accountancy, veterinary medicine and the law. Virginia Woolf hailed this measure as a milestone in the emancipation of the 'educated man's daughter', who could now earn a living and forge her own path free of parental control.[4] In truth, the largest group of professionally employed women was, as in earlier decades, teachers in elementary schools, yet notable advances were made in other occupations. The number of women practising medicine more than doubled from 1,200 to 2,800 between 1921 and 1931, whilst, from a lower base, increases were seen amongst dentists (296 to 394), barristers and solicitors (37 to 195), accountants (43 to 119) and architects (49 to 107).[5] Three women entered the prestigious administrative class of the Civil Service in 1925 and by the eve of the Second World War their ranks had swelled to forty-three.[6] For some contemporaries, these decades felt like a breakthrough era for professional women, who entered unclaimed fields of endeavour from broadcasting and retail management to insurance and land surveying. Reflecting in 1935 on changes since the First World War, the feminist Ray Strachey noted that 'instead of it being slightly disgraceful for a middle-class woman to take payment for her work, it began to be thought natural and right'.[7] This new breed of pioneering career woman formed clubs and associations, set up

specialist employment bureaux and offered advice and inspiration
to young graduates and school-leavers through an expanding genre
of career manuals, yearbooks and guides.[8]

Yet professional equality was still some way off. As in industry,
most salaried women earned less than their male counterparts and
were dramatically outnumbered at senior levels. Women accounted
for little more than 3 per cent of the senior Civil Service in 1939 and
only 4 per cent of all those training to become barristers between
the wars.[9] A mere handful of women held university chairs and
very few medics secured residential posts at top teaching hospitals.
In the late 1920s, only 300 of the 27,000 directors of listed
companies were women.[10] Some institutions held out completely.
Women remained barred from the Church, the Army, the London
Stock Exchange, the Diplomatic Service and the House of Lords.
A number of the medical schools which had opened their doors to
female students during the war voted to close them again in the
1920s.[11]

Without a doubt, the greatest limiting factor for women's career
progress between the wars was marriage. Paid work became the
norm for young, single women: only 12 per cent of unmarried
eighteen- to twenty-four-year-olds were *not* in regular employment
by 1931.[12] Yet the picture was almost exactly reversed for married
women, with less than one in ten returned as occupied in the 1931
census (although this figure naturally hid a great deal of casual
or seasonal employment). For the minority who *did* earn, there
was little change either in the kinds of jobs on offer or in regional
patterns of employment.[13] Working wives could still be found in
significant numbers in the Lancashire textile mills, where more
than one in four female weavers were married, although the loss
of overseas markets and the influx of cheap imports made these
skilled jobs increasingly precarious. Other familiar occupations in
which married women and widows were well represented included
laundry work, pottery manufacture, boot-making and the metal
trades.[14]

Some wives and mothers were restricted, as they had been
before the war, to casual work that was poorly paid, low in prestige

and could be easily fitted around domestic duties. Cleaning jobs were popular because they could often be done in early morning or evening shifts. Eleanor Barton of the Women's Co-operative Guild described the 'army of women cleaners' which crossed the river Thames every day around 6 p.m. after finishing their own housework to start jobs in City and West End offices.[15] Home-work also remained a significant source of income for mothers, despite the general movement towards factory organisation following the pre-war campaign against sweating. In his *New Survey of London Life and Labour*, Hubert Llewellyn Smith estimated that between 3,500 and 5,000 home-workers were still employed in London's tailoring trades and another thousand in dressmaking, mostly married women 'with domestic ties who are not in a position to give regular attendance in the employer's shop'.[16]

Prospects for middle-class wives and mothers were more promising in certain lines of work. Having been less conspicuous in the decades before the war, married women recovered some of their earlier presence in the medical profession. A 1928 survey of recently qualified medical school graduates found that nearly two-fifths of women who had married were still in practice.[17] Janet Vaughan, a pioneer in the science of blood transfusion and later principal of Somerville College, Oxford, pursued her medical research and clinical work as a mother of two young daughters in 1930s London. Writing in 1936, the South African psychologist Winifred de Kok insisted that medicine was an excellent career for the married woman, who could take time out to care for her family and re-enter the profession at a later date. De Kok had followed this pattern herself, temporarily giving up work to raise two children and subsequently re-establishing herself as a general practitioner.[18] Despite the financial risk involved, this was an increasingly popular speciality for female medics, with and without families, because of the freedom it offered from male-dominated bureaucracy. In the pre-National Health Service era, GPs were effectively small-business owners and could set their own hours, pay and working patterns.[19] Dentists could control their practices in a similar fashion. It was striking that in a survey of women's membership of professional associations in the 1920s, the highest ratio of married to unmarried women – roughly one in four – was found amongst dental practitioners.[20]

Self-employment was equally attractive to mothers in other middle-class occupations. The monthly journal of Soroptimist International, a voluntary organisation for business and professional women, listed the varied trades and services in which its married members were engaged in the 1930s, including music teachers, masseuses, painter-decorators, car dealers, elocutionists, lingerie specialists, theatre managers, restaurateurs and proprietors of shops, hotels and beauty parlours.[21] Marjory Allen, who had one daughter from her marriage to the socialist politician Clifford Allen, was a pioneering landscape architect, producing designs for urban roof-gardens from her home in the Surrey countryside.[22] Some of the earliest female lawyers went into partnership with husbands as a strategy for reconciling professional and family life. Mary Pickup was in her late thirties and had two children aged eight and five when she started her legal training in 1919. She was articled in her husband's firm of solicitors and joined him as a partner after qualifying three years later.[23] Maud Crofts married a fellow solicitor in 1922 and the two set up in partnership with Crofts' brother. She subsequently gave birth to two daughters but continued practising law, leaving the office early to meet the children from school.[24] Another high-profile working couple was John Spedan Lewis and his wife Sarah, who became deputy chairman and a director at her husband's eponymous major retail business, a job she continued to do through three pregnancies.[25]

Being one's own boss clearly made life easier for these women, but it was not impossible to combine family and career as an employee in a large organisation if one's talents were considered exceptional. Mary Somerville successfully negotiated paid maternity leave from her job as Head of Schools Broadcasting at the BBC in 1928–9. Eight years later, Mary Adams took up a senior post in the corporation's new television arm just six months after the birth of her daughter.[26] At the University of Cambridge in the 1930s, Joan Robinson navigated the tight-knit masculine world of the Economics Department as a mother of two, securing a permanent lectureship and laying the foundations of a career as an internationally recognised economic theorist.[27] In Oxford in 1938, the crystallographer and future Nobel laureate Dorothy Hodgkin became the first female fellow to give birth in post. Thanks to the enlightened attitude of the authorities at her college, Somerville, Hodgkin was not forced to resign and even received paid maternity leave, an arrangement repeated for her two subsequent pregnancies.[28]

*

These career women were, admittedly, far from typical. In other workplaces, married women found their paths blocked by a rising tide of formal restrictions. From the 1920s, local authorities applied marriage bars systematically against female teachers, medical officers and other municipal workers, whilst the Civil Service re-established its policy of excluding married women, temporarily suspended during the war, with immediate effect.[29] The London County Council pursued this course full throttle in March 1922, when it fired Dr Gladys Miall Smith following her marriage, as well as a number of married cleaners and charwomen on the council's payroll. In industry, many employers held with long-established custom and routinely dismissed women on marriage. Elsie Lee, who worked at Courtauld's rayon factory in Coventry, recalled that 'when you were married you couldn't go back & that was it. No married women. That was the rule.'[30] As feminists discovered with dismay, these restrictions were perfectly legal under the Sex Disqualification (Removal) Act. The legislation purported to make discrimination on the basis of marital status unlawful, but in practice employers were left with a free hand to dismiss or exclude married women as they wished. This became clear when fifty-eight married teachers fired by the Rhondda Education Authority in South Wales in 1923 brought a case against their employer, arguing that the council's actions were in breach of the 'letter and spirit of the 1919 Act'. The judge, however, thought differently and overturned their claim. His ruling established a narrow interpretation of the Act's provision on marriage, spelling out that whilst this did not disqualify a woman for employment, a married woman had no legal entitlement to keep her job.[31]

Given these practices, careers guidance often explicitly advised young women about occupations which could or could not be continued after marriage. Alix Kilroy and Evelyn Sharp, two of the earliest women to hold senior posts in Whitehall, wrote in 1936 that 'a very important point for girls who think of entering the administrative class is the Service attitude towards the marriage of women officers'.[32] This, they explained, was not absolute – there *was* discretion to waive the bar in individual cases – but any female civil servant wishing to stay on would need to make her case extremely persuasively. One woman who did so in 1934 was Miss E. G. Pearson, a highly experienced schools inspector who notified her superiors that she was soon to be married and requested that she be allowed to retain her post. Pearson had several facts on her side: she was already in her mid-forties and was therefore unlikely to require maternity leave, and she was extremely good at her job. Her line manager described Pearson as amongst 'the most efficient and valuable of my woman colleagues' and noted how unlikely they were to find anyone as well qualified to replace her. Pearson was allowed to stay.[33]

For working-class mothers doing routine manual work, exceptions were made on different grounds. The pre-war tradition of giving work to poor women without other breadwinners as a semi-charitable act continued to shape employer attitudes. The Labour politician Susan Lawrence successfully campaigned for the reinstatement of the charwomen sacked by the London County Council, a decision reached by the Council only after dozens of letters were received from the affected women describing their pitiful personal circumstances. Mrs A.'s husband had left her eight years earlier: 'I do not know where he is, dead or alive. All I get is what I work for.' Mrs C. was living apart from her violent husband, who had been convicted for assaulting her in 1911: 'I have received no maintenance or support whatever from him since.' According to Lawrence, 'these letters proved irresistible, and the decree of the Council was rescinded'.[34] Needy cases were given similar consideration by Civil Service employers, although complex rules governed the treatment of women in different situations, which ranged from widowhood, desertion, separation and divorce to the physical or mental disability of an incapacitated spouse.[35]

As in earlier decades, marriage bars offered employers a flexible method of managing the female workforce whilst containing labour costs. This was evident at the BBC, which, despite its self-image as a modern, forward-looking organisation, introduced both a marriage bar and a marriage tribunal in the 1930s to deliberate on cases where female employees planning to marry had indicated their wish to stay on. It awarded each applicant 'points' for various criteria including relevant experience, years of service, compassionate circumstances and 'character as bearing on the strain of combining married life with office work' – all matters which were discussed behind closed doors and without giving the applicant any right of reply. This allowed the BBC to employ older married women as cleaners and cloakroom attendants and to hold on to 'exceptional' women like Mary Somerville or Mary Adams. But it also enabled the corporation to dispense with the services of a large number of typists, secretaries and receptionists before they became promotable or pensionable.[36]

Such policies would have been universally condemned and vigorously resisted by trade unions if applied to married *men*, but general prejudice against working wives and mothers made them defensible in the case of women. Public opinion on this issue hardened at moments of economic crisis and high male unemployment, of which there were many between the wars. Sweeping public spending cuts in 1921, for instance, prompted Local Education Authorities to clamp down on the employment of married teachers, with 2,500 dismissed across England and Wales by the following August. There was strong pressure from schoolmasters and unmarried schoolmistresses for scarce jobs to be reserved for those with dependants or themselves to keep, a burden which it was assumed (often incorrectly) married women did not bear. The London County Council received forcefully worded letters arguing for the married woman 'to make way for the single girl who has to fight her way in the world', or insisting that 'husbands should be compelled to keep these women, not the public'.[37]

Censorious statements about 'selfish' women who worked despite having wage-earning husbands acquired greater force after 1930, as the economy slumped and male unemployment soared. The Open Door Council, a feminist body which campaigned for women's economic rights, noted the strength of popular feeling against 'two-income' families. Resentment ran especially high amongst the unemployed. To the jobless man, the Council wrote, 'it seems intolerable … that when there is apparently not enough work or pay to go around, a woman, a married woman with a husband in work, should be absorbing some of that work and money which he and his family so sorely need'.[38] The Council pointed out the irrationality of this stance, given that male workers rarely competed with married women for jobs and it was really the wage-earning woman's *husband* who posed the direct threat. Nonetheless, as unemployment figures pushed upwards, reaching a peak of 3 million in late 1932, the ideological tenet which held that men had a prior claim and a 'right' to provide for their families became further culturally entrenched.

In this, government policy played a major role. Social welfare legislation already assumed the dependence of wives, but the extended system of unemployment benefit in operation after 1931 gave women's inferior economic status a powerful institutional expression. Married women with regular work in industry who had kept up their National Insurance contributions were, like insured men, entitled to claim unemployment benefit, and by July 1930 significant numbers of them were doing exactly that.[39] Of the 200,000 women receiving payments that month, 46 per cent were married, the largest contingent being located in the ailing textiles sector where female unemployment ran significantly higher than male.[40] Officials refused to believe that all these claimants were genuine workers. The Ministry of Labour's accountant in Birmingham, Mr Postlethwaite, was convinced that abuse of the system was widespread. 'It is notorious,' he wrote in June 1930, 'that many married women do not desire work and are skilled in evading engagement. They pretend ignorance of any job for which they are submitted, or plead that it is unsuitable, e.g. for health reasons.'[41] A large section of these dole-seekers were young newly-weds who, he suggested, had husbands and homes to look after and no serious intention of re-entering the labour market. Yet under recently relaxed rules, such women – Postlethwaite dubbed them 'dowry cases' – were eligible to claim for up to two years.[42] He also reported cases of wage-earning mothers drawing unemployment benefit after childbirth instead of returning to work, because this brought in a higher income than their wages once childcare had been paid for. In another instance in Newcastle, a young mother made an unsuccessful claim having only worked for six weeks since her marriage, but later qualified for benefit after doing 'odd days as a shop assistant' in order to build up the required number of National Insurance stamps.[43]

This group was an obvious target when Ramsay MacDonald's Labour Cabinet began discussing ways to reduce pressure on the unemployment fund, now badly in deficit. A Royal Commission was appointed in autumn 1930 to review the operation of the entire system and amongst its recommendations were regulations designed to clamp down on the 'anomalies' presented by married women. As the majority report stated: 'It is clear that it is the exception rather than the rule for women after marriage to earn their living by insurable employment. It follows that in the case of married women as a class, industrial employment cannot be regarded as the normal condition.'[44]

Benefit should be limited, the report suggested, to the married woman who could convincingly demonstrate that she had not abandoned regular paid work for home-making and could 'reasonably expect to obtain insurable employment in the district in which she is residing'. The regulations introduced in autumn 1931 brought this recommendation into effect, resulting in the disallowance of more than 320,000 claims from married women over the next five years.[45] The reason for such a high refusal rate was the double trap in which claimants now found themselves, often forced to resign their jobs on marriage and then denied benefit on the grounds that they had no reasonable chance of obtaining employment as a married woman. Local officials interpreted the rules broadly, meaning that even textile workers who had been paying contributions for years stood at risk of losing their benefit. Pregnant women who had temporarily left their looms to give birth were especially vulnerable. In short, prejudice against married women in the labour market reinforced discrimination in the benefits system.[46]

Mass unemployment and the public response to it more generally helped to re-inscribe the identity of the 'worker' as male in the 1930s. The plight of men unable to fulfil their duty as family provider formed the focus of parliamentary debates, newspaper articles, philanthropic initiatives and social investigations throughout the decade. Hunger marchers took these grievances to the street, with wives and children present in a symbolic capacity as the unjustly deprived dependants of men. The best-publicised protest was the Jarrow Crusade of 1936, when 200 men tramped from the slump-hit town in the north-east to petition Parliament, a living tableau of dispossessed masculinity. The status of the unemployed married *woman*, by contrast, was deeply ambiguous. One influential study questioned whether in fact she truly existed. A wife's time could always be absorbed by housework or childcare, the authors reasoned, and under normal economic conditions she would anyway be supported by a male earner:

> The woman who is out of work, therefore, is not, on the whole, left stranded by unemployment as is the unemployed man; she has plenty to do, and looks perhaps as healthy or healthier, as happy as or happier than she did when she was working, so that the real problem is to increase the income brought in by her husband's wage sufficiently for it to be possible for her to reject definitely the alternative of going back to work, and settle down instead to make a home.[47]

Women workers were thus largely excluded from mounting public concern about the psychological impact of long-term unemployment. Alarm about the physical deterioration of workers and their families was considerable, but it was the wounds to the spirit inflicted upon men that were most vividly delineated in books like Walter Greenwood's *Love on the Dole* or George Orwell's iconic *The Road to Wigan Pier*, and in a new genre of social surveys investigating the lives of the unemployed, which often reproduced long, verbatim accounts from the lips of their – mostly male – subjects.[48]

This growing spotlight on how it *felt* to be without trade or occupation opened up a space for working-class men to narrate their experiences to a generally sympathetic if uneasy middle class. In summer 1933, the BBC's *Listener* magazine published a series of 'memoirs' penned by unemployed workers which described their traumatic loss of status in heart-wrenching terms: the soul-destroying search for work; the petty tyranny of labour exchange officials; the hated means test; and the shame of relying on the wages of wives or daughters. Some men found the reversal of roles in the home humiliating. A thirty-two-year-old skilled steelworker described his situation thus:

> Our child is still too young to realise that it is her mother who works. We carefully keep her from knowing it ... I have a wife and child to keep, but I cannot keep them ... I do the housework after my wife has left home at half-past seven in the morning, I read, I play with the child, I go out for walks in the evening after my wife has returned at half-past six. Is this a man's life?[49]

Another memoirist, a forty-nine-year-old skilled worker who had been jobless for three years, wrote: 'I think my wife looks on me now as a useless piece of goods, and worse than our old table.'[50]

Other husbands accepted their loss of status with greater equanimity. The novelist James Hanley met an unemployed coal miner in South Wales who regularly got up to cook breakfast, wash the children and send them off to school before cleaning the house. His wife commented that 'hundreds of men are doing the same thing', although she made it clear that her husband's domestic labour was entirely voluntary: 'I never ask him to do those things. He just did it himself.'[51] Few working wives could *rely* on unemployed spouses to take over household tasks and thus relieve their double burden. Many men preferred to spend their time at pubs, clubs or occupational centres for the unemployed, whilst others took up new hobbies or tended gardens or allotments. A minority became involved with the National Unemployed Workers Movement, a communist-led pressure group which demanded that government provide work at decent wages or adequate benefit to support a family. By staying connected to former workmates and asserting their right to maintenance and leisure, working-class men could thus preserve their self-image as providers and breadwinners, even when unemployed.[52]

The *Listener* memoirs included just one account by an unemployed woman: a forty-three-year-old unskilled factory hand and mother of six who was managing to survive through a combination of benefits, casual cleaning jobs and the wages of four earning children. It is a rare example of an extended testimony from a working-class mother reflecting on the pain of losing her livelihood:

> If I can get enough cleaning to do I shall give up the 'Labour' altogether and the factory. But I don't welcome the change after nearly nine years of work that I liked and did well. I hate this nothing-to-do. I am a strong woman and I can keep this little house clean with two hours' work a day. I liked having my work at the factory, although it meant eleven hours away from home every day and five on Saturday, and doing the cooking, washing and sewing for the week on Saturday afternoon and Sunday. But I liked doing it and I worked hard for the regular 30s; now there is nothing for me to do to earn the money we need for clothes and food. I must try 'charing'.[53]

Like the workless men who told their stories, regular paid employment had been a central part of this mother's identity and daily life. Yet it was significant that the *Listener* gave space not to a 'selfish' wife with a husband in work, nor to a skilled worker employed in industry since marriage. The writer was instead a deserted wife who had taken up factory employment only after the family's main breadwinner had absconded, and who was now more or less resigned to a life of casual charring. If her candid confession that she had *enjoyed* her job marked this woman's testimony out as unusual, her material situation – as a lone mother under intense pressure to earn to feed her family – was wholly unremarkable.

*

Discrimination against wives and mothers in the labour market did not go unchallenged between the wars. Feminist societies and professional women's organisations were deeply troubled by the manner in which employers and the State acted arbitrarily against married women. Bodies like the Open Door Council and Lady Rhondda's Six Point Group deployed liberal arguments first made by the mid-Victorian women's movement but now applied them explicitly to defend the *married* woman's right to earn. Marriage regulations, in their view, were objectionable because they removed a woman's freedom to decide for herself whether matrimony – and likely maternity – was compatible with continued employment. As Nancy Astor, the first woman to take her seat in Parliament, put it during a debate on marriage bars in the public service in 1927: 'We do not want the Government to tell us what we should do. It is a question between the woman and her husband, and has nothing to do with a third person outside.'[54] Feminists pointed out that employers did not *need* to introduce artificial barriers to protect themselves against inefficient married women: if a woman's work proved inferior following her marriage, she could be dismissed on the same grounds as any other under-performing employee.

Critics of the marriage bar particularly disliked the loss of privacy which its enforcement entailed. Women wishing to keep their jobs or seeking reinstatement were often required to disclose personal details regarding family finances, domestic difficulties, medical problems, even the state of their sex life. In 1925, the General Post Office re-engaged a former telegraphist after evidence was produced confirming that her marriage had been annulled due to non-consummation.[55] Similarly, divorced women could be readmitted to the Civil Service so long as they could prove that they were the injured party and that any adultery had been committed by their husband and not by themselves. Resentment towards unwelcome prying prompted some women to conceal their marriages or to cohabit with partners. Astor claimed that 'thousands of women nowadays are secretly married, or, worse still, living with the men they ought to be married to'.[56] It is impossible to know just how widespread such practices were, although anecdotal evidence suggests that secret marriages occurred across a range of workplaces. Three cases were exposed at the BBC in the 1930s, with the women involved immediately losing their jobs. A shop assistant employed at a Co-op in the Rhondda Valley was sacked after her manager received an anonymous letter tipping him off about her recent marriage.[57] Factory workers were also known to keep their employers in the dark about changes in marital status. Young women at Peek Frean's biscuit factory in Bermondsey in the late 1930s wore wedding rings on chains around their necks, carefully hidden under layers of clothing.[58] Pregnancy, of course, was harder to conceal.

To statements about fundamental rights, women's societies added pragmatic arguments. They emphasised the loss to the community of valuable expertise when teachers, doctors, health visitors and factory inspectors were routinely dismissed, and talked up the positive contribution that married women with families could make in these 'feminine' fields of work. In 1922, the Standing Joint Committee of Industrial Women's Organisations declared that 'no one would deny that a married woman is apt to be more successful in maternity and child welfare work than a single woman' because 'a mother will more easily have confidence and talk freely to a married woman'.[59] Some reiterated the pre-war eugenicist fear that 'racial' deterioration would follow should the State insist on preventing the most educated and energetic sections of the female population from reproducing. This line of reasoning could play into emerging pseudo-Freudian stereotypes of the older unmarried woman as a sexless, frustrated spinster. This image particularly attached itself to teachers between the wars, with some questioning the desirability of placing young girls under the care of women forced, in Vera Brittain's words, 'into a lonely and unnatural existence' by rigid marriage policies. Brittain suggested that the teaching profession badly needed 'the influence of a few married women teachers, leading a normal life and with children of their own'.[60] It would not be the last time that advocates of married women's work would take aim at the alleged inadequacies of those leading single, childless lives, either from choice or necessity.[61]

Critics of the marriage bar campaigned hard for its abolition throughout the period and achieved some local victories. Manchester City Council dropped its marriage regulation in 1928 following feminist pressure, whilst in Birmingham in 1931, a deputation of women's organisations persuaded the Public Health Committee to retract a marriage bar proviso included in a job advert for a Maternity and Child Welfare officer.[62] In 1934, the University of Liverpool reversed its earlier decision to dismiss Dr Margaret Miller, an eminent academic who had fallen foul of her institution's newly adopted marriage bar, and two years later the London County Council lifted its bar for teachers and doctors on the municipal payroll. From a national perspective, however, discrimination against married women remained rampant. A parliamentary effort in 1927 to abolish the marriage bar in the Civil Service and local government was easily defeated. Sir Robert Newman's Private Member's Bill was sponsored by an ex-suffragist organisation, the National Union of Societies for Equal Citizenship (NUSEC), and inspired some powerful speeches in the Commons. Yet only 147 MPs bothered to turn up to vote, splitting eighty-four to sixty-three against the bill. No government in power throughout this period felt moved to champion married women's workplace rights as a pressing policy objective.

One reason for this was the ambivalent attitude of working-class women's organisations, especially those linked to the Labour Party, which became the official opposition after 1918 and formed minority governments in 1923–4 and 1929–31. Women's position within the party improved after their partial enfranchisement. Women could become full members, gained formal representation on the party's main policymaking body, and were reorganised in women's sections which met annually at a national conference. Policy issues affecting women's status and welfare subsequently moved up Labour's agenda, but the rights of married women to work and earn did not figure especially prominently.[63] Labour women spoke out on particular cases, such as the dismissal of Dr Miall Smith and the London County Council charwomen in 1922, whilst female MPs including Susan Lawrence and Margaret Bondfield voted for Newman's bill against the marriage bar (although did not speak in the debate). Yet, as before the war, the position of socialist and trade unionist women on married women's employment was not enthusiastic and tended to focus on the wife or mother's *need* to earn rather than her inviolable *right* to do so. The Standing Joint Committee declared that the question was 'fundamentally an economic one and not a sex one'.[64] It was poverty, male unemployment and an inadequate social welfare system which posed the greatest threat to the security of working-class women and their families, not discrimination against wage-earning wives.

These mixed feelings were compounded by suspicion that the middle-class feminists leading the charge against the marriage bar had really only the interests of the professional career woman at heart. Such a charge was not wholly ungrounded. In arguing passionately for equal treatment, feminists did sometimes imply that all that was necessary to create a level playing field in the workplace was the removal of artificial barriers. They dwelt far less on domestic practicalities, presupposing that the working mother could easily organise childcare and housework by paying someone else to do it. Such assumptions might have been self-evident to women with sizeable salaries or private incomes, but they were far less so for those living on low earnings and in servantless homes. This tension between what Vera Brittain called 'middle-class theory and working-class anxiety' created wider divisions on the question of women's economic status.[65] There was particular animosity amongst trade unionist women towards the Open Door

Council, which took a principled stance against all sex-specific protective legislation, from restrictions on women's night work and employment in 'dangerous' trades to the exclusion of mothers from the workplace after childbirth. The Council opposed the (still unratified) Washington Convention on Maternity which sought to provide paid leave extending to six weeks, arguing that maternity leave should be voluntary rather than compulsory. What liberal feminists saw as intolerable interference with women's economic liberty, socialist and trade unionist women viewed as a crucial defence against exploitation.[66]

On the issue of unemployment benefit, Labour women were more assertive. They argued that cases of benefit abuse involving married women were rare and should not be used as a pretext for stopping payments to wives and mothers who were regular earners. Ex-suffragist and Labour councillor Clara Rackham wrote a minority report along these lines for the Royal Commission on Unemployment Insurance, in which she shrewdly pointed out the 'impossibility of judging a married woman's intention to work by her ability to obtain work, especially in a time of depression such as the present'.[67] This critique did not, however, prevent the Labour Cabinet from endorsing the position set out by the majority report. In April 1932, *Labour Woman* published an angry article by the trade unionist, Dorothy Elliott, who claimed that married women had been 'defrauded' by the new regulations. Elliott was incensed by the treatment handed out to women 'who have spent the whole of their working lives in industry and who have been contributors to the Unemployment Insurance Fund as long as it has been in existence'.[68]

Even this indignant statement did not amount to a full-throated endorsement of wage-earning by wives and mothers. The group which Rackham and Elliott primarily had in mind were the minority employed in such industries as textiles or pottery, where everyone agreed that a tradition of married women's work was long established. These women were thus genuine workers who deserved benefits, as their employment histories resembled the masculine norm of full-time, continuous earning over a lifetime.

Other married women, by implication, who earned casually and intermittently, fitting it in around family needs, could not be regarded as unemployed because they were not proper workers. Labour's Chief Woman Officer, Dr Marion Phillips, noted the existence of cases 'where there was undoubtedly a wrong position', with claimants 'who were not in the true sense available for employment' due to domestic responsibilities successfully drawing benefit.[69] By concurring that such claims be disallowed, Labour's female leadership tacitly accepted the logic underpinning the anomalies regulations, namely, that the 'normal' state of affairs for women was withdrawal from the labour market on marriage. Any casual, seasonal or informal labour that wives subsequently engaged in to supplement household income did not count as real 'work'.

*

What Labour women like Marion Phillips *really* cared about in the 1920s and 1930s was not the rights of working wives and mothers but measures which they had been demanding for decades: generous investment in maternal and child welfare services, State-funded allowances for mothers and wider housing and educational reforms which would support women as homemakers and nurturers of the next generation. Mothers who needed to earn should not be prevented from doing so, but the ultimate aim of a progressive social policy was to ensure that they didn't have to. This was why Labour women showed such little interest in the alternative model being developed in Bolshevik Russia, where collectivised childcare enabled mothers to continue working more or less continuously if they wished. 'I believe that British people will want to work out legal and economic independence for married women by some other method,' was the view expressed by Jennie Adamson, a former Labour councillor, when asked about the Soviet policy during a radio broadcast in 1932: 'The vast majority of married women in this country, though they have a growing interest in public affairs, prefer to be home-builders rather than to seek paid employment outside the home.'[70] It was also for this reason that Labour women forged alliances with figures like Eleanor Rathbone, who continued to champion State endowment of motherhood as President of NUSEC and, after 1929, as an independent Member of Parliament. Rathbone remained convinced that measures to support mothers in the home were the most effective means of advancing women's social and economic equality, an approach which she dubbed the 'new feminism' to distinguish it from the strict equal rights focus of bodies like the Open Door Council.[71]

Yet even with the enthusiastic backing of women in the Labour Party, family allowances moved no closer to becoming practical politics. Trade unionist leaders remained opposed to universal State-funded payments to mothers on the basis that they undermined wage bargaining, whilst ministers and officials took fright at the cost to the Exchequer at a time of economic downturn. Family allowances were controversial amongst feminists too, some of whom questioned the desirability of swapping women's dependence on a male breadwinner for a new kind of dependence on the State.[72] The more limited demand of pensions for widows enjoyed greater success, becoming official Labour policy in the early 1920s and enacted by Stanley Baldwin's Conservative government in 1925. The reform fell safely within existing welfare norms. A woman's entitlement relied on the absence of a male breadwinner and flowed from her deceased husband's National Insurance payments rather than from her own, or children's, needs, which meant that deserted, separated and unmarried mothers were usually ineligible to claim. Nonetheless, it did have the effect of giving some widows the option of withdrawing from paid work. According to census figures, the proportion of occupied widows fell between 1921 and 1931 from 26 per cent to 21 per cent.[73]

Services directly targeted at improving the physical welfare of mothers advanced in piecemeal fashion at municipal level, where working-class women were increasingly well represented as elected councillors, Poor Law Guardians and members of the committees created by the 1918 Maternal and Infant Welfare Act. Often acting in concert with non-party organisations like the National Council of Women and the Women's Institutes, Labour women used their presence in local government to push for more baby clinics, midwife and health-visiting services, home-help schemes and subsidised milk supplies for expectant mothers.[74] Activists were especially exercised by the shockingly high rates of maternal death during or following labour. Unlike the infant mortality figures, which continued to fall, the number of mothers perishing in childbirth actually rose in the 1920s, prompting trade unionist Gertrude Tuckwell to form a Maternal Mortality Committee with May Tennant, another veteran of the pre-war women's trade union movement, as its chair. This committee was highly effective in bringing its cause to the attention of government, aided by vocal advocacy inside Whitehall from Janet Campbell, now senior medical officer for Maternity and Child Welfare at the Ministry of Health. The development of new antibiotic drugs, together with improved midwife training and greater take-up of ante- and post-natal services, led to a dramatic decline in deaths caused by childbirth over the next twenty years.[75]

Statutory provision of birth control proved a more divisive issue. It was opposed by organisations such as the Mothers' Union and the Catholic Women's League on religious grounds as well as by sections of opinion within all three main political parties. Nevertheless, a minor victory was achieved in 1930 when the Labour government agreed to permit maternal and infant welfare clinics to advise married women on methods of family limitation 'in cases where further pregnancy would be detrimental to health'.[76] No such movement occurred on the more controversial question of abortion, despite efforts by a small feminist pressure group, the Abortion Law Reform Association, to push for decriminalisation in the later 1930s.[77] Whilst interwar women's organisations consistently framed maternal health as fundamental to women's status as citizens, they deployed the language of reproductive rights only tentatively.[78]

Instead, activists developed the rhetoric, first articulated before the war, which described the housewife as a 'worker' who required adequate conditions in which to perform her labour. Improving the quality and design of housing was an issue on which women's organisations campaigned vigorously, as they did on extending access to utilities such as piped water and electricity in slum districts or under-served rural areas.[79] The Electrical Association for Women was founded in 1924 to promote investment in infrastructure and raise awareness of the emancipatory possibilities of this new technology in the home. Its president, Caroline Haslett, called for 'scientific management' principles to be introduced to the humble kitchen, arguing that housewives would benefit from rational layouts, easy-to-clean floors and work surfaces, and from modern appliances such as gas cookers, refrigerators and electric kettles and irons.[80] By the 1930s, the Labour Party had made improving access to electricity a formal policy objective, partly on the strength of its appeal to female voters. Writing in *Labour Woman*, Herbert Morrison (who was shortly to become Labour's leader on the London County Council) explained how upgrading the nation's electricity supply was not just an issue for industry: it will 'give the housewife clean and pleasant lighting; it will cook; it will heat the flat iron; it will lighten labour through the vacuum cleaner; it will provide a fire which can be moved from room to room'.[81] In short, electricity would 'beautify the home', which now, more explicitly than ever before, was understood as the workplace in which wives and mothers did their most important, albeit unwaged, job.

*

This vision of professional housewifery was reinforced by a highly commercialised culture of home-making. Recipes, dress patterns, household tips and child-rearing advice became the staple fare of magazines like *Good Housekeeping*, launched in Britain in 1922, and the women's pages of broadsheet and tabloid newspapers, which the vast majority of the population now read on a daily basis.[82] Over half a million visitors flocked every year to the *Daily Mail's* Ideal Home Exhibition at Olympia, where they could see model house, fancy showrooms and stands displaying new furnishing trends and the latest gadgets.[83] It was the better-off middle classes who participated most actively in this emerging consumer culture in the 1920s. By the later 1930s, however, a wide variety of goods and commodities had moved within the reach of prosperous manual labourers as well as lower-salaried white-collar employees. For families with earners in secure, well-paid work, it was even possible to contemplate buying one's own home, facilitated by falling construction costs and easy mortgage terms. Private builders began to target this group as future residents of the new suburban estates and ribbon developments colonising the outskirts of towns in southern England. Between 1931 and 1938, owner-occupation amongst the manual working class doubled from around 9 per cent to nearly 18 per cent.[84] Couples could furnish their homes more ambitiously through the hire-purchase system, whereby large items were secured with a modest deposit and paid off in instalments. Credit of this kind had been available in earlier decades, but buying 'on the tick' became increasingly respectable, offered by all the major retail chains and aggressively promoted as the smart route to achieving one's dream lifestyle.[85]

This kind of aspirational marketing further entrenched the era's wider ideology of domesticity, which seemed to anchor women's lives in the home more than ever before. Yet what was striking about this modern ideal for the British housewife was its promise to reduce domestic drudgery and free women's time for other interests and pursuits. The corollary of being a 'worker' in the home was an entitlement to leisure outside it, a point reiterated repeatedly by interwar women's organisations seeking to engage and mobilise their growing memberships. Bodies like the Women's Institutes, the Townswomen's Guilds and the National Council of Women, alongside the women's sections of the three main political parties, held monthly meetings, evening lectures, study circles, amateur dramatics and excursions to places of interest, and encouraged women to take up voluntary or political work. The Townswomen's Guilds were created in 1929 to 'encourage the science and practice of homemaking and housecraft', but also to stimulate an interest in 'architecture, local history, folklore and natural history', and to make women aware 'of their opportunities and responsibilities as voters'.[86] One reader of *Labour Woman* described how she spent her leisure hours in the early 1930s, which included regular 'appointments' with the wireless and one night a week for politics:

The wonderful music and educative talks give me pleasant
half-hours of mental rest and recreation ... Having two young
children, I am unable to spend much time away from my home,
but our Women's Section claims my one 'evening out'. Here
I associate with kindred spirits, and enjoy the free interchange of
ideas, sympathy and understanding which always pervades the
atmosphere of these gatherings.[87]

Not all married women, of course, engaged in such worthy or
edifying pursuits, preferring to frequent the cinema, read penny
novels or listen to dance music on the wireless after the children
had gone to bed. The spare time of younger working women was
even more dominated by these new commercial leisure forms, from
dance halls and cheap fiction to shopping for ready-made clothes
and cosmetics.[88] The question for Pearl Jephcott, a youth worker
who ran evening clubs for working-class girls, was how these young
women would survive once they swapped the monotony of the
assembly line for married life in a suburban semi-detached house.
Jephcott worried that the girl who spent her days crouched over
a workbench and her evenings at the pictures 'is doing nothing
for her career and nothing to accustom her to the fact that when
she is married she will probably have to face a great many full and
uneventful hours'.[89] Leisure was important, she argued, because it
was only by training the mind and establishing wider interests that
young women could acquire the inner resources necessary to adjust
to the demands of modern domesticity.

This problem of the under-occupied housewife achieved a
moment of public prominence in 1938 when a young male physician
coined a term for it: 'suburban neurosis'. Stephen Taylor, a junior
medical officer at the Royal Free Hospital in London, described in
The Lancet a new type of patient whom he was regularly seeing at
his clinics. She was married, in her late twenties with one or two
children and complained of a range of indefinite symptoms, from
headaches and bloating to insomnia and loss of appetite. Taylor
thought these women were suffering from a nervous condition
peculiar to housewives leading isolated existences on new housing

estates. 'The small, labour-saving house, the small family, and the few friends,' he wrote, 'have left the women of the suburbs relatively idle. They have nothing to look forward to, nothing to look up to, and little to live for.' As Pearl Jephcott had feared, limited education and boring, repetitive work before marriage left such women ill-equipped to find pleasure in books or the arts, or to get involved in local politics or community associations, assuming such bodies existed amongst the rows of identikit houses. For Taylor, these urban developments were storing up major social problems for the future: 'We have allowed the slum which stunted the body to be replaced by a slum which stunts the mind.'[90]

The suburban neurosis diagnosis was questioned by Taylor's medical peers but its cultural purchase was considerable. Just a few months after the *Lancet* article appeared, the suicide of a married woman in Barnet was described at the inquest as a case of 'suburban neurosis', as was the tragedy of a young mother who shot herself at home in Carlisle in July 1939.[91] Some press coverage was sceptical, but it was striking how much public discussion of women's domestic lives was now imbued with the language of popular psychology. As one doctor cited in the *Daily Mirror* put it: 'Everybody left to themselves are inclined to become introspective – particularly women. The way to be happy is to form new interests, to stop thinking about yourself and your troubles.'[92] Newspaper editorials urged urban planners to give more thought to the role of communal spaces and of road and housing layouts in encouraging neighbourliness and reducing loneliness. The *Sunday Express* referred to a longing amongst housewives 'for the jolly atmosphere of the more closely-packed towns where they knew their neighbours from childhood'.[93]

Hardly anyone in these articles suggested that housewives might consider getting a job as a 'cure' for suburban neurosis. Taylor's recommendations included having more babies or joining a voluntary association, advice echoed by other doctors cited in the popular press. None of the handful of suburban housewives interviewed by the *Daily Express* in June 1938 voiced any burning desire for paid work to relieve their housebound existence. Mrs

Constance Colman, 'a pretty young mother' of baby twins in Harrow, told the newspaper that 'people sometimes ask if I don't get fed up looking after them. But I can't think of anything I'd rather do.'[94] Mrs Colman, however, did not speak for everyone. By the late 1930s, some firms in the light industries of the south of England and the Midlands – places exactly like Harrow, in fact – were relaxing their policies towards married women, allowing female employees to stay in post at least up to the birth of their first child. The General Electric Company in Coventry was known locally for its policy of keeping married women on, mostly young wives looking to put money towards a mortgage or furniture for their new homes.[95] Others reinstated older married women on a temporary basis. In 1937, for example, the Peek Frean biscuit factory started a register of seasonal workers to cover busy periods, which included many former employees who had previously left to get married but now jumped at the opportunity to earn some extra income.[96] Some retailers also adopted this practice, most notably the John Lewis Partnership, already well known to be a pioneering employer of women.[97] In September 1939, one of the bestselling women's magazines of the era, *Woman*, published a humorous poem on the theme of working wives, suggestive of a growing cultural presence for the woman who, like

> Mrs MacFee of gay Dundee
> Said housemaid's knee
> Hurt horriblee.
> She'd rather camp in office damp
> With rubber stamp
> And typist's cramp.[98]

Demand for the services of bored housewives like Mrs MacFee was still limited, with regular part-time work (as opposed to seasonal cover) particularly thin on the ground. Employers generally preferred to recruit full-time adult or juvenile labour, which in the 1930s was plentiful.[99] Yet it seems likely that many mothers with children at school or informal baby-minding services at hand would have welcomed a well-paid, part-time job in congenial surroundings, had one been available. Oral history testimonies lend support to this contention. A group of Birmingham housewives interviewed in the 1970s recalled how badly they had missed their jobs after getting married and how much they would have liked some gainful occupation. One policeman's wife recalled:

> I missed the company, the girls, the laughter, the singing. I only knew one person in Birmingham ... I used to walk up to Sparkbrook and see my husband on point duty – give him a sweet ... then come back ... I would have loved to have gone to work but my husband said the day you go to work is the day I stop at home so that was that ... I had hours to waste when I could have been doing something useful ... He wanted to take care of me, he undertook to take care of me.[100]

This statement points to an additional obstacle in the path of the interwar mother who wanted to work: the implacable opposition of husbands. Another Birmingham interviewee remembered covering her sister-in-law's job for a few mornings as a favour but dared not tell her husband: 'He said if you go to work I stop your money. It wasn't considered really right for a woman to go to work.'[101] Such men regarded their capacity to 'keep' a wife and family in a reasonable level of comfort on a single wage as a mark of respectability. This breadwinner ideology was hardly new, but by the later 1930s it had produced a peculiar paradox for housewives in the more prosperous working and lower-middle classes. Increasing numbers of men in secure, well-paid work were able to provide a reasonably high living standard for their families just at the moment when their wives had less reason – and perhaps less desire – to stay at home.

This was the ultimate legacy of the interwar decades for the working mother of the future. Mass unemployment and labour market discrimination constrained opportunities for paid work after marriage and maternity. Yet at the same time, important social and cultural developments were underway which prepared the ground for the major expansion in married women's work following the Second World War. The shrinking size of the family was key to this: despite the absence of reliable or easily accessible birth control, working-class couples increasingly practised family limitation, with the two-child ideal well established by the end of the 1930s. Fewer pregnancies and fewer mouths to feed relieved pressure on male breadwinners and housewives alike, who could now form achievable aspirations for buying modern homes, taking more holidays, and keeping their children at school for longer.[102] In some households, husbands would soon recognise that a second income earned by their wives could bring these aspirations closer to reality and perhaps lift some of the burden from their own breadwinning shoulders. This attitudinal shift amongst fathers was much remarked upon by observers of family life from the 1950s.

Between the wars, however, these emerging trends attracted only limited attention. This was due in part to the ongoing problems of unemployment and poverty, which remained pressing and acute for large sections of the population, and in part to the strong focus on maternal and child welfare pushed by women's organisations across the political spectrum.[103] It was the male worker and the professional housewife who supplied the dominant images of masculinity and femininity in the 1920s and 30s, not (as yet) the married couple who both worked outside the home. This would all change in the second half of the twentieth century. But first, the working mother's service and sacrifice were needed once again. In September 1939, Britain went to war.

6

The Reserve Army

A thirty-seven-year-old war worker from Oxford recorded the
following diary entry for Wednesday 9 February 1944:

> My baby woke me at 6. I got him his bottle & returned to bed
> & slept till about 7.15. Then he wanted to play. I sat him up in
> his cot, gave him a scarlet penguin … a wooden mallet & a tin.
> (I can sleep through bangings but not through howlings.) At
> quarter to eight I pulled myself out of bed, dressed him & put
> him on the floor to crawl around while I dressed myself. He
> enjoyed himself with the hanging brass handles of the bottom
> drawer of the chest. I put on an overall over my office clothes
> & took him down to the kitchen where he sat on my knee
> and had breakfast (scrambled egg, lease-lend orange juice,
> and bread & butter). Then I sat him in his chain-and-table,
> kissed him goodbye & went off to work, leaving him with a
> girl married to someone in the RAF. She looks after him and
> her own baby for me in the daytime, & shops & copes with
> the flat.

The diarist drove to her office job and returned shortly before seven
to a supper of cauliflower cheese and potatoes.

> I made a hot water bottle for myself & a … milk bottle for
> Tommy, brought him up, fed & changed him & played with

him a bit, jumped him up & down & talked to him & then tucked him in his cot. I rinsed the bottle & put it in water, said my prayers and went up to bed.[1]

This mother was describing her day at the behest of Mass Observation, an innovative social research organisation founded in 1937 to study the everyday lives of ordinary Britons. She was one of a thousand or so volunteers who kept diaries and replied regularly to monthly directives eliciting information on an eclectic range of subjects, from religious beliefs and courtship practices to eating and reading habits.[2] After September 1939, women's war work featured as a regular topic in the reports which Mass Observation produced for government and business, and in its punchy books for the general public.[3] These drew together volunteer testimonies, like the diary of the Oxford mother cited above, with ethnographic studies carried out by Mass Observation's own team of researchers, mostly young, well-educated men and women with left-of-centre ideals. These investigators went undercover in war factories, chatted to women outside labour exchanges and carried out fact-finding visits to newly opened day nurseries. They listened in to conversations on trams, in canteens and at the factory gate, and they watched women's interactions with managers, supervisors and workmates on the shop floor. Through these eclectic methods, Mass Observation collected a rich body of material illuminating women's experiences and attitudes towards paid work, and their hopes and fears about jobs, houses and bringing up children after the war.

These feelings mattered in wartime Britain because women's labour was badly needed. In December 1941, Winston Churchill's coalition government took the unprecedented step of conscripting single women into the armed services, civil defence and war industries, shortly afterwards extending this to married women without dependent children. Mothers were not compelled to register but nonetheless came under a great deal of moral – and, for some, economic – pressure to do so. At the height of the wartime mobilisation in mid-1943, at least 670,000 wives or widows with children under fourteen were in employment.[4] Given the sacrifice being demanded of every citizen, it suddenly became important to understand what women thought about State efforts to direct the female workforce, and to identify measures to keep that workforce toiling productively. Alongside the intelligence procured by Mass Observation, policymakers looked for answers in the work of the newly founded Wartime Social Survey and in numerous departmental investigations into childcare, absenteeism, working hours and shopping problems.[5] Together with the wealth of journalistic commentary and patriotic propaganda produced on these themes between 1939 and 1945, the lived experiences and interior worlds of working women moved more clearly into official view than at any time previously.

Questions about mobilising wives and mothers were lent particular urgency because this group, it was universally agreed, were the hardest to entice into the labour market and experienced stress from their 'double-job' as workers and homemakers. Policies familiar from the previous conflict, including the opening of day nurseries, reappeared in the 1940s with some new additions, most notably part-time work in industry. Protecting women's physical health remained a priority, but the earlier obsession with the maternal body was now superseded by a sharper focus on minds and morale. This partly reflected material improvements in the intervening period: female workers were better nourished in 1939 than in 1914, whilst factories were generally cleaner and safer working environments. But it also suggested the stirrings of a wider cultural transformation in which a space opened up for women to describe their *own* thoughts and feelings about work and family, and to be listened to by those in power. This was one product of the larger democratic forces unleashed by the Second World War, which endowed the aspirations of the ordinary man or woman with an elevated public status and would be translated politically by post-war Labour governments into universalist welfare reforms. By no means did mothers get to define the meaning of their working lives as a result. What women wanted, needed or desired was still interpreted by others with alternative objects in mind, be it boosting wartime production or stabilising the family. But at least those questions were now being asked. They would never go away.

*

Judged by the weight of numbers alone, the Second World War did not revolutionise the economic position of mothers. As in 1914, the vast majority of women with responsibility for dependent children did *not* seek paid work after September 1939. At its height, the participation rate for those falling into this category was around 13 per cent, with slightly higher rates for women aged between forty-one and fifty-nine.[6] Nevertheless, this marked a significant change in the composition of the female workforce, particularly in industry, where an estimated one-third of workers were mothers of children under fourteen.[7] Furthermore, there were 750,000 wage-earning wives in their forties and fifties, many of whom were likely to be mothers with older children still living at home. The overall proportion of all occupied women who were either married or widowed was around 40 per cent.[8] This was a major increase from the early 1930s and reflected the shifting age structure of the female workforce. In 1931, two-fifths of this workforce was aged between eighteen and twenty-four, a figure which dropped to just over a quarter by 1943. By contrast, the percentage of workers aged thirty-five to forty-four rose from 16 per cent to 26 per cent over the same period.[9] Put simply, greater numbers of older, married women were juggling regular paid work with significant caring and household duties during the war than at any previous time.

These working wives and mothers were not evenly distributed throughout the economy. Demand for their labour was high in munitions, where the female workforce soared to nearly 2 million, over two-fifths of whom were married. In other expanding sectors, such as agriculture, transport and local and central government, the proportion of married women hovered between 30 and 40 per cent.[10] Marriage bars were once again suspended for the duration across the Civil Service and in many private-sector workplaces, and in 1944 the marriage regulation was permanently abolished for teachers. The women's armed services, which were reconstituted on a much larger scale than between 1914 and 1918, were mostly the preserve of younger women who were willing to move to army camps or travel overseas. Yet significant numbers of married women were also recruited, including some who had served in the previous conflict and rejoined with their adult daughters in tow. In her celebratory book *British Women in War* (1940), the writer Peggy Scott included a photograph of a vigorous-looking middle-aged officer from the Auxiliary Territorial Service with a fresh-faced young woman standing beside her. The caption read: 'A sergeant mother giving instructions to her corporal daughter.'[11] A sizeable proportion of officers in the Women's Royal Naval Service were married women, including high-profile figures like the prime minister's daughter, Diana Churchill, who in 1940 was the wife of a government minister and had two small children. Several of the elite women aviators recruited to the Air Transport Auxiliary to ferry planes between factories and aerodromes were mothers. Margaret Fairweather was thirty-nine with an eight-year-old daughter when she signed up. Her colleague Gabrielle Patterson was a divorcee who had a son aged seven.[12]

From 1943, this small band of female pilots were employed on near-identical terms to their male counterparts and received equal pay. This was an exceptional arrangement, affecting no more than a hundred or so women, mostly from middle- or upper-class backgrounds who had taken up flying as a pastime in the 1930s. The majority of women war workers, whether married, single, mothers or childless, occupied a vastly inferior status. Their employment in industry followed the pattern of dilution and substitution worked out in the First World War, which enabled the use of female labour on skilled and semi-skilled work previously performed by men. As before, agreements between employers and trade unions were struck which allowed some women to receive the male rate for their work, but the purpose of these deals in the long term was to protect men's jobs and wage differentials. Women were admitted to the Amalgamated Engineering Union, the main craft union for skilled men, under this rationale in 1943. Male workers were often patronising or openly hostile to women, whilst employers could be just as unwelcoming and resistant to claims for equal pay, training or promotion.[13] Professionally qualified women often met with a cold reception when they offered their specialist skills for the war effort. 'Despite the fact that total war affects women equally with men,' one feminist wrote angrily in 1943, 'it is still regarded primarily as a man's war, in which women are permitted to share, though not as full and equal partners.'[14]

Official and semi-official propaganda naturally skirted over these tensions, depicting women war workers as unfailingly cheerful and eager to do their bit for the country. Photogenic and well-groomed young women supplied much of this imagery, but older mothers made prominent appearances too, in line with the State's drive to recruit more volunteers from this demographic after 1940. A great deal was made of Great War 'munitionettes' who had patriotically returned to their lathes, and of the heroic housewives who stepped forward for war service despite having homes to run. The writer J. B. Priestley paid extended tribute to the latter group in his richly illustrated *British Women Go to War* (1943), dramatising in word and image the 'double role' they were now playing. Of one photograph featuring a middle-aged munition worker, Priestley wrote:

> There is a sharp and piquant contrast between the severe and impersonal background of the drilling machine with its suggestion of a grim Machine Age, and her comfortable spectacled face and matronly aspect. She might be baking a pie for the family, but she is not, she is helping to construct a weapon of war with which to defend the home she has had to leave.[15]

In the character of another working-class mother, Mrs C. with a family of six children, Priestley detected the warrior spirit of Britain's Soviet ally:

> Surely there is something of the Stalingrad spirit about this heroic British working-class mother, who with a large young family to support, a home destroyed by the blitz, and a man's job added to all her maternal responsibilities, has more than fulfilled every

possible obligation and has successfully defied all the challenging circumstances as Stalingrad successfully defied the full fury of the Nazi hordes.[16]

This rousing statement was accompanied by two images: one of Mrs C. in factory garb repairing broken engine lamps for railway locomotives, the other of Mrs C. seated at a kitchen table surrounded by her brood. This sort of rhetoric was frequently found in recruitment posters and newsreels following Britain's alliance with the USSR in 1941, with Ministry of Information officials expressing the hope that British women would find inspiration in the example of their energetic Soviet sisters.[17]

Popular writing and propaganda placed themes of duty and patriotism to the fore, but in reality these were rarely the sole or even chief motives drawing mothers into the wartime workforce. Many women found it necessary to earn where their husbands or sons had been called up for military service. As in the previous conflict, separation allowances were often inadequate and wives looked for ways to supplement them. One thirty-year-old mother of two from Leeds told a Mass Observer in December 1939 that her husband would 'be mad' if he knew that she had gone out to work, but with only twenty-five shillings a week to live on, she felt there was no alternative.[18] Another housewife explained how she had been forced to look for munitions work after her eldest son, who had brought home £2 10s a week, was conscripted into the army. She had a twelve-year-old child and unemployed husband at home, so this was 'the only way I can manage'.[19] Later in the war, a social worker from Aberdeen told an official committee that it had been

the saddest thing to me to see girls whose husbands have gone into the Army, having to leave little children to go and do two or three hours charring in the morning and again in the evening, after they have put the children to bed, to get the extra money they have been missing, owing to the insufficiency of Army allowances.[20]

Working mothers did sometimes express a sense of national duty, but this was usually cited alongside more personal reasons for earning, including the desire to save up some money or to get a break from housework. As one tailoress who had returned to her old firm to make suits for discharged servicemen put it to a Mass Observation researcher: 'It isn't that I really wanted to work but they wanted me to go, and it seemed like letting the lads down if I didn't. After all, they'll want some clothes to come back to. Besides, the money'll be useful to set Thomas [her fourteen-month-old baby] on his feet later on.'[21] A mother of three from Staines, Mrs Felice MacDonald, told a public meeting that she had gone into a factory because

> I need something to do, and I honestly needed the money because you can't live on Army pay you know ... It seemed only right when my husband became a soldier that I should go and make munitions. It's nice work, and I like it, and am very proud of it because I've taken over a machine a woman has never taken over before.[22]

An equally varied set of motives were found amongst the canteen workers quizzed in a war factory in Wiltshire: 'the extra bit of money helps along' was one answer; 'I've always gone out to work' was another; a third replied, 'You get a bit of fun and it makes variety.'[23]

This last response – that work could be pleasurable – was repeated by numerous middle-aged women who came within earshot of wartime social investigators. Mass Observation often contrasted the boredom and impatience of the younger worker with the cheerful contentment of her older married peer. One forty-five-year old mother with grown-up children travelled twenty miles to her factory job because 'we get a good laugh here and a bit of fun'.[24] Another forty-year-old part-timer talked almost euphorically about her work: 'I thoroughly enjoy my four hours working in the afternoon. I'm all agog to get here. After all, for a housewife who's been a cabbage for fifteen years – you feel you've got out of the cage

and you're free.'[25] This notion of paid work as welcome recreation
was reiterated by Labour's Chief Woman Officer, Mary Sutherland,
at the end of the war. Speaking before a Royal Commission in
1945, Sutherland described what she believed was 'a growing feeling
arising out of wartime experience that if women have had their
babies fairly young, once they are a little older and at school and
off their hands, as it were, they would think it nice to be able to
take a job again.'[26] The Wartime Social Survey lent further credence
to this view. Amongst the 2,609 employed women questioned in
autumn 1943 on their post-war plans, those likeliest to express a
desire to continue working were married women aged thirty-five
to forty-four. Nearly half of all the working mothers surveyed said
that they would like to stay in paid employment.[27]

*

In the early phases of the conflict, how women felt about paid
work mattered chiefly because of the fraught politics surrounding
female conscription. Men began to receive call-up papers
immediately after Britain's declaration of war in September 1939,
and rules were subsequently hammered out to exempt workers in
reserved occupations deemed essential to the running of industry
at home. By contrast, no move was made to direct women into
war work before 1941. The rationale adopted by policymakers,
including the powerful figure of Ernest Bevin, the trade unionist
appointed Minister of Labour, was that women's services should be
voluntarily given, in the interests of both morale and productivity.
Tellingly, it was *men's* morale which was believed to be most at
threat from female conscription, with much emphasis laid on
maintaining conditions of 'normal' family life for fathers, husbands
and brothers serving in the armed forces. Yet Mass Observation
uncovered a great deal of anxiety amongst women too, who feared
being forced to move to another part of the country, to neglect
their families or to accept unpleasant jobs with uncongenial hours.
Whilst the abstract principle of compulsory national service won
general support, it was widely agreed that mothers could not be
compelled or even encouraged to do paid work unless the State was

prepared to relieve them of some of their domestic duties. As one thirty-five-year-old woman put it:

> They're all right provided they look after the children. I feel very strongly on that point. It's madness to expect a woman to go to work and not look after the children. And think of the mother coming [home] at 6.30 after a hard day's work and being expected to do the washing and mending and so on.[28]

These objections were raised again when conscription was finally phased in from March 1941 in response to mounting labour shortages. Initially, only registration at an employment exchange was required; this was followed in December by the call-up of single women aged between twenty and thirty, who were given a choice of employment in the armed services, civil defence or essential industry. In February 1942, the upper age limit was extended to forty and again the following year to fifty. Extensive debates were conducted at the Ministry of Labour regarding exemptions for married women, an issue on which Bevin's recently appointed Women's Consultative Committee weighed in heavily. Composed of female trade unionists, MPs, social workers and others with industrial experience, the Committee spent a great deal of time considering what sort of household responsibilities should excuse a woman from making herself available for paid work. There was broad consensus that caring for dependent children belonged to this category, but the leniency given to childless women making 'homes' for their husbands underlined the State's willingness to uphold the male breadwinner's traditional privileges, even though, as already noted, many servicemen's wives *needed* to work to supplement inadequate allowances.[29]

In truth, policymakers wanted to preserve the logic which regarded women as the eternal dependants of men whilst making it possible for a significant proportion of wives and mothers to enter the wartime workforce. The prime minister, Winston Churchill, made this clear in a secret memorandum to the Cabinet in November 1941, in which he noted that whilst married women were exempt from compulsion, they were free to volunteer and should be encouraged to do so in the strongest terms. 'Considerable emphasis should be laid,' he wrote, '... on the need for utilising the services of large numbers of married and older women. Employers should be urged to take all practicable steps to facilitate the employment of married women, and thereby to release mobile women for essential industry.'[30] Two measures were proposed to accelerate recruitment amongst this group: the expansion of nursery places and the extended use of part-time shifts. These steps, Churchill suggested, would enable married women to take up gainful employment without neglecting their 'domestic duties'. From this point on, driving up participation rates became official policy, but in practice, balancing the demands of production against the desire to protect home and family life from the strains of war proved far from straightforward. The practical needs of working mothers moved more squarely into focus, but only insofar as they could be reconciled with these twin objectives of the wartime State.

*

Nowhere was this tension more evident than in policy concerning childcare. On the eve of the war, public provision for wage-earning mothers was minimal, limited to piecemeal efforts at municipal level to establish day nurseries as part of wider programmes of infant welfare work. There were scarcely more than a hundred of these in operation by the late 1930s, whilst private nurseries and workplace crèches were similarly in short supply. The interwar campaign for nursery schools had made some modest advances, aided by inspiring pioneers such as Margaret and Rachel McMillan, who ran an 'open-air' school in Deptford where children could roam free in the generous outdoor gardens and shelters. But with their typically short opening hours and locations in the poorest urban communities, nursery schools did not – and were never intended to – provide routine childcare for mothers with jobs. Instead, most women used paid minders or relied on relatives and friends, just as they had in earlier decades.[31] These private arrangements continued to serve the childcare needs of the majority of mothers after 1939. The Wartime Social Survey found that the commonest form of childcare for under-fives was grandmothers, followed by neighbours and other family members. Those with older children largely left them to their own devices or asked a relative or friend to keep an eye on them after school.[32]

Policymakers debated how far to intervene in these existing childcare practices. Some officials favoured municipal action to extend private childminding by registering minders and subsidising their fees, or through the lighter-touch method of maintaining lists of women willing to undertake this work. These schemes largely foundered, either because mothers preferred to find their own trusted minders or because so many older women who might have stepped forward in earlier years were already engaged in paid war work. The indefatigable Felice MacDonald took her children to three separate minders, having failed to find anyone willing to look after them all together. This arrangement quickly broke down when 'the woman with my little girl decided to go to work herself, so I had to start looking round again'.[33]

In households where parents worked shifts, couples sometimes tried to cover childcare between them. One welfare worker described to the writer Amabel Williams-Ellis how 'mothers on night shift keep children up to school age in bed with them all day while they try to get some sleep, and at night the child is in bed again with Father'. As Williams-Ellis observed, these solutions were unreliable and produced high levels of stress for parents: 'This sort of thing is a patchwork that is bound to break down in case of illness and at best needs constant repair,' she wrote. 'To have to live by such a patchwork, as so many war workers do today, is terribly harassing.'[34]

Recognition of the ways in which war disrupted 'traditional' childcare practices reinforced arguments in favour of day nurseries in Whitehall. Ministry of Labour officials anticipated from the outset that increased nursery provision would be necessary to aid recruitment, but they encountered resistance from colleagues at the Ministry of Health, the department responsible for funding and inspecting nurseries, as well as many local authorities, who had to build and staff them. Their objections often focused on the purported risks of infection posed by congregating large groups of children together, although one of the Ministry of Labour's regional controllers thought that the opposition was also ideological. Local Medical Officers of Health, in her experience, were generally of the 'opinion that a mother's place is in the home where she should look after her own children'.[35] War conditions had seemingly done little to alter these ingrained prejudices against nursery provision.

These views were partially challenged by advocates of nursery care, such as Lady Reading, who pestered government ministers in her capacity as Chairman of the National Society of Day Nurseries from early 1940. Privately, she urged Bevin's predecessor, Ernest Brown, to recognise that married women's 'output and attendance would probably be much enhanced if they were free from the worry of looking after their children on odd days of illness or of wondering how they were getting on'.[36] Publicly, she presented a grandiose vision in which the war nursery became the blueprint for securing every child's birthright of 'health, opportunity and liberty' in the future.[37] At no point did Reading suggest that nurseries should provide a *permanent* service to working mothers. Many socialist women shared her hope that war nurseries would light the path to more progressive child welfare policies, but they were similarly silent or equivocal as to the desirability of mothers going out to work once peace returned. A Labour Party organiser in South Wales, Elizabeth Andrew, wrote to Bevin pressing for more nursery places to help mothers enter industry, but stressed only the benefits to children in the longer term. Tellingly, Andrew envisaged the war nurseries as 'forerunners of Nursery Schools all over the country' giving 'to every child a chance of full development in Mind and Body'. She did not make her case on the basis that mothers might need childcare in order to continue wage-earning after the war.[38]

By autumn 1941, however, the chief consideration in Whitehall was how to tap the last remaining reserve of labour, unconscriptable married women, for immediate war production. Bevin wrote to local authorities urging them to open nurseries, pointing out that 100 per cent grants were now available from the Exchequer to cover start-up and running costs. The difficulties of finding suitable premises and trained staff slowed progress in some areas, but provision did significantly expand as a result. By July 1943, there were 1,345 war nurseries with places for nearly 59,000 children. Just over a year later, provision had expanded to 72,000 full-time places, with an additional 138,000 part-time places in nursery schools and the nursery classes of elementary schools.[39] Children of all ages up to five were eligible, so long as their mothers were doing work of national importance, and parents contributed a flat rate of 1s per day for a full-time place, which included all meals. Nurseries occupied large residential houses, adapted pubs and halls, or purpose-built huts made from prefabricated materials, an innovation which greatly speeded up the construction process. Most were open for twelve hours, from around 7 a.m. to 7 p.m., allowing mothers to drop their children off on the way to work and pick them up at the end of the day.

Despite high-level ministerial backing, Ministry of Labour officials still struggled to convince sceptical local authorities of the need for nurseries. In some places, Medical Officers of Health pointed to low or erratic attendance as proof that demand simply did not exist for these expensive public institutions. This question of whether mothers actually *wanted* nurseries had been contested from the outbreak of the war. The Labour MP Ellen Wilkinson was convinced that they did, arguing in a 1940 article in the left-leaning *Picture Post* that women 'would be glad to go out to work if they were sure the children could be properly looked after'. She pointed to the system of nurseries and crèches put in place during the last war: 'The children had a good time, and the mothers' minds were at rest. These arrangements ought to be started now.'[40] Bevin broadly agreed that demand was likely to follow supply: once mothers knew that nursery places were available, they would step forward for war work. This contrasted with the position of many local authorities, who wanted to see concrete proof, including lists of names and addresses, that mothers would make use of a day nursery before committing any funds towards building it. Officials based at employment exchanges developed a more nuanced understanding of the difficulties of measuring demand. One regional controller in the North Midlands pointed out that many women, when asked about childcare needs, 'argue to themselves that if they say they cannot provide for their children they will be considered as not available for work and consequently reply that they can make satisfactory arrangements, whatever the difficulties may be'.[41] His counterpart at the Southern Divisional Office added that it was dangerous to rely on 'local opinion' regarding childcare preferences, as 'this opinion is very much coloured by the attitude of the person questioned towards Day Nursery provision. So that, if you take half a dozen people with similar experience of the neighbourhood and ask them their opinion, they will flatly contradict one another.'[42]

From mid-1941, official policy was to anticipate and stimulate demand by opening nurseries in areas where women's labour was urgently needed and where there were sizeable numbers of yet-to-be-mobilised married women. In many towns, nurseries filled up quickly, with long waiting lists reported in Leeds and Dewsbury and organised campaigns demanding more provision in Birmingham and parts of London.[43] Yet elsewhere, evidence of low take-up was troubling, leading to forty-three nursery closures and an insecure status for many more. Mass Observation sent researchers to explore the story behind these half-empty nurseries from the autumn of 1941. Their findings painted a complex picture of how mothers made decisions about engaging in paid work and arranging childcare under war conditions. Some women's answers implied not so much a dislike of day nurseries per se as a more general reluctance to take up war work due to the perceived needs of children or the opposition of husbands. One twenty-five-year-old mother in Cardiff told the researcher: 'My husband say[s] he'll come out of the army if I go into war work.'[44] Other women, by contrast, voiced more specific concerns about using nurseries, including familiar worries about infectious diseases and high-handed matrons. In some places, investigators found that nurseries were inconveniently located, poorly equipped and badly publicised, causing confusion amongst mothers as to their children's eligibility. Even staff at the Grangetown nursery in Cardiff, which was located in a prefabricated hut on a piece of wasteland, thought that its services were unenticing:

> You see the sort of position we've got, right on the edge like this, and the mists coming up behind us. If people round here don't know what we are it's no wonder. The Nursery School has got a big board up outside and a nice entrance and everybody in the neighbourhood knows about it. But we've got nothing like that.[45]

War nurseries varied greatly in quality and attractiveness, from well-resourced and spacious modern buildings to ill-furnished double-fronted houses on residential streets. The matron at Stoke Green nursery in Coventry, where places were unfilled, expressed her disappointment in the 'gloomy look of the rooms, as she wanted light-coloured floors for the children but could not persuade the council to do it'.[46]

There were additional practical problems for mothers who might have otherwise considered using the services of a nursery. Opening hours frequently did not align with factory shifts, forcing mothers to find friends or neighbours willing to cover the drop-off or pick-up – often at additional expense. Some local authorities arranged special buses to transport children to nurseries, but most did not, and in rural areas it was sometimes impossible to get children safely to nursery and mothers to work on time. Officials argued over the question of keeping nurseries open twenty-four hours so as to accommodate mothers working night shifts. The Ministry of Labour was keen in principle, but colleagues at the Ministry of Health objected on the grounds of added costs and the undesirability of prolonged separation of children from their parents. Night nurseries never took off, save for a few experimental 'children's hotels' which opened in Birmingham. The children of working mothers did, however, make up a sizeable proportion of those attending residential nurseries. Originating in the government's evacuation scheme for children living in areas at risk of bombardment, these institutions were caring for some 16,000 preschoolers by February 1944.[47] The most famous of these was the Hampstead nursery run by the psychoanalyst Anna Freud, whose wartime research would influence later thinking about children's emotional development and the employment of mothers with under-threes.[48]

Mothers with both preschoolers *and* school-aged children faced a particular quandary if they wanted to work. Even if the nursery adequately cared for babies and toddlers during the day, older children needed feeding at dinner time and supervision after school. One working mother with a four-year-old son in nursery school wrote anxiously to *Picture Post* in November 1941: 'What is going to happen to him when he turns five and is too old for nursery school care?' she asked. 'He'll be at day-school, of course, but what happens to him between school hours? Hundreds of working mothers want to know the answer.'[49] A mother interviewed by Mass Observation felt frustrated at the lack of care available for her son: 'I feel I should be doing something, it's getting on my nerves [but] he's too little to leave for all the time between when school ends and when I or his father would get in.'[50]

In response, the Ministry of Labour encouraged municipal authorities to tackle the dinner-hour problem by providing school meals on a more ambitious scale than before the war.[51] In Newcastle, children unable to go home at lunchtime could attend one of the city's twenty communal feeding centres. Meanwhile the Local Education Authority in Wolverhampton was supplying daily midday meals to 550 children by mid-1941, with plans for further expansion.[52] Policy debates on child health and nutrition were already moving towards a consensus in support of universal provision, and the 1944 Education Act placed a new duty on schools to provide a meals service. By October 1945, nearly 40 per cent of pupils in England and Wales were staying at school for dinner, a development which indirectly benefited working mothers, who no longer had to worry about providing midday meals (and some of whom later on got jobs as dinner ladies).[53]

After-school care, by contrast, was very patchily provided. Hertfordshire County Council was unusual for appointing a full-time officer to organise play-schemes across the district. The Deputy Educational Officer wrote to the Ministry in autumn 1941 noting that his investigations had revealed 'that the demand for this kind of Play Centre is very wide and that it is steadily growing in light of the number of women who have children of school age and who are going into war industries under your Ministry's plans'. Coordinating funding and staff to get these schemes off the ground was, however, proving difficult. Teachers were often dealing with class sizes of fifty or more as well as supervising during dinner hours and proved reluctant to provide additional childcare. The Hertfordshire officer urged Bevin to issue a high-level statement to generate much-needed political momentum for these initiatives, but such a statement was not forthcoming.[54] Compared to its proactive approach to nursery expansion, at least from 1941, the Ministry of Labour was curiously indifferent to the problem of after-school care. One possible explanation was that officials believed, not entirely without justification, that mothers could arrange a few hours of supervision for their older children more easily than finding a local minder for their under-fives. Another reason may have been the institutional energies flowing into the government's other major strategy to boost married women's employment: the promotion of part-time work.

*

Wives and mothers had frequently been employed on a less-than-full-time basis before 1939. Cleaning, charring, shop work and home-work were often casual, intermittent or seasonal in nature, performed on top of unpaid domestic duties. *Regular* part-time work, by contrast, was rare in pre-war industry and white-collar occupations, where five- or six-day working weeks of forty-eight hours were the norm for women and juveniles (who continued to be bracketed together in factory legislation).[55] The wartime demand for married women's labour altered this picture. For policymakers searching for ways to increase productivity without destabilising the traditional family unit, recruiting wives and mothers on part-time war work offered an elegant solution. By 1943, some

700,000 women, around 10 per cent of the female workforce, were employed part-time, most of them married women working morning or afternoon shifts in essential industries. Many popular commentators looked admiringly on this workplace innovation, presenting part-time work as an ideal choice for the hard-pressed mother who wanted to do her bit. *Picture Post*'s women's editor, Anne Scott-James, observed that 'this type of half-time job gives a housewife a feeling of security. She hasn't got to rush herself to death, or neglect the family. She still has half the day to shop, cook, clean the house and look after the children.'[56] J. B. Priestley suggested that part-timers were settled and reliable workers 'because they know they have something else to do besides looking after machines. Because the factory claims them only part of the day, they are willing to give it all the better service.'[57]

It was certainly true that women working part-time avoided some of the problems associated with full-time employment. Foremost amongst these was shopping, which under war conditions often involved queuing for several hours a day, two or three times a week. Even after rationing was introduced, housewives working ten-hour shifts found that they had little to choose from when they got to the shops, assuming they managed to do so before closing time. Despite pressure from government, retailers were reluctant to open for longer hours as the staffing costs usually outweighed any additional takings. Instead, many women rushed to the closest shopping areas during their lunch break, leaving themselves little time to eat or have a rest before the afternoon shift started up. More considerate employers altered start and finish times so as to enable married women to leave early, whilst a few even introduced 'official shopper' schemes involving volunteers fetching groceries for workers during factory hours. The most popular solution, however, was also the simplest: women took unauthorised absences from work, sometimes just for an hour or two, sometimes missing an entire shift. A major study carried out by the Ministry of Labour in 1943 found that absentee rates amongst women working full-time were nearly twice as high as those of men, with Saturday morning an especially common time to stay away.[58]

Absenteeism amongst part-timers, by contrast, was much lower, as women could generally do their shopping and catch up on housework before or after shifts. Some arranged job-shares with friends, one looking after both sets of children and preparing food whilst the other worked, with a handover at lunchtime.[59] In some rural areas, part-time work could be performed at home or within small groups of out-workers based in village halls or improvised 'depots'. Such schemes were actively promoted by the government from 1943, with employers encouraged to outsource simple assembly tasks which could be done on a kitchen table.[60] As one official wrote to the Ministry of Labour's regional controllers: 'In wartime home work has a new value. It relieves pressure at the factory and enables women with domestic responsibilities who live in districts remote from factories and women with young children who cannot take work away from home to be brought into production.'[61] Recruitment campaigns continued to prioritise conventional factory employment, but these out-working schemes did succeed in mobilising modest numbers of married women who might otherwise have remained outside the labour market. By official count, there were 2,877 home-workers and 17,194 out-workers employed on war production in September 1943, with the most popular schemes found in agricultural eastern counties like Norfolk and Cambridgeshire.[62]

Yet part-time arrangements did not answer every difficulty, either for government recruiters or for married women seeking work. In the first place, it was not available everywhere. Many employers in industry were resistant to taking on part-timers, dismayed by the additional paperwork, supervision and training which it entailed. Although in his 1941 memo Churchill had called for government to set an example, part-time arrangements progressed only slowly across the Civil Service and within local authorities, partly due to perceptions of white-collar work as less easily allotted into half-time shifts than routine manual labour.[63] Civil defence work in air-raid shelters and first-aid posts was typically part-time, but often involved evening or night shifts which many housewives could not manage on a regular basis. Interestingly, the mostly middle-aged *men* who took up these roles or volunteered for evening or weekend factory work, were referred to as 'spare-time' workers, so as to draw a clear line between them and the mass of married women in routine part-time employment.[64] Even middle-class women looking for a few hours of unpaid voluntary work sometimes struggled to find suitable employment. One Mass Observation diarist, a comfortably off young mother of two living in London, described her efforts in October 1940 to volunteer as a part-time ambulance driver, which were met 'with a series of rebuffs, complications of red tape, discouragement'. She finally found congenial work with a YMCA mobile canteen.[65] Others in her position joined the Women's Voluntary Service, which, under Lady Reading's stern leadership, organised over a million British housewives on useful tasks – from welcoming evacuees to collecting scrap metal – which would not take them away from their homes for too lengthy a time.[66]

Those who did manage to find suitable part-time work found that it could be just as stressful as full-time employment. Part-timers were not eligible for bonuses or overtime premiums, and their relatively small earnings meant that few felt justified in paying for nursery places or domestic help, which was difficult to find in any case. Policymakers and employers assumed that women on half-time shifts could largely be left to manage childcare, shopping and housework by themselves, which many successfully did, although sometimes at emotional cost. In March 1944, a Mass Observation investigator met 'Molly', who lived in a four-room flat in a London suburb with her baby son and husband, a factory foreman. Molly did a part-time clerical job between 8 a.m. and midday, leaving the baby with a neighbour and picking him up on her return. This left the afternoon free for cooking, cleaning and playtime. Despite this apparently convenient set-up, Molly was strung-out and unhappy, telling the investigator

> I do get fed up with it, I don't mind telling you, rushing home like this directly after work and have to start off cooking a dinner. It's not so bad today, he's being good ... But sometimes when I get him home he's a proper terror – won't let me get on with

a thing. It wasn't so bad when he just wanted a bottle, but now all this business, mashed vegetables and I don't know what, well, it's a lot isn't it? I wish I could find someone who'd give him his dinner, but there isn't anyone round here. I don't know what I'm going to do, I'm sure. I'll have to do something, that's certain. I can't go on like this...[67]

Another mother of two interviewed by Mass Observation, Mrs X of Willesden, seemed to be coping better with her part-time factory job and household duties – the investigator noted that her flat was 'spotlessly clean' – but the strain was obvious from her testimony:

It's all work, that's all there is. I get up soon after 7am, and get the children dressed and make them a hot drink and by 7.30am I am at my mother's. My mother gives the children their breakfast and takes Philip to school. I collect them later on in the day. From 2–4pm I tidy up the flat and get the dinner ready. And then I put Diane in the pram, and go to collect Philip from school. I do all my shopping on the way home. I give the children their tea and I let them play in the garden while I get on with the washing or ironing or mending. You know what it is with children. You're never finished. You're always on the go. And soon it's time to wash them, give them their supper, and put them to bed. There isn't much of an evening left. I try and do a little knitting in the evening, I knit all the socks and jerseys. Sometimes in the evening I get fed-up and want to pity myself. But I can't really. There must be many fixed the way I am.[68]

This pattern – of using relatives for informal childcare, fitting paid work in during school hours, and managing housework in the time that remained – became a familiar one for working-class housewives after the war. It would form the basis for much of the expansion of married women's employment in the 1950s. Yet even at the high point of State intervention during the war, the tensions of part-time work for mothers were apparent. Shorter, more flexible hours in the workplace became possible, but women were relieved of none of their responsibilities outside it.

*

One group of mothers struggled harder than most with reconciling paid work and family. Life was tough for women who had babies out of wedlock during the war. Illegitimacy rates nearly doubled from the level they had been in the 1930s, amounting to almost 300,000 births over the six years of the conflict. A large proportion of these, perhaps as many as a third, were to parents who subsequently married, but the remainder were the result of wartime affairs involving both single women and housewives, the latter of whom often already had children at home. Public opinion towards women who 'strayed' was mixed, stretching from thundering moral condemnation to sympathetic concern for their welfare and that of their babies. The press printed alarmist stories about 'good-time' girls who loitered outside army bases, whilst official rhetoric celebrating women's war service mostly ignored single mothers, their sexual transgressions viewed by State authorities as a threat to national unity and morale.[69] Meanwhile the National Council for the Unmarried Mother and her Child, alongside other voluntary agencies and a few progressively minded local authorities, did what they could to provide practical support to women who found themselves homeless, penniless and friendless on account of their 'disgrace'.[70]

As in earlier decades, most of the single women who fell pregnant were in paid work and needed to continue earning for as long as possible. There was still no statutory maternity pay beyond the modest benefit payable under National Insurance legislation, and the average working-class girl could expect only limited financial support from parents. An investigation carried out in early 1944 discovered that 30 per cent of unmarried expectant mothers worked to within four weeks of their due date, compared to just 5 per cent of their married peers. Half of all single mothers were earning again twelve weeks after childbirth, whereas over 90 per cent of married mothers were still at home with their newborns.[71] Wartime mobilisation presented particular difficulties for young women who fell pregnant, as many were living in hostels or lodgings in unfamiliar towns far from parents, siblings and friends. Many could not afford to throw in their jobs and return to their families, whilst others feared the reception they would receive if they did. Some girls were already pregnant when they left home, grasping war work as an escape route from small-minded relatives and judgemental neighbours. A survey of conditions in the Auxiliary Territorial Service found that of the single women discharged during the first five months of 1942 due to pregnancy, the proportion who had been pregnant on the day they signed up varied between 18 and 44 per cent.[72]

With so many young women on the move, government recognised that some sort of provision would be needed for unmarried mothers but was slow to act, partly from fear of drawing too much public attention to this wartime social 'problem'. When the Ministry of Health finally introduced a scheme for factory workers in autumn 1941, it was cloaked in the strictest secrecy, so much so that many of the social workers and welfare officers who might have made referrals did not know of its existence. The Ministry undertook to subsidise the expectant mother's accommodation and medical costs for two months before confinement and three or four months afterwards, during which time she and her baby would live in a voluntary home run by a moral welfare charity. Yet so poorly was the scheme publicised that in total it helped only thirty-six women. More successful were measures introduced for servicewomen, who were usually in greater financial difficulty due to the policy of early discharge with no return until at least six months after childbirth. Again, government trod slowly, anxious to avoid feeding public rumour about sexual laxity in the women's services, but good communication and coordination with voluntary agencies produced better results: some 2,000 women had been accepted onto the scheme by 1947, when it was wound down.

These measures were taken with the dual purpose of protecting official recruitment efforts from public scandal and rehabilitating young mothers who, it was assumed, would need to find paid work in order to support themselves after the birth of their babies. Yet only limited thought was given to women's housing and childcare needs. Servicewomen had little hope of reinstatement unless they could lodge their baby with a relative or a residential nursery and could demonstrate a flawless record of conduct before their pregnancy. Some were offered places on government training schemes, but the most obvious employment option for the unmarried mother was domestic service. With the wartime scarcity of servants, far more middle-class households were now willing to take unmarried mothers with babies in tow, although performing heavy domestic labour whilst tending to an infant made for a strenuous job. The other route was adoption, a process involving private and voluntary agencies of varying respectability and one looked upon with concern by the National Council, whose policy was to keep mother and child together wherever possible.[73] Yet for young women without family support and few employment or childcare options, adoption often seemed the only way out, heartbreaking as it was.

The position of a *married* woman who fell pregnant with another man's child could be more or less complicated depending on her circumstances. It is impossible to know what proportion of illegitimate births were to married mothers during the war, but records kept by the public health authority in Birmingham show that there were 520 such cases in the city in 1945. Over half of these were the wives of servicemen, including many who had married hastily at the outbreak of the war and spent much of the intervening period separated from their husbands. The rest, it transpired, were divorced, widowed or living apart from their spouse. It is not clear how many of this group were in paid employment, but it is likely than a large proportion were, given the inadequacy of army allowances and the conscription of childless wives. Young wives were often in a similar position to single girls: working full-time and with evenings to spare for dancing and drinking with men other than their husbands, including, from 1942, large numbers of US servicemen posted in Britain in anticipation of an Allied invasion of France.[74]

When husbands discovered their wives' infidelity they often insisted on adoption as the price of forgiveness, but there were cases where men accepted the new arrival into the family, frequently passing the baby off as their own. This was, however, rarely a possibility for women who fell pregnant as a result of affairs with one of the many thousands of African American soldiers or West Indian servicemen stationed in Britain during the war. Unless the child was exceptionally light-skinned, or some story could be concocted about an 'exotic' arm of the family, mothers could not conceal the parentage of their offspring.

Children of mixed marriages were not unusual in port cities like Liverpool, Cardiff or South Shields, which had sizeable populations of black merchant seamen from the late nineteenth century, or Sheffield, where male migrants from South Asia settled between the wars, finding work in the region's foundries, collieries and rolling mills.[75] One notable interracial marriage of the early twentieth century was that of Jamaican doctor and civil rights activist Harold Moody, who wed Olive Tranter, a white nurse in 1913. The couple worked together at Moody's medical practice in Peckham, south London, and had six children. Yet interracial sex was still largely taboo across 1940s Britain. Whether single or married, mothers with mixed-race children struggled to find lodgings or childcare and often faced prejudice in the workplace. The League of Coloured Peoples, a campaigning body founded by Moody, reported the experience of one unmarried mother in 1944: 'The news that Queenie has a coloured child has spread, and the girl is constantly taunted, and has on occasion had to leave her employment because of the unpleasant remarks that have been spoken and because of writing on cloakroom walls.'[76] The League also received letters from mothers asking for advice on adoption, such as Miss K. from Sevenoaks, who was looking for a home for her toddler son: 'I have to earn my living so cannot keep him myself,' she explained. 'This is a village where hardly anyone has seen a coloured person.'[77] Adoption societies often struggled to place these 'half-caste' children (as they were known in the derogatory language of the day), and many were sent instead to foster homes and voluntary institutions, some of which were well-run places while others were not. A small number migrated to the US after the war to join their African American fathers. Their mothers, in the meantime, looked to the future in a country now emerging from six years of mass mobilisation, collective sacrifice and personal upheaval.

*

There was no shortage of commentators willing to offer their take on the likely long-term effects of women's wartime employment. From as early as 1942, journalists, popular writers and politicians were pronouncing on how women's outlook would be permanently altered by the experience of war. Many described a growing self-confidence, a widening interest in politics and a collective determination that peacetime Britain would be a better, brighter place in which to make homes and start families. J. B. Priestley wrote that British housewives 'will no longer be content with what they had before the war. Drudgery, mean living, dwindling opportunities for themselves and their children, will be recognised for what they are, and they will be rejected.'[78] When it came to paid work, most agreed that women's primary focus would still be marriage and home-making, although a few observers detected a creeping desire for economic independence which could have significant consequences for post-war family life. Ellen Wilkinson thought that younger married women in particular 'dread the return to the little home' and felt increasingly conflicted about their future role:

> They have taken a real interest in their jobs. They feel a real thrill in the consciousness that they are working for their country. They don't want to go back to complete dependence upon a husband's income and therefore a husband's whim, yet at the same time an instinct makes them long for that home of their own. This is one of the real problems that will remain after the war, and it is very difficult to see what the solution will be.[79]

The writer Margaret Goldsmith agreed that young wives had 'acquired new habits of thought, new attitudes, a new emotional mechanism' through war work which were likely to resurface when, after the war, 'they are again forced to ask their husbands for every shilling they wish to spend'.[80]

Others, by contrast, suggested that it was the *older* married woman who would feel this urge most keenly. The economist Gertrude Williams thought that technological advances in the home would give increasing numbers of middle-aged housewives little to occupy them during the day. 'It is at this stage in her life, when she has launched her children in the world,' Williams argued, 'that the married woman might return to paid employment with profit both to herself and the community.'[81] In its 1944 book on demobilisation, *The Journey Home*, Mass Observation drew similar conclusions. Most women, it claimed, longed for conventional lives as housewives and mothers, with the exception of older part-time war workers who had enjoyed their four-hour stints in the factory 'with something approaching an ecstasy which neither strain nor fatigue can spoil'. For these women, the prospect of part-time work after the war had 'an almost romantic appeal'.[82]

Mass Observation's research on this subject included a directive sent to its volunteer panel in January 1944 inviting comment on the possibilities of married women's employment after the war. Although not representative of the population as a whole, the 168 replies preserved in the organisation's archive paint a revealing picture of the attitudes which a cross-section of British people expressed on questions concerning women, family and paid work towards the end of the war.[83] The feelings articulated by female correspondents were frequently more complex than those attributed to them by public experts, including Mass Observation itself. Many of the replies had a contemplative, discursive and undecided quality, perhaps best illustrated by the long, winding answer provided by one fifty-five-year-old housewife, who opened by stating her own strongly held view that home-making was 'a full-time job & those who wanted a career should choose between the two', but added quickly that 'other women might think differently' and then noted that 'to force square pegs into round holes does neither peg <u>or</u> hole any good'. Many women during the war, this writer observed, have 'found out they have abilities they never dreamed they possessed' and will find it hard

> to step down to domestic drudgery, to account for every penny handed to them, and to know they would give their children much better chances if they had 'kept their job'. Some women will in any case continue to work out of necessity, and others from choice, including 'clever' women who have grown skilled & happy in their jobs.

Despite this writer's personal preference for home-making, her general stance was one of tolerant respect for human differences: 'it's not every woman who <u>is</u> a home maker, it's not every woman who really likes to rear children, however much she may love them.'[84]

Most female directive-writers, like this one, were reluctant to conclude decisively either in favour of or against married women's work, and hedged their replies with multiple conditions and provisos. A common caveat concerned the care of children, particularly those below school age. Many respondents thought mothers ought to look after under-fives themselves, taking up paid work only at a later date. Others, however, wrote positively about the wartime nurseries and argued for ongoing State provision. The more left-leaning respondents cited the achievements of Soviet Russia on this front. One young married woman wrote that

> I feel sure arrangements could be made to secure them work which will fit in with household duties, & to ensure that their work at home is made easier by the provision of day nurseries, communal feeding centres etc. to enable them to work if they wish to. After all it is possible in Russia, why should it not be here?[85]

Exceptions were frequently made for the 'trained' woman or the woman with 'special gifts' whose labour was likely to be much needed after the war. Especially strong support was expressed by both male and female respondents for married women teachers, amplifying interwar concerns about the presence in classrooms of spinsters denied a 'normal sexual life'.[86] These replies also occasionally reiterated eugenicist arguments about the dangers of enforced celibacy. As one female teacher put it: 'we are not in a position to be able to dispense with the breeding of the better types.'[87]

A minority of writers explicitly advocated a married woman's 'right' to work and to receive equal pay. One young wife, working as a railway clerk, declared that she would 'leave the country' in the event of any post-war moves by the government to restrict women's employment: 'I hate and abominate all such sex distinction and I think it a scandal that at present women can be forced to work at less pay than men. Even if it didn't affect me personally it would madden me. I just explode inside at the thought of it.'[88]

Yet a number of those who agreed that married women were entitled to work did not see this in absolute terms, arguing that men deserved priority should large-scale unemployment reappear at the end of the war. One thirty-nine-year-old single woman declared that she believed 'absolutely in the right of every woman to undertake any job & be trained for it first on an equal footing', but subsequently opined that

> if there is to be a limited no. of jobs after the war, & these won't go around, then I think the best happiness of the majority of women is best going to be served by making the men the priority wage-earners, & that would mean limiting the no. of married women who wd be allowed to earn a wage.[89]

Others tempered their answers with observations of this kind, suggesting not only a high degree of uncertainty about post-war economic conditions but also the resilience of older cultural assumptions associating married women's work with male unemployment. Several male writers favoured equal pay purely on the grounds that it would protect men's wages and *discourage* employers from recruiting married women. Others thought that socialism was the only system capable of creating jobs for all.

Another notable tendency amongst female respondents was to reverse the logic of Mass Observation's question by reframing it as one about the housewife's 'right' to be supported in the home and to have access to leisure and interests outside it. A married clerical worker in her mid-forties adopted this view:

> I do not think any woman who is married should <u>have</u> to go out to work … If the wife really wants to do some work which is of interest to her, I think it a good thing for her to feel free to do so, provided she doesn't neglect the home too much, & that her husband really feels happy about it. (Husbands are getting used to it in wartime, & may be educated to agree to it in peace-time). I am sure <u>every</u> married woman needs at least some <u>interests</u> outside her home if she is to lead a full life.[90]

This line of thinking recalled interwar arguments about the housewife's status as a domestic worker with an entitlement to leisure. Yet unlike the situation in the 1930s, paid employment now featured explicitly as one of the options available to the married woman looking for useful ways to fill her spare time. A middle-class businesswoman reflected: 'I have never regarded one husband, one house, one garden and say two children as a full-time job for an energetic intelligent woman. Whether outside these cares she likes to do voluntary, paid, cultural, or any other kind of task besides is entirely up to her.'[91]

Several male respondents agreed that paid jobs could provide an enjoyable pastime for wives, keeping them 'fresh' and alleviating boredom. As one Cambridge undergraduate somewhat facetiously wrote: 'Let them if they want to. What's the odds to the way they work. In fact I think some work which meant meeting other people & not interfering with the housework would be a very good thing. Three afternoons a week or something.'[92]

This way of seeing married women's work as a pleasant diversion obscured the economic significance of a wife's wages, both to her family and to herself, and left the division of domestic labour largely untouched. Yet in other respects, this emerging narrative of paid work as useful leisure was highly significant. The married woman who worked not out of necessity but to please herself had provoked deep cultural ambivalence for most of the nineteenth and early twentieth centuries. Now she was beginning to be seen as an ordinary and harmless figure: a young wife or older mother who not unreasonably wanted to get out of the house and perhaps earn a few shillings to add to the family income. Most commentators at the time failed to register the importance of this shift, although Wilkinson and Goldsmith touched upon it when they predicted that British wives and mothers would no longer see their lives as tightly circumscribed by the duties owed to husbands and children. This emerging sensibility would play a crucial part in reconfiguring the landscape of paid work and family life for women in the post-war decades.

7

Put Money in Your Bag

In June 1947, the effects of the war were still being felt by Britons in their everyday lives. Rationing controls remained in force, bomb-devastated buildings stood unrepaired, nearly half a million servicemen were stationed overseas, and British wives and mothers were being courted once again by official recruiters for their labour. Reviving Britain's flagging economy was an urgent task for Clement Attlee's Labour government, in power following a landslide election victory two years earlier. The nation was deeply in debt to US creditors and had a worryingly large trade deficit, a result of poorly performing export industries and heavy reliance on imports for food and raw materials. This was the problem which the Ministry of Labour's high-profile Women in Industry campaign aimed to solve, boosting essential sectors by encouraging housewives who had only recently removed their overalls and put down their lathes to go back to the factory. Adverts were placed in the daily press; posters were emblazoned on buses, trams and billboards; displays were erected in shop windows; appeals were made through cinema newsreels and radio broadcasts; mobile vans toured the streets with loudspeakers whilst canvassers knocked on doors. In Yorkshire and Lancashire, where the push to get women into the cotton and wool mills was at its strongest, carnival floats were commandeered and fashion parades organised to drive home the national importance of the region's textile trade.[1]

The tone of the campaign was both rousing and apologetic. It channelled a familiar wartime rhetoric of patriotic service, impressing upon women the gravity of the nation's problems. 'We can't win back prosperity without the women's help,' one newspaper advert read: 'Britain is up against it. Try and free yourself for work, whole-time or part-time. In the next big effort, you can be one of the women who turn the tide of recovery.' The accompanying imagery was familiar, too: lots of smiling, middle-aged women cheerfully engaged in their work and enjoying a break from the domestic routine. But the campaign also acknowledged that housewives might feel that they had sacrificed enough and now deserved a rest. The Labour minister, George Isaacs, told BBC listeners that he was sorry the appeal had proved necessary. 'You did well – amazingly well – by your country during the war,' he said, 'and it seems a pity that there is again this urgent call for your help.'[2] Isaacs emphasised the short-term nature of the emergency, which required women's services for perhaps only six months or a year – just enough, as one colourful leaflet put it, for 'the strong pull over the hill'.[3] Britain's housewives were 'entitled to a respite' and, as Isaacs pledged later in the campaign, 'they would get it as soon as possible'.[4] A further caveat was entered: mothers of very young children would *not* be expected to respond to the call. It was more important, in Isaac's words, that they 'should be looking after their babes than volunteering to do a job outside the home'.[5]

This approach, of time-limited national service and the exemption of mothers, mirrored the logic behind the earlier wartime mobilisation. Yet in other ways, the 1947 campaign marked a clear departure. In his broadcast, Isaacs clarified that women were not being recruited to fill 'men's' jobs. 'During the war,' he remarked, 'women showed that they were able to do anything from chimney-sweeping to boiler-stoking. Now the jobs are on work which it has always been usual for women to do.'[6] This continuity with tradition, officials hoped, would make it easier to attract women to sectors where they may have worked before marriage, such as spinning, weaving, boot-making and laundry work. It also allowed policymakers to evade the ever-controversial question of equal pay. Unlike wartime munitions, the jobs on offer were not typically performed by men and therefore could not be considered 'equal work'.

If this part of the government's strategy sought to restore a pre-war pattern of employment, the explicit appeal to married women drew upon wartime predictions that older housewives would wish to keep working after demobilisation. These proved accurate. Middle-aged women with grown-up or school-age children predominated amongst volunteers for vacancies in essential export industries and expanding public services, including the new National Health Service. Most employers continued to see these women as a strictly temporary workforce, whilst policymakers similarly predicted that, once short-term economic difficulties were resolved and 'normal' conditions returned, the majority of wives would once again devote themselves to full-time domestic duties. These assumptions underpinned the new welfare state erected in the immediate post-war years, which, much like the old one, treated wage-earning wives as anomalies. What changed for mothers were the more generous policies supporting the family, which included free universal healthcare, plans for nursery school expansion and – at last – a system of family allowances, all measures intended to ease the housewife's burden, *not* to free her for paid work outside the home.

Yet there was another side to this social-democratic settlement. Women had begun to voice and act upon their desires for better health, wider interests, nicer homes and educational opportunities for their children in the years before the war, and by the late 1940s these aspirations were widely felt. Some observers tentatively suggested that the conditions were in place for a fundamental change in the pattern of women's lives. Perhaps, they wondered aloud, the experience of regular paid employment would no longer be terminated at marriage or first pregnancy. Perhaps mothers would find ways to re-enter the workplace when their children were a little older – to earn money of their own, to leave the housework for a few hours, perhaps even to reclaim something resembling a career. This vision was not as yet fully articulated, and only a minority of women were in a position to embrace it in austerity-era Britain. Nonetheless, the period between 1945 and 1951 was a crucial moment when interwar aspirations and wartime experiences were forged into a new model of working motherhood.

Judged this way, the language of temporariness employed during the 1947 recruitment drive was wildly off-beam, as was apparent to a few perceptive commentators at the time. Shortly after the launch of the campaign, a leading article in *The Economist* remarked that it was

> by no means clear whether the appeal for women is purely a short-term one, to tide over an immediate crisis, or whether there will be longer-term opportunities for women's employment. If the latter, then Government and industry will surely have to readjust their attitude to the question of women's employment as a whole.[7]

This turned out to be an accurate forecast, although policymakers and employers would not realise it for quite some time.

*

Married women were amongst the first to be released from wartime employment when peace returned. As expected, large numbers of housewives and younger newly-weds dutifully swapped paid work for full-time home-making. With the school leaving age raised from fourteen to fifteen under the 1944 Education Act, the overall size of the female workforce was further reduced, the number of women in paid work dropping by almost a million between the wartime peak of 1943 and the end of 1947. This dip, however, was short-lived. Women's participation rates subsequently rallied and by 1951, the year of the first post-war census, almost a third of the workforce was female, marking a restoration, more or less, of the position before war.[8] Most munition workers were required, as they had been in 1918, to give up their well-paid skilled jobs to returning servicemen and to move into sectors where women had previously been employed, such as textiles, clothing and

light engineering. This was counterbalanced by growing demand
for typists, secretaries and clerical workers and by opportunities
in professions linked to the expanding welfare state, such as
teaching, nursing and social work. Government tried again to
push demobilised women into domestic service, applying pressure
through the benefits system and establishing a National Institute
of Houseworkers, which trained women for jobs in private homes.
Despite these efforts to elevate its status, domestic service proved
even less popular amongst women in the late 1940s than it had
been twenty years before. By 1951, just 5.7 per cent of the female
workforce in England and Wales were servants in private houses,
a drop from more than 30 per cent half a century earlier.[9] Many
middle-class households had to look to foreign workers, including
young women entering Britain as 'au pairs', to meet their need for
waged domestic labour.

By far the most significant new feature of women's employment
was the growing participation rate of married women. In 1951 this
stood at more than double the level of two decades previously, with
around one in five wives now engaged in regular wage-earning,
comprising nearly half the overall female workforce. Mothers
of dependent children were, as before, in a minority, but only
just: one major survey from 1949 found that 45 per cent of married
women workers had children under fifteen, with the overall
employment rate amongst mothers standing at 19 per cent, which
was considerably higher than the 13 per cent recorded in 1943 at the
peak of the wartime mobilisation.[10] Regional differences were still
marked, with wage-earning by wives most common in areas where
their employment had long been 'customary', such as north-west
England, the East and West Ridings of Yorkshire and the Midlands.
Lower rates were recorded in regions such as Scotland, Wales and
the north-east of England.[11] Various factors lay behind the overall
upward trend, but underpinning it was an important demographic
fact: the pool of single women from which employers could recruit
was dwindling. A greater proportion of the female population was
now married, partly due to the flurry of weddings delayed by the
war, but also as a result of a longer-term rise in the marriage rate

and a fall in the average age at first marriage, a pattern which would only start to reverse in the early 1970s.

These broad trends provided the backdrop to the decision by the government to lift the marriage bar across most parts of the public sector, starting with teachers in 1944. Manpower shortages had led to a temporary suspension of marriage regulations in 1942 and a resultant increase in the numbers of married women teachers, a measure which feminist societies and women's teaching unions lobbied hard to be made permanent during the passage of the 1944 Education Act.[12] In this they were successful, although R. A. Butler, the Conservative minister overseeing the legislation, was persuaded not by principled arguments about equal opportunity but by the questionable claims made by his ministerial colleague, James Chuter Ede, about the undesirable influence of 'sex-starved spinsters' in girls' schools.[13] Nonetheless, recruiting qualified married women became an important focus for policymakers when the sharp spike in births at the end of the war created a staffing crisis in infant schools around 1948–9. The Ministry of Education estimated that it needed to enrol 6,000–8,000 women on teacher training courses every year to fill the gap. Given that the annual number of girls staying at school to the age of eighteen was only 10,000, such a target was obviously unrealistic and officials turned to the large pool of qualified women who had left the classroom to marry.[14] Luring them back became a major plank in the Ministry's recruitment strategy, and it would be deployed again in the 1960s when the baby boomers reached secondary-school age.

It was notable that these early efforts focused on teachers who had completed their families and, it was assumed, could arrange any necessary childcare without too much difficulty. Employing women through pregnancy was a much less attractive prospect, although one which some local authorities acknowledged would become increasingly common now that the marriage bar was gone. The London County Council was amongst the more generous employers, offering four weeks of maternity leave at full pay and nine weeks at half pay for women with at least a year's service, provided that they returned to work and stayed for a minimum of three months once the thirteen weeks had elapsed.[15] Other councils, by contrast, had to create maternity leave policies from scratch. In Salford in 1950, where the marriage bar had been rigorously enforced before the war, the Education Committee was flummoxed by a request from one of its teachers for a paid leave of absence to have a baby. Several male councillors opposed this, protesting that married teachers usually had husbands in secure jobs and that some might take the money and not return, a point to which their female colleague pragmatically retorted: 'if the authority wanted to retain married women it must make some recompense to them at such a time.'[16] Formal maternity leave policies became increasingly standard for female teachers over the following decades, but older attitudes regarding 'two-income' households and compulsory retirement on marriage evidently died hard.

The decision to abolish the marriage bar in the Civil Service was more prolonged. Wartime pressures forced government departments to relax their position on employing married women, and at least nineteen women in higher level grades had been allowed to keep their jobs after marriage, for the duration only.[17] Opinion was divided as to the desirability of regularising this arrangement when peace returned. Many departmental heads were deeply resistant, emphasising the disruption caused by married women who wanted time off at short notice to see husbands on army leave. On the staff side, there was strong opposition amongst the Post Office unions, who defended the marriage bar as a mechanism for protecting jobs and promotion routes for men and single women. Following pressure from Parliament, a joint committee was appointed in 1945 to review the implications of removing the marriage bar and its report appeared the following year. Officially, this report offered no recommendation, but privately senior officials advised the Labour Chancellor, Hugh Dalton, to adopt a compromise solution which would abolish the marriage bar for women in the administrative and professional grades but retain it for lower-level routine work, where regular turnover of staff was operationally advantageous.[18] Dalton was convinced by this proposal, but his Cabinet colleagues, including the prime minister, Clement Attlee, were not. Sanctioning sex discrimination at a time when the country urgently needed married women's labour was not good politics, Attlee argued, whilst the suggested compromise could be easily criticised for 'drawing an invidious distinction between different classes of women civil servants'.[19] It had to be complete abolition or nothing, the Cabinet concluded. Dalton was overruled and in September 1946 the marriage bar was removed across all grades of the home Civil Service.[20]

As in the case of teachers, this move did not signal any dramatic reversal in official attitudes towards working mothers. Just four of the thirty women for whom the marriage regulation had been waived since the early 1930s had given birth in post, and department chiefs did not expect an avalanche of demands for maternity leave once the bar had gone for good. The prospect of *some* increase in the number of pregnant employees was enough of a concern to prompt a proposal, presented to Dalton as part of the compromise solution, that retention be granted in the lower grades for women 'who marry in the later years of their service', that is, beyond normal childbearing age.[21] Yet the underlying assumption remained that most women would continue to resign, if not on marriage, then upon pregnancy, and the inconvenience to the Civil Service was likely to be minimal. Senior officials and Cabinet ministers were in agreement that married women who did stay on could expect no special allowances and that 'firmness should be shown in terminating the employment of married women whose domestic responsibilities were found to interfere with the efficient discharge of their duties'.[22] The abolition of the marriage bar might have made motherhood and Civil Service employment compatible in theory, but in practice Whitehall would remain an inhospitable environment for women juggling careers with caring responsibilities for some time to come.

*

The position in private industry was not quite as rigid, although it was still far from welcoming to the working mother. Private employers had adopted marriage bars unevenly in the 1920s and 1930s, but were forced, like the government, to drop them during the war. Some, including the BBC and the retail chemist Boots, decided not to reinstate marriage regulations, but others fully expected to return to the pre-war position. Investigating practices elsewhere, one official from the Treasury discovered that Unilever, ICI, the Bank of England and all the major railway companies regarded wartime arrangements as strictly temporary and had no plans to employ married women on a permanent basis.[23] Nonetheless, as the demand for labour intensified and the government exhorted private industry to make more use of women workers, this residual resistance began to break down. In key export sectors such as textiles, married women had remained a familiar presence for decades. Some factories tried to boost recruitment further by installing nurseries and staffed laundries on site or by making workers eligible for factory-owned housing.[24] Many of the problems which had dogged working women during the war, however, remained unsolved, including shopping for rationed foodstuffs. A housewife from London wrote to the *Daily Mirror* in July 1947 complaining about a greengrocer who had refused to sell her some oranges during her lunch break. He insisted that she return mid-afternoon to join the queue, an impossibility given the demands of her full-time factory job. A group of female trade unionists in Birmingham called for local employers to give all women in industry an hour off in the morning to do their shopping, arguing that such a move would encourage more housewives back to the factory.[25]

As during the war, part-time work offered one way round these difficulties. Although the government was anxious to register women for full-time work wherever possible, officials behind the 1947 campaign were conscious that many mothers were likely to want jobs with shorter hours which allowed time for housework and to see children off to school. An inquiry carried out by the Government Social Survey shortly after the campaign was launched confirmed this picture, estimating that around 350,000 unoccupied women were available for part-time work, compared to only 100,000 for full-time work.[26] Two of the three women featured in one recruitment leaflet were married part-timers. The first worked in the closing room of a boot factory, a job she had done before marriage. She explained cheerfully to the reader how her employers had 'arranged my working hours so that it is possible for me to take my child to the Nursery [School] and fetch her away in the late afternoon'. The second woman was a widowed laundress and mother of five whose working week consisted of two full days, two shorter days and a half-day on Mondays. Her two grown-up children helped with shopping, the next two 'make their beds every morning', whilst the youngest 'has a cup of tea ready for his mother at lunch-time'. This busy widow, the leaflet observed, 'plans her day to the last minute and finds she can fit in all her duties and still have time for leisure'.[27]

The experience of local labour exchanges during the 1947 campaign revealed further evidence of the popularity of part-time work. Women volunteering for full-time jobs predominated in textile areas such as Lancashire and Yorkshire, but nearly everywhere else part-timers were far more numerous. In Norwich, only twenty women had registered for full-time work by mid-July, compared to 114 for part-time. In Watford, six full-timers and forty-three part-timers had come forward, whilst in the Selly Oak district of Birmingham, the figures were sixty-two versus 262.[28] Firms offering part-time shifts had little difficulty filling vacancies. Two employers attending a week-long 'Women in Industry' exhibition at a showroom in Hendon, north London, recruited all the workers that they needed within two days.[29] Evening shifts were especially sought after. These were introduced initially by wool and cotton manufacturers but were quickly adopted by other industries where women were widely employed, including light engineering and food processing.[30] Women typically arrived at 5.30 or 6 p.m. and stayed for four hours, an arrangement which required special permission from the factory inspectorate until the government passed legislation in 1950 allowing all women to work until 10 p.m.[31] The other type of part-time employment was home-work, which, despite trade union grumbles, was actively promoted as part of the government's exports drive. An official inquiry in 1948 estimated that there were some 55,000–60,000 home-workers engaged in industries such as glove-making, hosiery, tailoring and dressmaking, as well as doing less familiar work, such as packing stationery and making Christmas crackers.[32]

According to the census, 12 per cent of the female workforce was working part-time by 1951, although this figure does not capture the large volume of casual and seasonal employment which continued to be done by married women as cleaners, childminders, landladies and hop-pickers. It seems likely that many more wives and mothers would have taken up regular part-time jobs in these immediate post-war years had employers been more enthusiastic about offering them. Managers disliked the extra paperwork and supervisory burden of organising multiple shifts, even though industrial research showed that part-timers were just as productive as those working standard full-time hours. Where part-time jobs *were* available, employers preferred to maintain the wartime pattern of morning and afternoon half-day shifts, even though many mothers wanted to work from 9 a.m. to 4 p.m., now they were freed from the house in the middle of the day thanks to the provision of school dinners. A Ministry of Labour official in Birmingham observed that whilst some employers were cooperative and flexible, others 'are not prepared to cause dissatisfaction amongst their full-time employees by having part-time workers coming and going to and from the factory at all hours of the day'.[33]

Many of the women who responded to the Ministry of Labour's appeal were disappointed to find so few part-time opportunities outside factory employment, having hoped for a nice 'clean' job in a shop or an office. Nor was home-work available to everyone who wanted it. Nine women in Welwyn Garden City volunteered for work that they could do at home, but were left empty-handed as there were no home-working schemes in operation in the district.[34] One housebound mother with a young baby in Nuneaton wrote to the *Daily Mirror* to express her frustration: 'If it is only counting screws or nuts, I'd do it. Or why don't firms lend typewriters to ex-typists and give them copying work to do? I've worked as a typist, book-keeper and general clerk, so surely someone could find me something to do even if it's only sticking labels on jam-jars.'[35]

This inflexibility on the part of employers helped to explain why the success rate for placing full-timers into jobs during the 1947 campaign was nearly twice that for part-timers, even though the latter volunteered in much larger numbers.[36]

The other major constraint on married women's employment, whether on a full- or part-time basis, was the availability of childcare. Most of the wartime nurseries closed quickly after the government withdrew its subsidy to local authorities, whilst nursery school places grew slowly, despite ambitious plans for expansion under the 1944 Education Act. Some provision was made in areas where essential export industries were located, but Ministry of Labour officials noted multiple cases of women turning down jobs or registering only for part-time hours due to childcare difficulties.[37] According to one 1951 estimate, there were publicly funded nursery places for just 1 per cent of Britain's under-fives, with priority given to 'social cases', typically the children of unmarried mothers, unsupported widows and deserted wives or children from 'broken' homes.[38] The problem extended to those with older children, too. The reason why so many women sought shifts which finished at 3 p.m. or 4 p.m. was to fit with school hours, as very few local authorities ran after-school clubs. There was also the perennial issue of the school holidays. One mother from west London wrote to the *Daily Mirror* in July 1947: 'Of all my many anxieties,' she explained, 'the school holidays present the biggest problem. For six or seven weeks in summer, three at Easter, two at Christmas and one at Whitsun I am at my wits' end to know what to do for my little girl, aged nine.'[39] The newspaper took up her plea, paying tribute to the 'tens of thousands' of housewives who would gladly answer the government's call 'IF THE COUNTRY WOULD LET THEM'. It continued:

> And they ask so little – somewhere to leave their children where they know they will be well looked after, the adjustment of working hours so that they get the children off to school or nursery before they go to work, and so they can get home in time to give husband and family their main evening meal.[40]

The government's response was lacklustre. Ministers reiterated that the recruitment drive was *not* asking mothers with very young children to register, so the question of nursery provision was not strictly relevant. Officials toyed with ideas for voluntary childminding schemes to tackle the after-school and holiday problem, but generally expected mothers to make their own arrangements, as they had before the war. A circular sent to editors of women's magazines offered a range of suggestions: 'It might be possible in some cases,' it noted, 'to solve the problem with the help of a grandparent, a neighbour, or an elder daughter or woman lodger employed in an office or shop and starting work at the same hour as the opening of the school.' The circular also floated as a scenario 'that two friends might agree that each of them will work half a week, and that, when one of them is working, the other will look after her household cares, including the "queuing" for her shopping'.[41] This laissez-faire attitude had not changed by early 1951, when investment in Britain's new defence programme stimulated further demand for women's labour in industry. Officials dismissed proposals for any kind of government-led initiative to meet childcare demands, one opining confidently that 'working mothers whose children go to school will generally prefer to solve their problems with the help of friendly neighbours, perhaps at some trifling cost, and will commonly be able to do so, at any rate so far as term-times are concerned'.[42]

*

The availability of flexible jobs and reliable childcare were crucial factors shaping the possibilities for married women's employment in these years. Yet they do not in themselves explain what motivated some women to seek paid work while others did not. There were still plenty of mothers who earned from economic necessity, including the familiar list of widows, unmarried mothers and divorced or deserted wives, although the numbers in absolute poverty had fallen as a result of more generous social welfare provision. Furthermore, the government's commitment to a policy of full male employment created a space for seeing wage-earning wives in a new light, as secondary earners who helped their families to enjoy higher living standards rather than 'parasites' dragging down wages. A study of social conditions in York in 1950 found that only one in ten wives worked where their breadwinning husbands had secure employment, but the reasons that this minority gave for wage-earning surprised the researchers. Over a third said that they worked 'to make ends meet', but the rest were earning not to secure basic subsistence but to buy 'luxuries' or to save for items of furniture, household appliances, family holidays and even cars.[43]

These material aspirations had been evident amongst some sections of the working class in the later 1930s, but low demand for married women's labour limited the scope for wives to realise such ambitions by bringing in a second wage. By 1950, this picture was changing. That mothers might work in order to save for mortgages or earn money for 'extras' was now recognised as a legitimate, if not yet widespread, phenomenon amongst women. The incentives of spending and getting would be fully felt in the later 1950s, when disposable incomes could be converted into washing machines, fridges, new clothes and better quality cuts of meat. In the immediate post-war years, these items could be obtained only with difficulty due to rationing and government controls prioritising consumer goods for export. Buying a car, for instance, involved putting one's name on a waiting list, and the whole process could take up to a year.[44] Officials behind the 1947 recruitment campaign were conscious that slogans which emphasised increased earning power – telling a woman to 'put money in your bag' by returning to industry, for instance – were risky when there were so few goods in the shops to buy.[45]

Awareness of these constraints was probably behind some of the 'pickiness' exhibited by women registering for part-time jobs. If there were no vacancies with convenient hours, no childcare on offer, and no obvious use for the additional income, many women may have decided that working was simply not worth their while. The relatively low wages on offer further tipped the scales, particularly when offset against the added costs of travelling to and from work. Reports from labour exchanges noted that married women often refused to take any job which incurred a bus fare.[46] Many feminists and trade unionists pressed the Labour government to legislate immediately on equal pay, arguing that it was insulting to launch a patriotic appeal to women whilst maintaining unjust wage differentials.[47] Yet, as previously noted, most of the industrial jobs on offer to married women were segregated from men's skilled jobs, meaning that the principle of equal pay for equal work would have been difficult to enforce even if conceded. This government inaction bothered middle-class professional women (who stood to gain most from equal pay in teaching and the Civil Service) more than it did the working-class housewife, although ministers did modestly increase married women's tax allowance for earned income in the 1948 Budget.[48]

Nonetheless, for some women, all these disincentives were outweighed by the appeal of controlling an independent income, however small. Wage-earning as a means of achieving financial autonomy within marriage had been noted by Clementina Black before the First World War, but this dynamic attracted renewed attention from researchers as they observed the rising numbers of married women in the workforce from the late 1940s. The sociologist Michael Young thought that husbands were handing over a lower proportion of their wage-packets to wives than in the past, possibly due to increased taxes on tobacco and alcohol, always the working man's heaviest items of personal expenditure. Despite the introduction of family allowances in 1945, many women found it impossible to save even a fraction of the housekeeping money for themselves once rent, food and other essentials had been paid for. Young speculated that this unequal distribution of resources within the household explained why more wives were seeking paid work, even though their families appeared to enjoy an adequate income.[49] Speaking on the same topic at a conference in 1951, the social scientist Gertrude Willoughby argued that wives who had earned high wages during the war resented now having to ask husbands every time they wanted a haircut or a new hat. The post-war housewife, Willoughby commented, 'continues to work, in part, for the psychological satisfaction of remaining independent'.

And, she added, 'it may well be that the work itself is interesting and gives her an opportunity of exercising gifts which are not used in the home circle'.[50]

*

Commentary of the kind provided by Willoughby began to chip away at the old moral distinction between mothers who 'needed' employment and those who 'wanted' to work for their own (selfish) reasons. Wartime rhetoric had already established new ways of talking about paid work as a pleasant, sociable and satisfying experience for the older married woman and this language continued to crop up in the popular press in the later 1940s. A long article in the *Daily Mail*, for instance, described a growing demographic of middle-aged mothers who 'enjoy going out' as factory workers, dinner ladies and cleaners now that their children were teenagers: 'They love getting away from their own pot-and-pan washing,' the paper observed. 'They enjoy the companionship, the jokes.'[51] The *Daily Mirror*'s industrial correspondent, Harold Hutchinson, was effusive about married women who had returned to the workplace as part-timers following the government's call:

> These women enjoyed their work – the younger ones because they earned a bit more to help out the family budget, the older ones because it gave them two precious gifts – friendship and a sense of being useful to the community. Don't believe that women don't want to get out of their homes for a few hours a day. They do. They like the sense of independence, the absence of loneliness, the extra money they can spend on their home or children, the sense of usefulness.[52]

Much of this press coverage echoed the official line by presenting married women's work as a time-limited phenomenon, required only to help the country through a tight economic spot.[53] But within certain policy circles, an alternative analysis was beginning to emerge. This linked the personal fulfilment which wives and mothers now gained from paid work to more fundamental shifts in women's lives in modern societies.

This viewpoint was aired most explicitly before the Royal Commission on Population, a body appointed in 1944 to investigate the factors behind Britain's falling birth rate.[54] The spectre of a shrinking population had sparked gloomy predictions of national decline for decades, but the terms of the debate shifted in the 1940s to give greater consideration to the role played by women's changing expectations in reducing average family size. This now stood at 2.2 children, a dramatic contrast to the mid-Victorian mean of five or six.[55] Widening employment opportunities for women as a cause or consequence of the falling birth rate emerged as one strand in the Commission's enquiries. This problem had been studied by statisticians and social investigators much earlier in the century, who discovered an intriguing variety of patterns in the fertility of wage-earning women. Wives employed in the textile industries were widely known to have smaller than average families, yet in other occupational groups, including home-workers, the correlation seemed to work in the other direction: here, wage-earning by mothers was common where families were large. The picture was different again in the middle classes. Many professional women were forced to remain childless through the operation of marriage bars, whilst others married late, thus reducing the possibility of having large families. But *non*-earning wives in the middle classes were increasingly limiting their families too, in some cases because women wanted more time for voluntary or unpaid political work. Mapping these patterns against male wages and local 'customs' governing family formation was fiendishly complex.[56]

Revisiting the question in the 1940s, experts still could not agree on the effect of employment on women's willingness to have children.[57] One witness, the Swedish social democrat Alva Myrdal, presented the Commission with an especially well-developed analysis based on the experience of her own country, where the birth rate had fallen even more precipitously than in Britain. A mother of three in her early forties, Myrdal had recently published *Nation and Family*, a lengthy study of the 'Swedish

Experiment in Democratic Family and Population Policy'. Central to her account was the growing desire amongst women to combine paid work with childbearing, a path which she had herself followed since marriage to the politician and economist Gunnar Myrdal twenty years earlier. Both husband and wife had been closely involved in policy debates in Sweden in the 1930s which resulted in legislation to protect married and pregnant women from dismissal and to establish their entitlement to maternity leave followed by reinstatement. Alva Myrdal argued that extending women's workplace rights was not a *threat* to the family unit but a means of preserving it, because now women could marry and bear children without fear of losing their jobs. 'More children can be expected from working wives,' she wrote, 'when they feel free to follow their own desires.'[58] Just as importantly, she noted, young women could plan their working and family lives with more confidence, including the tricky period in middle age when so many mothers found themselves unoccupied. Myrdal emphasised this point in her oral evidence to the Commission in March 1945, arguing that public policy had to 'find other ways of giving women a feeling that they have life tasks and opportunities'. Ensuring that mothers could continue with careers was one important aspect of the problem, but societies like Britain and Sweden, Myrdal thought, had 'only just touched on these deep questions'.[59] Finding ways to tackle the 'meaninglessness of the middle age for women' would become her major preoccupation in the 1950s.

Alva Myrdal's ideas influenced and were reinforced by the written submission made by the socialist Fabian Society. Envisaging the progressive, planned society of the future, this substantial document argued that whilst women would retain their 'special function of maternity', this role could not demand their full attention for more than a portion of the average female lifespan. Even if a mother had four children, each spaced two years apart, she would have completed the main business of bearing and rearing them within thirteen years. Like Myrdal, the Fabians wished to see workplace discrimination against married or pregnant women ended and an expansion of part-time opportunities for the mother 'who wanted to exercise both her functions', particularly in later life. Women's very status as citizens, they thought, was at stake: 'A democratic society cannot tolerate parasites, and married women who are not pulling their weight should be recognised as parasites.'[60]

This claim that something fundamental was changing in women's lives formed a major part of the Royal Commission's conclusions. The final report noted:

> It is clear that in general women today are not prepared to accept, as most women in Victorian times accepted, a married life of continuous preoccupation with housework and care of children, and that the more independent status and wider interests of women today, which are part of the ideals of the community as a whole, are not compatible with repeated and excessive childbirth.[61]

Younger women, the report observed, shuddered at the memory of their own childhoods, in which 'the life of the mother was one of unremitting toil and drudgery, without leisure, and frequently burdened with ill-health; and in which the older girls all too often had to sacrifice both play and school attendance to the demands of the home'.[62] Turning back the clock now was neither possible nor desirable. Any proposed measures to boost the birth rate needed to work within the grain of women's new aspirations.

Yet on the particular question of paid employment after marriage, the report was more equivocal. It recognised that the pursuit of 'outside interests' might include the carrying on of a career or the taking up of a part-time job in middle age, and it broadly welcomed the lifting of marriage bars. But the Commissioners did not follow Alva Myrdal or the Fabian Society's lead by advocating positive steps to help women reconcile paid work with childbearing. They took for granted that most women would continue to spend the greater part of their married lives fully occupied as mothers and housewives. The bulk of their recommendations aimed to improve women's quality of life *within* the context of this homemaker role, through providing more nursery school places, children's playgrounds, publicly subsidised home helps, babysitters, laundries and holiday schemes to give women an occasional rest from housework and childcare. Tellingly, such measures were framed as 'family services', as though the needs of mothers and children were self-evidently one and the same.[63]

*

The elision of mother and child's needs reflected the position of women more broadly in the post-war social settlement. By 1949, when the Royal Commission finally reported, Britain had a comprehensive welfare state which promised its citizens security 'from cradle to grave'. Stabilising family life was a central objective of Sir William Beveridge, whose famous 1942 report on social insurance provided a blueprint for the system of universal healthcare, secondary education, state pensions and income support implemented by the Labour government after the war. Beveridge recognised that a minority of women would continue to work for wages after marriage, but he made full-time home-making the norm to which the vast majority would subscribe. 'The attitude of the housewife to gainful employment outside the home is not, and should not, be the same as that of a single woman,' Beveridge wrote. 'She has other duties.'[64] Beveridge described the married couple as forming a 'team' with differentiated but complementary roles, an idea expressed in more homespun terms in his remarks to a working-class housewife published in the *Daily Mirror* in May 1945. Beveridge answered a range of questions about his policy proposals and then thanked his interrogator, Mrs Richards, for her time: 'Your time is just as valuable as mine,' he told her: 'You housewives have the most important job in the country, because if you didn't look after us and feed us, how could we men get on with our jobs.'[65] This belief in the value of women's unpaid work in the home, alongside longstanding concerns about shrinking family size, prompted Beveridge to include family allowances in his plan – although only after protests from female MPs and women's societies did the government agree to pay them directly to mothers rather than through the male wage packet.

These taxpayer-funded cash payments to mothers marked a new departure for British social policy. After decades of resistance from trade unionists and government actuaries, women would now receive a guaranteed income from the State in recognition of the costs incurred in bringing up their families.[66] Yet those who feared family allowances would erode men's role as providers need not have worried. The value of the allowance was set well below subsistence – just five shillings per week per child – and payments were made for second and subsequent children only. Traditional male incentives to earn therefore remained strong and were designed into other features of the Beveridge welfare state. Married women's pension entitlements continued to flow from their husbands' National Insurance contributions, and wives in insurable employment were exempt from paying their own contributions on the assumption that their earnings were supplementary to household income.[67] One small improvement was the extension of maternity benefit for insured women, which was paid at the rate of thirty-six shillings for up to a maximum of thirteen weeks. Mothers still, however, had no right to reinstatement at the end of that period.

If further evidence were needed of the anomalous status of wage-earning mothers in the post-war welfare state, it was amply supplied by policy on childcare. As previously noted, day nursery provision dramatically contracted after the war once the Treasury's grant was withdrawn from local authorities. A Whitehall circular of December 1945 set out the official position, which was 'positively to discourage mothers of children under two from going out to work', and to focus any spending on nursery schools, with their educational rather than day-care remit. Day nurseries were to become a residual service for children whose home conditions were 'unsatisfactory from the health point of view', or whose mothers were 'incapable for some good reason of undertaking the full care of their children'.[68] The only group of wage-earning women with any claim on nursery places were unmarried mothers, who, unlike wives married to male breadwinners, were positively encouraged to work. It was far better, policymakers argued, that these mothers should earn, both for their 'self-respect' and to avoid becoming a burden on taxpayers. As one Medical Officer of Health from Smethwick told a conference on childcare in 1951:

> The ideal is for the [unmarried] mother to earn her living in industry or commerce, placing her child in a day nursery in the morning and fetching him when she returns in the evening. By this means it is possible to give her an opportunity of bringing up her child in as normal a way as possible.[69]

Such a set-up was, by contrast, the opposite of 'normal' for mothers with husbands in work and no obvious economic need themselves to seek employment. When it came to childcare, *these* mothers were on their own. The same Medical Officer of Health went on:

> Many people would suggest that if the career mother wishes to park out her child for a substantial proportion of the day in order to devote herself to her career, she should at least be asked to pay the full cost, and should not expect the State or the municipality to subsidise her.[70]

A municipal officer from Guildford agreed: 'the woman who wanted to supplement her income to buy a new hat ... was not a deserving person to claim a place in a nursery for her child.'[71] In February 1947, councillors in Bethnal Green in east London took the step of formally excluding any mothers whose husbands earned more than £5 a week from using the district's three remaining nurseries.[72] Few argued for legal prohibition of married women's employment of the kind demanded by infant-welfare campaigners fifty years earlier. Nonetheless, this kind of institutionalised hostility towards nurseries as aids to the mother who, in the Smethwick officer's words, desired 'to have one's cake and eat it too', was as entrenched as it ever had been.

Some of the reasons for this, including the purported risks of infection and high staffing costs, were well established. Other arguments against collective day-care drew on fresh lessons from the wartime experience of evacuation as interpreted by a new type of childcare 'expert'. Adopting the lens of psychoanalytic theory, figures such as John Bowlby, Anna Freud, Susan Isaacs, Melanie Klein and Donald Winnicott concluded that the effects of separation on children had been deeply harmful, more so perhaps even than falling bombs. Their perception of the child as an emotionally fragile creature fuelled by irrational fears and inner conflicts was developed in the 1930s, but wartime evidence of behavioural problems amongst evacuees, including the much publicised incidences of bedwetting, gave greater power to their analyses.[73]

First-hand observations at the residential nursery which Freud ran with Dorothy Burlingham in Hampstead informed the pair's widely read 1943 book, *Infants without Families*. This described the emotional difficulties which resulted when children were forced to live outside a 'normal' home environment.[74] John Bowlby's writings echoed this message. Bowlby was already convinced of the damage caused by prolonged separation through his Child Guidance work in London and was deeply critical of the government's mass evacuation policy in 1939–40.[75] He worked as an army psychiatrist during the war but continued to publish research on child development and, in 1948, was commissioned by an Expert Committee of the World Health Organisation to survey the published literature on this topic. Bowlby's report, published in 1952 as *Maternal Care and Mental Health*, dwelt upon the detrimental impact of institutional care and the importance of a continuous maternal presence in early life for a child's healthy emotional development.

Bowlby's work did not have a direct impact on decision-making in Whitehall concerning the closure of the war nurseries. His ideas were more influential in relation to policy on children in care, where practice shifted away from placements in residential homes and towards individualised fostering arrangements.[76] Nonetheless, expert claims about the dangers of separation helped to reinforce existing arguments against public spending on nurseries in the mid- to late 1940s. They also confirmed the official view that nursery education should begin after the age of two and extend only for relatively short hours. A medical officer from Essex County Council told the 1951 childcare conference that one lesson of the war was that 'the average child of two years is not ready to leave his mother for the whole day with benefit to himself', and that even the three-year-old 'who is just learning to adapt himself to the outside world will miss his mother most at meal times and for a time it is better for him to go home for his midday meal'.[77] By the 1950s, Bowlby's theories about 'maternal deprivation' were core reading for those training in child welfare work or nursery education.[78]

Officials concerned with labour supply had to navigate these new ideas about child psychology as they managed the ongoing drive to get women back into industry. Given that mothers of preschool children were officially exempt from any obligation to volunteer, the government was off the hook in terms of nursery provision to aid recruitment. Yet official statements sometimes sent mixed messages. Dame Mary Smieton, a senior civil servant at the Ministry of Labour, went on the BBC radio programme *Woman's Hour* in 1950 in an effort to clarify the government's position. She rehearsed the 1945 policy on the care of children under two, which, she added, was based on 'authoritative advice'. But Smieton qualified this statement by arguing that the recent devaluation of the pound and an expanded defence programme meant Britain was 'not back to "normal peace time conditions"' and that 'the need for women in industry is as urgent today as it was [in 1947]'. She ended the broadcast on an ambiguous note:

> The Government doesn't forbid a mother of young children to work if she wishes. It says instead 'the place of a mother with children under two is at home'; to women with older children it says 'here are the facts about our economic needs, these needs are very great and there are urgent demands for women to work, but a woman's home responsibility is also great, and she has to decide for herself whether she can and should take on a job outside her home'.[79]

This ambiguity captured an important dynamic within Britain's new social democracy: the State could not – and would not – compel women to have more children or to stay at home full-time to look after them. But nor would it take any positive measures to help mothers combine paid employment with childbearing, the only exception to this rule being unmarried, divorced or deserted mothers, who might secure a nursery place on the strength of their status as 'social cases'. Otherwise, mothers had to arrange their own childcare, persuade employers to offer flexible hours, and find individual solutions to the problems of shopping and housework. Wives who wanted jobs could have them, but they could expect no support from the government in realising this desire.

*

This lack of governmental support, above anything else, explains why the majority of British mothers did *not* enter paid employment between 1945 and 1951. The abolition of marriage bars heralded a false dawn. One formal constraint on married women's work had been removed, but the structures which denied wives and mothers equal access to the labour market – low pay, non-existent childcare, rigid working hours – remained in place. Some feminists expressed dismay at the ways in which the nascent welfare state entrenched women's dependency. Elizabeth Abbott and Katherine Bompas of the Open Door Council protested that Beveridge's proposals perpetuated 'the denial of any personal status to a woman because she is married, the denial of her independent personality within marriage'.[80] Representatives of the National Council of Women similarly criticised Beveridge's treatment of wives as a special class with no independent entitlement to draw benefits or to receive them at the standard rate. Other women's organisations, however, welcomed the welfare reforms, interpreting them as proof that policymakers now took seriously the value of women's unpaid work in the home. The Women's Institutes rejoiced that 'housewives have come into their own at last!' following the publication of the Beveridge Report.[81] Labour women continued to press for investment in maternity services and nursery schools and for more

generous family allowances, but they nonetheless acknowledged
the major benefits of the expanded welfare state for working-class
housewives, especially the free medical care now available on the
NHS.[82] Despite ongoing rationing and the nation's economic
woes, the Labour Party's popularity with female voters held up well
between 1945 and 1950, suggesting that British women were not in
collective revolt against the post-war settlement which accorded
them a primary role as wives and mothers.[83]

Some housewives even reacted with indignation at the 1947
Women in Industry campaign, insisting that the State had
no business urging them to neglect their homes and children,
particularly at a time when men's hours had been getting shorter as
a result of trade union pressure. The *Daily Mail* ran a story about
widespread resistance towards government recruitment efforts
in the textile industries of Yorkshire and Lancashire. The paper
quoted the defiant words of Mabel Holroyd, a recently married
housewife from Pudsey: 'Five years in a mill before the war and
three years in a munition factory were enough for me,' she said.
'My job is in the home, and that's where I'm staying.'[84] Dorothy
Layton, President of the Women's Liberal Federation, wrote to
the Ministry of Labour in August 1947 to express her members'
disapproval of the campaign:

> Far too little importance is attached, we feel, to the influence
> on production and the national effort generally of a stable
> home, with well cooked food, and a wife or mother in the
> home when workers return who is not too irritable, tired and
> sick from the utter exhaustion of trying to do two jobs at the
> same time.[85]

Support amongst British women for the 'modern' ideal of full-time
housewifery was still very strong in the immediate post-war years.
How far the ideas of Bowlby or Winnicott reinforced these home-
centred values is uncertain, although many thousands of mothers
would have come into contact with the new child psychology
through Winnicott's popular radio talks on infant care, which the
BBC began broadcasting from 1943.[86] Winnicott received long,

appreciative letters from his listeners, although their tone suggested that what working-class housewives liked best about his talks was the way in which they seemed to validate already established mothering styles. Winnicott told women to trust in their 'natural' maternal instincts and to disregard old-fashioned advice about rigid feeding and sleeping regimes. By translating psychoanalytical theory into seemingly common-sense messages about warmth, intimacy and being emotionally available to one's child, these experts exerted a powerful influence over parenting norms in the post-war decades. Popularised through radio, newspapers and mass-circulation magazines, their authoritative claims helped to convince many mothers to abstain from paid work, at least until their children were at school.

Nonetheless, ideologies of domesticity and the cult of maternal love were not the only forces shaping the landscape of the post-war working mother. Women's decision-making about wage-earning took place within complex circumstances and contexts over which they often had limited control. Some embraced employment opportunities where the jobs on offer were attractive and where the additional income served a definite purpose. Others judged it not worth the time and effort. Mothers had always earned for a range of reasons, but what changed in the late 1940s was that motives other than the alleviation of poverty became increasingly visible to observers. This was due in part to the confluence of long-term demographic trends and the particular economic pressures of the period 1947–51. Together, these created an unprecedented situation in which married women's labour-force participation increased alongside full male employment. But this newfound visibility also stemmed from a heightened interest in women's subjective feelings about paid work. Evidence that wives and mothers enjoyed the sociability of the workplace, liked having a break from housework, wanted control of their own income, or took pride in earning 'extras' for the family, formed the basis for new ways of thinking and talking about married women's work. What emerged from these years immediately following the Second World War was a model of working motherhood which would remain culturally dominant until the 1970s.

PART THREE

The Best of Both Worlds, 1951–1970

8

Housewives' Choice

In 1954, the social researcher Pearl Jephcott moved into lodgings in Bermondsey, just south of the river Thames, with a brief to study the lives of the district's working wives. Jephcott was by then a seasoned interviewer, someone who was good at getting people to talk and who had a sensitive eye for the colour and texture of working-class communities. These qualities served her well in densely populated Bermondsey, where over half of all married women were in paid employment by the mid-1950s. Several thousand were part-timers at Peek Frean, an old family-owned firm of biscuit manufacturers which occupied a sprawling site next to the Southern Region railway line and became the focal point of Jephcott and her team's investigations.[1] Married women had always worked in this part of London, either as unskilled factory hands bottling jam, sorting rags, making tin boxes and packing chocolates, or as casually employed cleaners and home-workers. Some of these jobs survived into the 1950s: early-morning office cleaning, for instance, remained popular amongst mothers looking to work for only a few hours a day. But in most respects, the working wives interviewed by Jephcott looked dramatically different from their Victorian and Edwardian predecessors. Investigators before the First World War had discovered malnourished women labouring in dilapidated factories or foul-smelling attics, driven by poverty to accept whatever work they could get. Jephcott, by contrast, found smartly dressed, house-proud wives in excellent health looking for well-paid part-time jobs. These women could increasingly take their pick of employment, as local firms scrambled to recruit labour to meet booming consumer demand.

Under the conditions of greater prosperity which set in from the mid-1950s, the meanings attached to married women's work changed in important ways. Rather than supplementing an inadequate male wage (or substituting for a non-existent one), most of Jephcott's wives pooled their income with husbands who were in secure, regular employment. This included a large number of dock workers, whose earning power had been transformed by the guaranteed minimum wage introduced by the National Dock Labour Board, a body established in 1948 by the Labour government to tackle the problem of casualisation. As the 'bad old days' of sporadic, low-paid employment receded for their husbands, Bermondsey wives gravitated towards firms like Peek Frean, not with the threat of destitution at their backs, but with the prospect of a superior lifestyle in their sights. This was often articulated through the language of 'extras', which for one woman might mean nicer clothes or matching furniture, whilst for another could translate as a better cut of meat at the butchers or a week in a caravan by the sea with the kids. 'Certainly by the standards even of the immediate past, levels of living were vastly improved,' Jephcott commented. 'In general the spur was the determination to improve on the improvements.'[2]

Jephcott noticed something else about her research subjects. Many of them seemed to positively *enjoy* going out to work. Packing biscuits in a factory was not an exciting job, but it was highly sociable and a welcome break from the daily grind of housework and childcare. For a handful of women who had taken jobs on the advice of their doctor, paid work had an explicitly therapeutic purpose: 'I felt so heavy', 'I got morbid' and 'I worried so over little things' were how these interviewees described their former non-earning selves. Others explained that they worked to alleviate boredom and loneliness. 'I used to turn the room round just for something to do,' said one, whilst a mother of three living in a block of flats confessed that her evening job was primarily a means of getting out and meeting other people. These psychological benefits were inseparable from material ones, illustrated by the obvious pleasure which women took in bringing a second income into the home: 'You do feel nice when you get your bit of money on a Friday and know that you've earned it.' For some, contributing to the household budget was a route to higher status in the eyes of husband, children and community. Jephcott reflected on this:

> To be able to hold down a job at all in the competitive outside world was reassuring and something that not every married woman would dare to tackle. How important it sounded to say you '*must go in tomorrow,*' to talk of 'my mates' and to refer to rush jobs and overseas orders ... Merely to be moving in a wider circle than the domestic one was a mark of some distinction since, in a place like Bermondsey, housewives lead a very uniform existence.[3]

By making a place for paid work in their married lives, the women of Bermondsey seemed to have found an answer to the 'meaninglessness of middle age' diagnosed by Alva Myrdal before the Royal Commission on Population at the end of the war. In 1956, Myrdal expanded on her thesis by co-authoring *Women's Two Roles* with the sociologist Viola Klein, who would become a well-known, expert voice on the subject of women's work in these decades. The authors set out a model of phased life-stages for women which they dubbed the 'dual role'. Mothers in advanced industrial nations like Britain, Myrdal and Klein argued, were settling into a new pattern of paid work after marriage, encompassing a period of time out from the labour market for childbearing, followed by re-entry to the workplace, typically at the age of thirty-five or forty. The dual role, they believed, offered an ideal middle way between the 'irreconcilable alternatives' of continuous wage-earning and unrelieved housewifery:

> The Gordian knot of a seemingly insoluble feminine dilemma has been cut. The technical and social developments of the last

few decades have given women the opportunity to combine and to integrate their two interests in Home and Work ... No longer need women forgo the pleasures of one sphere in order to enjoy the satisfactions of the other. The best of both worlds has come within their grasp, if only they reach out for it.[4]

Jephcott struck a less utopian tone when writing up her Bermondsey findings, published in 1962 as *Married Women Working*, but she nonetheless shared Myrdal and Klein's view that something fundamental was shifting in women's working and family lives. Employment beyond marriage and motherhood, Jephcott suggested, was 'meeting deep-seated needs which are now felt by women in general in our society'.[5]

The claim that married women's work had become a permanent feature of modern societies was developed and amplified by a range of voices in post-war Britain. Politicians and civil servants pondered over it as they wrestled with labour-supply policies and future educational and training needs. Women's societies, employers' organisations and trade unions convened conferences on the subject. Newspapers and broadcasters ran lively features on working wives and advertisers began to address this group directly when marketing convenience foods and labour-saving devices for the home. Slowly but unmistakably, the wage-earning wife and mother was shedding her former status as a social problem and being reinvented as a social norm.

This transformation took place against the backdrop of full male employment and a growing economy, conditions that were crucial in securing a link in the public mind between married women's work, aspirational consumption and personal fulfilment. Pre-war critiques of working wives as economic 'parasites' did not disappear, whilst new ones lamented the obsession with getting and spending that was evident amongst newly affluent workers. As a defence, many women used the old language of material need to justify their decision to work, but this terminology was now more capacious: houses 'needed' televisions and washing machines, children 'needed' music lessons and new toys, families 'needed' cars and holidays away. Furthermore, it was increasingly conceded that mothers themselves 'needed' interests beyond the home for their mental well-being and self-esteem. Unlike the decades between the wars, paid employment now supplied a ready arena in which to pursue these psychological goals. In short, the mother who earned in order to give her children the best of everything and herself a richer inner life became a figure to be admired rather than condemned.[6]

Yet if a new moral economy of working motherhood took shape in the post-war decades, some women still found themselves positioned outside it. The dual role privileged a pattern of work predicated on a mother's return to the labour force when her children were judged old enough to be 'safely' left. This was neatly in line with the advice of psychoanalysts like John Bowlby, whose theory of maternal deprivation gained further purchase in the 1950s, even if it was never universally accepted. The dual role also let fathers and policymakers off the hook; if women re-entered the workplace only when their children were at school, and often did so on a part-time basis, then no change was needed either in men's primary identity as breadwinners or to the existing regime of minimal public investment in day-care. The minority of women who *did* earn continuously whilst their children were young were out of step with this emerging norm. Widowed, separated, divorced and unmarried mothers typically fell into this category, as did professional 'career women' and many migrant mothers born outside Britain. In summary, working motherhood became increasingly 'ordinary' in the 1950s and 1960s, but it was a narrowly conformist kind of ordinariness, like the narrowly conformist times which produced it.

*

This new era for working mothers opened at a moment when most families in Britain were experiencing significant material improvements in their daily lives. A comprehensive welfare state, universal secondary education, low unemployment and rising wages offered security and opportunity on an unprecedented scale.[7] More

people than ever before could afford mortgages, with 42 per cent of all
dwellings owner-occupied by 1960, whilst sustained investment by
local authorities expanded the stock of good quality social housing.[8]
Jephcott noted that about half of all homes in Bermondsey were
council-owned, and one in seven families lived in properties newly
built since the war.[9] As slums were cleared, New Towns sprang up
in places like Milton Keynes in Buckinghamshire and East Kilbride
in Scotland, offering urban city-dwellers modern homes, fresh air
and green spaces.[10] With greater disposable income, households
could spend more lavishly on fancy foods and new clothes and
acquire refrigerators and cars through hire-purchase schemes. The
social scientist Mark Abrams estimated that two-fifths of the average
family budget went on such 'luxuries' in the late 1950s, noting little
difference between the spending habits of working-class and middle-
class consumers.[11] A decade later, nearly two-thirds of households
had washing machines, three-quarters had a vacuum cleaner,
and nine in ten had a television.[12] Paid holidays were available to
nearly all workers in regular employment, and a small but growing
minority chose to take them abroad: 5 million Britons were doing
so by the close of the 1960s, with resorts in Spain and France at the
top of the list.[13] Day-to-day leisure was increasingly spent at home,
where couples watched television together, played with the kids or
pottered around on gardening or DIY tasks. Surveying these trends,
Abrams concluded that Britain was becoming a 'home-centred
society' with family, privacy and domesticity at its heart.

This turning inwards carried particular significance for women,
elevating and intensifying the 1930s ideal of the professional
housewife. Married women had always been responsible for
making the weekly budget stretch, but now they became arbiters of
lifestyle and controllers of taste. Family meals were to be not merely
nutritious but appetising and demonstrative of culinary skill.
Picking out home furnishings or even making them from scratch
was an invitation to show originality and flair. How a woman
organised the housework became an expression of her personality.
Mass-circulation magazines like *Housewife*, *Good Housekeeping* and
Woman's Own reinforced these messages with their cleaning tips,

recipes, knitting patterns, agony aunt columns and the barrage of advertising on every page. One magazine columnist, writing in 1957, urged her readers to remember that

> A woman's influence over the home is far greater than her husband's. He may be very much king of the castle, making all the decisions, disciplining the children and handling the accounts. But he does not rule over the atmosphere of the home. His wife does. She may do it deliberately, but usually it is an unconscious power that she wields. The home is built round her. She creates its predominant atmosphere, and sets its moods by her moods ... Don't forget the terrific responsibility of your importance to your family's behaviour. It's up to you to set the pattern.[14]

This sort of advice seemed to prescribe a life of immersive domesticity, yet it was imparted at the very moment that large numbers of housewives were starting to look for paid work outside the home. Employment rates amongst married women rose steadily through the 1950s, reaching 35 per cent in 1961 and 49 per cent a decade later, according to census data. The trend was especially marked amongst those aged forty-five to fifty-four, where the percentage of wives out at work doubled between 1951 and 1966 from a quarter to a half. Regional differences were still notable. In 1961, the lowest participation rate, just 12.2 per cent, was found in Port Talbot, South Wales, whilst the highest, almost 57 per cent, was in Burnley in Lancashire, suggesting the resilience of pre-war 'traditions' of married women's work. There were also socio-economic differences, with the wives of manual workers more likely to be earning than women married to professional men, employers or managers: some two-fifths of the former were in work, compared to less than a third of the latter.[15] Nonetheless, the direction of travel was upwards across all social classes, with a strong emphasis on part-time work. One in three female workers counted in the 1966 census was employed on a less than full-time basis.[16]

From the mid-1960s, reliable data on the employment of mothers became more widely available, showing strong evidence of Myrdal and Klein's dual-role pattern. A large-scale official survey overseen and analysed by Audrey Hunt in 1965 estimated that mothers made up a third of the female workforce, with the highest participation rates amongst those with school-aged offspring. Hunt found that 44 per cent of mothers with children aged five to fifteen were earning, compared to 21 per cent with three- or four-year-olds, and 15 per cent with under-threes. Part-time work was common amongst all married women, but especially so amongst mothers: only one in six full-timers were responsible for dependent children, compared to more than half the women working part-time. Of the non-earning women interviewed for the survey, half said it was 'practically certain' that they would return to paid employment at some point in the future and another third said it was 'likely'. Reflecting on these findings, Hunt commented: 'It seems likely that more and more women will regard it as natural to continue work after marriage at least until the birth of the first child, and to return to work when their children are old enough.'[17]

It might seem paradoxical that at the very moment that the housewife was culturally enthroned in her ideal home by magazines and advertisers, millions of married women were looking for jobs outside it. Yet, in truth, these phenomena were intimately interlinked. The working mother was also the home-centred mother in the sense that her earnings were frequently what enabled families to enjoy a higher level of domestic comfort. Study after study confirmed Jephcott's findings in Bermondsey. The National Council of Women investigated the reasons why so many wives were going out to work in a 1957 questionnaire, noting that 'good clothes for the family, toys for the children and television were mentioned in nearly every reply'.[18] Of the 200 married women interviewed in a Leicester hosiery factory in the early 1960s, only one in five claimed 'real need', with the remainder driven by hopes 'for a higher standard of living, viewed both in general terms and with reference to specific items'.[19] A middle-aged housewife in

Swansea told researchers that she would hate to give up her job because 'the extra money is putting us on our feet nicely. We saved up enough to go to take the children up to Butlin's at Pwllheli last August, and we had a really wonderful time.'[20] Retrospective accounts from Mass Observers writing in the early twenty-first century reinforce this picture. One former shop manager and mother of two from Brentwood decided to work at home in the 1950s as a dressmaker 'so that I could buy a car to take [the children] around in the school holidays'.[21] A retired doctor from Wigan remembered his mother doing part-time cleaning, factory and shop work throughout his childhood, noting that she 'saw the need to work because they had three young children and they wanted to make sure that they had an education, and also holidays and toys'.[22]

Most of this evidence was self-reported, what women *said* their wages were for. Some researchers tried to explore actual family income and expenditure and found a complex picture. Hunt discovered, for example, that households headed by a male manual worker were more likely to have a car where the wife earned, but this trend was not evident amongst non-manual workers. The sociologist Ferdynand Zweig also noticed higher levels of car ownership amongst the dual-earner couples whom he interviewed in the early 1960s, but in only two of his four case-study factories did a second income correlate with higher rates of home ownership.[23] Some of the differences in married women's employment across income groups were clearly related to the husband's earning power: where families could enjoy a superior standard of living on a single wage, mothers might very well choose not to work. Yet judgements about whether getting a job was 'worth it' were deeply subjective and contingent on multiple factors, including what sort of job with what sort of pay was on offer, and whether taking it would incur additional childcare and travel costs.

Working-class wives had, of course, weighed these factors carefully in the past, but heightened expectations about domestic comfort and opportunities for leisure recalibrated the scales.

What was deemed necessary for families to 'live decently' had changed, with goods once thought beyond ordinary reach now considered essentials. As Viola Klein put it: 'To the extent to which these and similar items of expenditure become part of people's normal standard of living, the "subsidiary" income contributed by a wife's earnings fulfils a need, even in a society such as ours in which primary poverty has practically vanished.'[24] This, Klein thought, was one explanation for the favourable view adopted by the husbands that she surveyed in 1958 on the subject of married women's work. Of those with wives working full-time, only 14 per cent expressed disapproval, whilst a mere 4 per cent objected where the job was part-time.[25] Under mounting pressure to give their families every creature comfort, men appreciated the help that an earning wife could offer. One thirty-year-old welder commented, 'With only one working in the house we wouldn't be able to get things we wanted and we wouldn't be able to go on holiday.' A forty-eight-year-old labourer explained how his wife's earnings enabled their daughter to stay in further education: 'It makes things easier in the home. My daughter has gone back to school and is now 17 and taking a special course which we couldn't afford otherwise.'

Husbands were increasingly willing to pitch in with housework and childcare if it freed their wives for paid work, a phenomenon largely limited before the 1950s to places like Lancashire, with its tradition of dual-earning marriages. The working wives in Zweig's affluent worker study were overwhelmingly positive about the assistance they received from their spouses, which ranged from cleaning windows and preparing meals to walking the children to school and covering bath and bedtime where wives worked evening shifts. 'He helps me out now since I came out,' one woman noted; 'I help him out, so he helps me out, fifty-fifty,' were the words of another.[26] Audrey Hunt's larger-scale survey did not paint quite such an egalitarian picture, noting that in many cases husbands' involvement rarely extended beyond doing a bit of washing-up. Nonetheless, over one in five helped with cooking, and one in seven lent a hand with washing, ironing and mending. 'Of course, a husband has to help out at home,' a plumber wrote in his reply to Klein's survey, 'but he's getting the benefit.'

*

Very few working-class housewives took on jobs unless the financial return was significant, but paid employment meant more to them than simply monetary gain. Distinctions between 'financial' and 'non-financial' motives quickly collapsed when women were invited to account for why they worked. Mrs Batty of Swansea, for example, wrote to *Woman's Own* in March 1957 enthusing about her new part-time job on multiple fronts:

> It means being up at and out by half-past six in the morning, but what fun it is! I meet people, have a chat, hear the news and have a glorious walk which is steadily reducing my ample figure. My savings are slowly rising and our family *will* be able to have holiday this year. My job? Delivering the morning papers![27]

The wives who replied to Viola Klein's 1958 survey cited similarly varied reasons for working or wanting to work, foremost amongst which was a desire for company, followed by the need for mental stimulus and enjoyment of one's job. One working-class housewife with nine children wrote, 'Oh, it would be smashing to get a break. To get away from this lot for an hour or two – it would be like heaven!' Another mother of three commented, 'It would break the monotony. I'd see more of life and get to know more people.' These sentiments were echoed by the Leicester hosiery workers, who emphasised the value of getting out during the day. Nearly two-fifths mentioned the 'depressing effect of unrelieved household activity', which the researchers linked to the fact that many were leading isolated lives in new housing estates on the outskirts of the city. Klein heard from married women who, like the cases discovered by Jephcott in Bermondsey, had looked for work following medical advice. One respondent employed as a domestic help told her, 'I am bad with nerves and it helps my health. The doctor told me to take a job; I don't really need to do it.'

These testimonies fed a growing unease about the psychological effects of all-absorbing housewifery. Like the suburban neurosis concept in the late 1930s, these concerns rested on shaky clinical evidence but gained popular purchase as families became more geographically mobile and less embedded in extended networks of kin.[28] Those studying the decline of the 'traditional' working class commented frequently on the lonely existence of mothers bringing up children without grandparents, siblings or trusted neighbours at hand. In their influential 1957 study, *Family and Kinship in East London*, Michael Young and Peter Willmott met Mrs Harper, a native of Bethnal Green who had moved twenty miles out to a new housing estate and hated it bitterly. She was alone all day with her husband at work and children at school and had tried and failed to befriend the woman next door. In the end, Mrs Harper got herself a part-time job: 'If I didn't go to work, I'd get melancholic,' she told Young and Willmott. 'It's like being in a box to die out here.'[29] In her 1966 book, *The Captive Wife*, Hannah Gavron similarly drew attention to the plight of the housebound mother, noting how many working-class women led an 'isolated, extremely family centred existence' and found their main contact to the outside world through television. A plumber's wife told Gavron, 'You've no idea what it's like to spend all day in one room, trying to keep the children quiet because the landlady can't bear noise. I feel like I'm in a cage.'[30]

Such unhappiness was interpreted by some advocates of married women's employment as proof that paid work had become positively necessary for a wife or mother's psychological well-being. Myrdal and Klein observed that many women 'pass through a phase of acute emotional crisis' when they realise they are no longer needed by their children, and are 'seized by a feeling of emptiness and lack of purpose'. They advised readers to plan actively for 'starting afresh at forty' as the best protection against a mental breakdown. 'Modern mothers who make no plans outside the family for their future,' they warned, 'will not only play havoc with their own lives but will make nervous wrecks of their overprotected children and of their husbands.'[31]

Few put it quite as baldly as this, but the notion that housewives were happier, 'fresher' and more contented when they had some kind of job outside the home was articulated across a range of settings. The Institute of Personnel Management issued a pamphlet in 1954 which concluded that the married woman who was employed part-time had 'the best of both worlds. She has the mental and emotional satisfaction so many women seek from their jobs, some financial independence ... companionship and new interests outside the home, and more in common with her older children when they too are working.'[32]

Around the same time, advertisers began to deploy positive images of working mothers in the pages of women's magazines. One such was 'attractive Mrs Valerie Pratt' of Hinckley in Leicestershire, who was featured in *Woman's Weekly* in 1956 drinking a mug of Cadbury's hot chocolate during her busy day running the family's two businesses and looking after her young children. Another advert in the same series depicted an equally cheerful Mrs Skeffington of Gloucestershire, a farmer's wife who settled down to her well-deserved cuppa after feeding pigs, bathing children and preparing rooms for lodgers.[33]

When US-based companies Avon and Tupperware brought their model of direct home-selling to Britain, they recruited housewife saleswomen through similarly aspirational messaging. One advert told the story of 'Mary', an average wife and mother who 'wanted to enlarge her outside interests' by becoming a Tupperware dealer, a job involving product demonstration at parties hosted in customers' homes. Mary, we learn from the advert, 'enjoys the sense of freedom and being "her own boss". She finds her life is much more interesting, and she has more conversation with her husband and more fun with her daughter.' In Mary's own words: 'The whole family benefit in so many ways. We've had holidays abroad on my earnings, and we're able to run a car.'[34] This marketing rhetoric rather overstated the thrill of selling plastic containers to one's friends, but in identifying part-time work with pleasure, sociability and material aspiration, Tupperware showed that it understood its target group perfectly. Here was a popular vision of working motherhood, not as a social evil or temporary wartime measure, but as a fun, stimulating way for women to get out of the house and earn some money for the family. In this vision, having a family *and* a job was becoming an ordinary, rather than a shameful, or heroic, act. 'Mary', the advert screamed, 'is someone like you!'

*

Most of the growth in married women's employment took place amongst older mothers, those 'starting afresh at forty', but there were signs that younger women were beginning to think differently about their future working and family lives. Most girls still expected to marry and most of them did: in 1970, only 8 per cent of women aged between forty-five and forty-nine had never been married.[35] But now that most marriage bars were gone, the trend towards staying in one's job until first pregnancy, evident in some workplaces in the later 1930s, became firmly established. The psychiatrist Eustace Chesser surveyed around 700 single women in the mid-1950s and found that over 60 per cent of those aged twenty or below wanted to continue working after marriage, as did nearly half of those aged between twenty-one and thirty.[36] Young women increasingly assumed that they would contribute alongside their husbands to the costs of setting up home rather than delaying marriage until they could afford to do so on a single male wage. The authors of a 1956 study which asked 600 schoolgirls to write essays about their future lives noted how many envisaged themselves continuing to earn for a period of time after getting married. One schoolgirl wrote: 'After my honeymoon I went back to work at the same firm for another three years, saving as hard as I could so that my husband and I would eventually be able to buy a house.'[37] The Marriage Guidance Council regarded this practice to be so commonplace by the late 1960s that it warned young couples against becoming too accustomed to life on two incomes. One 1968 pamphlet urged newly-weds to start saving for when the wife would be fully occupied at home: 'it is a fatal mistake to start living at a standard which you will not be able to maintain when there is only one of you working.'[38]

The period between getting married and leaving the labour market on pregnancy thus became a distinct phase in many women's post-war lives, although it was often not a very long one. The average age of first marriage for women in 1961 was twenty-three, while the average age for first pregnancy was not much higher.[39] Babies were more likely than not to be planned by these decades, a development reinforced by the growing availability of the contraceptive pill after 1963. This combination of early marriage and the trend towards small, efficiently spaced families meant that many younger women started to envisage a return to paid work in their thirties or forties, as Myrdal and Klein hoped they would. Half of the schoolgirls surveyed in 1956 said that they would take up employment when their children were old enough to be left, whilst Hunt found in 1965 that nearly three-quarters of non-working women in their twenties believed they would re-enter the labour market at some point. A group of working-class girls in Leicester, interviewed in the early 1960s about their hopes for the future, put marriage high on the list, but saw work as important too. In this they were influenced by the example of their mothers, most of whom were back at work in the hosiery, knitwear and boot factories of the district, although many girls rejected this kind of work for themselves. Their aspirations were for 'clean' jobs involving skills which they could fall back on in future years – for example, as hairdressers or nursery teachers – although in reality many ended up in factories or shops.[40]

Policymakers slowly began to wake up to the changing outlook of young women. In 1956, the government appointed a committee, chaired by the former editor of *The Economist*, Sir Geoffrey Crowther, to explore options for reforming educational provision for fifteen- to eighteen-year-olds. When it reported three years later, the Committee acknowledged that the pattern of women's lives had shifted, with recent demographic trends

> making it increasingly possible for marriage to mark not the end, but simply a break in a woman's career. Indeed it is no longer marriage itself, but child-bearing and child-care which

today signal a withdrawal from outside employment. How long a withdrawal? There is a period when part-time employment is possible, but not full-time. But when full allowance has been made for this … it remains true that the wife of today has a large number of years which she can devote to activities outside her home (whether 'gainful' or voluntary), and that the changed outlook of today makes her want to use them in this way.[41]

The school curriculum, it was suggested, should prepare girls for their 'careers' as wives and mothers but at the same time push them towards occupations which could be resumed in later years. The report noted with disapproval how few girls received vocational training once they were in the workplace: less than one in ten were on apprenticeships or day-release schemes, compared with around a third of boys. Yet it did not advocate any serious rethinking of the established pathways for girls leaving school, which were dominated by clerical and shop work for the majority who left at fifteen, and teaching, nursing and social work for those staying on until eighteen.[42] From the 1960s, further education colleges began to run 'refresher' training and short courses aimed at women returners, but again, mostly relating to occupations or trades where women's employment was already long established. In this respect, the growing popularity of the dual-role model reconfigured the *pattern* of women's working lives, but not the *types* of work they were doing.

Employers also played a role in shaping how young women imagined their futures as working wives and mothers. Many school-leavers would have been aware of older married women in the workplace (including, perhaps, their own mothers) and the expanding possibilities for part-time work. By the time Jephcott arrived in Bermondsey, Peek Frean was running no fewer than four different shifts to accommodate its married female workforce, whilst nearly two-thirds of wives at the hosiery factory studied by researchers in Leicester had negotiated some form of concession around hours. Hospitals and local authorities also began to embrace part-time working in order to attract back women with prior nursing, midwifery or health visiting experience. A survey from the early 1960s noted the case of a large general hospital where nurses were able to choose from a variety of start and finish times and to alternate evening and weekend shifts to suit them. At one county hospital, married women worked flexibly in pairs: 'they arrange their own duty rotas,' the survey's author explained, 'accepting responsibility for each others' children and changing to another duty period if the "paired" nurse is unable to attend.'[43] By the mid-1960s, a full third of all NHS nurses were working part-time.[44] Even the Civil Service experimented with part-time working, employing married women as typists, telephone operators and bookkeepers. They made up less than 5 per cent of the total central government workforce, but the numbers (34,000) were far from negligible.[45]

Some employers seemed positive about recruiting wives and mothers. When Viola Klein asked a sample of firms how they judged the performance of their married women employees, over half reported their attendance to be as good as or better than that of single women. Some suggested that married women were steadier, more conscientious workers, and one company with numerous offices in the London area thought that their age and maturity made them better at dealing with difficult customers. Yet much of this surface enthusiasm was undoubtedly connected to the fact that married women formed a relatively cheap and flexible labour force. Post-war housewives held some bargaining chips over hours and enjoyed greater latitude in moving between jobs than in earlier decades, but their position vis-à-vis employers was still weak compared to men and single women with unbroken employment records. Women returning to manual work after an extended break typically took jobs that were less skilled and lower paid than the ones they had held before marriage or childbirth, and the position of part-timers was especially precarious. These workers usually had poor job security and inferior promotion prospects, fewer holiday or sick pay entitlements, and were excluded from occupational pension schemes. In some workplaces they attracted animosity from full-timers, who felt that part-time employees were given lighter, easier work.[46]

Trade unions were often equally ambivalent towards the married woman worker. Women's union membership grew slowly in these decades, but overall rates of unionisation held steady at around 25 per cent, half the level amongst male workers.[47] Union officials blamed this on women's apathetic attitudes, although attention began to focus in the later 1960s on the reasons *why* women might be deterred from joining trade unions, from the male leadership's feet-dragging over equal pay in industry to the practical difficulties preventing mothers from attending union meetings held in the evening. Conditions of full employment weakened old arguments about married women as a threat to the male breadwinner's wage, but did not eliminate them completely. Some men feared that more part-time workers in industry would reduce opportunities for higher-paid overtime or lead to the loss of full-time jobs. In 1966, the General Post Office started to employ married women as part-time postal workers only after protracted negotiations with the unions.[48] In the 1970s and 1980s, growth in part-time jobs *would* outstrip full-time employment, but married women remained clustered in the lowest-paid sectors of the economy and were as much at the mercy of capitalist restructuring and deregulatory policies as the skilled male breadwinner.

*

If employers and trade unions sent mixed messages to working mothers, other voices in post-war Britain were openly hostile, and their objections ranged widely. Religious commentators lamented how materialist impulses were luring housewives into the labour market at the cost of family life and their own spiritual well-being. In his regular column in *Woman's Own* in 1959, the evangelical bishop David Sheppard noted disapprovingly that 'the children get their toys, but have to come home to no mother or to one who's tired out by a long day's work. A child needs his parents' companionship much more than the finest presents they can give him.'[49] Rosamond Fisher, wife of the Archbishop of Canterbury, expressed the same sentiment in the *Daily Express*: 'Mothers have allowed their pursuit of money to drive them into factories, shops and other work,' she said, 'and let them leave their children without a mother's love and understanding.'[50] The *Picture Post* journalist Venetia Murray questioned the motives of women who claimed to work to improve the family's standard of living. 'Their excellent reasons rang a little like excellent excuses,' Murray observed of the mothers she had interviewed for her article. 'It seemed there was just a shade of doubt, or guilt in their minds. That super electric train they gave Johnny for Christmas – how much was it really for him, and how much was it conscience money from the mother?'[51]

Other observers linked the employment of mothers to juvenile delinquency and child neglect, deploying the newly coined phrase 'latch-key kid', a popular shorthand for the schoolchild left to himself in an empty house while his mother worked. The well-known magistrate and philanthropist Basil Henriques described the plight of such children in some detail in a women's monthly magazine, *Modern Woman*, in 1961:

> Many mothers look on motherhood as secondary to earning money in a job … It means they are absent when they are most needed, especially after school when the child is itching to tell his mother about all the exciting things that have happened during the day. Now, he comes home to an empty house. He is lonely, bored and insecure, a prey to any temptation that comes along. Discipline has gone by the board. In my opinion, the 'latchkey' child – in one infant school, one-third of all the children under seven had latchkeys hanging round their necks – is the greatest disgrace in this country today. I believe there should be legislation forbidding employers to employ mothers of schoolchildren at the times they are needed in their homes.[52]

Further arguments against married women's employment invoked the husband's 'duty' to provide for his family on a single wage. 'Should a wife go out to work?' one *Daily Mirror* columnist asked readers rhetorically in 1952, following with his own response: 'As a husband with two children, steam begins to rise in me at the very thought. The answer is No. Emphatically No.'[53] Amongst the minority of husbands in Klein's 1958 survey who disapproved of working wives, the chief reason they gave was a conventional one – that a woman's place was in the home. One forty-three-year-old coal miner wrote, 'If the husband brings home a fairly good wage then the wife should be made to stay at home.'[54] Klein found working-class men in unskilled work to be the most hostile, although Hunt's 1965 survey revealed regional differences which mapped on to older patterns of women's employment. Male disapproval was highest in Wales, where wage-earning by mothers was rare before the Second World War, and lowest in Yorkshire and Lancashire, areas with long histories of married women's factory work.

Personal testimonies collected by Mass Observation reveal just how deep-seated men's feelings could be, sometimes as a result of parental influences or formative childhood experiences. A retired local government officer from West Sussex recalled that he had no doubt of his duties as a husband and father in the 1950s: 'I had a wife, three young sons, and a mortgage to support. To me it was the natural order of things. A man met a girl, married her, produced progeny and had obligations and responsibilities to honour. In my nuclear family it was what real men did.'[55] A widow and former civil servant from Essex explained how she agreed to stay at home because of her husband's memories of growing up in poverty with a working mother in the 1930s:

> When I was expecting our first child my husband asked me not to go out to work after she was born because of the problems he had experienced as a child, having to push his baby sister in her pram three miles each way morning and afternoon to and from an aunt and then make his way to school. This was because his mother had to go to work to help the family budget and the aunt was her only hope.[56]

The writer eventually returned to work when the eldest child was nineteen.

These testimonies demonstrate that there was no sweeping consensus in favour of working wives and mothers in the 1950s and 1960s. Yet opinion did shift towards greater approval of *older* married women returning to the workplace once their children were at school, particularly if they were working part-time. Less than 20 per cent of the women surveyed by Audrey Hunt in 1965 thought that mothers with school-age children 'ought' to stay at home, whilst as many as two-thirds agreed with the statement that 'a woman and her family both benefit if she does a job'. Amongst married women who already had part-time jobs, agreement topped 80 per cent.[57] It was a different story when it came to mothers with very young children; here, attitudes were far less tolerant, with over three-quarters of Hunt's sample agreeing that women with children below school age should stay at home to look after them.

The belief that women bore primary responsibility for the care of babies and toddlers was, of course, long established, but it was reinforced in the 1950s by the ongoing popularisation of the ideas of John Bowlby, Donald Winnicott and other experts writing from a psychoanalytical perspective. Having acquired prominence in the immediate post-war years, theories of maternal deprivation and attachment parenting circulated widely through mass-market paperbacks, advice columns in newspapers and magazines, and radio and television broadcasts.[58] These theories were presented to women as simple common sense, a re-articulation of the mother's 'natural' instincts towards her child. As Winnicott put it in one of his regular radio talks, 'The ordinary good mother knows without being told that during this time nothing must interfere with the continuity of the relationship between the child and herself.'[59] In his bestselling 1953 book, *Child Care and the Growth of Love*, Bowlby argued that this intense physical and emotional engagement was crucial to the successful achievement of becoming a mother; through it, a woman felt 'an expansion of her own personality in the personality of her child'. He suggested that mothers should be constantly available to their offspring for at least the first three years of life: 'The mothering of a child is not something which can be arranged by rota; it is a live human relationship which alters the characters of both partners.'[60]

Those warning women with young children against paid employment could draw on this authoritative language of psychoanalysis in these decades. Venetia Murray opened her *Picture Post* article with a quotation, printed in bold, by the child psychiatrist Dr Ronald McKeith. 'For a mother of children between five and ten years old to have to park her children and go to work is a moderate pity,' he wrote. 'But for a mother of a child under five to have to leave her baby is a tragedy that can have disastrous consequences.' McKeith was cited again later in the article, making the startling claim that separation of mother and infant 'may cause more lasting and irreparable damage to the child even than under feeding it through poverty'.[61] A similarly alarmist message was imparted by an unnamed 'leading psychiatrist' to readers of *Modern Woman* in 1960: 'The mother who insists on taking over the care of her baby from nanny in the evenings and at week-ends,' the author wrote, 'can seriously damage the emotional security of her child.' Even leaving a three- or four-year-old was likely to cause suffering. Readers were cautioned to

> be prepared for anything when you return. He may greet you with a warm hug but more likely he will keep you at a distance or reject you entirely. This is distressing for you, but remember he has been bewildered, anxious or even angered by your absence and it will take an hour, a day or perhaps weeks for him to accept you.[62]

The working mother should not be surprised, the author added, to find her child tearful and clingy, 'terrified that you will leave him again'.

*

It is hard to judge how far women took this kind of advice to heart. Most mothers bringing up children in the post-war decades would have encountered Bowlby or Winnicott's ideas in some form, such was their popular reach. Impressionistic evidence shows that they did sometimes figure in women's decision-making about whether (or when) to return to work. A graduate mother surveyed by Viola Klein in 1963, for instance, commented: 'One hears all the time that young children need the security of their mother's continual presence, and that consideration has prevented me from working, even part-time, until now.'[63] Six years later, a young wife who was expecting her first child told *Woman's Own* that she had decided to give up work once the baby was born, citing an experience, prior to marriage, of looking after a 'mentally-disturbed' boy for a family in France: 'He wet himself all the time, and couldn't talk properly,' she recalled. 'He was deprived of motherly love by being brought up by a series of au pair girls. I am determined not to make the same mistakes.'[64]

Yet if many women felt a sense of obligation to stay at home until their children were at school, 'Bowlbyism' (as feminists later dubbed it) was only one factor shaping their thinking. Even assuming suitable jobs with convenient hours were available locally, many mothers were still overburdened with housework and had limited childcare options. Government policy on day nurseries continued to follow the lines set out in the 1945 circular, which stipulated that places should be provided chiefly for special priority groups, such as unmarried mothers and widows, with mothers in 'normal' circumstances encouraged to care for their children full-time at home until at least the age of three. The number of local authority nursery places in England and Wales actually decreased – falling from 40,000 in 1950 to 28,000 in 1955 and 21,500 in 1963 – whilst the eligibility criteria were tightened towards the end of the decade.[65] Nursery schools took children from the ages of two to five, but expansion momentarily ground to a halt after 1960, with public spending focused instead on secondary education. These institutions were in any case not intended to serve as day-care for working mothers, with an exception made in 1964 for women responding to the government's call for qualified teachers to return to the classroom.[66] The strictly educational function of nursery schools was reiterated in uncompromising terms in Bridget

Plowden's influential report on preschool provision published three years later. 'While some mothers who are not obliged to work may work full-time, regardless of their children's welfare,' noted Lady Plowden, 'it is no business of the educational service to encourage these mothers to do so.'[67] Nursery schools did help some mothers to take part-time jobs, but, given that places existed for only 3 per cent of three- and four-year-olds in 1965, their numbers cannot have been very great.[68] Similarly, employer-run nurseries served only a tiny fraction of children. There were fifty-five factory crèches operating at the end of 1960, plus around a dozen nurseries located in hospitals, mainly for the use of nursing staff.[69]

If a married woman with preschool-aged children *did* decide that she wanted to work, her chances of finding suitable formal day-care were therefore extremely low. Most women looked instead, as they had in the past, to low-cost informal arrangements within the family and community. One 1963 study found that two-thirds of working mothers with children under five entrusted them to the care of female relatives (mostly grandmothers), neighbours or local minders.[70] A Mass Observer whose parents ran a pharmacy and optician's in the 1950s remembered as a young child being looked after 'by a fearsome woman with a huge cloud of black curly hair, she was a relative of my mother's family (an illegitimate cousin I think) and she lived with us for a while'.[71] In east London, the researcher Peter Townsend discovered an array of reciprocal arrangements and financial transactions between middle-aged mothers and their married daughters. There was a woman who cleaned an office every morning from 6 a.m. to 10 a.m., after which she took charge of her grandchildren while her two adult daughters went to work. They did her shopping for her on the way home.[72]

Some mothers were able to take babies or toddlers with them to work, such as the widow who told Mass Observation how she had wheeled the baby in his pram to her regular three-hour cleaning job in the mid-1950s, leaving an older son with his grandmother.[73] Similarly, a male informant recalled accompanying his mum to a large house in Leeds which she cleaned top to bottom every Friday:

> I was never allowed to help her in any way. I had to sit on the step outside and if it was raining I was allowed to sit next to the bins where there was a sort of lean-to-shelter. When mum had finished she would call me inside where I would sit, without a word being spoken, and have a cup of tea, a piece of brown bread and cheese, followed by a thin sliver of fruit cake.[74]

These arrangements had a major advantage over nurseries in that they usually incurred no expense, a serious consideration when women's wages in industry still hovered at about half the rate earned by men. Audrey Hunt found that over 70 per cent of working mothers with under-fives were paying nothing at all for their childcare in the mid-sixties.

Where informal arrangements were stable and long standing, or involved close relatives, working mothers seemed to attract little disapproval at a community level. Pearl Jephcott noticed the operation of 'family and class interpretations of what constitute proper care' amongst the housewives of Bermondsey, most of whom initially worked only early morning or evening shifts when their husbands were at home, switching to a short day – starting at 9.30 a.m. and ending at 4 p.m. – once the children were at school. The minority who *did* work during the day used relatives or trusted minders, but where a satisfactory solution could not be found, the mother simply stayed at home. Jephcott recounted an incident at Peek Frean's which demonstrated these local norms in action. A mother enquiring about a job left her one-year-old twins strapped in their pram on the street outside, where their insistent wailing quickly drew a crowd of concerned onlookers. Messengers were dispatched to seek out the mother, who eventually appeared, insisting

> these twins always did cry; that she knew what was best for her own kids, didn't she; and (presumably in justification of a

prospective evening job) that her husband could manage them much better than ever she could. The small drama lasted half an hour and revealed something of the attitudes aroused when a mother was held to be going out to work in circumstances not approved by local standards.[75]

In short, 'Bermondsey' rather than Bowlby determined what was acceptable maternal conduct in this working-class district.[76] Here wage-earning mothers were more likely to be guided by tacit community rules about what constituted 'good' mothering than by expert advice imparted in books and magazines.

In this respect, the availability of grandmothers as care-givers was probably a far stronger factor governing working-class women's decision-making over employment. As noted, grandmothers remained a chief source of support for their married daughters in many families, yet the ties of multigenerational reciprocity were not unbreakable. With families becoming more geographically dispersed, and older women themselves more likely to be back at work, mothers could not always draw on extended kin as they once had.[77] Some middle-aged women admitted bluntly that they did not want the burden of caring for grandchildren, either because of their own employment commitments or because they were looking forward to a rest in later life. A Bethnal Green mother complained to Young and Willmott about the noisy demands of her grown-up daughters, who came to her 'with all their troubles' including requests for baby-minding. 'I say when they're married, they've got to look after themselves. They've made their bed and they've got to lie on it.'[78] One woman from Oxford recalled her mother telling her: 'they're my children, I can get on with it.'[79] Policymakers often justified their limited investment in nursery provision by reference to the resilience of traditional forms of family-based care. Yet loosening ties of obligation between the generations and the changing nature of retirement and old age placed new pressures on the young post-war mother relying on 'granny' to lend a hand. These would intensify later in the century.

*

Despite the general material improvements experienced by Britons from the 1950s, there was always a minority of mothers who remained under acute economic pressure to earn, regardless of the age of their children. Estimating how many married women fell into this category is difficult, given how capaciously wives now referred to their 'need' for paid employment. The lazy or selfish husband who failed to provide for his family remained a familiar cultural stereotype, albeit one increasingly out of step with new ideals of home-centred fatherhood. The Labour MP Jean Mann thought there were still too many wives forced to earn because their husbands would not. 'It might be said,' she wrote in 1955, ' "Let her stay at home if the Brute takes advantage of her earnings to escape his own obligations!" But almost always the Brute has been the cause of driving her out to work.'[80] Memories of monstrous fathers and long-suffering mothers surfaced frequently in the accounts of those writing for Mass Observation many decades later. One informant described her father as a violent and controlling man who would spend the weekend drinking and 'sometimes come home and beat up practically the whole house'. She remembered seeing her mum, who worked full-time as a nurse, 'heavily pregnant crying in the kitchen because she didn't have enough money to pay the bills'.[81]

Other wives took on breadwinning responsibilities as a result of spousal unemployment or disability, as had been the case in previous decades. A Mass Observer who grew up in Barnsley in the 1950s recalled how her mother worked six days a week as a sub-postmistress after her father contracted TB and gave up his trade as a welder. This writer discovered much later that 10s of her mother's weekly income went on maintenance payments for an illegitimate daughter whom her husband had fathered with another woman.[82] The majority of breadwinning mothers, however, earned for the familiar reasons of widowhood, divorce or abandonment. The premature death of a male spouse was less common an experience than earlier in the century, but the number of widowed women of working age was still far from negligible; one study estimated that there were 175,000 widows bringing up a total of around 260,000 dependent children in the mid-1960s.[83] Employment rates remained high for this group. In Hunt's sample, 55 per cent of widows were working, compared to 45 per cent of married women with husbands still living. A widow's material situation could vary dramatically depending on the level of pension she drew from her deceased husband's National Insurance contributions, her own capacity for earning, plus any number of additional personal factors. A graduate wife explained to Viola Klein how her husband's death during the war had prompted her to train as a solicitor so that she might support her two young children:

> When I married I had not the slightest intention of pursuing a career. My husband had political ambitions and we both took it for granted that I should help him in any way that might present itself. It was only the necessity of earning my living, as a widow, that made me enter the profession which had been my husband's.[84]

By contrast, a Mass Observer growing up in Lancashire recalled her mother's struggle to find well-paid work following her father's unexpected death from a heart attack. Her mother had been a skilled cotton weaver before marriage, but the industry was in decline by the late 1950s and she was forced to take a job in a fish and chip shop, working mornings and lunchtimes. The writer, who had just left school when her father died, gave all her wages to her mother to help the family get by.[85]

Although low by later twentieth-century standards, marital breakdown was another event which pushed many mothers into the labour market. There were a quarter of a million separated wives and 55,000 divorced women heading households in the mid-1960s, often living in highly precarious economic circumstances.[86] The vulnerability of these groups was raised frequently by women's organisations during debates over divorce law reform, which culminated in the passing of landmark legislation in 1969 allowing couples to dissolve marriages on the basis of 'irretrievable breakdown'.[87] The Labour MP Edith Summerskill pointed out that few divorced wives were in a position to support themselves adequately, particularly if they had given up full-time wage-earning to bring up their children. 'The fact that the divorced wife and children are entitled to a maintenance allowance does not meet the case,' Summerskill insisted in 1967, 'for how many men can afford to support two families?'[88] She was right to worry, as in practice maintenance orders were difficult to enforce where husbands had remarried. Most divorced women had little option but to enter the labour market – 70 per cent had done so in Hunt's 1965 survey – or to find another male earner to support them.

Divorce could also carry a social stigma. Ferdynand Zweig met employers in the early 1950s who said they preferred not to employ a divorced woman, even if she had been listed as the injured party in the proceedings. Such judgemental attitudes could affect children. One Mass Observer remembered pitying a friend who had to 'fend for herself' after school because her divorced mother was out at work, and being shocked at the inadequacy of her friend's tea: 'a bowl with dry cornflakes in, with currants sprinkled on and then a hard lump of suet on top!'[89] Not everyone, however, was so censorious. Another writer wrote affectionately of her godmother, a divorcee with one child who worked full-time in a bank: 'we did all admire her achievement.'[90] By the 1970s and 1980s, more positive images of the divorced or separated mother began to supplant older stereotypes of the fallen woman or pitiable victim. Divorce rates shot up in these later decades in part because more women felt confident that they could support themselves outside an unhappy marriage.

The status of unmarried mothers was more ambiguous. Illegitimacy was generally low in the post-war decades, with over 90 per cent of births (if not conceptions) taking place within marriage, making the unmarried mother arguably an even more marginalised and transgressive figure than in earlier times. She was able to claim income support and family allowances if she had more than one child, and was, as noted earlier, at the front of the queue for local authority nursery places, where they were available. The National

Council for the Unmarried Mother and her Child thought that conditions had, in this respect, improved. The unmarried mother 'is no longer "ruined" as a matter of course, but can usually go back fairly easily, after her confinement, to whatever employment she had before', it noted in a 1957 report.[91] Yet unmarried mothers were usually ineligible for council housing and often ended up living at home, where they were expected to contribute financially and to defer to parental authority, a situation which could cause intergenerational tensions. A lucky few with private resources were better placed to retain some degree of independence, like Rosamund Stacey, the young, unmarried heroine of Margaret Drabble's 1965 novel, *The Millstone*. Rosamund continues writing her PhD after the birth of her baby, made possible by rent-free access to a flat in central London (belonging to her parents, who are conveniently located overseas) and paid help two days a week from 'an amiable fat lady named Mrs Jennings'.[92]

New mothers in less fortunate circumstances frequently turned, as they had before, to adoption. John Bowlby explicitly encouraged this practice in the case of unmarried mothers, who, he believed, were likely to be psychologically disturbed and unable to provide the continuous maternal care which an adoptive mother would supply. The number of adoptions rose slightly in the post-war decades, from 23,564 in 1945 to 24,861 in 1968, and young women continued to come under pressure to give their babies away, despite the introduction of a six-week cooling-off period under the 1949 Adoption of Children Act.[93] A long feature published in *Woman's Own* in 1966 quoted a teenager living in a Mother and Baby Home who had decided to put her ten-week-old infant up for adoption: 'I couldn't earn enough money to support her and my parents can't take on a new baby,' she explained. A local authority children's officer interviewed for the article suggested that this was the best course of action all round:

In our new home the babies will be looked after while the girls go to school or out to work. But once the day's business is over, each mother will be entirely responsible for her own baby ...

A girl who is tired will still have to get up at four o'clock in the morning if her baby is crying. Our idea is that within a few months the girls might realise that for their sakes and the babies' sakes, they should agree to adoption. If they keep their babies there is nothing for them but work and loneliness.[94]

She might have added poverty to this list, as it became clear by the later 1960s that families headed by lone mothers of all kinds – widowed, divorced, separated or never married – were far likelier to be struggling on low incomes than households containing a male adult earner. One in five such families were in receipt of means-tested social security, compared to just 3.5 per cent of all households containing dependent children.[95] Anti-poverty activists raised protests against welfare policies which ensnared lone mothers with impenetrable bureaucracy and perverse incentives around earning, while the rest of the population enjoyed ever-rising living standards.[96] These voices kick-started a debate which would run for the rest of the century over how lone mothers ought to be supported by the State and wider society, whether through government stepping into the male breadwinner's shoes, or by encouraging women to support themselves through paid work and providing the training, educational opportunities and nursery places which would actually enable them to do so.

*

A curious reversal took place in the popular meanings attached to working motherhood between the early 1950s and the late 1960s. What had only recently been considered harmful at worst and regrettable at best was rapidly becoming a new aspirational ideal for the modern woman with school-aged children. The earlier vision of the full-time housewife who worked in the home for her family did not lose its ideological power, but it was significantly reconfigured by the new form which married women's employment assumed in these decades. For the majority of working wives, wage-earning was now a genuine choice exercised without the threat of poverty looming overhead. It signalled that a family was doing well rather than badly, with husband and wife pulling together to give their children the best possible start in life. Imagery of paid work as an enjoyable pastime for patriotic housewives shed its wartime air of impermanence and was recast as an ordinary experience for the married woman returning to the workplace after a break. Plenty of voices railed against this dual-role model, but they increasingly belonged to the past. Alva Myrdal, Viola Klein and Pearl Jephcott, by contrast, seemed to point to the future with their claims about how paid work was meeting 'deep-seated needs' felt by women across social classes. Like earlier observers of married women's work, their analysis rested on empirical investigation, but rather than watching and inferring moral truths about their subjects, these researchers tried to understand what women themselves said and felt about their jobs. Feminist activists would push this commitment to giving women the space to narrate their own lives in more radical directions from the 1970s.

What these advocates of married women's work did not realise, or rather did not spell out explicitly, was just how reliant this vision of working motherhood was on the economic conditions which helped to produce it. Corresponding with a like-minded sociologist in the US in 1958, Klein acknowledged that she and Myrdal had assumed when writing *Women's Two Roles* that full employment would continue indefinitely. In the event of an economic downturn, Klein speculated, 'the picture may alter very considerably', with a resurgence of the traditional male breadwinner ideology and widespread dismissal of female workers.[97] Klein's predictions were, as it happened, wrong: when mass unemployment did return in the 1970s, it was *male* jobs that were most affected. Yet she was right to recognise, albeit in private, that the attitudinal shift regarding married women's employment was riding an economic wave which would eventually recede. How much of the positive feeling about working wives would wash away with it, no one yet knew.

Furthermore, the post-war model of working motherhood rested on women's acceptance of a bargain which opened up new employment opportunities without disturbing wider inequalities in the labour market and at home. Women settled for jobs which were less skilled and lower paid than the ones they had done before becoming mothers, and they continued to accept primary responsibility for childcare and housework. Most married women took this deal because it delivered a higher standard of living and better prospects for their children, and a slice of financial independence and psychological fulfilment for themselves. For women without male breadwinners, this deal was never on the table. Lone mothers found themselves standing outside looking in on the home-centred post-war family, just like other groups who failed to conform to its norms, including older unmarried women, women in same-sex partnerships and many of the migrant mothers who sought to make new lives in Britain in these decades.[98] Finally, the post-war ideal made little room for mothers who wished to pursue continuous careers offering progression and high earnings rather than 'little jobs' to be picked up and put down. This group formed a small, privileged minority of working mothers, but they voiced a dilemma which dogged middle-class women for the rest of the century: how easily could professional ambition be reconciled with the demands of family life?

9

Come Back

Shortly before Pearl Jephcott began her investigations in Bermondsey, a middle-class housewife in north London was writing up the findings of a very different kind of study. *Wives Who Went to College* explored the constricted lives and stunted careers of over a thousand graduate women surveyed by post in the early 1950s. Its author, Judith Hubback, was no professional social scientist, but a Cambridge history graduate in her mid-thirties with a comfortable home, three children and a husband employed in the senior Civil Service. The impulse behind the questionnaire, which Hubback stuffed patiently into envelopes at her kitchen table over the course of several weeks, was deeply personal.[1] She had married young, given up teaching after the birth of her first child, and now felt the lack of any meaningful career sorely. Trailing after her husband's job, Hubback had seized opportunities to work wherever she could: writing the odd article for the press, tutoring girls for university entrance, editing a few radio scripts for the BBC. But after ten years of a largely domesticated existence, she was ready to reassess her life choices – and those of nearly every graduate woman she knew.

The frustrations felt by housewives who had trained brains but no outlet for their use formed the central theme of *Wives Who Went to College*. As Hubback observed of her questionnaire respondents:

They were trying to be reasonable; some were fatalistic; others rueful; some, even, bitter. 'I certainly think it is a pity that so

many women, because they want a family, are more or less
forced to spend a large part of their time in domestic work,
when they might be doing something more socially useful and
satisfying' sums up what was said at greater length in many of
the letters.[2]

This sentiment resonated profoundly with Hubback's own
experience: 'To be as happy and useful as possible,' she wrote,
'women as well as men should use all their capacities to the
full. If one side of them is unused, it atrophies.'[3] For Hubback,
this meant making available more part-time professional work,
together with training courses for mothers returning to careers
or starting from scratch in their thirties or forties. Britain
simply could not afford to neglect this source of highly skilled
womanpower, she insisted. Graduate women today wished
to marry and have families, just like the rest of the female
population. Society would have to 'adjust itself to taking them
back, later in life, on a part-time basis'.[4]

Hubback's research caused quite a stir, first in 1954, when she
published a preliminary pamphlet summarising the findings, and
again three years later when the full-length book hit the shelves.[5]
Both were widely reviewed and commented upon in venues
ranging from the *Daily Mirror* to the *British Medical Journal*.
Scores of letters were published in the national and regional press
from readers passionately concurring or violently disagreeing with
Hubback's analysis, whilst Hubback herself was in high demand as a
speaker and received invitations to talk about her questionnaire on
radio and television.[6] *Wives Who Went to College* was read especially
carefully by the officers of bodies like the British Federation of
University Women and the Medical Women's Federation, who
were already conscious of the many difficulties faced by married
women in the professional workplace. One Cambridge graduate,
Diana Furley, was directly inspired by Hubback's book to set up
a part-time employment agency catering specifically for graduate
wives, matching them to jobs in which they could use their hard-
won qualifications.[7]

It might seem curious that a book about women graduates should have attracted so much attention at a time when little more than 7 per cent of the female population entered any form of post-eighteen education.[8] Yet this privileged group was articulate and well organised, and Hubback's findings touched a nerve. Media commentators latched onto *Wives Who Went to College* as a lively contribution to controversies over the purpose of expanded higher education for women in an era of early and near-universal marriage.[9] Some were fascinated by the female graduate's rapid metamorphosis from spinster bluestocking to womanly housewife, and expressed surprise that marriage rates and family size amongst Hubback's respondents were close to the national average. Reporting these findings, the *Daily Mail* reassured its female readers that intellect was no longer the turn-off to prospective husbands it once had been: 'Cheer up Portia!' shrieked the humorous headline, 'Cheer up you blonde and blue-eyed scientists, radiotherapists, doctors and female dons-to-be. The Girls with Brains are doing all right.'[10]

Others seized upon these high marriage rates as proof that degrees were 'wasted' on women and questioned whether taxpayers and parents should persist with such a poor investment. These latter voices, however, were in a minority and were undermined by survey data which revealed employment rates to be higher amongst graduate wives than married women without degrees.[11] Most of those who objected to Hubback's conclusions did so on different grounds, invoking the principle that higher education was an end in itself and socially beneficial even if the recipient never made direct use of it in the labour market. Graduate women who were fully occupied in their homes tended to be the most vocal in advancing this view. One of Hubback's respondents wrote: 'I feel very strongly, that running a house and caring for a husband and family is vastly more than "unmixed domesticity" and is a career and profession in itself.'[12] This position continued to find advocates throughout the 1950s and 1960s, but a consensus was undoubtedly building behind Hubback's prescriptions for flexible, part-time work for the graduate returner. Refresher training gradually became available for women looking to restart interrupted careers on a wider basis, alongside part-time and correspondence courses aimed at housewives looking for a second chance to train for a profession. Handbooks and guides with titles such as *Late Start*, *Comeback* and *Women Want to Work* provided practical advice, whilst employment agencies and registers sprang up around the country to find graduate wives suitable work.[13]

Just as jobs for lower-skilled mothers flourished under a set of benign economic conditions, so the growth in women's higher-level employment relied on broader structural changes in the labour market. Foremost amongst these was the massive demand for teachers, doctors, nurses and social workers created by the expansion of the welfare state, starting in the late 1940s but sustained for much of the next three decades. These professions underwent a striking transformation, from vocations designed for husbandless spinsters to ones deemed a natural fit for a mother seeking a career which could be picked up after a break. They remained closely identified with the 'caring' qualities which women were widely believed to possess, and girls entering post-compulsory education were channelled towards them.[14] By contrast, other expanding areas of professional employment, including the senior Civil Service, law, academia and higher levels of industry, were as unfriendly to women as they ever had been. Here, the unbroken, full-time career remained the dominant pattern, with successful female role models – married or single – thin on the ground.

These sexual divisions mirrored those in operation in the wider economy, where women were overwhelmingly concentrated in lower-paid jobs, and less prestigious grades and roles. Yet the position of the female graduate was, for obvious reasons, very different from that of the working-class school-leaver or the older housewife looking for shift work in a factory. Full employment and rising living standards reduced poverty and narrowed income inequality, but social class still mattered in post-war Britain. The majority of girls who stayed on to take A-levels and secured a place at university or teacher training college were from middle-class backgrounds, and the men whom they subsequently married were usually fellow graduates employed in professional or executive jobs. Observers often spoke of

Cotton workers in Oldham, c. 1900. Mothers were widely employed in the Lancashire textile industries, where they did skilled work and often received the same piece-rates as men.

In other industries, women typically did low-paid, unskilled work of the kind on offer at Fry's chocolate factory, Bristol, pictured here.

Some mothers worked in or close to their homes, like these lace drawers, photographed in the Narrow Marsh district of Nottingham in the 1890s.

Chain-making was another trade that women could practise in domestic workshops, watching their children at play or asleep nearby.

In 1906, social reformers photographed poor home-working mothers in order to draw public attention to the evils of low-paid, 'sweated' labour.

Items manufactured by mothers at home were often sold to well-heeled consumers. A box designed to hold chocolates or sweets might have ended up at an establishment like Birch's in the City of London.

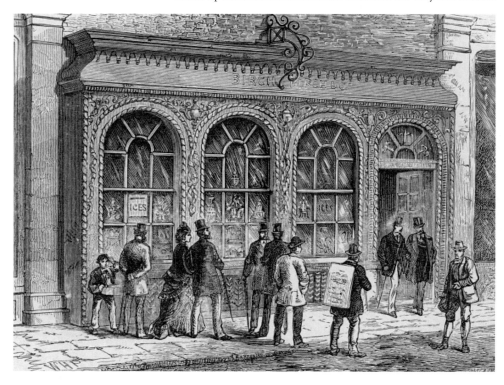

From the 1880s, a new cadre of female experts shaped public debate about women's industrial employment, including economist Clara Collet (top left), socialist intellectual Beatrice Webb (top right), trade unionist Clementina Black (bottom left) and factory inspector May Tennant (née Abraham) (bottom right).

Two images of Victorian working motherhood: Elizabeth Garrett Anderson (left),
the first woman to qualify as a doctor in Britain, pictured with her daughter, Louisa;
and Jane Senior (right), philanthropist, artist's muse and pioneering civil servant.

The General Post Office was the first government department to
employ women as clerks from the 1870s, an occupation considered
respectable enough for young, unmarried ladies to do.

Beauty, talent and popularity with paying audiences allowed actresses Ellen Terry (right) and Sybil Thorndike (below) to combine successful careers on the stage with marriage and motherhood.

Margaret MacDonald (left) and Mary Macarthur (right) were ambivalent about married women's work in industry but found ways to balance the demands of motherhood with their own political commitments in the labour and trade union movement.

A more typical occupation for middle- and upper-class ladies with time to spare was unwaged voluntary work amongst the poor.

Although never conscripted, wives and mothers were recruited into essential industries in large numbers during the First World War. Note the wedding ring on the hand of the woman (above) operating a chronometer, designed to measure the velocity of bullets. A group of older women push a trolley of shells ready for inspection (below).

Women retained their second-class status as workers after the
war, both in established trades such as pottery manufacturing in
Staffordshire (above), and on the assembly lines of booming light
industries in the Midlands and south of England (below).

Modern mothers: the opening up of professional opportunities for well-off middle-class women enabled some mothers to sustain careers in the 1930s, such as novelist E. M. Delafield (right) and doctor Winifred de Kok (below).

During the Second World War, over 1,300 government-funded
nurseries cared for the children of war workers, including
Mrs Donovan, photographed collecting her son after finishing
a shift in a Birmingham munitions factory.

Hundreds of women travelled from Britain's colonies to serve on the
home front. The Caribbean women pictured here were recruited to
the Auxiliary Territorial Service, which employed its members on a
wide range of tasks, from canteen work to operating anti-aircraft guns.

The 'Women in Industry' campaign (1947) tried to entice women, including many wives and mothers, back into factories in a bid to boost exports and remedy Britain's serious trade deficit in the immediate post-war years.

In 1956, Alva Myrdal (left) and Viola Klein (right) co-wrote *Women's Two Roles*, which predicted – correctly – that married women would increasingly wish to re-enter the labour market in later life after bringing up their children.

Schools were especially desperate for married women's labour in the 1960s. This leaflet, published by the London County Council, promised teachers good pay, refresher training and flexible hours.

Shirley Conran's best-selling *Superwoman* (1975) told women to cut back on housework but unintentionally gave rise to an unattainable ideal of professional and domestic perfection.

Margaret Thatcher, pictured in 1975, presented an image of successful working motherhood but did little as prime minister to help parents reconcile caring responsibilities with the demands of work.

For women with few social or educational advantages, work still meant low pay and little opportunity for training or progression. Working from home, which resurged in the 1970s and 1980s, remained one of the options available to mothers without reliable childcare.

Women, including migrant mothers who had settled in Britain, fought back against exploitation. Jayaben Desai, leader of the famous strike at Grunwick (1976–77), confounded popular stereotypes of South-Asian women as meek and docile.

NICOLA HORLICK
CAN YOU HAVE IT ALL?

HOW TO
SUCCEED IN
A MAN'S
WORLD

Asset manager and mother of six, Nicola Horlick was both celebrated
and vilified for her determination to 'have it all' in the late 1990s.

'graduate', 'educated' or 'professional' women as a group defined by their intellectual training rather than their class status, but they also assumed that members of this privileged group inhabited the world of the professional middle classes and would therefore apply a different calculus of decision-making from the working-class housewife when it came to paid work. This factored in school fees, the cost of domestic help, nannies and au pairs, plus the household's overall income tax liability. It also put most jobs involving manual labour out of bounds. One modern languages graduate wrote to *The Times* after reading Hubback's pamphlet to complain that she had failed utterly to find suitable part-time employment. 'The only work ever advertised in our local paper,' she added, 'is for a part-time barmaid, a position I should dearly love to hold, but conventions forbid.'[15]

Another aspect of the debate over graduate women's work centred on the psychological problem of reconciling professional ambition with the needs of husbands and children. The desire to have a 'career' was considered largely irrelevant to the mass of housewives taking jobs as cleaners, factory hands or shop assistants, but for women fortunate enough to have received an elite education, the position was not so clear. Judith Hubback argued for a middle way, advising wives to seek intellectually stimulating work which would not cause mental overstrain or risk domestic disharmony. Marriage and motherhood, she wrote, constituted a 'disability' to which the high-achieving female graduate must adapt 'as she would have to, for example, with deafness or blindness'.[16] For Hubback, happiness lay not in chasing professional glory in competition with husbands, but in accepting these limitations from the start. This ideology of compromise – of managing one's ambitions, adjusting to constraints and maintaining marital unity at all costs – was presented to the educated middle-class woman as the key to feminine fulfilment. By these means, Hubback concluded, might the young graduate mother be 'encouraged to see her life in proportion and to gain serenity in the process'.[17]

*

In no occupation was Hubback's logic more evident than in teaching. Britain's schools continued to suffer chronic staffing shortages throughout the 1950s, turning into a full-blown crisis in the early 1960s when children born during the immediate post-war baby boom reached secondary-school age.[18] The problem stemmed in part from the trend towards ever earlier marriage, which meant large numbers of women were leaving the profession each year to have babies: only half of all women entering teaching between 1957 and 1961 stayed for more than five years.[19] The problem, however, suggested its own solution, with policymakers turning, as they had in the late 1940s, to the pool of retired married women who were now in a position to return to their former profession. This group of mothers found themselves importuned by desperate head teachers, circularised by Local Education Authorities and subjected to patriotic government appeals on the radio and in the national press. David Eccles, the Conservative Minister for Education, launched a search for 50,000 teachers in December 1960, urging local authorities to tell married women that they 'will make every possible arrangement to suit their convenience so that they can fit in at least some teaching hours a week without neglecting their families'. These mothers, he added, 'are our only hope of bridging the gap'.[20] So dire was the situation that policymakers gave councils permission to expand nursery-school places for use as day-care by women who might otherwise be unable to return to the classroom.[21]

Alongside these recruitment efforts, courses were laid on in areas of high demand offering refresher classes as well as fast-track training to graduates who had not taught before.[22] The press took a lively interest in these housewife-students. The *Guardian* reported on a group enrolled on a correspondence course through the National Extension College, whose numbers included a retired doctor, a lawyer, an architect, a psychologist and a social worker, all now embarking on new careers as teachers.[23] A similar article in the *Telegraph* followed students attending a six-week course hosted in a disused church near Waterloo Station in London. This cohort included a parson's wife, a graduate who had married fresh from university and had never used her earlier training, and a mother of three whose parents had moved in to her home for childcare purposes while she revived her teaching career.[24] For some women, these opportunities were personally transformative. Reflecting on their week-long residential course at Madingley Hall in Cambridge, two graduate wives remarked on how 'exhilarating' it was 'to be able to give once again our whole minds to an intellectual pursuit'. Both were delighted to have found 'a worth-while job, which would provide a mental stimulus and also enable us to be at home with our children during the holidays'.[25]

By the mid-1960s, an occupation once considered the preserve of lifelong spinsters had been rebranded as the ideal career for the educated wife and mother. Married women had always maintained a presence in the profession, but in the post-war decades they achieved critical mass: in 1952, around a third of women teachers were married, and a decade later it was more than two in five.[26] The spread of part-time working helped to speed this trend. Numbers of part-time teachers more than doubled between 1957 and 1961, with some married women discovering that they could more or less dictate their own terms. One Mass Observer recalled that her children's school offered her a post teaching maths even though she had no prior training or experience. Casually mentioning her interest to the headmaster at the school gate, 'within 48 hours I had an interview at our local secondary & was offered a part-time job. They were desperate for Maths teachers!'[27] An arts graduate surveyed by Viola Klein in 1963 similarly confided that she

> never had the slightest difficulty in getting exactly the sort of employment I wanted on my own terms, e.g. it is an understood thing that I will not work when my own children are at home for their school holidays, as I put my duty as wife and mother first. My employers are extraordinarily considerate and understanding about this. I am always freed for my children's prize-givings & so on, without the slightest demur.[28]

The London County Council lured potential recruits with promises of paid training, part-time arrangements ranging from two hours to four days a week, authorised absences to deal with family emergencies, and maternity leave with half pay for eighteen weeks.[29]

Given the flexibility on offer, it was not surprising that a large proportion of the young women entering higher education in these decades ended up teaching, with over half enrolling directly on teacher training courses. Teaching was the most common destination for female graduates by some distance: 45 per cent of women with science degrees went into the classroom, whilst amongst those studying arts and humanities subjects, the proportion was closer to 60 per cent.[30] Girls with secondary-school education had always been pushed towards teaching as a 'respectable' feminine profession, but by the 1960s it was widely recognised as *the* career for the young woman who hoped to marry, have children and return to the workplace following an extended break. Viola Klein thought that teaching would continue to absorb two-thirds of all professionally qualified women for some time to come, because the period of training was relatively short, the pay was reasonably good and, following the extension of equal pay to public sector employees in 1955, on a par with men's, whilst working hours and vacations were 'generally felt to be better adjusted than most to marriage and family life'.[31] A grammar school headmistress who had trained in the 1920s believed that the profession's dramatic image change was all for the good. 'Teachers nowadays,' she remarked, 'are not marked out from the rest of the community. You can continue your work after marriage and that makes a lot of difference to women. And it is pre-eminently a job that lends itself to part-time work.'[32]

Not everyone, however, found it quite so easy to get back in. Training courses were not available everywhere, rural areas being particularly badly served, and nor were flexible employment arrangements embraced universally by heads. One science graduate explained to Viola Klein that she was teaching full-time purely because she had found it impossible to secure a job with shorter hours, whilst another graduate mother revealed that the local council had refused to approve her employment at a local technical college on a part-time basis.[33] Others complained that part-timers were frequently put on short-term contracts and were treated disdainfully by full-time colleagues. One graduate who was teaching physics at a grammar school described her good fortune in finding a head teacher who was 'most kindly disposed towards part-timers – and even says they have something positive to contribute towards the school'. This was not the case in her previous post, where she felt the headmaster 'actually disapproved of mothers doing part-time work but took me as he could not find anyone else'.[34] The London County Council met with resistance from full-time teaching staff when it drew up proposals in 1964 to make part-timers eligible for senior appointments. The secretary of the London Teachers Association argued that whilst the average teacher was perfectly happy to cover an occasional class for a part-time married colleague, 'his attitude would be very different if Mrs So-and-So held a special post with special allowance and still expected that concessions would be made for her domestic problems. Good will would vanish.'[35] Even mothers working full-time hours could encounter obstacles if they sought career progression, with some local authorities limiting the number of headships open to women. As late as 1973, only 7 per cent of women teaching in primary schools were head teachers, compared to almost 30 per cent of men. In secondary schools, three times as many men as women held headship posts.[36]

Furthermore, although teaching was frequently described as a 'popular' occupation for women, many of those entering it – or returning to it – did so with little sense of vocational commitment. This was especially true of graduates, who, unlike those with teaching diplomas, might have followed different careers before marriage or drifted into teaching due to a lack of realistic options elsewhere.[37] Some of these recruits were subsequently surprised to discover how much they enjoyed teaching. The Mass Observer snapped up by her children's headmaster recalled that she had 'vowed I'd never teach' on leaving university, but after a year in the classroom 'I found I could do it and I loved it'.[38] Others, however, had the opposite experience. A history graduate told Klein that she quit teaching in the mid-1930s because she disliked it and, having briefly returned – 'as requested in the press' – found she disliked it

'as much as ever & intend to stop at the end of the summer term'.[39]
Another respondent explained at length why she was only prepared
to offer supply teaching to a select group of schools, revealing
her highly attuned sense of social and professional distinction as
a university graduate. She would not take on 'infant teaching or
modern stream pupils' – referring to the non-selective secondary
modern schools created by the 1944 Education Act – and refused
'point blank to go on breaking up knife fights with the modern
stream (while making them copy out words of one syllable) or,
come to that, taking five-year-olds to the lavatory'.[40] Other
respondents seemed to share her assumption that having a degree
entitled them to higher-prestige jobs in grammar schools and sixth
forms, although few were quite so open about their aversion to
secondary moderns, where the majority of Britain's working-class
children were educated.[41]

It is difficult to know how far these sorts of individual preferences
and social prejudices thwarted efforts to entice graduate women
back to the classroom. In the early 1960s, full-timers were returning
at the rate of 3,500 a year, a figure which officials thought could
not be increased any further unless more part-time work were
made available.[42] Others suggested that higher salaries and better
pensions, new teaching methods, more professional development
opportunities and greater scope to work in mixed-sex schools
would help to attract married women into, or back to, teaching.[43]
But by the end of the decade, a sharper critique began to form of
how women's wider career prospects were being strangled at birth
by the excessive emphasis placed on teaching. Analysing data from
a major study of graduates who completed their degrees between
1960 and 1966, the sociologist Anne Poole raised questions about
the under-utilisation of women's skills in other fields, as well as the
unequal division of domestic labour in the home. Teaching was 'so
well-adapted to the problems of working mothers', Poole wrote,

> that it has actually served to dampen the demands of highly
> educated women for changes in other occupations, or in
> domestic structures which would further their occupational

chances in other fields. In effect, teaching provides a safety valve which allows the status quo both in other fields of employment and in domestic arrangements to be preserved.[44]

Many women genuinely enjoyed teaching and did not regard it as a second-best option, but Poole's analysis was essentially correct. It suited government to push women into teaching at a time of pressing labour shortages in Britain's schools, and it suited middle-class men to have such a career path open to their well-educated wives, a path which would not inconvenience them too much domestically nor challenge their own professional status or superior earning power.

*

Medicine was another profession in which women's presence was long established and growing in the post-war period. Around 9,000 women were in active medical practice in the early 1950s, growing to nearly 13,000 two decades later, by which time women represented around a fifth of all qualified doctors.[45] The barriers to entry were considerably higher than in teaching, with a much lengthier training and most medical schools still enforced an unofficial quota on female applicants, ranging from 15 per cent in London to a more generous 30 per cent at some provincial universities.[46] The rationale behind such policies stemmed in large part from the trend for early marriage, with some claiming that this made women's medical education an even riskier investment than in earlier decades. Others, including the highly vocal Medical Women's Federation, argued to the contrary that policymakers, medical schools and NHS employers needed to adjust to women's changing aspirations for marriage *and* a career.[47]

In fact, female medics married later than average, usually after qualifying, whilst the number of working mothers in the profession was far from negligible. A major study published in 1963 found that nearly two-thirds of female medics with children under five were still working (17 per cent full-time and 46 per cent part-time), whilst over four-fifths of mothers with school-aged children were actively

practising (30 per cent full-time and 51 per cent part-time).[48] Viola
Klein noted that of all professional working mothers, medics were
the most likely to pursue their careers continuously rather than take
an extended break followed by re-entry to the workplace.[49] This
divergence from the 'returner' model was partly explained by the
strong vocational commitment which medics acquired over long
years of training at public expense, as well as their awareness of how
easily a doctor's clinical knowledge could become out of date. The
Medical Women's Federation urged its members in 1950 'to keep in
touch with any part-time work while bringing up children' and to
avoid lengthy intervals without practice of any kind.'[50] A mother of
three surveyed by Klein put it in similar terms: 'as far as medicine
is concerned, it is vital that there should be no complete break in
employment at any time for more than a very few months in my
opinion.'[51]

Some women achieved this continuity, as earlier generations
had, through the relative flexibility of running a general practice in
or close to their homes. Over 50 per cent of practising doctors who
were married with children worked in this speciality, compared to
just a third of single women.[52] One GP explained to Klein how she
had kept her career going through four pregnancies by alternating
between full- and part-time work and by limiting the size of her
patient list.[53] By contrast, less than one in five medical mothers were
found in hospital medicine, a far more challenging field due to the
long hours and the requirement of living in residential quarters
(or close enough to respond quickly when on call). In 1954, a male
correspondent in the *British Medical Journal* told female hospital
doctors that they must pull their weight by taking a fair share of
night shifts, insisting that no mother should be permitted to opt
out 'because, for instance, the baby has a whooping cough'.[54] One
young wife who had negotiated just such a concession testified to
the hostile reaction of her male colleagues. 'Perhaps one should say
that this attitude should be ignored,' she reflected, 'but sometimes
it becomes so strong as to be really hurtful, and is the sort of thing
that tends to take the joy out of work and to make one feel one
would do better as a full-time housewife.'[55]

Others looked to part-time employment as a means of keeping their careers going through the most intensive years of child-rearing. This typically included GP locum work, running family planning or baby clinics, carrying out school medical inspections or assisting with medical research.[56] Much of this work was not terribly interesting or prestigious, and offered little prospect of career advancement or long-term job security. One mother of three employed as a medical officer told Klein that she was the only woman in her county with a permanent part-time post in public health, and she felt 'very lucky to get it'.[57] The London County Council employed 350 part-time doctors, but all were on temporary contracts with no pension rights. At the highest levels of the profession, consultants usually held part-time posts in the NHS which they supplemented with lucrative private work, but to achieve this privileged position involved a long stint of hospital posts, further postgraduate training and possibly moving one's family to another part of the country. Female medics did reach these heights but in far smaller numbers and at a slower rate than their similarly qualified male peers, whilst women with families were far less likely to progress. A survey of 171 women trained at the University of Sheffield between 1933 and 1957 found that only five married women had held consultant status during their careers, compared to twenty-seven of the unmarried women in the sample.[58] 'Had I remained single I would have continued "up the ladder" to a consultantship,' one working mother was quoted in another study. 'I am still employed in the career for which I trained although not at the level which I originally envisaged.'[59]

Growing evidence of blockages to women's progression did, however, eventually prompt action. Rosemary Rue, a senior medical officer at the Oxford Regional Hospital Board, established a pioneering scheme in the mid-1960s for talented female doctors looking for flexible pathways into the senior ranks of specialist hospital medicine. Conscious of how mothers with small children could get stuck in dead-end jobs, and bearing a few battle scars on this front herself, Rue organised a series of salaried placements matching female trainees to consultants in their preferred specialities.[60] The placements were in hospitals located close to the women's homes and demanded a non-residential commitment of four half-days a week, 'an amount satisfactory for training purposes and a sufficient commitment for a woman throughout the year'.[61] Rue's scheme exceeded expectations, was much copied elsewhere and prepared the ground for an official memorandum on the re-employment of women doctors issued by the Department of Health in 1969.[62] This urged hospital boards to provide postgraduate training on a part-time basis and to create part-time registrar and consultant posts which would attract women into specialities experiencing staffing problems. Whilst progress on the ground was uneven over the following years, government had at least recognised the need, as one official put it, 'to educate the medical profession to accept married women who are only able to work part time'.[63]

*

Widening opportunities for mothers in teaching and medicine formed part of a larger expansion of professional employment within the post-war welfare state. The growth of publicly funded social services drove up demand for staff trained in social work, youth work, probation work, child welfare work and care of the elderly and disabled, all fields in which single women had made their mark and now married women were eager to do the same. Calls went out to provide training for women wishing to take up or return to these occupations and new courses were laid on to meet the demand. Bromley Technical College, for instance, launched a two-year diploma in social work in 1966 aimed specifically at married women, taught between 10.15 a.m. and 3.20 p.m. to fit with school hours. The College of Further Education in Stevenage started a similar programme, receiving 200 applications for its ten local authority-funded places in the first year.[64] One of Viola Klein's survey respondents expressed her satisfaction at being able to retrain and find a part-time job in a county mental hospital after seventeen years at home. 'My non-professional friends envy me for the ease with which I have re-obtained employment of great interest so late in life,' she wrote.[65]

This correspondent *was* in fact lucky to secure a permanent part-time post, as such jobs were rare. This was despite staffing shortages, a growing supply of qualified women returners, and the recommendations of a government-appointed committee on social work training chaired by the veteran reformer, Eileen Younghusband. Her influential 1959 report suggested that greater use of part-time employees could help replenish the profession, a cause taken up by the newly established Association of Part-time Social Workers.[66] But when the Association surveyed its 200-odd members a year later, it found that most female part-timers were clustered in a narrow range of fields, including citizens' advice bureaux, psychiatric social work and hospital almoning, and that requests for flexible hours were usually met with strong resistance.[67] One woman had asked whether a job with hours of 9 a.m. to 5 p.m. could be slightly reduced to a 4 p.m. finish, but was flatly refused. Those looking to work half-days, or to work full-time during school terms with time off over the summer, got nowhere.[68]

The dominant view in the profession seemed to be that social work was a full-time occupation and those who were unwilling to commit to it on that basis should consider doing voluntary work instead, which, after all, was always available to the married woman with time on her hands.[69] Younghusband might have unintentionally reinforced this position in her arguments for more rigorous training, better-defined career structures and enhanced pay to elevate the status of social work as a unified profession. None of these reforms were incompatible with the employment of married women, but they had the effect of consolidating promotion routes for men, whose presence in senior management grew in the 1960s, and sharpening the once blurry line between paid and unpaid social welfare work which women had leveraged creatively in earlier decades.[70]

Architecture was another profession expanding fast thanks to a booming economy and public investment in schools, hospital buildings, council homes and New Towns. The vast majority of architects were male, but by the early 1960s attention was beginning to turn, as elsewhere, to the married woman returner. The Architectural Association, the profession's chief training body,

launched an exploratory survey on the subject overseen by Anne
Acland, who had herself successfully re-established a career after
an extended period keeping house for her husband, the radical
politician Sir Richard Acland.[71] Unsurprisingly, refresher training
and flexible hours were at the top of the wish-list for those hoping
to follow her example, although a few women did manage to
keep their practices going through the years of child-rearing. One
member of the East Surrey branch of the British Federation of
University Women told a conference that architecture was 'the
easiest of all [professions] to take up and put down again. She had
trained about 25 years ago and had been in both full and part-
time work. She was never out of work and was always doing a job
she liked.'[72] A handful of working mothers gained real prominence
as architects, such as Nadine Beddington, Jane Drew and Alison
Smithson. They nonetheless had to fight hard to get work beyond
designing kitchens and house extensions, which male colleagues
and clients assumed was a woman's natural domain. Beddington
used her senior position at a leading footwear retail chain, Freeman,
Hardy & Willis, to hire women as part-time assistant architects,
but she acknowledged that most employers preferred to use male
full-timers and did so wherever possible.[73]

The dynamics were similar in other prestigious and well-
paid occupations, where lip-service was paid to the principle of
employing married women but few practical steps taken to make
it a reality. In the mid-1960s, women made up less than 1 per cent
of chartered surveyors, accountants, auctioneers, estate agents,
electrical and mechanical engineers, and only 3.5 per cent of
practising lawyers.[74] In universities, women composed around a
sixth of junior lecturers but just 2 per cent of professors.[75] Only one
in twenty women held any kind of managerial post in industry, and
in some sectors the proportion was closer to one in a hundred.[76]
Women were largely absent from the boardrooms of big business,
accounting for 2.5 per cent of the membership of the Institute
of Directors, whilst their representation in the higher reaches of
Whitehall edged up extraordinarily slowly, from 7 per cent in 1950
to 8.4 per cent in 1968.[77] Replying to a query from Viola Klein, a

Civil Service spokeswoman confirmed that married women were eligible for graduate-level posts in home departments, but added that part-time employment was unavailable and there was no automatic right of return for those taking an extended break to have children.[78]

Maternity leave, career breaks and flexible working opportunities were generally rare in these sought-after jobs, however well qualified the applicant. One mother with a science PhD told Klein how she had been forced to give up a permanent university lectureship after her request for shorter hours was turned down. She retained access to library and laboratory facilities, but found it impossible to continue her research with no salary or proper standing. 'Unless the university changes its policy concerning part time staff,' she commented, 'I see no way round the situation.'[79] In over-subscribed professions like academia and law, women were competing for entry-level posts alongside a ready supply of similarly qualified men – who, it was reasonable to assume, were unlikely to take five or ten years out of their careers to bring up children, or to request part-time hours if and when they returned. It was not difficult to see why, unless there was a serious shortage of strong male candidates, employers might plump for those they believed would cause least disruption to long-established modes of working. Heavily pregnant women were viewed as strange, slightly terrifying phenomena in most corporate workplaces. The journalist Drusilla Beyfus, who had three children in the late 1950s and early 1960s, recalled how 'men colleagues treated you as if you were on fire; they always seemed afraid that you might have the baby in the office, so the relief on their faces when you finally left for hospital was considerable'.[80] Yet it was not simply the administrative inconveniences of organising part-time jobs or reintegrating returners that preserved the masculine tone of boardrooms and executive suites. Culturally entrenched stereotypes and prejudices against *all* women in positions of authority compounded the problem.

This was most starkly apparent in sectors reliant on scientific and technological expertise, such as chemicals, electronics, engineering, pharmaceuticals and multiple branches of applied research. Demand for skilled workers in these fields ran high in the 1960s, but opportunities for women were few and far between. Of some 34,000 managers with scientific or technical qualifications employed in industry in 1961, just 370 – or 0.01 per cent – were women.[81] Many observers located the root of the problem in poor science teaching in girls' schools, which limited the number of female applicants to university courses and in turn the supply of qualified science teachers.[82] Yet ambitious girls had little incentive to train for a career in which prospects seemed so limited. The various experts and bodies giving evidence to the Robbins Committee on Higher Education in 1961–2 made uninspiring suggestions for how better use might be made of female scientists. The Nobel Prize-winning physicist John Cockcroft thought that married returners could 'go into technician jobs, not on the highest grades, but they can nevertheless be of great value. They can certainly go back to teaching, that is easy.'[83] The Royal Society similarly pointed to 'much-needed scientific supporting work … in which a family woman could immediately become valuable scientifically, for example, as a scientific research assistant to those undertaking pioneering research'.[84]

Even this sort of lower grade, ancillary work was largely unavailable, as the social scientist Nancy Seear discovered when she investigated women's positions in a handful of large firms, including well-known names like ICI, Pfizer and Hoover. Wives and mothers, she found, were rarely seen in the intermediate grades and were practically non-existent in line management. Some companies formally excluded women from executive posts and promotion routes and paid them less than men doing the same job.[85] Many of the senior men interviewed by Seear's team expressed profound animosity towards the idea of being managed by a woman. One announced that he 'would chuck it' if a woman were put in charge of his department, whilst another thought such an appointment would be an 'indictment of [the] men employed'.[86] When pressed on the reasons for this hostility, a manager at an electronics firm said, 'Goes back to primitive man. Puritan background. Built in over thousands of years.'[87] Very few of these men had working wives, although they often expressed career ambitions for their daughters – just not in industry. An ICI manager thought that if one of his daughters acquired a science degree, he would advise she go into teaching, as it was a 'useful social service' and 'does suit women'. She should avoid ICI at all costs, he warned, because the 'attitude to women is medieval'.[88]

*

Bodies like the British Federation of University Women and the Medical Women's Federation were anxious, above all, to support women's *careers*, which they associated with the acquisition of skill and responsibility, and with continuity and progression over time. But in truth, a great deal of the paid work undertaken by graduate women bore few of these features. Many of the specialist employment agencies serving this group offered little more than supply teaching or miscellaneous secretarial work.[89] Viola Klein was struck by how much intermittent home-working was being undertaken by graduate women, from indexing and proofreading to tutoring, typing and translating. Several respondents to her 1963 survey described their efforts to earn an income from freelance journalism or by writing fiction, but for every Katharine Whitehorn or Margaret Drabble there were hundreds of others who struggled to secure regular remunerative work. One graduate housewife related how she had 'dabbled in "writing" & was local government correspondent for the local paper for four years & wrote on & off', but was now 'bored to death doing bits of jobs'. At her most desperate moment, she placed an advert in a newspaper and received one offer to sell knitwear garments to retail traders, a job which left her out of pocket after six months.[90]

The lengths to which these housebound graduate mothers went to find even the most mundane jobs suggests the extent of their personal frustrations. Many agreed with Hubback that unrelieved domesticity was doubly cruel to those who had abandoned professional careers for marriage. In a review of *Wives Who Went to College*, the novelist Ruth Adam observed that we are so used to its being the common lot of an educated woman that we hardly realise what its frustration and wretchedness can be. If you translate it into male terms, and think how a skilled architect must feel, perhaps in prison, doing an unskilled labourer's job, day in day out, for years at a stretch, you realise it better.[91]

Boredom with housework was not, of course, the exclusive preserve of the graduate, as occasionally pointed out by acerbic columnists in the tabloid press.[92] Yet this group did feel especially aggrieved by the shortage of jobs in which they could use their hard-won qualifications. They yearned, as one woman wrote to *The Times*, 'for a temporary change of environment, with the companionship of kindred spirits and the possibility of sharpening their ever-rusting wits in the company of their intellectual equals or superiors'.[93]

This restlessness explained why some graduate mothers doggedly persisted with paid work even when the financial return was negligible. A vet assisting part-time in her husband's practice in Wrexham, for example, calculated that she earned £600 per annum, of which £510 went on expenses and tax. A doctor who took up part-time locum work after having a third baby actually found herself £30 in the red once she had paid for domestic help, installed a telephone, bought a car for professional purposes and re-subscribed to the British Medical Association.[94] One woman told Klein that she enjoyed her teaching job but sometimes felt like giving up 'because it costs me so much to keep on with it'.[95] There were other cases, however, where the mother's salary made a more substantial contribution or provided much-valued 'extras': one journalist informed Klein that she had 'always written for money to pay school fees, uniforms, and my own clothes'.[96] Yet, as in working-class households, very few graduate wives were breadwinners for their families, whilst professional women's earning power more generally was far inferior to men's. Women accounted for only one in twenty earners in the average 'top' salary range of £2,000–3,000 in the mid-1960s.[97]

Furthermore, it was tacitly understood that any additional costs – childcare, housekeeping, transport, lunches or personal grooming – incurred by a wife going out to work had to be met from her potential earnings. This logic applied equally in non-professional households, but mothers doing unskilled manual jobs were unlikely to engage nannies or cleaners, run a car or require a wardrobe of smart clothes for the office. Middle-class women, by contrast, took for granted that substantial expenditure to replace themselves in the home would be a necessary corollary of getting a job. Grumbles about the unaffordability of reliable domestic help were near-universal amongst this group in the 1950s and 1960s, with many wives expressing nostalgia for the pre-war days of residential domestic service. Some attempted to recreate these arrangements by engaging an 'au pair'. These young European women were an increasingly common presence in the post-war middle-class home, visiting Britain to learn English and receiving bed, board and pocket money in exchange for helping with children and light chores. Au pairs were, on the face of it, cheaper than housekeepers, but their ill-defined status, somewhere between guest and servant, created tensions and misunderstanding on both sides.[98] Furthermore, the average au pair stayed for only a year and could add to household running costs in unpredictable ways. According to one working mother, they were 'exceedingly extravagant with hot water, heat, electricity, and everything else including the telephone. This adds up, since you can't "tick" the au pair girl off like you can your family, because the au pair leaves you.'[99]

One group of professional women were so incensed by the myriad financial disincentives impeding their ability to work that in 1967 they set up a Women's Taxation Action Group (WOTAG). This body campaigned against joint taxation of married couples and lobbied for tax relief for those employing domestic help, arguing that such reforms were necessary to encourage highly qualified women back into the workplace.[100] These efforts met with a mixed reception, attracting some positive press commentary but less sympathy from Labour ministers, who defended the principle of progressive taxation and observed that only the tiny minority of couples with an income in excess of £5,000 paid significantly more under joint assessment.[101] The government had a point: these professional women earned far above the average salary and *chose* to live in large houses and to send their children to expensive private schools. Yet WOTAG was correct to identify the basic injustice of treating a woman's earnings as an extension of her husband's income, an issue that was only partly rectified by the introduction of optional separate assessment in 1971.[102]

They were also right that government inaction on tax relief risked undercutting wider efforts to recruit women to short-staffed sectors. Two husbands wrote to the Medical Women's Federation in the mid-1960s expressing outrage at the situation in which their highly qualified wives found themselves. Harold Leigh's wife worked as a GP in Letchworth, employing a full-time nanny and a resident 'charlady-cook-housekeeper', as well as temporary cover when the nanny went on holiday. None of these expenses were tax deductible, meaning that they absorbed almost her entire salary. 'This gives women doctors little encouragement,' Leigh commented, 'at a time when there is supposed to be a shortage of doctors.'[103] Julius Silman calculated that his wife's net earnings as a hospital consultant were 'less than the lowest-grade cleaner receives' and far lower than the wages they paid a nanny to look after their two-year-old daughter. As a family they were not short of money, but Silman thought that there was

> a psychological effect derived from the feeling that for her skill and services there is virtually no financial reward. Out of a sense of frustration, my wife is now considering reducing her hours of work, at a time when the medical services cannot find sufficient consultants of adequate calibre to fill all the vacancies ... This is a great waste and probably represents a greater 'brain drain' than any other form.[104]

These correspondents fell into the category of 'enlightened' husbands, men who were proud of their wives' accomplishments and keen to support their professional ambitions. Yet it was notable that neither questioned the basic assumption that childcare and housework were a married woman's responsibility, something which she either had to do herself or pay someone else to do out of her earnings. Judged as a proportion of a wife's salary, these costs probably did appear demoralisingly high to many graduate women. Viewed alternatively as a joint expense which enabled *both* spouses to follow fulfilling careers, they might not have looked so bad. Very few married couples, however, were thinking in these terms in the 1960s. The concept of the 'dual-career marriage' was in its infancy, a term coined by husband-and-wife sociologists Robert and Rhona Rapoport to describe an exceptional group of men and women who (like themselves) had cast off conventional expectations about gender roles at home and work. The Rapoports saw such high-achieving couples as 'partners in social innovation', modelling a future in which both spouses would advance professionally and grow personally, each tuned in to the temperamental differences and emotional needs of the other.[105] These husbands and wives, the Rapoports observed, tended to share household chores, took equal responsibility for bringing up their children, and made financial decisions jointly. As a result, they enjoyed 'an enriched family life through each partner doing the things they are better at rather than just the things that go with their sex role whether they like it or not'.[106]

Such couples did exist in post-war Britain, but the idea that marital harmony was possible, perhaps even enhanced, when both spouses pursued serious careers was a radical one for the 1960s. It fundamentally challenged the dual-role model, which relied on the wife's willingness to step back from her job for five, ten or fifteen years, and to return on terms which were compatible with the demands of home and family. The small number of women who rejected this compromise, seeking instead continuous, high-level careers on the same basis as their husbands, were anomalous figures and attracted ambivalent press commentary. The *Guardian*, for instance, reported the Rapoports' optimistic findings in 1969 but ran a case study alongside the main article featuring 'James' and 'Claire', whose dual-career marriage was hardly a picture of egalitarian bliss. The couple had two children and were both hospital consultants employed full-time in the same speciality, although Claire had initially progressed faster. That period in their marriage was, she recalled, 'a very difficult time indeed' which James coped with 'by making derogatory comments about the set-up in which she was working'. James resented having to 'bath the children and go shopping for tea towels and crockery', chores he felt distracted him from work and which he 'wouldn't have to do if Claire didn't have a career'. Claire equally felt that, professionally, she would have done 'even better on her own'. Despite their supposed flexibility of roles at home, Claire was solely responsible for managing the au pair and planning meals, and revealed that she was often tired or depressed. The couple had minimal leisure, hardly ever entertained and counted few friends outside their small professional circle. The case study ended on a decidedly negative note: 'One way and another, James sighs, we see so little of each other that we need an agenda when we do.'[107]

*

The uneasy relationship between professional ambition and conventional femininity lent the dilemmas of the graduate mother a distinctive flavour in the post-war period. In earlier decades, most middle-class women had to choose between family and career; now the problem was how to combine both without losing, to use Hubback's phrase, 'serenity in the process'. Such mothers were prevented by their education and class from seeking a job in a factory or a shop, but they were also largely excluded from top posts in the most interesting and well-remunerated professions. Staying at home as a full-time housewife remained, of course, a respectable option and one widely embraced by graduate women, especially those married to men in occupations where the services of a supportive and presentable wife were advantageous.[108] Some of the non-working respondents to Klein's 1963 survey were deeply invested in this alternative 'career' as the wives of parsons, diplomats, senior managers and university dons, although it was possible to detect a hint of defensiveness in their replies. One maths graduate wrote rather acidly that she had never been 'gainfully employed' but was at present 'fully employed as mother, housewife, doctor's receptionist, telephonist, gardener, seamstress, tailoress & specialist in house decoration. All done for the love of a wonderful husband and children.'[109]

By the mid-1960s the belief that full-time housewifery constituted a waste of the educated woman's capacities was widely voiced, not least by female graduates themselves, whose numbers were growing following the publication of the influential Robbins report on higher education in 1963.[110] On the face of it, these post-war graduates were more fortunately placed than their pre-war counterparts: marriage bars had gone and equal pay was established in the public sector, whilst part-time work and opportunities to retrain were on the increase. Yet the select band of mothers who had managed – through private incomes, perseverance or both – to pursue careers before the 1950s enjoyed certain advantages. Keeping servants had been a middle-class norm between the wars, as a result of which married women were relieved of a great deal of household labour which twenty years later would fall to their daughters to do for themselves. One GP and mother of four recalled in 1965 that when she started her practice thirty years earlier, she had 'resident nannies, a maid, daily helps. No young professional woman can possibly afford that now.'[111] Paid domestic work would revive again from the 1980s, driven by growing demand from middle-class professionals and new waves of global migration.[112] In the decades in between, however, graduate wives discovered with dismay that working-class women were reluctant to scrub their floors or wash their dishes unless the wages on offer were high and the hours convenient. Amongst Hubback's sample, fewer than one in six had a residential domestic helper (in half of the cases this was an au pair), and over a quarter did their housework entirely unaided. Hubback described this as one of the ways in which 'social democracy' had hurt the middle classes, with married women feeling the worst effects. 'The position of the educated wife and mother,' she wrote, 'has altered more, in relation to what she would have expected before the Second World War, than has that of her husband.'[113]

In addition to enjoying greater domestic help, earlier generations were unburdened by psychoanalytic prescriptions concerning the continuous maternal care of small children. Before the 1950s, women of the upper and middle classes, whether working or leisured, routinely used nurses, nannies and boarding schools, with prolonged separation of parents and offspring carrying little social stigma. Some families continued these traditions well into the post-war period; it remained standard, for instance, for diplomatic wives to accompany husbands overseas and leave their children in English boarding schools. Yet middle-class women were increasingly exposed to the new popular orthodoxies, perhaps to a greater extent than their working-class counterparts. Viola Klein commented that 'Bowlby and other psychoanalytical theories are, of course, read more by educated women than by others,' whilst the social worker Phyllis Willmott thought the influence was direct in the case of her own profession.[114] Trained to avoid separating children from their mothers in their casework, social workers 'not surprisingly perhaps, show awareness of this potential danger themselves'. They seemed, Willmott observed, 'overanxious to practise what in a way they used to preach', hence their reluctance to work while their children were young.[115]

Given these conflicting pressures on graduate women, it is not difficult to see how a book like *Wives Who Went to College* gained such cultural purchase in the post-war decades. It called for women to make a wider contribution to society in line with their intellectual capacities, but at the same time urged them to seek balance in their personal lives. It was, Hubback wrote, for each woman 'to face the difficulties involved in combining marriage, motherhood and individualism and to work out her own solution in terms of her own circumstances, character and endowment'.[116] Many graduate women appear to have taken this advice, reining in their ambitions and adjusting to the constraints of juggling family and career. One mother told Klein that she had tried to avoid losing momentum in her academic career following marriage, but now accepted that her current role as a temporary lecturer was the best she could expect. Her contract would soon end, at which point 'I shall at least feel that I have had a few years congenial work & company again, & feel grateful for it'.[117] In a similar vein, a female doctor writing to the *British Medical Journal* in 1954 explained how she felt content to serve 'in the humble, but very useful, position of school medical officer and medical officer at a maternity and child welfare clinic' rather than compete for higher-level posts. Young women going into medicine, she thought, 'should be encouraged to marry and make full use of their experience both as doctors and as well-balanced women, not to put all their energies into their careers'.[118]

Even as they lobbied for equal pay, part-time employment opportunities, training and tax reforms, professional women's organisations endorsed this ideology of compromise and self-restraint. The Medical Women's Federation thought that female undergraduates should be urged to 'take a sensible look at their circumstances and plan to make these compatible with their professional ambitions'.[119] Similarly, the British Federation of University Women took for granted that the duties of marriage and motherhood placed special difficulties in the way of female graduates which did not affect their male peers: 'They are women; and that means that they have a double contribution to make. They have their contribution through their professional work, and they have their contribution as wives and mothers.'[120] Most commentators agreed with Hubback that harmonising the demands of family and career was ultimately the responsibility of women themselves. This impulse to personalise the problem, framing it as an issue about individual commitment rather than external constraints, was strongly evident in debates about graduate women's employment throughout the 1950s and 60s.[121] Most professional women believed that there were limits to how much help they could reasonably demand from employers, husbands or the State in solving their dilemmas. Second-wave feminists would challenge this mentality just a decade later, arguing that women needed to see those dilemmas as the products of a patriarchal society and to resist them collectively. Yet the assumptions they were up against, that the successful working mother was one who overcame adversity through an exceptional blend of personal qualities, were already running deep in the culture. Her strength of character, resilience and drive would inspire and torment successive generations of middle-class women for many years to come.

10

Newcomers

When Doreen Phillips arrived in London in 1964 with a baby on one arm and a small child gripping her other hand, everything seemed dismal and dark. Accustomed to year-round sunshine in her native Guyana, Doreen found fault at every turn, from the shabby rooms occupied by her husband and eldest son, who had migrated to Britain before her, to the strangeness of the London Underground. 'I used to stand at the top of the escalator looking down,' she recalled, 'asking, "do I have to go on that?"' Finding work was easy – 'as long as you were prepared to do the menial jobs' – and Doreen soon started an evening shift in a sweet factory, with a neighbour watching the children while she was out. She was dismayed by the racial prejudice that she found there:

> The Blacks were on one side, the Whites were on one side. We sort of got all the worst bits to do, the sweeping up and things. We were packing sweets, they were packing the sweets, handling the things, but all the dirty jobs the Blacks were doing. Then they would use remarks like 'What's smelling like that?', you know, them sorts of things because they used to say Black people stink.

By speaking up and standing her ground, Doreen got herself moved to a better job in the factory, although she remained ever-conscious of her status as a 'dark stranger', as the title of one influential study of Commonwealth immigration put it, in an overwhelmingly white society. Doreen could at least draw for emotional sustenance and practical aid on Caribbean friends in London:

> We used to visit each other's homes, you didn't need appointments, you walked in, you're in one room, you sit together round the paraffin heater, you put the kettle on the paraffin heater, you make tea. You keep my children, I keep yours ... We used to arrange to pick up each other's children from school, you pick up mine today, I pick up yours tomorrow.[1]

Doreen's testimony, recorded in the early millennium, bore the classic hallmarks of the migrant narrative: a long journey, shock and dislocation on arrival, a lasting sense of living between two worlds but belonging to neither, and the comforting embrace of the tightly knit communities which migrants quickly built for themselves within a hostile host nation.[2] Travelling to Britain after the 1962 Immigration Act, which limited the eligibility of 'coloured' colonial subjects, Doreen was classed as a dependant of her husband. Yet like most migrant mothers, she fully expected to work, earn and save. There was no 'dual role' for women like Doreen, who were far less likely than white, British-born mothers to take an extended break from paid employment for child-rearing and home-making. A survey carried out in the mid-1970s found that nearly three-quarters of Caribbean women in Britain were wage-earning, compared to the national average of 45 per cent.[3] In inner London, foreign-born mothers with children under the age of one were twice as likely as their British-born counterparts to be working, and four times as likely to be working full-time.[4]

Migrant women often took up occupations identified with particular ethnic groups – Irish and Caribbean nurses in the NHS, Bangladeshi machinists in the garment industry – where they frequently found themselves, like Doreen, directed into the lowest paid or least congenial tasks, emptying bedpans in hospitals, sweeping factory floors or moving around heavy equipment on twilight cleaning shifts in offices. Part of the reason for these distinctive work histories was the combination of economic pressure and material aspiration which made wage-earning central to the lives of post-war migrants. High rents, childminding fees and remittances sent to extended kin overseas translated into long hours of paid work, with some women juggling multiple jobs alongside evening classes or studying for correspondence courses. Many migrant couples dreamed of acquiring land or starting businesses when they returned to their homeland, a shared goal powerful enough to convince more conservative-minded husbands to let their wives earn, even where it went against time-honoured tradition. These dynamics played out in different ways for women from the Asian subcontinent, depending on religion, community norms and local labour market opportunities. A Muslim wife from rural Pakistan living in Bradford might find it impossible to do anything but poorly paid home-work, whereas a Punjabi Sikh in Southall could be spending long hours away from her family mopping the concourses at Heathrow airport. A tiny elite of highly educated Indian women found higher-level work, although rarely in line with their qualifications. Sheela Banerjee's mother, a high-caste Hindu from West Bengal who arrived in Britain in 1968, studied chemistry at night school because employers would not recognise the degree she had already earned in the subject in India.[5]

The other major factor shaping migrant women's lives was racial prejudice. This affected black and Asian migrants profoundly, in the workplace, in the housing market and in everyday struggles over shopping, finding childcare or accessing public services. As a Guyanese of African descent, Doreen's experience was distinct from that of the Irish, Polish and other Europeans arriving in large numbers from the late 1940s, whose white faces made them a more suitable class of migrant in the eyes of the host population. Biological theories of race were officially discredited by the post-war decades, yet crude racial stereotypes persisted, both in the vernacular language of the shop floor and in expert diagnoses of the 'problems' associated with particular migrant communities. Childrearing practices amongst Caribbean and West African families caused particular concern to doctors, social workers and health visitors, who berated mothers for their heavy use of unregistered childminders and failure to offer the always-available maternal care prescribed by authorities like John Bowlby.

All this made it impossible for working mothers from Britain's former colonies to become 'ordinary' in the way that the white, British-born mother was increasingly able to do in the booming economy of the 1950s and 1960s. Much comment on migrant lives was cast in the mould of the pre-war social investigator who studied the urban poor through observation and moral inference. Although many migrant communities sustained a rich cultural and intellectual life, it was only in later decades that personal memoirs and oral history projects began to recover their experiences from the bottom up.[6] These revealed that, material and cultural differences aside, paid work often held a similar mix of meanings for migrant women as it did for white, British-born mothers, from the need to put food on the table and pay the rent, to a desire for independence, professional achievement or simply something to do beyond housework and childcare. Yet for contemporaries, the fault-lines of race and diverse histories ran deep, excluding migrant mothers from the more positive images and understandings of working motherhood which were moving to the fore in public debate. The 'good' working mother, it seemed, was the white working mother.[7]

*

Migrants formed a major part of the workforce long before the era of mass immigration following the Second World War. The Irish arrived in large numbers in the nineteenth and early twentieth centuries as both seasonal workers and permanent residents, the men filling jobs in agriculture, construction and general labouring, the women entering domestic service, nursing and unskilled factory work. Jews from Russia and Eastern Europe formed the next largest grouping, with many women helping husbands to run small businesses or earning their own living as tailoresses or domestic servants. Thousands of well-educated Jewish women fleeing Nazi persecution were directed into the latter occupation in the 1930s as a condition of their admission to Britain.[8] This included Austrian-born Viola Klein, who arrived in London in 1938 with a PhD in French literature, multiple languages and several years of writing and editing under her belt. She found herself working as a lowly governess-housekeeper for a family in Hammersmith before eventually escaping to study at the London School of Economics, aided by a scholarship from the Czechoslovakian government-in-exile.[9]

The demands of the wartime State for labour deepened the ethnic diversity of the British population further, with several hundred women recruited from the colonies to the Auxiliary Territorial Service in 1943–4, joining much larger numbers of Caribbean servicemen employed in the RAF. Some of these black Britons encountered racial discrimination when they tried to sign up, including women who had been born in Britain and grown up there. Amelia King, an east Londoner, was turned away for a post in the Land Army because of the colour of her skin, whilst Lilian Bader, a native of Liverpool with a Barbadian father, was forced to leave her canteen job for the same reason, although she subsequently found work and rose through the ranks of the WAAF.[10]

This picture changed in important ways from the late 1940s. The Irish presence, already standing at half a million by 1951, continued to grow at a rate of 50,000 or more per year for the rest of the decade.[11] They were joined by 80,000 Poles, Latvians, Balts, Yugoslavs and Ukrainians recruited by the British as 'displaced persons' from refugee camps across Austria and Germany, most of whom were eventually given permanent resident status as European Volunteer Workers (EVW).[12] This scheme, launched to fill urgent labour shortages in the British economy, was extended to include Italians, around 14,000 of whom came for work between 1946 and 1951, whilst the Polish Resettlement Act of 1947 enabled a further 120,000 Polish war veterans and their families to make Britain their home.[13] From 1948, migrant numbers were swelled by substantial flows from the British Commonwealth, including colonies still under British rule as well as newly independent states. In the mid- to later 1950s, 20,000 people arrived annually from the Caribbean islands, rising to over 60,000 in 1961, a year which also saw 21,000 Indians, 22,000 Pakistanis and 6,300 Cypriots land on British soil.[14] Between 1951 and 1971, the proportion of the population of England and Wales born overseas grew from 4.3 per cent to 6.4 per cent, representing an increase in numbers from 1.9 million to 3.1 million.[15]

These newcomers did not share an identical legal status. The Europeans were mostly 'alien' guest-workers with no automatic right to settle permanently. Commonwealth migrants, by contrast, were entitled under the terms of the 1948 British Nationality Act to live, work and vote in Britain, rights which Irish citizens continued to enjoy even after Ireland's exit from the Commonwealth in 1949. This liberal, open-door policy was driven by economic and political self-interest, adopted at a time of desperate labour shortages and a new threat to Britain's global prestige in the form of Cold War superpower rivalry between the US and the Soviet Union. Ministers and officials hoped that both problems could be solved by creating a universal category of citizenship for all subjects born within the British Commonwealth. Not only would this shore up the historic ties of empire, but it would allow for a modest flow of temporary migrants to help revive Britain's flagging economy and under-staffed welfare state. What policymakers did not foresee was just how many Commonwealth citizens would assert their rights by seeking new lives for themselves and their families in Britain. As early as the mid-1950s, plans were afoot within Whitehall to apply controls, resulting in a string of legislation which, piece by piece, rolled back the inclusive, colour-blind provisions of the 1948 Act.[16]

Most newcomers found homes in cities and large towns, especially London, where one in ten of the population was born outside the UK by 1961. Ten thousand Caribbean migrants, four-fifths of them Jamaican, settled in Brixton alone, dwelling alongside 9,000 Irish, 2,000 Cypriots and 1,400 migrants from the Asian subcontinent.[17] Northern industrial towns like Bradford, Leeds, Derby and Rochdale became prime destinations for Pakistanis in the 1950s and 1960s, whilst Leicester in the Midlands saw a dramatic growth in its migrant population between 1968 and 1978, when

some 20,000 East African Asians arrived from Kenya, Tanzania,
Malawi and Uganda following the end of British colonial rule in
those countries. With the exception of the Irish, men outnumbered
women in the early phases of post-war migration. Some had served
in the army or industry during the war and were returning to a
country they already knew, whilst others left villages and townships
for a land they had only read about in books or located on the map.
By the early 1960s, this pattern had changed, with large numbers
of wives and children travelling to join male kin, prompted by new
immigration rules making it difficult for Commonwealth citizens
to enter except for purposes of family reunion. Between 1962 and
1965, some 90 per cent of new migrants from Commonwealth
countries were the dependants of men already working in Britain.[18]
As these families earned and saved, bought houses and sent their
children to local schools, started up small businesses and established
places of worship, the transformative impact of immigration on
British society began to be felt. Women's labour, paid and unpaid,
stood at the heart of this transformation.

*

Maira Curran was amongst the many thousands of young women
who left Ireland's green hills and sluggish economy in the 1940s
and 1950s to begin nursing careers in Britain. Born in Clonakilty,
County Cork, as Maira O'Rourke, Curran had spent much of her
childhood and youth in institutions under the care of the Catholic
Church, but aged twenty she boarded a ship to Liverpool, followed
by a train to Cardiff, where a job awaited her at a small private
hospital run by nuns. Curran's sheltered upbringing was exposed
on her very first day, when the matron lifted the bedclothes from
a patient and Curran found herself faced with the male anatomy
in all its glory. 'Well, I never knew that men and women were
different,' Curran recalled, 'and I let out a scream. She put her hand
across and slapped me round the face and said, "Control yourself,
Nurse O'Rourke." She didn't know why I was screaming, and
I never told her, but I shall never forget that though, when I saw
that, oh my God, you know.'[19] Teased and taunted for nine months

by patients whose English accents she struggled to understand, Curran completed her training and moved to the Royal Northern Hospital in London where, feeling isolated and bullied, she began to entertain suicidal thoughts. Things looked brighter following another transfer, this time to a convalescent hospital in Southgate, but after two years Curran swapped nursing for nannying, eventually marrying a widower with four children and then having another five of her own.

The demands of family left Curran little choice but to give up paid work, but others travelling the same path from Ireland took advantage of the part-time nursing opportunities now available in the NHS. Siobhan, a nurse interviewed about her post-war experiences in the early 2000s, had managed by working night shifts, which solved the problem of paying for a minder but was less than ideal for her marriage. 'It was hard,' Siobhan recalled of the bargain she struck with her husband. 'He'd come in and I'd just walk out the door.' Another interviewee, Roisin, negotiated a similar arrangement: 'I couldn't have done it without him but I did a lot of preparation in the week for the weekend, like I'd make a casserole on the Friday for lunch and I'd get the children ready for bed before I went to work and then I would be back the next morning about half past eight.' Some returned to nursing once their children were at school, like Una, who was promoted to senior management by the time she retired, aged sixty-five. 'I did have a long career,' she remembered with satisfaction, 'I loved it.'[20] Margaret Collins from County Tyrone trained in Scotland, moved to London for a post in Fulham and left nursing in the 1950s when she started a family. Once her youngest was of school age, Collins made use of her former skills by getting a job as a home help. 'I thought I'll do this for a year or two until he's at secondary school,' she remembered, 'and it ended up I was there fourteen years!'[21]

These testimonies affirmed nursing's reputation as a relatively secure, flexible and 'respectable' occupation for female migrants, and one in which their labour was badly needed. The British government actively courted girls like Maira, Siobhan, Una and Margaret, placing adverts in the Irish press promising free passage, good wages and subsidised accommodation, and sending over Ministry of Labour officials to interview nervous candidates in provincial hotels. These efforts produced almost 1,200 recruits in 1947, whilst later arrivals swelled their numbers to the point that nearly 12 per cent of all nurses in Britain were Irish-born by the early 1970s.[22] Even so, nursing was not the largest occupation for this group of female migrants. According to the 1951 census, around one in five of all Irish-born women working in Britain were nurses, some way behind the two-fifths employed in 'personal service', a broad category comprising cleaning, charring, laundry work, waitressing, cooking and domestic labour in private homes.[23] This kind of routine, low-skilled work was readily available in Ireland, but officials investigating the causes of mass emigration in the 1950s found that many young women preferred to do it in England, drawn by the prospect of better wages and a more exciting social life, as well as the possibility of moving into higher-status clerical or shop work. 'The domestic worker in Great Britain gets recognition as a human being while she does not get it here,' was the conclusion of the Irish Housewives Association, submitting evidence to an official commission in 1948.[24] Mary Galvin's experience as a cleaner in London in the late 1930s and 1940s did not quite bear this out, a period in which she was juggling three part-time jobs with the care of a young family:

> I used to go to one job at half-past six to eight o'clock in the morning, come home, have a cup of tea, and at nine o'clock I'd go and clean out a pub. At two o'clock I'd go to a shop in Bayswater and I'd clean that up and at 3 o'clock I went down to a café at Westminster Hospital and I worked there until 8 o'clock. I went from work to bed. I'd be so tired I wouldn't want to do anything else, after slaving all day.[25]

What struck Galvin most keenly was the lack of friendliness from her managers and co-workers, not one of whom would pause to say good morning when she arrived for her shift. Nonetheless, in material terms the move paid off. By the late 1950s, Mary was living in a home that she owned. 'That's because I was working, and my husband and then three in me family was working and two going to school.'[26]

Surveying the Irish presence in these decades, some observers suggested that very little now distinguished these migrants from British-born locals. In 1955, an inter-departmental working party endorsed exemptions for Irish nationals from immigration controls on the grounds that they were not, 'whether they like it or not – a different race from the ordinary inhabitants of Great Britain'.[27] A study published eight years later agreed that, tired clichés about drunken 'Paddies' aside, the Irish were far from a marked-out minority. For many employers, the author concluded, 'the Irish are no longer regarded as an exceptional group'.[28] Female migrant memories, however, do not tell such a sanguine story. Nursing recruits in the late 1940s often struggled to find posts in the 'better class' of hospital, relegated instead to working in mental asylums, sanatoria for tubercular patients or hospitals in remote rural locations. Emer recalled the nastiness of one English matron during her training:

> They used to teach us all this stuff about hygiene, cleaning baths and all this, the sister holding up a box of Vim and then she should say, 'Of course you Irish girls wouldn't know about this.' The knife sticking in all the time, you know.[29]

Such experiences were not confined to nurses. Miriam James came over from Dublin in 1949 to work as a switchboard operator, but was prevented from covering for a colleague who answered the telephone because the boss didn't like her accent. 'Most of his customers and friends seemed to like talking to me,' she recalled, 'but I think he thought it wasn't good for his image to have an Irishwoman on the telephone. That was the first occasion on which I was rejected as an Irish person, and it was a very salutary lesson.'[30]

Ignorant and hurtful claims about the Irish being dirty or ill-educated diminished over time, particularly as the skill and dedication of thousands of Irish NHS nurses became more widely known to the general public. Nonetheless, Irish migrants encountered prejudice right through the post-war decades, sometimes targeted against their Catholicism, or, from the late 1960s, laced with anger about the Troubles in Northern Ireland and IRA bombings on British soil. Anti-Irish feeling could complicate the process of finding rental accommodation, always tough for any family with young children, but doubly so for Irish mothers. As one woman recalled:

> Oh you couldn't get a place, there's no way you could get a place, once you had children. I mean, even if you had two children they wouldn't let you in, and once you were Irish, once they heard the accents, that was it. They didn't want you, they just didn't.[31]

Notices in the windows of lodging houses stipulating 'no Irish' eventually disappeared, but the sense of separateness felt by Irish newcomers, of being unwanted strangers who did not quite belong, took longer to fade.

*

A similar ambiguity existed in relation to the temporary foreign workforce recruited to plug gaps in essential industries after the war. These 'displaced persons' were not native English speakers and had no long history of migration to Britain like the Irish. Yet their white European lineage made them, in the eyes of some observers (especially those fearful about falling birth rates), suitable candidates for long-term settlement and integration. European migrants benefited from 'the lack of a conspicuous badge of different origin and greater experience in knowing how to work the machinery of urban life', as one expert put it in the late 1950s.[32] Newspaper coverage of the 'Balt Cygnets', the first tranche of Latvian, Lithuanian and Estonian women recruited as domestic workers in British hospitals, was strikingly upbeat, noting their smart clothes, strong physiques and the approval which they won amongst employers, some of whom described them as 'first-class workers'.[33] An official at the Ministry of Labour thought these young women 'would be rapidly assimilated' and perhaps even marry and settle permanently, forming 'a valuable addition to our man-power and a not undesirable element in our population'.[34]

Migrant testimonies add shade to this rosy picture. Many of those recruited under the European Volunteer Worker scheme were dismayed by the run-down hostels and disused barracks in which they were received on arrival, and hated the strange-tasting food, strict curfew rules and single-sex dorms. Male workers were eventually permitted to bring dependants, although the scarcity of decent family housing severely limited the number that could be accommodated. The official policy on female recruitment was to take only young women without husbands or children, although some married couples were engaged as 'linked' workers, the men employed mostly as miners or agricultural labourers whilst the wives were dispatched to the cotton mills of Lancashire and the West Riding. The rules concerning pregnant volunteer workers was harsh during the first year of the scheme: those whose pregnancies had been concealed at interview or missed during medical examinations were to be sent back to the refugee camps which they had come from. 'These persons can make no valuable contribution to the industry of this country,' one Ministry of Health official argued, grouping unmarried mothers with tubercular workers and those carrying venereal diseases. 'They represent a serious menace to their associates and an undue burden on our already overstrained health services.'[35] By April 1948, thirty-three pregnant women had been deported to Germany under these rules. By contrast, expectant mothers who conceived *after* arrival in Britain, or who had husbands already in the country, were generally allowed to stay. In the Lancashire mills, with their long tradition of married women's work, such mothers were even cautiously welcomed by employers desperate to fill vacancies. A Ministry of Labour official noted that mill-owners were 'finding these women excellent workers and are prepared to retain them in their employment so long as the women are fit for work and to undertake to find employment for them afterwards'.[36]

This more flexible attitude was borne out by the experiences of Italian migrants in the north-west of England. Marina travelled from Italy to Manchester in 1953 with her husband, where they were both employed full-time in the textile industry until the birth of their first child. Marina kept working until six months into her pregnancy, took two years out of the labour market and then returned to a full-time day shift whilst her husband worked nights. Another Italian millworker, Gabriella, described how she adopted a similar pattern of shift-work in the 1960s,

> so we could take care of the children, and my sister in law would keep them in between shifts, because she lived not far from me. When I went out I would leave them with her and go to work. Then he [my husband] would come back, pick them up and take them home. Ah, a bit of sacrifice for the children, what else to do?[37]

Dual-earning couples were also common amongst Polish migrants, especially where men struggled to find well-paid work or had suffered physical or mental trauma from their war service. In Leicester, Polish women joined the thousands of British housewives looking for full- or part-time work in the city's hosiery factories. Jaroslaw, a war veteran, recalled that his wife's earnings were nearly equal to his, making money tight when babies arrived and she withdrew temporarily from employment: 'We had to depend on the wives working. So, if any of our wives got pregnant at that time, it was a disaster! ... But somehow we managed.'[38]

One further group of European migrants were the Cypriots, although as Commonwealth citizens their status differed from the volunteer workers or Polish veterans. Numbers peaked around the time that Cyprus won its independence from Britain in 1959–60, with men arriving first, leaving the under-developed agricultural economy of their homeland to open cafes, restaurants and clothing workshops in places like Haringey and Islington in north London. Their wives and children followed, swelling the Cypriot-born population to more than 170,000 by the early 1980s, three-quarters of whom were Orthodox Christians from the Greek south and the rest Muslims from the Turkish north.[39] Official statistics recorded low rates of employment amongst wives, but much female labour was informal or unregistered: helping to run small businesses, working sewing machines in family enterprises or finishing garments at home. By tradition, a Greek-Cypriot woman was expected to obey her husband and safeguard the family honour through her virtue and modesty. This could create tensions or even provoke violence where wives took paid employment outside the tight-knit Greek-Cypriot community. Writing in the early 1980s, a community activist recounted the story of Yiota, whose husband regularly beat her if she came home late from her factory job: 'He calls her a "whore". But she wants to stay with him. She has a small child and could not cope on her own.'[40] Yet in other cases, wives gained greater power in the household by bringing in a second income. Their earnings might contribute to the purchase of property back in Cyprus or effect a family move to a desirable outer London suburb like Finchley or Barnet.

For many European migrant mothers, juggling family and work was not a wholly dissimilar experience from that of their British-born counterparts. Men generally retained their status as breadwinners, but paid employment amongst wives allowed for a higher standard of living and, in some households at least, a re-ordering of power between husbands and wives. It was the case that differences of language, culture and religion made it difficult for these migrant mothers to feel just like any other ordinary British housewife. Stereotypes of filthy, uncivilised 'foreigners' continued to circulate in popular culture and everyday life. 'We've got to remember they're peasants!' one woman told a newspaper when asked about the Italians in her neighbourhood. 'They are terribly noisy, blaring radios, shouting across the street, lounging around.'[41] Yet despite all this, European migrants could generally feel confident about their long-term prospects in post-war Britain. It was a very different story for so-called 'coloured immigrants' travelling from former colonies in the Caribbean, Africa and South Asia.

*

Adah, the heroine of Buchi Emecheta's semi-autobiographical novel, *Second-Class Citizen*, arrives in Britain in the early 1960s as a well-educated and ambitious young Nigerian with high hopes for the future. Securing a good job as a senior assistant at North Finchley Library, Adah quickly becomes the family breadwinner, supporting her husband, Francis, with his legal studies and paying a minder to look after their two small children. Repeated pregnancy and Francis's abusive behaviour, however, compounded by constant childcare and housing worries, quickly take their toll on Adah's spirits. When Francis burns the book manuscript Adah has been lovingly drafting in precious snatches of free time, she leaves him, becoming a single mother of five struggling for survival in the precarious labour market and labyrinthine welfare system of post-war London.[42] Race is an unmistakable presence throughout the novel, as Adah resists what so many of her fellow black migrants seemed to have accepted with resignation: that they cannot have what white Britons take as their entitlement, be it a skilled job with secure prospects, or a comfortable home and high-quality education for their children. At one moment in *Second Class Citizen*, Adah sits in an NHS maternity ward following the birth of her third baby, humiliated at having to wear an ugly hospital gown whilst the mothers around her show off the pretty nightdresses that their relatives have brought them. Why shouldn't Adah enjoy such simple pleasures? Why should the colour of her skin disqualify her from having nice things, or her husband from getting a well-paid and respected job, or her children from living in decent housing?

Other black migrants felt a similar sense of shock. Travelling on British passports, speaking English and schooled as children in the history and traditions of the 'mother country', they were disturbed at the hostility which their presence provoked amongst landlords, neighbours, employers and co-workers. Adah knew she was lucky to get her librarian post, having refused Francis's demand that she apply to the local shirt-making factory for 'the type of job

considered suitable for housewives, especially black housewives'.[43]
It was more typical for those equipped with qualifications to find
no outlet for them in Britain. Cecelia Wade, who migrated from
Montserrat in 1956, proudly presented her teaching credentials at a
labour exchange only to be told by the woman behind the counter,
'Oh, you were a teacher back home were you? Well you won't get
a job teaching here!'[44] Even the routine 'little jobs' which enabled
Bermondsey housewives to earn money for extras were not always
available to black migrants, as one Caribbean mother discovered
when she applied for work: 'I went to Peek Freans that used to have
loads of part-time jobs and this woman said to me "We've got jobs,
yes, but we can't give it to your people." '[45]

White women helped to police racial boundaries in the workplace
in other ways. One labour exchange official referred to a firm
'where the director has told me that no coloured girl will ever enter
his doors because, if this happened, half his machine girls would
leave'.[46] A manager at a food-processing factory in south London
which had started to employ Caribbean women remarked, 'I don't
know how much our girls will stand, and we can't afford to lose our
white labour.'[47] Some employers capitulated to demands from their
existing workforce for separate toilet facilities for the newcomers,
who, it was claimed, had poor hygiene habits – washing their feet
in the sink, for instance, or cleaning false teeth. Other complaints
included Caribbean women's 'bizarre' dress and their tendency to
keep their hats on indoors.[48] Investigating these dynamics in the
early 1960s, the sociologist Sheila Patterson observed that tensions
were minimised where managers discriminated against black
workers, keeping the proportion of non-white labour below 10 per
cent and protecting promotion routes for white locals. She also
found that animosity could gradually break down over time. In
one light-engineering firm studied by Patterson, a group of white
workers were invited to a Caribbean wedding 'and quite enjoyed
themselves', according to the manager. At another firm, it became
standard practice to present any black worker leaving to have a
baby with a layette of bedlinen funded by a collection from her
workmates, just as would happen for any expectant white mother.[49]

Yet racial prejudice remained rife across large sections of the British economy. Black women rarely got jobs as waitresses or shop assistants for fear that customers would not like it: 'I think a woman might object if they were served by a coloured girl in corsetry,' as one retailer put it.[50] Migrants were instead employed out of sight as kitchen hands, cleaners or domestic assistants in hotels and restaurants. A survey of Jamaicans in the British workforce in 1966 found that just 2 per cent of women in the sample – and none of the men – had office jobs, typically as typists or telephone operators.[51] One manager of a laundry in Brixton explained why black women did not hold any clerical posts in his firm: 'The public might object and a coloured girl in the office might feel awkward on her own. It's easy enough to get clerks anyway.'[52] Employers in short-staffed parts of the public sector, by contrast, could not be so picky. Large numbers of Caribbean men and women were recruited for jobs on London's public transport system and in NHS hospitals, in the latter case hired directly through overseas schemes. The first recruitment campaign for Caribbean nurses was launched in Barbados in 1949, with others following soon after. By the mid-sixties, some 5,000 Jamaican nurses alone were employed in the NHS, whilst Daphne Steele had become the nation's first black matron, a post she occupied at St Winifred's Hospital in Ilkley, Yorkshire.[53] At the close of the decade, black and minority ethnic nurses made up a quarter of NHS hospital staff.[54]

Like their white colleagues, Caribbean nurses took advantage of flexible shift patterns to juggle paid work with caring for children. Morvia Gooden's mother, for instance, came to Britain in 1960, working as a nursing auxiliary by night and taking charge of her five children during the day. Gooden recalled a happy childhood but was ever conscious of 'the exceedingly tangible hostility to our very presence in the country'.[55] Interactions with patients could contribute to this feeling of unease. One nurse employed in Fulham remembered that 'some of the patients were nice and some of them were horrible … They don't want you to come near, they don't want you to touch them … If you tell anything to them they will complain to the matron and you will get the sack.'[56] How common such encounters were for black nurses is unclear. Patterson investigated the situation at three hospitals in south London, where matrons claimed to have encountered only a 'bare handful' of difficult patients over a ten-year period, a finding which Patterson thought threw 'a rather strange light' on the assertions of employers concerning black workers in other public-facing occupations.[57]

Discrimination from co-workers and line managers was more of a problem. Those training to become State-Enrolled Nurses (SEN), a qualification which took two years to complete rather than the three required for State-Registered Nurse (SRN) status, found themselves lumped with repetitive low-grade tasks and disadvantaged in relation to promotion prospects. The distinction between these two qualifications was not always explained to overseas recruits, who only realised that they were on an inferior career track once in post. Some Irish nurses got caught out this way, but it affected many more Caribbean applicants, who expressed bitterness at their treatment by NHS employers in later life. 'A lot of us fell for that. If we were given a chance at the time to sit the test to do SRN a lot of us would have got through. We were sort of cheap labour really,' one post-war recruit recalled.[58] Another remembered with anger how her request to resume SRN training following a break to have a baby was flatly refused by the ward sister:

> I will never, ever forget it. It was really hurtful. What did I want to do that for? I'm good as I am, and all this nonsense. And of course when you've got, at that time of your life, when you've got children to take on and somebody says things like that to you, it does knock you back, so I never just started that again.[59]

Nonetheless, even with these barriers to career progression in place, black nurses could find some satisfaction in their new-found earning power and professional status. Nancy Foner, an anthropologist studying the Jamaican community in London in the early 1970s, reported much contentment amongst the working wives. 'Many nurses' auxiliaries and ward orderlies talked with enthusiasm and pride about their dealings with hospital patients and the services they provide for the old and sick,' she noted, whilst 'those in catering often described the new dishes they had learned to prepare, and many women boasted of the sewing skills they had acquired in England.'[60] Foner remarked upon the intriguing situation which migration had produced for some married couples, whereby husbands suffered a loss of occupational status whilst their wives experienced the reverse, although both earned considerably more than would have been possible in the Caribbean. Mrs Inwood, a nurse who had been a non-earning housewife before migrating, described how her husband had swapped a clerical job for skilled factory work in London but subsequently gave it up to work on the buses, where the hours were more flexible. This enabled him to look after their children while Mrs Inwood worked her nursing shifts. Her satisfaction with this arrangement was obvious. She regarded it as a vast improvement on her life in Jamaica, where 'a woman's place was in the home and husbands didn't want their wives to work'.[61]

*

Sharing childcare was an obvious strategy for dual-earning migrant couples. Yet, just as British housewives discovered, not all men were willing or able to shoulder this responsibility. In *Second-Class Citizen*, Francis takes over domestic duties when Adah starts her library job, but makes it clear that he considers this a strictly temporary arrangement: 'Who is going to look after your children for you?' he asks her after a few weeks.[62] Later, Adah becomes eligible as a single mother for a place at the local authority nursery, but in the meantime is forced to rely on Trudy, a childminder who allows Adah's children to play near contaminated water from the toilet in a rubbish-cluttered yard. In West Africa or the Caribbean, mothers would have called upon extended kin to share the care of children, just as white working-class mothers habitually left their offspring with grandmothers or trusted neighbours. But in Britain, migrants had to build these support networks from scratch. Sometimes they did this with success. Patterson noted the existence of 'cellular' households in Brixton in which 'there is usually one woman who acts as unofficial baby-minder for other women who go out to work', whilst Caribbean women like Doreen Phillips recalled the warm reciprocity amongst fellow migrants.[63] Such arrangements were not, however, available universally and many mothers were constrained in their choice of minder depending on what they could afford and who was available. As one mother recalled, 'It was hard bringing up two children in one room. You get up in the morning, take them down to the childminder at 6 o'clock in the morning. No choice you have to ... It was rough, there was no other way. I had to start at 7. You have to work.'[64]

From the 1960s, child welfare experts expressed mounting concern about the high proportion of minders not registered with local authorities, both white and black, looking after migrant children.[65] Simon Yudkin, a well-known paediatrician, noted the case of 'Mrs M', a migrant from Trinidad, who was minding up to eleven children in her damp, poorly ventilated basement, heated by an unguarded oil stove. The room contained five cots which, Yudkin commented, 'one might think are there to allow the children to rest but are, in fact, mainly used for the purpose of incarcerating the children'.[66] The sociologists Brian and Sonia Jackson described conditions in the homes of the minders they visited in the late 1960s as akin to 'Hogarth's London or Rowntree's York'. In one case, seven children sat at a table 'being fed from the same bowl with the same spoon. Each pair of enormous eyes followed the spoon hungrily. It was like a scene from Dickens.' In another home, rows of carrycots containing small babies were 'parked like packaged battery chickens in a garage', whilst in a third, the children were left by the minder on 'an old white linen sheet in her sort-of-front-hall for twelve hours a day'.[67]

Both Yudkin and the Jacksons acknowledged the difficult material circumstances that many migrant families were in and criticised policymakers for failing to invest in nursery provision and training for childminders. Yet these more nuanced aspects of their research were not always appreciated by the press, which preferred to run alarmist headlines about neglectful working mothers casually dumping their babies upon ill-qualified minders in dilapidated houses. Accidents involving Caribbean children injured by faulty oil stoves received particular attention, reinforcing widely held assumptions about the squalid conditions in which migrants supposedly chose to live. In truth, racial discrimination against black tenants was rife, worse even than that suffered by the Irish, with most finding it impossible to secure good-quality, spacious accommodation at an affordable rent. Investigating the cramped, poorly maintained rooms in which numerous Caribbean families were living in Notting Hill, Pearl Jephcott thought 'that so few smell sour or are even mildly unpleasant is a tribute to the housewives'.[68] Furthermore, and despite frequent claims to the contrary, Caribbean mothers *did* express discontent with minding arrangements and many removed their children in cases where the care received was obviously inadequate. As one woman recalled, 'When my children were younger, I couldn't work really because I find out that the lady that looked after them wasn't looking after them as how I thought she should. So I give up work, but things got very difficult for me.' Another mother left her baby with a neighbour, but 'one day a white lady said to me, "Linda is better off with you." So you could read between the lines. She was the shopkeeper, so I packed it in … It's no good idea to give your children out.'[69]

Yet for women who had come to Britain specifically to earn, staying at home to care for children in a bedsit or two-roomed flat was not an attractive or viable prospect. Some decided instead to leave children with relatives in the Caribbean or West Africa, sending for them once their employment and housing situation was more secure. A 1961 study estimated that around 10,000 children were living with extended family in Jamaica due to the migration of parents to Britain. One case noted was that of Mrs Rocco, 'a small, bright-eyed, dark-skinned woman' who had left her four children with their grandmother in Jamaica while she worked long hours at a dry-cleaner's in London and attended night school every evening. Another case described was that of Mrs Wilson, a mother with six children in the West Indies and a baby in London, who was working as a maid and planned to 'make good' so that she and her husband could bring their two eldest to Britain and enrol them in school.[70]

Sending children to live with extended kin whilst parents searched for work was a long-established Caribbean practice, but observers in Britain, especially those subscribing to psychoanalytic theories of maternal deprivation, looked on it with disapproval. Jephcott noted the case of four-year-old Lallie, living in a bedsit in Notting Hill and soon to travel to the West Indies to make room for a new baby sibling. 'By English norms the distress that lies ahead of poor Lallie, and its possible consequences to her in later life, do not bear thinking about,' Jephcott wrote. 'On the other hand the migrants themselves plainly attach less importance than we do to the risk of separating children from their parents, though they do worry should the children fall ill.'[71] The painful testimonies of some of those left behind suggest that Jephcott's fears were not entirely misplaced.[72] It is striking, nevertheless, how few British commentators recognised the structural similarities with their own nation's time-honoured traditions of child–parent separation. It was a black Caribbean economist, R. B. Davison, who suggested in 1966 that leaving children with grandparents was quite normal for Caribbean mothers, 'just as some people in England leave their children for extended periods in boarding schools'.[73]

Instead, experts in Britain insisted on framing the 'problem' of child-parent separation as peculiar to certain migrant communities. This included the placing of children in private foster homes, a practice closely identified with the 10,000–15,000 West African students temporarily resident in the UK in the 1960s and early 1970s.[74] Amongst these students were significant numbers of married couples, the husbands typically enrolling on medical or legal degrees, the wives registering for nursing or teaching diplomas. Adah and Francis were one such couple in *Second-Class Citizen*, although Adah resists her husband's wish to see their children fostered with an English family. 'No African child lives with his parents,' Francis tells Adah. 'It is not convenient; it is not possible. There is no accommodation for it. Moreover, they won't learn good English. They are much, much better off with an English woman.'[75] Many West African parents shared Francis's view, placing newspaper adverts for foster homes in places like Essex or Kent, easily accessible from London where the majority of migrants were studying. Reliable figures are hard to come by, but one estimate put the number of African children in private foster care at around 5,000 by the late 1960s. Official policy towards these private arrangements was initially tolerant, with ministers eager to see British-educated Africans occupying positions of authority in newly independent ex-colonies. Local authorities, who were forced to step in when fostering arrangements broke down, tended to be less sanguine. One study in Kent discovered cases where children were happy, well cared for and visited frequently by their parents, but documented many more where white foster-mothers were neglectful or racially prejudiced towards their charges, or, conversely, where the English family alienated the child from its parents and cultural heritage in a bid to effect a permanent adoption.[76]

Surveying the full range of West African and Caribbean parenting practices, some experts concluded that the black migrant family was intrinsically dysfunctional, with inadequate mothering at the heart of the problem.[77] Black mothers, it was argued, failed to appreciate or prioritise the emotional needs of their children, putting them at greater risk of developing psychological problems and underperforming at school. Working for pay was not in itself identified as the source of the deficiency. Rather it was the intensity of the black mother's commitment to studying, training or earning, and her willingness to consider 'harmful' childcare solutions in order to realise that commitment, which indicated a lack of proper maternal feeling.[78] Welfare officials were often incredulous when mothers turned up asking for help with childcare to enable them to study or work. A social worker in south London, for instance, described how she had dealt with a young Caribbean mother who wished to put her small children temporarily into foster care so that she could leave her abusive partner, train as a nurse and build a more secure home for her family: 'I tried to make her see that now was the time the children, all under three years old, needed her most and that nursing was not compatible with motherhood.' The social worker flatly refused the request and did not raise alternative possibilities, such as a place in a day nursery or part-time training options, leaving the mother to manage entirely on her own.[79]

Even the black mother who *did* stay at home with her child, or worked only part-time, was found wanting when held up to the standards of intensive and continuous maternal care prescribed by psychoanalysts like Bowlby and Winnicott. West African and Caribbean mothers were criticised by health visitors and GPs for not kissing, cuddling or talking to their babies, for failing to give them stimulating toys and for refusing to take them out regularly for excursions. Shrewder observers noted that migrant families lacked space in their tiny bedsits for boisterous games or large quantities of toys, whilst mothers had to carry prams and shopping bags up and down multiple flights of creaky stairs every time they wanted to go out.[80] Anthropologists, meanwhile, emphasised how African child-rearing traditions prioritised alternative ways of expressing love, such as bathing, grooming and hair care, and how parents saw little value in speaking to infants who could not themselves yet speak.[81] Emecheta's heroine Adah voices her puzzlement over

> this ritual of talking to a baby who either did not understand or in most cases did not know what to make of it. In England they said it was very good to chatter to your child, even when it was a few hours old, so she too started doing it, but would make sure that none of her people were around. They might well think her a witch, talking to something that did not answer back.[82]

Over time, welfare officers in Britain became more sensitive to these kinds of cultural differences, although racial discrimination remained an everyday experience for black migrants trying to access public services. In truth, many of the 'problems' associated with the Caribbean or West African family were symptomatic of poor housing conditions, overstretched social services and inadequate childcare provision, exacerbated by racism in the workplace and rental market. The black mother who worked to give her children a better future and for her own independence and satisfaction was, in many respects, not so very different from the white, British-born mother who embraced the 'dual role' for the very same reasons. The white mother, however, could largely avoid public censure by staying at home until her children were at school, by taking a part-time job and using a grandmother to help with childcare, and by conforming to 'correct' mothering styles. Doing so limited her earning power and perpetuated an unequal division of labour in the home, but it also paraded the racial privilege of whiteness – the privilege of being a first-class, rather than second-class citizen. Towards the end of Emecheta's novel, Adah enjoys a brief period of being 'a real housewife', staying at home with her fourth baby whilst Francis goes out to work to support them:

> She had been reading a great number of women's magazines, and was surprised to read of mothers saying that they were bored just being housewives. She was not that type of woman. There were so many things she planned to do, and she did them. She knitted endless jumpers and cardigans for everybody, including thick, big ones for Francis. It was a way of telling him that that was all she asked of life. Just to be a mother and a wife.[83]

*

The South Asian women who travelled to Britain in ever-growing numbers from the 1960s were widely assumed to be what Adah craved, just mothers and wives. Cultural stereotypes of the meek, demure Indian or Pakistani woman flowed from popular beliefs about the region's religious traditions and 'backward' social practices, although few Britons had any detailed understanding of the complex history of the subcontinent before, during or after Britain's two centuries of colonial rule. It was true that South Asian women were far less likely than black female migrants to take jobs in public transport or the NHS, or to look for the sort of factory jobs attractive to white housewives. Asian *men* were increasingly found in these sectors; in the textile mills of Bradford, Oldham, Rochdale and Blackburn, night shifts might be filled almost entirely by teams of Pakistani men.[84] Their wives, by contrast, were constrained by the requirements of *izzat*, a concept which the British-Asian feminist Amrit Wilson described as 'the sensitive and many-faceted male family identity which can change as the situation demands it – from family pride to honour to self respect, and sometimes to pure male ego'.[85] Zubeida, who came to live in Colindale, north London, in the mid-1960s following an arranged marriage, described how her husband made his expectations of her clear:

> He was very handsome and he was very good to me. But one thing about our Asian men is that they think it a matter of pride that their women must not go out to work. But the problem for us is one of loneliness. At least if a woman goes out to work she can escape that – her mind is occupied, she does not long so much for her home in Pakistan. When I first came my husband did not want me to go out to work. It is true there was a lot of housework but I used to be very lonely. Everyday I used to cry.[86]

Other South Asian women arriving in Britain experienced a similar sense of isolation, deprived of the consoling presence of a large network of female kin. In places like Mirpur in rural Pakistan, women tended to crops or livestock together, visited each other's houses daily and provided mutual support through marriage, childbirth, illness and old age. In Bradford or Tower Hamlets, by contrast, Muslim wives were rarely seen outside, observing purdah as best they could in small terraced houses by sending husbands out for shopping and using back alleys to visit female friends, should they be fortunate enough to have any living close by. One woman remembered travelling once a month by taxi to join her husband on his regular shopping trips to Bradford, but she was forbidden from making any purchases herself:

> I wasn't allowed to go into the shops in those days. It was only men who usually go into the shop, they don't like their women going in front of everybody else, so it is his job. He used to bring everything that I needed. I just had to tell him if I was short of anything.[87]

Not all husbands could afford to keep their wives entirely secluded, especially if they nursed dreams of returning to Pakistan or Bangladesh to buy land or start businesses. Some wives therefore took in home-work or found jobs in Asian-run firms as a culturally acceptable means of earning. Migrant women workers were in high demand in the east London and West Midlands clothing industries, where Asian entrepreneurs competed for major contracts from high-street retailers. Studying Asian clothing firms in the 1970s and early 1980s, the Bengali-born radical economist Swasti Mitter argued that 'access to cheap female labour, normally at extremely low rates of pay, is often the only advantage these employers have over their white counterparts'.[88] She quoted one factory owner who spoke in patronising and paternalistic terms about his workers:

> I see the majority of women working for me as benefiting from my job offer. They are all illiterate and have no skills, hence no British factory will make use of them … I see myself providing a little extra for them; a place of work where they meet women in similar situations as themselves. Their £20 a week will help towards the family income, and we are like a big family here.[89]

This 'family' atmosphere included phone calls from management to husbands or fathers when female employees complained or tried to assert themselves on the shop floor. As Mitter saw it, this kind of patriarchal control negated the independence and self-esteem which wage-earning might have otherwise offered these women. 'The servility, subservience and passivity that the communities expect of wives towards their husband, daughters-in-law towards fathers-in-law in the home,' Mitter noted, 'were reproduced to an important extent in factories.'[90]

Yet South Asian women working for white employers were rarely better off. Sikh and Hindu husbands tended to be more tolerant than Muslim men about wives taking jobs outside the home, although wage packets usually had to be handed over and the type of work available for women without language skills or recognised qualifications was typically unskilled and poorly paid. A long article in the feminist periodical *Spare Rib* described the case of Mrs A., a Punjabi Sikh living in two rooms in a terraced house in Southall, west London, with her husband and two sons. Mrs A. was employed as a cleaner at Heathrow airport, rising at 4 a.m. to catch her bus and working an eight-hour day with only one twenty-minute break. Unlike the white women who cleaned the toilets, Mrs A. was not allowed to sit down at quiet moments during her shift. When asked about her dreams for the future, Mrs A. simply replied, 'I'd like to work in the lavatory, at least I can sit down.'[91] Mrs T. was in a similar situation, getting up at 4.30 a.m. to clean a transport cafe on the M4 motorway for 42p an hour. Her husband, who worked six days a week in a local factory, took their four-year-old son to his childminder and Mrs T. would collect him on her way home, a journey involving a two-mile walk to the bus stop because the cafe only provided transport for employees early in the morning. Catching the bus, picking up her son and getting back to their cramped bedsit took £3 out of Mrs T.'s £11 weekly wages. Neither woman belonged to a trade union, Mrs T. because none existed at her workplace, and Mrs A. because of difficulties with language.

Over time, the position of South Asian wives and mothers did slowly improve. Contrary to prevailing stereotypes, most women were keen to learn English in order to get better jobs and to avoid having to rely on husbands or children to translate when out shopping or dealing with welfare officials. Employers, local authorities, adult education colleges and community projects laid on special classes, although some wives preferred to learn from already fluent husbands, school-aged children or friends. Younger women generally found it easier to adapt, such as Harbhanan, a Punjabi from East Africa who moved to London in 1963 aged fourteen. At first she stayed at home to help her mother, but after a few years started working as a machinist at Marks & Spencer, where her fiancé, who had migrated from India, was also employed. With his help, Harbhanan learned to speak English and remained at Marks & Spencer for twelve years after marriage, leaving the children in the care of her mother-in-law, who lived with the family.[92]

By the later 1970s, South Asian women were becoming increasingly visible in trade union activism and industrial action, including the high-profile dispute at the Grunwick film-processing plant in north-west London in 1976. In August of that year, Jayaben Desai, a married mother of two in her forties, led the walk-out of more than a hundred female workers, who were angered by the rigid discipline and derogatory treatment they received at the hands of the management. Like Desai, most of the striking women were from middle-class Hindu families in East Africa, where they had enjoyed relatively privileged lives before the introduction of 'Africanisation' policies following the end of British colonial rule.[93] Such women were unwilling to allow white, middle-aged men to order them around, or tell them when they could or could not go to the toilet. As Desai famously told the plant manager, Malcolm Alden: 'What you are running is not a factory, it is a zoo. But in a zoo there are many types of animals. Some are monkeys who dance on your fingertips. Others are lions who can bite your head off. We are those lions, Mr Manager.'[94] Although the strike ultimately failed, the widely publicised images of sari-wearing protesters on picket lines, together with Desai's defiant leadership, shook the assumptions which many white Britons held about the 'passive' or 'docile' South Asian woman.

*

The working wives and mothers of Britain's Caribbean, West African and South Asian migrant communities shared much common ground with their white counterparts in the post-war decades. The expectation that women bore primary responsibility for childcare and housework was entrenched in migrant and host populations alike, limiting women's access to well-paid jobs or satisfying careers. The pressures on migrant women to earn were typically greater, but their motivations for seeking work were not so very far apart. Migrant mothers wished to improve their family's standard of living, give their children the best possible start in life, and find satisfaction and interest for themselves through paid employment. Insofar as black and Asian women's voices can be heard in the historical record, they often sounded a familiar note. One Caribbean mother interviewed in Birmingham in the late 1970s recalled the boredom she felt when not working: 'I used to clean the house over and over again, you know, everything was spotless and I used to do all myself up for him coming home from work in the evening and I get sick of it.' An Asian home-worker told the same researcher of how dearly she desired an outside job: 'At home you're just by yourself and you're stuck. Outside you meet more people. You enjoy yourself more. You go out and you get fresh air and you meet so many people, you know, and you enjoy it.' Her non-working neighbour took the same view: 'all I know is that I want to work – just go out and do something, anything so long as you're out of the house. You get so bored, homesick, doing the same job all the time.'[95]

Yet despite these areas of shared experience, both expert and popular opinion towards Commonwealth migrants dwelt on difference, looking upon these newcomers as unwelcome strangers rather than ordinary men and women trying to make better lives for themselves and their families. The more optimistic commentators suggested that racial prejudice resulted from ignorance and would ease over time, helped by friendly adjustments made on both sides. Yet older forms of racial thinking, including hierarchical ideas about 'inferior' and 'superior' races, lingered on in debates over population and immigration, as did public squeamishness over interracial contact: according to a 1958 Gallup poll, 70 per cent of Britons disapproved of mixed marriages.[96] This surfaced in the racist behaviour of some childminders, foster-mothers and health professionals. Caribbean mothers often worried that minders were leaving their children's nappies unchanged throughout the day, a suspicion confirmed by Brian and Sonia Jackson's investigations. One woman openly admitted her visceral disgust for this part of the job: 'It's these black bottoms, I can't stand. I mean, with shit on ... I can manage it all right with my own. Funny, somehow it's only smelly black bottoms. They fair make me sick.'[97] A study of Caribbean families in Paddington in the mid-1960s interviewed two local GPs who 'obviously had personal difficulties in dealing with coloured people'. One described the 'Negro odour' as disturbing to his white patients whilst the other said 'the darker the colour the deeper the neurosis'.[98]

These doctors formed an extreme minority, with most of their colleagues showing some empathy for their Caribbean patients, if mixed with condescension. Many white Britons struggled with the idea that black or Asian people could be their equals, especially the generations who had grown up in a world in which the white man's dominion over subject races was considered natural and just. These highly charged psychic legacies of empire help to explain why white Europeans could be regarded as more 'suitable' migrants, despite their status as foreign nationals.[99] Most Commonwealth migrant memoirs contain stories of racist encounters, from discriminatory treatment by employers or landlords to physical violence on the street. When Sheela Banerjee's mother and two aunts arrived in Britain in 1968, the effects of Enoch Powell's inflammatory 'Rivers of Blood' speech were palpable every time they stepped outside their front doors. 'I felt afraid whenever I saw the young men, in large boots, with their heads shaved,' Banerjee's mother recalled, remembering how a Bengali friend was dragged from a car and punched, whilst her sisters were spat at by passengers from a passing bus.[100]

Black and Asian migrants organised to protect their communities and to demand equal treatment from police, employers and welfare officials, with mothers often in the frontline of these movements. They joined trade unions and fought exploitation in the workplace, ran supplementary schools to expose how mainstream education

failed their children, and created bodies like Southall Sisters and the
Organisation for Women of Asian and African Descent (OWAAD)
to expose how sexism and racism were deeply interlinked.[101] As
a result, subsequent generations of black and minority ethnic
mothers found it a little easier to be 'ordinary' as they went about
their working and family lives, although racial discrimination and
injustice would remain a central part of their experience well into
the twenty-first century.

PART FOUR

Doing the Impossible, 1971 to the Present

11

Superwomen

'Three political statements point the way to the liberation of housewives,' wrote the feminist Ann Oakley in 1974. 'The housewife role must be abolished. The family must be abolished. Gender roles must be abolished.' Her words came at an eventful time for British women: six years after the famous equal pay strike by machinists at Ford's in Dagenham, five years after the first national Women's Liberation Conference in Oxford, and just a year before Parliament would pass legislation outlawing sexual discrimination in the workplace.

The publication of Oakley's fiery tome, simply entitled *Housewife*, signalled the coming of age of a new generation of feminists who were determined to expose and dismantle the patriarchal order. Society, she argued, conditioned women to identify as housewives, thus condemning them to a life of psychological and physical isolation. Housework was 'directly opposed to the possibility of human self-actualization' and any woman who claimed to enjoy it was suffering from false consciousness. 'It is not merely what a woman wants that is at issue,' Oakley insisted, 'but what she is induced to want, and what she is prevented – by social attitudes – from believing she can have, or be.' To embrace housewifery was 'a form of antifeminism', a dangerous 'rationalization of an inferior status'. Above all, mothers must stop teaching their daughters to do housework. 'A sense of *excitement* must be communicated about the areas of self-realization which lie beyond the kitchen door.'[1]

A year later, the journalist Shirley Conran published her bestselling *Superwoman: Every Woman's Book of Household Management*. Where Oakley's polemic simmered with barely concealed rage, *Superwoman's* register was humorous and practical, sharing tips on everything from buying in bulk for the freezer to getting stubborn stains out of curtains. Yet in seeking to remove housework from the altar of woman's destiny, Conran occupied common ground with Oakley. 'The purpose of this book,' she told readers, 'is to help you do the work you don't like as fast as possible, leaving time for the work you enjoy.' Labour-saving gizmos, quick fixes and delegating tasks to others were nothing to be ashamed of in Conran's philosophy. Imperfection was unavoidable and to be embraced. Disregard what you're *supposed* to do, she advised breezily, consider what you *can* avoid doing, and then do everything else as quickly as possible. Women, Conran argued, must step off the treadmill of housework and remember this simple motto: 'Life is too short to stuff a mushroom.'[2]

For all their differences of genre and tone, *Housewife* and *Superwoman* were products of the same historical moment. By the mid-1970s, women born after the Second World War had reached adulthood and were beneficiaries of the NHS, the 1944 Education Act and, for a growing minority, the expansion of higher education. Marriage remained the most popular setting in which to start a family, but women were now delaying this life event until their later twenties, often following a period of cohabiting with boyfriends or fiancés.[3] Wage-earning after marriage and maternity was more common than ever, with an especially striking rise in the employment of mothers with under-fives. In 1976, about a quarter of women with preschool-aged children were working, more than double the figure fifteen years earlier.[4] This included a growing number returning to paid work between having babies instead of taking an extended break in line with the 1950s dual-role model. By the end of the decade, one in four mothers re-entered the labour market within a year of giving birth, and one in six within six months, in some cases assisted by new maternity laws compelling employers to hold jobs open for their pregnant employees.[5]

These rising participation rates were associated with a dramatic expansion of part-time work, which now accounted for over two-fifths of all female employment and remained closely associated with mothers: nearly 70 per cent of all wage-earning mothers were employed on a part-time basis by 1977.[6]

This growing presence of mothers in the workplace was interpreted by some as evidence of a new spirit of confidence and self-assertion amongst women. Men still dominated at the top of business, industry and the professions, but their monopoly on power looked increasingly unsteady. Feminists refused to accept that pay differentials, blocked promotion routes and discrimination against women were 'natural' or defensible features of a labour market which privileged male wages and careers. The official ideology of equal opportunities enshrined in the Equal Pay Act (1970) and the Sex Discrimination Act (1975) was in this respect both cause and consequence of a wider shifting mood. If mothers in the 1950s had talked more freely about their desire for paid work, their 1970s counterparts began to add the language of rights to the mix. Women not only 'needed' paid work for their self-esteem and self-respect, they were entitled to it.

Yet feminism was not the only driver of rising maternal employment rates across the decade. Within the expanding vocabulary around women's work, the old association between wage-earning by mothers and economic pressure on families regained some of its former prominence. High inflation, the return of mass male unemployment and growing rates of marital breakdown meant that more mothers were stepping into the breadwinner's shoes. One study estimated in 1971 that around 2 million women were the chief earners for their households.[7] Under these conditions, part-time employment carried very different meanings from the sociable little jobs which affluent housewives had taken up in the 1950s. Many private employers treated their part-time workforce in ways reminiscent of the late-Victorian sweated industries, including a resurgence in the use of home-workers on pitifully low wages. Even mothers with educational qualifications or professional training employed in the more secure public sector found that going part-time or seeking 'flexible' hours usually translated into a worse job with inferior pay.

On top of all this was the problem named in books like *Housewife* and *Superwoman*. Too many women were still caught in the emotional snares of domesticity, believing themselves uniquely responsible for making the home a warm and inviting place for husbands and children. Feminism was a powerful cultural force in the 1970s, but its influence was never universal. Without banishing the myth of womanly duty, and without forcing men to take their equal share in the family and household roles, wage-earning would continue to saddle mothers with a double burden rather than offer real liberation.

*

Many of those drawn to the women's movement in the 1970s had lived this myth from the inside. By her mid-twenties, Ann Oakley had acquired a husband, two children and a house in Chiswick which she kept clean 'in the classic mould of the houseproud housewife with severe obsessional tendencies'. Her first baby was born in 1967 and the second less than a year later, an experience which plunged her into a deep state of depression. Oakley felt 'exhausted and incapable', and her life seemed devoid of meaning. 'What was it all for? How could I go on?' she asked herself, getting through the day with the help of five or six tablets of Valium. Oakley felt her economic dependence keenly, with 'its connotation of secondariness, of belonging to someone else and not to myself'. These intense years of motherhood when she should have felt fully alive 'spelled instead a kind of death'.[8] Yet her misery eventually turned to clarity, and in 1969 Oakley started a sociology PhD, studying women's attitudes to housework. Over the next four and a half years, she worked evenings, weekends and during snatches of time when her husband was at home, completing the manuscript which would become *Housewife*. In a twist on authorial tradition, in the preface Oakley thanked her family 'for the experience of my own oppression as a housewife'. Without it, she observed, 'I would never have wanted to write the book in the first place'.

In some respects, Oakley was following a path well-trodden by Judith Hubback in the 1950s and Hannah Gavron in the 1960s, who had similarly investigated other women's conflicts as a means of better understanding their own situation. Gavron never found a resolution to hers, committing suicide only weeks after finishing the manuscript of *The Captive Wife*, which was published posthumously in 1966 and read widely within the nascent women's movement.[9] Yet the critiques of domesticity produced by feminists in the 1970s departed from these post-war precedents in important ways. Their tone was less measured, the descriptions less restrained, and the prescribed solutions less optimistically reformist. Giving voice to women's personal experiences and intimate feelings was a means of laying bare their collective oppression. It would reveal how patriarchy was everywhere – inside the family, inside the home, even inside the head. Many of the leading voices of Women's Liberation in Britain were formed politically by the revolutionary milieu of the 1960s and viewed women's unwaged work as a crucial piece in the puzzle of how capitalism reproduced itself. Saying that women were born to look after homes and families was not merely perpetuating a lazy stereotype. Such beliefs about sexual difference were key to the historical subordination of one half of the human race.[10]

Encouraging women to describe their ambivalence formed a key part of the fight-back. The feminist academic Dorothy Hobson interviewed young mothers in Birmingham in the mid-1970s, carefully noting their nervous laughter, tense silences, stray thoughts and barely articulated feelings. The sense of isolation was overwhelming, with most of her sample spending every day alone with children, rarely going out with spouses or meeting up with friends. One mother told Hobson that she had lost touch with old workmates, knew none of her neighbours and now relied on the radio and TV as her 'only connection ... with the outside world'. These women recognised that their husbands enjoyed a privileged status, experiencing the home as a place of relaxation and freedom rather than endless unpaid labour, but they saw little hope that this would ever change. When men clock off at work, one mother commented, 'what they do then it's up to them. I mean if they don't want to help the wife, I mean nobody can force them to and they can just sit down all night if they want to and do what they like.' This spirit of defeat extended to her own compulsive attachment to cleaning, a task which could hardly be contained to the hours between nine and five. If her child spilt sugar on the floor before bedtime, the mother commented, she could not wait until the morning to clear it up. 'Well, I can't sit and look at it, it would worry me to death all night ... I wouldn't be able to relax all night till I'd done it.'[11]

Helpful husbands who might lend a hand with the washing-up were not the answer to these women's problems. Liberation was what was required, and not only from housework but from the unexamined assumption that women bore primary responsibility for the care of young children. Feminists railed against theories of maternal attachment, which had done more, as one book put it, 'to keep mothers at home than any chauvinist husband'.[12] Ann Oakley thought that the ideal of boundless mother-love popularised by experts like John Bowlby reinforced fathers' exclusion from care-giving and bred feelings of inadequacy in women.[13] Interviewing young suburban wives in London, the researcher Susannah Ginsberg discovered that many punished themselves for not feeling 'the correct emotions' towards their children. They interpreted their irritation and boredom when at home all day as proof that they had failed as mothers.[14] The pseudoscience lending authority to such notions was deplorable, argued sociologist Patricia Morgan in her hard-hitting critique of Bowlby's maternal deprivation theory. His ideas had been latched onto by men in power because they endorsed a traditional role for women as 'the tender Madonna shielding the delicate impressionable young from the sordid world in the haven of each home'.[15]

Feminists might have overstated the particular influence of Bowlby, but they found ample evidence of women struggling under the pressure to be a 'good' mother. Jean, a former factory worker at home with two preschool children, told Ginsberg:

I don't feel I should go to work ... it's a matter of conscience really. In one way you think, well I could do with going out to work, not just for money, for my mind's sake. It drives me up the wall sometimes when I'm shut in ... then again I think I've had them, they're <u>mine</u> and <u>I</u> should look after them.[16]

Another interviewee regretted taking a job, which she felt was tantamount to an admission of defeat in her role as a mother: 'because I've gone out to work I feel as though I'm giving up [on] the problems of coping with two young children.'[17] Such conflicts had been experienced by working mothers before the 1970s, but maternal 'guilt' had never been articulated so openly and extensively, spilling out of feminist publications and consciousness-raising groups into the mainstream women's media. 'Why does a working mum feel guilty?' asked Claire Rayner, a mother of three who had worked continuously since marriage, to readers of *Woman's Own* in 1970.[18] Patricia Keiran included a lengthy reflection on this question in her popular book, *How Working Mothers Manage*:

> It's all very well for experts to tell us how the work force of this country would crumble without us; that there are still positions crying out to be filled, you still feel guilty when you leave the house in the morning, instead of waving the family off. Often it's irrational; even if no one is complaining, you still feel guilty. You feel you ought to be there.[19]

Shirley Conran told readers of *Superwoman* that guilt was impossible to avoid altogether. 'You have been conditioned to feel guilty. Accept it.' The trick for the working mother was how to keep her guilt under control, remembering that children could be equally damaged by 'smother-love' and end up resenting a mother who made 'gargantuan sacrifices' for her family.[20] These kinds of questions, about whether working mothers helped or harmed their children, would be revisited endlessly in women's magazines, newspapers and popular books for the rest of the twentieth century and well into the twenty-first.

For feminists of the 1970s, the dual-role solution favoured by their post-war predecessors was no solution at all. Alva Myrdal and

Viola Klein had argued in *Women's Two Roles* that portioning life into distinct phases – of work, home-making and work again – removed the dilemma of choice: women could have family *and* meaningful employment, if not at the same time. Yet viewed through the lens of radical sexual politics two decades later, this prescription seemed woolly and insipid. It presented women with a false image which was ideologically tooled, as one feminist put it, to 'mesh their new role in the workforce with their continuing responsibilities as mothers and housewives'.[21] Far from enjoying the best of both worlds, the dual role lumped women with housework and childcare in their prime of life and released them middle-aged into a labour market in which only the least interesting and lowest-paid jobs were on offer. The growth in married women's employment, Oakley argued, had left the old sexual divisions essentially untouched:

> In terms of the work they do, in terms of the patterns of their work-careers, in terms of the financial benefits which accrue to them as a result of work, the roles of men and women in the world of work remain differentiated. Women's defining role is a domestic one.[22]

This realisation inspired some feminists to take up the cause of Wages for Housework, protesting against how women's domestic labour was valued in advanced capitalist societies. The visionary aims of the campaign, which included a string of strike actions involving thousands of women withdrawing their labour from the home, won followers across the US, Australia and Western Europe. But it also attracted critics within the women's movement, who argued that any system of payment for housework would only entrench existing sexual divisions.[23] Wages for Housework was also problematic because it seemed to deny the emancipatory potential of paid work, a key battlefront for feminists of all ideological stripes in the 1970s. Even those hoping to see capitalism swept away recognised that waged labour offered women *some* degree of economic independence and created a basis for collective action.

'Locked away at home,' the sociologist Anna Pollert argued, 'women, however radical, end up in a consciousness that is "imprisoned" ... With women at work there *is* the possibility to develop such an alternative.'[24]

*

The struggle for women's workplace rights had been sustained by alliances of women MPs, trade unionists and professional bodies throughout the post-war decades, but the pace quickened dramatically from the late 1960s. The fight for equal pay in private industry was finally won in 1970 through a combination of organised pressure from below and strategic considerations in government, including Britain's impending entry to the European Common Market, whose member states were bound by the equal-pay clause in its founding Treaty of Rome.[25] European legal norms provided helpful leverage for advocates of further legislative action, including the two bills which eventually passed into law in 1975 as the Sex Discrimination Act (SDA) and the Employment Protection Act (EPA). As a result of these reforms, basic wage rates improved and equal pay provisions were added to collective wage agreements in unionised industries, leading to a narrowing of the gender pay gap from around 50 per cent to 40 per cent by April 1975.[26] Discrimination against married or pregnant women was made unlawful, whilst female employees with two years of full-time service (or five years part-time) became eligible for fourteen weeks of statutory maternity pay, plus the right to reinstatement for up to twenty-nine weeks after the birth of their baby.[27]

Many feminists picked holes in the legislation, pointing to employers who evaded the Equal Pay Act by quietly re-grading jobs, and to the cautiousness of industrial tribunal and county court rulings on sex discrimination cases.[28] Nonetheless, enshrining the principle of sex equality in law had a wider symbolic importance and provided a basis for further reform, although these were admittedly slow to materialise. The Equal Pay Act was amended in 1983 to cover work of 'equal value', making it somewhat easier for those in jobs typically performed by women to bring claims.

It took another ten years before statutory maternity leave was extended, and another decade after that for men to win two weeks' paid paternity leave, a demand first issued by the National Council for Civil Liberties in the mid-1970s.[29]

Women's access to training improved more rapidly over the course of the decade. The Sex Discrimination Act forced employers to open up male-only programmes to both sexes, whilst increased government funding flowed into initiatives targeting the older female returner. New Opportunities for Women (NOW) were short courses aimed at building women's confidence and skills for professional employment, whilst Wider Opportunities for Women (WOW) provided placements for women in a variety of manual and semi-skilled jobs.[30] These schemes tended to push participants towards 'traditional' areas of employment – education, clerical work, typing, catering – but they could provide a crucial boost for women trying to kick-start careers. One Mass Observer who had qualified as a nurse before marriage described how she applied to multiple training schemes in the late 1970s following ten years of full-time motherhood. 'Eureka!' she wrote, 'I was offered a place on all three courses, very good for the morale.' She opted for health visiting and secured employment immediately after completing her qualification, eventually landing a well-paid policy-level job at the Ministry of Health in London.[31] Growing State spending on public services created further opportunities for women to train for interesting and well-paid jobs in these kinds of welfare professions. Some of them experienced considerable social mobility as a result.[32]

Women's position advanced more generally in the professional workplace, albeit only gradually. New bodies sprang up pushing for equality across a range of fields: Women in Publishing, Women in Media, Women in Banking and Finance, Women in Medicine, Women in Dentistry, Women in the Civil Service, Women in Management and the Company of Women in Architecture were all founded between 1969 and 1985.[33] Women's share of these occupations inched up over the same period, in most cases from a stubbornly low base. By 1980, nearly a quarter of practising doctors and 17 per cent of dentists were female, whilst women comprised

27 per cent of those in the training grades of the senior Civil Service and 21 per cent of newly qualified accountants.[34] The proportion of female solicitors more than doubled from the late 1960s, reaching over 7 per cent by 1977, just below the 8 per cent figure for women barristers.[35] This changing picture reflected a narrowing gender gap in higher education, with overall participation rates now hovering around 14 per cent of the population, and women's share of undergraduate places rising to around a third. The new polytechnics created by Harold Wilson's Labour government had a major hand in this, particularly for older women returning to education, but women's representation at the ancient universities of Oxford and Cambridge also improved as a string of all-male colleges went mixed.[36] Teaching was still a common destination for the female graduate but less markedly so than previously, a result of lower birth rates, cuts to teacher-training budgets and the opening up of opportunities elsewhere under the influence of the Sex Discrimination Act.[37] Female students increasingly expressed indignation at sex-specific careers advice or adverts for graduate-entry schemes which invited men only to apply.[38]

Added to this, the dual-career family was no longer the curiosity it once was. Nearly 40 per cent of marriages now contained two earners, a trend which Rhona and Robert Rapoport, revisiting their pet subject in the late 1970s, attributed in large part to women's changing aspirations. 'Increasingly, women have a work-role as part of their self-conception,' they argued. 'Whatever part economic motives may play in taking and sustaining a job, women expect and find other satisfactions too.'[39] This claim found support in the growing tendency for professionally qualified women to delay childbirth and thereafter avoid extended breaks from work. The authors of a 1980 study on women in the professions found that two-thirds of accountants were back at work within two years, whilst dentists rarely took off longer than a year and in most cases were practising again within six months. There were major advantages to this pattern, the authors suggested: 'Women who become mothers at thirty years of age or more have had an opportunity to establish themselves in their career. They will have reaped benefits in terms of training, experience and promotion which puts them in a good competitive position.'[40] A survey of women's careers at the BBC revealed a similar pattern, with those in senior management more likely to have babies in their thirties and to take statutory maternity leave before resuming highly valued careers.[41]

For some expert commentators observing these developments, the evidence seemed to point to ever greater egalitarianism between the sexes. In their 1973 book, *The Symmetrical Family*, the sociologists Michael Young and Peter Willmott argued that society was evolving steadily towards a convergence in men and women's roles, driven by new technologies at home and work and by the ideology of feminism, which they described as a 'great agent of change'.[42] As women's educational attainment further improved and as a wider range of well-paid and interesting employment opportunities came within their grasp, fewer wives, they predicted, would settle either for full-time domesticity or housework plus a little job. Addressing a conference on recent trends in women's employment in 1976, the researchers Peter Moss and Nickie Fonda agreed that the principle of equality was destabilising the existing gender order. 'The whole process of ideological and attitudinal change, about the role and position of women in the home and society,' they argued, 'may be expected to continue and become increasingly influential in shaping women's expectations, aspirations and values.'[43]

*

Optimism like that shown by Peter Moss and Nickie Fonda rested on the belief that a pioneering minority of dual-career couples pointed the way to the future of the majority. Yet in truth, the path to equality was strewn with obstacles, not least the small matter of childcare. The highest earning professional mothers, like elite mothers before them, could generally pay for nannies to look after their children while they worked (although they continued to grumble over the hit which this outlay made on their salaries). Interviewed shortly after becoming Secretary of State for Education in autumn 1970, Margaret Thatcher explained how, when her twins were young, she 'always had a good nanny. Any working mother *must* have competent and reliable domestic help, and be prepared for emergencies.'[44] The barrister Barbara Mills agreed: 'You must have a nanny who can change a wheel and mend a washing machine, someone who has practical brains.' She dismissed one girl after three weeks 'because she kept saying, "That's not my job." It's impractical to have people around who say, "That's not my job."'[45] A survey of female doctors found that around a quarter used nannies, reflecting the long hours that were habitual in hospital medicine.[46] Beulah Bewley, a distinguished epidemiologist with five children, bought a seven-bedroomed house in the 1970s and engaged a daily cleaner for three hours every morning and another domestic help for the afternoons: 'she would be there when the children came home from school, a sort of surrogate granny who was there to see they had something to eat and to talk to them.'[47]

These expensive solutions were off limits for most mothers, who turned instead to childminders or informal care in the family, often reducing their hours and commuting time or working at home. One 1980 study estimated that 15–20 per cent of wage-earning mothers regularly took their children with them to work instead of paying for care.[48] A Mass Observer remembered going on home visits with her chiropodist mother during the school holidays, sitting in a locked car with her three-year-old sister and a stash of sweets and comics. Sometimes they spent the day with their father, also a chiropodist, playing games and reading books in the back office, 'interspersed with chatting to the beautician who shared the premises and to the man who ran the wood yard next door and visiting the newsagents for more sweets and comics'.[49]

The multi-generational structure of many South Asian households meant that older female kin, where present, were often available for regular childminding duties, enabling their adult daughters or daughters-in-law to go out to work. A supervisor interviewed at the General Electric Company in Coventry in the late 1970s attributed the high rate of return after maternity leave amongst her South Asian workers to this factor.[50] Amongst the general population, however, grandmothers were more likely than ever before to be employed themselves – by 1984, well over half of all women in their fifties were working – or enjoying peaceful retirements away from extended family.[51] Elderly parents eventually became care-receivers rather than care-givers, presenting a burden which adult daughters had dutifully shouldered for decades but now felt more keenly as opportunities for career progression and retraining improved. One professional working mother surveyed in the late 1970s noted how she had gradually increased her hours as her sons grew up, but 'I am now a little alarmed to find that an aged mother is the next item on my life-and-work see-sawing agenda'.[52]

High-quality and affordable nursery provision was in as short supply as it ever had been. The number of places in local authority nurseries dropped in the early 1970s, standing at around 30,000 by 1977, equivalent to one place for every thirty preschoolers. Nursery schools expanded modestly, but most of the 200,000 children in attendance had part-time places and stayed for an average of two or three hours a day, which had limited value for the working mother.[53] Provision varied between local authorities, tending to be higher in inner cities or areas with long histories of married women's work, although pressure on budgets gave little scope for ambitious spending on preschool care. Islington Borough Council provided one place for every sixteen children under five; in Waltham Forest there was a place for one in every fifty-three. In Oxfordshire, by contrast, only three council nurseries were in operation, offering ninety-five places to a preschool population of around 40,000.[54] It was still difficult to secure a nursery place without pleading some special circumstances. As one matron in Hackney put it: 'you've got to have a real problem to get your child a place – unmarried, divorced, a battered or handicapped child, a handicapped parent or particularly bad housing conditions. If you can't produce that sort of evidence you haven't a hope.'[55] Even mothers who could prove such hardship were often turned down. In 1974, there were 12,000 'priority cases' languishing on local authority waiting lists.[56]

Advocates of public investment in preschool care were vocal about these failings and some were prepared, at last, to argue that working mothers deserved support in their own right, regardless of whether they demonstrated special need. In *Nurseries Now*, a group of prominent childcare experts argued that the intolerable strain on mothers looking after young children single-handed formed the basic case for better State provision. Nurseries, they claimed, had an essential part to play in advancing gender equality and giving women real choice in how to organise their lives: 'In a society which is committed by legislation to ending sex discrimination and promoting equal opportunities, the provision of comprehensive nursery services should be a fundamental social priority.'[57] This echoed the position adopted by the Equal Opportunities Commission, the body set up to enforce the Sex Discrimination Act, and a growing number of forward-looking local authorities, trade unionists and progressively minded academics.[58] The psychologist Jack Tizard, who created the Thomas Coram Research Unit in 1973 as a pioneering research centre on children and the family, urged government to listen to what mothers said they wanted instead of clinging to bogus claims about the harmful effects of nursery care. 'Since very many parents who have the welfare of their children very much at heart would make use of day care if they could,' Tizard wrote, 'the onus is on those who think it would be wrong to do so to support their views with evidence. This they have so far failed to do, relying instead on doctrine and false analogy.'[59] Feminists gave even higher priority to women's needs when debating childcare, pressurising local authorities or running their own nurseries, like the childcare centre opened at 123 Dartmouth Park Hill in Highgate in 1972. Its founders explained their rationale:

> Many mothers would like to work, others must for financial reasons – all are faced with the practical burden of arranging suitable child-care. All are faced with the more intolerable emotional burden of guilt placed on them by a society which has built a myth around motherhood and dumped it on all women regardless of their individuality.[60]

Slowly, childcare was becoming a feminist issue.

These views crept into central government thinking in the late 1970s through the work of the Central Policy Review Staff (CPRS), a small, recently established unit with a remit to promote strategic thinking across Whitehall. In 1978, the team published a major report on services for children of working mothers, commissioned by the Labour government as part of its wider review of the social policy landscape. The CPRS report took for granted that significant numbers of women with under-fives went out to work and would continue to do so, suggesting that government needed to 'take a fundamental look' at how it supported these families. 'Hitherto,' it noted, 'the (convenient) assumption has been that the parents, and in particular the mother, can normally cope unaided with a child's first 5 years of life with a certain amount of fairly elementary help on health and development, together with some part-time nursery education for children over three'.[61] This assumption was no longer valid. Serious investment was now required in preschool day-care and nursery education, as well as in after-school and holiday care for older children. The whole system should be better coordinated and 'aimed more at the needs of the working mother'.[62] Kate Jenkins, one of the civil servants behind the report, advised her boss to present it to ministers not as 'a study of the rights or wrongs of working mothers with young children nor of the virtues or otherwise of nursery education or day nurseries', but as a pragmatic response to shifting social norms, 'a study of the practicalities of making arrangements for the children involved in the most effective way possible with particular emphasis on the need for coordination and the most effective use of all available resources'.[63]

The CPRS's ambitious recommendations failed to win ministerial backing at a time of heavy retrenchment in government spending, but it is doubtful that the political will to implement them existed in Whitehall in any case. Labour's home secretary, Merlyn Rees, advised caution when he wrote to the prime minister in July 1978. 'A major switch of resources,' he noted, 'would in any event raise important questions of principle about the extent to which the Government ought to finance programmes designed to make it easier for women to go out to work.' This was a subject which Rees thought should be discussed 'in the context of family policy generally'.[64] Thus, despite growing pressure from childcare campaigners and feminists, there was still little official appetite for funding preschool services explicitly as an aid to working mothers. Government policy remained wedded to low-cost solutions, such as encouraging an expansion of childminding, and largely ignored the growing evidence that parents wanted day nurseries and universal, full-time nursery education.[65]

Employers hardly rushed to fill the gap. As in previous decades, workplace crèches tended to be available only where recruiting full-time female staff posed a serious operational problem. A clothing factory in Newry in Northern Ireland, for instance, ran a subsidised nursery for its machinists as a result of acute labour shortages in the early 1970s. 'Girls get married and leave and there is a lot of competition for women workers round here,' the firm's director remarked. 'We were trying to buy back our trained labour. We wrote to the girls who had left, told them about the nursery and invited them back.'[66] Few employers envisaged nurseries as a long-term investment in women's careers or a means of signalling a wider commitment to equal opportunities. The Inland Revenue established a crèche at its Cardiff offices in July 1973 but closed it three years later and shelved plans for another nursery in Croydon.[67] A BBC nursery at Pebble Mill Studios in Birmingham had an even shorter lifespan, opening for just ten months from October 1974. A study of women in senior management at the corporation noted widespread dismay at the decision to close it and a strong feeling that 'a forward-thinking employer with positive policies for the welfare of its staff would be able to see the increasing need for nursery provision and act on that need'.[68] In 1978, a group of female employees took matters into their own hands and started campaigning internally for a crèche at the BBC's headquarters in west London, a demand that was finally granted in 1990.[69]

Voluntary self-help was another option for parents, as exemplified in the Pre-School Playgroup Association, an organisation founded in 1961 by middle-class mothers frustrated by the shortage of nursery schools for their children. Membership grew dramatically in the 1970s, although the short sessions meant that playgroups could only form one part of any childcare solution for the working mother.[70] Some women, however, found convenient part-time employment actually running the playgroups. One Mass Observer who had worked as a nursery nurse before marriage explained that organising the playgroup in her village was the only job she could realistically take on, as she had a young son and no car. Her husband thought she was devoting too much time to the playgroup in exchange for a very low wage, but she used her skills later on to get more secure work in a university crèche: 'I was much better off and learned to drive!'[71] Other Women's Liberation groups followed the example set by the Dartmouth Park Hill nursery and set up their own childcare centres, supported in many cases by grants from sympathetic local authorities.[72]

In the absence of comprehensive, well-funded nursery services, finding reliable childcare was a constant worry for mothers in the 1970s. Reflecting on the complex patchwork of care which characterised her childhood, the chiropodist's daughter quoted earlier admitted that she had not 'quite appreciated the scope of support or the logistics involved in the day-to-day, week-by-week organisation of this'. She and her sister were looked after by neighbours and au pairs, attended playgroups, caught lifts to school with friends and spent time with 'a succession of 5 long-haired and smiling girls in their late teens who were paid to keep us entertained in school holidays and who freed up my parents for evenings out'. Her mother was mostly responsible for orchestrating these arrangements, as well as acting as business manager for her husband's practice and dealing with all money matters, shopping and housework.[73] A small number of men were prompted by the feminist politics of the era to reassess their less than equal contributions in the home, but there was little evidence of any general shift in the division of domestic labour between husbands and wives.[74] Even amongst highly paid dual-career couples who outsourced these tasks to others, the burden of finding and managing domestic help typically fell to women. The journalist Drusilla Beyfus recalled how she spent 'endless time worrying about the nanny's health and happiness', and went to great lengths to ensure domestic harmony during her absences for work. On the eve of one business trip, Beyfus wrote '*twelve* closely typed pages of instructions such as "No butter on the potatoes for Jason" '.[75] Shirley Conran found the annual churn of arriving and departing au pairs too much of a strain and decided to teach her children to cook instead, reasoning 'I don't change the children every year'. The money saved enabled Conran to buy a fridge-freezer and a dishwasher, neither of which, she further observed, were 'likely to have an affair with my husband'.[76]

*

Stress became the companion to guilt for the working mother of 1970s Britain. The double burden of wage-earning and housework was nothing new, but it was felt more acutely by women who held rising expectations for their lives in an era of feminism and equal opportunities. The Rapoports observed that many professional women clung on to their careers 'by not admitting when they are fatigued, or overcompensating and becoming "superworkers", allowing themselves less leeway than male colleagues – to prove that they can "do it" '.[77] A schoolteacher interviewed in the late 1970s described how her efforts to juggle career and family were tearing her in two:

> You try to find the other character, that of a teacher, before you get to school ... and sometimes you feel that really is quite a task especially if you've had a bit of an upset with one of your own children ... It's very near schizophrenia ... you fulfil your role as a mother, carry on your own hobbies, if you've got time for any ... and then you teach children what to do. Even at school there's no getting away from it ... you know you dash off to the shops at dinner-time to get something for tea ... it never ends.[78]

For another respondent, her biggest fear was the children getting ill, or worse still, falling ill herself. 'If I ever get poorly ... you know you can see the house literally coming down about your ears. The pattern ... the routine you've built up to keep one step ahead of everything just falls apart.'[79] Drusilla Beyfus recalled the precarious nature of her domestic arrangements at this time: 'I don't know how it appeared to others, but the edifice was always on the verge of collapse. The whole undertaking felt threatened, night and day. I thought I was going to blow into a million fragments.'[80]

This was not what Shirley Conran had in mind when she enjoined readers of *Superwoman* to refrain from stuffing mushrooms. Her intention was to give women freedom to *enjoy* life; hours not spent on housework could be redeployed to more pleasurable, meaningful activities. Yet by the later 1970s, the stressed-out working mother was well on her way to becoming a media cliché. In March 1977, the *Daily Mail* ran a long article on 'the women who work too hard', which featured the views of a distinguished Cambridge medic, Ivor Mills. Professor Mills was convinced that fertility problems and nervous breakdowns were increasing amongst working wives. In language strikingly reminiscent of Henry Maudsley, the Victorian psychiatrist with whom Elizabeth Garrett Anderson had locked horns back in the 1870s, Mills claimed that 'when a woman's mental arousal is too high she loses her libido (sex drive), starts to row with her husband and then the family breaks up'. He cited the case of a mother who started regular evening shifts in a factory, moved up to full-time employment and soon found it impossible to sit down and relax with her three children when not at work. 'So she joined a social club, began organising social events and so it went on, until she was also heavily committed with the local football supporters' club.' Rows with her husband followed and then serious illness. 'If only women would recognise their limits before it's too late,' Mills concluded sadly.[81]

These kinds of claims did not go unchallenged. The next day the newspaper published a riposte to Mills from another doctor, who argued, like proponents of the 'suburban neurosis' theory in the late 1930s, that the greater risk to women's mental health was 'the stress of being confined to a Waites-style two-up and two-down modern villa, with nobody to talk to all day long, and with nothing but the radio for company'.[82] Yet if concern about depressive housewives deepened in the 1970s, so did unease about the price being paid by women chasing career success in a world still very much designed for men. One senior civil servant, a mother in her mid-thirties with two small children, thought that her job had become 'generally busier, more stressful and more competitive' and was 'beginning to feel that the Service is no place for any human being, male or female, who doesn't want to work fourteen hours a day, six days a week, most of the time high on adrenalin'.[83] Barbara Mills believed the Bar was unforgiving to the working mother, 'because you simply have to be there, at the Old Bailey at 10 a.m. with your head screwed on to your shoulders and quite unemotional, and if your child is being operated on that day that is just hard luck'. Yet it was a sacrifice which she was prepared to make. 'I have made it my business to put 105 per cent of effort in this respect,' she explained. 'You cannot fail to turn up in court because your child's not well. You cannot bring a trial to a halt.'[84]

Part-time employment, Judith Hubback's preferred solution to the graduate mother's dilemma in the 1950s, was slowly becoming more possible in the professions but was still rare at senior levels. Less than 2 per cent of posts in the higher administrative grades of the Civil Service were held by part-timers in 1978. One woman who had temporarily reduced her hours between having two babies judged it a 'serious mistake' in career terms: 'while the Civil Service can organise part-time working in some posts, one's credibility declines very markedly.'[85] A female barrister who had entered the profession once her children were at school commented, 'You can't do part-time work at the Bar – there is such pressure of space for chambers that people would become resentful of someone only using her chambers part of the time. The clerks would not care for it either and they are the ones who get in the work for their barristers.'[86] Any deviation from the expected way of doing things required enormous tact and self-discipline, as exemplified by the senior civil servant who persuaded her superiors to agree to flexible hours. As described by the researchers who recorded her case: 'she had latitude to negotiate with colleagues that meetings involving her be held only at specific times, that colleagues were to contact her at home, and that subordinates had to hold the office in her absence.'

Other women brokered similar deals with their departments, all agreeing that 'the success of the arrangement depended on their ability to count on the goodwill of colleagues and that the goodwill depended on their being seen not to be cutting corners'. The result, the researchers concluded, 'was that they purchased their flexibility at the cost of intensive work both in the office and in the evenings at home'.[87]

*

Some of the most stressed-out working mothers of the 1970s were not, in fact, high-flying professionals, but belonged to the growing ranks of women bringing up their children alone. Half of the 150,000 lone mothers in the workforce in 1971 were employed full-time, a figure significantly higher than the 29 per cent of wage-earning mothers in two-parent households.[88] By the end of the decade, one in three lone mothers was divorced, reflecting the relaxation of the divorce laws but also a greater confidence on the part of women that economic survival might be possible without a male breadwinner. A Mass Observer recalled how, when her marriage fell apart in the early 1970s, she was able to train as a teacher and find secure employment which fitted with her children's school hours. The training college, she recalled, was 'very understanding' and allowed her to bring her sons to class when childcare failed.[89] A mother of two, interviewed in the late 1970s, explained how she had walked out on her husband (who 'wouldn't work, see') and found herself a succession of jobs: at a pen factory, a jam factory, on the tramways, at the zoo, on a farm – 'all sorts'.[90] Much of the stigma and secrecy surrounding unmarried motherhood, adultery and marital breakdown was lifting by these years. References to children born 'out of wedlock' fell out of fashion, whilst the National Council for the Unmarried Mother and her Child changed its name to the snappier One Parent Families.[91]

Yet if stories of resilience and self-sufficiency became more common, it was still difficult for lone mothers to achieve a decent standard of living through paid work. In two-parent households, only 5 per cent of primary earners brought home less than £20

a week, but in lone-parent families the figure was 70 per cent.[92]
Some lone mothers took jobs in order to supplement benefits,
but wages above £2 resulted in a downward adjustment, meaning
there was little incentive for mothers to work unless they could
find especially well-paid employment and had reliable childcare.[93]
For others, dependence on the State was intolerable, such as
divorced mother-of-three Mrs Barron, who described her string of
'unpleasant experiences' with benefit officials in the early 1970s: 'I
will never, never apply for Social Security again no matter what
the circumstances,' Mrs Barron pledged, choosing instead to finish
fishing rods at home in her front room for £8 a week.[94] Flaws in
the benefits system formed the most pressing problem identified
by the Committee on One Parent Families, appointed in 1969 to
investigate the difficulties experienced by this group. Reporting in
1974, the Committee recommended more generous allowances for
mothers and stronger enforcement of maintenance payments by
fathers. It also argued in favour of giving women greater freedom
to choose whether or not to work outside the home. 'Many lone
mothers who at present remain on supplementary benefit are
anxious to work,' the Committee observed,

> and we have no doubt that, financial considerations apart, many
> of them would benefit psychologically and socially as well.
> They would gain not only in the opportunities of wider and
> more varied social contact through their workmates, but also
> in confidence of their ability to support themselves once their
> children were no longer dependent on them.[95]

A more flexible system could provide support to mothers unable to
access higher paid work and allow for 'a steadier graduation from
dependence on State support to independence and self-support'.

These humane conclusions were widely welcomed by social
policy experts and anti-poverty campaigners, but fell foul of public-
spending cuts in the later 1970s. Lone mothers did gain from a
general rise in the value of child benefit and from new rules which
made this group eligible at last for council properties, although

plenty of applicants were still turned away.[96] A Mass Observer remembered her mother's housing problems following the failure of her marriage. Her application to the council was rejected when officials learned that she was living temporarily in her own mother's house. This they regarded as an entirely satisfactory long-term arrangement, showing little sympathy for a single mother's desire for independence.[97] The position of lone *fathers*, who headed around 10 per cent of one-parent households, was wholly different. Unlike mothers, fathers were required to register as job-seekers before claiming supplementary benefits, which only 7 per cent received.[98] This low figure was explained in part by men's greater earning capacity, but also by the power of ingrained assumptions that men 'should' work, regardless of their domestic circumstances. Over three-quarters of people surveyed for a study of 'motherless families' agreed that a lone father with children under five ought to get a job, compared to only 14 per cent who took the same position on lone mothers. 'A man can't take on a woman's role,' one respondent commented, 'he can't become a mother.' Another remarked: 'A man should be encouraged to go out to work. After all he is not a woman and he should not be expected to fill a woman's role.'[99]

*

These opinions about lone fathers underlined the resilience of the male breadwinner ideal in the late twentieth century. Yet the meanings attached to women's earnings – even low, part-time earnings – *were* subtly shifting. Post-war housewives might have underplayed how much their families relied on a second wage to maintain a high standard of living, but their 1970s counterparts were less able, and perhaps less willing, to do the same. By the end of the decade, a working mother typically contributed only 20 per cent of earned household income, but this figure concealed the important part which women's wages could play in keeping their families above the poverty line.[100] Male wages continued to rise, but so did unemployment and inflation, with restructuring across large swathes of industry reducing job security for skilled workers.

Women were also affected by these developments, but the loss of female manufacturing jobs was offset by major growth in the service industries – catering, cleaning, waitressing, secretarial work, shop work – and a resurgence of home-working, particularly in the garment trades of London, Yorkshire and the West Midlands. Part-time employment outstripped growth in full-time jobs by some margin, increasing by over a third between 1971 and 1981. By the latter date, a total of 3.8 million women had part-time jobs.[101]

The post-war pleasure culture of part-time employment did not disappear entirely for these workers. One mother of four explained how she went into a tobacco factory initially 'to get some toys for Christmas for my children' but stayed on because 'it was fun like, meeting so many people after being on your own at home with the children'.[102] A Mass Observer described the 'five happy years' she spent working for a pharmacist who allowed her to adjust her hours around family commitments: 'If there was a dental appointment, OK ... Daughter trotted off to school, no prob. I dropped her off, went to work until 3.30 and collected her ... It was an absolute treat, to pay bills on time, and have money for riding lessons, pretty clothes and days out.'[103]

Yet by the 1970s, the typical part-timer had little latitude in picking and choosing where and when she would work. She was less likely than her post-war counterpart to have a husband in a secure, well-paid job or an employer willing to accommodate her preferences. As firms restructured, employing part-time staff became a means of reducing labour costs and creating more 'flexible' workforces. Married women were valuable to employers not, as in the 1950s, because of an undersupply of full-time workers, but because they were cheap and dispensable. Part-timers could be recruited in periods of high demand and released when trade slackened; they could be integrated around new technologies and rationalised production processes; or they could substitute permanently for full-time staff. Veronica Beechey and Tessa Perkins found evidence of all three strategies in their landmark study of part-time work in Coventry. Exploring women's employment in textiles, confectionery, telecommunications, car manufacturing and the city's hospitals, schools and social care system, the authors found a mix of practices but in all cases part-time work was organised to suit employers, 'with little or no consideration of women's needs'. Britain was witnessing, they concluded grimly, 'the development of a new form of work which is highly exploitative and heavily gender-specific'.[104]

This changing picture was reflected in women's own accounts of their part-time jobs, which struck a strikingly downbeat note. A lollipop lady surveyed by Beechey and Perkins explained how she worked four half-hour shifts a day on an hourly wage of 79p, helping children from multiple schools across a busy T-junction. She did not qualify for the pension scheme or for overtime and was not paid for the twenty minutes between her two lunchtime shifts. It was often lonely work and downright unpleasant when the weather was bad. The job fitted with her own daughter's school hours, but rushing back and forth for short bursts of activity was stressful. She had taken the school-leaving exam in her native Ireland and worked before marriage as a nurse, but felt it was too late now to retrain for her former profession.[105] A thirty-nine-year-old dinner lady was equally unenthusiastic about her job, working in a school from 12 noon to 2.45 p.m. five days a week for £16, or less once her bus fares were taken into account. Her supervisor was difficult when she needed to take time off for family emergencies and the work itself was hot and tiring: preparing the meals, serving through the hatch, washing up and sterilising utensils. She took the job because she needed something which would keep the school holidays free and 'there was nothing else'. When asked whether there were any aspects of the job that she enjoyed, the dinner lady responded: 'I don't really like it at all.'[106]

The dramatic growth of part-time work was an important factor behind the gender pay gap, which persisted despite the introduction of equal pay legislation in 1970. Part-timers were earning just 58 per cent of men's full-time hourly rate by the early 1980s and only four-fifths of the hourly wages of full-time female workers.[107] Mothers were amongst the worst off, as they tended to work shorter hours and were typically found in unskilled or semi-skilled service jobs where it was difficult to prove pay discrimination due to the absence of men. The Low Pay Unit, a pressure group established to defend the rights of low-paid workers, was vocal on these gender inequalities, pointing out that in only 3 per cent of the occupational categories dominated by men did weekly average earnings slip below £40, compared to in three-quarters of the jobs typically performed by women. To make matters worse, part-timers working less than sixteen hours a week had fewer protections from unfair dismissal and did not qualify for statutory maternity leave.[108]

Anti-poverty campaigners registered particular alarm at the rising numbers of low-paid home-workers, some even warning of a return of Victorian-style sweated labour. Home-working had never completely disappeared from the economy, but its reappearance at a time of industrial restructuring and high unemployment revived old fears of the harm which casual earning by married women did to wages and full-time skilled jobs. Feminists challenged these claims by going into homes to interview and photograph low-paid women workers, just as Clementina Black and her trusty team of investigators had done in the 1890s and 1900s. There they discovered many of the same dynamics at play – low skills, lack of childcare, health problems, poor housing – as well as new factors, including the language barriers and cultural and religious norms which governed women's employment in many South Asian households. Researchers in the 1970s were less high-handed than their early twentieth-century counterparts, seeking to give their subjects a voice and to attend to the complexity of their experience.[109] In feminist hands, visual representations of home-working were critical, creative and multi-layered. The artist Margaret Harrison produced *Homeworkers* in 1977, a large canvas mixing stencilled text, photography and newspaper clippings, and which juxtaposed small manufactured items with details of the pay received by the worker and the price at which they were sold, a strategy strikingly similar to the placards on display at the Sweated Industries Exhibition of 1906.[110]

Efforts to organise home-workers were also more successful. Homeworking action groups were launched across London and

in Leicester, bringing the problem of low wages to the attention
of local authorities and providing practical help to women unsure
of their employment rights. Initiatives were set up to tackle
isolation, like the women's group for Urdu-speaking home-workers
at Saltley Action Centre in Birmingham, or the experimental
cooperatives formed by Asian garment workers in Greenwich.[111]
Most importantly, the trade union movement swung behind
these campaigns, the Trades Union Congress dropping its earlier
ambivalence towards home-workers and issuing a major statement
on the subject in 1978. This called for government action to curb
low pay and strengthen health and safety protections for employees
working at home.[112] Drives to unionise home-workers also bore
some fruit. Helen Eadie established a branch of the General and
Municipal Workers Union amongst glove-workers in Torrington,
Devon, which quickly secured a major wage rise for its members
and improved holiday pay.[113]

In short, if low wages and insecurity presented a growing problem
in the 1970s, women were better equipped to fight back than they
had been in the bad old days of sweating. Their membership of
trade unions slowly increased over the decade – almost 27 per cent
of unionists were female by 1975 – and women were more assertive
in pushing male colleagues to prioritise issues of sex discrimination
and pay inequality.[114] Women took the lead in a number of high-
profile industrial actions, including the equal pay strike at Ford's in
Dagenham and the famous walk-out at Grunwick led by Jayaben
Desai and her South Asian comrades. Contract night-cleaners in
London made further headlines with their campaign against low
pay and poor conditions. One strike at a large government office in
Fulham lasted for three weeks, with the pickets preventing any post
being delivered or supplies entering the building. Aided by feminist
activists and the Civil Service Union, the cleaners successfully
negotiated a wage increase, sick pay, two weeks of paid holiday
and recognition for their union, the Cleaners' Action Group.
May Hobbs, a key figure in the campaign, described how the
Group took on a wider support function for its members: 'We get
cleaners phoning up and telling us about their housing problems,

the difficulties they're having with their kids, as well as asking us questions about welfare benefits to which they are entitled.'[115]

All this seemed to bear out the feminist claim that paid work – even low-paid, menial work – created the potential for women to develop a collective political consciousness. Reflecting on the tobacco factory workers she had met in Bristol, Anna Pollert declared:

> Together at work women break out of their isolation. However much they remain cut off, both ideologically and in practice from the world of men, they are *still* in that same world of wage labour. More than this, they share their world with one another as women; they can build up confidence, share problems, have a laugh, learn collectively.[116]

Pollert observed a multitude of small acts of assertion performed by women on the shop floor: reading magazines whilst on the clock, handing round family photographs, chatting about the news, doing quizzes, or 'switching off' from supervisory dictates and retreating into private mental worlds. The older mothers in the workforce, she noted, commanded a substantial degree of respect and deference from management and were more confident than their younger peers in answering back. They unnerved younger male staff by teasing and scolding them like children, and 'as for the male chargehands, they could have been their husbands, and were treated as such'.[117] Pollert saw in these behaviours a source of power which might be harnessed not only to fight exploitative low wages but to resist 'the sexual oppression which cuts right across the home and the work-place'.[118] This was the spark which feminism could provide, stirring the smouldering ashes of women's everyday experiences of subordination into a burning blaze of righteous anger.

*

Just how fiercely this fire burned in British women during the decade of Women's Liberation is difficult to say. For activists like

Ann Oakley, feminism's impact was direct and transformative, altering irrevocably her politics, relationships and whole way of being in the world. For most of the female population, feminism's influence was more diffuse. It was an uneven cultural presence, a backdrop of ideas encountered intermittently in newspaper articles or on television, a topic for passing conversation rather than an all-absorbing, animating force. Even amongst well-educated baby boomers, the demographic best represented in the 1970s women's movement, feminism's appeal could be muted. Mary Ingham made contact with her grammar-school classmates in 1977, the year in which they all turned thirty, and found feminism to be 'a minority obsession'. Most suburban housewives, she wrote, 'my peers at home among them, dismissed "women's lib" as extremist nonsense'. Ingham remembered the publication of Germaine Greer's iconic text *The Female Eunuch* – 'its strange bodystocking cover haunting bookshops everywhere' – but she never actually read it and found only one school friend who had.[119] Long-established professional women's organisations regarded the language and style of Women's Liberation as dangerously radical. The President of the National Federation of Business and Professional Women told her annual conference in 1970 that their association could 'show that women can have confidence without emotionalism, realism without revolution and femininity without feminism'.[120] In a televised debate with the feminist Juliet Mitchell four years later, the Conservative MP Sally Oppenheim accused Women's Liberation of trivialising the issue of sex equality through its obsession with 'bra-burning' and other outlandish political stunts.[121]

Yet feminism had always been a broad church in Britain and arguably became broader still in the 1970s. There can be no doubt that the ideology of equal opportunities moved up the political agenda and began to shape employment practices in this decade, even if wage differentials, occupational segregation and residual sexist attitudes continued to hold women back. Mothers struggled to access reliable childcare, but at least they now had a statutory entitlement to maternity pay and to reclaim their jobs. When she surveyed working wives in 1960, Viola Klein found 'no trace of feminist egalitarianism' and little talk of 'emancipation' in the replies;[122] twenty years later, it was possible to detect a greater sense of individualism and self-assertion in women's answers when asked why they worked. A mother interviewed in inner London in 1979 said that she did it for 'independence – continuing with something. I'm interested in the work. It's good for me. Also, I'm not in a pigeon-hole as "John's mother".' Another wanted 'freedom of mind, independence, money, we've all benefitted because I'm happier', whilst a third went out to work for 'complete freedom, feeling myself normal again. Stimulation, friendship, proving myself.'[123] Reflecting on her life as a GP and young mother in the 1950s, Jill Parker recalled how she was 'always so apologetic about the children ... there was a definite feeling that you were very much in a man's world and you had to bend over backwards to be reliable so that nobody would say, "Oh God, she's got *children*." '[124] If she were doing it now, Parker thought, 'I'd be bolder. I'd say: "You're jolly lucky to have me! *And* I've got these wonderful children." '

Parker added a less cheerful coda to this statement which pointed to the new challenges facing working mothers in the 1980s and beyond. 'I do think that the person who has done the worst disservice to women is Superwoman,' she observed. 'Whereas I had to be apologetic, now women have to be *super*. This is the difference. I have never tried to do everything. I do not sew on buttons.'[125] Shirley Conran's playful caricature had, it seemed, unintentionally morphed into an unattainable ideal. In 1990, Conran published a new edition of her household manual which she called *Down With Superwoman* so as to ensure no misinterpretation of her message. The original title, she explained, 'was used ironically to demolish a myth' – that of the 'demanding, exhausting, super-achiever that threatened to depress our lives'. It was now necessary, she commanded, 'to forget SUPERWOMAN' and remember that the real achiever was the woman 'who avoids doing too much'.[126] Few working mothers would find it possible to follow this new mantra at the end of the twentieth century.

12

Doing It All

In December 2000, the critic and commentator Allison Pearson created the character of Kate Reddy, a permanently overstretched working mother, in her weekly *Daily Telegraph* column. Reddy was a City fund manager juggling a demanding job with two high-spirited children, a surly nanny and a resentful husband, whilst managing her own guilty conscience and physical fatigue. In 2002, Pearson made Reddy the heroine of a full-length novel, *I Don't Know How She Does It!*, which sold millions of copies in Britain and overseas, was serialised on radio and later turned into a Hollywood film. In the months following the book's publication, Pearson toured literary festivals and television studios across the UK and the US (where the book also won a huge following) and received thousands of emails from readers expressing gratitude for her witty and sensitive portrayal of the dilemmas facing contemporary women. Reviewers dubbed Pearson's book a leading example of 'mum-lit', a variant on the 'chick-lit' genre sweeping commercial fiction in the 1990s, and described Kate Reddy as the working mother's Bridget Jones.[1]

Why did *I Don't Know How She Does It!* touch such a nerve? The novel was undoubtedly topical, distilling a decade or more of popular stereotypes of career women, from the heroines of movies such as *Baby Boom* (1987) or *Working Girl* (1988) to media caricatures of Nicola Horlick, the asset manager and mother of six who declared in her 1997 memoir that women could and should 'have it all'.[2] But

Kate Reddy's life also exposed the darker side of pursuing success and advancement in the corporate world. Pearson depicts the City as a bastion of misogyny and machismo, where entertaining clients at lap-dancing clubs is routine and women returning from a few short months of maternity leave find they are no longer assigned to the more prestigious accounts. Kate notes how her male colleagues litter their desks with family photographs whilst mothers at the firm hide them away, fearful that their commitment to the job will be questioned. Her schedule is relentless and spills into evenings and weekends, enabled by mobile phones and new teleworking technologies. Kate's genteel architect husband is always telling her to slow down, as does her weed-smoking mini-cab driver and mothers at her children's school, who cannot understand why she hasn't gone part-time. Kate knows that she is pushing herself too hard but feels trapped: 'the age of working to live instead of living to work,' she reflects wistfully, 'feels far away in a land where district nurses arrived by Morris Traveller and televisions glowed like embers. I don't know anyone at the office who eats with their kids in the week now.'[3]

Pearson's novel also ventured into sexual politics, a fraught ideological terrain around the turn of the millennium. By encouraging women to cast off traditional gender roles and aim for the skies, had seventies feminists simply prescribed a new set of impossible ideals for mothers? Kate remembers how she used to believe in the equality of the sexes, 'with all the passionate certainty of someone very young who knew absolutely everything and therefore nothing at all'. Now she is not so sure. 'It was a nice idea, equality: noble, indisputably fair. But how the hell was it supposed to work?'[4] Leaving her son and daughter every morning for work produces painful emotions which Kate fights to control. Their need for her, she reflects, 'is like the need for water or light. It has a devastating simplicity. It doesn't fit any of the theories about what women are supposed to do with their lives.'[5] Yet Kate values her independence and the feeling of competence and authority that her career gives her. She is terrified by the thought of her mother's life, tied down by housework, childcare and intermittent casual jobs.

Kate really does want to Have It All. But, as Pearson frequently quipped in her interviews and columns, for mothers on the cusp of the twenty-first century, 'having-it-all' meant 'doing-it-all' as well.[6]

From one perspective, it was odd that a highly paid city executive became a cultural touchstone for British working mothers. Reddy was hardly a representative figure. Women were dramatically outnumbered by men in the senior ranks of business and the professions right through the 1980s and 1990s, with the financial services sector especially notorious for its sexist culture. Pearson's novel did resonate, however, with the growing numbers of women hovering in mid-level managerial or professional jobs, who recognised elements of Kate's struggle to keep her career going whilst marshalling husbands, nannies, cleaners, school pick-ups, birthday parties and visits from the in-laws on the home front. In truth, however, the lives of most working mothers looked nothing like Kate Reddy's in the late twentieth century. As in previous decades, far more typical was the mother employed part-time in cleaning, catering, retail or low-level office work, who had no money to spare for expensive childcare or lunchtime dashes to the L.K. Bennett sale.

Some observers suggested that women's opportunities in the labour market had further polarised under the free-market policies of the Conservative governments of Margaret Thatcher (1979–1990) and John Major (1990–1997). An expanding class of high-earning, career-orientated graduates appeared to be breaking away from the mass of women with few educational qualifications who were stuck in low-paid employment. Tony Blair's New Labour government tried to temper this trend after 1997 with measures to tackle low pay, broaden access to higher education, get lone parents into work and provide affordable and high-quality childcare to everyone who needed it. Yet income inequality continued to grow into the early twenty-first century and social mobility stalled. These social cleavages were reflected in the fracturing of feminist activism, where it seemed increasingly impossible to build a unified movement amongst women in such vastly different material circumstances and with diverse experiences.

Polarisation, however, was not the whole story. If Kate Reddy was the privileged, middle-class face of working motherhood, her emotional conflicts and physical exhaustion were more widely shared. The popular clichés of women spinning plates, juggling balls and battling against the clock struck a chord because many mothers felt that their lives *were* defined by tension and stress: the stress of making ends meet; the stress of finding reliable childcare; the stress of competing for careers designed for men with full-time wives; the stress of looking after elderly parents, staying in touch with friends and remembering important birthdays; the stress of keeping everyone happy. Working mothers had always experienced some of these pressures, alongside the feelings of maternal guilt and inadequacy which feminists had theorised and critiqued in the 1970s. Yet the mismatch between women's ever-growing desire for independence and fulfilment on the one hand, and labour market restructuring and the rolling back of the State on the other, created an especially toxic mix from the 1980s. No one seriously questioned a mother's right to re-enter the workplace by the end of the century, or even to aspire to something resembling a career. Stress was the price which women paid for that acceptance, and it was a cost which they largely bore alone.

*

With anti-discrimination and equal opportunities firmly established in law, reconciling family and career *should* have become easier for women in the 1980s and 1990s. Some employers appeared genuinely keen to embrace the equality agenda, pioneering a range of initiatives designed to attract and support female staff. In banking, NatWest devised a much publicised 'retainer' scheme which allowed women to work two-week refresher periods each year whilst bringing up their families, leading in many cases to eventual reinstatement.[7] In 1981, Thames Television established a Women's Committee and appointed an equal opportunities advisor following an internal review of women's career progress in the organisation. BP followed suit the following year by sponsoring a network for women in senior posts which held regular lunchtime seminars and organised specially tailored training sessions. Government meanwhile inaugurated a 'programme of action' to support women's careers in the Civil Service.[8] Around the same time, some technology firms started experiments in remote working, using cable networks to set programmers and analysts up with terminals in their homes, a convenient arrangement for many women with small children. International Computers Limited (ICL) led the field in promoting this new style of working, employing around 300 home-based staff, mostly women, by the late-1980s. *The Times* ran an interview with Diana Hill, who managed ICL's home-workers and had herself been working remotely since 1972. Pictured next to a computer in her home office in Stratford-upon-Avon, and with her ten-year-old daughter looking cheerfully on, Hill explained the company's approach: 'We try to ensure that it is not a backwater for those who want to mark time. Some don't want the responsibility but working from home can still provide an opportunity to progress in your career in the organisation. It is a career and not just an area for pin money.'[9]

These corporate initiatives gathered pace after 1990, when a government task force led by Elspeth Howe, a former deputy chair of the Equal Opportunities Commission, published its influential report, *Women On Top*. The report predicted that 80 per cent of those entering the labour market over the next five years would be women, mostly older returners with 'major family responsibilities'.[10] A sharp decline in the number of school-leavers meant that employers would have to compete harder to recruit and retain the most talented candidates, which they were urged to do through a range of woman-friendly policies – everything from mentoring programmes and board-level champions to better maternity packages and flexible working schemes. *Women on Top* led to the creation of an employer-led campaign, Opportunity 2000, whose sixty-one founder members pledged to adopt best practice and set targets for promoting women to senior posts.[11] John Major's Conservative government backed the campaign and added its own initiatives, hosting a series of conferences aimed at women returners, opening 'opportunity shops' across the country to provide information about training, and setting up a working group chaired by Gillian Shephard, Secretary of State for Employment, to bring 'fresh ideas' to women's issues in government.[12]

Gender equality in the workplace continued its slow advance over these decades. By 1990, women made up more than 14 per cent of practising barristers and 19 per cent of practising solicitors, whilst one in five middle-managers were female, a four-fold increase from the early 1970s. Women accounted for 35 per cent of those in higher management at the BBC and more than two in five of recruits to the prestigious fast-stream programme of the Civil Service.[13] Helen Wilkinson, a researcher at the think tank Demos, declared that a 'genderquake' was underway in 1990s Britain: 'The cultural and economic enfranchisement of women is deep-rooted and irreversible,' she argued, pointing to evidence of young women's desire for 'greater autonomy and the chance to develop identities through work', and to strong female role models in the media, from pop singer Madonna to Detective Chief Inspector Jane Tennison, the character played by Helen Mirren in the long-running television series *Prime Suspect*.[14] Asked in 1997 to name the prominent women they most admired, a group of sixth-form schoolgirls put barrister Cherie Blair in first place, followed by Princess Diana, Margaret Thatcher, Nicola Horlick and the actress Nicole Kidman. One seventeen-year-old explained why she found the prime minister's wife such an inspiration: 'She is successful, having her own career and looking after her children. She must be under pressure but the image she portrays is one of a happy, ordered and stable family life. These days girls want to have it all, and women like her prove it's possible.'[15]

Such upbeat talk, however, obscured the many obstacles still blocking women's paths as they aimed for the top of their professional fields. Women's presence in the senior Civil Service doubled between 1984 and 1995, but still stood at only 10 per cent, with just two female permanent secretaries in post across the whole of Whitehall.[16] A paltry 7 per cent of university professors were female in the mid-1990s, and only six universities were headed by female vice-chancellors.[17] Women composed almost two-thirds of

NatWest's workforce in 1996, but only a quarter of its managerial staff, a finding which cast some doubt upon the effectiveness of the equality policies proudly unveiled by large employers.[18] In practice, part-time and 'flexible' working schemes often enticed women onto less prestigious and decelerated career tracks. Mothers who returned immediately from maternity leave on a full-time basis had the best chance of maintaining their position and securing further promotion, but over half returned instead to part-time jobs.[19] A survey of home-working computer programmers in the early 1980s found that average pay was lower than that received by on-site staff and in a large number of cases home-workers had fewer employee benefits or rights. A majority of the sample, who were mostly women in their thirties with children under five, felt that their prospects for career advancement were poor.[20] Even so, clinging on to a career by working reduced hours or at home was judged preferable by many mothers to resigning altogether. Yet like the graduate wives who had resumed their professions after a five- or ten-year break in the 1950s and 1960s, the trade-off was slower progression with many senior-level posts effectively out of reach.

Equal opportunities or 'diversity' policies could thus feel like corporate window-dressing to women who watched less talented male peers promoted ahead of them. Whilst employers now had to respect women's maternity rights, few provided generous leave packages or helped with childcare. In 1979, just 10 per cent of working mothers received more than the statutory minimum maternity pay, and by 1990 this had inched up to 14 per cent, in most cases offered by public sector employers under pressure from their unionised workforce. Less than 4 per cent of mothers reported any assistance from employers with childcare costs or provision of workplace nurseries.[21] Opportunity 2000 campaigners increasingly made the 'business case' for action, arguing that women's knowledge and skills were a resource requiring long-term investment, but in practice most employer-sponsored schemes threw the initiative on to women themselves. It was the ambitious career woman's *own* responsibility to build networks, seek out mentors and make a success of the flexible working arrangements now so generously on offer. And it was *her* job to organise childcare, which for the highest-flying professional mothers meant, as in earlier times, a succession of nannies, mothers' helps and resident au pairs. The market for this kind of waged domestic labour surged in the late twentieth century to meet expanding demand from dual-career households. The economist Alison Wolf, who had a young family in south London in the early 1980s, remembered 'days when I used to come home to a kitchen full of socialising nannies and assorted small children'.[22] A 1994 study estimated that between a third and a half of all professional couples with preschool children employed a nanny, in many cases drawing upon global care chains through which women from poorer countries travelled to Britain for work, often leaving their own children behind.[23] Following the temporary decline in domestic service in the middle of the century, well-off white women were once more issuing orders to employees in their homes, albeit in a very different social and cultural climate.

A growing self-help literature offered advice to these professional working mothers on how to cope with the multiple demands on their time and emotional energies. The journalist Libby Purves warned against constantly ringing home during the day or talking about one's children with male colleagues, and she suggested dealing with any genuine domestic crises covertly, pleading a migraine if necessary to effect an early exit from the office.[24] In her *Working Mother's Survival Guide*, the barrister Jill Black listed a range of desirable qualities for the woman juggling family and career, from 'good health' and 'perseverance and optimism' to 'plenty of stamina and the ability to make do with very little sleep'. If working from home, she observed, 'you need to have the self-discipline to shut yourself away and keep at it even if the utility room is stuffed full of dirty washing and it sounds as if the nanny is murdering the baby'.[25] Penny Vincenzi briskly told readers of her 1984 parenting guide to make up their minds about going back to work, find a 'smashing substitute' to look after the children, and then 'stick to it and shut up about it'.[26] These guides were cast in Shirley

Conran's *Superwoman* mould, counselling against perfection and advising women through witty, personalised and often irreverent prose to protect their sanity and health by *not* trying to do it all. But these books tended nonetheless to reinforce the assumption that women were solely responsible for the success or failure of any attempted career re-launch after childbirth. Husbands were mostly background figures whose approval was necessary but from whom little could be expected by way of active support. As Jill Black saw it, the working mother's requirement from her spouse was simple: 'no sabotage'.[27]

There was, in fact, very limited evidence that British fathers had turned over a new leaf when it came to taking a regular share in housework or childcare. Most men now routinely attended the birth of their children and took some time off immediately afterwards, although very few were offered paid paternity leave by their employers.[28] Time-use surveys showed a small increase in the amount of unpaid domestic labour performed by husbands, from 26 per cent in 1974 to 37 per cent just over a decade later, with the greatest help given by men whose wives worked full-time.[29] Yet this upswing in male involvement was often limited to washing-up after dinner, supervising bath-time or taking the children to the park at the weekend, and rarely encompassed any reduction in men's working hours to fit around domestic tasks. Less than 10 per cent of the male workforce was employed part-time, and this was mostly older men starting to wind down for retirement. Amongst fathers on high or middle incomes, the proportion working part-time stayed below 5 per cent right through the 1990s.[30] Media pronouncements of the dawning of the age of the New Man created an illusion of change not matched by the reality. Some sociologists even wondered whether women overstated the extent of spousal help in order to deny their own feelings of frustration, projecting instead an image of marital harmony based on the mythical possession of 'an apron-clad domesticated husband'.[31] By contrast, one working mother interviewed in the early 1980s was under no such delusions: 'I'd like to be a man,' she told the researcher. 'It must be lovely just to go out to work and come home, and have a wife and children at home, it must be gorgeous for them.'[32]

*

Some men, of course, *were* willing to support their wives' careers. One Mass Observer growing up in the 1980s remembered 'lots of conversations about money (and the lack thereof), but never did my dad ever consider suggesting that my mum stay at home to bring us up. I was always very aware that Mum and Dad were equals.'[33] Yet the confident predictions made by Rhona and Robert Rapoport back in the late 1960s that egalitarian role-sharing would become the marital norm proved hopelessly optimistic. Instead, mothers became experts in the management of time, by no means an unfamiliar role but one made ever more challenging in an era of instant digital communication and the intensification of work. Social forecasters suggested that Western societies were shifting from an 'industrial to a post-industrial order of time', creating new pressures and strains as people struggled to cope with a '24/7' world.[34] Women, it was noted, suffered especially badly, one survey revealing that 86 per cent of women in full-time work felt that they never had enough time to get things done.[35] A similar poll in the magazine *Good Housekeeping* inspired Allison Pearson to write her column about Kate Reddy. Readers were asked what they wanted for Mother's Day and the most popular answer, Pearson was shocked to discover, was a modest few hours to themselves. 'I thought about my life and the lives of my friends with young children,' she reflected, 'and I realized we were all being driven crazy by the pressure we were under juggling work and family.'[36] *I Don't Know How She Does It!* was Pearson's attempt to critique this intolerable situation for mothers, exemplified by the strenuous, non-stop life of Reddy, who 'counts seconds like other women count calories'.

Concern for the well-being of women pushing themselves to the limit was frequently discussed alongside the concept of 'work–life balance'. This term entered the popular lexicon from the mid-1990s, often presented as an ideal for *all* workers to strive towards but especially women with heavy domestic responsibilities. Shirley Conran took up the cause of work–life balance, swapping the playful tone of *Superwoman* for more sombre reflections on the 'dark, enlarging cloud of stress' which she saw overshadowing Britain.[37] Conran hosted a conference on this topic at the Savoy Hotel in autumn 1999 under the auspices of Mothers in Management, the body she had founded the previous year to promote flexible working practices for women. She went on to establish the Work–Life Balance Trust in 2001.[38]

Yet for some women hungry for career success, a more pressing question was whether they had time to have babies at all. The medic Beulah Bewley encountered this 'bio-panic' amongst the female trainees that she mentored in the 1980s, a time when increasing numbers of professional women were postponing pregnancy until their mid-thirties or even later.[39] The overall birth rate, already in decline, hit a low in 2001, whilst childlessness doubled, running highest amongst women with university degrees and professional qualifications.[40] Advances in fertility treatments, including *in vitro* fertilisation, gave women greater confidence to delay childbearing until after they had established themselves in their careers. In 1993, to great media fanfare, a fifty-nine-year-old businesswoman gave birth to twins using donor eggs fertilised by her partner's sperm.[41] Emerging egg-freezing technologies created the possibility, as one medical expert speculated in the mid-1990s, for 'a young woman lawyer of twenty, who wanted to delay having children until she is 45, and a barrister or a QC, having some of her ovarian tissue frozen down for twenty years. She could then use it, mixed with her future partner's sperm, to have a baby when she is ready.'[42]

These developments undoubtedly gave some women more options in terms of exactly how and when to fit having children into their lives, although in doing so they strengthened the perception that maternity was fundamentally antithetical to high-level professional success. Most women did *not*, in fact, want to delay childbearing until their forties and felt they had little choice but to accept the consequences of having babies earlier. Some went further, swapping high-level corporate jobs for full-time domesticity or less frenetic part-time work, in many cases establishing home-based businesses that were more compatible with the demands of family life.[43] The heroine of Maeve Haran's 1991 novel, *Having It All*, does exactly this, quitting her career as a television executive in London for an East Sussex cottage with herbaceous borders and a more flexible role running a local recruitment agency for mothers looking for part-time jobs. It is also the solution which Kate Reddy eventually embraces at the end of *I Don't Know How She Does It!*, moving her family to rural Derbyshire where she uses her city contacts to save an ailing toy company. Real-life 'mumpreneurs', as the media quickly dubbed them, included Lisa Burke, who left her job as a manager at Tupperware on pregnancy but launched a comeback in 1993 with a new business selling aromatherapy products, adapting Tupperware's home-demonstrating method.[44] In 1999, Julia Macquisten created Body Back, a fitness company aimed at new mothers wanting to get into shape, whilst nursing her own new-born at home in rural Hampshire. Florence Ducret-Blagburn founded her company, Bonne Nuit, after spotting a gap in the market in Britain for French-style baby sleeping bags, whilst mother-of-three Mandy Haberman was inspired to design a spill-proof toddler cup when she watched her friend's child pour Ribena all over their pale carpet. By 2001, the Anywayup cup was enjoying global sales of 10 million a year.[45]

Most mothers were neither as energetic nor as successful as these career women-turned-business owners. Many had, in fact, stepped off the corporate treadmill precisely to escape the relentless pressure to compete, make profits and deliver results. Catherine Hakim, a leading expert on women's employment in the 1990s and early 2000s, interpreted this behaviour as revealing of important differences of outlook and orientation, not only between the sexes, but between different groups of women. In an article published in the *Daily Mail* in March 1996, she argued that at least two-thirds of the female population had no interest in prioritising career over family and that 'no matter what carrots are offered, some women will always want to stay at home'.[46] According to Hakim, in an era of anti-discrimination legislation and the pill, the choice which most women made to fit their jobs around family needs – and to accept lower pay and slower progress as a result – reflected genuine preferences. Feminists might have opened the door to workplace equality in the 1970s, she argued, but they were mistaken if they assumed that every woman wanted to walk through.[47]

Hakim's analysis proved popular with right-wing think tanks and commentators anxious about the erosion of 'family values', but dividing women into categories based on fixed, unchanging preferences masked the deeper dynamics shaping women's feelings and attitudes towards work.[48] The feminist writer Rosalind Coward was struck by how many of the mothers she interviewed in the early 1990s expressed ambivalence about the professional workplace: the egotistical power games they were forced to play, the demand for long hours and total commitment, and the shabby treatment of women, especially those with children. If mothers threw in their jobs, perhaps it was a consequence of intolerable late-capitalist work cultures rather than the timeless pull of maternity? One woman explained how she gave up an academic research career because of the toxic atmosphere of her university department: 'I couldn't stand the way it *mattered* so much to the individuals if they had more papers published than anyone else. And I couldn't stand their need to put other people down.' A BBC film editor reduced her working hours because of the posturing and politicking of her male colleagues. 'I'm just not like that. In fact, I hate it. I don't want to be judged on my personality.' Reading such views as proof that women wanted, in their heart of hearts, to be traditional housewives, was simplifying a complicated issue. 'The portrayal of spectacular career renunciations in the media,' Coward wrote, 'has obscured the real issues around mothering and work, and distorted the dilemmas and decisions of most ordinary women.'[49]

Tabloid newspapers, however, could not resist the temptation to draw battle-lines between working and non-working mothers, a topic which garnered ever more coverage as the 1990s progressed. The *Daily Mail* ran a piece under the headline 'The Mothering Wars' which described the resentment felt by full-time housewives towards their professional peers. 'Working mothers are very good at making you feel valueless,' said one. 'At the school gate it is very much us and them. They look different. They have different clothes. I would like them to know that staying at home with the children has been the hardest work I have ever done.' This was followed by a quote from a working mother explaining how she tried to maintain 'good relations' by offering regularly to babysit.[50] Other newspapers took aim at professional women who cynically paraded their offspring in public. 'For a particular kind of determined and hard-headed career woman,' the *Express* journalist Jane Gordon wrote, 'the mother-with-Trophy-Child trick is an ideal way of softening her image and broadening her appeal.'[51] Nicola Horlick was counted amongst this group, attacked by Gordon for appearing at press conferences with her youngest child in a pram after being fired in a very public fashion from Morgan Grenfell in late 1997.

Alongside her status as a celebrated role model, Horlick attracted immense volumes of bile from newspaper columnists in the late 1990s, who criticised her hair, her clothes and the hyper-efficiency with which she organised her home life. One male reviewer was repelled by the self-satisfied tone of Horlick's memoir, *Can You Have It All?*, and commented that, were she a character in a novel, readers would be anticipating her well-deserved downfall in the final chapter: 'There are few human frailties to endear her to us. Like baked Alaska, she's cold in the middle.'[52] The *Daily Mirror* columnist Sue Carroll described Horlick as 'a control freak who juggled her existence with military precision', whilst Topaz Amoore at the *Express* held her up as a warning to women about the perils of chasing a high-powered career: 'We can't have it all, even if we think we should be able to,' Amoore proclaimed. 'Just because the cult of uber-banker Nicola Horlick suggests you can be a leading fund manager and bring up a herd of children, there's no need to fall for it.'[53]

These writers found something disturbing, unnatural even, in how Nicola Horlick pursued power in the boardroom whilst enjoying the pleasures of a full family life. Her determination, quite unapologetically, to have both broke the existing mould of professional women's lives, in which compromise, demotion or stasis had, since the 1960s, been the price willingly paid for hanging on to the threads of a career after motherhood. Horlick was a threatening figure in the eyes of women because her success implied that the superwoman lifestyle *was* possible if a mother worked hard enough to achieve it: Sue Carroll found her perfection 'galling'. But Horlick was an even more dangerous prospect for men. She unsettled the status quo whereby most of the serious female competition in the professional workplace conveniently disappeared or went part-time in their thirties. Powerful women had always disorientated men in authority, but powerful women with small children threw them into a panic.

*

It was perhaps reassuring all round that women like Nicola Horlick were few and far between in the 1980s and 1990s. The most towering female presence of this period, Margaret Thatcher, was a mother but her twins were fully grown adults by the time she became Conservative Party leader in 1975, whilst her businessman husband, Denis, was helpfully retired. As prime minister, Thatcher was thus able to channel elements of strong, modern career womanhood without affronting more traditionally minded voters with unsavoury images of breastfeeding or nappy-changing at Downing Street. In the past, Thatcher had been fairly relaxed about her status as a working mother, telling the press that she 'should vegetate if I were left at the kitchen sink all day' and that she didn't believe the family 'suffers at all through my political ambitions'.[54] But once in power, Thatcher did very little to champion other women's opportunities in the workplace. There was no substantial public investment in nursery provision, no strengthening of maternity rights, and no tax relief for women spending large portions of their salaries on childcare. Thatcher explicitly disavowed feminism, depicting 'Women's Libbers' as radical left-wing extremists. She poured scorn upon Labour's decision to focus on 'women's issues' during one of its press conferences at the 1983 election. 'We were amazed,' Thatcher later wrote. 'As we joked about it I said to my male colleagues at the briefing session: "If they have their way, you'll soon be having the babies." '[55]

Thatcher's wider economic policies hit mothers working in lower-skilled occupations hard, as a wave of public services were contracted out to private providers. Some 70 per cent of the public-sector jobs selected for so-called 'competitive tendering' in the 1980s were held by women, including thousands of dinner ladies, cleaners and home helps.[56] Black and minority ethnic women were over-represented in these kinds of jobs due to enduring racial discrimination in other parts of the labour market. In 1982, over a quarter of the female workforce was employed in white-collar clerical work, but amongst Caribbean women the figure was just 11 per cent.[57] Once the Fair Wages Resolution put in place by the post-war Labour government was swept away in 1983, contractors were under no obligation to offer the better wages and conditions which workers had received when employed directly by the State. The abolition of the Wages Councils, the successors of the Edwardian trade boards which had set minimum rates for many of the lowest-paid workers, left these women at risk of even greater exploitation. Trade unionists tried to fight back, including the hundreds of cleaners who picketed the gates at Barking Hospital in 1984 after their employer, Crothall's, slashed pay by a third following the renegotiation of its NHS contract.[58] Yet unions struggled to recruit these precarious workers at a time of rising unemployment and government legislation imposing tighter restrictions on industrial action. The difficulty of getting by on low wages prompted some mothers to take up sex work as a better-paid alternative, either on the street or at home whilst children were at school. Young women from the provinces, many of whom had children to support, travelled to King's Cross in London in the 1980s to pick up trade, where they were known colloquially as 'Thatcher's Girls'.[59]

All lower-income women suffered from a social security system which continued to treat wives as the dependants of men regardless of their actual economic or domestic circumstances. This affected mothers especially badly when unemployment soared in the early 1980s to 13 per cent, in part as a result of the Conservative government's aggressive policies to curb inflation. From 1983, anyone

claiming unemployment benefit was required to supply details of
what arrangements they had in place for the care of dependants
should a job be offered, a question which was notionally gender-
neutral but obviously targeted at mothers with small children.
The Equal Opportunities Commission argued that demanding
such information was indirect discrimination which might have
the effect of discouraging unemployed women from applying for
a benefit to which they were fully entitled.[60] The following year,
wives with husbands who were earning were made ineligible for
places on job creation schemes, a form of discrimination which the
Department of Employment argued was justified as such women
did not 'need' to support themselves.[61]

With major industries such as coal mining, steel and ship-
building in recession and millions of school-leavers and skilled
men out of work, the principle that these groups should be ahead
of married women in the queue for available jobs commanded a
fair degree of public support in the early 1980s. The commentator
Ronald Butt thought that, given present economic circumstances,
'the essential question is who is *not* to work'. High amongst his
possible candidates were low-skilled women who had a valuable
task to do at home bringing up their families. Butt wanted to see
an allowance paid to these mothers to remove the incentive to go
out to work and free up jobs for men and single women.[62] The
letters pages of the broadsheet and tabloid press saw an airing of
similar views. A resident of Penzance wrote to *The Times* suggesting
that a 'benevolent dictator' might ease the pain of the unemployed
by cutting numbers of married women working in 'schools, local
government, commercial offices, chain-stores, indeed in every kind
of shop and establishment in a typical High Street'.[63] An angry
reader from Romford told the *Daily Mirror* that he had counted
eight married women working on the tills at his local supermarket
the other day: 'With so many school-leavers needing jobs this
seems wrong.'[64]

Proposals to ration employment in this manner were reminiscent
of the interwar decades, when 'greedy' married women were attacked
for taking work from single women and male breadwinners. Yet

conditions in the 1980s were very different. Sex discrimination legislation meant there could be no return to the era of formal marriage bars, whilst it was not just middle-class feminist societies who now objected indignantly to the suggestion that wives and mothers should forfeit their jobs. One woman told the *Mirror* that she was 'sick of reading criticisms of married women who work'. Her husband, she explained, did not earn enough to cover bills and 'keep two 6ft sons in school. I don't sit and sweat in an outdated factory in summer or freeze there in winter for fun or pin money.'[65] Another wrote: 'I'd be happy to give up my job if Mrs Thatcher will give up hers.'[66] The researcher Sue Sharpe estimated that fewer than one in ten of the women she interviewed for her 1984 study of working mothers were willing to leave employment, even if they had no financial need to earn.[67]

In truth, Conservative governments did not expect Britain's mothers to retreat en masse to the kitchen. The 'hard-working families' who featured so prominently in Thatcherite rhetoric in the 1980s relied on women's earnings as well as men's and were appealed to as such. 'People don't go out to work for the Chancellor of the Exchequer,' Thatcher said in one speech, choosing her words carefully. 'They go out to work for their family, for their children, to help look after their parents.'[68] Most mothers in lower- or middle-income households were not thinking in terms of high-powered careers, but they did desire greater economic independence. The sociologist Jan Pahl noticed this dynamic in her 1989 study of how married couples managed their finances. Two-thirds of wives agreed that it was important 'to have some money you know is your own'. In the words of one interviewee: 'it gives you a feeling of independence – a feeling you're not absolutely reliant on your husband. You feel you're somebody – more confident.'[69] The wives who were working, Pahl found, had more control over household income, in some cases maintaining separate bank accounts and taking responsibility for particular items of expenditure. Mrs K., a nurse, described how much she valued having her own earnings, recalling the very different situation in her parents' marriage: 'Father had the money, mother had none. He was the boss. He totally controlled his wife through his control over money.'[70] Mrs K. later told Pahl about the secret savings account which she kept without her husband's knowledge – 'for an emergency'.

As became increasingly evident from the 1970s, rising rates of divorce and family breakdown made women more conscious of the risks of lifelong dependency on a male earner and more assertive in seeking ways to avoid it. A Mass Observer from Cumbria worked shifts in a local pub while her children were young but later decided to train as a nurse, which she did in the face of open opposition from her husband. 'I remember getting home at 9pm,' she wrote, 'everyone sitting in front of the TV since 4.30pm and my husband looking over his shoulder and telling me to hurry up with dinner [as] they were all starving!' When she asked why he refused to do his share of housework now that she was working, he said 'it was because I had to make up the difference between what he earned and what I earned'. Those words, she explained, proved 'the death knell of the marriage', reverberating in her head for five years until she felt sufficiently financially secure to walk out.[71] Another Mass Observer remembered the string of part-time jobs which his mother did in the late 1970s and 1980s, including working the till at a cash and carry, doing the electoral roll and taking on intermittent cleaning shifts and secretarial work. As a child, he was told that these earnings were for 'holiday money and "extras"' but he later learned that his father was having an affair and that his mother wanted an income of her own so as to build up savings which would eventually enable her to leave the marriage, which she did in the early 1990s.[72]

Recession and deteriorating job security for men left some mothers little choice but to become the main earners for their families. This role reversal was not always unwelcome for women, although husbands often felt differently. *The Times* profiled one couple in 1983, Sue and John Tanner, who lived in Scunthorpe with their two school-aged sons. Sue had been a full-time housewife but started working as a welfare rights officer just before John was made redundant from his local government job. Sue confessed:

> I do get quite a kick out of being the one who brings home the money, and it's nice coming home to a cooked meal … When you are at home with the children, there are always a hundred things you should be doing. You never actually relax … Out at work, the lunch hour is *yours* – time out for yourself.

John, who was photographed in the garden wearing an apron, said that he enjoyed spending more time with the children and learning how to make pastry and keep chickens, but he found the isolation and loss of status hard to take. 'Your wife comes home from work and says: "Had an interesting day?" You say: "I cleaned the upstairs lavatory," and suddenly realize how boring you've become!' John concluded, 'It's quite fun, as long as it doesn't go on too long.'[73] Male unemployment could create even greater tensions in some ethnic-minority households. The economist Swasti Mitter described how the recession of the early 1980s threw thousands of Bangladeshi men in Tower Hamlets out of work when clothing factories closed down or shifted production to cheap female home-workers. 'The response was near-panic in a community which prided itself on "self-reliance",' Mitter told a conference in 1985. 'In many families it is the women who ended up being the sole breadwinners, while frightened immigrant men tried to sort out the non-payment of tax and National Insurance contributions with the authorities for the employment they had had in the previous two decades, in the twilight economy.'[74]

There were limits to how much pleasure women could take from stepping into the breadwinner's shoes when the employment on offer was poorly paid home-work. With trade union support, some progress was made under Labour in the late 1970s in setting up an Advisory Committee on Home-Working to look into pay, employment rights and health and safety protections for those handling hazardous materials at home. Thatcher's new Conservative government, however, was sceptical that manual home-work was on the rise or that legislative action was necessary. It drew this conclusion despite volumes of evidence to the contrary presented before a House of Commons Select Committee in 1980–1, whose minutes read like a curious replay of early twentieth-century debates over 'sweating'. One notable parallel was the invited testimony of three home-workers, who were more poised and articulate than their Edwardian counterparts but painted a similarly bleak picture of housebound working lives. Jan Fahey sewed shoes with her three-year-old son underfoot:

> I try and put in as many hours as I can during the day, they are sort of irregular hours. I cannot sit down for more than two hours at a time to work at it because there are so many interruptions in looking after a small child, you know, plus the fact that you are at home. So being at home all day you think you have to run the home as a housewife as well, which makes it doubly worse because you are doing two jobs instead of one.

Her house was always cluttered with boxes of thread, fabric and half-finished products.

> I put linings into shoes and make bars and things so there is a lot of mess. It is difficult because I try to keep the mess down as much as I can because of my son, if I do not, he is in the habit of spreading it all around the carpet, so I try to keep it in one particular area but it is very difficult.

The work could also be dangerous. Mrs Fahey explained that the cut on her nose was from the knife on the machine supplied by the firm. It operated on a spring 'and if you pull it too hard it is in the habit of coming forward'. The Committee also heard from Jane James, who was currently making baby slipper-socks at 70p for a dozen. She told MPs that her preference was to go out to work but she felt restricted by her children's school hours: 'Who is going to give you work 9 till 12, then from 1.15 to 3.15?' she asked. 'What job can you get doing that with three months' school holidays?' Mrs

James calculated that it would cost her £7.70 in bus fares to get to her nearest city, which made anything other than very well-paid work economically unviable.[75]

All three witnesses wanted to see their employment status regularised so that they could enjoy a secure income, receive sick pay and take time off for holidays without fear of losing work. Mrs Forbes, a skilled machinist who moved to home-working when her health failed, said that she felt like a 'prisoner' waiting for a job to arrive. 'You dare not go out because if they come up and you are out someone else gets that work because it is urgent, so you stay in. I cannot even go for a walk with the dog because I am afraid to be away from the house.' The Committee echoed these demands in its final report but the government was unconvinced.[76] The Secretary of State for Employment, Norman Tebbit, took the view that home-working was an atypical form of employment and that many home-workers 'no doubt prefer to be self-employed'. No action was to be taken until a clearer picture of the problem had been established.[77] To this end, the government commissioned a major survey, published after lengthy delays in 1987, which appeared to show that traditional manual home-work was losing ground to start-up businesses, freelancers, computer programmers and managers working 'flexibly'.[78] These findings further convinced ministers and officials that intervention was unnecessary, although activists hotly disputed this, arguing that the survey underplayed the constraints pushing women into low-paid work and presented a misleadingly rosy image of conditions for white-collar homeworkers.[79] This latter group, they pointed out, were often similarly isolated and underpaid, prone to depression and paralysed by unpredictable fluctuations in workload.[80] Trade unionists and the campaigning organisation HomeWorkers Worldwide continued to push for better protections into the 1990s and new millennium.[81] The meanings of home-work for mothers, it seemed, were as contested at the end of the twentieth century as they had been at the beginning.

*

When Labour re-entered office in May 1997 under the leadership of Tony Blair, it felt like a turning point for women. One of Labour's first acts was to establish a Women's Unit in Whitehall with a remit to promote gender equality policies across government, championed by a dedicated Minister for Women. A national consultation exercise, *Listening to Women*, was launched to find out what policies British women wanted to see prioritised, amongst which childcare, better parental leave and flexible working came out top. Over the next five years, Labour acted on all of these fronts, publishing a National Childcare Strategy, providing enhanced maternity pay and longer maternity leave, introducing two weeks of paid paternity leave for fathers, and giving carers a right to request flexible working arrangements from their employers. In addition, the government appointed a taskforce on equal pay, sponsored initiatives to help aspiring women entrepreneurs, and offered support to lone parents trying to get into work. In 2002, Cabinet minister Tessa Jowell described New Labour as 'the most feminist government in history'.[82]

This newfound policy commitment to gender equality was certainly due in part to feminist influences inside the party, figures such as Harriet Harman, Clare Short and Diane Abbott, Britain's first black woman MP, as well as the other ninety-eight Labour women MPs elected in the 1997 landslide.[83] Around a third of these MPs were beneficiaries of all-women shortlists, a policy introduced to make the party less masculine in appearance and more appealing to female voters, whose support had been crucial in securing John Major's narrow election victory for the Conservatives five years earlier. There was thus a strong element of electoral calculation behind Labour's new 'feminised' image, prompting some to ask how radical the government was actually prepared to be on gender equality. The Women's Unit adopted a consensual style of policymaking encapsulated in its bland slogan, 'Better for Women is Better for All', and echoed in the language used by the holders of the Minister for Women brief.[84] Jowell rather contradicted her later statement when she described herself as a 'post-feminist' in an interview in December 2000. 'I support feminist views, such as equal pay or the right of women to be safe – but we've moved on from that,' she said. 'I don't believe that the relationship between men and women is any longer adequately defined as men's oppression of women.' Jowell insisted that Labour was not trying to push women into the workplace, but simply offering a choice: 'The most important job that any woman does is to be a mother, but what most women want is to work too. They combine a career with bringing up children for 15 years, so we have to put a framework in place which makes that possible.'[85]

The central pillar in this framework was Labour's National Childcare Strategy. Launched in 1998 with a Green Paper, *Meeting the Childcare Challenge*, this flagship policy was intended to reverse decades of under-investment in services for under-fives and meet a mounting parental demand for high-quality and affordable day-care. Emphasis was placed on creating new places through substantial grant-making and by giving parents tax credits or vouchers to spend as they wished on childcare. This led to major increases in provision. In 1997 there were 5.5 preschoolers for every full-time nursery or childminder place; this number had fallen to 4 by 2003, and 3.4 in 2008. The proportion of under-twos in childcare rose from a quarter to nearly 40 per cent during Labour's period in government, whilst take-up of subsidised places for three- and four-year-olds ran at over 80 per cent.[86] This marked a serious advance on the situation under John Major, who had experimented cautiously with a parental voucher scheme in 1995 as an alternative to major public spending on nurseries.[87] Yet Labour's Strategy was built on similar market principles, requiring parents to 'package' services from a mixed economy of providers across the private and voluntary sectors, as well as to draw upon traditional family-based care. The government saw its task as one of developing capacity within this existing system and filling gaps for families in the most deprived areas. As it turned out, low-income parents were the least likely to make use of new childcare services, partly because tax credits were paid only to those already in work, whereas many mothers felt unable to apply for jobs without having already arranged childcare.[88]

There was a further tension in Labour's National Childcare Strategy. Was it intended to meet the working mother's need for affordable day-care or to advance a more traditional welfare commitment to stabilising the family and tackling poverty? The language of *Meeting the Childcare Challenge* slipped constantly between these objectives. Labour's policy, this document declared, was about 'meeting the needs and enhancing the opportunities of children and their families'. It would give children 'the best start in life' and parents 'genuine choices'. Britain's under-fives would reap the developmental benefits of high-quality care, whilst the economy would gain from getting more parents into work. Only towards the end of the executive summary did the Green Paper explicitly acknowledge that 'offering equal opportunities for parents, especially women' formed part of the Strategy's agenda.[89] As some feminist critics pointed out at the time, Labour was more comfortable invoking the cosy communitarian language of children and families than talking about structural inequalities between the sexes.[90] Despite parading its radical reforming credentials as 'New' Labour, there were clear ideological continuities between Blairism and the party's earlier tendency to view the interests of women and families as one and the same thing.

Labour's record on supporting working mothers was also doubtful when it came to women trapped in low-paid, low-skilled jobs. The introduction of a National Minimum Wage in 1999 was intended to tackle the problem of in-work poverty, but one of the major drivers of low wages – the culture of contracting out – continued unabated. When the journalist Polly Toynbee went undercover to investigate Britain's low-pay economy in 2002 she found it impossible to get a routine job at a school, hospital or municipal building in which she would be directly employed by the State. Everyone – dinner ladies, cleaners, NHS porters, assistants at the shiny new nursery at the Foreign Office – worked for a private contractor of some kind. Toynbee thought that these companies cynically exploited mothers, keeping shifts below the threshold at which women would qualify for various employment protections and State benefits, and offering minimal training or progression because they knew women were desperate enough to accept these conditions. Everyone she met at an induction session for new recruits to ServiceTeam, a private contractor in Lambeth, complained about the pay on offer 'but because of children no one here had any choice but to take it'.[91] Even under Labour's system of tax credits, a working mother on the minimum wage would struggle to pay for childcare, limiting the range of jobs she could feasibly take on. Toynbee discovered that women working the early morning cleaning shift at Guy's Hospital were aware of higher wages on offer in the West End but took the lower rate because it meant they could walk to work from nearby estates rather than pay for public transport.

By the early millennium, an increasing chorus of critics was asking whether Labour really had 'delivered' for women. On the one hand, evidence of women's professional advancement was abundant. Ten years on from the 1997 landslide, women had achieved or were approaching critical mass across a range of fields: they composed over 40 per cent of the medical and legal professions, over a third of secondary school head teachers and more than a quarter of senior managers in the Civil Service.[92] Girls were outperforming their male peers at school and were more likely to go on to university: 38 per cent of female school-leavers progressed to higher education, some seven points higher than the participation rate for boys.[93] On the other hand, women were at greater risk of poverty for the same reasons as fifty or a hundred years before, namely, their low earning power and broken employment histories, their stronger likelihood of having to bring up their children alone, and the fact that so many women faced old age without an adequate State or occupational pension.[94] Alison Wolf suggested in 2006 that these developments had effectively divided women into two categories: 'A minority of well-educated women have careers,' she asserted, 'a majority do jobs, usually part-time, to make some money.' Echoing Catherine Hakim's analysis from the mid-1990s, Wolf argued that it made little sense to discuss 'women' in general, given the gulf of experience and opportunity separating these groups:

For the former, there is very little, if any, disadvantage
associated simply with being a woman. If they are equally
qualified and willing to put in the hours, they can do as well
as any man. But for the majority of women, this sort of life
remains a fantasy. Their families are their top priority, they dip
in and out of the labour market, and they are concentrated in
heavily feminized occupations, such as retailing, cleaning and
clerical work.[95]

Wolf's later study of the lives of female high-fliers seemed to confirm
this picture. 'Educated successful women today have fewer interests
in common with other women than ever before,' she concluded.[96]

Wolf was undoubtedly right to point to serious material
inequalities dividing women in the late twentieth century, yet
disparities of wealth, education and lifestyle had always shaped
women's lives, including the lives of working mothers. Both Hakim
and Wolf overplayed the uniformity of female experience before
the social changes of the 1970s and underestimated the conflicts
involved in juggling family and work *across* income brackets and
occupational hierarchies. In her 1984 study of working mothers,
Sue Sharpe agreed that women with less formal education 'usually
approach motherhood with fewer reservations and leave work, often
thankfully, with no immediate prospect of going back', but their
subsequent experiences, she noted, 'help to promote their return to
work and their reluctance to leave again'. Housebound working-
class mothers were just as frustrated as their middle-class peers
and equally keen to work. 'You do not need special qualifications
to experience social deprivation at home,' Sharpe wrote, 'all you
need are small children, no income, little adult company, and few
outside activities.'[97]

Nor were professional women immune to downward mobility as
a consequence of motherhood. One former City worker explained
to Mass Observation how she had resigned from her job to
accompany her husband overseas and bring up two children; now,
aged forty and keen to return, she felt that only low-paid clerical

work awaited her. She regretted her original decision to enter such a family-unfriendly occupation. 'The cleverest thing I could have done is train as a teacher or planned a career that was more flexible when I wanted to have children.'[98] Yet even these public sector professions, so key to women's career and social mobility in the post-war decades, placed heavy demands on mothers as spending cuts and market reforms intensified over the course of the 1980s and 1990s. Many teachers, doctors, social workers and lecturers experienced this as a form of de-professionalisation, citing mounting managerial oversight, excessive workload and a loss of autonomy in their day-to-day work.[99] Some were made redundant, others resigned when the pressure got too much. One university lecturer, who lost her job following an internal review by management consultants, moved into charity work and counselling after failing to find another professional role. She described in an interview how sorely she felt the loss of status:

> After doing something that allowed you to gain expertise and be a player out there in the world, what's expected of you and available to you now is just to do caring way below your skillset without power or status. What you brought to the professions as a female was at least recognised and remunerated in a male world, you weren't a housewife, but now it just feels like being put back in my box.[100]

*

The fear of being put back in one's box haunted millions of working mothers at the end of the twentieth century, whether they were negotiating million-pound accounts in the Square Mile like Kate Reddy or dishing out dinners to schoolchildren in Lambeth. Despite massive asymmetries of wealth, income and opportunity, these mothers were united in taking on a life of stress in return for acceptance of their presence in the labour market. Hardly anyone questioned women's 'right' to work by the late 1990s, when raising maternal employment rates, especially amongst lone mothers, had explicitly become an object of public policy, a position previously unknown in peacetime. Yet there remained limits to what employers, government and wider society were willing to do to help mothers to exercise that right, whether through the redesign of corporate career structures, public investment in childcare or equal sharing by fathers of domestic labour. The title of Pearson's novel, *I Don't Know How She Does It!*, was clichéd but hit its target by invoking the tension that was inherent in the working mother's situation. The playful phrase acknowledged the reality of women's workplace advancement whilst expressing mirthful incredulity that it should be possible at all. Mothers, of course, knew exactly how they did it, and the price that they paid.

Conclusion

'To be a mother', the critic Jacqueline Rose wrote recently, 'is to be saturated with the good and evil of the day.'[1] In the later nineteenth century, where this book opened, working mothers were mostly saturated with the evil, standing as an emblem of social and economic harm. A century later, working mothers had become, if not a symbol of all that was good in womanhood, then at least an acceptable – ordinary, even – version of it. A number of conditions had to fall into place to bring this transformation about. First, a mother's waged labour had to be in demand from employers. Second, her family had to be reasonably small and her health moderately strong. Third, her husband, if she possessed one, had to recognise the benefits of a second income to his own comfort and status. Finally, mothers had to feel able to claim a life of their own and to insist that society affirm the legitimacy of that life.

Wage-earning was not the only means by which women sought and won this kind of autonomy over the course of the twentieth century, but for many it proved the most effective defence against the servility imposed on them by marriage and domesticity. Paid work provided a source of selfhood and meaning not just for the privileged minority of women pursuing well-remunerated careers, but for mothers across social classes and ethnicities. A desire for independence and fulfilment was most clearly articulated by women in the period after 1945, yet aspiration, pride in skill and pleasure in earning could be glimpsed in the accounts of even the most poorly paid mothers in Victorian industry. Women's assertiveness and self-esteem were bolstered by enfranchisement in 1918 and by the social and political changes which slowly and unevenly improved their material security and physical welfare over the next two decades. The urgent needs of the wartime State and concern over declining birth rates made understanding women's complex feelings about paid work and family an official priority in the 1940s.

It was amidst the booming economy and consumerism of the post-war decades, however, that the moral distinction once tightly drawn between mothers who 'needed' to work and those who merely 'wanted' to broke down. This, rather than the later era of feminism and equal opportunities, was the watershed moment for working mothers in Britain. It was in these years that a second income in the family became a mark of prosperity rather than a source of shame, and that claims about the psychological satisfactions of paid work for mothers gained broad acceptance. Demands for workplace equality, maternity rights, family-friendly working practices and public investment in childcare all flowed from this fundamental shift. Rather than occasioning moral panic, the return to work after childbearing was an increasingly unremarkable step in the life-course of the average modern woman. Once that fact was established, it became possible to argue for more radical measures to secure mothers not just a greater foothold in the labour market, but an equal one.

This, however, mothers did not get – and still do not have. Across the nineteenth and twentieth centuries, women's earning power remained dramatically lower than men's and vast areas of skilled and professional employment were off limits to them, initially through trade union agreements and formal bars, and later through employment practices and cultural norms which protected male privilege. These affected *all* women, but they hit mothers hardest, who were always likelier to work part-time, earn less and advance at a slower pace than their unmarried or childless counterparts. Working mothers were best supported by the State at moments when their labour was badly needed, as exemplified by the war nurseries or the subsidised nursery-school places designed to entice women teachers back to the classroom in the 1960s. Feminist arguments for day-care as the key to giving mothers real choices were only articulated clearly from the 1970s and were viewed uneasily by policymakers. Even under New Labour's bold childcare policies in the late 1990s, gender equality objectives occupied an ambiguous place alongside traditional concerns for the welfare of families and children.

Private employers similarly pursued their self-interest with regard to female workers. In the 1950s, companies like Peek Frean in Bermondsey engaged married women on part-time shifts as a solution to the shortage of full-time recruits, but firms only became truly enthusiastic about part-timers from the 1970s, when changing dynamics in the global economy put a premium on cheap and 'flexible' workforces. Around the same time, the resurgence of home-working and expansion of the service sector created jobs which mothers could fill, but this occurred within the larger context of creeping precarity and low pay, trends which persist in the 'gig economy' of the twenty-first century. In the corporate world, equality campaigners have advocated for the business benefits of retaining experienced female staff through generous maternity packages, family-friendly hours and sustained career support. But there are limits to how much traction such arguments can achieve when even higher-paid professionals lack job security and when long-term careers with a single employer are unusual for men, let alone for mothers.

Furthermore, in large bureaucracies where promotion pathways continue to exist, some mechanism for discarding employees before they reach senior grades is still necessary, and whilst marriage bars are now unlawful, wastage through maternity offers a convenient alternative. In 2013, a number of feminist pressure groups formed the Alliance Against Pregnancy Discrimination in the Workplace to highlight the problem of pregnancy-related redundancies, worryingly on the rise as companies shed staff in the economic downturn. Unlike the 1930s or the early 1980s, proposals to ration employment for the benefit of male breadwinners were notably absent in the immediate aftermath of the 2007 financial crisis.

Yet the pernicious practices of maternity discrimination, affecting more than 50,000 women annually, leave mothers in little doubt as to their inferior and conditional status in many workplaces.[2]

In short, becoming 'ordinary' reduced the stigma experienced by mothers who worked for pay, but it did not bring them equality and it came with costs. In pursuing their double lives since the late nineteenth century, mothers have been forced to strike a number of bargains: with employers and trade unions; with the State; with partners and children; and with themselves. Women's presence in the labour market expanded without seriously disturbing men's monopoly on the highest-paid jobs or reversing their exemption from domestic labour in the home. What Beatrice Webb in 1918 called the 'principle of the vested interest of the male' survived intact right through the interwar and post-war decades. Mothers were channelled into traditionally feminised sectors and encouraged from the 1950s to embrace the phased dual-role model rather than compete with men for continuous careers. Even highly educated graduates overwhelmingly accommodated themselves to this reality, swapping ambition for 'serenity' and weaving narratives about helpful partners who did so much more than the next woman's husband. The sex equality legislation of the 1970s dealt a blow to the ideological foundation of masculine privilege but did not cause it to crumble completely. The British economy remained highly segregated by gender, with women concentrated in lower-paid, lower-skilled sectors and under-represented at the upper levels of management and the professions. This pattern was starkly revealed in 2017, when legislation forcing large employers to report their gender pay gap figures exposed the extent to which women still clustered at the bottom of organisations. At Ryanair, the most extreme case, the pay gap stood at 72 per cent amongst UK-based staff, reflecting how women accounted for two-thirds of lower-paid cabin crew but only eight of the airline's 500 or more pilots. Amongst Britain's major banks, pay differentials ranged from 54 per cent at JP Morgan, to 36 per cent at Goldman Sachs and 29 per cent at HSBC, figures explained for the most part by the numerical dominance of men in senior roles and the higher bonuses paid to male employees.[3]

Observing these enduring inequalities, some contemporary observers conclude that women ultimately lack men's commitment to paid work. As Catherine Hakim argued in the mid-1990s, the doors to professional success were flung open by the social and cultural changes of the later twentieth century, but women seemingly refused to walk through, prioritising the needs of family instead. A new version of this argument was made recently by the commentator David Goodhart, who suggests that the careerist obsessions of a high-achieving feminist elite have been allowed to obscure the more conservative attitudes held by the majority of British women. Rather than privileging equal opportunities and childcare policies which benefit this vocal minority, government ought to focus on stabilising families and restoring the breadwinning incentives which Goodhart sees as integral to the self-esteem of working-class men. Such a move would signal 'a broader view of women's interests' and create 'a more benign environment for family life'.[4] It is certainly true that feminists have in recent decades challenged a historically entrenched model of family which took segregated roles for granted and maintained powerful expectations of women as unpaid care-givers. But the problem with Goodhart's analysis is that, like Hakim's, it presents workplace equality as the sectional interest of a small elite rather than a right historically denied to women across social classes and ethnicities. Slotting women into rival camps as strident careerists or traditional homemakers flattens what are often complicated feelings about ambition, power, love and obligation. Any sense that women's attitudes might be dynamic rather than fixed is lost, whilst the psychic adjustments that mothers make *every day* to accommodate the needs of others are hidden beneath the fiction of unrestrained freedom and choice.

This book has tried to restore some shade and texture to the picture by setting the lives of British working mothers in historical perspective and by asking what it was possible to say or think or claim about those lives over time. David Goodhart belongs to a long line of expert voices purporting to interpret what paid work means to mothers and what constitutes 'women's interests'. In writing

Double Lives, I have resisted the temptation to join him, taking the view that it is not the historian's job to reveal essential truths about women's desires, past or present, or to generalise about paid work as either 'good' or 'bad' for mothers, families or the nation at large. Yet if there is one point upon which history *can* instruct us, it is that mothers do not 'choose' to be paid less than men, or to have less interesting jobs, or to wield less economic power collectively in society. For much of the nineteenth and twentieth centuries, women's worlds were shaped by a labour market founded on sexual difference, a welfare state which institutionalised the dependency of wives, and a wider culture which prized devoted mothering and housewifery as the apotheosis of femininity. What is astonishing is not that mothers accepted their second-class status in the workplace for so long, but that they pushed back against it at all.

Many features of that social order are now gone. Working motherhood does not today attract the violent hostility or pangs of conscience that it summoned in late Victorian hearts and minds. Mothers are an everyday presence in most workplaces, with nearly three-quarters of women with dependent children now in employment.[5] If equality still proves elusive, a woman's need or desire to return to work after having children is recognised as a legitimate aspiration rather than an unnatural urge or anti-social act. Yet it *is* still a double life that working mothers are forced to live, and a stressful and often lonely one at that. In 1912, the avant-garde feminist periodical *The Freewoman* posed a fundamental question about the divided loyalties felt by mothers: 'To whom is her first duty, herself or the coming generation?' Its answer was radical then and remains radical now: 'We hold, that her first, second, and third duty is to herself, and, that duty being fulfilled, she will have done her duty to the coming generation.'[6]

Notes

1 This account is based on census, birth, marriage and death records available at www.ancestry.co.uk, and on Isabella Killick's testimony to the House of Lords Select Committee on the Sweating System, which she gave on 24 April 1888. See *Report of the Select Committee of the House of Lords on the Sweating System: First Report* (HMSO 1888), pp. 150–1.

2 For a good overview of the types of paid work performed by women at the beginning of the twentieth century, see *The Occupations of Women According to the Census of England and Wales, 1911: Summary Tables Arranged and Compiled by L Wyatt Papworth and Dorothy M Zimmern* (London, 1914).

3 John McKay, 'Married women and work in nineteenth-century Lancashire: the evidence of the 1851 and 1861 census reports' in Nigel Goose, ed., *Women's work in industrial England: regional and local perspectives* (Hatfield, 2007), pp. 164–181. The extent to which census data undercounted married women's employment in the post-1850 period should not, however, be overstated, as recently argued by Edward Higgs and Amanda Wilkinson in 'Women, occupations and work in the Victorian censuses revisited', *History Workshop Journal*, 87, Spring 2016, pp. 17–38.

4 The census recorded marital status but it did not provide aggregate data on women's maternal status before the 1960s. We can gain a very rough idea of the numbers of wage-earning mothers for the early twentieth century by using childbearing age as a proxy. In 1901, 918,000

married and widowed women were recorded as occupied in England and Wales, of which some 450,000 were aged between nineteen and forty-four. Given that only around 11 per cent of married couples were childless at this time, it can be safely assumed that a large majority of these working wives were also mothers. As this figure does not include older mothers, unmarried mothers in paid work or working mothers whose occupations were not recorded by the census, the true number is therefore likely to have been significantly greater.

5   There is a large literature on the emergence of the breadwinner family, but see Sara Horrell and Jane Humphries, 'Women's Labour Force Participation and the Transition to the Male-Breadwinner Family, 1790–1865', *Economic History Review*, second series, 48 (1995), pp. 89–117, and Sara Horrell and Jane Humphries, 'The origins and expansion of the male breadwinner family: the case of nineteenth century Britain', *International Review of Social History*, supplement, 5 (1997), pp. 25–64; Colin Creighton, 'The rise of the male breadwinner family: a reappraisal', *Comparative Studies in Society and History*, 38 (1996), pp. 310–37, and 'The rise and decline of the "male breadwinner family" in Britain', *Cambridge Journal of Economics*, 23 (1999), pp. 519–41.

6   Mass Observation Project, Autumn 2014 Directive, observer F5576, dated 6 January 2015.

7   Office for National Statistics, *Mothers in the Labour Market, 2011* (ONS, 31 March 2011).

8   Office for National Statistics, *Families and the Labour Market: England 2018* (October 2018).

9   Pay gap figure from Fawcett Society, *Gender Pay Gap Reporting Deadline Briefing 2019* (April 2019).

10 The scholarly literature is vast, but for key interpretations see Alice Clark, *The Working Life of Women in the Seventeenth Century* (London, 1919); Ivy Pinchbeck, *Women Workers and the Industrial Revolution, 1750–1850* (London, 1930); Eric Richards, 'Women in the British Economy since about 1700: An Interpretation', *History*, 59 (1974), pp. 337–47; Sally Alexander, 'Women's work in nineteenth-century London' in Juliet Mitchell and Ann Oakley, eds, *The Rights and Wrongs of Women* (London, 1976), pp. 59–111; Louise Tilly and Joan Scott, *Women, Work and Family* (London, 1978); Pat Hudson and Maxine Berg, 'Rehabilitating the industrial revolution', *Economic History*

Review, 45 (1992), pp. 25–50. A good general survey is provided by Jane Rendall, *Women in an Industrializing Society: England 1750–1880* (Oxford, 1990).

11 Mabel Atkinson, 'The economic foundations of the women's movement' in Sally Alexander, ed., *Women's Fabian Tracts* (London, 1988), p. 15.

12 Eleanor Rathbone, *The Disinherited Family* (London, 1924), p. vii.

13 For the concept of 'family strategies', see Jane Humphries, *Childhood and Child Labour in the British Industrial Revolution* (Cambridge, 2010).

14 Carolyn Steedman, *Landscape for a Good Woman* (London, 1989), p. 12.

15 For working-class autobiography, see David Vincent, *Bread, Knowledge and Freedom: A Study of Nineteenth-Century Working Class Biography* (London, 1982); Humphries, *Childhood and Child Labour*; and Emma Griffin, *Liberty's Dawn: A People's History of the Industrial Revolution* (London, 2013).

16 Mrs Carl Meyer and Clementina Black, *Makers of Our Clothes: A Case for Trade Boards* (London, 1909), p. 10.

17 Gillian Sutherland, *In Search of The New Woman: Middle-Class Women and Work in Britain, 1870–1914* (Cambridge, 2015); Christine Etherington Wright, *Gender, Professions and Discourse: Early Twentieth-Century Women's Autobiography* (Basingstoke, 2009); Martha Vicinus, *Independent Women: Work and Community for Single Women, 1850–1920* (London, 1985).

18 Female rate-payers were eligible to stand for election to School Boards, created by the 1870 Education Act to oversee the provision of universal elementary schooling, and from 1875 to serve as Poor Law Guardians. However, only after the local government franchise was extended in 1894 were *married* women eligible for these posts. It was also in 1894 that women, both married and single, were allowed to stand for election to parish rural district and urban district councils, and in 1907 women became eligible for office in borough and county councils.

19 See, for example, Rosalind Gill, 'Culture and Subjectivity in Neoliberal and Postfeminist Times', *Subjectivity*, 25 (2008), pp. 432–445, and Zoe Young, *Women's Work: How Mothers Manage Flexible Working in Careers and Family Life* (Bristol, 2018).

20 A development which is explored and explained in Laura King's excellent *Family Men: Fatherhood and masculinity in Britain, 1914–1960* (Oxford, 2015).

21 Chris Belfield, Richard Blundell, Jonathan Cribb, Andrew Hood, Robert Joyce, Agnes Norris Keiller, *Two decades of income inequality in Britain: The role of wages, household earnings and redistribution* (IFS, 2017), Appendix, pp. 13–14. See also Richard Hall, 'The Emotional Lives and Legacies of Fathers and Sons in Britain, 1945–1974' (unpublished PhD thesis, University of Cambridge, 2019).

I BREAD AND BUTTER

1 Hansard Parliamentary Debates, House of Commons, 10 May 1844.

2 George Newman, *Infant Mortality: A Social Problem* (London, 1906), p. 120.

3 Ada Nield Chew, 'All in the Day's Work: Mrs Bolt' in *The Englishwoman* (1912), reprinted in Doris Nield Chew, ed., *Ada Nield Chew: The Life and Writings of a Working Woman* (London, 1982), pp. 161–6.

4 Ellen Barlee, *A Visit to Lancashire in December 1862* (London, 1863), p. 27.

5 Mary Merryweather, *Experience of Factory Life* (London, 1862), p. 30.

6 In his sample of households in Preston, Michael Anderson found that 17 per cent of wives employed in factories had a non-earning grandmother resident, whilst 28 per cent had at least one other non-earning adult resident in the household, either a relative or a lodger, who was a potential minder. See *Family Structure in Nineteenth-Century Lancashire* (Cambridge, 1971), p. 74.

7 Newman, *Infant Mortality*, pp. 124–5.

8 M. L. Walker, 'Women and Children in Dundee', *Charity Organisation Review*, 27 (1910), pp. 31–42.

9 Hansard Parliamentary Debates, House of Commons, 15 March 1844.

10 Judy Lown, *Women and Industrialization: Gender at Work in Nineteenth-Century England* (Cambridge, 1990), p. 146. The factory inspector Adelaide Anderson noted an 'instinctive prejudice in favour of individual care by nurses' amongst factory mothers. A. M. Anderson, 'Memorandum on the Employment of Mothers in Factories and Workshops' in *Report of the Inter-Departmental Committee on Physical Deterioration: Volume I* (HMSO, 1904, Cd. 2175), p. 128.

11 One factory inspector visiting cotton mills in Manchester in 1847 judged over a quarter of female operatives to be married women, a finding broadly confirmed by later census data. In Oldham the figure was as high as 46 per cent in 1851, whilst in Blackburn the proportion rose from 24 per cent to 30 per cent over the following two decades. A further 5 per cent were widows. See Margaret Hewitt, *Wives and Mothers in Victorian Industry* (London, 1958), pp. 13, 15.

12 Royal Commission on Labour, *The Employment of Women: Reports by Miss Eliza Orme, Miss Clara Collet, Miss May Abraham and Miss Margaret Irwin* (HMSO, C.6894, 1893), p. 63. For the complex gendered division of labour in the potteries, see Richard Whipp, *Patterns of Labour: Work and Social Change in the Pottery Industry* (London, 1990).

13 Women's Industrial Council, *The Occupations of Women According to the Census of England and Wales, 1911: Summary Tables Arranged and Compiled by L Wyatt Papworth and Dorothy M Zimmern* (London, 1914). See also Patricia E. Malcolmson, *English Laundresses: A Social History, 1850–1930* (Chicago, 1986).

14 *The Employment of Women: Reports*, pp. 33–4.

15 Ibid., p. 237.

16 B.L. Hutchins, 'Statistics of Women's Life and employment,' *Journal of the Royal Statistical Society*, 72 (1909), p. 213. Married women suffered from poor health as well, but were more likely to develop chronic debilitating conditions caused by repeated pregnancy and inadequate diet. If food was scarce, mothers typically prioritised the needs of male breadwinners and children over their own.

17 The New Poor Law (1834) stipulated that outdoor relief should not be given to persons deemed fit to work, although this rule was widely disregarded at local level. Efforts in the 1870s to reduce the provision of outdoor relief to the able-bodied were largely successful, although policy towards married women and widows was complex and practices varied a great deal between areas. See Pat Thane, 'Women and the Poor Law in Victorian and Edwardian England', *History Workshop Journal*, 6 (1978), pp. 29–51; Lynn Hollen Lees, *The Solidarities of Strangers: The English Poor Laws and the People, 1700–1948* (Cambridge, 1998); Anna Clark, 'The new poor law and the breadwinner wage: contrasting assumptions', *Journal of Social History* 34 (2000), pp. 261–82.

18 Lown, *Women and Industrialisation*, p. 110.

19 Quoted in Michael Hiley, *Victorian Working Women: Portraits from Life* (London, 1979), p. 91.

20 Judith Walkowitz, *Prostitution and Victorian Society: Women, Class and the State* (Cambridge, 1980), p. 156.

21 Julie Marie Strange, *Fatherhood and the British Working Class, 1865–1914* (Cambridge, 2015).

22 Elizabeth Roberts, 'Working wives and their families' in Theo Barker and Michael Drake, eds, *Population and Society in Britain, 1850–1980* (London, 1982), p. 152.

23 *The Employment of Women: Reports*, p. 23.

24 Clementina Black, ed., *Married Women's Work: Being the report of an enquiry undertaken by the Women's Industrial Council* (London, 1983, first published 1915), p. 23.

25 Ibid., p. 88.

26 Ibid., p. 6.

27 Fabian Women's Group, *Summary of Eight Papers and Discussions upon the Disabilities of Mothers as Workers* (London, 1910), p. 28.

28 Anna Clark, 'The rhetoric of Chartist domesticity: gender, language and class in the 1830s and 1840s', *Journal of British Studies*, 31 (1992), quotes at p. 83 and p. 72. Clark points out that many Chartist women reinforced this ideology by framing their waged labour as degrading and exploitative rather than drawing upon male conceptions of artisanal skill and control over the labour process; see p. 81.

29 Cited by Carol E. Morgan, *Women Workers and Gender Identities, 1835–1913: The Cotton and Metal Industries in England* (London, 2001), p. 47.

30 Hansard Parliamentary Debates, House of Commons, 15 March 1844.

31 Beatrice Webb, *My Apprenticeship* (London, 1926), p. 183.

32 Anna Davin, 'Imperialism and Motherhood', *History Workshop Journal*, 5 (1978), pp. 9–65; Jane Lewis, *The Politics of Motherhood: Child and Maternal Welfare in England, 1900–1939* (London, 1980); Ellen Ross, *Love and Toil: Motherhood in Outcast London, 1870–1918* (Oxford, 1993).

33 Pat Thane, *Foundations of the Welfare State* (second edn, London, 2016).

34 Royal Commission on Labour, *Fifth and Final Report* (C.7421, 1894), p. 3.

35 Royal Commission on Labour, *Minutes of Evidence, with appendices, taken before Group C* (C.6708, 1892), p. 327.

36 Ibid., pp. 366, 367.

37 Ibid., p. 369.

38 One historian describes Collet as 'widely regarded from the 1890s as *the* English expert on aspects of women's work and wages'. See Peter Groenewegen, 'Introduction: Women in Political Economy and Women as Political Economists in Victorian England' in Peter Groenewegen, ed., *Feminism and Political Economy in Victorian England* (Aldershot, 1994), p. 3. On ideological divisions over the appointment of the first lady factory inspectors, see Ruth Livesey, 'The politics of work: feminism, professionalisation and women inspectors of factories and workshops', *Women's History Review*, 13 (2004), pp. 233–62.

39 For some stimulating perspectives on how historians might read the gender and class dynamics produced by this late-nineteenth-century tradition of social investigation, see Ross McKibbin, 'Social Class and Social Observation in Edwardian England', *Transactions of the Royal Historical Society*, 28 (1978), pp. 175–99; Ross, *Love and Toil*, pp. 18–26; and Gabrielle Mearns, '"Long Trudges Through Whitechapel": The East End of Beatrice Webb's and Clara Collet's Social Investigations', *19: Interdisciplinary Studies in the Long Nineteenth Century*, 13 (2011) DOI: http://doi.org/10.16995/ntn.634.

40 Anderson, 'Memorandum on the Employment of Mothers', p. 125.

41 *The Employment of Women: Reports*, p. 306.

42 *Report of the Proceedings of the National Conference on Infantile Mortality* (London, 1906), p. 230.

43 Celia Briar argues convincingly that the Act treated widows little differently from the Poor Law. The reason for including women in the schemes was 'not to preserve their skills as workers but because they were semi-destitute through the lack of a male "breadwinner"'. Celia Briar, *Working for Women? Gendered Work and Welfare Policies in Twentieth-Century Britain* (London, 1997), p. 16.

44 Evidence of J. G. Newey, 2 April 1907, *Report from the Select Committee on Homework* (HMSO, 1907), p. 143.

45 Briar, *Working for Women?* p. 23.

46 John Burnett, 'Report as to the Condition of Nailmakers and Small Chainmakers in South Staffordshire and East Worcestershire, 1888' in *Report of the Select Committee of the House of Lords on the Sweating System: Fifth Report* (HMSO, 361, 1890), p. 12.

47 *The Employment of Women: Reports*, p. 22.

48 Mrs Player and Mrs J. R. MacDonald, 'Wage-Earning Mothers', *The Labour Leaflet* (No. 3, March 1911), p. 2.

49 Jose Harris, *Unemployment and Politics: A Study in English Social Policy, 1886–1914* (Oxford, 1972); Marjorie Levine-Clark, *Unemployment, Welfare, and Masculine Citizenship: 'So Much Honest Poverty' in Britain, 1870–1930* (Basingstoke, 2015).

50 Black, *Married Women's Work*, p. 14. See also Ada Meyer and Clementina Black, *Makers of Our Clothes: A Case for Trade Boards* (London, 1909), pp. 149, 183.

51 For historical accounts which situate married women's employment within wider family 'strategies', see Jane Humphries, *Childhood and Child Labour in the British Industrial Revolution* (Cambridge, 2010); Ross, *Love and Toil*; Andrew August, 'How Separate a Sphere? Poor Women and Paid Work in Late-Victorian London', *Journal of Family History*, 19 (1994), pp. 295–309.

52 *The Employment of Women: Reports*, p. 53.

53 *National Conference on Infantile Mortality*, p. 230.

54 For an insightful discussion of 'custom' in the US context, see Alice Kessler Harris, *A Woman's Wage: Historical Meanings and Social Consequences* (Kentucky, 1990). For cultural understandings of gender in the industrial workplace more broadly, see Sonya Rose's seminal *Limited Livelihoods: Gender and Class in Nineteenth-Century England* (London, 1992).

55 *The Employment of Women: Reports*, p. 283. For the prevalence of husbands employing their wives as assistants in the pottery industry around Stoke on Trent, see Whipp, *Patterns of Labour*, chapter 2.

56 Walker, 'Women and Children in Dundee', p. 38.

57 Anderson, 'Memorandum on the Employment of Mothers in Factories', p. 126.

58 Black, *Married Women's Work*, p. 7.

59 Ada Nield Chew, 'A Daughter's Education', *Common Cause*, 13 June 1913, in Nield Chew, ed., *Life and Writings*, pp. 176–80.

60 Black, *Married Women's Work*, p. 4.

61 For feminist arguments about married women's property rights, see Ben Griffin, *The Politics of Gender in Victorian Britain: Masculinity, Political Culture, and the Struggle for Women's Rights* (Cambridge, 2012).

62 For these debates, see Carol Dyhouse, *Feminism and the Family in England, 1880–1939* (Oxford, 1989), chapter 2; Jane Lewis, 'Models of equality for women: the case of state support for children in twentieth-century Britain' in Gisela Bock and Pat Thane, eds, *Maternity and Gender Policies: Women and the Rise of the European Welfare States 1880s–1950s* (London, 1991), pp. 73–92, and Pat Thane, 'Visions of gender in the making of the British welfare state: the case of women in the British Labour Party and social policy, 1906–1945' in same volume, pp. 93–118; and Susan Pedersen, *Family, Dependence, and the Origins of the Welfare State: Britain and France, 1914–1945* (Cambridge, 1993), pp. 32–59.

63 *Report of the Inter-Departmental Committee on Physical Deterioration*, p. 49.

64 *The Employment of Women: Reports*, p. 53.

65 Player and MacDonald, 'Wage-Earning Mothers', p. 2.

66 The Fabian economist Sidney Webb regarded this latter factor as operational in determining women's wages, writing in 1891: 'it is impossible to overlook the effect of the fact that the woman has something else to sell besides her labour' – by which he meant sex (*Economic Journal*, 1 [1891], p. 660). Testing this claim is not straightforward, given the difficulties of mapping the extent and geographical distribution of sex work accurately over time.

67 W. S. Jevons, 'Married women in factories', *Contemporary Review*, 41, January 1882, p. 37.

68 *National Conference on Infantile Mortality*, p. 17.

69 Edgar S. Kemp, 'Baby-minding', *Charity Organisation Review*, 36 (1914), pp. 133–8.

70 The best general overview is still Carol Dyhouse, 'Working-class mothers and infant mortality in England, 1895–1914', *Journal of Social History*, 12 (1978), pp. 248–67, but see also Melanie Reynolds, *Infant Mortality and Working-Class Child Care, 1850–1899* (Basingstoke, 2016).

71 Mrs H. J. Tennant, 'Infant Mortality and Factory Labour – I' in Thomas Oliver, ed., *Dangerous Trades: The Historical, Social, and Legal Aspects of Industrial Occupations as Affecting Health, by a Number of Experts* (London, 1902), p. 73.

72 A good summary of the position of this group can be found in Jessie Boucherett and Helen Blackburn, *The Condition of Working Women*

and the Factory Acts (London, 1896). For these distinct feminist positions on the question of protective legislation, see Rosemary Feurer, 'The Meaning of "Sisterhood": the British Women's Movement and Protective Labour Legislation', *Victorian Studies*, 31 (1988), pp. 233–60; Ellen Mappen, 'Strategies for Change: Social Feminist Approaches to Problems of Women's Work' in Angela V. John, *Unequal Opportunities: Women's Employment in England, 1800–1918* (Oxford, 1986), pp. 235–59; and Malcolmson, *English Laundresses*, chapter 3.

73 From the summer of 1898, women were barred from certain processes in white lead factories and became subject to monthly medical examinations in potteries which used lead for glazing purposes. These rules were based on medical evidence apparently pointing to women's greater susceptibility to health risks arising from lead exposure, although cases of poisoning amongst men rose dramatically as male was substituted for female labour following the rule changes. See Barbara Harrison, *Not only the 'dangerous trades': Women's work and health in Britain, 1880–1914* (London, 1996); Carolyn Malone, 'The Gendering of Dangerous Trades: Government Regulation of Women's Work in the White Lead Trade in England, 1891– 1898', *Journal of Women's History*, 8 (1996), pp. 1–35.

74 Clara Collet, 'The collection and utilisation of official statistics bearing upon the extent and effects of the industrial employment of women', *Journal of the Royal Statistical Society*, 61 (1898), pp. 219– 70. Recent historical analysis of infant mortality similarly explores the interplay of environmental, demographic and socio-economic factors, with particular emphasis placed on the health of pregnant women and nursing mothers, although the relationship between the latter and female employment remains complex. See Robert Milward and Frances Bell, 'Infant Mortality in Victorian Britain: The Mother as Medium', *Economic History Review*, 54 (2001), pp. 699–733.

75 *Report of the Inter-Departmental Committee on Physical Deterioration*, p. 47.

76 Ibid., p. 49. For the complexities of government action to 'protect' women workers by restricting their labour, see Jane Lewis and Sonya Rose, '"Let England Blush": Protective Labor Legislation, 1820–1914' in Ulla Wikander, Alice Kessler-Harris and Jane Lewis, eds, *Protecting Women: Labor Legislation in Europe, the United States*

and Australia, 1880–1920 (Urbana & Chicago, 1995), pp. 91–124, and Barbara Harrison and Helen Mockett, 'Women in the Factory: The State and Factory Legislation in Nineteenth-Century Britain' in Lynn Jamieson and Helen Corr, eds, State, Private Life and Political Change (Basingstoke, 1990), pp. 137–62.

77 Lewis, Politics of Motherhood; Deborah Dwork, War is good for babies and other young children: A history of the infant and child welfare movement in England 1898–1918 (London, 1987).

78 National Conference on Infantile Mortality, p. 182. Melanie Reynolds cites evidence of Yorkshire mothers in the later nineteenth century taking their babies to the factory, where they would sleep in baskets next to their looms between feeds, but it is difficult to assess how widespread this practice might have been. See Reynolds, Infant Mortality and Working-Class Child Care, chapter 2.

79 Leo Chiozza Money, Riches and Poverty (London, fourth edn, 1908), p. 169.

80 A few members of the Fabian Women's Group floated the idea, although not in any detail, of a scheme of State maintenance for women 'during the period when her motherhood incapacitates her'. See introductory lecture by Mrs Pember Reeves in Fabian Women's Group, Summary of Eight Papers, p. 5.

81 See Thane, 'Visions of gender in the making of the British welfare state'.

82 Margaret Llewelyn Davies, Maternity: Letters from Working Women (London, 1915).

83 There is ample evidence that many working-class housewives regarded full-time home-making as preferable to the double burden of waged work. See Elizabeth Roberts, A Woman's Place: An Oral History of Working-Class Women, 1900–1940 (Oxford, 1984) and Joanna Bourke, 'Housewifery in working-class England, 1860–1914', Past & Present, 143 (1994), pp. 167–97.

2 THE ESSENTIAL ELEMENT OF EVIL

1 Daily News, 8 June 1906, p. 9.

2 Richard Mudie-Smith, 'Foreword' in Handbook of the Daily News Sweated Industries Exhibition (London, 1906), p. 10.

3 By foregrounding the lives of home-working mothers and the claims made about them, this chapter builds upon important

scholarship linking women's work, sweating and minimum wage legislation, including: Deborah Thom, 'Free from chains? The image of women's labour in London, 1900–1920' in David Feldman and Gareth Stedman Jones, eds, *Metropolis London: Histories and representations since 1800* (London, 1989), pp. 85–99; Sheila Blackburn, *A Fair Day's Wage for a Fair Day's Work? Sweated Labour and the Origins of Minimum Wage Legislation in Britain* (Aldershot, 2007); Jenny Morris, *Women Workers and the Sweated Trades: The Origins of Minimum Wage Legislation* (Aldershot, 1986); Sonya Rose, *Limited Livelihoods: Gender and Class in Nineteenth-Century England* (London, 1992), chapter 4; and Kristina Huneault, *Difficult Subjects: Working Women and Visual Culture, Britain 1880–1914* (Farnham, 2002). For earlier sweating debates see Duncan Bythell, *Sweated Trades: Outwork in Nineteenth-Century Britain* (London, 1978); James Schmiechen, *Sweated Industries and Sweated Labour: The London Clothing Trades* (Urbana, 1984); and Helen Rogers, 'The Good are not always powerful, nor the powerful always good: The politics of women's needlework in mid-Victorian London', *Victorian Studies*, 40 (1997), pp. 589–623.

4 This was the title of chapter one in Clementina Black's *Sweated Industry and the Minimum Wage* (London, 1907).

5 Twenty-seven per cent of shirt-makers and 24 per cent of tailoresses fell into this category. Figures derived from *The Occupations of Women According to the Census of England and Wales, 1911: Summary Tables Arranged and Compiled by L Wyatt Papworth and Dorothy M Zimmern* (London, 1914).

6 For a helpful overview of the major home-working trades employing women see Shelley Pennington and Belinda Westover, *A Hidden Workforce: Homeworkers in England, 1850–1985* (Basingstoke, 1989).

7 John Burnett, 'Report as to the Condition of Nailmakers and Small Chainmakers in South Staffordshire and East Worcestershire, 1888' in *Report of the Select Committee of the House of Lords on the Sweating System: Fifth Report* (HMSO, 361, 1890), p. 6.

8 *Report from the Select Committee on Homework* (HMSO 218, 1907), p. 103.

9 Royal Commission on Labour, *The Employment of Women: Reports by Miss Eliza Orme, Miss Clara Collet, Miss May Abraham and Miss Margaret Irwin* (HMSO, C.6894, 1893), p. 294.

10 See evidence of Malcolm Delevingne, *Select Committee on Homework* (1907), p. 8. Clara Collet thought that there were 300,000 homeworkers in the clothing trades alone.

11 Margaret Irwin, 'The Problem of Home Work', *Westminster Review*, November 1897, p. 54.

12 Evidence of Robert Graves, *Select Committee on Homework* (1907), p. 75.

13 Evidence of Mrs Isabella Killick, *Select Committee of the House of Lords on the Sweating System: First Report* (HMSO 240, 1888), p. 150.

14 *Report by Miss Constance Williams and Mr. Thomas Jones on the effect of outdoor relief on wages and the conditions of employment* in *Royal Commission on the Poor Laws and Relief of Distress: Appendix volume XVII* (HMSO, Cd 4690, 1909). Quotation is from 'Interim Report No.1', p. 10.

15 As David Feldman argues, racial stereotypes of the 'mercenary' and 'unscrupulous' Jew substituted for serious analysis of Jewish entrepreneurship, a phenomenon which would resurface in the 1970s and 1980s in relation to the 'ethnic economy' taking shape following mass migration from the Asian subcontinent. See *Englishmen and Jews: Social Relations and Political Culture 1840–1914* (London, 1994).

16 Which is not to say that the subject of immigrant labour fell out of discussion, as an examination of parliamentary debates reveals. See, for example, the Second Reading of the Sweated Industries Bill in the House of Commons, Hansard, 21 February, 1908.

17 *Select Committee on Home Work* (1907), p. 22.

18 Ibid., p. 113.

19 See the evidence of Mabel Vines, factory inspector at the Home Office, *Select Committee on Home Work* (1907), p. 64.

20 Ibid., p. 119.

21 Ibid., p. 140.

22 Ibid., p. 73.

23 *The Employment of Women*, p. 273.

24 Ibid., p. 63.

25 *Select Committee of the House of Lords on the Sweating System: First Report*, pp. 153–4.

26 *Select Committee of the House of Lords on the Sweating System: Fifth Report* (HMSO, 361, 1890), p. 37.

27 *Report from the Select Committee on Homework* (HMSO, 1908), p. 4.

28 *Select Committee on Homework* (1907), p. 25.

29 Ibid., p. 75.

30 Testimony of Miss Edith Lawson, *Select Committee on Homework* (1908), p. 131.

31 Mrs Hylton Dale, *Child Labor Under Capitalism* (London, 1908). The Women's Industrial Council carried out a study of child labour in the late 1890s. See Edith Hogg, 'School Children as Wage Earners', *The Nineteenth Century*, vol. 42, 1897, pp. 235–44.

32 *Select Committee on Home Work* (1907), p. 116.

33 Clementina Black, 'Suggested Remedies', *Handbook of the Daily News Sweated Industries Exhibition* (London, 1906), p. 24.

34 Irwin, 'The Problem of Home Work', p. 553.

35 *Select Committee on Home Work* (1907), p. 133.

36 *Report on the effect of outdoor relief on wages and the conditions of employment.*

37 The Poplar figure is from Eric Horne, 'Outwork and Relief in Poplar Union', a report included in the appendices of the report cited in the previous footnote. The West Ham figure, which was 2.5 per cent, is from Edward Howarth and Mona Wilson, *West Ham: A Study in Social and Industrial Problems: Being the Report of the Outer London Inquiry Committee* (London, 1907), p. 268.

38 Case recorded by G. Rose Armstrong in 'Artificial Flowers' file, records of the Women's Industrial Council, WIC/F/2, The Women's Library, London School of Economics.

39 Case recorded in 'Boxes' file, WIC/F/1.

40 *Select Committee on Home Work* (1907), p. 22.

41 Ibid., p. 37.

42 *Select Committee on Home Work* (1908), p. 244.

43 Barbara Caine, 'Beatrice Webb and the "Woman Question"', *History Workshop Journal*, 14 (1982), pp. 23–43; Deborah Epstein Nord, *The Apprenticeship of Beatrice Webb* (Basingstoke, 1985).

44 *Select Committee of the House of Lords on the Sweating System*, p. 330.

45 Beatrice Potter, 'The Lords and the Sweating System', *The Nineteenth Century*, June 1890, pp. 893.

46 Beatrice Webb, 'Women and the Factory Acts' (London, 1896), p. 14.

47 *Royal Commission on Labour: Fourth Report* (C.7063, 1892), pp. 301–2.

48 Sidney Webb and Beatrice Webb, *Industrial Democracy* (London, 1897), p. 764. The radical economist J. A. Hobson had floated the idea of a national minimum wage first. For more on the Webbs'

position on women's work and wages, see Morris, *Women Workers and the Sweated Trades*, pp. 178–9; Chris Nyland and Gaby Ramia, 'The Webbs and the Rights of Women' in Peter Groenewegen, ed., *Feminism and Political Economy in Victorian England* (Aldershot, 1994), pp. 110–46; Blackburn, *A Fair Day's Wage for a Fair Day's Work?* (Aldershot, 2007), chapter 3.

49 *Royal Commission on Labour: Fourth Report*, p. 299.

50 The classic works on this progressive moment are P. F. Clarke, *Liberals and Social Democrats* (Cambridge, 1978); Michael Freeden, *The New Liberalism: An Ideology of Social Reform* (Oxford, 1978); and Jose Harris, 'Political Thought and the Welfare State, 1870–1940: An Intellectual Framework for British Social Policy', *Past & Present*, 135 (1992), pp. 116–41.

51 Other notable members of the committee were the radical Liberal Charles Trevelyan, who had toured North America and Australasia with the Webbs in 1898–9, and Charles Masterman, another 'New' Liberal who was close to the Webbs and committed to social reform.

52 Sheila Blackburn, 'Ideology and Social Policy: The Origins of the Trades Boards Act', *Historical Journal*, 34 (1991), pp. 43–64.

53 *Select Committee on Home Work* (1908), p. 6.

54 A. G. Gardiner, introduction to Black, *Sweated Industry*, p. xxiv.

55 For three excellent discussions, see Ellen Ross, ed., *Slum Travellers: Ladies and London Poverty, 1860–1920* (London, 2007); Seth Koven, *Slumming: Sexual and Social Politics in Victorian London* (London, 2006); and Ruth Livesey, 'Reading for Character: Women Social Reformers and Narratives of the Urban Poor in Late Victorian and Edwardian London', *Journal of Victorian Culture*, 9 (2004), pp. 43–67.

56 Judith Walkowitz superbly dissects this cultural hybridity in *City of Dreadful Delight: Narratives of Sexual Danger in Late-Victorian London* (London, 1992). See also Deborah Epstein Nord, *Walking the Victorian Streets: Women, Representation and the City* (London, 1995), chapter 7. For growing media interest in stories about women's work, see Carolyn Malone, 'Sensational Stories, Endangered Bodies: Women's Work and the New Journalism in England in the 1890s', *Albion*, 31 (1999), pp. 49–71.

57 Edith Hogg, 'The fur-pullers of south London', *The Nineteenth Century*, 42, 1897, pp. 734–43. See also Ada Meyer and Clementina

Black's account of an expedition into the home-working districts of south London at the beginning of *Makers of Our Clothes: A Case for Trade Boards* (London, 1909).

58 'Baby's Heritage', *The Woman Worker*, 3 July 1908, pp. 125–6.

59 *The Woman Worker*, No. 1, September 1907, p. 2.

60 My analysis in this and the following two paragraphs builds upon Kristina Huneault's wonderful book, *Difficult Subjects: Working Women and Visual Culture*. Huneault's discussion of women's factory work implies that such images, in contrast to home-work, usually depicted younger unmarried women. It was, of course, much easier for artists to indicate the maternal status of home-workers through visual clues in the domestic interior, notably the presence of children. I have not located any images of pregnant workers, either in factories or at home.

61 T. J. Edelstein, '"They Sang the Song of the Shirt": The Visual Iconology of the Seamstress', *Victorian Studies*, 23 (1980), pp. 183–210.

62 Judith Walkowitz, 'The Indian woman, the flower girl, and the Jew: photojournalism in Edwardian London', *Victorian Studies*, 42 (1998), pp. 3–46; Thomas Prasch, 'Photography and the image of the London poor' in Debra Mancoff and Dale Tela, eds, *Victorian urban settings: Essays on the nineteenth-century city and its contexts* (New York, 1996), pp. 179–94.

63 See Seth Koven's brilliant analysis of the scandal which engulfed Thomas Barnardo over posed photographs of 'ragged' children in the 1870s in *Slumming*, pp. 88–139.

64 'Talking to the Princess', *Daily Mirror*, 17 May 1906, p. 5.

65 'Sweating Exhibition: A Throng of Visitors', *Daily News*, 5 May 1906, p. 9.

66 *Handbook of the Daily News Sweated Industries Exhibition*, p. 12.

67 See Ruth Livesey's sensitive discussion of this observational mode in 'Reading for Character'.

68 My reading of the evidence follows Huneault's analysis of the Exhibition, and that of Jane Beckett and Deborah Cherry, eds, *The Edwardian Era* (Oxford, 1987), pp. 70–87, more closely than that of Sheila Blackburn, who suggests that the workers 'were no longer represented, as they had been in the popular poems, paintings and plays of the past, as uncomplaining and inert victims; they were

active participants in a dynamic, living spectacle' (*Fair Day's Wage*, chapter 4).

69 Vynne had not seen the London Exhibition, but rather a provincial version modelled along the same lines in Bristol. See also Collet, *Select Committee on Home Work* (1907), p. 45.

70 *Select Committee on Home Work* (1908), p. 86.

71 Ibid., p. 125.

72 *Select Committee on Home Work* (1907), p. 150. See also Black's long and detailed description of the intricate process of matchbox making in 'Match-Box Making at Home', *The English Illustrated Magazine*, May 1892, pp. 625–9.

73 Case filed under 'Boots and Shoes' in WIC/F/1.

74 Case filed under 'Artificial flowers' in WIC/F/2.

75 *Select Committee on Home Work* (1908), p. 129.

76 Hansard Parliamentary Debates, House of Commons, 28 April 1909.

77 Jessica Bean and George Boyer, 'The Trade Boards Act of 1909 and the Alleviation of Household Poverty', *British Journal of Industrial Relations*, 47 (2009), pp. 240–64.

78 Constance Smith, 'The Working of the Trade Boards Act in Great Britain and Ireland', *Journal of Political Economy*, 22 (1914), pp. 605–29.

3 SERVING TWO MASTERS

1 Diary entry for 28 July 1894. Webb's diaries have been fully digitised by the London School of Economics and are accessible at https://digital.library.lse.ac.uk/collections/webb.

2 Diary entry for 20 June 1891.

3 Diary entry for 28 July 1894.

4 All quotes in this paragraph are from the above 28 July 1894 entry.

5 Diary entry for 21 October 1891. For Webb's relationship with Chamberlain, see Barbara Caine, *Destined to be Wives: The sisters of Beatrice Webb* (Oxford, 1986), pp. 77–80.

6 For Webb's early social work, see Deborah Epstein Nord, *The Apprenticeship of Beatrice Webb* (Basingstoke, 1985). For singleness and the public-spirited, middle-class woman, see Martha Vicinus, *Independent Women: Work and Community for Single Women, 1850–1920* (London, 1985).

7 Diary entry for 1 March 1896.

8 The most thorough biography of Garrett is still Joan Manton's
Elizabeth Garrett Anderson (London, 1958), but for more recent studies
which place her life in wider networks of kin and the social, political
and economic developments of her day, see Elizabeth Crawford,
Enterprising Women: The Garretts and their Circle (London, 2002)
and Jenifer Glynn, *The Pioneering Garretts: Breaking the Barriers for
Women* (London, 2008).

9 Elizabeth Garrett to Millicent Fawcett, 25 December 1870, in
Autograph Letters Collection, 9/10, The Women's Library, London.

10 Garrett to James Skelton Anderson, 4 Jan 1871.

11 Garrett to Skelton Anderson, 30 December 1870.

12 Garrett to Skelton Anderson, 31 December 1870.

13 Garrett to Skelton Anderson, 28 December 1870.

14 Ibid.

15 Skelton Anderson to Garrett, 3 January 1871. Their daughter, Louisa,
destroyed most of her parents' correspondence to each other after
writing her own memoir of Elizabeth. The picture which emerges of
their marriage is inevitably shaped by this significant absence.

16 *Daily Telegraph*, 9 January 1871, p. 5; 'Female Medical Education,'
Bradford Observer, 14 January 1871, pp. 2–3.

17 *Berkshire Chronicle*, 14 January 1871, p. 8.

18 *Bradford Observer*, 14 January 1871, p. 3.

19 As quoted in the *Dundee Advertiser*, 9 January 1871, p. 2.

20 Manton, *Elizabeth Garrett Anderson*, p. 217.

21 Ibid. p. 174; Louisa Garrett Anderson, *Elizabeth Garrett Anderson*
(London, 1939), p. 192.

22 Manton, *Elizabeth Garrett Anderson*, p. 234.

23 Ibid., p. 248.

24 For Victorian domestic ideology see Leonore Davidoff and Catherine
Hall, *Family Fortunes: Men and women of the English middle class
1780–1850* (London, 2002, revised edn) and Ben Griffin, *The Politics
of Gender in Victorian Britain: Masculinity, Political Culture and the
Struggle for Women's Rights* (Cambridge, 2012).

25 A wealthy father could rely on the law of equity by setting up a trust
which would protect a daughter's estate when she married, but it did
not protect her earnings nor give her the same rights as an unmarried
woman over her property. In many cases *husbands* were themselves
trustees. See Griffin, *The Politics of Gender*, p. 83.

26 For more on the economic position of propertied married women, see Mary Shanley, 'One Must Ride Behind: Married Women's Rights and the Divorce Act of 1857', *Victorian Studies*, 25 (1982), pp. 355–76; Lee Holcombe, *Wives and Property: Reform of the Married Women's Property Law in Nineteenth-Century England* (Toronto, 1983); Ben Griffin, 'Class, gender and Liberalism in Parliament, 1868–1882: the case of the Married Women's Property Acts', *Historical Journal*, 46 (2003), pp. 59–87; R. J. Morris, *Men, women and property in England, 1780–1870* (Cambridge, 2005).

27 Despite concerns expressed by contemporaries about growing numbers of spinsters in the population, the vast majority of women *did* in fact marry. In 1871, nearly 90 per cent of women aged between forty-five and forty-nine were or had been married. See Mary Shanley, *Feminism: Marriage and the Law in Victorian Britain, 1850–95* (Princeton, 1989), p. 9.

28 For the plight of the middle-class spinster seeking paid work, see Lee Holcombe, *Victorian Ladies at Work: Middle-class working women in England and Wales, 1850–1914* (London, 1973) and Ellen Jordan, *The Women's Movement and Women's Employment in Nineteenth-Century Britain* (London, 1999).

29 Henry Maudsley, 'Sex in Mind and in Education', *Fortnightly Review*, April 1874, pp. 466–83. For debates concerning women's access to higher education, see Carol Dyhouse, *No Distinction of Sex? Women in British Universities, 1870–1939* (London, 1995).

30 Josephine Butler, *The Education and Employment of Women* (London, 1868), p. 10.

31 Anne Bridger and Ellen Jordan, *Timely Assistance: The Work of the Society for Promoting the Training of Women, 1859–2009* (Ashford, 2009).

32 Harriet Taylor Mill's essay, *The Enfranchisement of Women*, was published under her husband John Stuart Mill's name in the *Westminster Review*, 55 (1851), pp. 298–311.

33 These observations are found in *Women and Work* (London, 1857), which Bodichon published before her marriage and under her maiden name of Barbara Leigh Smith. Bodichon's father, the radical MP Benjamin Smith, had refused to marry her mother, Anne Longden, in protest against the legal disabilities of married women. At the time of writing, Barbara Bodichon had already met Eugene Bodichon, a

French physician and ethnographer, whom she wed on 2 July 1857, and the couple lived in Algiers for six months of the year. They did not have children, but Barbara Bodichon continued her activism for women's rights alongside landscape painting, in which she had some critical and commercial success.

34 Bessie Rayner Parkes, 'What Can Educated Women Do?', *The English Woman's Journal*, 1 January 1860, p. 293.

35 Bessie Rayner Parkes, *Essays on Women's Work* (London, 1865), p. 35.

36 Ibid., pp. 216–7.

37 John Stuart Mill, *The Subjection of Women* (London, 1869), p. 92.

38 For an eccentric account of Taylor and Mill's working partnership, see Jo Ellen Jacobs, *The Voice of Harriet Taylor Mill* (Bloomington, 2002).

39 Leigh Smith, *Women and Work*, p. 18.

40 Although it is important to note that not all supporters of reform of the laws governing marriage were suffragists. Some, such as Caroline Norton and Eliza Lynn Linton, believed that women *were* inferior to men but recognised that husbands did not always meet their responsibilities and therefore wives needed legal protection over their property and children.

41 Ginger Frost, *Living in Sin: Cohabiting as Husband and Wife in Nineteenth-Century England* (Manchester, 2008), chapters 8 and 9.

42 Sandra Stanley Holton, *Suffrage Days: Stories from the Women's Suffrage Movement* (London, 1996), chapter 1.

43 Annie Besant, *An Autobiography* (London, 1893), p. 218. For an important account of the contribution made by Besant and other free-thinking women to the evolution of feminism in Britain, see Laura Schwartz, *Infidel Feminism: Secularism, religion and women's emancipation, England, 1830–1914* (Manchester, 2013).

44 Elizabeth Garrett Anderson, 'Sex in Mind and Education: A Reply', *Fortnightly Review*, May 1874, pp. 582–94.

45 In 1908, Garrett Anderson joined the Women's Social and Political Union, the militant wing of the suffrage movement of which her daughter Louisa was then an enthusiastic supporter. She resigned, however, three years later and considered Louisa's militancy, which resulted briefly in imprisonment in 1912, misguided.

46 Letter to *The Times*, 5 August 1873, p. 3.

47 Mary Ann Elston, 'Women Doctors in the British Health Services: A Sociological Study of their Careers and Opportunities' (unpublished doctoral thesis, University of Leeds, 1986).

48 Mary Scharlieb, *Reminiscences* (London, 1924).

49 It is possible that the high demand for trained female medics in the colonies offered European women more flexibility in arranging their domestic lives. Tending only to women and children, such female doctors were unlikely to be regarded as a threat to male medics, while their work in many respects resembled that of missionaries' wives, whose presence in the overseas empire was long established.

50 Margaret Todd, *Sophia Jex-Blake* (London, 1918), p. 503.

51 Jennian F. Geddes, 'Louisa Garrett Anderson (1873–1943), surgeon and suffragette', *Journal of Medical Biography*, 16 (2008), pp. 205–14. For the complex meanings of women's same-sex relationships, see Martha Vicinus, *Intimate Friends: Women Who Loved Women, 1778– 1928* (London, 2004) and Sharon Marcus's groundbreaking *Between Women: Friendship, Desire, and Marriage in Victorian England* (Oxford, 2007).

52 Helen Glew, *Gender, Rhetoric and Regulation: Women's Work in the Civil Service and the London County Council, 1900–55* (Manchester, 2016).

53 Holcombe, *Victorian Ladies*, p. 210. For growing employment opportunities in white-collar work, see Gillian Sutherland, *In Search of the New Woman: Middle-Class Women and Work in Britain, 1870–1914* (Cambridge, 2015), chapters 5 and 6; Gregory Anderson, ed., *The White-Blouse Revolution: Female Office Workers since 1870* (Manchester, 1988); Meta Zimmeck, 'Jobs for the girls: the expansion of clerical work for women, 1850–1914' in A. John, ed., *Unequal Opportunities: Women's Employment in England, 1800–1918* (Oxford, 1986), pp. 153–77; and 'The "new woman" in the machinery of government: a spanner in the works?' in Roy MacLeod, ed., *Government and Expertise: Specialists, administrators and professionals, 1860–1919* (Cambridge, 1988), pp. 185–202.

54 This perception was reinforced from the 1890s by the practice of paying a 'marriage gratuity' – akin to a dowry – to women who had been in government employment for at least six years in lieu of a pension when they retired to marry.

55 Senior's experiences have come to light only relatively recently following the discovery of her personal papers in a trunk in an attic.

See Sybil Oldfield, *Jeanie, an 'Army of One': Mrs Nassau Senior 1828–1877. The First Woman in Whitehall* (Brighton, 2008). The quote is from a letter to her son, Walter (p. 194).

56 Quoted in Mary Drake McFeely, *Lady Inspectors: The Campaign for a Better Workplace, 1893–1921* (London, 1991), p. 59.

57 *Final Report of the Royal Commission on Superannuation in the Civil Service* (HMSO, 1903, Cd 1744), p. xii.

58 Holcombe, *Victorian Ladies*, p. 203.

59 Clara Collet, *Educated Working Women: Essays on the Economic Position of Women Workers in the Middle Classes* (London, 1902), p. 13.

60 For the experiences of this group, see Sutherland, *In Search*, chapter 2.

61 Dina Copelman, *London's Women Teachers: Gender, class and feminism 1870–1930* (London, 1996). See also Alison Oram, *Women Teachers and Feminist Politics 1900–1939* (Manchester, 1996).

62 Andrews was an alumnus of Bedford College and married Richard Withiel in 1888 when she was thirty-five. She went on to found the Association of Assistant Mistresses, serving as its president in 1896–7. After missing out on the headship at Notting Hill in 1901, Marion Withiel moved to a job at the Teachers Registration Council and ended her career as an inspector of girls' secondary schools. Her husband died in 1901 and no children are mentioned in the obituary printed in *Notting Hill High School Magazine*, March 1925, pp. 15–17. See also Josephine Kamm, *Indicative Past: A Hundred Years of the Girls' Public Day School Trust* (London, 1971), p. 100 and Sutherland, *In Search*, p. 31.

63 For women's professional status in academia, see Dyhouse, *No Distinction*; Fernanda Perrone, 'Women Academics in England, 1870–1930', *History of Universities*, XII, 1993, pp. 339–67; and Sutherland, *In Search*, pp. 36–7. Sutherland notes that the tutorial system at Oxford and Cambridge offered some teaching opportunities for women following marriage (especially if they married a don), but these were on a casual, part-time basis and carried no job security or promotion prospects.

64 For Church, see the evocative memoir written by her son, Richard Church, *Over the Bridge: An Essay in Autobiography* (London, 1955), and Copelman, *London's Women Teachers*.

65 An illuminating snapshot of practices in local authorities at this time is provided in the confidential 'Memorandum on the Employment of

Married Women as Teachers in Public Elementary Schools' produced by an official at the Board of Education and dated 30 November 1909. See ED 24/418, The National Archives (TNA), Kew.

66 Oram, *Women Teachers* (Manchester, 1996).

67 For widening opportunities for women in journalism, see Linda H. Peterson, *Becoming a Woman of Letters: Myths of Authorship and Facts of the Victorian Market* (Princeton, 2009) and Barbara Onslow, *Women of the Press in Nineteenth-Century Britain* (Basingstoke, 2000).

68 Parkes, *Essays*, pp. 120–21.

69 Viola Meynell, *Alice Meynell: A Memoir* (London, 1929).

70 Besant, *Autobiography*, pp. 84–5.

71 Meynell, *Alice Meynell*, p. 89.

72 David Garnett, *The Golden Echo* (London, 1953), pp. 53–4. For Constance Garnett's wider life and career as a translator, see also Richard Garnett, *Constance Garnett: A Heroic Life* (London, 1991) and Carolyn Heilbrun, *The Garnett Family* (London, 1961). Garnett's elder sister was the trade unionist and social investigator, Clementina Black.

73 Emily Crawford, 'Journalism as a Profession for Women', *Contemporary Review*, September 1893, pp. 370–71.

74 Millicent Garrett Fawcett, *What I Remember* (London, 1924).

75 Tracy C. Davis, *Actresses as Working Women: Their social identity in Victorian culture* (London, 1991); Sos Eltis, 'Private Lives and Public Spaces: Reputation, Celebrity and the Late Victorian Actress' in Mary Luckhurst and Jane Moody, eds, *Theatre and Celebrity in Britain 1660–2000* (Basingstoke, 2005), pp. 169–88. For Terry and Thorndike, see also Sandra Richards, *The Rise of the English Actress* (Basingstoke, 1993).

76 Nicola Phillips, *Women in Business 1700–1850* (London, 2006); Hannah Barker, *The Business of Women: Female Enterprise and Urban Development in Northern England, 1760–1830* (Oxford, 2006); Karen Pearlston, 'Married women bankrupts in the age of coverture', *Law & Social Inquiry*, 34 (2009), pp. 265–99. I am grateful to Ben Griffin for this latter reference.

77 Ivy Pinchbeck, *Women Workers and the Industrial Revolution 1750–1850* (London, 1981 [1930]), pp. 8–9.

78 Beatrice Webb, 'Pages from a Work-Girl's Diary', *The Nineteenth Century*, September 1888, pp. 301–14. For a wider picture of women as small-business owners, see Alison Kay, *The Foundations of Female Entrepreneurship: Enterprise, Home and Household in London, c.1800–1870* (London, 2009).

79 Perilla Kinchin, 'Cranston [Married name Cochrane], Catherine [Kate], 1849–1934', *Oxford Dictionary of National Biography*, 25 May 2006, https://www.oxforddnb.com/view/10.1093/ref:odnb/9780198614128.001.0001/odnb-9780198614128-e-56587. See also Eleanor Gordon and Gwyneth Nair, 'The economic role of middle-class women in Victorian Glasgow', *Women's History Review*, 9 (2000), pp. 791–814.

80 Kate Elms, 'International Women's Day: Ellen Nye Chart, actress turned manager of Brighton's Theatre Royal' (12 March 2015), blog post for The Keep, accessed 11 December 2017; http://www.thekeep.info/international-womens-day-ellen-nye-chart-actress-turned-manager-brightons-theatre-royal/.

81 Women's role as investors has only recently been uncovered through pioneering historical research. See Josephine Maltby and Janette Rutterford, '"She possessed her own fortune": Women investors from the late nineteenth century to the early twentieth century', *Business History*, 48 (2006) pp. 220–53; Janette Rutterford and Josephine Maltby, '"The widow, the clergyman and the reckless": women investors in England, 1830–1914', *Feminist Economics*, 12 (2006), pp. 111–38; Anne Laurence, Josephine Maltby and Janette Rutterford, eds, *Women and their Money 1700–1850: Essays on women and finance* (London, 2009).

82 For women's growing activism, power and authority in the sphere of social welfare work, see Frank Prochaska, *Women and Philanthropy in Nineteenth-century England* (Oxford, 1980); Anne Summers, 'A home from home: women's philanthropic work in the nineteenth century' in Sandra Burman, ed., *Fit Work for Women* (London, 1979), pp. 33–63; and Anne Summers, *Female Lives, Moral States: Women, Religion and Public Life in Britain, 1800–1930* (Newbury, 2000).

83 Margaret Bateson, *Professional Women upon their Professions* (London, 1895), p. 51. For women's position in local government, see Patricia Hollis, *Ladies Elect: Women in English Local Government, 1865–1914* (Oxford, 1987).

84 Lucy Herbert, *Mrs Ramsay MacDonald* (London, 1924), pp. 19, 22.
85 Edith Morley, ed., *Women Workers in Seven Professions* (London, 1914), p. 36.
86 Ibid., p. 162.
87 Ibid., p. 163.
88 Sheila Rowbotham, *Dreamers of a New Day: Women Who Invented the Twentieth Century* (London, 2010), chapter 6; Lucy Delap, *The Feminist Avant-Garde: Transatlantic Encounters of the Early Twentieth Century* (Cambridge, 2007).
89 For the character of these debates outside Britain, see Ann Taylor Allen, *Feminism and Motherhood in Western Europe, 1890–1970: The Maternal Dilemma* (Basingstoke, 2005), and Gisela Bock, ed., *Maternity and Gender Policies: Women and the Rise of the European Welfare States, 1880s–1950s* (London, 1991).

4 TEMPORARY PATRIOTS

1 This account of Christina MacLennan's story is constructed from her WRNS service record and the military record of her husband, John MacLennan, both held at The National Archives (TNA), Kew (ADM 318/142 and WO 374/45017).
2 Susan Pedersen, *Family, Dependence, and the Origins of the Welfare State: Britain and France 1914–1945* (Cambridge, 1993), p. 89. The proportion of all adult women occupied in paid work rose from 31 per cent at the beginning of the war to 37 per cent by November 1918.
3 The best general accounts of women's war work in Britain are Deborah Thom, *Nice Girls and Rude Girls: Women Workers in World War I* (London, 2000); Angela Woollacott, *On Her Their Lives Depend: Munitions Workers in the Great War* (London, 1994) and Gail Braybon, *Women Workers in the First World War* (London, 1981).
4 Millicent G. Fawcett, 'Equal Pay for Equal Work', *Economic Journal*, 28 (March 1918), p. 2.
5 Speech reported in 'Labour In Session', *The Times*, 23 January 1917, p. 5.
6 Mary Macarthur, 'The Women Trade Unionists' Point of View' in Marion Phillips, ed., *Women and the Labour Party* (London, 1918), p. 20.
7 This important insight is made in Thom, *Nice Girls*, chapter 8.
8 Pedersen, *Family, Dependence*, p. 90.

9 Figures cited by Woollacott, *On Her Their Lives Depend*, p. 24.

10 See, for example, Monica Cosens, *Lloyd George's Munition Girls* (London, 1916); Naomi Loughnan, 'Munition Work' in Gilbert Stone, ed., *Women War Workers* (London, 1917), pp. 25–45; Agnes K. Foxwell, *Munition Lasses: Six Months as a Principal Overlooker in Danger Buildings* (London, 1917).

11 Peggy Hamilton, *Three Years or For the Duration: The Memoirs of a Munition Worker, 1914–1918* (London, 1978).

12 Ibid., p. 36.

13 Cosens, *Lloyd George's Munition Girls*, pp. 58–9.

14 David Kenyon, *First World War National Factories* (Historic England Research Report Series 076, 2015), pp. 29–30.

15 Woollacott, *On Her Their Lives Depend*, p. 64.

16 See Angela Woollacott, 'Maternalism, professionalism and industrial welfare supervisors in World War I Britain', *Women's History Review*, 3 (1994), pp. 29–56.

17 For Barker, see Thom, *Nice Girls*, pp. 156–7. For growing concern over the welfare of women workers, see also Hilary Marland and Vicky Long, 'From Danger and Motherhood to Health and Beauty: Health Advice for the Factory Girl in Early Twentieth-Century Britain', *Twentieth Century British History*, 20 (2009), pp. 454–81.

18 Elizabeth Gore, *The Better Fight: The Story of Dame Lilian Barker* (London, 1965), p. 68.

19 Ibid., p. 83.

20 Anonymous, 'Some Thoughts on Factory Life', *The Englishwoman*, January 1919, p. 18.

21 See Gail Braybon and Penny Summerfield, *Out of the Cage: Women's Experiences in Two World Wars* (London, 1987). Thom gives greater emphasis to the negative aspects of women's munition work in *Nice Girls*, yet still notes that her interviewees said that they had generally enjoyed their work.

22 As the authors note in *Out of the Cage*, oral historians only began to interview war workers in the 1970s, which resulted in a greater number of testimonies from women who had been young and unmarried at the time.

23 The estimate is made by Pedersen, *Family, Dependence*, p. 91, based on evidence to the government's War Cabinet Committee in 1918.

24 There was no formal conscription of women for war work, although measures were temporarily enforced to prevent munition workers leaving their jobs once they had taken up employment.

25 Pre-war restrictions limiting women's working hours were relaxed, meaning that most munition workers were on twelve-hour shifts in 1915–16, and many worked at night or on Sundays. In September 1916, working hours for women were limited to sixty hours per week, and eight-hour shifts became more common, although night working was still permitted.

26 Health of Munition Workers Committee, *Final Report* (1918, Cd 9065), Appendix B (II) 'General Findings of Inquiries into the Health of Women Munition Workers', p. 146.

27 Ibid., Appendix B (I) 'A Further Inquiry into the Health of Women Munition Workers', p. 137.

28 'From the Inside of a Munitions Court' by 'CW' in *The Woman Worker*, January 1917, p. 6.

29 Interview with Dorothy Haigh, Imperial War Museum, DSR 000734/07.

30 Health of Munition Workers Committee, *Final Report*, p. 24.

31 *The Woman Worker*, May 1917, p. 9.

32 L. K. Yates, *The Woman's Part: A Record of Munitions Work* (London, 1918), p. 49.

33 W. Leslie MacKenzie, *Scottish Mothers and Children* (Dunfermline, 1917), p. 329.

34 Janet Campbell, *Report on the Physical Welfare of Mothers and Children: England and Wales*, Volume II (1917).

35 Sylvia Pankhurst, *The Home Front: A Mirror to Life in England during the World War* (London, 1932), p. 174.

36 Campbell, *Report on the Physical Welfare*.

37 For the wartime pledges, see Pedersen, *Family, Dependence*, pp. 83–4, and Thom, *Nice Girls*, pp. 57–8.

38 *Report of the War Cabinet Committee on Women in Industry* (1919, Cmd 135), p. 152.

39 For women's trade unionism, see Thom, *Nice Girls*, chapter 5.

40 Not all mothers were married to men serving away from home. Military conscription was introduced in January 1916 for single men aged between eighteen and forty-one and extended to married men in April, but certain workers were exempt due to their value to the

war industries on the home front. These were mostly skilled manual occupations, such as engineering and mining, but also included some white-collar occupations in central and local government. In total, around half of all adult males did *not* serve in the armed forces.

41 Kenyon, *First World War National Factories*, p. 29.

42 'General Findings of Inquiries into the Health of Women Munition Workers', p. 146. See also the evidence of Miss Constance Smith, Senior Lady Factory Inspector, to the Physiological Sub-Committee of the War Cabinet Committee, 21 November 1918, MUN 5/88/342/17.

43 For infant mortality during the war, see J. M. Winter, 'The Impact of the First World War on Civilian Health in Britain', *Economic History Review*, 30 (1977), pp. 487–503, and Linda Bryder, 'The First World War: Healthy or Hungry?', *History Workshop Journal*, 24 (1987), pp. 141–57.

44 Evidence of Dr Thomas O'Neill to to the Physiological Sub-Committee of the War Cabinet Committee, 7 November 1918, MUN 5/88/342/17.

45 See Bonnie White, *The Women's Land Army in First World War Britain* (Basingstoke, 2014); Gill Clarke, *The Women's Land Army: A Portrait* (Bristol, 2008); and Susan Grayzel, 'Nostalgia, Gender, and the Countryside: Placing the "Land Girl" in First World War Britain', *Rural History*, 10 (1999), pp. 155–70.

46 See Pamela Horn, *Rural Life in England in the First World War* (Dublin, 1984), chapter 6, and Nicola Verdon, 'Left out in the cold: Village women and agricultural labour in England and Wales during the First World War', *Twentieth Century British History*, 27 (2016), pp. 1–25.

47 Campbell, *Report on the Physical Welfare*, p. 125.

48 Viscountess Wolseley, *Women and the Land* (London, 1916).

49 Maggie Andrews, 'The WI's rural retailing and markets 1915–1939: A First World War legacy', *History of Retailing and Consumption*, 1 (2015), pp. 89–104.

50 Lucy Noakes, *Women in the British Army: War and the gentle sex, 1907–1948* (London, 2006).

51 This finding is based on a preliminary examination of the military service records recently released by The National Archives. More research is required to establish a fuller picture of the marital and maternal status of the women who joined the auxiliary services.

52 Not all of these women were new recruits: there were 12,000 women employed on the railways before July 1914, and 1,200 on trams (figures from Woollacott, *On Her Their Lives Depend*, p. 26).

53 This Committee was appointed in September 1918 to consider men and women's pay in industry, but its lengthy final report represented a major intervention into wider policy debates about women's economic status during and after the war.

54 *Report of the Committee on Women in Industry: Appendices, Summaries of Evidence, &c* (Cmd 167, 1918), pp. 135–7.

55 Irene Osgood Andrews and Margaret A. Hobbs, *Economic Effects of the World War upon Women and Children in Great Britain* (Oxford, 1921). See also the oral evidence of the National Union of Railwaymen and the written evidence of the Municipal Tramways Association in *Report of the War Cabinet Committee: Summaries of evidence*, pp. 135–8.

56 War Office, *Women's War Work* (September 1916), p. 6, copy in MUN 5/70.

57 Speech by Ben Roberts, cited in Helen Fraser, *Women and War Work* (London, 1918), pp. 121–2.

58 Mrs C. S. Peel, *How We Lived Then: A Sketch of Social and Domestic Life in England during the War* (London, 1929), p. 67.

59 Michael MacDonagh, *In London during the Great War: The Diary of a Journalist* (London, 1935), see entry for 7 August 1916.

60 Cited in Diana T. Wilkins, 'Communal Housekeeping', *The Englishwoman*, December 1917, p. 222.

61 See *Report of the War Cabinet Committee*, pp. 149, 165.

62 Wilkins, 'Communal Housekeeping', p. 222.

63 Furse had two children: Peter (born 1902) and Paul (1904), whom she had been left to bring up alone following the death of her husband, the portrait artist Charles Wellington Furse, just days after Paul's birth. Both sons were naval cadets by the time Furse took up her WRNS post. Chalmers Watson also had two sons, aged seven and four in 1914. Denman had a son and daughter aged nine and seven. Tennant's children were born in 1897, 1899, 1903, 1904 and 1913. Her eldest son, Henry, was killed in action in May 1917. Lyttelton had two grown-up children: Oliver (b. 1893) and Mary (b. 1895), and a third child, Anthony (b. 1900) had died aged eighteen months.

64 It also didn't hurt that her other brother was Eric Geddes, the Director General of Military Railways and Transportation in France, reporting directly to Field Marshal Haig.

65 See the description of women's voluntary war work in Lady Randolph Churchill, ed., *Women's War Work* (London, 1916).

66 The best analysis of how suffragists reconfigured notions of women's citizenship during the war is Nicoletta Gullace, *The Blood of Our Sons: Men, Women and the Renegotiation of British Citizenship during the Great War* (Basingstoke, 2002).

67 V. de Vesselitsky, *The Homeworker and Her Outlook: A Descriptive Study of Tailoresses and Boxmakers* (London, 1916).

68 Pankhurst, *The Home Front*, p. 166.

69 Pedersen, *Family, Dependence*, p. 109.

70 Andrews and Hobbs reported anecdotal evidence that some married jute workers in Dundee left their jobs and lived off their allowances (*Economic Effects of the World War*, p. 77).

71 'The Women's Labour League and the Welfare of the Soldier's Family', *Labour Woman*, January 1915, pp. 269–71; Marion Philips, 'The Soldier's Wife', *Labour Woman*, August 1915, p. 314.

72 Allowances were administered by the 50,000 volunteer workers of the Soldiers' and Sailors' Family Association until December 1916, when the scheme was taken over by the newly established Ministry of Pensions.

73 See Pankhurst, *The Home Front*, p. 83.

74 Janis Lomas, 'Soldiering On: War Widows in First World War Britain' in Maggie Andrews and Janis Lomas, eds, *The Home Front in Britain: Images, Myths and Forgotten Experiences since 1914* (Basingstoke, 2014), pp. 39–56. See also Ministry of Health, *Survey of Relief to Widows and Children* (Cd 744, 1920).

75 Cited by Woollacott, *On Her Their Lives Depend*, p. 148.

76 Ginger Frost, *Illegitimacy in English law and society, 1860–1930* (Manchester, 2016), chapter 2.

77 Gore, *The Better Fight*, p. 76.

78 Molly Izzard, *A Heroine in Her Time: A Life of Dame Helen Gwynne-Vaughan, 1879–1967* (London, 1969), p. 160.

79 Pankhurst, *The Home Front*, p. 183.

80 'War Babies', *Labour Woman*, May 1915, p. 299.

81 'The Saving of Life', *Labour Woman*, March 1915, pp. 279–80.

82 'The Loss Of Young Life', *The Times*, 25 June 1915, p. 5. The speaker was a Mr Pett Ridge, probably William Pett Ridge, the novelist and philanthropist.

83 Cited in Winter, 'Impact of the First World War', p. 498.

84 Jane Lewis, *The Politics of Motherhood: Child and Maternal Welfare in England, 1900–1939* (London, 1980).

85 'Saving of the Race', *The Times*, 11 May 1917, p. 9.

86 'The New Motherhood', *The Times*, 19 May 1917, p. 3.

87 Health of Munition Workers Committee, *Memorandum No. 4: Employment of Women* (Cd 8185, January 1916), p. 3.

88 *The Position of Women After the War: Report of the Standing Joint Committee of Industrial Women's Organisations presented to the Joint Committee on Labour Problems After the War* (London, 1918), p. 10.

89 Rhoda Adamson and H. Palmer Jones, 'The Work of a Department for Employing Expectant Mothers in a Munitions Factory', *British Medical Journal*, 21 September 1918, pp. 309–10.

90 Mary Deacon, 'Employment of Pregnant Women in Munitions Factories', *The Lancet*, 7 September 1918, pp. 311–12.

91 Ernestine Mills, 'Mothers in Factories', *The Englishwoman*, January 1919, pp. 9–11.

92 *Report of the Committee on Women in Industry: Appendices, Summaries of Evidence*, p. 16.

93 F. E. Dawson, 'Report on the Industry and Motherhood Enquiry: Part III', *Women's Industrial News*, July 1918, p. 16.

94 *Report of the Committee on Women in Industry: Appendices, Summaries of Evidence*, p. 38.

95 Ministry of Reconstruction, *Report of the Women's Employment Committee* (Cd 9239, 1919), p. 6.

96 Evidence of Dr A. Fulton to the Physiological Sub-Committee of the War Cabinet Committee, 7 November 1918, MUN 5/88/342/17.

97 'Day Nurseries', joint memorandum by the National Society of Day Nurseries and the National Association for the Prevention of Infant Mortality to the Local Government Board, n.d., in MH 55/694.

98 The speaker was Mr E. Pelham. See minutes of the Welfare Advisory Committee at the Ministry of Munitions, June 10 1918, MUN 5/93.

99 'Report on the Advantages and Disadvantages of Industrial Creches' by Welfare Advisory Committee to Winston Churchill, Minister of Munitions, n.d. [August 1918?], MUN 5/93.

100 Evidence of Dr G. W. N. Joseph, to the Physiological Sub-Committee of the War Cabinet Committee, 5 November 1918, MUN 5/88/342/17, p. 36.

101 *Report of War Cabinet Committee*, p. 245.

102 Evidence of Mrs Davies to the Physiological Sub-Committee of the War Cabinet Committee, 6 November 1918, MUN 5/88/342/17, p. 57.

103 Evidence of Dr John Robertson to the Physiological Sub-Committee of the War Cabinet Committee, 9 November 1918, p. 6.

104 *Report of War Cabinet Committee*, p. 236.

105 Marion Phillips, 'Co-operative Housekeeping and Housing Reform', *Labour Woman*, February 1918, p. 256.

106 For Rathbone, see Susan Pedersen's definitive biography, *Eleanor Rathbone and the Politics of Conscience* (London, 2004).

107 *Report of War Cabinet Committee*, p. 306.

108 Maude Royden, 'The Woman's Movement of the Future' in Victor Gollancz, ed., *The Making of Women: Oxford Essays in Feminism* (London, 1917), p. 142.

109 Eleanor Rathbone, 'The Remuneration of Women's Services', *Economic Journal*, 27 (March 1917), p. 67.

110 Margaret Llewelyn Davies, 'The Claims of Mothers and Children' in Phillips, *Women and the Labour Party*, p. 33.

111 Royden, 'Woman's Movement,' p. 143.

112 Evidence of NUWSS, *Report of the Committee on Women in Industry: Appendices, Summaries of Evidence*, p. 36.

113 Letter from J. E. Price, *The Woman Worker*, March 1919, p. 3.

114 These were part of a series of adverts from former women war workers which the *Daily Express* offered to publish for free. They included many munition workers looking for skilled manual work in industry. See 13 December 1918, p. 7.

115 Deborah Cohen, *The War Come Home: Disabled Veterans in Britain and Germany, 1914–1939* (London, 2001), p. 4. For the complex system of pensions available to disabled veterans, see Niall Barr, *The Lion and the Poppy: British Veterans, Politics, and Society, 1921–1939* (London, 2005), pp. 120–21.

116 For a rich analysis of the breadwinner 'logic' shaping post-WWI social policy, see Pedersen, *Family, Dependence*, pp. 120–30.

117 *Report of the Committee on Women in Industry*, p. 265.

118 Barr, *Lion and the Poppy*, p. 121.

119 League of Nations, *International Labour Conference: First Annual Meeting, October 29th – November 29th 1919* (ILO, 1919): full text of the proceedings is available here: http://www.ilo.org/public/libdoc/ilo/P/09616/09616(1919-1).pdf.

120 See Addison's comments as quoted in the Commons debate on the International Labour Conference in Hansard, 27 May, 1921, vol. 142, no. 64.

121 *Memorandum by the Government Actuary on the Washington Draft Convention concerning the employment of women before and after childbirth*, dated 28 June 1920 (Cmd 1293, 1921). See also the confidential report circulated to Cabinet by one of the government delegates, George Barnes MP: 'International Labour Conference, Washington: Supplementary Report by Mr GN Barnes', dated 7 February 1920, LAB 14/332.

5 MODERN MOTHERS

1 Alison Light, *Forever England: Femininity, literature and conservatism between the wars* (London, 1991); Nicola Beauman, *A Very Great Profession: The Woman's Novel, 1914–1939* (London, 1983); Rosa Maria Bracco, *Merchants of Hope: British Middlebrow Writers and the First World War, 1919–1939* (Oxford, 1993).

2 Violet Powell, *The Life of a Provincial Lady: A Study of E.M. Delafield and her Works* (London, 1988).

3 For young women's employment opportunities between the wars, see Selina Todd, *Young Women, Work and Family in England, 1918–1950* (Oxford, 2005); Miriam Glucksmann, *Women Assemble: Women Workers and the New Industries in Inter-war Britain* (London, 1990); and T. J. Hatton and R. E. Bailey, 'Female Labour Force Participation in Interwar Britain', *Oxford Economic Papers*, 40 (1988), pp. 695–718.

4 Virginia Woolf, *Three Guineas* (London, 1938).

5 Figures as cited by Ray Strachey in *Careers and Openings for Women: A Survey of Women's Employment and a Guide for those seeking Work* (London, 1935), p. 44.

6 R. K. Kelsall, *Higher Civil Servants in Britain: From 1870 to the Present Day* (London, 1955), chapter 9.

7 Strachey, *Careers and Openings*, p. 17.

8 For professional women's networks, see Helen McCarthy, 'Service clubs, citizenship and equality: gender relations and middle-class associations between the wars', *Historical Research*, 81 (2008), pp. 531–52; Linda Perriton, 'Forgotten Feminists: the Federation of British Professional and Business Women, 1933–1969', *Women's History Review*, 16 (2007), pp. 79–97; and Kaarin Michaelsen, '"Union is

Strength": The Medical Women's Federation and the Politics of Professionalism, 1917–30' in Krista Cowman and Louise A. Jackson, eds, *Women and Work Culture: Britain c.1850–1950* (Aldershot, 2005), pp. 161–76.

9 Patrick Polden, 'Portia's Progress: Women at the Bar in England, 1919–1939', *International Journal of the Legal Profession*, 293 (2005), pp. 293–338.

10 Vera Brittain, *Women's Work in Modern England* (London, 1928), p. 39.

11 Carol Dyhouse, 'Women Students and the London Medical Schools, 1914–39: The Anatomy of a Masculine Culture', *Gender & History*, 10 (1998), pp. 110–32.

12 Strachey, *Careers and Openings*, p. 31.

13 For a good overview, see Diana Gittins, *Fair Sex: Family Size and Structure, 1900–1939* (London, 1982), chapter 4.

14 *A Study of the Factors which have operated in the past and are operating now to Determine the Distribution of Women in Industry* (HMSO, Cmd 3508, 1929). Married women and widows made up 40 per cent of all female laundry workers, almost a third of pottery operatives, and between a quarter and a fifth of those employed in boot factories and the metal trades.

15 The comments were made during a BBC broadcast. See 'The Family Purse', *Listener*, 9 March 1932, pp. 342–4.

16 H. Llewellyn Smith, *The New Survey of London Life & Labour: Volume II, London Industries* (London, 1931), p. 259.

17 'Women Medical Students', *The Times*, 31 May 1928, p. 10.

18 Winifred de Kok, 'Medicine' in Margaret I. Cole, ed., *The Road to Success: Twenty Essays on the Choice of a Career for Women* (London, 1936), pp. 33–44.

19 A 1936 poll of graduates from St Mary's medical school found that nearly two in five female graduates had chosen careers in this speciality, as cited by Anne Digby in *The Evolution of British General Practice, 1850–1948* (Oxford, 1999), p. 163. Similar dynamics can be found amongst veterinary practitioners. See Julie Hipperson, 'Professional Entrepreneurs: Women Veterinary Surgeons as Small Business Owners in Interwar Britain', *Social History of Medicine*, 31 (2018), pp. 122–39.

20 Charlotte Haldane, *Motherhood and Its Enemies* (London, 1927), p. 107.

21 Derived from author's analysis of issues of *The British Soroptimist* between 1930 and 1939.

22 Hal Moggridge, 'Allen [née Gill], Marjory, Lady Allen of Hurtwood, 1897–1976', *Oxford Dictionary of National Biography* (Oxford, 2007).

23 Obituary in *The British Soroptimist*, April 1938, p. 29.

24 Biography of Maud Crofts, published by First 100 Years, 5 July 2016. Available at: https://first100years.org.uk/maud-crofts/.

25 Judy Faraday, 'A Kind of Superior Hobby: Women Managers in the John Lewis Partnership, 1918–1950' (unpublished MPhil thesis, University of Wolverhampton, 2008).

26 Kate Murphy, 'A Marriage Bar of Convenience? The BBC and Married Women's Work, 1923–1939', *Twentieth Century British History*, 25 (2014), pp. 533–61.

27 Nahid Aslanbeigui and Guy Oakes, *The Provocative Joan Robinson: The Making of a Cambridge Economist* (London, 2009).

28 Georgina Ferry, *Dorothy Hodgkin: A Life* (London, 1998).

29 Alison Oram, *Women Teachers and Feminist Politics 1900–1939* (Manchester, 1996); Helen Glew, *Gender, Rhetoric and Regulation: Women's Work in the Civil Service and the London County Council, 1900–55* (Manchester, 2016).

30 Notes from undated interview with Mrs Elsie Lee (b. 1910) in papers of Josie Castle, sociologist, on Coventry women's employment, MSS.266/3/1/1-15, Modern Records Centre, University of Warwick. See also Josie Castle, 'Factory work for women: Courtaulds and GEC between the Wars' in Bill Lancaster and Tony Mason, eds, *Life and Labour in a Twentieth Century City: The Experience of Coventry* (Coventry, 1986), pp. 133–71, and Mike Savage, 'Trade Unionism, Sex Segregation, and the State: Women's Employment in "New Industries" in Inter-War Britain', *Social History*, 13 (1988), pp. 209–30.

31 A further claim, brought by a married teacher in Dorset in 1925 and backed by the National Union of Teachers, was upheld but subsequently dismissed on appeal. See Rosa Matheson, 'The Marriage Bar', *Who Do You Think You Are? Magazine*, 12 March 2019.

32 Alix Kilroy and Evelyn Sharp, 'The Civil Service' in Cole, *Road to Success*, p. 55.

33 E. G. Pearson to Mr Duckworth, 15 May 1934, and Duckworth to Mr R. S. Wood, 16 May 1934, in ED 23/282, The National Archives (TNA), Kew. An official report in 1946 found that of thirty cases in

which the bar had been waived, only five involved women below the age of thirty and in only four cases did the retained employee take maternity leave. See *Marriage Bar in the Civil Service: Report of the Civil Service*, National Whitley Council Committee (HMSO, Cmd 6886, 1946), p. 7.

34 Susan Lawrence, 'Keeping the London Schools Clean', *Labour Woman*, April 1922, p. 57.

35 For a thorough analysis of how these cases were dealt with, see Glew, *Gender, Rhetoric and Regulation*, chapter 7.

36 See Murphy, 'A Marriage Bar of Convenience?'

37 Cited in Alison Oram, 'Serving two masters? The introduction of a marriage bar in teaching in the 1920s' in London Feminist History Group, eds, *The Sexual Dynamics of History: Men's power, women's resistance* (London, 1983), p. 141.

38 Open Door Council, *The Married Woman: Is She a Person?* (London, 1934), p. 8.

39 In July 1930, of a population of 14 million women aged eighteen to sixty-four, 2.88 million women were insured; 800,000 of these were married. See *First Report of the Royal Commission on Unemployment Insurance* (HMSO, Cmd 3872, 1931), p. 43.

40 'Married Women in Receipt of Unemployment Benefit: Memorandum by the Minister of Labour', 14 July 1930, p. 4, CAB 24/213, TNA.

41 'Title to Benefit – Married Women', memorandum sent by Postlethwaite to Mr Bebb at Ministry of Labour, 4 June 1930, LAB 2/1597/1/F3243/1931/Amended, TNA.

42 In March 1930, the Labour government abolished the 'genuinely seeking work test' from the insurance system, following pressure from trade unionists and sections of the parliamentary party. This led to a rise in claims from both men and women and intensified fears about potential abuse.

43 Memorandum to Mr Paxon at the Ministry of Labour, dated 18 October 1930, LAB 2/1597/1/F3243/1931/Amended, TNA.

44 *First Report of the Royal Commission on Unemployment Insurance*, p. 43.

45 J. D. Tomlinson, 'Women as "Anomalies": The Anomalies Regulations of 1931, their background and implications', *Public Administration*, 62 (1984), pp. 423–7. For the historical background and wider fears about abuse of the system, see Alan Deacon, *In Search of the*

Scrounger: The Administration of Unemployment Insurance in Britain, 1920–1931 (London, 1976).

46 For a detailed analysis of the policy debate over married women's entitlement to unemployment benefit, see Susan Pedersen, *Family, Dependence and the Origins of the Welfare State, Britain and France 1914–1945* (Cambridge, 1993), pp. 297–307. An amendment was introduced in 1934 to make it easier for women to claim in areas such as Lancashire where married women were ordinarily employed in industry, but married women's claims continued to be disallowed to the tune of 3,000–4,000 per month in 1934–5 (Pedersen, p. 305). For discrimination against married textile workers, see Rex Pope, 'Unemployed women in inter-war Britain: the case of the Lancashire weaving district', *Women's History Review*, 9 (2000), pp. 743–59.

47 The Pilgrim Trust, *Men Without Work* (Cambridge, 1938), p. 232.

48 See, for instance, Edward Wight Bakke's *The Unemployed Man: A Social Study* (London, 1933). For a brilliant analysis of the gender dynamics of how unemployment was experienced by men, see Sally Alexander, 'Men's Fears and Women's Work: Responses to Unemployment in London between the Wars', *Gender and History*, 12 (2000), pp. 401–25.

49 The memoirs were subsequently published in H. L. Beales and R. S. Lambert, *Memoirs of the Unemployed* (London, 1934). The BBC also broadcast the voices of the unemployed on air: see Felix Greene, ed., *Time to Spare: What Unemployment Means, by eleven unemployed* (London, 1935).

50 Beales and Lambert, *Memoirs*, p. 105.

51 James Hanley, *Grey Children: A Study in Humbug and Misery* (London, 1937).

52 Neil Penlington, 'Masculinity and Domesticity in 1930s South Wales: Did Unemployment change the domestic division of labour?', *Twentieth Century British History*, 21 (2010), pp. 281–99.

53 Beales and Lambert, *Memoirs*, p. 87.

54 House of Commons debate on the Married Women (Employment) Bill, Hansard, 29 April 1927.

55 Glew, *Gender, Rhetoric and Regulation*, pp. 221–2.

56 Quoted in Murphy, 'A Marriage Bar of Convenience?,' p. 541.

57 Rosemary Crook, '"Tidy Women": women in the Rhondda between the wars', *Oral History*, 10 (1982), pp. 40–46.

58 Glucksmann, *Women Assemble*. See also the case of an office worker cited in Teresa Davy, ' "A Cissy Job for Men; A Nice Job for Girls": Women Shorthand Typists in London, 1900–1939' in Leonore Davidoff and Belinda Westover, eds, *Our Work, Our Lives, Our Words: Women's History and Women's Work* (Basingstoke, 1986), pp. 124–44.

59 'The Employment of Married Women', *Labour Woman*, March 1922, p. 36.

60 Brittain, *Women's Work*, p. 67. The dangerous spinster teacher was also a prominent theme in Haldane, *Motherhood and its Enemies*.

61 For prejudice against older unmarried women, see Kath Holden, *The Shadow of Marriage: Singleness in England, 1914–1960* (Manchester, 2007) and Alison Oram, 'Repressed and Thwarted, or Bearer of the New World? The Spinster in Inter-war Feminist Discourses', *Women's History Review*, 1 (1992), pp. 413–34.

62 *The British Soroptimist*, March 1931, p. 3.

63 Pamela Graves, *Labour Women: Women in British Working-Class Politics, 1918–1939* (Cambridge, 1994).

64 'The Employment of Married Women', p. 37.

65 Vera Brittain, 'Women in Industry: Restrictive Legislation Again' in *Manchester Guardian*, 8 December 1927, reprinted in Paul Berry and Alan Bishop, eds, *Testament of a Generation: The Journalism of Vera Brittain and Winifred Holtby* (London, 1985), p. 111.

66 For a flavour of these opposing viewpoints, see Open Door Council, *Restrictive Legislation and the Industrial Woman Worker: A Reply by the Open Door Council* (London, 1928).

67 *First Report of the Royal Commission on Unemployment Insurance*, p. 63.

68 Dorothy Elliott, 'Married Women Defrauded', *Labour Woman*, April 1932, pp. 56–7.

69 'That Anomalies Bill', *Labour Woman*, August 1931, p. 119.

70 'Marriage a la Mode', *Listener*, 6 April 1932, pp. 510–11.

71 Susan Pedersen, *Eleanor Rathbone and The Politics of Conscience* (London, 2004), pp. 176–98.

72 Ada Nield Chew, 'Family Endowment: Another View', *The Woman's Leader*, 15 September 1922, pp. 261–2. For an exhaustive analysis of the policy debate over endowment in the 1920s and 30s, see Pedersen, *Family, Dependence*, chapters 3–5.

73 Strachey thought that pensions were a factor in this decline, see *Careers and Openings*, p. 29.

74 Pat Thane, 'What Difference Did the Vote Make?' in Amanda Vickery, ed., *Women, Privilege and Power: British Politics, 1750 to the Present* (Stanford, 2001), pp. 253–88. For a detailed account of how Labour women were able to leverage local government funding in different settings, see Michael Savage, *The Dynamics of Working Class Politics: The Labour Movement in Preston, 1880–1940* (Cambridge, 1987).

75 Jane Lewis, *The Politics of Motherhood: Child and Maternal Welfare in England, 1900–1939* (London, 1980). See also Violet Markham, *May Tennant: A Portrait* (London, 1949).

76 Caitriona Beaumont, *Housewives and Citizens: Domesticity and the Women's Movement in England, 1928–64* (Manchester, 2013), chapter 3.

77 The 1861 Offences Against the Person Act made the procurement of abortion illegal under any circumstances. This was modified by the 1929 Infant Life (Preservation) Act, which permitted medical abortion in cases where the life of the mother was at risk, but this, with the exception of insanity, was defined in narrow, physiological terms.

78 Stephen Brooke, '"A New World for Women"? Abortion Law Reform in Britain in the 1930s', *American Historical Review*, 106 (2001), pp. 431–59.

79 Beaumont, *Housewives and Citizens*, chapter 6. See also essays in Paul Brassley, Jeremy Burchardt and Karen Sayer, eds, *Transforming the Countryside: The Electrification of Rural Britain* (Abingdon, 2016).

80 Suzette Worden, 'Powerful Women: Electricity in the Home, 1919–40' in Judy Attfield and Pat Kirkham, eds, *A View from the Interior: Women and Design* (London, 1989), pp. 131–50.

81 Herbert Morrison, 'Labour's Bold Policy for Electricity and Transport', *Labour Woman*, September 1932, pp. 136–7.

82 Judy Giles, 'Professionalising the Housewife, 1920–50' in Krista Cowman and Louise Jackson, eds, *Women and Work Culture: Britain c.1850–1950* (Aldershot, 2005), pp. 70–86; Adrian Bingham, *Gender, Modernity, and the Popular Press in Inter-War Britain* (Oxford, 2004), chapter 3.

83 Deborah Sugg Ryan, *The Ideal Home Through the 20th Century* (London, 1997).

84 See Peter Scott, 'Marketing mass home ownership and the creation of the modern working-class consumer in inter-war Britain', *Business History*, 50 (2008), pp. 4–25, and his *The Triumph of the South: A Regional Economic History of Early Twentieth-Century Britain* (Aldershot, 2007).

85 Peter Scott, 'Mr Drage, Mr Everyman, and the Creation of a Mass Market for Domestic Furniture in Inter-war Britain', *Economic History Review*, 62 (2009), pp. 802–27. This democratisation did not yet extend to motor cars, due to the peculiarities of the business model pursued by manufacturers in the UK. See Sue Bowden and Paul Turner, 'The Demand for Consumer Durables in the United Kingdom in the Interwar Period', *Journal of Economic History*, 53 (1993), pp. 244–58.

86 Quoted in Mary Stott, *Organisation Woman: The Story of the National Union of Townswomen's Guilds* (London, 1978), pp. 23–4.

87 'Correspondence', *Labour Woman*, November 1932, p. 171. For further evidence of working-class women's reading habits and political work, see the extracted letters from members of the Women's Cooperative Guild in Margaret Llewelyn Davies, ed., *Life As We Have Known It: The Voices of Working-Class Women* (London, 1931 [1977]), pp. 127–43.

88 For moral panics about young women, see Billie Melman, *Women and the Popular Imagination in the Twenties: Flappers and Nymphs* (Basingstoke, 1988) and Bingham's more measured conclusions in *Gender, Modernity and the Popular Press*.

89 Pearl Jephcott, *Clubs for Girls* (London, 1943), p. 17.

90 Stephen Taylor, 'Suburban Neurosis', *The Lancet*, 26 March 1938, pp. 759–61. For more on Taylor, see Ali Haggett, *Desperate Housewives, Neuroses and the Domestic Environment, 1945–70* (London, 2012), pp. 26–7, and Rhodri Hayward's penetrating analysis of the medical and intellectual influences shaping Taylor's thought in 'Desperate Housewives and Model Amoebae: The Invention of Suburban Neurosis in Inter-War Britain' in Mark Jackson, ed., *Health and the Modern Home* (London, 2007), pp. 1–17.

91 'Doctor Has Plan For Lonely Wives of Suburbs', *Daily Mirror*, 9 June 1938, p. 5; 'Wife lonely in suburb shoots herself', *Daily Express*, 18 July 1939, pp. 1–2.

92 'Doctor Has Plan'. For the growth of popular psychology, see Mathew Thomson, *Psychological Subjects: Identity, Culture and Health in Twentieth-Century Britain* (Oxford, 2006).

93 'Women Homesick in the Suburbs', *Sunday Express*, 7 May 1939, p. 17.

94 Mary Welsh, 'Happy housewives say "suburban neurosis" is all nonsense', *Daily Express*, 10 June 1938, p. 5.

95 Castle, 'Factory work for women', p. 149.

96 Pearl Jephcott, Nancy Seear and John Smith, *Married Women Working* (London, 1962), p. 66. See also Glucksmann, *Women Assemble*, pp. 42–3.

97 Faraday, 'A Kind of Superior Hobby'.

98 Diana Kaye, 'Sisters under the skin', *Woman*, 9 September 1939, p. 15.

99 Savage, 'Trade unionism'.

100 Catherine Hall, 'Married women at home in Birmingham in the 1920s and 1930s', *Oral History*, 5 (1977), p. 73.

101 Ibid., p. 74.

102 Kate Fisher, *Birth Control, Sex and Marriage in Britain, 1918–1960* (Oxford, 2007). Claire Langhamer, 'The Meanings of Home in Post-War Britain', *Journal of Contemporary History*, 40 (2005), pp. 341–62.

103 For the dominance of the 'social problem' paradigm in 1930s Britain, see Jon Lawrence, 'Class, "Affluence" and the Study of Everyday Life in Britain, *c*.1930–64', *Cultural and Social History*, 10 (2013), pp. 273–99.

6 THE RESERVE ARMY

1 Directive: January 1944, Day Survey from Mass Observer 1578, Mass Observation Archive, University of Sussex Special Collections, SxMOA/1/3/75.

2 There is a large scholarly literature on the history of Mass Observation and the nature of its research. The most comprehensive are Nick Hubble, *Mass Observation and Everyday Life: Culture, History, Theory* (Basingstoke, 2006) and James Hinton, *The Mass Observers: A History, 1937–1949* (Oxford, 2013).

3 Mass Observation was formally contracted in April 1940 by the Home Intelligence Section at the Ministry of Information to provide regular reports on the state of public morale. The 1943 book, *War Factory*, was based on research commissioned by a firm manufacturing radar equipment, Ekco Ltd, and many other wartime surveys were funded by the Advertising Services Guild, an association of eight advertising agents. For some of the tensions within MO's research

objectives and its relationships with government and business, see
Penny Summerfield, 'Mass Observation: Social Research or Social
Movement?' *Journal of Contemporary History*, 20 (1985), pp. 439–52.

4 This figure, from a 1943 Ministry of Labour memorandum, is
likely to be an underestimate, as it counted two part-time workers
as a single worker. Memorandum by the Minister of Labour and
Man Power to War Cabinet, 22 October 1943, CAB 66/42/22, The
National Archives (TNA), Kew.

5 The Survey was established by the Ministry of Information to
carry out studies involving statistically representative samples
of the population. This contrasted with MO's idiosyncratic and
ethnographic style. For in-depth analysis of these investigations,
see Penny Summerfield, *Women Workers in the Second World
War: Production and Patriarchy in Conflict* (Abingdon, 1984),
which is still the best single-volume account of women's wartime
employment. For the Wartime Social Survey, see Frank Whitehead,
'The Government Social Survey' in Martin Bulmer, ed., *Essays on
the History of British Sociological Research* (Cambridge, 1985), pp.
83–100.

6 CAB 66/42/22.

7 Geoffrey Thomas, *Women at Work: The attitudes of working women
toward post-war employment and some related problems. An inquiry
made for the Office of the Minister of Reconstruction* (Wartime Social
Survey, June 1944).

8 CAB 66/42/22.

9 Figures from Summerfield, *Women Workers in the Second World
War*, p. 31.

10 CAB 66/42/22.

11 Peggy Scott, *British Women in War* (London, 1940).

12 Julie Fountain '"The Most Interesting Work a Woman can Perform in
Wartime": The Exceptional Status of British Women Pilots during the
Second World War', *Cultural and Social History*, 13 (2016), pp. 213–29.

13 For discriminatory practices in industry, see Summerfield, *Women
Workers*, chapter 7 and Richard Croucher, *Engineers at War*
(London, 1982).

14 Vera Douie, *The Lesser Half: A survey of the laws, regulations
and practices introduced during the present war which embody
discrimination against women* (London, 1943), p. 85.

15 J. B. Priestley, *British Women Go to War* (London, 1943), pp. 34–5.

16 Ibid., p. 38.

17 For an illuminating analysis of this trend, see Chloe Ward, '"Something of the Spirit of Stalingrad": British women, their Soviet sisters, propaganda and politics in the Second World War', *Twentieth Century British History*, 25 (2014), pp. 435–60. For propaganda aimed at working women more generally, see Susan Carruthers, 'Manning the factories: propaganda and policy on the employment of women, 1939–47', *History*, 75 (1990), pp. 232–56.

18 Tom Harrisson, 'Working Women in this War', December 1939, Mass Observation File Report 15B.

19 'Women in Wartime', Mass Observation File Report 290, July 1940, p. 22.

20 Oral evidence of Mrs Dugald Baird to the Royal Commission on Population, 27 October 1944, RG 24/9, TNA.

21 Quoted by Irene Claydon in her report, 'Municipal Nurseries in Leeds', sent to Harrisson, 4 June 1942. Mass Observation Topic Collection: Day Nurseries, 19-1-F.

22 Unidentified newspaper clipping of article by Hilde Marchant, probably January 1942, in Mass Observation Topic Collection: Day Nurseries, 19-1-F.

23 Cited in Dorothy Sheridan, ed., *Wartime Women: An Anthology of Women's Wartime Writing for Mass-Observation, 1937–1945* (London, 1990), p. 162.

24 Ibid., p. 164.

25 Mass Observation, *The Journey Home* (London, 1944), p. 58.

26 Oral evidence of Mary Sutherland to Royal Commission on Population, 4 March 1945, RG 24/9, TNA.

27 Thomas, *Women at Work*.

28 'Manpower and Conscription', Mass Observation File Report 1009, December 1940.

29 See Summerfield's discussion of this Committee's work in *Women Workers*, pp. 43–53.

30 'Man Power: Memorandum by the Prime Minister', dated 27 November 1941, CAB 66/20/14.

31 For a good summary of the state of provision in the late 1930s, see Angela Davis, *Pre-school childcare in England, 1939–2010: Theory, practice and experience* (Manchester, 2015).

32 Thomas, *Women at Work*.

33 Unidentified newspaper clipping of article by Hilde Marchant.

34 Amabel Williams-Ellis, *Women in War Factories* (London, 1943), p. 85.

35 Mrs K. M. Stirling to Miss E. Whyte, 9 October 1941, LAB 26/58, TNA.

36 See summary of Reading's meeting with Brown in minutes by R. M. Gould [March 1940?], LAB 26/57, TNA.

37 Lady Reading, 'While Mothers Work', *Picture Post*, 20 July 1940, pp. 23–4.

38 Elizabeth Andrew to Bevin, 26 November 1940, LAB 26/58, TNA.

39 Summerfield, *Women War Workers*, p. 120.

40 Ellen Wilkinson, 'Women in War', *Picture Post*, 9 March 1940, p. 24.

41 'Day Nurseries and School Meals for the Children of Married Women Workers', memorandum from North Midlands Divisional Controller to Ministry of Labour, 15 April 1941, LAB 26/58.

42 Memorandum from Mr A. Barratt Brown, Southern Divisional Office, to Ministry of Labour, 13 May 1941, LAB 26/58.

43 Sheila Ferguson and Hilde Fitzgerald, *Studies in the Social Services* (HMSO, 1954), p. 189.

44 'Day Nurseries – Demand', report from Cardiff dated 10 March 1942, Mass Observation, Topic Collection: Day Nurseries, 19-1-D.

45 'Grangetown Day Nursery', handwritten report dated 9 February 1942, Mass Observation, Topic Collection: Day Nurseries, 19-1-D.

46 'Coventry, Wartime Day Nursery', report dated 23 November 1941, Mass Observation, Topic Collection: Day Nurseries, 19-1-D.

47 Residential nurseries served families in a range of circumstances, including cases of destitution, death of one or both parents, serious illness of the mother, or an impending confinement where there were no relatives or friends on hand to look after older children. 'Work'-related reasons accounted for only 15 per cent of applications for nursery places amongst families in London in 1940, but 51 per cent by 1942. See Ferguson and Fitzgerald, *Studies in the Social Services*, p. 230.

48 For a good overview of the wartime residential nurseries, see Ferguson and Fitzgerald, *Studies in the Social Services*, chapter 7, and Davis, *Pre-school Childcare*, chapter 2.

49 Letter from Mrs J. Simms, *Picture Post*, 29 November 1941, p. 3.

50 Cited by Summerfield, *Women War Workers*, p. 40.

51 After 1906, the provision of school meals grew significantly following mounting concern about the physical health of the nation's children, but they were not universally provided and central government subsidies to local authorities were tightly controlled. Between the wars, the vast majority of schoolchildren continued to go home for their midday meal.

52 Memo from Divisional Office in Newcastle, dated 25 April 1941 and Memo from Divisional Office in Birmingham, dated 14 May 1941, both in LAB 26/58, TNA.

53 John Welshman, 'School meals and milk in England and Wales, 1906–45', *Medical History*, 41 (1997), p. 27. State-subsidised 'British Restaurants', which were serving more than 600,000 meals a day during the war, also relieved some women from the burden of cooking for husbands in the middle of the day, as did workplace canteens, which grew in number during the war. See Nadja Durbach, 'British Restaurants and the Gender Politics of the Wartime Midday Meal' in Sandra Dawson and Mark Crowley, eds, *Home Fronts: Britain and the Empire at War* (Woodbridge, 2017), pp. 19–36.

54 J. L. Langland to G. H. Ince, 3 November 1941, LAB 26/58, TNA.

55 The 1937 Factories Act prescribed forty-eight hours as the legal maximum for these groups. These restrictions were relaxed during the war and by 1942 it was not unusual for women in Royal Ordnance Factories to be working fifty-five hours or more.

56 Anne Scott-James, 'Recruiting Van Draws Women to War Work', *Picture Post*, 6 June 1942, pp. 14–15.

57 Priestley, *British Women*, p. 58.

58 For a good overview of wartime shopping problems, see Summerfield, *Women Workers*, chapter 5.

59 Political and Economic Planning, *Planning: Special issue on part-time employment and woman power*, no. 185, 10 February 1942, p. 15.

60 In September 1943, the Ministry of Production produced an illustrated booklet for employers which explained the possibilities for making use of home-workers and out-workers. All the workers featured in the accompanying photographs were women. See *Outwork: A Method of Utilising Non-Factory Labour* (1943), copy in LAB 8/1283, TNA.

61 'Regional Controllers' Conference: Part-Time Employment, Home Work and Depot Work', draft paper sent by Mr McAlpine to Mary Smieton, 29 March 1943, LAB 8/703, TNA.

62 W. P. N. Edwards to Mrs M. A. Patterson, 4 September 1943, LAB 8/703, TNA.

63 See, for instance, memorandum by Ann Patterson, 'Part-time work in Local Authorities' Offices', dated 10 May 1943, LAB 8/703, TNA.

64 See the discussions amongst officials about the scope for recruiting 'spare-time' workers in 1942–3 in LAB 8/703, TNA.

65 Mass Observation, 'Women in Wartime', p. 260.

66 The most penetrating account of the WVS's war work is James Hinton, *Women, Social Leadership and the Second World War: Continuities of Class* (Oxford, 2002).

67 Typed document entitled 'Molly' and dated March 1944, Mass Observation, Topic Collection: Family Planning, 3-2-C.

68 'Mrs X, Burrows Rd, Willesden', dated 2 May 1944, Mass Observation, Topic Collection: Family Planning, 3-2-A.

69 Wendy Webster, '"Fit to Fight, Fit to Mix": sexual patriotism in Second World War Britain', *Women's History Review*, 22 (2013), pp. 607–24; Sonya Rose, 'Girls and GIs: Race, Sex, and Diplomacy in Second World War Britain', *International History Review*, 19 (1997), pp. 146–60.

70 Much of the discussion in this and the following four paragraphs draws upon Ferguson and Fitzgerald, *Studies in the Social Services*, chapter 3, and Pat Thane and Tanya Evans, *Sinners? Scroungers? Saints? Unmarried Motherhood in Twentieth-Century England* (Oxford, 2012), chapter 3.

71 Ferguson and Fitzgerald, *Studies in the Social Services*, p. 25.

72 *Report of the Committee on Amenities and Welfare Conditions in the Three Women's Services* (Cmnd 6384, 1942), pp. 49–50.

73 The Adoption of Children (Regulation) Act, passed in 1939 but not enforced until 1943, ruled that only local authorities and approved adoption societies could arrange adoptions, but informal and unregulated adoptions continued to take place and unmarried mothers were sometimes pushed by doctors, midwives and voluntary workers towards this option. See Thane and Evans, *Sinners? Scroungers? Saints?*, pp. 79–80.

74 David Reynolds, *Rich Relations: The American Occupation of Britain, 1942–1945* (London, 1995). Husbands posted overseas were suspicious of these 'bloody Yanks', with their flashy uniforms and deep pockets, although one study of wartime adultery found that three-quarters

of the men involved were in fact British civilians. See Allan Allport, *Demobbed: Coming Home after the Second World War* (London, 2009), p. 93.

75 Laura Tabili, *Global Migrants, Local Culture: Natives and Newcomers in Provincial England, 1841–1939* (Basingstoke, 2011); David Holland, 'The social networks of South Asian migrants in the Sheffield area during the early twentieth century', *Past & Present*, 236 (2017), pp. 243–79.

76 Cited by Lucy Bland in her pioneering study, 'Interracial Relationships and the "Brown Baby Question": Black GIs, White British Women, and Their Mixed-Race Offspring in World War II', *Journal of the History of Sexuality*, 26 (2017), p. 436. See also Bland's full-length book, *Britain's 'Brown Babies': The stories of children born to black GIs and white women in the Second World War* (Manchester, 2019), and Wendy Webster, *Mixing It: Diversity in World War Two Britain* (Oxford, 2018), pp. 210–20.

77 Ibid., p. 441.

78 Priestley, *British Women*, p. 57.

79 Wilkinson quoted by Margaret Goldsmith, *Women at War* (London, 1943), pp. 189–90.

80 Margaret Goldsmith, *Women and the Future* (London, 1946), pp. 14, 16.

81 Gertrude Williams, *Women and Work* (London, 1945), p. 127.

82 Mass Observation, *The Journey Home*, p. 58.

83 Mass Observation's panellists were diverse but what might be described as the educated lower middle classes (for example, schoolteachers, clerks, technicians, managers) were over-represented. More men than women responded regularly to directives.

84 Directive: January 1944, reply from Panel Member 1061.

85 Reply from Panel Member 3545.

86 This phrase was used by panellist 1688, a male radio operator who was married and in his early thirties.

87 Reply from Panel Member 2992.

88 Reply from Panel Member 1673.

89 Reply from Panel Member 1039.

90 Reply from Panel Member 1637.

91 Reply from Panel Member 3474.

92 Reply from Panel Member 2971.

7 PUT MONEY IN YOUR BAG

1 The most detailed account of the campaign is William Crofts, *Coercion or Persuasion? Propaganda in Britain after 1945* (London, 1989), but see also Susan Carruthers, 'Manning the factories: propaganda and policy on the employment of women, 1939–47', *History*, 75 (1990), pp. 232–56.

2 'Isaacs sorry he has to ask women to work', *Daily Mail*, 2 June 1947, p. 3.

3 'There's a Worried Man Who'd Like to Talk to YOU' leaflet, LAB 8/1485, The National Archives (TNA), Kew.

4 'Work In Vital Industries', *The Times*, 4 October 1947, p. 4.

5 'Broadcast by Rt Hon GA Isaacs MP, Minister of Labour and National Service on Sunday 1st June 1947', LAB 8/1485.

6 Ibid.

7 'The Use of Womanpower', *The Economist*, 152, 7 June 1947, p. 880.

8 For a useful overview of the position after the war, see Gerry Holloway, *Women and Work in Britain since 1840* (Abingdon, 2005), chapter 10.

9 Kathleen E. Gales and P. H. Marks, 'Twentieth Century Trends in the Work of Women in England and Wales', *Journal of the Royal Statistical Society*, 137 (1974), p. 64.

10 R. K. Kelsall and Sheila Mitchell, 'Married women and employment in England and Wales', *Population Studies* 13 (1959), pp. 19–33, based on data collected in David Glass's 1949 social mobility study.

11 'Defence programme – Supply and demand for women workers', paper prepared for the Women's Consultative Committee at the Ministry of Labour, 21 November 1951, LAB 26/286.

12 Harold Smith, 'The Womanpower Problem in Britain during the Second World War', *Historical Journal*, 27 (1984), pp. 925–45. There were 33,000 married women teachers by April 1945.

13 Memo from James Chuter Ede dated 6 March 1944, 'Note on Mr Hamilton Kerr's Amendment', ED 136/467.

14 See, for example, 'More Teachers', *The Times*, 17 June 1948, p. 5; ' "Equal Chance" for Women Teachers', *Manchester Guardian*, 7 July 1949, p. 2; and 'Training Scheme for Teachers', *Manchester Guardian*, 29 July 1948, p. 2.

15 Memo by Dorothy Hacket, 'Practice of certain Outside Employers in this Country, and of certain Foreign and Dominion Governments' dated November 1945, T 275/132.

16 'Teacher's Baby Sets a Problem', *Manchester Guardian*, 13 January 1950, p. 4.

17 *Marriage Bar in the Civil Service: Report of the Civil Service National Whitley Council Committee* (HMSO, Cmnd 6886, August 1946), p. 6.

18 Covering note from Sir Alan Barlow to the Chancellor, dated April 1946, 'Employment of Married Women in Established Civil Service Posts', T 275/134.

19 Cabinet Conclusion, 9 September 1946, CAB 128/6/18.

20 The Foreign Office, which decided in 1946 to admit women to its senior branch, secured an exemption and operated a marriage bar for all grades of female staff until the early 1970s. See Helen McCarthy, *Women of the World: The Rise of the Female Diplomat* (London, 2014).

21 See Minutes of a Meeting of the Official Side, 17 December 1945, T 275/132, and Barlow's subsequent covering note to the Chancellor.

22 Cabinet Conclusion, 9 September.

23 Hacket, 'Practice of certain Outside Employers in this Country'.

24 'More Women Needed In Industry', *The Times*, 30 January 1948, p. 4; 'Factory is Going All Out for the Target – a House', *Daily Mirror*, 23 January 1948, p. 5.

25 *Daily Mirror*, 16 July 1947, p. 2; 'Hour to Shop would put women into industry', *Daily Mirror*, 1 July 1947, p. 3.

26 Geoffrey Thomas, *Women and Industry: An inquiry in to the problem of recruiting women to Industry carried out for the Ministry of Labour and National Service* (Government Social Survey, March 1948).

27 'There's a Worried Man Who'd Like to Talk to YOU'.

28 See Eastern Regional Office to E. P. Moriarty at Ministry of Labour, 14 July 1947 and T. H. Fielding at the Birmingham Regional Office to Moriarty, 14 July 1947, LAB 12/417.

29 'Return of Women to Industry – Hendon District Campaign', dated 7 October 1947, LAB 12/417.

30 'Evening Shifts – A Valuable Part-Time Scheme', *Women In Industry Campaign Bulletin*, No. 9, 15 September 1947, LAB 8/1485.

31 Celia Briar, *Working for Women? Gendered Work and Welfare Policies in Twentieth-Century Britain* (London, 1997), p. 94.

32 'Outworkers and Homeworkers: notes for deputation from TUC on Thursday 26th January, 1950', LAB 8/1283.

33 See W. Simm at the Bristol Regional Office to Miss Waters, 16 Sep 1947, LAB 8/1485.
34 See letter from the manager of St Alban's Employment Exchange to H. J. Caradine, 1 August 1947, LAB 12/417.
35 *Daily Mirror*, 16 July 1947, p. 2.
36 In total, 35 per cent of the 8,270 part-timers registered by labour exchanges were placed in jobs, compared to 62 per cent of the 5,917 full-timers. See 'Recruitment of Women to Industry Campaign – June to September 1947', LAB 12/417.
37 See, for example, letter from the manager of St Albans Employment Exchange to H. J. Caradine, 8 September 1947, and Manager of Ipswich Employment Exchange to Caradine, 8 September 1947, LAB 12/417.
38 Hilda Menzies, 'The Day Care of Children Apart from their Parents' in *Journal of the Royal Sanitary Institute*, 71 (1951), p. 248.
39 *Daily Mirror*, 16 July 1947, p. 2.
40 Harold Hutchinson, 'Women and Work: What the People Say', *Daily Mirror*, 19 July 1947, p. 2.
41 Undated Circular from L. H. Hornsby [May 1947?], LAB 12/421.
42 'Child-care Implications of the Defence Programme', note by R. L. Bicknell to Mary Smieton dated 13 January 1951, LAB 26/286.
43 B. Seebohm Rowntree and G. R. Lavers, *Poverty and the Welfare State: A third social survey of York dealing only with economic questions* (London, 1951), chapter 7.
44 For an evocative picture of these years, see David Kynaston, *Austerity Britain: 1945–51* (London, 2007).
45 Notes of a Fourth Meeting of the Committee on the Recruitment of Women to Industrial Employment, 10 March 1947, LAB 8/1485.
46 See, for example, memo from London Regional Office dated 12 September 1947, LAB 8/1485.
47 See transcript of 'Recruitment of Women For Industry: Meeting 15 May 1947' in LAB 12/421, at which the junior Labour minister, Ness Edwards, was forced to answer repeated questions about equal pay from a range of feminist societies and women's organisations.
48 This reform was called for and subsequently welcomed by the *Daily Express* (see 'Opinion', 15 March 1948, p. 2, and 'First Capital Levy', 7 April 1948, p. 1), but otherwise did not appear to generate a great deal

of publicity or interest. There is little evidence that it made much practical difference to levels of labour-force participation.

49 Michael Young, 'Distribution of Income within the Family', *British Journal of Sociology*, 3 (1952), pp. 305–21.

50 Gertrude Willoughby, 'The Social and Economic Factors Influencing the Employment of Married Women' in *Journal of the Royal Sanitary Institute*, 71 (1951), p. 240.

51 Anne Temple, 'Council of Seven Women report on: Wives who go to work', *Daily Mail*, 26 August 1948, p. 2.

52 Hutchinson, 'Women and Work'.

53 See, for example, 'Five wives demand apology', *Daily Mail*, 31 December 1948, p. 3.

54 The best overview of the wider significance of the Commission is Pat Thane, 'Population Politics in Post-War British Culture' in Becky Conekin, Frank Mort and Chris Waters, eds, *Moments of Modernity: Reconstructing Britain, 1945–1964* (London, 1999), pp. 114–33.

55 The Victorian figure is misleading in the sense that the distribution of family size was very wide, with no more than 10 per cent of couples falling into any one category. By contrast, 50 per cent of those marrying between 1925 and 1929 had either one or two children. See *Royal Commission on Population: Report* (HMSO, Cmnd 7695, 1949), p. 26.

56 See the authoritative discussion of these issues in Simon Szreter, *Fertility, Class and Gender in Britain, 1860–1940* (Cambridge, 1996), especially pp. 490, 499–500 and 504–5. For middle-class women, see Sian Pooley, 'Parenthood, child-rearing and fertility in England, 1850–1914', *History of the Family*, 18 (2013), pp. 83–106.

57 See especially the first session of evidence involving the demographer David Glass and Mr R. R. Kuczynski (Minutes of Evidence, 7 July 1944, RG 24/9). This issue was also addressed in passing by witnesses before the Royal Commission on Equal Pay (1944–46). The economist Roy Harrod noted that one argument against equal pay was to ensure that 'motherhood as a vocation is not too unattractive financially compared with work in the professions, industry or trade', cited by Denise Riley, *War in the Nursery* (London, 1986), p. 167.

58 Alva Myrdal, *Nation and Family: The Swedish Experiment in Democratic Family and Population Policy* (London, 1941), p. 417.

59 Minutes of Evidence, 2 March 1945, RG 24/9.

60 The submission can be found in the volume of written evidence to the Commission (RG 24/11), but it was also published as *Population and the People: A National Policy* (London, 1945).

61 *Royal Commission on Population: Report*, p. 148.

62 Ibid., p. 147.

63 For an insightful discussion of these tensions within post-war pro-natalism, see Riley, *War in the Nursery*, chapter 6.

64 William Beveridge, *Social Insurance and Allied Services* (HMSO, Cmd 6404, 1942), p. 50.

65 'Mrs Richards took a deep breath', *Daily Mirror*, 7 May 1945, p. 7.

66 For the wartime evolution of policy debates over family allowances, see Susan Pedersen, *Family, Dependence and the Origins of the Welfare State, Britain and France 1914–1945* (Cambridge, 1993), pp. 327–36.

67 Wage-earning wives could opt in to the social insurance system but, as with the 1911 legislation, had to build up their entitlements from scratch following marriage and received a lower rate of benefit.

68 Joint circular issued by the Ministry of Health and the Ministry of Education, 'Nursery Provision for Children Under Five', dated 14 December 1945. A copy can be found in LAB 8/2627.

69 Hugh Paul, 'Day Nurseries', *Journal of the Royal Sanitary Institute*, 71 (1951), p. 234.

70 Ibid., p. 235.

71 Ibid., p. 251.

72 'No nurseries for working mothers with £5 husbands', *Daily Mirror*, 28 February 1947, p. 3.

73 For an excellent analysis of the origins and impact of this new form of expertise see Michal Shapira, *The War Inside: Psychoanalysis, Total War and the Making of the Democratic Self in Post-War Britain* (Cambridge, 2013).

74 Anna Freud and Dorothy Burlingham, *Infants Without Families: The Case For and Against Residential Nurseries* (London, 1943).

75 'Child Guidance' was the term given to a type of child welfare work established in Britain in the 1920s by pioneering child psychologists which focused on emotional rather than physical well-being. Child Guidance formed part of a wider 'mental hygiene' movement which promoted a preventative approach to mental health issues. See John

Stewart, *Child Guidance in Britain, 1918–1955: The Dangerous Age of Childhood* (London, 2013).

76 This shift was instigated by the 1946 report of a committee on children in care (chaired by Myra Curtis, a former civil servant and Principal of Newnham College, Cambridge, and known as the Curtis Report) and the subsequent Children's Act (1948). Under the Act, each local authority had to establish a Children's Committee and appoint a trained Children's Officer to ensure that the developmental needs of children in care were being met.

77 Menzies, 'Day Care of Children Apart from their Parents', p. 248.

78 Angela Davis, *Pre-school childcare in England, 1939–2010: Theory, practice and experience* (Manchester, 2015).

79 Transcript of broadcast dated 5 October 1950, 'Day Nurseries: Can we get more facts', LAB 26/286. Privately, Smieton pushed against the restrictive policy on nurseries adopted by the Ministry of Health, writing to a colleague: 'The manpower situation does not permit us to agree whole-heartedly with this line, and it does make it the more desirable, therefore, that reasonable provision of nurseries should be available for those mothers who do respond to the national need for their services.' (Smieton to Barnes, 31 August 1951, in same file).

80 Cited by Caitriona Beaumont, *Housewives and Citizens: Domesticity and the Women's Movement in England, 1928–1945* (Manchester, 2013), pp. 122–3.

81 Beaumont, *Housewives*, p. 120.

82 For an insightful discussion of how women were affected by the postwar welfare reforms, see Sheila Blackburn, 'How useful are feminist theories of the welfare state?', *Women's History Review*, 4 (1995), pp. 369–94.

83 James Hinton, 'Essay in Labour Statistics: Women and the Labour vote, 1945–50', *Labour History Review*, 57 (1992), pp. 59–66.

84 Graham Stanford, 'I'm through with the din and dirt of the mill', *Daily Mail*, 29 April 1947, p. 2.

85 Dorothy Layton to L. H. Hornby, 12 August 1947, LAB 12/421.

86 Michal Shapira, 'Psychoanalysts on the radio: Domestic citizenship and motherhood in postwar Britain' in Joanne Regulska and Bonnie G. Smith, eds, *Women and Gender in Postwar Europe: From Cold War to European Union* (London, 2012), pp. 71–86.

8 HOUSEWIVES' CHOICE

1 Jephcott was based at the Department of Social Administration at the London School of Economics and worked on the study with Nancy (later Baroness) Seear, an expert in industrial welfare work, and John H. Smith, a relatively young academic who had recently completed his sociology doctorate at LSE.

2 Pearl Jephcott, with Nancy Seear and John H. Smith, *Married Women Working* (London, 1962), p. 102. The social anthropologist Raymond Firth, who was conducting his own fieldwork in Bermondsey at the time, noted a similar sense of optimism about improving conditions. See Jon Lawrence, *Me, Me, Me? The Search for Community in Post-War England* (Oxford, 2019), chapter 2.

3 Jephcott, *Married Women Working*, p. 108.

4 Viola Klein and Alva Myrdal, *Women's Two Roles: Home and Work* (London, 1968 [1956]), p. xvi.

5 Jephcott, *Married Women Working*, pp. 100–101.

6 For a pioneering study of some of these themes, see Dolly Wilson, 'A New Look at the Affluent Worker: The Good Working Mother in Post-War Britain', *Twentieth-Century British History*, 17 (2006), pp. 206–29. This chapter builds upon, develops and extends Wilson's important insights into the post-war wage-earning mother. See also Helen McCarthy, 'Social Science and Married Women's Employment in Post-War Britain', *Past & Present*, 233 (2016), pp. 269–305 and 'Women, Marriage and Paid Work in Post-War Britain', *Women's History Review*, 26 (2017), pp. 46–61.

7 Unemployment never exceeded 2.6 per cent between 1951 and 1969 and fell below 2 per cent for eleven of these nineteen years. See 'Unemployment statistics from 1881 to the present day', *Labour Market Trends*, January 1996, pp. 5–18.

8 Aled Davies, '"Right to Buy": The Development of a Conservative Housing Policy, 1945–1980', *Contemporary British History*, 27 (2013), pp. 421–44.

9 Jephcott, *Married Women Working*, pp. 54–5.

10 Mark Clapson, *Invincible green suburbs, brave new towns: Social change and urban dispersal in postwar England* (Manchester, 1998); Lynn Abrams, Barry Hazley, Valerie Wright and Ade Kearns, 'Aspiration, Agency, and the Production of New Selves in a Scottish New Town,

c.1947–c.2016', *Twentieth-Century British History*, 29 (2018), pp. 576–604.

11 Mark Abrams, 'The Home-Centred Society', *Listener*, 26 November 1959, pp. 914–15.

12 Pat Thane, 'Family Life and "Normality" in Postwar British Culture' in Richard Bessel and Dirk Schuman, eds, *Life After Death: Approaches to a Cultural and Social History of Europe during the 1940s and 1950s* (Cambridge, 2003), pp. 193–210.

13 Office for National Statistics, *Travel Trends 2010* (2010), p. 14.

14 Monica Dickens, 'It's the woman who makes the home', *Woman's Own*, 11 April 1957, p. 24.

15 The exact figures were 41.8 per cent for wives of manual workers; 28.3 per cent for women married to professional men; and 31.1 per cent for the wives of employers or managers.

16 The figures in this paragraph refer to England and Wales and are taken from Kathleen E. Gales and P. H. Marks, 'Twentieth Century Trends in the Work of Women in England and Wales', *Journal of the Royal Statistical Society*, 137 (1974), pp. 60–74.

17 Audrey Hunt, *A Survey of Women's Employment* (Government Social Survey, HMSO, 1968), p. 8.

18 'The Employment of married women with children: a survey', *Women in Council* (April 1957), pp. 68–9.

19 R. K. Brown, J. M. Kirkby and K. F. Taylor, 'The employment of married women and the supervisory role', *British Journal of Industrial Relations*, 2 (1964), pp. 23–41.

20 Colin Rosser and Christopher Harris, *The Family and Social Change: A Study of Family and Kinship in a South Wales Town* (London, 1965), p. 232.

21 The testimonies quoted in this chapter are from part two of a directive issued in autumn 2014 by the Mass Observation Project which asked respondents for their memories and views on various themes relating to parenting and work. See *Mass Observation Project, Autumn 2014 Directive (Working Families)*, Mass Observer H260.

22 Mass Observer M3231.

23 Ferdynand Zweig, *The Worker in an Affluent Society: Family Life and Industry* (London, 1961).

24 Viola Klein, *Working Wives: The Survey of Facts and Opinions Concerning the Gainful Employment of Married Women in Britain* (London, 1960),

p. 26. The link between married women's earnings and consumer spending was made by participants in other post-war social surveys, including the working wife interviewed by Raphael Samuel in Stevenage who said: 'you've just got to compete with the Joneses here, whether you like it or not.' Cited by Lawrence, *Me, Me, Me?*, p. 98.

25 Viola Klein, *Britain's Married Women Workers* (London, 1965), p. 65.

26 Zweig, *The Worker in an Affluent Society*, pp. 176–7. For more on men's growing involvement with domestic labour, see Laura King, *Family Men: Fatherhood and masculinity in Britain, 1914–1960* (Oxford, 2015), and Angela Davis and Laura King, 'Gendered Perspectives on Men's Changing Familial Roles in Postwar England, *c*.1950–1990', *Gender & History*, 30 (2018), pp. 70–92.

27 *Woman's Own*, 14 March 1957, p. 7.

28 For an insightful discussion of the development of this critique within professional medical circles, see Frederick Cooper, 'Medical Feminism, Working Mothers, and the Limits of Home: Finding a Balance Between Self-Care and Other-Care in Cross-Cultural Debates about Health and Lifestyle, 1952–1956', *Palgrave Communications* (2016), DOI: 10.1057/palcomms.2016.42.

29 Michael Young and Peter Willmott, *Family and Kinship in East London* (London, 1957), p. 133. For more on the Bethnal Green study, see Jon Lawrence, 'Inventing the "Traditional Working Class": A Re-Analysis of Interview Notes from Young and Willmott's *Family and Kinship in East London*', *Historical Journal*, 59 (2016), pp. 567–93.

30 Hannah Gavron, *The Captive Wife* (London, 1966), p. 118. In his book, *Me Me Me?*, Jon Lawrence shows how 'community' was not, as some social scientists feared, disappearing, but working-class people became more selective about their social and kinship networks and this might have intensified the sense of isolation experienced by housebound mothers. The evidence for this, however, is not conclusive: in their post-war study of Croydon, two medical researchers found scant evidence that non-working wives suffered from mental health problems at a higher rate than working ones. See E. H. Hare and G. K. Shaw, *Mental Health on a New Housing Estate: A Comparative Study of Health in Two Districts of Croydon* (Oxford, 1965), p. 60.

31 Myrdal and Klein, *Women's Two Roles*, p. 23.

32 E. M. Harris, *Married Women in Industry* (Institute of Personnel Management, Occasional Papers, 1954), p. 28.

33 The adverts appeared in the issues for 14 January and 18 February 1956.

34 'Mary's wonderful world as a Tupperware Dealer', *Daily Mirror*, 28 January 1967, p. 12.

35 Claire Langhamer, *The English in Love: The Intimate Story of an Emotional Revolution* (Oxford, 2013), pp. 4–5.

36 Eustace Chesser, *The Sexual, Marital and Family Relationships of the English Woman* (London, 1956).

37 Joyce Joseph, 'A Research Note on Attitudes to Work and Marriage of Six Hundred Adolescent Girls', *British Journal of Sociology*, 12 (1961), pp. 176–83.

38 Angela Reed, *The £.s.d of Marriage* (London, 1968), p. 47.

39 Ruth Hancock, Rachel Stuchbury and Cecilia Tomassini, 'Changes in the distribution of marital age differences in England and Wales, 1963–1998', *Population Trends* (Winter 2003), pp. 19–25. The age at which women had their first child fell from just under twenty-six to just under twenty-four by 1970. See House of Commons Library, *Olympic Britain: Social and Economic Change since the 1908 and 1948 London Games* (2012), p. 23.

40 Henrietta O'Connor and John Goodwin, 'Girls' Transitions to Work and Adulthood in the 1960s' in Christopher Pole, Jane Pilcher and John Williams, eds, *Young People in Transition: Becoming Citizens?* (Basingstoke, 2005), pp. 52–73.

41 Central Advisory Council for Education, *15 to 18* (HMSO, 1959), chapter 3, paragraph 48.

42 For an excellent exploration of gendered career advice and pathways open to young women in the 1950s, see Stephanie Spencer, *Gender, Work and Education in Britain in the 1950s* (Basingstoke, 2005).

43 Mrs B. A. Bennett, 'Part-time nursing employment in Great Britain', *International Labour Review*, April 1962, p. 351.

44 Veronica Beechey and Tessa Perkins, *A Matter of Hours: Women, Part-time Work and the Labour Market* (Cambridge, 1987), p. 28.

45 Jean Hallaire, *Part-Time Employment: Its Extent and Problems* (Paris, 1968), p. 18.

46 Klein noted some of these features of part-time work in *Britain's Married Women Workers*, chapter 3.

47 Sarah Boston, *Women Workers and the Trade Unions* (London, 1987), chapter 10.

48 See the correspondence for 1965–6 in LAB 8/3224, The National Archives (TNA), Kew.

49 Reverend David Sheppard, 'The love of money', *Woman's Own*, 24 January 1959, p. 34.

50 'Mothers told, "Don't work"', *Daily Express*, 27 March 1953, p. 3.

51 Venetia Murray, 'The Children of Mothers Who Work', *Picture Post*, 7 January 1956, p. 7.

52 Basil Henriques, 'Children need more discipline', *Modern Woman*, November 1961, p. 52.

53 Claud Morris, 'What! My wife go out to work?', *Daily Mirror*, 28 April 1952, p. 2.

54 Klein, *Britain's Married Women Workers*, p. 69.

55 Mass Observer H1543.

56 Mass Observer R1760.

57 Hunt, *Survey of Women's Employment*, p. 189.

58 For the cultural reach of Bowlby, see Michal Shapira, *The War Inside: Psychoanalysis, Total war, and the Making of the Democratic Self in Postwar Britain* (Cambridge, 2013) and Mathew Thomson, *Lost Freedom: The Landscape of the Child and the British Post-War Settlement* (Oxford, 2013).

59 Cited by Thomson, *Lost Freedom*, p. 90.

60 John Bowlby, *Child Care and the Growth of Love* (London, 1953), both quotes at p. 77.

61 Murray, 'Children of Mothers'.

62 'You can't be a part-time mother', *Modern Woman*, December 1960, pp. 60–61, continued pp. 88–90.

63 Viola Klein Papers (VK), University of Reading Special Collections, Box 26, questionnaire no. 191.

64 Jane Deverson, 'When the Honeymoon is Over', *Woman's Own*, 27 September 1969, pp. 31–2, 37, 39.

65 Policy memorandum 'Provision of day nurseries for young children' dated 4 January 1965, MH 156/30, TNA.

66 Ibid.

67 Cited in Angela Davis, *Pre-school childcare in England, 1939– 2010: Theory, practice and experience* (Manchester, 2015), p. 130. See also this earlier statement by a civil servant at the Ministry

of Education to his colleague at the Ministry of Labour: 'Whilst it may be true that the facilities offered by nursery schools and classes can often ease the problems of working mothers, the primary purpose of nursery education is to meet the children's needs and not to facilitate employment ... it would not be right to extend a child's attendance irrespective of whether he is ready for it. It is very necessary not to lose sight of the distinctive purposes of nursery education.' V. H. Stevens to B. M. Grainger, 30 January 1962, LAB 8/2627.

68 The estimate is Tessa Blackstone's in *A Fair Start: The Provision of Pre-School Education* (London, 1971), and she included private nurseries and nursery schools.

69 'Provision of Care of Children of Working Mothers', briefing paper dated February 1962 in LAB 8/2627. For hospital crèches, see M. M. Perry to O'Brien, 17 June 1963, enclosing 'Paper on "The Employment of Women"' in MH 156/99.

70 Simon Yudkin and Anthea Holme, *Working Mothers and their Children: A study for the Council for Children's Welfare* (London, 1963), chapter 3. See also Peter Townsend, *The Family Life of Old People* (London, 1957).

71 Mass Observer L4071.

72 See Pat Thane, *Old Age in English History: Past Experiences, Present Issues* (Oxford, 2000), chapter 21.

73 Mass Observer F1373.

74 Mass Observer H5603.

75 Jephcott, *Married Women Working*, p. 157.

76 Firth also noted the power of local norms and social practices. See Jon Lawrence, 'Languages of place and belonging: anthropological versus vernacular understandings of communal life in mid-twentieth-century Bermondsey, London' in Stefan Couperus and Harm Kaal, eds, *(Re)Constructing Communities in Europe, 1918–1968* (London, 2016), pp. 19–44.

77 Rosser and Harris noticed this in Swansea: 'The geographical dispersal of related households over separate neighbourhoods, and farther, has limited the more extensive development of this grandmotherly role just at the time when the incidence of married women working is increasing substantially – as more and more women come to adopt the point of view advocated by Myrdal and Klein. That grandmothers

are not more readily available to help is one of the strains of the contemporary system.' Rosser and Harris, *The Family and Social Change*, p. 191.

78 Cited in Lawrence, 'Inventing the "Traditional Working Class"'.

79 Cited in Angela Davis, 'Women's experiences of combining childcare and careers in postwar Oxfordshire, *c.*1940–1990', *The Local Historian*, 43 (2013), p. 21.

80 Jean Mann, 'Should married women go out to work? The Penalties and the Awards', *Marriage Guidance*, April 1955, p. 4.

81 Mass Observer B42.

82 Mass Observer E743.

83 Margaret Wynn, *Fatherless Families* (London, 1964), p. 18.

84 VK Papers, box 27, questionnaire no. 382.

85 Mass Observer H2639.

86 Figures from Wynn, *Fatherless Families*, p. 18.

87 Before 1969, couples still had to prove fault on the part of one or the other party, usually adultery, cruelty, insanity or desertion. The new legislation introduced 'no-fault' conditions for divorce which could be demonstrated by husband and wife having lived apart for two years, or for five if one or the other did not consent to the divorce petition. The legislation actually came into effect in January 1971.

88 Edith Summerskill, *A Woman's World: Her Memoirs* (London, 1967), p. 239.

89 Mass Observer C3513.

90 Mass Observer O3436.

91 Cited by Pat Thane, 'Unmarried motherhood in twentieth-century England', *Women's History Review*, 20 (2011), p. 21.

92 Margaret Drabble, *The Millstone* (London, 1965).

93 See Thane, 'Unmarried motherhood'.

94 Chiquita Sandilands, 'It could never happen to me...' *Woman's Own*, 2 April 1966, pp. 16–19.

95 Wynn, *Fatherless Families*, p. 24.

96 See, for instance, Dennis Marsden, *Mothers Alone: Poverty and the Fatherless Family* (London, 1969).

97 Klein to Henry David, 29 March 1958, VK Papers, 4/2.

98 For single women, see Kath Holden, *The Shadow of Marriage: Singleness in England, 1914–1960* (Manchester, 2007). For women in same-sex

partnerships, see Rebecca Jennings, *Tomboys and Bachelor Girls: A lesbian history of post-war Britain* (Manchester, 2007).

9 COME BACK

1 Judith Hubback, *From Dawn to Dusk: Autobiography of Judith Hubback* (Illinois, 2003), p. 122. As she later reflected: 'I would be tapping into a subject of general interest to many women and their partners, but I also knew that I would be working towards finding out more about my own dissatisfactions, under cover of researching in a sociologically respectable way.'

2 Judith Hubback, *Wives Who Went to College* (London, 1957), p. 54.

3 Ibid., pp. 1–2.

4 Judith Hubback, 'Some Graduate Wives: Work and Children', *Manchester Guardian*, 10 July 1954, p. 4.

5 This appeared as *Graduate Wives* (1954), published by a think tank, Political and Economic Planning.

6 For the book's reception, see Helen McCarthy, 'Social Science and Married Women's Employment in Post-War Britain', *Past & Present*, 233 (2016), pp. 269–305.

7 Joan Little, 'Professional Part-Timers', *Guardian*, 5 September 1962, p. 6.

8 In 1961 in England and Wales, the proportion of women in the relevant age group starting full-time university degrees was 2.4 per cent, less than half the figure for men. Another 4–5 per cent were enrolled on teacher training courses, with a very small additional number studying in Further Education Colleges on a full- or part-time basis. See *Committee on Higher Education* (The Robbins Report), Appendix I (HMSO, Cmnd 2154-I), p. 15.

9 For this wider context, see Peter Mandler, 'The Two Cultures Revisited: The Humanities in British Universities Since 1945', *Twentieth Century British History*, 26 (2015), pp. 400–23, and 'Educating the Nation II: Universities', *Transactions of the Royal Historical Society*, 25 (2015), pp. 1–26; and Carol Dyhouse, *Students: A Gendered History* (London, 2006).

10 Iris Ashley, 'Brains do help', *Daily Mail*, 18 March 1957, p. 8.

11 Fifty-one per cent of married women who had stayed in education beyond nineteen were gainfully employed in 1965, compared to 42

per cent of those leaving school between the ages of sixteen and eighteen, and 36 per cent of those leaving school at fifteen. Married women with higher qualifications were also more likely to be working full-time: 31 per cent versus 21 per cent and 20 per cent. See Audrey Hunt, *A Survey of Women's Employment: Volume II* (Government Social Survey, HMSO, 1968), Table A5.

12 Hubback, *Wives*, p. 55.

13 Penelope Labovitch and Rosemary Simon, *Late Start: Careers for Wives* (London, 1966); Women's Information and Study Centre, *Comeback: A guide for the educated woman returning to work* (London, 1965); Women's Employment Federation, *Women Want to Work* (London, 1964).

14 These occupations required a significant period of training towards a formal qualification but as yet only medicine was unambiguously a 'graduate' profession. Some teachers and social workers held undergraduate degrees, but these were not necessary for entry until at least the 1980s.

15 'Women Graduates', *The Times*, 23 April 1957, p. 7. For broader accounts of the resilience of class in post-war Britain, see Selina Todd, *The People* (London, 2014) and Jon Lawrence, *Me, Me, Me? The Search for Community in Post-war England* (Oxford, 2019).

16 Hubback, *Wives*, p. 93.

17 Ibid., p. 66.

18 The number of pupils in secondary schools more than doubled between 1946 and 1961 from 1.3 million to 3.2 million. See Paul Bolton, *Education: Historical Statistics* (House of Commons Library, 2012), p. 6.

19 Geoffrey Partington, *Women Teachers in the 20th Century in England and Wales* (Windsor, 1976), p. 89.

20 Roy Hash, 'Come Back, Mrs Teacher – for £5 a day', *Daily Mail*, 6 December 1960, p. 4.

21 See copy of circular 8/60 issued by the Ministry of Health in MH 156/100, the National Archives (TNA), Kew.

22 See Nancy Seear's overview in *Re-entry of women to the labour market after an interruption in employment* (OECD, n.d.), chapter 2.

23 Ruth Elliot, 'Mainly for Women', *Guardian*, 21 May 1965, p. 10.

24 Virginia Waite, 'How a Home and Teaching Fit Together', *Daily Telegraph*, 7 July 1965, p. 15.

25 Margaret Maries and Kay Leadbetter, 'Housewives into Teachers', *University Women's Review*, 50 (1960), pp. 6–7.

26 Partington, *Women Teachers*.

27 Mass Observation Project (MOP), Autumn 2014 Directive (Working Families), Mass Observer L2281.

28 Questionnaire no. 696, Viola Klein Papers (VK), University of Reading, Box 28.

29 London County Council, *Teaching Opportunities for Married Women in London* (n.d.). Copy in VK Papers, 17/1.

30 *Committee on Higher Education* (The Robbins Report), Appendix Two (B) (HMS) (Cmnd 2154 I-II), p. 150.

31 Viola Klein, 'The demand for professional womanpower', *British Journal of Sociology*, 17 (1966), p. 184. Following years of campaigning by women's organisations, the Conservative government introduced legislation in 1955 to equalise pay in public sector employment. It was implemented in stages over the course of seven years and affected 140,000 teachers as well as female civil servants in grades where men were employed on the same work.

32 ' "New Women" of the twenties are near retirement now', *Manchester Guardian*, 8 November 1957, p. 5.

33 Questionnaires nos 680 and 542 in VK Papers. See also Thelma A. Hunter, 'Part-time teaching: neglect of the graduate wives', *Manchester Guardian*, 22 June 1956, p. 5.

34 Questionnaire no. 692, VK Papers, Box 28.

35 Roy Nash, 'Would you work for a part-time boss?' *Daily Mail*, 18 June 1964, p. 10.

36 Partington, *Women Teachers*.

37 As Pat Thane writes: 'Teaching was the career *expected* of the standard middle-class Girton graduate at least up to the 1960s; it was what many parents and teachers thought that a university education for a woman was for.' Pat Thane, 'Girton Graduates: earning and learning, 1920s–1980s', *Women's History Review*, 13 (2004), pp. 347–61. See also Sarah Aiston, 'A Good Job for a Girl? The Career Biographies of Woman Graduates of the University of Liverpool post-1945', *Twentieth Century British History*, 15 (2004), pp. 361–87.

38 Mass Observer L2281.

39 Questionnaire no. 745, VK Papers, Box 29.

40 Questionnaire no. 750, VK Papers, Box 29.

41 The 1944 Education Act established a three-tiered system of secondary education comprising selective grammars, non-selective secondary moderns and a small number of technical schools. The Crowther report noted how few graduates of either sex taught outside grammar schools or the independent sector. In 1958, just under 14 per cent of full-time female teachers in secondary moderns were graduates. For men, the proportion was 19 per cent. See Central Advisory Council for Education, *15 to 18* (HMSO, 1959), p. 96. Keith Kelsall also noted important class differences within the profession in his 1963 study for the Ministry of Education, *Women and Teaching* (HMSO, 1963), p. 14.

42 Oral evidence from the National Advisory Council on the Training and Supply of Teachers in *Committee on Higher Education* (The Robbins Report), Evidence – Part One: Volume F (Cmnd 2154 XI).

43 See, for example, M. Collins, ed., *Women Graduates and the Teaching Profession: Report of a Working Party of the British Federation of University Women* (Manchester, 1964).

44 R. K. Kelsall, Anne Poole and Annette Kuhn, *Graduates: The Sociology of an Elite* (London, 1972), p. 153.

45 Mary Ann Elston, 'Women Doctors in the British Health Services: A Sociological Study of their Careers and Opportunities' (unpublished doctoral thesis, University of Leeds, 1986), pp. 57, 63.

46 Ibid.

47 The Federation had a Standing Committee on the Work of Married Medical Women, and a Watching Committee on Part-Time Work, which merged in 1953. The Federation's extensive activities around the employment of married women are detailed in its archives, held at the Wellcome Library (SA/MWF).

48 Margot Jefferys and Patricia Elliott, *Women in Medicine: The results of an inquiry conducted by the Medical Practitioners' Union in 1962–63* (London, 1966).

49 See Constance Arregger, ed., *Graduate Women at Work: A Study by a Working Party of the British Federation of University Women* (Newcastle, 1966), chapter 8.

50 Minutes of the Committee on Part Time Work, 15 December 1950, SA/MWF/G.8.

51 Questionnaire no. 779, VK Papers, Box 29.

52 Jefferys and Elliott, *Women in Medicine*, p. 16.

53 See questionnaire no. 665, VK Papers, Box 28.

54 Letter from C. M. Ottley, *British Medical Journal*, 12 June 1954, clipping in papers of Judith Hubback, 7JUH/3, The Women's Library, London.

55 Medical Women's Federation, *Survey of the Completed Questionnaires Relating to Medical Women who Qualified in 1933 and 1948* in SA/ MWF/J.3/1, p. 28.

56 See, for example, 'Council Meeting, Nottingham, May 25 and 26, 1951: Report of the Committee on Part-Time Work' in SA/ MWF/G.14.

57 Questionnaire no. 535, VK Papers, Box 27.

58 Audrey W. M. Ward, 'Women Doctors Graduating at Sheffield, 1933–1957', *The Medical Officer*, 28 November 1969. See also Morag Timbury and Maria Ratzer, 'Glasgow medical women 1951–4: Their contribution and attitude to medical work', *British Medical Journal* (10 May 1969), pp. 372–4.

59 Arregger, *Graduate Women at Work*, p. 14.

60 Rue had been forced to abandon her training at the Royal Free Hospital in 1949 after getting married, but was able to take the University of London external degree and qualify in Oxford in 1951. She started clinical work but was dismissed when the hospital found out that she had a husband and a small baby. Rue switched to general practice and, following a debilitating bout of polio and the breakdown of her marriage, moved into hospital administration in 1965.

61 Rosemary Rue, 'Employment of Married Women Doctors in Hospitals in the Oxford Region', *The Lancet*, 10 June 1967, pp. 1,267–8.

62 For imitators, see Michael Essex-Lopresti, 'Recruitment of Doctors for Hospital Service', *The Lancet*, 25 July 1970, pp. 204–6; Kerry Bluglass, T. Leslie Dunn and F. W. Gastoni, 'Married women doctors' training and re-employment schemes in the West Midlands Region, with particular reference to psychiatry', *Medical Education*, 10 (1976), pp. 297–301. For the internal discussions leading to the 1969 circular, see papers in MH 149/322 and MH 149/323, TNA.

63 'Interpretation of HM69(6)' note by Annette Rawson dated 18 June 1970 in MH 149/323, TNA.

64 Seear, *Re-entry of women to the labour market*.

65 Questionnaire no. 740, VK Papers, Box 29.

66 *Report of the Working Party on Social Workers in Local Authority Health and Welfare Services* (Ministry of Health, 1959).

67 Dating from the 1890s, the role of the hospital almoner was to provide pastoral care to patients, typically involving home visiting or referrals to charities and other services. It was an almost exclusively feminised profession. Klein discovered that 99.5 per cent of the 1,200-strong membership of the Institute of Almoners was female in the mid-1960s.

68 Phyllis Willmott, *The Part-Time Social Worker* (1963), typescript copy in VK Papers, 17/1.

69 For a statement of this view, see letter from F. W. Brackstone, Public Relations Officer for the Education Welfare Officers' National Association in *Manchester Guardian*, 16 May 1959, p. 6. Many women did indeed switch to voluntary work after marriage, as a study of students taking Birmingham's social work courses revealed: see Winifred E. Cavenagh, *Four Decades of Students in Social Work* (Birmingham, 1956).

70 Kathleen Lyons, 'Dame Eileen Younghusband (United Kingdom), President 1961–1968' in *Social Work and Society* (2008): https://www.socwork.net/sws/article/view/102/391. For the 'male threat', see Ronald G. Walton, *Women in Social Work* (London, 1975), chapter 15.

71 Mary Green, 'They laughed when she went back to work', *Sunday Telegraph*, 23 Feb 1964, p. 16. See also 'Women Architects', *The Times*, 24 December 1963, p. 7.

72 BFUW, 'The Occupational Outlook for Graduate Women: Interim Report on One-Day Conference, Saturday October 31 1964', p. 30. Copy in Papers of the Medical Women's Federation, SA/MWF/J.9.

73 'Nadine Beddington, FRIBA, puts the case for the woman architect' in *Set Square*, August 1966, pp. 9–10. Clipping in Papers of the Medical Women's Federation, SA/MWF/L.6.

74 Klein, 'Demand for professional womanpower'.

75 Political and Economic Planning, *Women and Top Jobs: An Interim Report* (1967), p. 10.

76 Audrey Hunt, *A Survey of Women's Employment* (HMSO, 1968), p. 11.

77 IoD figure from *Women and Top Jobs*. Civil Service figures from R. K. Kelsall, *Higher Civil Servants in Britain: From 1870 to the Present Day*

(London, 1955), chapter 9, and Michael Fogarty, Isobel Allen and Patricia Walters, *Women in Top Jobs, 1968–1978* (London, 1981), p. 36.

78 Miss E. M. Young to Viola Klein, 16 April 1963, VK Papers, 6/1.

79 Questionnaire no. 292, VK Papers, Box 26.

80 Cited in Valerie Grove, *The Compleat Woman: Marriage, Motherhood, Career: Can she have it all?* (London, 1987), p. 207.

81 Nancy Seear, Veronica Roberts and John Brock, *A Career for Women in Industry?* (London, 1964), p. 1. For the fascinating story of how women were marginalised during the early phases of computing in Britain see Marie Hicks, *Programmed Inequality: How Britain discarded women technologists and lost its edge in computing* (Cambridge, MA, 2017).

82 See, for example, Dame Kitty Anderson, *Women and the Universities: A Changing Pattern* (London, 1963).

83 *Committee on Higher Education* (The Robbins Report), Evidence Part I – Volume A (Cmnd 2154-VI), p. 295.

84 Ibid., pp. 305–6.

85 Seear et al., *A Career for Women*.

86 Twenty-five of the sixty men interviewed said they would be happy to be managed by a woman if she were suitably qualified, but the remainder expressed ambivalence or outright opposition; see Seear et al., *A Career for Women*, p. 80. The man who said he would 'chuck it' was from Allen and Hanburys Ltd, see fieldnotes for Manager No. 8 in 7BNS/a/2/2, Papers of Baroness Nancy Seear, The Women's Library, London.

87 Manager No. 6 at Mullard Radio Valve Company, 7BNS/A/2/08.

88 Manager No. 10, 7BNS/A/2/06.

89 One such agency, Freelance Work for Women, gave examples of recently filled posts in its newsletter for summer 1968, which included part-time secretarial work for a number of charities, a firm of solicitors, an ambassador, a script-writer, a composer and an author, as well as catering businessmen's lunches, testing recipes for cookbook publishers, typing theses, scripts and engineering specifications, coding and editing market research questionnaires, translating Norwegian knitting patterns into English and showing American students around London. See *Freelance Work for Women Newsletter*, June/July 1968, copy in Papers of the Medical Women's Federation, SA/MWF/L.15.

90 Questionnaire no. 430, VK Papers, Box 27.

91 Ruth Adam, 'Problems of the Wives Who Went to College', *Church of England Newspaper*, 25 October 1957, clipping in Papers of Judith Hubback, Scrapbook 9, 7JUH/4, The Women's Library, London. See also Elizabeth Gundrey, 'Women in Society', *Sunday Times*, 21 July 1963, p. 21.

92 See, for example, 'Marjorie Proops lectures on the love life of a female egg head!', *Daily Mirror*, 25 September 1957, p. 11.

93 'Women Graduates', *The Times*, 26 April 1954, p. 7 (letter from J. P. A. Fenley).

94 These cases were collected by the Medical Women's Federation as part of its wider inquiry into the finances of professional women in the mid-sixties. See Patricia Edwards to Jean Lawrie, 1 May 1965, and Anne Mathieson to Lawrie, 5 April 1965, in SA/MWF/L.4.

95 Questionnaire no. 726, VK Papers, Box 29.

96 Questionnaire no. 263, VK Papers, Box 26, and no. 755, Box 29.

97 Above this level, female earners were even rarer. The ratio of women to men amongst those earning £3,000–£4,999 was 1:33, and for £5,000 or above it was 1:41. See Political and Economic Planning, *Women in Top Jobs: Interim Report* (1967).

98 For these dynamics, see Sheila Williams and F. D. Flower, *Foreign Girls in Hendon: A Survey* (Hendon Overseas Friendship Association, 1961) and Anne Glidewell, '"Au pair" and others', *Guardian*, 17 March 1961, p. 12.

99 Note by Annette Rawson to Mr S. I. Smith, 8 September 1970, MH 149/324.

100 WOTAG was an initiative of the Inter-Professional Working Party set up in 1965 by the Medical Women's Federation as a forum for representatives of women across a range of professions. See minutes for 28 November 1967 in SA/MWF/L.1/2.

101 For press commentary, see 'The wages of virtue', *The Economist*, 20 December 1969, p. 72, and Jill Tweedie, 'A taxing problem for working wives', *Guardian*, 16 March 1970, p. 9. For the government position, see Miss D. E. Chapman, private secretary to the Chancellor of the Exchequer, to R. P. W. Shackleton, President of the Association of Anaesthetists in August 1969, MH 149/323.

102 From 1971, a married woman could choose to have her earned income assessed as though she were a single person if her husband

agreed. The couple lost their married person's allowance as a result, making this option attractive only to those on fairly high incomes. The Inland Revenue continued to correspond solely with husbands in relation to their wives' tax affairs until 1978. See House of Commons Library, *Tax and Marriage* (Research Paper 95/87, July 1995).

103 Harold Leigh to Jean Lawrie, 17 February 1965, SA/MWF/L.4.

104 Julius Silman to Jean Lawrie, 7 April 1966, SA/MWF/L.6.

105 See Robert Rapoport and Rhona Rapoport, 'Work and Family in Contemporary Society', *American Sociological Review*, 30 (1965), pp. 381–94; Rhona and Robert Rapoport, *Dual Career Families* (London, 1971), and *Dual-Career Families Re-examined: New Integrations of Work & Family* (London, 1976).

106 Quoted in Laurence Dobie, 'Working Partnership', *Guardian*, 11 December 1969, p. 9.

107 Ibid.

108 See, for example, J. M. and R. E. Pahl, *Managers and their Wives: A study of career and family relationships in the middle class* (London, 1971). This phenomenon was theorised by Hannah Papanek as the 'two-person career' in 'Men, Women, and Work: reflections on the two-person career', *American Journal of Sociology*, 78 (1973), pp. 852–72, and later by feminist scholars as the 'incorporated wife'. See Hilary Callan and Shirley Ardener, eds, *The Incorporated Wife* (London, 1984), and Janet Finch, *Married to the Job: Wives' incorporation in men's work* (London, 1983).

109 Questionnaire no. 815, VK Papers, Box 29.

110 When the Committee on Higher Education reported in 1963, Robbins recommended an immediate and significant expansion in the number of university places which were to be made available to 'all who were qualified for them by ability and attainment'. The government accepted these proposals and the number of students obtaining degrees each year more than doubled between 1960 and 1970, from 22,500 to nearly 52,000. Women's share of these qualifications also grew, from 25 per cent to over 30 per cent.

111 Virginia Waite, 'A woman doctor's dilemma – getting home help for 24 hours a day', *Daily Telegraph*, 6 October 1965, p. 15.

112 Nicky Gregson and Michelle Lowe, *Servicing the Middle Classes: Class, gender and waged domestic labour in contemporary Britain* (London,

1994). See also Lucy Delap, *Knowing their Place: Domestic Service in Twentieth-Century Britain* (Oxford, 2011).

113 Hubback, *Wives*, p. 82.

114 Viola Klein to Miss Almond, 31 July 1963, VK Papers, 13/1.

115 Willmott, *The Part-Time Social Worker*, p. 4.

116 Hubback, *Wives*, p. 87.

117 Questionnaire no. 570, VK Papers, 13/3.

118 Letter from Hazel B. Baker, *British Medical Journal*, June 1954, clipping in Papers of Judith Hubback, 7JUH/3.

119 Jean E. Lawrie, Muriel Newhouse and Patricia M. Elliott, 'Working Capacity of Women Doctors', *British Medical Journal*, 12 February 1966, pp. 409–12.

120 Arregger, *Graduate Women at Work*, p. xvi.

121 Viola Klein, 'A Double Life', *Manchester Guardian*, 30 October 1964, p. 10.

10 NEWCOMERS

1 Doreen's story is one of many accounts from elderly Caribbean migrants collected in Z. Nia Reynolds, *When I Came to England: An oral history of life in 1950s and 1960s Britain* (London, 2001).

2 The best general account of the migrant experience published in recent years is Clair Wills, *Lovers and Strangers: An Immigrant History of Postwar Britain* (London, 2017).

3 D. J. Smith, *Racial Disadvantage in Britain: The PEP Report* (1977).

4 Peter Moss, 'The Current Situation' in Nickie Fonda and Peter Moss, eds, *Mothers in Employment* (1976), p. 21.

5 Sheela Banerjee, '"It's been bittersweet": three Indian women on 50 years in the UK', *Guardian*, 29 December 2018, https://www.theguardian.com/lifeandstyle/2018/dec/29/bittersweet-three-indian-women-50-years-in-uk?CMP=Share_iOSApp_Other.

6 As Clair Wills notes of official and public texts about migrants: 'these records offer plenty of insight into and information about attitudes towards the newcomers … But in order to tell us anything about the immigrants themselves they need to be held up before a mirror, and interpreted for what they tell us but do not say.' Wills, *Lover and Strangers*, p. xx.

7 For a thoughtful analysis of how visions of the post-war family were racially inflected, see Wendy Webster, *Imagining Home: Gender, 'Race' and National Identity, 1945–1964* (London, 1998).

8 Bob Moore, 'Areas of Reception in the United Kingdom, 1933–1945' in Werner E. Mosse, ed., *Second Chance: Two Centuries of German-speaking Jews in the United Kingdom* (Tübingen, 1991), pp. 69–80.

9 E. Stina Lyon, 'Viola Klein: Forgotten Émigré Intellectual, Public Sociologist and Advocate of Women', *Sociology*, 41 (2007), pp. 829–42.

10 Stephen Bourne, *Motherland Calls: Britain's Black Servicemen & Women, 1939–1945* (Stroud, 2012). See also Wendy Webster, *Mixing It: Diversity in World War Two Britain* (Oxford, 2018).

11 Enda Delaney, *Demography, State and Society: Irish Migration to Britain, 1921–1971* (Liverpool, 2000); Wills, *Lovers and Strangers*, p. xii.

12 Diana Kay and Robert Miles, *Refugees or migrant workers? European Volunteer Workers in Britain, 1946–51* (London, 1992); John Allan Tannahill, *European Volunteer Workers in Britain* (Manchester, 1958), p. 3.

13 Kathy Burrell, 'Male and Female Polishness in Post-war Leicester: Gender and its Intersections in a Refugee Community' in Wendy Webster and Louise Ryan, eds, *Gendering Migration: Masculinity, Femininity and Ethnicity in Post-War Britain* (Aldershot, 2008), pp. 71–88; Flavia Gasperetti, 'Italian women migrants in post-war Britain: the case of textiles workers, 1949–1961' (unpublished PhD thesis, University of Birmingham, 2012).

14 R. B. Davison, *West Indian Migrants: Social and Economic Facts of Migration from the West Indies* (London, 1962), p. 4.

15 Office for National Statistics, '2011 Census analysis: immigration patterns of non-UK-born populations in England and Wales in 2011' (ONS, 2013).

16 One of the best recent accounts of the politics of immigration policy in this period is Kennetta Hammond Perry, *London Is the Place for Me: Black Britons, Citizenship, and the Politics of Race* (Oxford, 2016).

17 Sheila Patterson, ed., *Immigrants in London: Report of a study group set up by the London Council of Social Service* (London, 1963), p. 8.

18 Wills, *Lovers and Strangers*, p. 240.

19 Pam Schweitzer, ed., *Across the Irish Sea* (Age Exchange Theatre, 1989), p. 59.

20 All three testimonies can be found in Louise Ryan, 'Becoming Nurses: Irish Women, Migration and Identity Through the Life Course' in Ryan and Webster, eds, *Gendering Migration*, pp. 129–30.

21 Mary Lennon, Marie McAdam and Joanne O'Brien, *Across the Water: Irish Women's Lives in Britain* (London, 1988), p. 106.

22 Ryan, 'Becoming Nurses', p. 121.

23 See Appendix in John Archer Jackson, *The Irish in Britain* (London, 1963), pp. 198–9; 22.4 per cent of women were in the 'professions', the vast majority of whom would have been nurses or midwives, although this category might also have included some teachers and a small number of higher professionals. For men, the largest categories were metal manufacturing, construction, unskilled labouring and transport.

24 Delaney, *Demography, State and Society*, p. 185.

25 Schweitzer, *Across the Irish Sea*, p. 71.

26 Ibid., p. 72.

27 Cited in Delaney, *Demography, State and Society*, p. 209.

28 Jackson, *The Irish in Britain*, p. 108.

29 Ryan, 'Becoming Nurses', p. 126.

30 Lennon et al., *Across the Water*, p. 66.

31 Ibid., p. 145.

32 See W. J. M. MacKenzie's foreword in Tannahill, *European Volunteer Workers in Britain*, p. vi.

33 Kay and Miles, *Refugees or migrant workers?*, p. 51.

34 Foreign Labour Committee paper, 'Recruitment of Displaced Persons from Germany for Work in British Hospitals', dated September 1946, The National Archives (TNA), LAB 8/90.

35 L. J. Edwards to Ness Edwards, 12 August 1947, TNA, HO 213/1001.

36 B. P. Boyes to Mrs E. McKenzie, 17 November 1947, TNA, HO 213/1001.

37 These Italian migrant testimonies were collected by Gasperetti in 'Italian women migrants in post-war Britain'.

38 Burrell, 'Male and Female Polishness', p. 81.

39 The British Cypriot population also includes small minorities of Armenians, Maronites and Latins (i.e. members of the Roman Catholic Church).

40 Flora Anthias, 'Sexual Divisions and Ethnic Adaptation: The Case of Greek-Cypriot Women' in Annie Phizacklea, ed., *One Way Ticket: Migration and Female Labour* (London, 1983), p. 83.

41 Cited in Gasperetti, 'Italian women migrants in post-war Britain', p. 63.

42 Buchi Emecheta, *Second-Class Citizen* (London, 1974). Adah's story after leaving Francis forms the narrative of Emecheta's first novel, *In the Ditch* (London, 1972).

43 Emecheta, *Second-Class Citizen*, p. 38.

44 From Notting Dale Urban Studies Centre and Ethnic Communities Oral History Project, *Sorry, No Vacancies: Life Stories of Senior Citizens From the Caribbean* (London, 1992), cited by Perry, *London is the Place for Me*, p. 86.

45 Elyse Dodgson, *Motherland: West Indian Women to Britain in the 1950s* (London, 1984), p. 35.

46 Political and Economic Planning, *Racial Discrimination* (London, 1967), p. 63.

47 Sheila Patterson, *Dark Strangers: A sociological study of the absorption of a recent West Indian group in Brixton, south London* (London, 1963), p. 104.

48 Racial prejudice was directed against men as well, of course. A manager at a firm of cleaners told a researcher in the early 1960s that he would try any 'likely-looking coloured applicants' but 'some of the men who've applied are really vicious-looking and would terrify the girls, so I wouldn't take them'. Patterson, *Dark Strangers*, p. 109.

49 Ibid., pp. 110–11.

50 Political and Economic Planning, *Racial Discrimination*, p. 44.

51 Davison, *West Indian Migrants*.

52 Patterson, *Dark Strangers*, p. 108.

53 Jane Cummings and Laura Serrant, 'BME nurses and midwives instrumental in shaping the NHS of today' (March 2018), available at: https://www.england.nhs.uk/blog/bme-nurses-and-midwives-instrumental-in-helping-shape-the-nhs-of-today/.

54 Stephanie Snow and Emma Jones, 'Immigration and the National Health Service: putting history to the forefront' (*History & Policy*, 2011), available at: http://www.historyandpolicy.org/policy-papers/papers/immigration-and-the-national-health-service-putting-history-to-the-forefron.

55 Morvia Gooden, 'A personal story of Black History in the NHS' (October 2016). Available at: https://www.leadershipacademy.nhs.uk/blog/personal-story-black-history-within-nhs/.

56 Dodgson, *Motherland*, p. 33.

57 Why, Patterson wondered aloud, 'will the public accept coloured doctors, nurses, postmen, ticket collectors, and sanitary inspectors, while flinching, or being supposed to flinch, from coloured teachers, policemen, meter-readers, shop assistants, receptionists, and even garbage collectors?' Patterson, *Dark Strangers*, pp. 129–30.

58 Dodgson, *Motherland*, p. 33.

59 Linda McDowell, *Working Lives: Gender, Migration and Employment in Britain, 1945–2007* (Chichester, 2013), p. 113.

60 Nancy Foner, *Jamaica Farewell: Jamaican migrants in London* (London, 1979), p. 69.

61 Ibid., pp. 116–17.

62 Emecheta, *Second-Class Citizen*, p. 43.

63 Patterson, *Immigrants in London*, p. 36.

64 Dodgson, *Motherland*, p. 40.

65 Following the Nurseries and Child-Minders Regulation Act of 1948, childminders were required to register with local authorities, submit to regular inspections of their homes and not exceed a specified maximum number of children permitted to be under their care at any one time.

66 Simon Yudkin, *0–5: A Report on the Care of Pre-School Children* (National Society of Children's Nurseries, 1967), pp. 61–2.

67 Brian Jackson, 'The Childminders', *New Society*, 26 (1973), pp. 521–3. See also Sonia Jackson, *The Illegal Childminders: A report on the growth of unregistered child-minding and the West Indian community* (Priority Area Children, Cambridge Educational Development Trust, n.d.), and Brian and Sonia Jackson, *Childminder* (London, 1979).

68 Pearl Jephcott, *A Troubled Area: Notes on Notting Hill* (London, 1964), p. 49.

69 Both cited in Dodgson, *Motherland*, p. 41. See also the Caribbean women interviewed by Karen Stone in the late 1970s, who frequently expressed frustration with their limited childcare options and a strong preference for day nurseries. Karen Stone, 'Motherhood and Waged Work: West Indian, Asian and White Mothers Compared' in Phizacklea, *One Way Ticket*, pp. 33–52.

70 R. B. Davison, *Black British: Immigrants to England* (Oxford, 1966), pp. 139, 142.

71 Jephcott, *A Troubled Area*, pp. 88–9.

72 See, for instance, Mary Chamberlain, 'Narratives of Caribbean families in Britain and the Caribbean' in Harry Goulborne and Mary Chamberlain, eds, *Caribbean Families in Britain and the Trans-Atlantic World* (Oxford, 2001), pp. 117–32; Floella Benjamin, *Coming to England* (London, 1995), pp. 34–6.

73 Davison, *Black British*, p. 118.

74 The analysis in this and the next paragraph builds on Jordanna Bailkin's brilliant account of West African fostering in *The Afterlife of Empire* (Berkeley, 2012), chapter 5.

75 Emecheta, *Second-Class Citizen*, p. 45.

76 See Vivien Biggs, 'Private fostering' in June Ellis, ed., *West African Families in Britain* (London, 1978), pp. 74–95.

77 As Bailkin explains, researchers disagreed over the source of this supposed dysfunction, with some seeing the problem as unsuccessful efforts by migrants to transport their 'indigenous' customs to Britain, and others arguing that it was produced by the migration process itself (*Afterlife of Empire*, pp. 178–9).

78 For contemporary perspectives on 'pathological' black mothering, see Katrin Fitzherbert, *West Indian Children in London* (London, 1967); G. Stewart Prince, 'Mental health problems in pre-school West Indian children' in *Maternal and Child Care*, 3 (1967), pp. 483–6; and Margaret Pollak, *Today's Three Year Olds in London* (Lavenham, 1972).

79 Fitzherbert, *West Indian Children*, p. 106. See also Biggs, 'Private Fostering', and Jackson, *Illegal Childminders*, who remarks: 'Theoretically, a deserted wife or unmarried mother is entitled to stay at home to look after her children. Many social workers and Health Visitors find it hard to understand why few West Indian women, in contrast to English women in the same position, are prepared even to consider this solution.' *Illegal Childminders*, p. 6.

80 See for example, Patterson, *West Indian Immigrants*; Jephcott, *A Troubled Area*; and Catriona Hood, T. E. Oppe, I. B. Pless and Evelyn Apte, *Children of West Indian Immigrants: A Study of One Year Olds in Paddington* (London, 1970).

81 See, for instance, June Ellis, 'The Child in West African society' in Ellis, *West African Families*, pp. 39–55.

82 Emecheta, *In the Ditch*, p. 14.

83 Emecheta, *Second-Class Citizen*, pp. 173–4.

84 See Wills, *Lovers and Strangers*, chapter 11.

85 Amrit Wilson, *Finding a Voice: Asian Women in Britain* (London, 1978), p. 31.

86 Ibid., p. 17.

87 Cited by Wills, *Lovers and Strangers*, p. 323.

88 Swasti Mitter, 'Industrial restructuring and manufacturing homework: immigrant women in the UK clothing industry', *Capital and Class*, 27 (1986), p. 59.

89 Ibid., pp. 55–6.

90 Ibid., p. 57.

91 'Lottery of the Lowest: Asian Families in Southall', *Spare Rib*, No. 17 (October 1973), pp. 17–19.

92 McDowell, *Working Lives*, p. 138.

93 Many Indians living in newly independent African states such as Kenya, Tanzania, Zambia and Malawi left when policies were introduced restricting their citizenship rights. Under colonial rule, the position of East African Indians had been relatively favourable, with many running successful businesses and living in large houses with African servants. Shortly after Idi Amin's seizure of power in Uganda in 1971, all Asians were ordered to leave the country within ninety days, with around 27,000 admitted to Britain.

94 For Asian women's workplace activism, see Sundari Anitha and Ruth Pearson, *Striking Women: Struggles and strategies of South Asian women workers from Grunwick to Gate Gourmet* (London, 2018); Sundari Anitha, Ruth Pearson and Linda McDowell, 'From Grunwick to Gate Gourmet: South Asian Women's Industrial Activism and the Role of Trade Unions', *Revue Française de Civilisation Britannique*, 13 (2018), DOI: 10.4000/rfcb.1790; and the wonderful website created by Anitha and Pearson, http://www.striking-women.org/, as part of their AHRC-funded project 'Striking Women: South Asian workers' struggles in the UK labour market from Grunwick to Gate Gourmet'.

95 All cited in Stone, 'Motherhood and Waged Work', pp. 38–9.

96 Ruth Glass, *Newcomers: The West Indians in London* (London, 1960), pp. 247–8; see also Clive Webb, 'Special Relationships: mixed-race couples in post-war Britain and the United States', *Women's History Review*, 26 (2017), pp. 110–29.

97 Jackson, 'The Childminders', p. 521.

98 Hood et al., *Children of West Indian Immigrants*, p. 64.

99 For a thoughtful account of this post-imperial 'trauma' thesis, see Bill Schwarz, *The White Man's World* (Oxford, 2012), especially pp. 10–13.
100 Banerjee, '"It's been bittersweet"'.
101 For this activism and critique, see Beverly Bryan, Stella Dadzie and Suzanne Scafe, *The Heart of the Race: Black Women's Lives in Britain* (London, 1985), and Valerie Amos and Pratibha Parmar, 'Challenging Imperial Feminism', *Feminist Review*, 1 (1984), pp. 3–19.

11 SUPERWOMEN

1 Ann Oakley, *Housewife* (London, 1974), chapter 6.
2 Shirley Conran, *Superwoman: Every Woman's Book of Household Management* (London, 1975), p. 1.
3 The age of first marriage fell to its lowest point (twenty-two for women and twenty-four for men) in the early 1970s and thereafter steadily rose. For these social changes, see Jane Lewis, *The End of Marriage? Individualism and Intimate Relations* (Cheltenham, 2001).
4 *Services for Young Children with Working Mothers: Report by the Central Policy Review Staff* (July 1978), copy in CAB 184/396, p. 38.
5 Angela Davis, *Pre-school childcare in England, 1939–2010: Theory, practice and experience* (Manchester, 2015), p. 3.
6 Peter Moss, 'Parents at Work' in Peter Moss and Nickie Fonda, eds, *Work and the Family* (London, 1980), pp. 22–67.
7 Diana Gittins, *The Family in Question: Changing households and familiar ideologies* (Basingstoke, 1985), p. 123.
8 These quotations are from Oakley's later autobiographical work, *Taking it Like a Woman* (London, 1984).
9 See Jeremy Gavron's moving memoir of his mother's life and academic work in *A Woman on the Edge of Time* (London, 2015).
10 An exemplary statement of socialist feminism in this period is Sheila Rowbotham, Lynne Segal and Hilary Wainwright, *Beyond the Fragments: Feminism and the making of socialism* (London, 1979). See also Sheila Rowbotham, *Promise of a Dream* (London, 2000). For an insightful discussion of feminist thought and activism on domestic labour in the 1970s, see Sarah Stoller, 'Forging a Politics of Care: Theorizing Household Work in the British Women's Liberation Movement', *History Workshop Journal*, 85 (2018), pp. 95–119.

11 Dorothy Hobson, 'Housewives: isolation as oppression' in Women's Studies Group (Centre for Contemporary Cultural Studies, University of Birmingham), *Women Take Issue: Aspects of Women's Subordination* (London, 1978), pp. 79–95, quote at p. 88.

12 Lindsay Mackie and Polly Pattullo, *Women at Work* (London, 1977), pp. 117–18.

13 Ann Oakley, 'The Myth of Motherhood', *New Society*, 26 February 1970, pp. 348–50.

14 Susannah Ginsberg, 'Women, Work and Conflict' in Nickie Fonda and Peter Moss, eds, *Mothers in Employment* (London, 1976), pp. 75–88.

15 Patricia Morgan, 'Exploding the medical myths of maternal deprivation', *The Times*, 17 January 1975, p. 11. See also her *Child Care: Sense and Fable* (London, 1975).

16 Ginsberg, 'Women, Work and Conflict', p. 77.

17 Ibid., p. 84.

18 Claire Rayner, 'Why does a working mum feel guilty?' *Woman's Own*, 10 October 1970, p. 63.

19 Serialised in 'Guilt: the working mother's big problem', *Woman's Own*, 29 November 1969, pp. 6–7.

20 Conran, *Superwoman*, pp. 147–8.

21 Elizabeth Wilson, *Only Half-Way to Paradise: Women in Postwar Britain, 1945–1968* (London, 1980), p. 40.

22 Oakley, *Housewife*, p. 73.

23 Ellen Malos, *Housework and the Politics of Women's Liberation* (Bristol, 1977).

24 Anna Pollert, *Girls, Wives, Factory Lives* (Basingstoke, 1981), p. 239.

25 Laura Levine Frader, 'International Institutions and Domestic Reform: Equal Pay and British Membership in the European Economic Community', *Twentieth Century British History*, 29 (2018), pp. 104–28.

26 Alison Mitchell, 'The consequences of the Equal Pay Act' in Frank Field, ed., *Are Low Wages Inevitable?* (Nottingham, 1977), pp. 67–76; A. Zabalza and Z. Tzannatos, *Women and Equal Pay: The Effects of Legislation on Female Employment and Wages in Britain* (Cambridge, 1985).

27 Patricia Hewitt, *A Step-By-Step Guide to Rights for Women* (London, 1975).

28 See, for instance, P. Byrne and Joni Lovenduski, 'Sex Equality and the Law in Britain', *British Journal of Law and Society*, 5 (1978), pp. 148–65; Nickie Fonda, 'Current Entitlements and Provisions: A Critical Review' in Fonda and Moss, *Mothers in Employment*, pp. 39–53.

29 For the NCCL demand, see 'And father is left holding the baby', *Daily Express*, 11 October 1976, p. 3. For historical trends in leave policies, see OECD Family Database, 'Detail of Changes in Parental Leave by Country', available online: https://www.oecd.org/els/family/PF2_5_Trends_in_leave_entitlements_around_childbirth_annex.pdf.

30 *Training for Equality: A Survey of Vocational Training Initiatives for Women in the United Kingdom* (1979), copy in the archives of the Medical Women's Federation, Wellcome Library, SA/MWF/J.22.

31 Mass Observation Project (MOP), Autumn 2014 Directive (Working Families), Mass Observer L1991.

32 Eve Worth, 'Women, Education and Social Mobility in Britain during the Long 1970s', *Cultural and Social History*, 16 (2019), pp. 67–83.

33 Helen McCarthy, *Girlfriends in High Places: How women's networks are changing the workplace* (London, 2003).

34 Mary Ann Elston, 'Women Doctors in the British Health Services: A Sociological Study of their Careers and Opportunities' (unpublished doctoral thesis, University of Leeds, 1986), p. 63; Michael Fogarty, Isobel Allen and Patricia Walters, *Women in Top Jobs, 1968–1979* (London, 1981), p. 38; Rosalie Silverstone and Audrey Ward, eds, *Careers of Professional Women* (London, 1980), pp. 19, 89.

35 '75 Years of women solicitors', 19 December 1997, BBC News, available online: http://news.bbc.co.uk/1/hi/uk/40448.stm; Mackie and Pattullo, *Women at Work*, p. 74.

36 In 1979, women's representation amongst newly admitted graduates was 36 per cent at Oxford and 29 per cent at Cambridge (Fogarty et al., *Women in Top Jobs*, pp. 40–41). For the decision to go mixed, see Nancy Weiss Malkiel, *'Keep the Damned Women Out': The Struggle for Coeducation* (Princeton, 2016).

37 R. K. Kelsall, 'Teaching' in Silverstone and Ward, *Careers of Professional Women*, pp. 185–206. Peter Mandler suggests that women's participation rates would have been higher had graduate employment prospects in teaching remained buoyant, although we might reasonably assume that the opening up of other professional

career-paths compensated somewhat for this, given how many female graduates had previously entered teaching with little vocational commitment (see chapter 9). Mandler's suggestion that the deteriorating public image of university students deterred some middle-class girls from applying is intriguing although difficult to demonstrate statistically. See Peter Mandler, 'Educating the Nation: II. Universities', *Transactions of the Royal Historical Society*, 25 (2015), pp. 1–26.

38 Carole Dyhouse, *Students: A Gendered History* (London, 2006), p. 115.

39 Rhona Rapoport and Robert Rapoport, eds, *Working Couples* (London, 1978), p. 14.

40 Silverstone and Ward, *Careers of Professional Women*, p. 210.

41 Fogarty et al., *Women in Top Jobs*. W. W. Daniel's study, *Maternity Rights* (Policy Studies Institute, 1980) found that women in management or professional jobs were the most likely to return full-time, whilst women in unskilled jobs were the most likely to return on a part-time basis.

42 Michael Young and Peter Willmott, *The Symmetrical Family: A Study of Work and Leisure in the London Region* (London, 1973), p. 277.

43 Fonda and Moss, *Mothers in Employment*, p. 132.

44 'Mrs Thatcher's double image', *Business and Professional Woman*, Autumn 1970, p. 4.

45 Valerie Grove, *The Compleat Woman: Marriage, Motherhood, Career: Can she have it all?* (London, 1987), pp. 133–4.

46 Mary Ann Elston, citing a 1986 survey, in *Desk Study of the Impact of Increasing Numbers of Women Doctors on the Medical Workforce* (NHS Executive, March 1996).

47 Grove, *Compleat Woman*, p. 74.

48 Moss, 'Parents at Work'.

49 Mass Observer F4813.

50 Interview with personnel officer at GEC, Stoke works, 4 August 1980, in records of the Coventry Part-Time Employment Survey, Modern Records Centre, University of Warwick, SN 5490, MSS.278/1/4/3.

51 Department for Work and Pensions, *Employment statistics for workers aged 50 and over* (November 2015), available online: https://assets. publishing.service.gov.uk/government/uploads/system/uploads/ attachment_data/file/568240/employment-stats-workers-aged-50-and-over-1984-2015.pdf. For retirement in the 1970s, see Pat Thane,

Old Age in English History: Past Experiences, Present Issues (Oxford, 2000), p. 424.

52 Joan Wheeler-Bennett, ed., *Women at the Top: Achievement and Family Life* (London, 1977), p. 23.

53 These figures are from *Services for Young Children with Working Mothers: Report by the Central Policy Review Staff* (July 1978).

54 *Services for Young Children.* For regional variation in day-care provision, see also Vicky Randall, *The Politics of Child Daycare in Britain* (Oxford, 2000), and Angela Davis, *Pre-school childcare in England,* and her article 'Women's experiences of combining childcare and careers in postwar Oxfordshire, *c.*1940–1990', *The Local Historian*, 43 (2013), pp. 14–25.

55 Mackie and Pattullo, *Women at Work*, p. 121.

56 Ibid.

57 Martin Hughes, Berry Mayall, Peter Moss, Jane Perry, Pat Petrie and Gill Pinkerton, *Nurseries Now: A Fair Deal for Parents and Children* (London, 1980), p. 32.

58 For the emergence of this 'under-fives lobby', see Randall, *Politics of Daycare,* chapter 3.

59 Jack Tizard, 'Effects of Day Care on Young Children' in Fonda and Moss, *Mothers in Employment*, p. 70.

60 'Not So Much a Day Nursery...' *Spare Rib*, October 1973, p. 33. As Randall explains in *The Politics of Daycare,* feminist views on State-provided nurseries were complex, with some expressing ambivalence towards what they saw as overly rigid, hierarchical and socially conservative approaches to childcare. Others were ambivalent about motherhood more generally, influenced by radical critiques of reproduction, heterosexuality and the nuclear family.

61 *Services for Young Children*, p. 11.

62 Ibid., p. 20.

63 Kate Jenkins to Kenneth Berril, 10 July 1978, CAB 184/601.

64 Minute on 'Children Under Five' by the Home Secretary to the Prime Minister, 14 July 1978, CAB 184/601.

65 Jane Lewis, 'The Failure to Expand Childcare Provision and to Develop a Comprehensive Childcare Policy in Britain during the 1960s and 1970s', *Twentieth-Century British History*, 24 (2013), pp. 249–74. Margaret Thatcher noted parental demand for nursery schools whilst Secretary of State for Education but advocated expansion of part-time

places for purely educational purposes, not as day-care for working mothers. See Anna Danziger Halperin, '"Cinderella of the Education System": Margaret Thatcher's Plan for Nursery Expansion in 1970s Britain', *Twentieth-Century British History*, 29 (2018), pp. 284–308.

66 'Industry holds the baby: how employers are helping working mothers', *Business and Professional Woman*, Spring 1970, pp. 7–9.

67 Fogarty et al., *Women in Top Jobs*, p. 76.

68 Ibid., pp. 192–3.

69 Suzanne Franks, 'Attitudes to women in the BBC in the 1970s', *Westminster Papers*, 8 (2011), p. 137.

70 Davis, *Pre-school childcare*.

71 Mass Observer I1610.

72 Here, the Labour-controlled Greater London Council led the field, funding 12 per cent of all full-time childcare places in the city by 1986. Stephen Brooke, 'Space, Emotions and the Everyday: The Affective Ecology of 1980s London', *Twentieth Century British History*, 28 (2017), p. 111.

73 Mass Observer F4813.

74 For anti-sexist men, see Lucy Delap, 'Feminism, masculinities and emotional politics in the late twentieth century', *Cultural and Social History* 15 (2018), pp. 571–93.

75 Grove, *Compleat Woman*, p. 209.

76 Conran, *Superwoman*, p. 43.

77 Rapoport and Rapoport, *Working Couples*, p. 14.

78 Cited in Katherine Clarricoates, 'All in a Day's Work', in Dale Spender and Elizabeth Sarah, eds, *Learning to Lose: Sexism and Education* (London, 1980), pp. 73–4.

79 Ibid., p. 78.

80 Grove, *Compleat Woman*, p. 213.

81 John Stevenson, 'The women who work too hard', *Daily Mail*, 23 March 1977, p. 11.

82 'Are you taking on too much?' *Daily Mail*, 24 March 1977, p. 12.

83 Fogarty et al., *Women in Top Jobs*, p. 63.

84 Grove, *Compleat Woman*, pp. 133, 139.

85 Fogarty et al., *Women in Top Jobs*, p. 68.

86 Mackie and Pattullo, *Women at Work*, pp. 89–90.

87 Fogarty et al., *Women in Top Jobs*, pp. 71–2.

88 Moss, 'Parents at Work'.

89 Mass Observer F3641. New educational and employment opportunities were pivotal in the decision to leave unhappy marriages as described by several of the women interviewed by Eve Worth in 'Women, Education and Social Mobility', p. 75.

90 Pollert, *Girls, Wives, Factory Lives*, p. 122.

91 Pat Thane, 'Unmarried motherhood in twentieth-century England', *Women's History Review*, 20 (2011), pp. 11–29.

92 *Report of the Committee on One-Parent Families: Volume I* (Cmnd 5629, HMSO, July 1974), p. 257.

93 Ibid., p. 250. In 1972, only 15 per cent of lone mothers claiming supplementary benefit were in work.

94 Cited in Marie Brown, *Sweated Labour: A Study of Homework* (London 1974), p. 22.

95 *Report of the Committee on One-Parent Families*, p. 412.

96 For the impact of the report, see Pat Thane and Tanya Evans, *Sinners? Scroungers? Saints? Unmarried Motherhood in Twentieth-Century England* (Oxford, 2012), chapter 7.

97 Mass Observer M5198.

98 *Report of the Committee on One-Parent Families*, p. 250.

99 Victor George and Paul Wilding, *Motherless Families* (London, 1972), quotations at pp. 40 and 45.

100 Moss, 'Parents at Work', p. 51.

101 Veronica Beechey and Tessa Perkins, *A Matter of Hours: Women, Part-time Work and the Labour Market* (Cambridge, 1987), p. 30.

102 Pollert, *Girls, Wives, Factory Lives*, p. 109.

103 Mass Observer B1180.

104 Beechey and Perkins, *A Matter of Hours*, pp. 1, 6. Other feminist analyses of the changing labour market in the 1970s include Jennifer Hurstfield, *The Part-Time Trap* (London, 1978) and Irene Bruegel, 'Women as a reserve army of labour: a note on recent British experience', *Feminist Review*, 3 (1979), pp. 12–23.

105 Questionnaire completed in June 1981, records of the Coventry Part-Time Employment Survey, Modern Records Centre, University of Warwick, SN 5490, MSS.278/1/2/1.

106 Questionnaire filled in by General Assistant, School Meals, SN 5490, MSS.278/1/2/1.

107 Celia Briar, 'Part-Time Work and the State in Britain, 1941–87' in Barbara D. Warme, Katharina L. P. Lundy and Larry Lundy, eds,

Working Part-Time: Risks and Opportunities (New York, 1992), pp. 75–86.

108 Chris Pond and Steve Winyard, 'A profile of the low paid' in Field, ed., *Are Low Wages Inevitable?*, pp. 19–34.

109 See, for example, Sheila Allen and Carol Wolkowitz, 'Homeworking and the Control of Women's Work' in Feminist Review, ed., *Waged Work: A Reader* (London, 1986), pp. 238–64; Emily Hope, Mary Kennedy and Anne De Winter, 'Homeworkers in North London' in Diana Leonard Barker and Sheila Allen, eds, *Dependence and Exploitation in Work and Marriage* (London, 1976), pp. 88–108.

110 The work is held at Tate Britain: https://www.tate.org.uk/art/artworks/harrison-homeworkers-t13631.

111 For Saltley, see 'Application for grant: Saltley Action Centre, to examine working conditions of Asian homeworkers, 1976–77' in CK 3/91, The National Archives, Kew. For cooperatives, see *Report of the National Homeworking Conference 1985* (Greater London Council, 1985) at London Metropolitan Archives, GLC/DG/PUB/01/190/U0477.

112 *Homeworking: A TUC Statement* (1978).

113 Ibid., Appendix E.

114 Sarah Boston, *Women Workers and the Trade Unions* (London, second edn, 2015), p. 293.

115 May Hobbs, 'Raising Wages at a Stroke: the Night Cleaners' in Field, ed., *Are Low Wages Inevitable?*, p. 46.

116 Pollert, *Girls, Wives, Factory Lives*, pp. 239–40.

117 Ibid., p. 153.

118 Ibid., p. 240.

119 Mary Ingham, *Now We Are Thirty: Women of the Breakthrough Generation* (London, 1981), pp. 132–3.

120 *Business and Professional Woman*, Summer 1970, p. 11.

121 'Argument: Women's Rights' (BBC, first broadcast 21 March 1974). The programme forms part of the BBC's excellent archive collection on second-wave feminism: http://www.bbc.co.uk/archive/70sfeminism/10409.shtml.

122 Viola Klein, *Working Wives: The Survey of Facts and Opinions Concerning the Gainful Employment of Married Women in Britain* (London, 1960).

123 Moss, 'Parents at Work', p. 56. Jon Lawrence notes the influence of the women's movement amongst many of the working-class and lower-middle-class women studied by the sociologist Ray Pahl in Sheppey, Kent, in the early 1980s, a phenomenon which Lawrence describes as 'a new vernacular feminism'; see Lawrence, *Me, Me, Me?* pp. 167, 170–1. See also the thoughtful analysis of this theme in Emily Robinson, Camilla Schofield, Florence Sutcliffe-Braithwaite and Natalie Thomlinson, 'Telling Stories about Post-war Britain: Popular Individualism and the "Crisis" of the 1970s', *Twentieth Century British History*, 28 (2017), pp. 268–304.

124 Grove, *Compleat Woman*, p. 230.

125 Ibid., p. 233.

126 Shirley Conran, *Down with Superwoman: The Guide for Everyone who Hates Housework* (London, 1990), p. 2.

12 DOING IT ALL

1 For media coverage of the novel, see, for example, Joan Smith, 'Big house, big salary, big fuss', *Independent*, 6 July 2002; Caroline Gascoigne, 'Life's a Bitch', *Sunday Times*, 21 July 2002; Justine Picardie, 'Kate Reddy's big dilemma', *Daily Telegraph*, 29 June 2002; and Isabel Wolff, 'In praise of chick-lit', *Evening Standard*, 14 July 2003.

2 Nicola Horlick, *Can You Have It All? How to Succeed in a Man's World* (London, 1997).

3 Allison Pearson, *I Don't Know How She Does It!* (London, 2002), p. 220.

4 Ibid., p. 190.

5 Ibid., pp. 165–6.

6 Joanne Hawkins, 'Sunday Life: Now we know how she does it', *Sun Herald* (Australia), 6 July 2003.

7 David Clutterbuck, 'A baby need not cost you your job', *The Times*, 15 December 1983, p. 23.

8 Frances Tomlinson, 'What do women's groups offer?' *Women and Management Review*, 2 (1987), pp. 238–48; Celia Briar, *Working for Women? Gendered Work and Welfare Policies in Twentieth-Century Britain* (London, 1997), p. 144.

9 Caroline Berman, 'How to make the homework pay', *The Times*, 4 October 1988, p. 33. See also Ursula Huws, *The New Homeworkers: New technology and the changing location of white-collar work* (London, 1984).

10 The Hansard Society, *The Report of the Hansard Society Commission on Women at the Top* (London, 1990), p. 2.

11 Business in the Community, *Opportunity Now: 20th Anniversary Review* (2011), available at http://www.globaldiversitypractice.co.uk/downloadsarea/5892_Opps_Now_20th_Anniversary_Review.pdf.

12 Briar, *Working for Women*, p. 124; 'Minister attacks slow progress for women', *Guardian*, 18 November 1992, p. 4.

13 Hansard Society, *Women at the top*, pp. 47, 53, 35, 69 respectively.

14 Helen Wilkinson, *No Turning Back: Generations and the Genderquake* (London, 1994), p. 1.

15 Lewis Smith, 'The women schoolgirls see as their role models', *Daily Express*, 10 September 1997, p. 21.

16 Michael White, 'Jobs for the boys slowly whittled away', *Guardian*, 30 March 1995, p. 6.

17 James Meikle, 'And then there were six', *Guardian*, 29 April 1997, p. 6.

18 Jill Papworth, 'Are women still being squeezed?' *Guardian*, 26 October 1996, p. 252.

19 Susan McRae, *Maternity Rights in Britain* (London, 1991), p. x. See also Sarah Stoller, 'Finding the Balance: Working Parents and the "Family Friendly" Private Sector' (unpublished paper delivered at North American Conference on British Studies, Providence, November 2018), and Stoller's forthcoming doctoral thesis on the evolution of the 'working parent' (Berkeley, 2020).

20 Huws, *The New Homeworkers*.

21 McRae, *Maternity Rights*, p. xxxiii.

22 Alison Wolf, *The XX Factor: How Working Women are Creating a New Society* (London, 2013), p. 73.

23 Nicky Gregson and Michelle Lowe, *Servicing the Middle Classes: Class, gender and waged domestic labour in contemporary Britain* (London, 1994); Barbara Ehrenreich and Arlie Russell Hochschild, eds, *Global Woman: Nannies, Maids and Sex Workers in the New Economy* (London, 2003).

24 Libby Purves, *How Not to Be A Perfect Mother* (London, 1984).

25 Jill Black, *The Working Mother's Survival Guide* (London, 1989), pp. 3, 11.

26 Penny Vincenzi, *There's One Born Every Minute* (London, 1984), p. 61.

27 Black, *Working Mother's Survival Guide*, p. 6.

28 Nine per cent of new mothers surveyed in 1990 said that their husbands or partners had taken paid paternity leave (McCrae, *Maternity Rights*, p. xliii). For fathers' presence at childbirth, see Angela Davis, *Modern Motherhood: Women and Family in England, 1945–2000* (Manchester, 2012).

29 Cited by Shirley Dex and Heather Joshi, 'Careers and motherhood: policies for compatibility', *Cambridge Journal of Economics*, 23 (1999), p. 648.

30 Chris Belfield, Richard Blundell, Jonathan Cribb, Andrew Hood, Robert Joyce and Agnes Norris Keiller, *Two decades of income inequality in Britain: the role of wages, household earnings and redistribution* (IFS, 2017), Appendix, pp. 13–14.

31 Jacqueline Burgoyne, 'Rethinking the Family Life Cycle: Sexual Divisions, Work and Domestic Life in the Post-war Period' in Alan Bryman et al., eds, *Rethinking the Life Cycle* (Basingstoke, 1987), p. 79.

32 Sue Sharpe, *Double Identity: The Lives of Working Mothers* (London, 1984), p. 25.

33 Mass Observation Project (MOP), Autumn 2014 Directive (Working Families), Mass Observer F5186.

34 Demos Quarterly 5 (1995), *The Time Squeeze*, p. vii. See also Patricia Hewitt, *About Time: The Revolution in Work and Family Life* (IPPR, 1993).

35 Bob Tyrell, 'Time in our lives: facts and analysis on the 1990s' in *The Time Squeeze*, pp. 71–80.

36 Interview with Allison Pearson, no date but from around the time of the novel's publication: https://www.penguinrandomhouse. com/books/128882/i-dont-know-how-she-does-it-by-allison-pearson/9780375713750/. She first wrote on this issue in early 2000: 'The living hell of today's working mother', *Evening Standard*, 5 April 2000. See also, 'Look, can we cut to the chase?' *Daily Telegraph*, 4 December 2000, p. 14.

37 Shirley Conran, 'Turning the tide of stress', *Observer*, 29 August 1999, p. 29.

38 Sarah O'Grady, 'Let's all unite to make life a little less taxing for working mothers', *Daily Express*, 1 October 1999, p. 39.

39 Valerie Grove, *The Compleat Woman: Marriage, Motherhood, Career: Can she have it all?* (London, 1987), p. 76. By the mid-1990s, the average age for degree-educated women to give birth to their

first child was thirty. See Office of National Statistics release, 'Mean age of mother at age of first child, by highest achieved educational qualification, 1996–2016, England and Wales' (10 September 2018).

40 Pat Thane, *Happy Families? History and Family Policy* (London, 2011); Richard Ford, 'Women delay starting families', *The Times*, 23 June 1994, p. 6.

41 'Woman of 59 gives birth to twins', *The Times*, 27 December 1993, p. 1.

42 Aileen Ballantyne, 'My baby's brave new world', *The Times*, 4 January 1994, p. 11.

43 Patricia Lewis, '"Mumpreneurs": Revealing the Post-feminist Entrepreneur' in Patricia Lewis and Ruth Simpson, eds, *Revealing and Concealing Gender: Issues of Visibility in Organisations* (Basingstoke, 2010), pp. 124–38.

44 Wendy Smith, 'Not to be sniffed at', *Guardian*, 18 March 2000, p. 49.

45 Angharad Lynn, 'Forward march of the mumpreneurs', *Daily Express*, 28 June 2001, pp. 43–5.

46 Catherine Hakim, 'Why so many long to look after a home and a family', *Daily Mail*, 29 March 1996, pp. 14–15.

47 See also Catherine Hakim, 'Grateful slaves and self-made women: fact and fantasy in women's work orientations', *European Sociological Review*, 7 (1991), pp. 101–21; 'Five feminist myths about women's employment', *British Journal of Sociology*, 46 (1995), pp. 429–55; and *Work-Lifestyle Choices in the 21st Century: Preference Theory* (Oxford, 2000).

48 For right-wing commentary, see, for example, Jill Kirby, *Broken Hearts: Family Decline and the Consequences for Society* (Centre for Policy Studies, 2002); Rebecca O'Neill, *The Fatherless Family* (Civitas, 2002).

49 Rosalind Coward, *Our Treacherous Hearts: why women let men get their way* (London, 1993), p. 20.

50 Janice Walmsley, 'The Mothering Wars', *Daily Mail*, 5 May 1992, p. 14.

51 Jane Gordon, 'The trophy child, a ghastly trend?', *Daily Express*, 19 April 1997, p. 13.

52 Naim Attallah, 'What you lose when you have it all', *Daily Express*, 17 October 1997, p. 65. See also the nasty piece by Jasper Gerard, 'The high-flier heading for a crash-landing', *Daily Express*, 20 January 1997, p. 11.

53 Topaz Amoore, 'Farewell Superwoman, you can never have it all', *Daily Express*, 9 October 1999, p. 23. Revealingly, in her column on Horlick, Carroll confessed that she only warmed to her after reading about her nightly vigil at Great Ormond Street, where Horlick's eldest daughter Georgie had been treated for leukaemia before her tragic death in November. Sue Carroll, 'Brave Nicola really is a superwoman', *Daily Mirror*, 2 December 1998, pp. 8–9.

54 Cited in John Campbell, *Margaret Thatcher, Volume 1: The Grocer's Daughter* (London, 2000), p. 112.

55 Margaret Thatcher, *The Downing Street Years* (London, 1993), p. 296.

56 Polly Toynbee, *Hard Work: Life in Low-Pay Britain* (London, 2003).

57 Gail Lewis, 'Black women's employment and the British economy' in Winston James and Clive Harris, eds, *Inside Babylon: The Caribbean Diaspora in Britain* (London, 1993), pp. 73–96.

58 The Labour-run Greater London Council pushed back by improving the fair wages clauses in its own cleaning contracts and announcing its intention to bring all cleaning services back in-house. See GLC, *London Industrial Strategy* (1985), chapter 5.

59 Eileen McLeod, *Women Working: Prostitution Now* (London, 1982); Judith Walkowitz, 'Feminism and the Politics of Prostitution in King's Cross in the 1980s', *Twentieth Century British History*, 30 (2019), pp. 231–63.

60 Adrienne Gleeson, 'Offensive question to find who holds the baby', *The Times*, 5 February 1983, p. 17. Official unemployment figures further undercounted women because so many had insufficient National Insurance contributions to qualify to claim benefit in their own right. See Sylvia Walby, 'Spatial and historical variations in women's unemployment and employment' in The Lancaster Regionalism Group, ed., *Localities, Class and Gender* (London, 1985), pp. 164–5.

61 Briar, *Working for Women?* p. 133.

62 Ronald Butt, 'The women whose workplace is in the home', *The Times*, 16 December 1982, p. 12; and 'Don't shriek about a little competition', *The Times*, 24 February 1983, p. 10.

63 'Sack these greedy women', *The Times*, 7 August 1980, p. 16.

64 *Daily Mirror*, 19 August 1981, p. 19; see also letters page for 22 May 1981, p. 26.

65 *Daily Mirror*, 25 August 1981, p. 17.

66 *Daily Mirror*, 9 October 1981, p. 12.

67 Sharpe, *Double Identity*, p. 90.

68 Cited in Jon Lawrence and Florence Sutcliffe-Braithwaite, 'Margaret Thatcher and the decline of class politics' in Ben Jackson and Robert Saunders, eds, *Making Thatcher's Britain* (Cambridge, 2012), pp. 132–47.

69 Jan Pahl, *Money and Marriage* (Basingstoke, 1989), p. 130.

70 Ibid., p. 74.

71 Mass Observer B42.

72 Mass Observer D4736.

73 Veronica Groocock, 'A man about the house', *The Times*, 6 May 1983, p. 9.

74 Greater London Council, *Report of the National Homeworking Conference* (1985), p. 5.

75 *House of Commons Select Committee on Employment, Session 1980–1981: Homeworking*, Minutes of Evidence for 28 April 1981.

76 House of Commons, *First Report from the Employment Committee (Session 1981–2): Homeworking* (November 1981).

77 House of Commons, *Third Special Report from the Employment Committee (Session 1981–2): Homeworking* (31 March 1982).

78 The research was conducted by Catherine Hakim, who would later argue that women's employment choices reflected genuine preferences. C. Hakim, *Home-Based Work in Britain: A Report on the 1981 Homeworking Survey and the DE research programme on homework* (Department of Employment: London, 1987).

79 For evidence of how Hakim's research inhibited action on health and safety protections, see paper entitled 'Homeworkers' circulated for discussion by members of the Health and Safety Commission, dated April 1987 in EF 7/2250 HSC, The National Archives, Kew.

80 Huws, *New Homeworkers*, and see also Huws' remarks in Greater London Council, *Report of the National Homeworking Conference* (1985), pp. 8–9.

81 TUC, *No Sweat! Why Britain's one million homeworkers need a new deal* (London, 1996); HomeWorkers Worldwide, *Subject to Status: An investigation into the working lives of homeworkers in the UK* (Leeds, 2007).

82 Tessa Jowell, 'We are the most feminist government in history', *Guardian*, 15 April 2002.

83 For women's position in the Labour Party in this period, see V. Atkinson and J. Spear, 'The Labour Party and Women: Policies and Practices' in M. J. Smith and J. Spear, eds, *The Changing Labour Party* (London, 1992), pp. 151–67; Sarah Childs, 'The New Labour women MPs in the 1997 British Parliament: issues of recruitment and representation', *Women's History Review*, 9 (2000), pp. 55–73; Sylvia Bashevkin, 'From tough times to better times: feminism, public policy, and New Labour politics in Britain', *International Political Science Review*, 21 (2000), pp. 407–24.

84 Judith Squires and Mark Wickham-Jones, 'Mainstreaming in Westminster and Whitehall: From Labour's Ministry for Women to the Women and Equality Unit' in Karen Ross, ed., *Women, Politics and Change* (Oxford, 2002), pp. 57–71.

85 'Labour's very own domestic goddess', *Daily Telegraph*, 2 December 2000, p. 10.

86 Kitty Stewart, *Labour's Record on the Under-Fives: Policy, Spending and Outcomes, 1997–2010* (LSE Working Paper, 2013), pp. 35–6. Available at: http://sticerd.lse.ac.uk/dps/case/spcc/wp04.pdf.

87 Ben Jackson, 'Free markets and feminism: the neoliberal defence of the male breadwinner model in Britain, *c.*1980–1997', *Women's History Review*, 28 (2019), pp. 297–316.

88 Jane Lewis, 'Developing Early Years Childcare in England, 1997–2002: The Choices for (Working) Mothers', *Social Policy and Administration*, 37 (2003), pp. 219–38.

89 Department for Education and Employment, *Meeting the Childcare Challenge* (1998), Executive Summary.

90 See, for example, Jane Franklin, 'After modernisation: gender, the third way and the new politics' in Anna Coote, ed., *The New Gender Agenda* (London, 2000), pp. 15–22.

91 Toynbee, *Hard Work*, p. 99.

92 Equality and Human Rights Commission, *Sex and Power 2008* (September 2008); Wolf, *The XX Factor*, p. 21.

93 Stijn Broecke and Joseph Hamed, *Gender Gaps in Higher Education Participation* (Department for Innovation, Universities and Skills, 2008).

94 Fran Bennett and Mary Daly, *Poverty Through a Gender Lens: Evidence and Policy Review on Gender and Poverty* (Oxford, 2014).

95 Alison Wolf, 'Working girls', *Prospect*, 121 (2006), pp. 28–33.

96 Wolf, *XX Factor*, p. 13.

97 Sharpe, *Double Identity*, pp. 41, 43.

98 Mass Observer M3055.

99 Eve Worth, 'A Tale of Female Liberation? The Long Shadow of De-Professionalisation on the Lives of Post-War Women', *Revue Française de Civilisation Britannique*, 13 (2018) DOI: 10.4000/rfcb.1778

100 Cited in Worth, 'A Tale of Female Liberation', p. 11.

CONCLUSION

1 Jacqueline Rose, *Mothers: An Essay on Love and Cruelty* (London, 2018), p. 130.

2 In July 2019, government announced measures to strengthen legal protections for pregnant women, mothers on maternity leave and those recently returned to the workplace, which were cautiously welcomed by equality campaigners. 'Pregnant women and new parents to get enhanced redundancy protections' (Press Release, Department for Business, Energy and Industrial Strategy, 22 July 2019).

3 Figures cited in Sarah Butler, 'The UK companies reporting the biggest gender pay gaps', *Guardian*, 5 April, 2018. Direct sex discrimination continues to play a part in sustaining the pay gap, as revelations concerning senior pay at the BBC in 2017–18 amply demonstrated. Explaining the persistence of vertical and horizontal gender segregation in the labour market and how this, alongside sex discrimination, affects pay is not straightforward, but see Equality and Human Rights Commission, *The Gender Pay Gap* (Research Report 109, 2017).

4 David Goodhart, 'The alpha female is squeezing out families', *Sunday Times*, 12 March 2017.

5 In England in 2018, 74 per cent of mothers were in employment, compared to just under 70 per cent for women without dependent children, whilst nearly three-quarters of two-parent families have both parents in work. Employment rates amongst mothers overtook those for women without dependent children in 2010, although only five in ten working mothers work full time, compared to seven in ten working women without dependent children. See Office for National Statistics, *Families and the Labour Market: England 2018* (October 2018).

6 'To What End in Life?', *The Freewoman*, 22 February 1912, p. 262.

Bibliography

MANUSCRIPT AND ARCHIVAL SOURCES

Letters of Elizabeth Garrett Anderson, Autograph Letters Collection, The Women's Library, London School of Economics

Papers of Josie Castle, sociologist, on Coventry women's employment, Modern Records Centre, University of Warwick

Records of the Coventry Part-Time Employment Survey, Modern Records Centre, University of Warwick

Records of the Greater London Council, London Metropolitan Archives

Interview with Dorothy Haigh, Imperial War Museum

Papers of Judith Hubback, The Women's Library, London School of Economics

Papers of Viola Klein, University of Reading

Mass Observation Archive: Directive, January 1944, File Report 15B, File Report 290, Topic Collection: Day Nurseries, Topic Collection: Family Planning

Mass Observation Project: Autumn 2014 Directive, Part 2 (Working Families)

Records of the Medical Women's Federation, Wellcome Library, London

The National Archives, Kew

Papers of Baroness Nancy Seear, The Women's Library, London School of Economics

Records of the Women's Industrial Council, The Women's Library, London School of Economics

OFFICIAL PUBLICATIONS (LISTED BY DATE)

Select Committee of the House of Lords on the Sweating System: First Report (240, 1888)

Select Committee of the House of Lords on the Sweating System: Fifth Report (361, 1890)

Royal Commission on Labour, *Minutes of Evidence, with appendices, taken before Group C* (C.6708, 1892)

Royal Commission on Labour, *Fourth Report* (C.7063, 1892)

Royal Commission on Labour, *The Employment of Women: Reports by Miss Eliza Orme, Miss Clara Collet, Miss May Abraham and Miss Margaret Irwin* (C.6894, 1893)

Royal Commission on Labour, *Fifth and Final Report* (C.7421, 1894)

Final Report of the Royal Commission on Superannuation in the Civil Service (Cd 1744, 1903)

Report of the Inter-Departmental Committee on Physical Deterioration: Volume I (Cd 2175, 1904)

Report from the Select Committee on Homework (HMSO, 1907)

Report from the Select Committee on Homework (HMSO, 1908)

Royal Commission on the Poor Laws and Relief of Distress: Appendix volume XVII (Cd 4690, 1909)

Health of Munition Workers Committee, *Memorandum No. 4: Employment of Women* (Cd 8185, January 1916)

Health of Munition Workers Committee, *Final Report* (Cd 9065, 1918)

Report of the Committee on Women in Industry: Appendices, Summaries of Evidence, &c (Cmd 167, 1918)

Report of the War Cabinet Committee on Women in Industry (Cmd 135, 1919)

Ministry of Reconstruction, *Report of the Women's Employment Committee* (Cd 9239, 1919)

Ministry of Health, *Survey of Relief to Widows and Children* (Cd 744, 1920)

Memorandum by the Government Actuary on the Washington Draft Convention concerning the employment of women before and after childbirth, dated 28 June 1920 (Cmd 1293, 1921)

A Study of the Factors which have operated in the past and are operating now to Determine the Distribution of Women in Industry (Cmd 3508, 1929)

First Report of the Royal Commission on Unemployment Insurance (Cmd 3872, 1931)

Report of the Committee on Amenities and Welfare Conditions in the Three Women's Services (Cmnd 6384, 1942)

Beveridge, William, *Social Insurance and Allied Services* (Cmd 6404, 1942)

Thomas, Geoffrey, *Women at Work: The attitudes of working women toward post-war employment and some related problems. An inquiry made for the Office of the Minister of Reconstruction* (Wartime Social Survey, June 1944)

Marriage Bar in the Civil Service: Report of the Civil Service National Whitley Council Committee (Cmd 6886, 1946)

Thomas, Geoffrey, *Women and Industry: An inquiry into the problem of recruiting women to Industry carried out for the Ministry of Labour and National Service* (Government Social Survey, March 1948)

Royal Commission on Population, *Report* (Cmnd 7695, 1949)

Ferguson, Sheila and Fitzgerald, Hilde, *Studies in the Social Services* (HMSO, 1954)

Central Advisory Council for Education, *15 to 18* (HMSO, 1959)

Report of the Working Party on Social Workers in Local Authority Health and Welfare Services (HMSO, 1959)

Kelsall, R. K., *Women and Teaching* (HMSO, 1963)

Committee on Higher Education (The Robbins Report), *Appendix I* (Cmnd 2154-I, 1963)

Hunt, Audrey, *A Survey of Women's Employment* (Government Social Survey, HMSO, 1968)

Report of the Committee on One-Parent Families: Volume I (Cmnd 5629, July 1974)

Services for Young Children with Working Mothers: Report by the Central Policy Review Staff (HMSO, July 1978)

House of Commons Select Committee on Employment, *Session 1980–81: Homeworking, Minutes of Evidence* (1981)

House of Commons, *First Report from the Employment Committee (Session 1981–2): Homeworking* (November 1981)

House of Commons, *Third Special Report from the Employment Committee (Session 1981–2): Homeworking* (March 1982)

Hakim, Catherine, *Home-Based Work in Britain: A Report on the 1981 Homeworking Survey and the DE research programme on homework* (Department of Employment, 1987)

House of Commons Library, *Tax and Marriage* (Research Paper 95/87, July 1995)

'Unemployment statistics from 1881 to the present day', *Labour Market Trends* (January 1996)

Elston, Mary Ann, *Desk Study of the Impact of Increasing Numbers of Women Doctors on the Medical Workforce* (NHS Executive, March 1996)

Department for Education and Employment, *Meeting the Childcare Challenge* (Green Paper, 1998)

Equality and Human Rights Commission, *Sex and Power 2008* (September 2008)

Broecke, Stijn and Hamed, Joseph, *Gender Gaps in Higher Education Participation* (Department for Innovation, Universities and Skills, 2008)

Office for National Statistics, *Travel Trends 2010* (2010)

Office for National Statistics, *Mothers in the Labour Market, 2011* (31 March 2011)

Bolton, Paul, *Education: Historical Statistics* (House of Commons Library, 2012)

Office for National Statistics, '2011 Census analysis: immigration patterns of non-UK-born populations in England and Wales in 2011' (2013)

Department for Work and Pensions, *Employment statistics for workers aged 50 and over* (November 2015)

Equality and Human Rights Commission, *The Gender Pay Gap* (Research Report 109, 2017)

Office of National Statistics, 'Mean age of mother at age of first child, by highest achieved educational qualification, 1996–2016, England and Wales' (10 September 2018)

Office for National Statistics, *Families and the Labour Market: England 2018* (October 2018)

NEWSPAPERS, PERIODICALS AND MAGAZINES

Berkshire Chronicle
Bradford Observer
British Medical Journal
The British Soroptimist

Business and Professional Woman
Charity Organisation Review
Contemporary Review
Dundee Advertiser
Daily Express
Daily Mail
Daily Mirror
Daily News
Daily Telegraph
The Economist
The English Illustrated Magazine
The English Woman's Journal
The Englishwoman
Fortnightly Review
The Freewoman
Independent
International Labour Review
Journal of the Royal Sanitary Institute
Labour Woman
The Lancet
The Listener
London Evening Standard
Manchester Guardian
Marriage Guidance
Modern Woman
New Society
The Nineteenth Century
Observer
Picture Post
Prospect
Spare Rib
Sun Herald
Sunday Express
Sunday Times
The Times
University Women's Review
Westminster Review
Woman

The Woman Worker
The Woman's Leader
Woman's Own
Women in Council
Women's Industrial News

PUBLISHED PRIMARY SOURCES

No author, *Report of the Proceedings of the National Conference on Infantile Mortality* (London, 1906)

Anderson, Kitty, *Women and the Universities: A Changing Pattern* (London, 1963)

Andrews, Irene Osgood and Hobbs, Margaret A., *Economic Effects of the World War upon Women and Children in Great Britain* (Oxford, 1921)

Arregger, Constance, ed., *Graduate Women at Work: A Study by a Working Party of the British Federation of University Women* (Newcastle, 1966)

Atkinson, Mabel, 'The economic foundations of the women's movement,' in Sally Alexander, ed., *Women's Fabian Tracts* (London, 1988 [1914])

Bakke, Edward Wight, *The Unemployed Man: A Social Study* (London, 1933)

Barker, Diana Leonard and Allen, Sheila, eds, *Dependence and Exploitation in Work and Marriage* (London, 1976)

Barlee, Ellen, *A Visit to Lancashire in December 1862* (London, 1863)

Bateson, Margaret, *Professional Women upon their Professions* (London, 1895)

Beales, H. L. and Lambert, R. S., *Memoirs of the Unemployed* (London, 1934)

Beechey, Veronica and Perkins, Tessa, *A Matter of Hours: Women, Part-time Work and the Labour Market* (Cambridge, 1987)

Benjamin, Floella, *Coming to England* (London, 1995)

Besant, Annie, *An Autobiography* (London, 1893)

Black, Clementina, *Sweated Industry and the Minimum Wage* (London, 1907)

—, ed., *Married Women's Work: Being the report of an enquiry undertaken by the Women's Industrial Council* (London, 1983 [1915])

Black, Jill, *The Working Mother's Survival Guide* (London, 1989)

Blackstone, Tessa, *A Fair Start: The Provision of Pre-School Education* (London, 1971)

Boucherett, Jessie and Blackburn, Helen, *The Condition of Working Women and the Factory Acts* (London, 1896)

Bowlby, John, *Child Care and the Growth of Love* (London, 1953)

Brittain, Vera, *Women's Work in Modern England* (London, 1928)

Brown, Marie, *Sweated Labour: A Study of Homework* (London 1974)

Brown, R. K., Kirkby, J. M. and Taylor, K. F., 'The employment of married women and the supervisory role', *British Journal of Industrial Relations*, 2 (1964), pp. 23–41

Bruegel, Irene, 'Women as a reserve army of labour: a note on recent British experience', *Feminist Review*, 3 (1979), pp. 12–23

Butler, Josephine, *The Education and Employment of Women* (London, 1868)

Byrne, P. and Lovenduski, Joni, 'Sex Equality and the Law in Britain', *British Journal of Law and Society*, 5 (1978), pp. 148–65

Callan, Hilary and Ardener, Shirley, eds, *The Incorporated Wife* (London, 1984)

Campbell, Janet, *Report on the Physical Welfare of Mothers and Children: England and Wales, Volume II* (1917)

Cavenagh, Winifred, *Four Decades of Students in Social Work* (Birmingham, 1956)

Chesser, Eustace, *The Sexual, Marital and Family Relationships of the English Woman* (London, 1956)

Chew, Doris Nield, ed., *Ada Nield Chew: The Life and Writings of a Working Woman* (London, 1982)

Churchill, Lady Randolph, ed., *Women's War Work* (London, 1916)

Cole, Margaret I., ed., *The Road to Success: Twenty Essays on the Choice of a Career for Women* (London, 1936)

Collet, Clara, *Educated Working Women: Essays on the Economic Position of Women Workers in the Middle Classes* (London, 1902)

—, 'The collection and utilisation of official statistics bearing upon the extent and effects of the industrial employment of women', *Journal of the Royal Statistical Society*, 61 (1898), pp. 219–70

Collins, M., ed., *Women Graduates and the Teaching Profession: Report of a Working Party of the British Federation of University Women* (Manchester, 1964)

Conran, Shirley, *Superwoman: Every Woman's Book of Household Management* (London, 1975)

—, *Down with Superwoman: The Guide for Everyone who Hates Housework* (London, 1990)

Coote, Anna, ed., *The New Gender Agenda* (London, 2000)

Cosens, Monica, *Lloyd George's Munition Girls* (London, 1916)

Coward, Rosalind, *Our Treacherous Hearts: Why women let men get their way* (London, 1993)

Dale, Mrs Hylton, *Child Labor Under Capitalism* (London, 1908)

Daniel, W. W., *Maternity Rights* (London, 1980)

Davies, Margaret Llewelyn, ed., *Life As We Have Known It: The Voices of Working-Class Women* (London, 1977 [1931])

—, *Maternity: Letters from Working Women* (London, 1915)

Davison, R. B., *Black British: Immigrants to England* (Oxford, 1966)

Demos Quarterly 5, *The Time Squeeze* (1995)

Douie, Vera, *The Lesser Half: A survey of the laws, regulations and practices introduced during the present war which embody discrimination against women* (London, 1943)

Drabble, Margaret, *The Millstone* (London, 1965)

Ellis, June, ed., *West African Families in Britain* (London, 1978)

Emecheta, Buchi, *In the Ditch* (London, 1972)

—, *Second-Class Citizen* (London, 1974)

Fabian Women's Group, *Summary of Eight Papers and Discussions upon the Disabilities of Mothers as Workers* (London, 1910)

Fawcett, Millicent Garrett, 'Equal Pay for Equal Work', *Economic Journal*, 28 (March 1918), pp. 1–6

—, *What I Remember* (London, 1924)

Feminist Review, *Waged Work: A Reader* (London, 1986)

Field, Frank, ed., *Are Low Wages Inevitable?* (Nottingham, 1977)

Finch, Janet, *Married to the Job: Wives' incorporation in men's work* (London, 1983)

Fitzherbert, Katrin, *West Indian Children in London* (London, 1967)

Fogarty, Michael, Allen, Isobel and Walters, Patricia, *Women in Top Jobs, 1968–1978* (London, 1981)

Foner, Nancy, *Jamaica Farewell: Jamaican migrants in London* (London, 1979)

Foxwell, Agnes K., *Munition Lasses: Six Months as a Principal Overlooker in Danger Buildings* (London, 1917)

Fraser, Helen, *Women and War Work* (London, 1918)

Freud, Anna and Burlingham, Dorothy, *Infants without families: The case for and against residential nurseries* (London, 1943)

Gavron, Hannah, *The Captive Wife* (London, 1966)

George, Victor and Wilding, Paul, *Motherless Families* (London, 1972)

Glass, Ruth, *Newcomers: The West Indians in London* (London, 1960)

Goldsmith, Margaret, *Women at War* (London, 1943)

—, *Women and the Future* (London, 1946)

Gollancz, Victor, ed., *The Making of Women: Oxford Essays in Feminism* (London, 1917)

Greene, Felix, ed., *Time to Spare: What Unemployment Means, by eleven unemployed* (London, 1935)

Grove, Valerie, *The Compleat Woman: Marriage, Motherhood, Career: Can she have it all?* (London, 1987)

Haldane, Charlotte, *Motherhood and Its Enemies* (London, 1927)

Hallaire, Jean, *Part-Time Employment: Its Extent and Problems* (Paris, 1968)

Hamilton, Peggy, *Three Years or For the Duration: The Memoirs of a Munition Worker, 1914–1918* (London, 1978)

Hanley, James, *Grey Children: A Study in Humbug and Misery* (London, 1937)

Hansard Society, *The Report of the Hansard Society Commission on Women at the Top* (London, 1990)

Harris, E. M., *Married Women in Industry* (London, 1954)

Herbert, Lucy, *Mrs Ramsay MacDonald* (London, 1924)

Hewitt, Patricia, *A Step-By-Step Guide to Rights for Women* (London, 1975)

—, *About Time: The Revolution in Work and Family Life* (London, 1993)

Hood, Catriona, Oppe, T. W., Pless, I. B. and Apte, Evelyn, *Children of West Indian Immigrants: A Study of One Year Olds in Paddington* (London, 1970)

Horlick, Nicola, *Can You Have It All? How to Succeed in a Man's World* (London, 1997)

Howarth, Edward and Wilson, Mona, *West Ham: A Study in Social and Industrial Problems: Being the Report of the Outer London Inquiry Committee* (London, 1907)

Hubback, Judith, *Wives Who Went to College* (London, 1957)

Hughes, Martin, Mayall, Berry, Moss, Peter, Perry, Jane, Petrie, Pat and
  Pinkerton, Gill, *Nurseries Now: A Fair Deal for Parents and Children*
  (London, 1980)
Hurstfield, Jennifer, *The Part-Time Trap* (London, 1978)
Huws, Ursula, *The New Homeworkers: New technology and the changing
  location of white-collar work* (London, 1984)
Ingham, Mary, *Now We Are Thirty: Women of the Breakthrough
  Generation* (London, 1981)
Jackson, Brian and Jackson, Sonia, *Childminder* (London, 1979)
Jackson, John Archer, *The Irish in Britain* (London, 1963)
Jackson, Sonia, *The Illegal Childminders: A report on the growth
  of unregistered child-minding and the West Indian community*
  (Cambridge, n.d.)
Jefferys, Margot and Elliott, Patricia, *Women in Medicine: The results of
  an inquiry conducted by the Medical Practitioners' Union in 1962–63*
  (London, 1966)
Jephcott, Pearl, *Clubs for Girls* (London, 1943)
—, Seear, Nancy and Smith, John, *Married Women Working*
  (London, 1962)
—, *A Troubled Area: Notes on Notting Hill* (London, 1964)
Joseph, Joyce, 'A Research Note on Attitudes to Work and Marriage of
  Six Hundred Adolescent Girls', *British Journal of Sociology*, 12 (1961),
  pp. 176–83
Kelsall, R. K., *Higher Civil Servants in Britain: From 1870 to the Present
  Day* (London, 1955)
— and Mitchell, Sheila, 'Married women and employment in England
  and Wales', *Population Studies*, 13 (1959), pp. 19–33
—, Poole, Anne and Kuhn, Annette, *Graduates: The Sociology of an Elite*
  (London, 1972)
Kirby, Jill, *Broken Hearts: Family Decline and the Consequences for Society*
  (London, 2002)
Klein, Viola, *Working Wives: The Survey of Facts and Opinions
  Concerning the Gainful Employment of Married Women in Britain*
  (London, 1960)
—, *Britain's Married Women Workers* (London, 1965)
—, 'The demand for professional womanpower', *British Journal of
  Sociology*, 17 (1966), pp. 183–97

Labovitch, Penelope and Simon, Rosemary, *Late Start: Careers for Wives* (London, 1966)

League of Nations, *International Labour Conference: First Annual Meeting, October 29th – November 29th 1919* (ILO, 1919)

MacDonagh, Michael, *In London during the Great War: The Diary of a Journalist* (London, 1935)

MacKenzie, W. Leslie, *Scottish Mothers and Children* (Dunfermline, 1917)

Mackie, Lindsay and Pattullo, Polly, *Women at Work* (London, 1977)

McLeod, Eileen, *Women Working: Prostitution Now* (London, 1982)

McRae, Susan, *Maternity Rights in Britain* (London, 1991)

Malos, Ellen, *Housework and the Politics of Women's Liberation* (Bristol, 1977)

Markham, Violet, *May Tennant: A Portrait* (London, 1949)

Marsden, Dennis, *Mothers Alone: Poverty and the Fatherless Family* (London, 1969)

Mass Observation, *The Journey Home* (London, 1944)

Merryweather, Mary, *Experience of Factory Life* (London, 1862)

Meyer, Mrs Carl and Black, Clementina, *Makers of Our Clothes: A Case for Trade Boards* (London, 1909)

Meynell, Viola, *Alice Meynell: A Memoir* (London, 1929)

Mill, John Stuart, *The Subjection of Women* (London, 1869)

Mitter, Swasti, 'Industrial restructuring and manufacturing homework: immigrant women in the UK clothing industry', *Capital and Class*, 27 (1986), pp. 37–80

Money, Leo Chiozza, *Riches and Poverty* (London, fourth edn, 1908)

Morgan, Patricia, *Child Care: Sense and Fable* (London, 1975)

Morley, Edith, ed., *Women Workers in Seven Professions* (London, 1914)

Moss, Peter and Fonda, Nickie, eds, *Work and the Family* (London, 1980)

Mudie-Smith, Richard, ed., *Handbook of the Daily News Sweated Industries Exhibition* (London, 1906)

Myrdal, Alva, *Nation and Family: The Swedish Experiment in Democratic Family and Population Policy* (London, 1941)

— and Klein, Viola, *Women's Two Roles: Home and Work* (London, 1968 [1956])

Newman, George, *Infant Mortality: A Social Problem* (London, 1906)

Oakley, Ann, *Housewife* (London, 1974)

—, *Taking it like a woman* (London, 1984)

Oliver, Thomas, ed., *Dangerous Trades: The Historical, Social, and Legal Aspects of Industrial Occupations as Affecting Health, by a Number of Experts* (London, 1902)

O'Neill, Rebecca, *The Fatherless Family* (London, 2002)

Open Door Council, *The Married Woman: Is She a Person?* (London, 1934)

—, *Restrictive Legislation and the Industrial Woman Worker: A Reply by the Open Door Council* (London, 1928)

Pahl, Jan, *Money and Marriage* (Basingstoke, 1989)

— and Pahl, R. E., *Managers and their Wives: A study of career and family relationships in the middle class* (London, 1971)

Pankhurst, Sylvia, *The Home Front: A Mirror to Life in England during the World War* (London, 1932)

Papanek, Hannah, 'Men, Women, and Work: reflections on the two-person career', *American Journal of Sociology*, 78 (1973), pp. 852–72

Parkes, Bessie Rayner, *Essays on Women's Work* (London, 1865)

Patterson, Sheila, *Dark Strangers: A sociological study of the absorption of a recent West Indian group in Brixton, south London* (London, 1963)

—, ed., *Immigrants in London: Report of a study group set up by the London Council of Social Service* (London, 1963)

Pearson, Allison, *I Don't Know How She Does It!* (London, 2002)

Peel, Mrs C. S., *How We Lived Then: A Sketch of Social and Domestic Life in England during the War* (London, 1929)

Phillips, Marion, ed., *Women and the Labour Party* (London, 1918)

Phizacklea, Annie, ed., *One Way Ticket: Migration and Female Labour* (London, 1983)

Pilgrim Trust, *Men Without Work* (Cambridge, 1938)

Political and Economic Planning, *Women and Top Jobs: An Interim Report* (London, 1967)

—, *Racial Discrimination* (London, 1967)

—, *Planning: Special issue on part-time employment and woman power* (London, February 1942)

Pollak, Margaret, *Today's Three Year Olds in London* (Lavenham, 1972)

Pollert, Anna, *Girls, Wives, Factory Lives* (Basingstoke, 1981)

Priestley, J. B., *British Women Go to War* (London, 1943)

Prince, G. Stewart, 'Mental health problems in pre-school West Indian children' in *Maternal and Child Care*, 3 (1967), pp. 483–6

Purves, Libby, *How Not to Be A Perfect Mother* (London, 1984)

Rapoport, Robert and Rapoport, Rhona, *Dual Career Families* (London, 1971)

—, 'Work and Family in Contemporary Society', *American Sociological Review*, 30 (1965), pp. 381–94

—, *Dual-Career Families Re-examined: New Integrations of Work & Family* (London, 1976)

—, eds, *Working Couples* (London, 1978)

Rathbone, Eleanor, *The Disinherited Family* (London, 1924)

Reed, Angela, *The £.s.d of Marriage* (London, 1968)

Rosser, Colin and Harris, Christopher, *The Family and Social Change: A Study of Family and Kinship in a South Wales Town* (London, 1965)

Rowbotham, Sheila, Segal, Lynne and Wainwright, Hilary, *Beyond the Fragments: Feminism and the making of socialism* (London, 1979)

Rowntree, B. S. and Lavers, G. R., *Poverty and the Welfare State: A third social survey of York dealing only with economic questions* (London, 1951)

Scharlieb, Mary, *Reminiscences* (London, 1924)

Scott, Peggy, *British Women in War* (London, 1940)

Seear, Nancy, *Re-Entry of women to the labour market after an interruption in employment* (OECD, n.d.)

—, Roberts, Veronica and Brock, John, *A Career for Women in Industry?* (London, 1964)

Sharpe, Sue, *Double Identity: The Lives of Working Mothers* (London, 1984)

Silverstone, Rosalie and Ward, Audrey, eds, *Careers of Professional Women* (London, 1980)

Smith, Barbara Leigh, *Women and Work* (London, 1857)

Smith, Constance, 'The Working of the Trade Boards Act in Great Britain and Ireland', *Journal of Political Economy*, 22 (1914), pp. 605–29

Smith, D. J., *Racial Disadvantage in Britain: the PEP Report* (London, 1977)

Smith, Hubert Llewellyn, *The New Survey of London Life & Labour: Volume II, London Industries* (London, 1931)

Spender, Dale and Sarah, Elizabeth, eds, *Learning to Lose: Sexism and Education* (London, 1980)

Standing Joint Committee of Industrial Women's Organisations,
　　*The Position of Women After the War: Report of the Standing Joint
　　Committee of Industrial Women's Organisations presented to the Joint
　　Committee on Labour Problems After the War* (London, 1918)
Stone, Gilbert, ed., *Women War Workers* (London, 1917)
Strachey, Ray, *Careers and Openings for Women: A Survey of Women's
　　Employment and a Guide for those seeking Work* (London, 1935)
Summerskill, Edith, *A Woman's World: Her Memoirs* (London, 1967)
Tannahill, John Allan, *European Volunteer Workers in Britain*
　　(Manchester, 1958)
Thatcher, Margaret, *The Downing Street Years* (London, 1993)
Todd, Margaret, *Sophia Jex-Blake* (London, 1918)
Tomlinson, Frances, 'What do women's groups offer?', *Women and
　　Management Review*, 2 (1987), pp. 238–48
Townsend, Peter, *The Family Life of Old People* (London, 1957)
Toynbee, Polly, *Hard Work: Life in Low-Pay Britain* (London, 2003)
TUC, *Homeworking: A TUC Statement* (1978)
—, *No Sweat! Why Britain's one million homeworkers need a new deal*
　　(London, 1996)
Vesselitsky, V. de, *The Homeworker and Her Outlook: A Descriptive Study
　　of Tailoresses and Boxmakers* (London, 1916)
Vincenzi, Penny, *There's One Born Every Minute* (London, 1984)
Walton, Ronald, *Women in Social Work* (London, 1975)
Webb, Beatrice, 'Women and the Factory Acts' (London, 1896)
—, *My Apprenticeship* (London, 1926)
Webb, Sidney and Webb, Beatrice, *Industrial Democracy* (London, 1897)
Wheeler-Bennett, Joan, ed., *Women at the Top: Achievement and Family
　　Life* (London, 1977)
Wilkinson, Helen, *No Turning Back: Generations and the Genderquake*
　　(London, 1994)
Williams, Gertrude, *Women and Work* (London, 1945)
Williams, Sheila and Flower, F. D., *Foreign Girls in Hendon: A Survey*
　　(London, 1961)
Williams-Ellis, Amabel, *Women in War Factories* (London, 1943)
Wilson, Amrit, *Finding a Voice: Asian Women in Britain* (London, 1978)
Wolseley, Viscountess, *Women and the Land* (London, 1916)
Women's Employment Federation, *Women Want to Work*
　　(London, 1964)

Women's Industrial Council, *The Occupations of Women According to the Census of England and Wales, 1911: Summary Tables Arranged and Compiled by L Wyatt Papworth and Dorothy M Zimmern* (London, 1914)

Women's Information and Study Centre, *Comeback: A guide for the educated woman returning to work* (London, 1965)

Women's Studies Group (Centre for Contemporary Cultural Studies, University of Birmingham), *Women take Issue: Aspects of Women's Subordination* (London, 1978), pp. 79–95

Woolf, Virginia, *Three Guineas* (London, 1938)

Wynn, Margaret, *Fatherless Families* (London, 1964)

Yates, L. K., *The Woman's Part: A Record of Munitions Work* (London, 1918)

Young, Michael, 'Distribution of Income within the Family', *British Journal of Sociology*, 3 (1952), pp. 305–21

—, *Family and Kinship in East London* (London, 1957)

— and Willmott, Peter, *The Symmetrical Family: A Study of Work and Leisure in the London Region* (London, 1973)

Yudkin, Simon, *0–5: A Report on the Care of Pre-School Children* (London, 1967)

— and Holme, Anthea, *Working Mothers and their Children: A study for the Council for Children's Welfare* (London, 1963)

Zweig, Ferdynand, *The Worker in an Affluent Society: Family Life and Industry* (London, 1961)

PUBLISHED SECONDARY SOURCES

Abrams, Lynn, Hazley, Barry, Wright, Valerie and Kearns, Ade, 'Aspiration, Agency, and the Production of New Selves in a Scottish New Town, *c.*1947–*c.*2016', *Twentieth Century British History*, 29 (2018), pp. 576–604

Aiston, Sarah, 'A Good Job for a Girl? The Career Biographies of Woman Graduates of the University of Liverpool post-1945', *Twentieth Century British History*, 15 (2004), pp. 361–87

Alexander, Sally, 'Women's work in nineteenth-century London' in Juliet Mitchell and Ann Oakley, eds, *The Rights and Wrongs of Women* (London, 1976), pp. 59–111

—, 'Men's Fears and Women's Work: Responses to Unemployment in London between the Wars', *Gender and History*, 12 (2000), pp. 401–25

Allen, Ann Taylor, *Feminism and Motherhood in Western Europe, 1890–1970: The Maternal Dilemma* (Basingstoke, 2005)

Allport, Allan, *Demobbed: Coming Home after the Second World War* (London, 2009)

Amos, Valerie and Parmar, Pratibha, 'Challenging Imperial Feminism', *Feminist Review*, 1 (1984), pp. 3–19

Anderson, Gregory, ed., *The White-Blouse Revolution: Female Office Workers since 1870* (Manchester, 1988)

—, 'The "new woman" in the machinery of government: a spanner in the works?' in Roy MacLeod, ed., *Government and Expertise: Specialists, administrators and professionals, 1860–1919* (Cambridge, 1988), pp. 185–202

Anderson, Michael, *Family structure in nineteenth-century Lancashire* (Cambridge, 1971)

Andrews, Maggie, 'The WI's rural retailing and markets 1915–1939: A First World War legacy', *History of Retailing and Consumption*, 1 (2015), pp. 89–104

—, and Lomas, Janis, eds, *The Home Front in Britain: Images, Myths and Forgotten Experiences since 1914* (Basingstoke, 2014)

Anitha, Sundari and Pearson, Ruth, *Striking women: struggles and strategies of South Asian women workers from Grunwick to Gate Gourmet* (London, 2018)

—, and McDowell, Linda, 'From Grunwick to Gate Gourmet: South Asian Women's Industrial Activism and the Role of Trade Unions', *Revue Française de Civilisation Britannique*, 13 (2018), DOI: 10.4000/rfcb.1790

Aslanbeigui, Nahid and Oakes, Guy, *The Provocative Joan Robinson: The Making of a Cambridge Economist* (London, 2009)

August, Andrew, 'How Separate a Sphere? Poor Women and Paid Work in Late-Victorian London', *Journal of Family History*, 19 (1994), pp. 295–309

Bailkin, Jordanna, *The Afterlife of Empire* (Berkeley, 2012)

Barker, Hannah, *The Business of Women: Female Enterprise and Urban Development in Northern England, 1760–1830* (Oxford, 2006)

Barker, Theo and Drake, Michael, eds, *Population and Society in Britain, 1850–1980* (London, 1982)

Barr, Niall, *The Lion and the Poppy: British Veterans, Politics, and Society, 1921–1939* (London, 2005)

Bashevkin, Sylvia, 'From tough times to better times: feminism, public policy, and New Labour politics in Britain', *International Political Science Review*, 21 (2000), pp. 407–24

Bean, Jessica and Boyer, George, 'The Trade Boards Act of 1909 and the Alleviation of Household Poverty', *British Journal of Industrial Relations*, 47 (2009), pp. 240–64

Beauman, Nicola, *A Very Great Profession: The Woman's Novel, 1914–1939* (London, 1983)

Beaumont, Caitriona, *Housewives and Citizens: Domesticity and the Women's Movement in England, 1928–1945* (Manchester, 2013)

Beckett, Jane and Cherry, Deborah, eds, *The Edwardian Era* (Oxford, 1987)

Belfield, Chris, Blundell, Richard, Cribb, Jonathan, Hood, Andrew, Joyce, Robert and Keiller, Agnes Norris, *Two decades of income inequality in Britain: The role of wages, household earnings and redistribution* (London, 2017)

Bennett, Fran and Daly, Mary, *Poverty Through a Gender Lens: Evidence and Policy Review on Gender and Poverty* (Oxford, 2014)

Bessel, Richard and Schuman, Dirk, eds, *Life After Death: Approaches to a Cultural and Social History of Europe during the 1940s and 1950s* (Cambridge, 2003)

Bingham, Adrian, *Gender, Modernity, and the Popular Press in Inter-War Britain* (Oxford, 2004)

Blackburn, Sheila, 'Ideology and Social Policy: The Origins of the Trades Boards Act', *Historical Journal*, 34 (1991), pp. 43–64

—, 'How useful are feminist theories of the welfare state?', *Women's History Review*, 4 (1995), pp. 369–94

—, *A Fair Day's Wage for a Fair Day's Work? Sweated Labour and the Origins of Minimum Wage Legislation in Britain* (Aldershot, 2007)

Bland, Lucy, 'Interracial Relationships and the "Brown Baby Question": Black GIs, White British Women, and Their Mixed-Race Offspring in World War II', *Journal of the History of Sexuality*, 26 (2017), pp. 424–531

—, *Britain's 'Brown Babies': The stories of children born to black GIs and white women in the Second World War* (Manchester, 2019)

Bock, Gisela and Thane, Pat, eds, *Maternity and Gender Policies: Women and the Rise of the European Welfare States 1880s – 1950s* (London, 1991)

Boston, Sarah, *Women Workers and the Trade Unions* (London, second edn, 2015)

Bourke, Joanna, 'Housewifery in working-class England, 1860–1914', *Past & Present*, 143 (1994), pp. 167–97

Bourne, Stephen, *Motherland Calls: Britain's Black Servicemen & Women, 1939–1945* (Stroud, 2012)

Bowden, Sue and Turner, Paul, 'The Demand for Consumer Durables in the United Kingdom in the Interwar Period', *Journal of Economic History*, 53 (1993), pp. 244–58

Bracco, Rosa Maria, *Merchants of Hope: British Middlebrow Writers and the First World War, 1919–1939* (Oxford, 1993)

Briar, Celia, *Working for Women? Gendered Work and Welfare Policies in Twentieth-Century Britain* (London, 1997)

Braybon, Gail, *Women Workers in the First World War* (London, 1981)
— and Summerfield, Penny, *Out of the Cage: Women's Experiences in Two World Wars* (London, 1987)

Bridger, Anne and Jordan, Ellen, *Timely Assistance: The Work of the Society for Promoting the Training of Women, 1859–2009* (Ashford, 2009)

Brooke, Stephen, ' "A New World for Women"? Abortion Law Reform in Britain in the 1930s', *American Historical Review*, 106 (2001), pp. 431–59

—, 'Space, Emotions and the Everyday: The Affective Ecology of 1980s London', *Twentieth Century British History*, 28 (2017), pp. 110–42

Bryan, Beverly, Dadzie, Stella and Scafe, Suzanne, *The Heart of the Race: Black Women's Lives in Britain* (London, 1985)

Bryder, Linda, 'The First World War: Healthy or Hungry?' *History Workshop Journal*, 24 (1987), pp. 141–57

Bryman, Alan et al., eds, *Rethinking the Life Cycle* (Basingstoke, 1987)

Bythell, Duncan, *Sweated Trades: Outwork in Nineteenth-Century Britain* (London, 1978)

Caine, Barbara, 'Beatrice Webb and the "Woman Question"', *History Workshop Journal*, 14 (1982), pp. 23–43

Campbell, John, *Margaret Thatcher, Volume 1: The Grocer's Daughter* (London, 2000)

Carruthers, Susan, 'Manning the factories: propaganda and policy on the employment of women, 1939–47', *History*, 75 (1990), pp. 232–56

Childs, Sarah, 'The New Labour women MPs in the 1997 British Parliament: issues of recruitment and representation', *Women's History Review*, 9 (2000), pp. 55–73

Church, Richard, *Over the Bridge: An Essay in Autobiography* (London, 1955)

Clapson, Mark, *Invincible green suburbs, brave new towns: social change and urban dispersal in postwar England* (Manchester, 1998)

Clark, Alice, *The Working Life of Women in the Seventeenth Century* (London, 1919)

Clark, Anna, 'The rhetoric of Chartist domesticity: gender, language and class in the 1830s and 1840s', *Journal of British Studies*, 31 (1992), pp. 62–88

—, 'The new poor law and the breadwinner wage: contrasting assumptions', *Journal of Social History*, 34 (2000), pp. 261–82

Clarke, Gill, *The Women's Land Army: A Portrait* (Bristol, 2008)

Clarke, P. F., *Liberals and Social Democrats* (Cambridge, 1978)

Cohen, Deborah, *The War Come Home: Disabled Veterans in Britain and Germany, 1914–1939* (London, 2001)

Conekin, Becky, Mort, Frank and Waters, Chris, eds, *Moments of Modernity: Reconstructing Britain, 1945–1964* (London, 1999)

Cooper, Frederick, 'Medical Feminism, Working Mothers, and the Limits of Home: Finding a Balance Between Self-Care and Other-Care in Cross-Cultural Debates about Health and Lifestyle, 1952–1956', *Palgrave Communications* (2016), DOI: 10.1057/palcomms.2016.42.

Copelman, Dina, *London's Women Teachers: Gender, class and feminism 1870–1930* (London, 1996)

Cowman, Krista and Jackson, Louise A., eds, *Women and Work Culture: Britain c.1850–1950* (Aldershot, 2005)

Crawford, Elizabeth, *Enterprising Women: The Garretts and their Circle* (London, 2002)

Creighton, Colin, 'The rise of the male breadwinner family: a reappraisal', *Comparative Studies in Society and History*, 38 (1996), pp. 310–37

—, 'The rise and decline of the "male breadwinner family" in Britain', *Cambridge Journal of Economics*, 23 (1999), pp. 519–41

Crofts, William, *Coercion or Persuasion? Propaganda in Britain after 1945*
    (London, 1989)
Crook, '"Tidy Women": women in the Rhondda between the wars',
    Oral History, 10 (1982), pp. 40–46.
Croucher, Richard, *Engineers at War* (London, 1982)
Danziger Halperin, Anna, '"Cinderella of the Education
    System": Margaret Thatcher's Plan for Nursery Expansion in 1970s
    Britain', *Twentieth Century British History*, 29 (2018), pp. 284–308
Davidoff, Leonore and Hall, Catherine, *Family Fortunes: Men and
    women of the English middle class 1780–1850* (London, 2002,
    revised edn)
Davidoff, Leonore and Westover, Belinda, eds, *Our Work, Our Lives,
    Our Words: Women's History and Women's Work* (Basingstoke, 1986)
Davies, Aled, '"Right to Buy": The Development of a Conservative
    Housing Policy, 1945–1980', *Contemporary British History*, 27 (2013),
    pp. 421–44
Davin, Anna, 'Imperialism and Motherhood', *History Workshop Journal*,
    5 (1978), pp. 9–65
Davis, Angela, *Modern Motherhood: Women and Family in England,
    1945–2000* (Manchester, 2012)
—, 'Women's experiences of combining childcare and careers in
    postwar Oxfordshire, c.1940–1990', *The Local Historian*, 43 (2013),
    pp. 14–25
—, *Pre-school childcare in England, 1939–2010: Theory, practice and
    experience* (Manchester, 2015)
— and King, Laura, 'Gendered Perspectives on Men's Changing
    Familial Roles in Postwar England, c.1950–1990', *Gender & History*,
    30 (2018), pp. 70–92
Davis, Tracy C., *Actresses as Working Women: Their social identity in
    Victorian culture* (London, 1991)
Deacon, Alan, *In Search of the Scrounger: The administration of
    unemployment insurance in Britain, 1920–1931* (London, 1976)
Delaney, Enda, *Demography, State and Society: Irish Migration to Britain,
    1921–1971* (Liverpool, 2000)
Delap, Lucy, *The Feminist Avant-Garde: Transatlantic Encounters of the
    Early Twentieth Century* (Cambridge, 2007)
—, *Knowing their Place: Domestic Service in Twentieth-Century Britain*
    (Oxford, 2011)

—, 'Feminism, masculinities and emotional politics in the late twentieth century', *Cultural and Social History*, 15 (2018), pp. 571–93

Dex, Shirley and Joshi, Heather, 'Careers and motherhood: policies for compatibility', *Cambridge Journal of Economics*, 23 (1999), 641–59

Digby, Anne, *The Evolution of British General Practice, 1850–1948* (Oxford, 1999)

Dodgson, Elyse, *Motherland: West Indian Women to Britain in the 1950s* (London, 1984)

Durbach, Nadja, 'British Restaurants and the Gender Politics of the Wartime Midday Meal' in Sandra Dawson and Mark Crowley, eds, *Home Fronts: Britain and the Empire at War* (Woodbridge, 2017), pp. 19–36

Dwork, Deborah, *War is good for babies and other young children: A history of the infant and child welfare movement in England 1898–1918* (London, 1987)

Dyhouse, Carol, 'Working-class mothers and infant mortality in England, 1895–1914', *Journal of Social History*, 12 (1978), pp. 248–67

—, *Feminism and the Family in England, 1880–1939* (Oxford, 1989)

—, *No Distinction of Sex? Women in British Universities, 1870–1939* (London, 1995)

—, 'Women Students and the London Medical Schools, 1914–39: The Anatomy of a Masculine Culture', *Gender & History*, 10 (1998), pp. 110–32

—, *Students: A Gendered History* (London, 2006)

Edelstein, T. J., '"They Sang the Song of the Shirt": The Visual Iconology of the Seamstress', *Victorian Studies*, 23 (1980), pp. 183–210.

Ehrenreich, Barbara and Hochschild, Arlie Russell, eds, *Global Woman: Nannies, Maids and Sex Workers in the New Economy* (London, 2003)

Eltis, Sos, 'Private Lives and Public Spaces: Reputation, Celebrity and the Late Victorian Actress' in Mary Luckhurst and Jane Moody, eds, *Theatre and Celebrity in Britain 1660–2000* (Basingstoke, 2005) pp. 169–88

Feldman, David, *Englishmen and Jews: Social Relations and Political Culture 1840–1914* (London, 1994)

Ferry, Georgina, *Dorothy Hodgkin: A Life* (London, 1998)

Feurer, Rosemary, 'The Meaning of "Sisterhood": the British Women's Movement and Protective Labour Legislation', *Victorian Studies*, 31 (1988), pp. 233–60

Fisher, Kate, *Birth Control, Sex and Marriage in Britain, 1918–1960* (Oxford, 2007)

Fountain, Julie, '"The Most Interesting Work a Woman can Perform in Wartime": The Exceptional Status of British Women Pilots during the Second World War', *Cultural and Social History*, 13 (2016), pp. 213–29

Frader, Laura Levine, 'International Institutions and Domestic Reform: Equal Pay and British Membership in the European Economic Community', *Twentieth Century British History*, 29 (2018), pp. 104–28

Franks, Suzanne, 'Attitudes to women in the BBC in the 1970s', *Westminster Papers*, 8 (2011), pp. 123–42

Freeden, Michael, *The New Liberalism: An Ideology of Social Reform* (Oxford, 1978)

Frost, Ginger, *Living in Sin: Cohabiting as Husband and Wife in Nineteenth-Century England* (Manchester, 2008)

—, *Illegitimacy in English Law and Society, 1860–1930* (Manchester, 2016)

Gales, Kathleen E. and Marks, P. H., 'Twentieth Century Trends in the Work of Women in England and Wales', *Journal of the Royal Statistical Society*, 137 (1974), pp. 60–74

Garnett, David, *The Golden Echo* (London, 1953)

Garnett, Richard, *Constance Garnett: A Heroic Life* (London, 1991)

Gavron, Jeremy, *A Woman on the Edge of Time* (London, 2015)

Geddes, Jennian F., 'Louisa Garrett Anderson (1873–1943), surgeon and suffragette', *Journal of Medical Biography*, 16 (2008), pp. 205–14

Gill, Rosalind, 'Culture and Subjectivity in Neoliberal and Postfeminist Times', *Subjectivity*, 25 (2008), pp. 432–45

Gittins, Diana, *Fair Sex: Family Size and Structure, 1900–1939* (London, 1982)

Glew, Helen, *Gender, Rhetoric and Regulation: Women's Work in the Civil Service and the London County Council, 1900–55* (Manchester, 2016)

Glucksmann, Miriam, *Women Assemble: Women Workers and the New Industries in Inter-war Britain* (London, 1990)

Glynn, Jenifer, *The Pioneering Garretts: Breaking the Barriers for Women* (London, 2008)

Goose, Nigel, ed., *Women's work in industrial England: regional and local perspectives* (Hatfield, 2007)

Gordon, Eleanor and Nair, Gwyneth, 'The economic role of middle-class women in Victorian Glasgow', *Women's History Review*, 9 (2000), pp. 791–814

Gore, Elizabeth, *The Better Fight: The Story of Dame Lilian Barker* (London, 1965)

Goulborne, Harry and Chamberlain, Mary, eds, *Caribbean Families in Britain and the Trans-Atlantic World* (Oxford, 2001)

Graves, Pamela, *Labour Women: Women in British Working-Class Politics, 1918–1939* (Cambridge, 1994)

Grayzel, Susan, 'Nostalgia, Gender, and the Countryside: Placing the "Land Girl" in First World War Britain', *Rural History*, 10 (1999), pp. 155–70

Gregson, Nicky and Lowe, Michelle, *Servicing the Middle Classes: Class, gender and waged domestic labour in contemporary Britain* (London, 1994)

Griffin, Ben, 'Class, gender and Liberalism in Parliament, 1868–1882: the case of the Married Women's Property Acts', *Historical Journal*, 46 (2003), pp. 59–87

—, *The Politics of Gender in Victorian Britain: Masculinity, political culture, and the struggle for women's rights* (Cambridge, 2012)

Griffin, Emma, *Liberty's Dawn: A People's History of the Industrial Revolution* (London, 2013)

Groenewegen, Peter, ed., *Feminism and Political Economy in Victorian England* (Aldershot, 1994)

Gullace, Nicoletta, *The Blood of Our Sons: Men, Women and the Renegotiation of British Citizenship during the Great War* (Basingstoke, 2002)

Haggett, Ali, *Desperate Housewives, Neuroses and the Domestic Environment, 1945–70* (London, 2012)

Hakim, Catherine, 'Grateful slaves and self-made women: fact and fantasy in women's work orientations', *European Sociological Review*, 7 (1991) pp. 101–21

—, 'Five feminist myths about women's employment', *British Journal of Sociology*, 46 (1995) pp. 429–55

—, *Work-Lifestyle Choices in the 21st Century: Preference Theory* (Oxford, 2000)

Hall, Catherine, 'Married women at home in Birmingham in the 1920s and 1930s', *Oral History*, 5 (1977), pp. 62–83

Hancock, Ruth, Stuchbury, Rachel and Tomassini, Cecilia, 'Changes in the distribution of marital age differences in England and Wales, 1963–1998', *Population Trends* (Winter 2003), pp. 19–25

Harris, Alice Kessler, *A Woman's Wage: Historical Meanings and Social Consequences* (Kentucky, 1990)

Harris, Jose, *Unemployment and Politics: A Study in English Social Policy, 1886–1914* (Oxford, 1972)

—, 'Political Thought and the Welfare State, 1870–1940: An Intellectual Framework for British Social Policy', *Past & Present*, 135 (1992), pp. 116–41

Harrison, Barbara, *Not only the 'dangerous trades': Women's work and health in Britain, 1880–1914* (London, 1996)

Hatton, T. J. and Bailey, R. E., 'Female Labour Force Participation in Interwar Britain', *Oxford Economic Papers*, 40 (1988), pp. 695–718

Hayward, Rhodri, 'Desperate Housewives and Model Amoebae: The Invention of Suburban Neurosis in Inter-War Britain' in Mark Jackson, ed., *Health and the Modern Home* (London, 2007), pp. 1–17

Heilbrun, Carolyn, *The Garnett Family* (London, 1961)

Hewitt, Margaret, *Wives and Mothers in Victorian Industry* (London, 1958)

Hicks, Marie, *Programmed Inequality: How Britain discarded women technologists and lost its edge in computing* (Cambridge, MA, 2017)

Higgs, Edward and Wilkinson, Amanda, 'Women, occupations and work in the Victorian censuses revisited', *History Workshop Journal*, 87 (2016), pp. 17–38

Hiley, Michael, *Victorian Working Women: Portraits from Life* (London, 1979)

Hinton, James, 'Essay in Labour Statistics: women and the Labour vote, 1945–50', *Labour History Review*, 57 (1992), pp. 59–66

—, *Women, Social Leadership and the Second World War: Continuities of Class* (Oxford, 2002)

—, *The Mass Observers: A History, 1937–1949* (Oxford, 2013)

Hipperson, Julie, 'Professional Entrepreneurs: Women Veterinary Surgeons as Small Business Owners in Interwar Britain', *Social History of Medicine*, 31 (2018), pp. 122–39

Holcombe, Lee, *Victorian Ladies at Work: Middle-class working women in England and Wales, 1850–1914* (London, 1973)

—, *Wives and Property: Reform of the Married Women's Property Law in Nineteenth-Century England* (Toronto, 1983)

Holden, Kath, *The Shadow of Marriage: Singleness in England, 1914–1960* (Manchester, 2007)

Holland, David, 'The social networks of South Asian migrants in the Sheffield area during the early twentieth century', *Past & Present*, 236 (2017), pp. 243–79

Hollis, Patricia, *Ladies Elect: Women in English local government, 1865–1914* (Oxford, 1987)

Holloway, Gerry, *Women and Work in Britain since 1840* (Abingdon, 2005)

Holton, Sandra Stanley, *Suffrage Days: Stories from the Women's Suffrage Movement* (London, 1996)

HomeWorkers Worldwide, *Subject to Status: An investigation into the working lives of homeworkers in the UK* (Leeds, 2007)

Horn, Pamela, *Rural Life in England in the First World War* (Dublin, 1984)

Horrell, Sara and Humphries, Jane, 'Women's Labour Force Participation and the Transition to the Male Breadwinner Family, 1790–1865', *Economic History Review*, second series, 48 (1995), pp. 89–117

—, 'The origins and expansion of the male breadwinner family: the case of nineteenth century Britain', *International Review of Social History*, supplement, 5 (1997), pp. 25–64

Hubback, Judith, *From Dawn to Dusk: Autobiography of Judith Hubback* (Illinois, 2003)

Hubble, Nick, *Mass Observation and Everyday Life: Culture, History, Theory* (Basingstoke, 2006)

Hudson, Pat and Berg, Maxine, 'Rehabilitating the industrial revolution', *Economic History Review*, 45 (1992), pp. 25–50

Humphries, Jane, *Childhood and Child Labour in the British Industrial Revolution* (Cambridge, 2010)

Huneault, Kristina, *Difficult Subjects: Working Women and Visual Culture, Britain 1880–1914* (Farnham, 2002)

Izzard, Molly, *A Heroine in Her Time: A Life of Dame Helen Gwynne-Vaughan, 1879–1967* (London, 1969)

Jackson, Ben, 'Free markets and feminism: the neoliberal defence of the male breadwinner model in Britain, *c.*1980–1997', *Women's History Review*, 28 (2019), pp. 297–316

— and Saunders, Robert, eds, *Making Thatcher's Britain* (Cambridge, 2012)

Jacobs, Jo Ellen, *The Voice of Harriet Taylor Mill* (Bloomington, 2002)

James, Winston and Harris, Clive, eds, *Inside Babylon: The Caribbean Diaspora in Britain* (London, 1993)

Jennings, Rebecca, *Tomboys and Bachelor Girls: A lesbian history of post-war Britain* (Manchester, 2007)

John, Angela V., *Unequal Opportunities: Women's Employment in England, 1800–1918* (Oxford, 1986)

Jordan, Ellen, *The Women's Movement and Women's Employment in Nineteenth-Century Britain* (London, 1999)

Kay, Alison, *The Foundations of Female Entrepreneurship: Enterprise, Home and Household in London, c.1800–1870* (London, 2009)

Kay, Diana and Miles, Robert, *Refugees or migrant workers? European Volunteer Workers in Britain, 1946–51* (London, 1992)

Kelsall, R. K., *Higher Civil Servants in Britain: From 1870 to the Present Day* (London, 1955)

Kenyon, David, *First World War National Factories* (Historic England Research Report Series 076, 2015)

King, Laura, *Family Men: Fatherhood and masculinity in Britain, 1914–1960* (Oxford, 2015)

Koven, Seth, *Slumming: Sexual and Social Politics in Victorian London* (London, 2006)

Kynaston, David, *Austerity Britain: 1945–51* (London, 2007)

Lancaster, Bill and Mason, Tony, eds, *Life and Labour in a Twentieth Century City: The Experience of Coventry* (Coventry, 1986)

Lancaster Regionalism Group, ed., *Localities, Class and Gender* (London, 1985)

Langhamer, Claire, *The English in Love: The Intimate Story of an Emotional Revolution* (Oxford, 2013)

—, 'The Meanings of Home in Post-War Britain', *Journal of Contemporary History* 40 (2005), pp. 341–62

Laurence, Anne, Maltby, Josephine and Rutterford, Janette, eds, *Women and their Money 1700–1850: Essays on women and finance* (London, 2009)

Lawrence, Jon, 'Class, "Affluence" and the Study of Everyday Life in Britain, c.1930–64', *Cultural and Social History*, 10 (2013), pp. 273–99

—, 'Inventing the "Traditional Working Class": A Re-Analysis of Interview Notes from Young and Willmott's *Family and Kinship in East London*', *Historical Journal*, 59 (2016), pp. 567–93

—, 'Languages of place and belonging: anthropological versus vernacular understandings of communal life in mid-twentieth century Bermondsey, London' in Stefan Couperus and Harm Kaal, eds, *(Re)Constructing Communities in Europe, 1918–1968* (London, 2016), pp. 19–44

—, *Me, Me, Me? The Search for Community in Post-War England* (Oxford, 2019)

Lees, Lynn Hollen, *The Solidarities of Strangers: The English Poor Laws and the People, 1700–1948* (Cambridge, 1998)

Lennon, Mary, McAdam, Marie and O'Brien, Joanne, *Across the Water: Irish Women's Lives in Britain* (London, 1988)

Levine-Clark, Marjorie, *Unemployment, Welfare, and Masculine Citizenship: 'So Much Honest Poverty' in Britain, 1870–1930* (Basingstoke, 2015)

Lewis, Jane, *The Politics of Motherhood: Child and Maternal Welfare in England, 1900–1939* (London, 1980)

—, *The End of Marriage? Individualism and Intimate Relations* (Cheltenham, 2001)

—, 'Developing Early Years Childcare in England, 1997–2002: The Choices for (Working) Mothers', *Social Policy and Administration*, 37 (2003), pp. 219–38

—, 'The Failure to Expand Childcare Provision and to Develop a Comprehensive Childcare Policy in Britain during the 1960s and 1970s', *Twentieth Century British History*, 24 (2013), pp. 249–74

Lewis, Patricia and Simpson, Ruth, eds, *Revealing and Concealing Gender: Issues of Visibility in Organisations* (Basingstoke, 2010)

Light, Alison, *Forever England: Femininity, literature and conservatism between the wars* (London, 1991)

Livesey, Ruth, 'The politics of work: feminism, professionalisation and women inspectors of factories and workshops', *Women's History Review*, 13 (2004), pp. 233–62

—, 'Reading for Character: Women Social Reformers and Narratives of the Urban Poor in Late Victorian and Edwardian London', *Journal of Victorian Culture*, 9 (2004), pp. 43–67

London Feminist History Group, eds, *The Sexual Dynamics of History: Men's power, women's resistance* (London, 1983)

Lown, Judy, *Women and Industrialization: Gender at Work in Nineteenth-Century England* (Cambridge, 1990)

Lyon, E. Stina, 'Viola Klein: Forgotten Émigré Intellectual, Public Sociologist and Advocate of Women,' *Sociology*, 41 (2007), pp. 829–42

McCarthy, Helen, *Girlfriends in High Places: How women's networks are changing the workplace* (London, 2003)

—, 'Service clubs, citizenship and equality: gender relations and middle-class associations between the wars', *Historical Research*, 81 (2008), pp. 531–52

—, *Women of the World: The Rise of the Female Diplomat* (London, 2014)

—, 'Social Science and Married Women's Employment in Post-War Britain', *Past & Present*, 233 (2016), pp. 269–305

—, 'Women, Marriage and Paid Work in Post-War Britain', *Women's History Review*, 26 (2017), pp. 46–61

McDowell, Linda, *Working Lives: Gender, Migration and Employment in Britain, 1945–2007* (Chichester, 2013)

McFeely, Mary Drake, *Lady Inspectors: The Campaign for a Better Workplace, 1893–1921* (London, 1991)

McKibbin, Ross, 'Social Class and Social Observation in Edwardian England', *Transactions of the Royal Historical Society*, 28 (1978), pp. 175–99

Malcolmson, Patricia E., *English Laundresses: A Social History, 1850–1930* (Chicago, 1986)

Malkiel, Nancy Weiss, *'Keep the Damned Women Out': The Struggle for Coeducation* (Princeton, 2016)

Malone, Carolyn, 'The Gendering of Dangerous Trades: Government Regulation of Women's Work in the White Lead Trade in England, 1891–1898', *Journal of Women's History*, 8 (1996), pp. 1–35

—, 'Sensational Stories, Endangered Bodies: Women's Work and the New Journalism in England in the 1890s', *Albion*, 31 (1999), pp. 49–71.

Maltby, Josephine and Rutterford, Janette, '"She possessed her own fortune": Women investors from the late nineteenth century to the early twentieth century', *Business History*, 48 (2006), pp. 220–53

Mandler, Peter, 'Educating the Nation: II. Universities', *Transactions of the Royal Historical Society*, 25 (2015), pp. 1–26

—, 'The Two Cultures Revisited: The Humanities in British Universities Since 1945', *Twentieth Century British History*, 26 (2015), pp. 400–23

Manton, Joan, *Elizabeth Garrett Anderson* (London, 1958)

Marcus, Sharon, *Between Women: Friendship, Desire, and Marriage in Victorian England* (Oxford, 2007)

Marland, Hilary and Long, Vicky, 'From Danger and Motherhood to Health and Beauty: Health Advice for the Factory Girl in Early Twentieth-Century Britain', *Twentieth Century British History*, 20 (2009), pp. 454–81

Mearns, Gabrielle, '"Long Trudges Through Whitechapel": The East End of Beatrice Webb's and Clara Collet's Social Investigations', *19: Interdisciplinary Studies in the Long Nineteenth Century*, 13 (2011), DOI: http://doi.org/10.16995/ntn.634

Melman, Billie, *Women and the Popular Imagination in the Twenties: Flappers and Nymphs* (Basingstoke, 1988)

Milward, Robert and Bell, Frances, 'Infant Mortality in Victorian Britain: The Mother as Medium', *Economic History Review*, 54 (2001), pp. 699–733

Mockett, Helen, 'Women in the Factory: The State and Factory Legislation in Nineteenth-Century Britain' in Lynn Jamieson and Helen Corr, eds, *State, Private Life and Political Change* (Basingstoke, 1990), pp. 137–62

Morgan, Carol E., *Women Workers and Gender Identities, 1835–1913: The Cotton and Metal Industries in England* (London, 2001)

Morris, R. J., *Men, women and property in England, 1780–1870* (Cambridge, 2005)

Morris, Jenny, *Women Workers and the Sweated Trades: The Origins of Minimum Wage Legislation* (Aldershot, 1986)

Mosse, Werner E., ed., *Second Chance: Two Centuries of German-speaking Jews in the United Kingdom* (Tübingen, 1991)

Murphy, Kate, 'A Marriage Bar of Convenience? The BBC and Married Women's Work, 1923–1939', *Twentieth Century British History*, 25 (2014), pp. 533–61

Noakes, Lucy, *Women in the British Army: War and the gentle sex, 1907–1948* (London, 2006)

Nord, Deborah Epstein, *The Apprenticeship of Beatrice Webb* (Basingstoke, 1985)

—, *Walking the Victorian Streets: Women, Representation and the City* (London, 1995)

O'Connor, Henrietta and Goodwin, John, 'Girls' Transitions to Work and Adulthood in the 1960s' in Christopher Pole, Jane Pilcher and John Williams, eds, *Young People in Transition: Becoming Citizens?* (Basingstoke, 2005), pp. 52–73

Oldfield, Sybil, *Jeanie, an 'Army of One': Mrs Nassau Senior 1828–1877: The First Woman in Whitehall* (Brighton, 2008)

Onslow, Barbara, *Women of the Press in Nineteenth-Century Britain* (Basingstoke, 2000)

Oram, Alison, 'Repressed and Thwarted, or Bearer of the New World? The Spinster in Inter-war Feminist Discourses', *Women's History Review*, 1 (1992), pp. 413–34

—, *Women Teachers and Feminist Politics 1900–1939* (Manchester, 1996)

Partington, Geoffrey, *Women Teachers in the 20th Century in England and Wales* (Windsor, 1976)

Pearlston, Karen, 'Married women bankrupts in the age of coverture', *Law & Social Inquiry*, 34 (2009), pp. 265–99

Pedersen, Susan, *Family, Dependence, and the Origins of the Welfare State: Britain and France, 1914–1945* (Cambridge, 1993)

—, *Eleanor Rathbone and the Politics of Conscience* (London, 2004)

Penlington, Neil, 'Masculinity and Domesticity in 1930s South Wales: Did Unemployment change the domestic division of labour?' *Twentieth Century British History*, 21 (2010), pp. 281–99

Pennington, Shelley and Westover, Belinda, *A Hidden Workforce: Homeworkers in England, 1850–1985* (Basingstoke, 1989)

Perriton, Linda, 'Forgotten Feminists: the Federation of British Professional and Business Women, 1933–1969', *Women's History Review*, 16 (2007), pp. 79–97

Perrone, Fernanda, 'Women Academics in England, 1870–1930', *History of Universities*, XII, 1993, pp. 339–67

Perry, Kennetta Hammond, *London Is the Place for Me: Black Britons, Citizenship, and the Politics of Race* (Oxford, 2016)

Peterson, Linda H., *Becoming a Woman of Letters: Myths of Authorship and Facts of the Victorian Market* (Princeton, 2009)

Phillips, Nicola, *Women in Business 1700–1850* (London, 2006)

Pinchbeck, Ivy, *Women Workers and the Industrial Revolution 1750–1850* (London, 1981 [1930])

Polden, Patrick, 'Portia's Progress: Women at the Bar in England, 1919–1939', *International Journal of the Legal Profession*, 293 (2005), pp. 293–338

Pooley, Sian, 'Parenthood, child-rearing and fertility in England, 1850–1914', *History of the Family*, 18 (2013), pp. 83–106

Pope, Rex, 'Unemployed women in inter-war Britain: the case of the Lancashire weaving district', *Women's History Review*, 9 (2000), pp. 743–59

Powell, Violet, *The Life of a Provincial Lady: A Study of E.M. Delafield and her Works* (London, 1988)

Prasch, Thomas, 'Photography and the image of the London poor' in Debra Mancoff and Dale Tela, eds, *Victorian urban settings: Essays on the nineteenth-century city and its contexts* (New York, 1996), pp. 179–94

Prochaska, Frank, *Women and Philanthropy in nineteenth-century England* (Oxford, 1980)

Randall, Vicky, *The Politics of Child Daycare in Britain* (Oxford, 2000)

Regulska, Joanne and Smith, Bonnie G., eds, *Women and Gender in Postwar Europe: From Cold War to European Union* (London, 2012)

Rendall, Jane, *Women in an Industrializing Society: England 1750–1880* (Oxford, 1990)

Reynolds, David, *Rich Relations: The American Occupation of Britain, 1942–1945* (London, 1995)

Reynolds, Melanie, *Infant Mortality and Working-Class Child Care, 1850–1899* (Basingstoke, 2016)

Reynolds, Z. Nia, *When I Came to England: An oral history of life in 1950s and 1960s Britain* (London, 2001)

Richards, Eric, 'Women in the British Economy since about 1700: An Interpretation', *History*, 59 (1974), pp. 337–47

Richards, Sandra, *The Rise of the English Actress* (Basingstoke, 1993)

Riley, Denise, *War in the Nursery* (London, 1986)

Roberts, Elizabeth, *A Woman's Place: An Oral History of Working-Class Women, 1900–1940* (Oxford, 1984)

Robinson, Emily, Schofield, Camilla, Sutcliffe-Braithwaite, Florence and Thomlinson, Natalie, 'Telling Stories about Post-war

Britain: Popular Individualism and the 'Crisis' of the 1970s',
  Twentieth Century British History, 28 (2017), pp. 268–304

Rogers, Helen, 'The Good are not always powerful, nor the powerful
  always good: The politics of women's needlework in mid-Victorian
  London', *Victorian Studies*, 40 (1997), pp. 589–623

Rose, Sonya, *Limited Livelihoods: Gender and Class in Nineteenth-
  Century England* (London, 1992)

—, 'Girls and GIs: Race, Sex, and Diplomacy in Second World War
  Britain', *International History Review*, 19 (1997), pp. 146–60

Ross, Ellen, *Love and Toil: Motherhood in Outcast London, 1870–1918*
  (Oxford, 1993)

—, ed., *Slum Travellers: Ladies and London Poverty, 1860–1920*
  (London, 2007)

Ross, Karen, ed., *Women, Politics and Change* (Oxford, 2002)

Rowbotham, Sheila, *Promise of a Dream* (London, 2000)

—, *Dreamers of a New Day: Women Who Invented the Twentieth Century*
  (London, 2010)

Rutterford, Janette and Maltby, Josephine, '"The widow, the clergyman
  and the reckless": women investors in England, 1830–1914', *Feminist
  Economics*, 12 (2006), pp. 111–38

Ryan, Deborah Sugg, *The Ideal Home Through the 20th Century*
  (London, 1997)

Savage, Michael, *The Dynamics of Working Class Politics: The Labour
  Movement in Preston, 1880–1940* (Cambridge, 1987)

—, 'Trade Unionism, Sex Segregation, and the State: Women's
  Employment in "New Industries" in Inter-War Britain', *Social
  History*, 13 (1988), pp. 209–30

Schmiechen, James, *Sweated Industries and Sweated Labour: The London
  Clothing Trades* (Urbana, 1984)

Schwartz, Laura, *Infidel Feminism: Secularism, religion and women's
  emancipation, England, 1830–1914* (Manchester, 2013)

Schweitzer, Pam, ed., *Across the Irish Sea* (London, 1989)

Scott, Peter, 'Marketing mass home ownership and the creation of
  the modern working-class consumer in inter-war Britain', *Business
  History*, 50 (2008), pp. 4–25

—, 'Mr Drage, Mr Everyman, and the Creation of a Mass Market for
  Domestic Furniture in Inter-war Britain', *Economic History Review*,
  62 (2009), pp. 802–27

—, *The Triumph of the South: A Regional Economic History of Early Twentieth-Century Britain* (Aldershot, 2007)

Shanley, Mary, 'One Must Ride Behind: Married Women's Rights and the Divorce Act of 1857', *Victorian Studies*, 25 (1982), pp. 355–76

—, *Feminism: Marriage and the Law in Victorian Britain, 1850–95* (Princeton, 1989)

Shapira, Michal, *The War Inside: Psychoanalysis, Total War and the Making of the Democratic Self in Post-War Britain* (Cambridge, 2013)

Smith, Harold, 'The Womanpower Problem in Britain during the Second World War', *Historical Journal*, 27 (1984), pp. 925–45

Smith, M. J. and Spear, J., eds, *The Changing Labour Party* (London, 1992)

Snow, Stephanie and Jones, Emma, 'Immigration and the National Health Service: putting history to the forefront' (History & Policy, 2011)

Spencer, Stephanie, *Gender, Work and Education in Britain in the 1950s* (Basingstoke, 2005)

Stewart, John, *Child Guidance in Britain, 1918–1955: The Dangerous Age of Childhood* (London, 2013)

Stewart, Kitty, *Labour's Record on the Under-Fives: Policy, Spending and Outcomes, 1997–2010* (LSE Working Paper, 2013)

Stoller, Sarah, 'Forging a Politics of Care: Theorizing Household Work in the British Women's Liberation Movement', *History Workshop Journal*, 85 (2018), pp. 95–119

Summerfield, Penny, *Women Workers in the Second World War: Production and Patriarchy in Conflict* (Abingdon, 1984)

—, 'Mass Observation: Social Research or Social Movement?' *Journal of Contemporary History*, 20 (1985), pp. 439–52

Summers, Anne, 'A home from home: women's philanthropic work in the nineteenth century' in Sandra Burman, ed., *Fit Work for Women* (London, 1979), pp. 33–63

—, *Female lives, moral states: Women, religion and public life in Britain, 1800–1930* (Newbury, 2000)

Sutherland, Gillian, *In Search of The New Woman: Middle-Class Women and Work in Britain, 1870–1914* (Cambridge, 2015)

Steedman, Carolyn, *Landscape for a Good Woman* (London, 1989)

Stott, Mary, *Organisation Woman: The Story of the National Union of Townswomen's Guilds* (London, 1978)

Strange, Julie Marie, *Fatherhood and the British Working Class, 1865–1914* (Cambridge, 2015)

Szreter, Simon, *Fertility, Class and Gender in Britain, 1860–1940* (Cambridge, 1996)

Tabili, Laura, *Global Migrants, Local Culture: Natives and Newcomers in Provincial England, 1841–1939* (Basingstoke, 2011)

Thane, Pat, 'Women and the Poor Law in Victorian and Edwardian England', *History Workshop Journal*, 6 (1978), pp. 29–51

—, *Old Age in English History: Past Experiences, Present Issues* (Oxford, 2000)

—, 'What Difference Did the Vote Make?' in Amanda Vickery, ed. *Women, Privilege and Power: British Politics, 1750 to the Present* (Stanford, 2001), pp. 253–88

—, 'Girton Graduates: earning and learning, 1920s–1980s', *Women's History Review*, 13 (2004), pp. 347–61

—, *Happy Families? History and Family Policy* (London, 2011)

—, 'Unmarried motherhood in twentieth-century England', *Women's History Review*, 20 (2011), pp. 11–29

—, *Foundations of the Welfare State* (second edn, London, 2016)

— and Evans, Tanya, *Sinners? Scroungers? Saints? Unmarried Motherhood in Twentieth-Century England* (Oxford, 2012)

Thom, Deborah, 'Free from chains? The image of women's labour in London, 1900–1920' in David Feldman and Gareth Stedman Jones, eds, *Metropolis London: Histories and representations since 1800* (London, 1989), pp. 85–99

—, *Nice Girls and Rude Girls: Women Workers in World War I* (London, 2000)

Thomson, Mathew, *Psychological Subjects: Identity, Culture and Health in Twentieth-Century Britain* (Oxford, 2006)

—, *Lost Freedom: The Landscape of the Child and the British Post-War Settlement* (Oxford, 2013)

Tilly, Louise and Scott, Joan, *Women, Work and Family* (London, 1978)

Todd, Selina, *Young women, work and family in England, 1918–1950* (Oxford, 2005)

—, *The People* (London, 2014)

Tomlinson, J. D., 'Women as "Anomalies": The Anomalies Regulations of 1931, their background and implications', *Public Administration*, 62 (1984), pp. 423–7

Verdon, Nicola, 'Left out in the cold: Village women and agricultural labour in England and Wales during the First World War', *Twentieth Century British History*, 27 (2016), pp. 1–25

Vicinus, Martha, *Independent Women: Work and Community for Single Women, 1850–1920* (London, 1985)

—, *Intimate Friends: Women Who Loved Women, 1778–1928* (London, 2004)

Walkowitz, Judith, *Prostitution and Victorian Society: Women, class and the state* (Cambridge, 1980)

—, *City of Dreadful Delight: Narratives of Sexual Danger in Late-Victorian London* (London, 1992)

—, 'The Indian woman, the flower girl, and the Jew: photojournalism in Edwardian London', *Victorian Studies*, 42 (1998), pp. 3–46

—, 'Feminism and the Politics of Prostitution in King's Cross in the 1980s', *Twentieth Century British History*, 30 (2019), pp. 231–63

Ward, Chloe, ' "Something of the Spirit of Stalingrad": British women, their Soviet sisters, propaganda and politics in the Second World War', *Twentieth Century British History*, 25 (2014), pp. 435–60

Warme, Barbara D., Lundy, Katharina L. P. and Lundy, Larry, eds, *Working Part-Time: Risks and Opportunities* (New York, 1992)

Webb, Clive, 'Special Relationships: mixed-race couples in post-war Britain and the United States', *Women's History Review*, 26 (2017), pp. 110–29

Webster, Wendy, *Imagining Home: Gender, 'Race' and National Identity, 1945–1964* (London, 1998)

—, ' "Fit to Fight, Fit to Mix": sexual patriotism in Second World War Britain', *Women's History Review*, 22 (2013), pp. 607–24

—, *Mixing It: Diversity in World War Two Britain* (Oxford, 2018)

—, and Ryan, Louise, eds, *Gendering Migration: Masculinity, Femininity and Ethnicity in Post-War Britain* (Aldershot, 2008)

Welshman, John, 'School meals and milk in England and Wales, 1906–45', *Medical History*, 41 (1997), pp. 6–29

Whipp, Richard, *Patterns of Labour: Work and Social Change in the Pottery Industry* (London, 1990)

White, Bonnie, *The Women's Land Army in First World War Britain* (Basingstoke, 2014)

Whitehead, Frank, 'The Government Social Survey' in Martin Bulmer, ed., *Essays on the History of British Sociological Research* (Cambridge, 1985), pp. 83–100

Wikander, Ulla, Kessler-Harris, Alice and Lewis, Jane, eds, *Protecting Women: Labor Legislation in Europe, the United States and Australia, 1880–1920* (Urbana & Chicago, 1995)

Wills, Clair, *Lovers and Strangers: An Immigrant History of Postwar Britain* (London, 2017)

Wilson, Dolly, 'A New Look at the Affluent Worker: The Good Working Mother in Post-War Britain', *Twentieth Century British History*, 17 (2006), pp. 206–29

Wilson, Elizabeth, *Only Half-Way to Paradise: Women in Postwar Britain, 1945–1968* (London, 1980)

Winter, J. M., 'The Impact of the First World War on Civilian Health in Britain', *Economic History Review*, 30 (1977), pp. 487–503

Wolf, Alison, *The XX Factor: How Working Women are Creating a New Society* (London, 2013)

Woollacott, Angela, *On Her Their Lives Depend: Munitions Workers in the Great War* (London, 1994)

—, 'Maternalism, professionalism and industrial welfare supervisors in World War I Britain', *Women's History Review*, 3 (1994), pp. 29–56

Worth, Eve, 'A Tale of Female Liberation? The Long Shadow of De-Professionalisation on the Lives of Post-War Women', *Revue Française de Civilisation Britannique*, 13 (2018) DOI: 10.4000/rfcb.1778

—, 'Women, Education and Social Mobility in Britain during the Long 1970s', *Cultural and Social History*, 16 (2019), pp. 67–83

Wright, Christine Etherington, *Gender, Professions and Discourse: Early Twentieth-Century Women's Autobiography* (Basingstoke, 2009)

Young, Zoe, *Women's Work: How Mothers Manage Flexible Working in Careers and Family Life* (Bristol, 2018)

Zabalza, A. and Tzannatos, Z., *Women and Equal Pay: The Effects of Legislation on Female Employment and Wages in Britain* (Cambridge, 1985)

Zimmeck, Meta, 'Jobs for the girls: the expansion of clerical work for women, 1850–1914' in John, A., ed., *Unequal Opportunities: Women's Employment in England, 1800–1918* (Oxford, 1986), pp. 153–77

UNPUBLISHED PHD AND MA THESES

Elston, Mary Ann, 'Women Doctors in the British Health Services: A Sociological Study of their Careers and Opportunities' (unpublished doctoral thesis, University of Leeds, 1986)

Faraday, Judy, 'A Kind of Superior Hobby: Women Managers in the John Lewis Partnership, 1918–1950' (unpublished MPhil thesis, University of Wolverhampton, 2008)

Gasperetti, Flavia, 'Italian women migrants in post-war Britain: The case of textiles workers, 1949–1961' (unpublished PhD thesis, University of Birmingham, 2012)

Hall, Richard, 'The Emotional Lives and Legacies of Fathers and Sons in Britain, 1945–1974' (unpublished PhD thesis, University of Cambridge, 2019)

Acknowledgements

As a parent, the labour of writing a book requires other labours to be lifted from one's shoulders, at least temporarily, and so my first and greatest debt is to the network of family, friends, nannies and nursery staff who have shared in the care of my two daughters over the best part of the last decade. During that time, my husband and I have had the extraordinarily good fortune of being able to pay for high-quality childcare whilst drawing upon grandparents living reasonably close by for babysitting and school runs and for general back-up and morale-boosting when disaster struck (as it often did). It is more conventional for an acknowledgements page to open with expressions of gratitude to funders, colleagues and editors, but in truth, I simply would not be a professional historian who happens also to be a mother without this infrastructure of love, luck and social privilege behind me. There would be no *Double Lives* had I not these resources with which to manage my own double life.

Funders, colleagues and editors must, of course, also receive their due, and I thank wholeheartedly everyone who has helped me on the journey to producing this book. A large portion of my research was conducted during a year of sabbatical leave at Queen Mary University of London in 2014–15, whilst the award of a Mid-Career Fellowship from the British Academy in 2017–18 provided precious time away from teaching and administration for drafting the final manuscript. I am grateful to the many archivists who assisted me at the Women's Library, the University of Reading Special Collections, the Modern Records Centre at the University of Warwick, the London Metropolitan Archives, The Keep at the University of Sussex, The Wellcome Library and The National Archives in Kew.

Colleagues and friends have given generously of their time in reading chapters in draft, and my thanks go to Lucy Delap, Ben Griffin, Peter Mandler, Sarah Mrkusic and Susan Pedersen for their careful commentary and feedback. The ideas behind the book have been shaped and enriched over the years by conversations with Emily Baughan, Cait Beaumont, Lawrence Black, David Cannadine, Laura Carter, Deborah Cohen, John Goodwin, Emma Griffin, Matthew Hilton, Christina von Hodenberg, Laura King, Sarah Knott, Claire Langhamer, Jon Lawrence, Stina Lyon, Linda McDowell, Henrietta O'Connor, Guy Ortolano, Laura Paterson, Chris Renwick, Emily Robinson, Caroline Rusterholz, Tehila Sasson, Leonora Saunders, Camilla Schofield, Alexandra Shepard, Sarah Stoller, Florence Sutcliffe-Braithwaite, Pat Thane, Natalie Thomlinson, Eve Worth and Zoe Young, and by lively discussions at the universities of Birmingham, Cambridge, Glasgow, Kent, Oxford, Westminster and York, at Queen Mary University of London and Northwestern University, and at the North American Conference on British Studies. The arguments and analyses developed in this book build upon a rich and extensive scholarship on women's labour, and I have tried to do some justice to the groundbreaking work of historians in this field, present and past, in my endnotes and bibliography. All errors, omissions and shortcomings remain my own.

My agent Andrew Gordon and editor Michael Fishwick have been faithful champions of *Double Lives* and I pay tribute to their enduring commitment to publishing and promoting both women's history and women historians. It has been a huge pleasure to work with Lauren Whybrow at Bloomsbury, who has overseen the production of the book with unfailing efficiency and cheerfulness, and with Kat Ailes, whose brilliant copy-editing whipped the manuscript into shape in the later stages.

Finally, I extend my eternal gratitude to my husband, James Mather, who is a devoted father, loyal friend, loving companion and the sharpest-eyed critic I know.

Index

A Note on the Author

Helen McCarthy is University Lecturer in Modern British History at the University of Cambridge and a Fellow of St John's College. Her first book was *The British People and the League of Nations* and her second book, *Women of the World: The Rise of the Female Diplomat*, won Best International Affairs Book at the Political Book Awards 2015.

@HistorianHelen

A Note on the Type

The text of this book is set Adobe Garamond. It is one of several versions of Garamond based on the designs of Claude Garamond. It is thought that Garamond based his font on Bembo, cut in 1495 by Francesco Griffo in collaboration with the Italian printer Aldus Manutius. Garamond types were first used in books printed in Paris around 1532. Many of the present-day versions of this type are based on the *Typi Academiae* of Jean Jannon cut in Sedan in 1615.

Claude Garamond was born in Paris in 1480. He learned how to cut type from his father and by the age of fifteen he was able to fashion steel punches the size of a pica with great precision. At the age of sixty he was commissioned by King Francis I to design a Greek alphabet, and for this he was given the honourable title of royal type founder. He died in 1561.